WHEELS *of* CHANGE

WHEELS *of* CHANGE

FROM ZERO TO 600 M.P.H.

THE AMAZING STORY OF CALIFORNIA AND THE AUTOMOBILE

KEVIN NELSON

Berkeley, California

San Francisco, California

Library of Congress Cataloging-in-Publication Data

Nelson, Kevin, 1953-
Wheels of change from zero to 600 m.p.h. : the amazing story of California and the automobile / Kevin Nelson.
p. cm.
Includes bibliographical references and index.
ISBN 978-1-59714-113-0 (pbk. : alk. paper)
1. Automobiles--California--History. 2. Automobiles--Social aspects--California. 3. California--Social life and customs. I. Title.
TL24.C2N45 2009
629.209794--dc22
2008047911

Cover Design: theBookDesigners
Interior Design/Typesetting: theBookDesigners

Orders, inquiries, and correspondence should be addressed to:
Heyday Books
P. O. Box 9145, Berkeley, CA 94709
(510) 549-3564, Fax (510) 549-1889
www.heydaybooks.com

Printing and Binding: Thomson-Shore, Dexter, MI

10 9 8 7 6 5 4 3 2 1

PHOTO CREDITS

COVER: © **iStockphoto INTERIOR PAGES: THIS PAGE:** © **Shutterstock**
PAGE VII (next to Introduction): © **Corbis PART OPENER 1:** © **San Diego Historical Society**
PART OPENER 2: © **Corbis PART OPENER 3:** © **Corbis PART OPENER 4:** © **Corbis**

PHOTO INSERT 1: Courtesy of the National Park Service, Yosemite National Park (Baum, RL 01876); © San Diego Historical Society; Courtesy of The Huntington Library, San Marino, California; Courtesy of the archives at the Pasadena Museum of History; Courtesy of The Bancroft Library, University of California, Berkeley; Center for Sacramento History, Dolores Greenslate Collection, 1980/038/011; Herald Examiner Collection/Los Angeles Public Library; Herald Examiner Collection/Los Angeles Public Library; Herald Examiner Collection/Los Angeles Public Library; Herald Examiner Collection/Los Angeles Public Library; © San Francisco History Center, San Francisco Public Library; © Corbis; Courtesy of The Huntington Library, San Marino, California; © Corbis; © Corbis; © Getty Images; Herald Examiner Collection/Los Angeles Public Library; © Corbis; © San Francisco History Center, San Francisco Public Library; © Corbis; © Corbis; © Corbis; © Corbis

PHOTO INSERT 2: Herald Examiner Collection/Los Angeles Public Library; Courtesy of The Bancroft Library, University of California, Berkeley; © Corbis; Hollywood Citizen News/Valley Times Collection, Los Angeles Public Library; © Wally Parks NHRA Motorsports Museum; © Courtesy of Sam Barris, www.barris.com; © Corbis; © Corbis; Hollywood Citizen News/Valley Times Collection, Los Angeles Public Library; © Corbis; Herald Examiner Collection, Los Angeles Public Library; Herald Examiner Collection/Los Angeles Public Library; © Courtesy of Pebble Beach Concours d'Elegance; Hollywood Citizen News/Valley Times Collection, Los Angeles Public Library; © Corbis; Courtesy of The Bancroft Library, University of California, Berkeley; © Corbis; © Corbis; Photograph by William Claxton / Courtesy Demont Photo Management, LLC; © Corbis

Dedicated to Randy Breckenridge;

and to all the people whose lives ended, too soon, in a car

CONTENTS

A 1954 Chevrolet Bel Air Coupe at the El Monte Drive-In.

INTRODUCTION

This is a story about cars, California and perhaps surprisingly, youth and the passions of the young.

Craig Breedlove was in his twenties searching for more meaning in his life when he decided to quit his job as a firefighter and take on what many regarded as a ridiculous quest: break the world land speed record. All his life Breedlove had been into machines, and as the youngest member of the Idlers car club in southern California, he was hungry to own his first car. He begged his parents until finally they relented and let him have one—a beat-down '34 Ford. Immediately the thirteen-year-old took apart the engine and began rebuilding it to make it run better.

Phil Hill had him beat, though. Hill got his first car when he was twelve. It was a Model T, and his doting Aunt Helen bought it for him. Too young to drive legally on the streets, Hill went off-road and merrily flung his souped-up T around the backroads of Santa Monica Canyon. Hill learned to drive with such verve and intelligence that the Italians, who admired both of these qualities, later recruited him for their Ferrari factory racing team. After thriving on the California sports car circuit, Hill became the first American Formula One champion and one of the finest Grand Prix drivers ever.

Both Hill and Breedlove are part of the California car story, a story dominated by teenagers and young people. The Beach Boys, a band with a pretty good fix on the passions of teenagers, particularly California teenagers, recorded a tribute song to Breedlove and his quest called "Spirit of America." The song appeared on the 1963 *Little Deuce Coupe* album, which features a candy blue custom rod on the cover. Hill and Breedlove both drove hot rods and the Beach Boys sang about them, but the hot rod craze did not begin with any of them—not by a long shot.

It began after World War II, when all the American boys who had gone off to war came back home, rejoining all the American boys who were too young to fight. All these boys and war-weary men—and plenty of girls and women too, riding around, partying it up, having the time of their lives—started taking to the streets in their hotted up home-built Fords and Chevys and Dodges (but mainly

Fords—the hot-rodder's car of choice). There was such a groundswell of interest in these fast and wild cars and the fast and wild kids who were speeding around in them that a twenty-one-year-old ex-GI, Robert Petersen, decided to start a new magazine devoted to the pastime. He called it *Hot Rod*.

Petersen sold the premiere issue of *Hot Rod* for a quarter apiece at the world's first hot rod show at the National Guard Armory at Exposition Park in Los Angeles in January 1948. The show's organizers wouldn't let him sell the magazine inside, so he stood on the steps outside the armory trying to get people to buy a copy. Many of them did—so many, in fact, that by the next year Petersen had established another magazine, *Motor Trend*, and he was off and running in his new career as a magazine publisher, a career that would bring him prodigious wealth and success.

Petersen is one more part of the California car story, as is his buddy Wally Parks, who could not stop fiddling with machines. When he was in the South Pacific in the Navy during the war he installed a V-8 engine with open exhaust pipes into his jeep, making it a jeep hot rod. Fittingly, Parks, who founded the National Hot Rod Association, the governing body of drag racing in North America, was the first person to use the term "drag race" in print, writing in a 1939 issue of the monthly newsletter of the Southern California Timing Association.

Parks and others formed the Southern California Timing Association in the late 1930s because they wanted tighter controls on the breakneck racing that was going on at Muroc Dry Lake, El Mirage Dry Lake, and other dry lakes in the Mojave Desert. These dry lakes are another reason why the California car story is so unique and filled with such lively and unpredictable personalities. Young red-hots burning to go fast showed up at the dry lakes in their raked Model Ts (Breedlove, after he turned sixteen, raced at El Mirage) and challenged whoever was there, gunfighter-style. Sometimes cars raced five abreast on the mile-long timing trap, spinning out and bumping against one another and sending up plumes of dust and smoke into the desert sky.

Of course, it wasn't just crazy kids who were doing this; Hollywood big shots such as Clark Gable and Gary Cooper raced at Muroc too. Gable and Cooper were authentic he-men on screen and off, squiring around the world's most beautiful and glamorous women in the world's most beautiful, glamorous, and expensive cars. After Cooper bought a one-of-a-kind Duesenberg roadster, Gable, his rival as the screen's top leading man in the late 1930s, decided he had to have one too. So he ordered one built exactly like Cooper's except that, as Gable joked, his Duesenberg was *longer*.

Nearing the end of his great career, Gable judged a Concours d'Elegance automobile show in Beverly Hills in the late 1950s with a young television actor who also had an interest in cars and going fast. His name was Steve McQueen.

The star of two of the greatest chase sequences ever filmed—the motorcycle jump in *The Great Escape* and the Dodge Charger–Mustang GT face-off in *Bullitt,* shot on the streets of San Francisco—was only then just starting to discover the joys of driving sports cars. Imported sports cars also took off after World War II, when all those GIs returning home discovered that the United States didn't have a sports car of its own—nothing to match the quick and fun British-made Triumphs and MGs they had seen and driven overseas. In the years to come, more quick and fun imports from Europe—Mercedes, Porsches, Ferraris—arrived in California, and the California sports car racing scene became like nowhere else on the planet.

More than ninety thousand people—*ninety thousand!*—watched Phil Hill race his Ferrari against other Ferraris, Triumphs, and homemade "backyard specials" in a 1952 race at Golden Gate Park in San Francisco. But Golden Gate Park was only one stop on the circuit; others were Torrey Pines in San Diego, Palm Springs, Santa Barbara, and the most beautiful and exciting road race in America, the Pebble Beach Road Race. These races are no more, of course, but the world-famous Concours d'Elegance luxury automobile show at Pebble remains a stylish carryover from those days.

In October 1955 the city of Salinas was hosting a sports car race, and James Dean, having just seen a sneak preview of his latest movie, *Rebel Without a Cause*, decided to enter his new Porsche Spyder in it. Blasting out of Los Angeles late in the morning, he was nearing San Luis Obispo when he crashed into another car at high speed on the highway and died instantly. When he was alive James Dean was famous for about nine months. But in death his fame may never die, and his story—like those of McQueen, Gable, Cooper, and other Hollywood fast-car guys—is part of the California automobile story too.

America's first sports car, introduced in 1953, was the Corvette, and it was Chevrolet's answer to all those exotic, low-slung imports invading these shores after the war. The man who designed the Corvette—and invented, among many other things, tail fins for Cadillacs—was Harley Earl, and he's a big part of this book as well.

Born and raised in California, Earl first made a name for himself by designing customs for Hollywood stars looking for unique motorized statements. One of the cars he designed for high-living comedian Fatty Arbuckle came with a cocktail bar and a toilet. The Cadillac he built for screen cowboy Tom Mix had a leather saddle mounted on the roof. The startling originality of his designs, a mix of Old World European flair with Hollywood razzamatazz, drew the attention of General Motors, which hired him to oversee the first styling department of any major car manufacturer in America. He became America's first professional automobile designer and, without doubt, this country's most influential ever. During his career he supervised the styling of every make and model produced by GM, some 40 to 50 million cars.

Earl said once that every car he designed had a trace of the old Santa Monica Road Race in it—the race he had watched as a boy, growing up in southern California in the years before the First World War. Like Pebble Beach, the Santa Monica Road Race took place on the streets of the city, where people ordinarily drove their cars (and, at the time, their horse-drawn buggies). And in 1912, when Barney Oldfield was the biggest name in car racing and one of America's most famous men, 150,000 spectators from around the world came to the tiny beach community of Santa Monica to see him in action.

There was nobody like Barney; refer to him only by his first name and the guy on the barstool next to you would know instantly who you were talking about. When Barney arrived in California for the first time—he eventually settled in Beverly Hills—he was twenty-five years old and known around the world as the cigar-chewing "Mile-a-Minute Man," the first to crack 60 miles per hour in an automobile on a racetrack. At the time, people regarded a mile a minute in an automobile as something akin to suicide on wheels, because it was. On the track or off, cars were dangerous. They represented freedom, but freedom came with a price. They hurt and killed people. They belched smoke and fire, arrived abruptly in an explosive volley of sound, and scared horses. Besides all that, at least in the early years, only rich folks could afford to own them.

One would have been hard pressed to find a city more hostile to the automobile than San Francisco. If a car stalled on a hill and the driver had to get out and push it, those walking by often ignored him and refused to lend a helping hand. Anyone with the dough to own a car—or "horseless carriage," as they were called then—deserved what he got. Push it yourself, Buster. But public sentiment began to change after the horrific events of the 1906 earthquake, when, as one newspaper put it, the "devil wagons turned into chariots of mercy," transporting victims away from the fires at lifesaving speed and performing other duties vital to the rescue effort.

Women also became early advocates of these strange, unsettling, status quo-disturbing machines. Unlike horses, which were physically difficult for them to control, women could more easily handle automobiles, especially with the demise of the hand crank and the advent of the electric starter. Alice Ramsey became the first woman to drive cross-country from New York to San Francisco, a truly heroic feat considering that in 1909 very few of her female contemporaries drove at all. The twenty-two-year-old wife and mother was determined to prove that women could manage these new machines, not just ride in them as passengers, and women at the helm of automobiles became a potent symbol for suffragists in California and around the United States campaigning for the right to vote.

There has never been a time of innocence for the automobile. It has always engendered strong feelings and controversy. It has always been a source of pride and envy and joy and criticism and experimentation and romance, always been at the center of enormous social change. In 1901, when this book begins, there were only a few hundred automobiles in California, and the fastest ones barely traveled faster than a person walking on foot. By 1965, when this book ends, millions of cars roamed the roads and highways of the state, and Craig Breedlove's jet-powered Spirit of America had gone 600 miles per hour, faster than a .30 caliber bullet shot from a rifle.

That is what this book is about. How we got from there to here, and what happened in between. How Californians changed the automobile—and how the automobile changed California.

Save for electricity and possibly the computer, no modern invention has changed our lives so fully as the automobile. Cars were new technology at the birth of the twentieth century and as is so often the case with new technology, teenagers embraced it. One of those teens was Carl Breer, and this story of love and loss and triumph and upheaval begins with him.

Proud of their machine: San Diego mechanics, circa 1911.

PART ONE
THE ANCIENT WORLD

ONE
Blacksmith's Son

In the dying years of the nineteenth century, a whip-smart teenager named Carl Breer set out on a bicycle ride that would change his life. His trip began at his home on South San Pedro Street, between Second and Third Streets in the young and ambitious city of Los Angeles, and carried him to a park in the hills north of downtown.

Slender of build and of medium height, with dark wavy hair, Carl loved the outdoors almost as much as he loved tinkering with things. A typical day for him consisted of school followed by chores around the house: chopping wood for the kitchen stove or helping his father and brothers at the family smithy. He pumped the bellows to get the furnace burning hotter or swung a sledgehammer to sharpen the worn edges of plowshares and shape new metal wagon wheels. "We would build fires around the wheel tires to expand them so that we could slip them over the wood rim wheels," he recalled, "then shrink them tight with cooling streams of water so as not to burn and ruin the wood rim."

But when work and school were done, he liked to hop on his bike and pedal off for open spaces, traveling down the block past the Empire Steam Laundry and Sanders Warehouse. On this day he likely steered clear of La Grande Station, a few blocks away. The Moorish-style domes of La Grande suggested exotic splendor, but it was really just a hard-working train depot, the railroad hub of the city. Whistles blowing, axles squeaking, black columns of smoke spiraling into the air, locomotives came and went all day and night, pulling long strings of rattling cars going west to Santa Monica and San Pedro Bay, south to the tiny coastal hamlets of Long Beach and San Diego, north to San Francisco and Sacramento, and east to the faraway cities of Chicago and New York. Travelers departed for these places every day, but in this growing city of one hundred thousand, more people always seemed to be arriving than leaving, and outside the station on Santa Fe Street a line of surrey cabs waited to take these new arrivals to their hotels.

Almost certainly Breer on his bike also stayed away from Spring Street, just a few short blocks from his house going west past old St. Vibiana's Cathedral with the bones of the martyr buried in the altar. Spring Street was the liveliest scene in town.

Here cometh the iceman in the ice wagon, carrying scales and a hook under his seat and a couple of tons of ice in his hooded rear compartment. There went the pie man in the pie wagon, taking his fresh-baked cherry and peach pies to cafés and grocers, followed by the butcher and his daughter looking for a place to stop on the street to sell pork chops, mutton, and steaks right out of the back of their wagon. Then there were the sandwich sellers in their lunch wagons, shopkeepers delivering dry goods, farmers in their sturdy green Studebaker wagons overflowing with hay, open-air four-horse coaches carrying a half-dozen passengers, even larger Concord coaches pulled by six heavy-breathing horses, and all manner of other vehicles—buggies, surreys, coupes, shays, cabs—streaming up and down the street with little regard for those crossing on foot or riding a bike. If the horses and wagons didn't get you—look out!—here came the trolley with its wobbly overhead guide lines and its dual tracks running down the center of the street. It was the tank wagon's job to water the dirt streets to keep the dust down, but with all the hooves and wagon wheels constantly chewing things up, there was plenty of dirt and dust to go around.

Those who wished to flee the hubbub of downtown found respite in the green, uncluttered hills of Elysian Park, and this was where Breer headed. "The habitués of this park are the lovers of wild nature," wrote one newspaper correspondent, "who repeatedly seek its delightful drives, high above all the surrounding country, that they may enjoy its exhilarating air, its rugged hillsides and sheltered nooks." Despite its charms, though, relatively few people came to Elysian, owing to the fact that after they took one horse cab to get there they had to pay for another to pass through the front gate at the top of the hill. "They sit in the car and look at the beautiful Fremont Gate, with its broad driveway and stair; with its green, flower-decked terraces rising one above the other; and at the steep hillside beyond. Its beauty is satisfying, [but] rather than pay an extra carfare, they pass on." What they missed when they did this were exquisite views of the San Gabriel Mountains and to the west, the slender shapes of the Channel Islands amidst the darkened blue spaces of ocean.*

From these heights one could also look down and see a water storage reservoir, a "reservoir like an island lake, surrounded by tree-clad hills. It is a restful spot that lends a charm to the place." After drinking in the views at the top of the hill, Breer and his brother Bill and another boy who had come on this trip with them followed their curiosity down to the reservoir to see what they could discover there. When they poked their heads inside the pumping plant, its chief engineer, Fred J. Fisher, a kindly-looking man with thick eyebrows, deep-set eyes, and a waxed, upward-curling mustache, invited them in for a tour.

The youngest of the three boys quickly began to ask questions. "As we walked around," remembered Carl, "my eye caught notice of a bi-polar direct current

---

* The city that Breer biked through has been transformed, of course. Elysian Park is the site of Dodger Stadium. La Grande Station has vanished, although there is still a working railyard there. The Breer family smithy would be located today in the Little Tokyo District. While the Cathedral of St. Vibiana remains standing, the 1994 Northridge earthquake dealt it a hard blow and its eventual fate may be the wrecker's ball.

generator, sitting on a high bracket on the wall. It was operated by overhead leather belts running from a counter shaft driven by a Pelton water wheel." Recognizing that any boy who could spot a bi-polar direct current generator, and who knew what it did, was one worth cultivating, the chief engineer explained that he had, in fact, built the generator himself. Carl responded with enthusiasm: "I was thrilled to learn that Mr. Fisher had personally built this electric generator in this very plant, set it up, and used the force of the water from the reservoir above to operate it so that he could light up all the dark corners in this remote pumping plant both day and night."

Even as an adult, Breer referred to Fred Fisher as Mr. Fisher, a sign of his respect for him. Fisher was that rarest of adults, one who truly took the thoughts and aspirations of a young person seriously, and he engaged the boy in a discussion about the developing science of electricity that probably bored Breer's brother and friend. "Before I left I was itching to build a machine of my own, one that could make electricity to light up an electric light bulb," Carl said. Even more important, he had found "a life-long friend, and I was befriended like an adopted son."

From then on, every day after school and chores, he rode the five miles over to Elysian Park to visit the wondrous pumping plant. "Fisher's plant was filled with engineering innovations," Breer recalled. "For example, another Pelton water wheel operated Fisher's stand-by engine lathe, which he used when some minor repair parts were quickly needed. What a unique setup! When things were running smoothly Mr. Fisher had spare time for his own use." The older man felt the boy's excitement, and he showed Carl how to operate the lathe. Carl in turn used it to build an electric generator of his own. "What a thrill it was," he exulted, "to see electric bulbs glow from electricity generated by the machine I built."

But the boy's experiments did not end there. The house on San Pedro, the first brick house in the city of Los Angeles, did not have electricity. Nor, for that matter, did the blacksmith shop run by his father, known to all as "Iron Louis" for his thick, hard chest and powerful arms that easily handled the twelve-pound sledge his son struggled with. The house also lacked a toilet, which was out back in the yard near the fruit trees and an earthen swimming pool that the children played in during the summer. Although indoor plumbing was out of his range, Carl, with Mr. Fisher's backing, felt growing confidence in his electrical abilities. He installed his self-built generator, wired the brick house on San Pedro Street, and brought electric light to the Breer household for the first time.

He was fourteen.

What distinguished it from the homemade ragtag experimentals was that the Duryea Manufacturing Company of Peoria, Illinois, owned by the famous Duryea brothers, Charles and Frank, had built the car. Frank Duryea had won what is generally regarded as America's first automobile road race, besting a handful of electrics and foreign gas models (including two by Karl Benz) in a Thanksgiving Day 1895 race around the snow-laden streets of Chicago. Afterward the Duryeas established a factory and formed their own manufacturing company, and this three-wheeler, delivered by train to the coast, was their latest model: "light and graceful in appearance, and weighing only seven hundred pounds. There are two seats, back to back, with room for two people in the front and three behind. The automobile is steered and the speed regulated by a single lever, manipulated by one of the people on the front seat. The small but powerful gasoline motors develop six horsepower. The fuel is ordinary gasoline, such as can be purchased at any country store. Enough can be carried to run 150 miles without refilling the tank."

The arrival of a Duryea motor wagon in town was newsworthy enough to merit a long article in the paper with an accompanying illustration. This drawing shows a family of three with a boy in the back and his father and mother in front. The man is bearded and wears a suit and hat. The woman also has a hat on, although hers appears to have flowers on top of it, and she is wearing a long, full dress that covers her shoes and whose sleeves extend all the way to her wrists. Interestingly, she is the one in the illustration gripping the lever and steering the vehicle, suggesting that this new form of motorized transportation was going to appeal not just to husbands but to their wives as well.

The excitement caused by the arrival of the Duryea was tempered somewhat by the fact that its owner, S. R. Henderson, didn't know how to drive it. By the next month, though, after taking some lessons in the country, Henderson was spotted all around town sporting about in his new three-wheeler. His abilities on the rise, Henderson soon did what many would regard as the next most logical thing. He took his new buggy down to Agricultural Park—now Exposition Park, near the University of Southern California—to see how fast it would go. The fairgrounds there had a mile-long oval dirt track, which, though normally used for horse racing, seemed suitable for an automobile test of speed. No official time for the Duryea was recorded, but it must have disappointed Henderson to some degree because soon after this he placed an order with an Eastern company for an eleven-toothed sprocket. The purpose of the sprocket: boost his vehicle's speed.

It's not clear if Carl Breer ever saw Henderson's Duryea around town, although he may have. One account says that he even saw the great Frank Duryea drive through the city on a promotional tour for his cars, and that this event inspired him to build his own horseless carriage. But if this did occur, it was not inspiring enough for Breer to mention it in his autobiography, written in the 1960s after a long and innovative career as a Chrysler engineer. Apart from his parents and family, the one clear source of early inspiration he cited was Fred Fisher. With the water district engineer providing advice and assistance but mostly staying out of the way, the teenager moved forward with his plan to build a steam-powered car.

Breer settled on steam locomotion because he and Fisher understood it best of all. More than any other mechanical process, steam power drove the nineteenth century, giving birth to factories and powering the machines in those factories. A steamship had brought his parents, Julia and Louis Breer, from their native Germany to America, and on days when he had nothing better to do their youngest son could go down to the First Street Bridge and sit and watch steam locomotives huff and puff in and out of La Grande. The logic of the time said that steam should power automobiles, and in many cases it already did. Steam wagons for transportation and hauling appeared before either gasoline or electric cars.

There were plenty of examples of steam engines around for Carl to observe and draw ideas from. Though it was a little inconvenient, because you had to first boil the water to get it going and then you had to constantly refill the tank with water, a steam engine was quieter and less confusing than those noisy, smelly gas engines. It also required fewer moving parts than gas, and the parts were simpler to put together and cheaper to make. So, steam it was.

With Carl's brother Bill pitching in money and a pair of skilled hands, they bought a small foot-powered lathe and installed it in an empty adobe hut on the South San Pedro Street property. All the work they did was powered by hand or foot. Carl built a workbench, cut through the shingle roof of the adobe, put in a skylight to help them see better. He found a description of the technical details of a steam engine in a magazine and, based on this article, made a dimension drawing of a two-cylinder, double-acting steam motor. He then made drawings of the individual parts and carved these parts out of sugar pine and poplar wood. But when he took these parts to a foundry to be cast into steel, the men there couldn't do the job on the trickier pieces such as the cylinder block. So the youngster took over. "I asked if I could give it a try. I made the cores, set the mold, and luckily was successful in getting a nice satisfactory cylinder casting. This was my first obstacle to overcome." Carl and Bill machined the rods and other parts on their foot-powered lathe, and forged the steel crankshaft using the anvil in their father's blacksmith shop.

These obstacles overcome, "proud I was the day...I took the completed engine to Fred Fisher's plant in Elysian Park to check it out and see the valve gear in operation," said Carl. This may have been when Mr. Fisher or Bill snapped the Kodak picture of Carl standing next to his shiny new creation. Then seventeen, he appears stiff and uncomfortable in front of the camera. His hair is parted in the middle and he is unsmiling. His greasy, oil-spattered work coat is buttoned at the neck, which only adds to his look of discomfort. But sticking out of the long sleeves of his coat are his hands, which give a better sense of the liveliness of his personality. They appear larger and yet more delicate than normal. Clearly, give that boy something to do with his hands, namely a machine, and he was happy.

Mr. Fisher admired the engine so far, but they were still a long way from having a finished automobile. Carl placed an order with a Buffalo company for running gear, and another order from a different company for a steel boiler. He bought these two items, plus the gauges and chassis, and hired out the painting and upholstery.

Otherwise, he built the entire car himself. To heat the boiler, he created an unusual Bunsen-style burner of his own design. But in order to make this design work, thousands of tiny holes had to be drilled into the inner steel chambers of the piece. Yet there was no practical way to power a drill in the adobe, so he concocted a smaller version of the Pelton water wheel system at Mr. Fisher's plant, running a hose from the outdoor faucet of the brick house into the adobe and using this water pressure to operate a high-speed drill. This drill allowed him to cut the holes needed.

While Carl was building his car, his father was making plowshares and wagon springs in the smithy next door, doing work that had been done for hundreds of years and had hardly changed in all that time. What his son was doing, of course, would ultimately render his father's trade extinct. But at the time an automobile was pure novelty, a curiosity. Those people who cared enough to peek their heads into the adobe hut must have been amused and a little flabbergasted at the sight of this two-cylinder steam engine lodged inside a black wooden carriage. Carl fashioned the body out of poplar and ash, and then sent it out to the carriage maker for trimming the upholstery and paint.

"Finally the day arrived," he said, "to see if this masterpiece would run. It was a late fall afternoon in 1901, in the yard by the blacksmith shop, that I started up the burner. It worked. Pressure showed on the steam gauge, and the water level in the water level gauge bobbed up and down to indicate activity....I nervously got up in the seat and pushed on the throttle. The car suddenly leaped forward in action," and he was on his way. Driving!

Is there anything more nerve-wracking and exciting than driving an automobile for the first time? But something wasn't right. Every time Carl opened the throttle, the car lunged forward. The same when he put it in reverse. He couldn't get the thing out of the yard before he had to stop, get out, and adjust the overactive throttle. Night fell by the time the car was ready to go again, and he had to wait until the next morning to take it out on the street.

"On this next attempt when I dared to take the car out on the street, what a thrill it was to drive along quietly, without hoof clatter." Quiet his engine may have been, but certainly not his brother and the rest of the family who came out to watch and go on rides. This must have been when Iron Louis and Julia Breer sensed, if they hadn't already, that their son's destiny was going to carry him far away from the little blacksmith shop on South San Pedro.

Upon hearing that his prize pupil's invention had finally taken to the road, Mr. Fisher could not contain his excitement. On Sunday he raced over to the Breers on his bicycle to see for himself and take a ride. After Carl proudly did the honors first, he asked Mr. Fisher if he wished to give it a go himself. Mr. Fisher naturally said yes, and he and Carl exchanged seats—Carl jumping down and climbing onto the passenger side, Mr. Fisher sliding into the driver's seat and taking the tiller in hand.

But when he drove onto South San Pedro, a narrow two-lane dirt road with deep gutters on both sides, he became confused about how to operate the controls and ran the vehicle into a ditch, breaking the right front axle.

"I never wanted that to happen," said Mr. Fisher sadly. "I would not have had that happen for anything."

His friend felt even worse than he did. "I never forgot the expression on his face," Carl said. "My heart went out to him."

Fortunately they were only a block away from home. They left the car in the ditch and walked back to the house to grab some tools and rope and to harness up the unexciting but reliable Fanny. When they got back to the car, they lodged a board under the right wheel for traction and attached a line from the rear of the vehicle to the horse. She dragged the steamer out of the ditch and pulled it back to the house as the men walked quietly alongside.

TWO

A Day at the Races

So this was at the core of it, how a world of horses ultimately became a world of automobiles: one man, usually young and quite often a teenager, by himself or with other young men, tinkering with a machine in the communal pleasures of a garage. But garages as we know them today did not exist when Carl Breer built his "steam chariot," as he liked to call it. He did his tinkering in an adobe hut with a high-speed drill whose power source was the water faucet outside, and this was where he, Fanny, and the devastated Mr. Fisher brought his broken vehicle. In a week or so the youngster repaired the car and although Breer does not say so in his autobiography, one has to believe he gave his friend and teacher a second try at the tiller, and that Mr. Fisher redeemed himself with a joyous run down South San Pedro and beyond.

"The sense of freedom that came from one's first ride in a horseless carriage, going faster and bouncing higher, and buying fuel from grocery stores in five-gallon tin cans was a new thrill," Breer wrote. "The physical strain in the horseless carriage was much higher, but the exhilaration of being your own master was well worth it in spite of the fact that a horse and buggy gave one a more comfortable ride. Also in those days came the interest—as well as the need—to become interested in learning about the mechanical things under the hood. Soon you became your own mechanic, a far cry from grooming and hitching a horse."

A born tinkerer, Breer improved his machine by adding a foot-operated steam whistle and installing an extra gas tank for long trips into the San Gabriel Mountains. (Steamers used gasoline or kerosene as fuel and for the burner and pilot light.) He put in the gas tank at four in the morning one spring day so that he and Bill could go trout fishing on the San Gabriel River near Azusa. They left home around sunrise, spent the day on the river, got back by nightfall. "It gave me a lot of satisfaction and delight just to think we were able to drive some thirty-five miles over dirt roads and return and still have plenty of time to wade the stream and flycast for fish. This wouldn't have been possible by horse or buggy."

The traditional family trek to Santa Monica Canyon went much faster as well, though sometimes Carl and Bill hit bumps in the road that would've bounced them through the roof of the steamer if there'd been one. Finding gas was also an adventure. Gasoline was a waste product of a then much more coveted commodity, kerosene, which people used for lighting and cooking. The storekeepers who carried gasoline, and there weren't many, sold it in five-gallon tin cans for less than a dollar, well below the price of kerosene.

As pleasurable as these trips were, though, Carl had more on his mind than just fun. His goal was to attend Stanford, and he felt he stood a better chance of being admitted if he first obtained some work experience outside his father's smithy. So, in the summer of 1902, he applied for a job at the Auto Vehicle Company, which had just opened an office on North Main Street in Los Angeles. Although new, the company did not lack for ambition. With some $250,000 in backing (its directors included the socially prominent president of California Bank, W. F. Botsford), it soon intended to begin manufacturing a touring car to be called "the Tourist."

The day of his interview Carl parked his steamer out front and went in to speak to a Mr. Ford (no relation to Henry), the head of the service department, explaining that he was looking for a job in automobiles. Carl added that he had brought his homemade steamer along with him as a kind of job reference.

Mr. Ford went outside for a look. Then he took a test-drive around the neighborhood with Carl sitting beside him showing him how to work the controls. When they were done, Mr. Ford told him, "You can come to work tomorrow," and hired him on the spot.

The job paid thirty cents an hour, pretty good pay for a teenager in 1902, and it did indeed lead to college as Carl had hoped, although not in the way he expected. Stanford's engineering department refused to recognize his high school course work, saying that before it would accept him he needed to take four more years of accredited science classes. This hardly seemed fair, so Carl and a teacher he knew from Commercial High drove over to the Throop Polytechnic Institute in Pasadena—now the California Institute of Technology, or Caltech—to see if someone there could help him. A math and engineering professor listened to Carl and, somewhat like Mr. Ford at the Tourist factory, decided to take a spin in the chariot to check out the boy's story. Afterward the professor consulted with a few colleagues and the president of the university and they unanimously agreed to admit him. Not only that, at Throop he could fulfill Stanford's admission requirements in one year, not four years. Carl took the offer.

That fall he started at Throop, mostly riding the trolley but occasionally commuting from his parents' house in his steamer. A member of the first generation of American teenagers to drive and own their own automobiles, Breer engaged in what would become a familiar rite of passage for every generation to come: going on a date in a car. One particular Saturday night the date was a double, and after leaving South San Pedro he swung by his buddy Walter Vail's house to pick him up. Like Carl, Walter was dressed to the nines in a starchy tuxedo, and the two of them rattled off to the Pintaresca Hotel in Pasadena to a dance. Since the chariot could only seat two people at a time, Walter jumped down at a street corner and caught the trolley while Carl went to pick up his date, Jenny McClain. At the hotel everyone hooked up again, and Carl and Jenny and Walter and his date talked and laughed and danced till midnight. When the festivities ended Carl drove Jenny home and Walter bid his lady adieu, waiting at the Pintaresca for Carl to pick him up for their return trip to Los Angeles.

But on the way back from Jennie's house Carl crossed over the railroad tracks on Colorado Street and ominously, "something gave way." What this something was he wasn't sure, but it prevented his car from going forward. "I stopped and discovered that I could only drive in reverse, therefore I had to proceed to our meeting place driving backwards. Here Walter happily greeted me thinking that I was just showing off on my return to pick him up. I told Walter that I seemed to have picked up something that cut off my forward-going valve gear." Unwilling to leave the steamer in Pasadena, but not relishing the prospect of driving to Los Angeles in reverse, the two went backward long enough to find a house and stable. They knocked on the door and woke up the owner, who generously loaned Carl a pair of overalls and a lighted place to work. Carl slipped into the overalls, grabbed the wrench and screwdrivers he carried in the seat pockets of the steamer, and eyeballed the problem: "A quick exploration indicated that I had picked up a length of bailing wire which had caught on the chain, wrapped itself around the engine shaft, and broken off the two adjacent eccentric rods operating the forward-going valve gear." In plain terms that meant a few hours of dirty work, some skinned knuckles and colorful language, and when the forward-going valve gear was going forward once more, the sun was on its way up on Sunday morning.

Carl fired up the burner, Walter climbed aboard, and they were off and running again, but not for long. The car broke down several more times on the way back, and Carl had to jiggle with this and jimmy with that. More than once they both had to get out and push, all the while trying not to get their tuxedos dirty. Carl took Walter home first, as was only right, and his pal slyly climbed up the outer porch of his house and sneaked into his bedroom without his parents ever finding out what time he had really returned home. Carl pulled it off too. His parents were still asleep when he tiptoed into his bedroom, shed his shirt and tux, and flopped into bed.

Despite an occasional bump or two in his social life, Breer's career path led him to Stanford and beyond. He fulfilled his requirements and graduated from Caltech, moved on to Stanford, studied engineering, and graduated from there as well. After gaining more car experience in California he went off to Detroit and joined Studebaker before finding a home at Chrysler. His five-decade career at the company more than justified the faith of Mr. Fisher and other adults who took the young boy's ideas seriously. He was among those who brought automobiles from the days of horseless carriages into the modern era, helping to develop such innovations as hydraulic brakes, which prevented accidents and saved lives. His design of the Chrysler Airflow in the 1930s pioneered streamlining in automobiles to lessen wind resistance to improve gas mileage and performance.

But it all started for him—and so many others yet to come in this wide-sweeping, many-peopled narrative—in sunny, out-of-the-way California, specifically southern California. While attending Caltech, the young Breer continued to work part-time at the Auto Vehicle plant, which served as the hub of the emerging Los Angeles automobile scene. Another Caltech mechanical engineering whiz, Waldeman Grant Hansen, who was a few years older than Breer, built the first gas automobile ever seen at the university, a long, wild-looking machine with giant wheels and no housing for the motor or any of its parts. After leaving school Hansen apprenticed at a Pasadena machine shop and liked the company so much he bought it. The Auto Vehicle Company in turn bought him out and installed the two-cylinder engine he had developed into the Tourist. One part of Hansen's job for the company was to test its cars on the hills and grow their reputation at the races at Agricultural Park. After being beaten by an Oldsmobile in one early race, Hansen, described by a modern writer as "Southern California's first hot-rodder," got up to his elbows in grease and in true hot rod fashion found a way to goose more speed from the engine. His hopped-up Tourist dusted the Olds in the rematch by going around the mile-long track in twenty-six minutes, or 26 miles per hour.

Auto Vehicle produced twelve Tourists in 1902, its first year of operation. The next year saw the arrival of Walt Moreland, a talented Riverside car man. He improved on Hansen's original one-cylinder Tourist design with a more advanced two-cylinder model. In two years the company was producing one hundred and fifty cars and trucks annually and doing enough business to move to a roomier building on South Main and Tenth. One of the company's chief selling points was the fact that its cars were made locally, not imported from the Midwest or East, and buyers did not have to pay as much or wait as long for delivery. "Our factory is open for your inspection," beckoned an advertisement. "Come and see us make them." At its peak the Auto Vehicle Company was the most successful California carmaker of this era, producing five hundred Tourists a year and cultivating homegrown talent such as Breer, Hansen, and Moreland.

Nearby on Bruno Street was Western Iron Works, run by William Woodward, who built gasoline engines for automobiles. So did Alfred Stewart of Stewart's Automobile Machine Works. Interested in an electric? Try the Electric Carriage Works on East Seventh, run by the Hafer brothers. Another brother combo, Alonzo and Stanley Smith of the Smith Automobile and Machine Company, built a motorcar they called the "Smithmobile." Robert Shepherd of Stephenson Avenue named his self-built vehicle "the Shepmobile." And despite the failure of the Erie-Sturgis, Sam Sturgis kept building cars at his shop on West Fifth, recruiting his brother William to work with him. Their touring car prototype, "the Rocket," never went into production as they hoped, but their customers still brought them repair and custom jobs.

Los Angeles policeman J. E. Fay also built cars, or at least one anyhow. "Police Officer J. E. Fay is the proud possessor of an automobile made by himself," a newspaper reported. "The construction of the horseless carriage has occupied nearly all of his spare time for the past two years." All that work produced some nice touches, such as having the rear seat fold forward out of sight to convert easily into a stylish single-seater. But like other backyard mechanics Fay had his share of problems, once accidentally sticking the car in reverse and backing it into the side of his barn. Another time the engine dropped a rod on the street and a horse had to tow the car back home.

Common as they were, such mishaps did not dent the enthusiasm of the many people who wished to drive and ride in these newfangled contraptions. These included the wealthiest citizens of Los Angeles, men such as J. Philip Erie and his financial partner in the Erie-Sturgis, C. H. Albers, who formerly managed the St. Louis Merchants Exchange. Whatever S. R. Henderson did for a living, it must've paid handsomely because it took a considerable bankroll to buy a brand-new Duryea and ship it two thousand miles west to Los Angeles. This was in fact how wealthy Californians bought their automobiles: by special order. The manufacturer then made it custom for them.

One assumes that bank president W. F. Botsford owned a Tourist since he was one of the financial backers of the Auto Vehicle Company, but he also drove a fully-appointed electric Woods Victoria Stanhope that set him back the royal sum of twenty-four hundred dollars. Battery-powered electrics were quiet, odorless, and a snap to operate. Eventually, though, the battery lost its charge, and with few places to charge it out in the country, electrics quickly gained a reputation as town cars. Nevertheless they tended to sell for more than their gas and steam counterparts. Mrs. M. F. Monroe paid $2,100 for her electric Waverly Stanhope, compared to $1,650 for a sturdy gas Winton and a little over a grand for a lightweight steamer on sale at the Locomobile Company of the Pacific.

What made these purchases so extravagant, beyond their prices, was that they were essentially toys—vehicles for entertainment, pleasure-mobiles. Virtually no one bought autos solely for transportation. Even physicians, who sometimes made house calls in their new vehicles, mainly used them for recreation. If you were serious about getting somewhere, and especially if you were serious about getting there on time, you took a horse and buggy. But if you wanted to have fun, a gay old time with friends and family, you hopped in your Waverly or Winton or Locomobile and baby, you hit the road.

"It is interesting to live in the time when some ancient, world-wide custom is giving way before something new," noted an observer in 1901, and this was certainly part of the appeal of automobiles too. They were modern and new and carried a romantic allure.

People, rich people anyhow, were discovering the pleasures of driving an automobile for the first time. They organized automobile parties and caravanned to the theater, took out-of-town visitors on a spin around the park, went on moonlight runs around the city, explored the countryside on Sundays. Naturally those who loved to drive formed clubs, and these clubs became an active part of the scene too. Founded in 1900, the Automobile Club of Southern California originally functioned much like a social club, bringing together members of the upper crust who wished to go on motorized tallyhos. (The Automobile Club of San Francisco also formed that year; it has now evolved into AAA of Northern California, Nevada, and Utah. The two clubs have since broadened their reach and purpose and are now the largest automobile clubs in the country.)

It is tempting to see all this activity as the dawn of California's and America's car culture, which it was. But no one then would have ever used such a term because no such thing existed. The word "car," for one, was short for carriage, which was a vehicle pulled by a horse. And in the early 1900s the future caropolis of Los Angeles was little more than a backwater, for automobiles and most everything else. If you were looking for urban action and sophistication, the place to go was San Francisco. Most eastern tourists hit the Barbary Coast city first and then, if they had time, took the train down to Los Angeles almost as an afterthought. This was what Barney Oldfield did the first time he came to California.

Stocky and solidly built with wavy light brown hair neatly combed and parted in the middle, the twenty-five-year-old Oldfield arrived in San Francisco in November 1903, already recognized as the most famous and glamorous racecar driver in the world. Fittingly a sixty-five-member brass band greeted him and his two cars, Bullet and Baby Bullet, when they disembarked at the Ferry Building after their cross-bay ferry ride from Oakland. The welcome so delighted Barney that he invited every member of the band to join him for dinner and drinks at the Palace Hotel on Market Street, where he was staying. The band accepted the offer, and Barney picked up the entire tab for the evening and threw in a big tip for the wait staff on top of it.

That was Barney in a nutshell—a man of grand gestures and grand feelings who knew how to seize the moment, on and off the racetrack. A former elite bicycle and motorcycle racer, the Ohio native had become the first person in history to drive a car faster than a mile a minute. The Mile-a-Minute Man had done this the year before, piloting an experimental car built by the aspiring Michigan automobile entrepreneur, Henry Ford. (In January 1904, a few months after Oldfield's appearance in California, Ford himself would set the world land speed record of 91.37 miles per hour in one of his cars.) Since that day Barney had made himself into the most popular figure in the emerging new sport of motor racing, wowing thousands around the country and setting records wherever he went.

It was no mystery why fans loved him. He wasn't some blueblood like so many others associated with automobiles; every bit of his money and fame he had earned, and he had done it not just by consistently driving faster than anyone else but by giving people a show. His presence alone made things big. If it was small, he made it big; if it was big, he made it bigger. Just by showing up in Bullet or Baby Bullet or whatever he happened to be driving at that moment, he could turn a meaningless county fair race around a dump of a horse track into an event, something to watch, a place to be. And the people who came out to see him walked away afterward feeling good about themselves, feeling uplifted as if they'd witnessed something and somebody truly special, and they had.

"How do I feel to ride faster than the wind?" Oldfield told a reporter. "I do not stop to analyze my feelings anymore. You may think you have an idea of what racing at a mile a minute means, but you haven't. It means flying; you have every sensation of falling, of being hurled through space, and the landscape rushing to you gives you a feeling that you cannot shake off. To ride faster than man ever rode before, to feel that space is being cut down. These things are worth feeling, and there is an ecstasy in the drive that tingles through every fiber of your being."

Tingling and fully alive, in his athletic prime, the Devil Wagon Man drove fast and cut down the space in front of him. The risks he took formed part of his appeal—why men of all classes and women both scarlet and refined sought out the pleasure of his company. Here was this handsome, fresh-scrubbed man from the nation's heartland doing things in an automobile nobody had ever done before, and laughing in the face of death.

People regarded a mile a minute in an automobile as suicide on wheels. The spitting and growling Bullet raced against other angry machines on dirt tracks chewed up by horses, with turns too sharp for automobiles and straights too narrow for the crowd of vehicles clattering down them. No driver wore a helmet, and if his open cockpit car rolled, nothing protected his head or body from a violent collision with the earth. Roll bars did not exist. Rearview mirrors were still years away from being invented. Drivers wore goggles because if they did not they wouldn't have been able to see a thing with the dirt and gravel being kicked up by the spinning wheels and the clouds of dust and exhaust in the air. Barney wore no protective jumpsuit; he raced in a sweater and street clothes, as did his competitors. Shoulder harnesses and safety belts did not commonly exist, and even if they had, drivers would have refused to wear them. The thinking was that they needed to be free to get away from the machine, not strapped to it, which made sense on some level because crashes so often ended in fiery gas explosions. Poorly made tires wore out quickly under the heat and pressure, and blowouts occurred frequently. The primitive braking and handling capabilities of these machines put still more pressure on the men trying to control them. If a driver couldn't hold a turn and didn't smash into another car as he skidded across the dirt, he barreled through the low wooden rail around the track. And on the other side of this fence, scrambling frantically to get out of the way, were spectators. Watching an auto race could be as dangerous as driving in one.

Only a couple of months earlier at a race in Detroit, a rear tire on Barney's car had burst and his vehicle crashed through a fence, hitting and killing a spectator. Oldfield broke a rib and cracked and chipped several teeth in the crash, and in the gloomy aftermath he briefly considered quitting racing while he still could. This he did not do—it was how he made his living—but out of the ruins came an idea. From then on he drove with an unlit cigar in his mouth to ease the pounding on his teeth and jaw caused by the intense vibration of his car.

His trademark cigar clenched between his teeth, Barney set a slew of records at the two-day meet at Ingleside Racetrack in San Francisco, a dirt horse track in the southwestern reaches of the city. After that the two Bullets and their Kingpin

Chauffeur—you'd be rich if you had a sawbuck for every nickname the press and promoters hung on Oldfield—boarded the Southern Pacific with the idea of doing the same thing all over again at a twenty-thousand-dollar meet at Agricultural Park.

Like Ingleside, Agricultural Park mainly featured the ponies, although S. R. Henderson had taken his Duryea there and it had hosted "the mobes" (short for "mobile") since 1900. The fairgrounds oval was made of dirt with a grassy pasture in the center; this was where the horses grazed when they weren't racing. The white wooden fence encircling the track was about three feet high, low enough for the spectators (mostly boys and men, but some women too) to lean out over the top of it and cheer on their favorite as the cars poured down the homestretch past the grandstands to the finish.

The earliest motor races puzzled gamblers because they couldn't figure out how to place odds on them. "If anybody will tell you within forty rods what these new-fangled things are going to do," said one bookmaker, "then we'll offer odds on them. But we can't place any bets on them at this stage of the game." Unlike horses, the mobes moved erratically, and no one could predict with any certainty what they'd do. "The engine-propelled vehicles would move around the circle in a pretty bunch, then one would fall away behind, but let itself out afterward enough to lead at the finish. Under high speed they were as uncertain as a flea's movements." Their jitterbugging, coupled with the smoke and hissing and popping noises they made, upset two-footed and four-footed creatures alike. One morning the mobes entered the racing grounds at the same time as the horses, and the animals reacted as if they'd seen the devil on wheels. Several reared up, and one bolted off dragging its carriage and injuring its driver.

But horseless carriage racing proved to be popular with the public, and promoters started organizing more events for them. Early automobilists disagreed strongly over which locomotion was best—gas, steam, or electric—and each method had its impassioned advocates. Taking advantage of this controversy, Agricultural Park staged a head-to-head showdown between a steamer and an electric that turned out to be not much of a contest. The steamer whipped past the quarter-mile pole in thirty-two seconds and finished the mile in just over two minutes, easily drubbing the electric. But the main complaint that day wasn't about the lack of competition; it was about how the track was pushing its beer sales too hard and not serving enough sandwiches. "The edible accompaniment served with drinks has dwindled from a fairly generous lunch almost to the microscopic point," grumbled one attendee. "The sandwiches are served on a ratio of 16 to 1—sixteen beers to one sandwich."

So many beer-soaked patrons leaving Agricultural Park after a race may have been one reason why the Chamber of Commerce passed a resolution urging the city to crack down on reckless drivers, recommending a speed limit of four miles per hour on the busiest streets. In Pasadena, police on bicycles rode alongside automobiles trying to get them to slow down. In another effort to curb speeders, one officer stood on one end of a street, clicking a stopwatch when a fast-moving car came through. Another officer with a stopwatch stood at the end of the speed trap, timing the vehicle as it passed by. If it was going too fast it was hailed down and cited.

But there were no speed limits at the racetrack, and pretty soon the bookmakers, who were quick studies, figured out how to set odds and stir up action. With money coming into the sport, to go along with the heaping amounts of pride and ego already there, both winners and losers started fiddling with their machines to make them go faster. This competition pushed automobile development forward. From the beginning of automobiles to today, if some new innovation appears in a passenger car, an early form of it almost certainly appeared first in a racecar, years before.

The excitement of watching moving vehicles compete against one another dates back to the chariot races of ancient Rome. But those races, like the buggies at Agricultural Park, were horse-powered, not machine-powered. Machine racing was new and modern too, and this added to the excitement felt by the thousands of people who showed up on November 20 to watch Barney Oldfield's Los Angeles racing debut. Though faster than Ingleside, Agricultural Park was considered to have a slower racing surface than the tracks of the East, and the gambling touts did not expect to see any records set. But the Mile-a-Minute Champion did not become who he was by disappointing people, and when the starter's gun sounded, off he went in an explosion of smoke and fury. "We just jump in and let 'er rip," said Barney, describing his racing style. He could have added "in a cloud of dust" because as the Bullet burst from the line, dust hung in the air like smoke at a fireworks display.

Racing alone, with no one to push or distract him, Barney hugged the inner rail on the straight and slid toward the outer fence on the first turn, pushing hard down the backstretch with streams of dust and smoke trailing behind. Fans stood along the railing on the inside and outside of the track all the way around, waving and cheering him on. A policeman shooed two boys off the fence where they were sitting. They could have reached out and touched the Bullet as it sped past them on the rail, spraying dirt. Not only that, they could actually see Barney's goggled and expressionless face as he drove past, his hair whipped back with the force of the onrushing air, his clothes pressed against him, his teeth chomping that cigar. They saw all that and pressed closer to the rail as the Bullet rumbled down the homestretch past the grandstand and the finish pole.

Every eye turned expectantly toward the timing stand. As if in response, the officials quickly posted the time, sending murmurs of disbelief around the stands: a new world record! Barney had clocked the mile in just over fifty-five seconds! But wait, he wasn't done yet; he was going around again, blowing down the straight through the dust that still hung in the air from when he started. "The mist of dust rises up and you feel alone with the machine in the swirling fog you left when you were around there before," said Barney, describing what it was like to drive through these clouds. "The exhilarating effect is immense." Exhilarating but dangerous. Dust hurt his ability to see and stung his face like tiny flying insects. "If there are other machines on the track, the dust whips you like a lash."

At the quarter-mile pole Barney hugged the fence so close, said a writer, "it seemed as if he must scrape the paint." On the straightaway he was going so fast that "if Barney's hat should blow off, he could catch it on the next lap before it hit the ground." But, said the writer—ripping off lines like this, alas, without a byline—there was no way to prove the claim because Barney wasn't wearing a hat.

"It looked this way: a flash of white shirt down the backstretch, a dark streak on the horizon across the fields, a cloud of dust far up the track, and before you could lean over the rail to see, a rushing mighty wind swashing by under the wire and everybody beginning to shout. That is what it was like to see Barney Oldfield do a mile in 55."

Going faster than any nag had ever run at Agricultural Park and more than twice as fast as Waldeman Grant Hansen's Tourist, Barney pointed the Bullet toward home. "All sensation is exaggerated," he said about the rush of this moment. "You have the feeling a bird on the wing must have...Why, it's flying, man."

After he flew past the timers' stand this second time, a moment of dramatic tension followed. The posting took longer to come up. Even the dust hanging over the track seemed suspended in air, as if it were waiting for the final result before deciding whether or not to come down. Then the number went up on the board: fifty-five seconds flat, even faster than the first lap. A new world record...*again!*

A shout went up from all over, and people could not hold back any longer, pouring out of the grandstands onto the track. They hopped the railing on both sides and ran across the dirt past some cops who were supposed to keep them away. But the numbers were too great, and their enthusiasm too high. Hundreds of grinning, yelling, arm-waving fans swarmed the Bullet, now resting contentedly in the middle of the track, its labors done for the day. Even the timers got caught up in the excitement, rushing down from their section to find Barney and pat him on the back and shake his hand. Goggles now up on his forehead, his face splattered with dirt except for an owl-like whiteness around his eyes, still working his cigar, he laughed and went along with the celebration as two men tried to pick him up and carry him around on their shoulders.

This may have been the moment when the Human Comet fell in love with California—a place where you could race all year round, where the winning pots were big and getting bigger, and where the timers were so supportive. But for now he had other places to go and more records to set, and before long he blew town, although he was certain to return again (and certain to return to this story again).

THREE

The Impossible Journey

While Barney Oldfield was getting to know California and vice versa, another hard-driving chauffeur, L. L. Whitman, was returning to the state after completing the third coast-to-coast automobile trip in history.

Today the word "chauffeur" has come to mean a hired driver, usually for the rich, but originally it meant the same thing as "driver," with no class associations attached. Lester Lee Whitman—that was his full name, although the newspapers invariably called him L. L. in the custom of the time—was a chauffeur in the original sense, a man who was happiest and most at ease in society when he was far away from it. Some people are just like that: born to roam, born to drive. Whitman was one of them.

Born and raised in Maine, Whitman first arrived in California in the spring of 1901 just shy of his fortieth birthday. Characteristically—because if there ever was a man who loved to drive, he was it—almost as soon as he landed in Pasadena he was heading for the hills in a De Dion Bouton motorette, a sprightly 3½-horsepower French make. A leader in the formative days of the automobile, France hosted the world's first authentic road race (Paris to Bordeaux, 1895), built slick little runners like the De Dion Bouton, and enriched the language of motoring. "Automobile" is a French word. So are "marque," "garage," and "chauffeur."

Whitman was not the first to drive to Yosemite Reserve in an automobile; no one knows who that was. Two San Jose brothers, F. H. and A. E. Holmes, may have been the first from the Bay Area to travel there by car, ignoring the warnings of friends and family worried about the trip because of its danger. Only horses and mules had gone up the narrow dirt switchbacks that snaked up the mountains of the central Sierra. If the brakes on their Stanley Steamer gave out or their tiller broke or their forward-going valve gears chose not to go forward, they'd be in big trouble—trouble that could land them at the bottom of a cliff. Ultimately the brothers survived the journey and arrived in Yosemite Valley in the summer of 1900, about the same time that two southern California motorists also appeared there.

Yosemite was not yet a national park, and its magnificent isolation could be breached only after a hard and dusty two-day ride over the mountains by stagecoach or horse and buckboard. Oliver Lippincott, an artist, photographer, and prominent member of the Automobile Club of Southern California, and another club member drove their vehicles up from Los Angeles to the tiny lowlands town of Raymond, between Merced and Fresno. From Raymond, the jumping-off point for early automobilists into Yosemite, they followed the same route as the Holmes brothers, crawling up the old Wawona Road into the granite throne room of Yosemite Valley.

Before entering the valley, though, they took a side trip over to Glacier Point on the Glacier Point Road. When they reached the overlook with its sensational view of Half Dome and the high country, in true tourist fashion they pulled out their cameras and took pictures. But these early car tourists did something no tourists can do today: drive to the very edge of the Glacier Point cliff. In front of them, only mountains and sky; below them, a sheer drop of thousands of feet. In one of the few photographs that survive from this period, a man, almost certainly Lippincott, poses with his automobile, proudly sitting inside it. Half Dome looms grandly in the background. Next to Lippincott are a strategically placed American flag, furled around a pole, and the man's wife, who's wearing a sour expression as if she's fed up with her husband's posturing and ready to be done with the whole pompous business. But, as proud (or vain) as the man may be, he hasn't let the moment go entirely to his head. Lodged behind the vehicle's rear right tire is a block of wood to stop the wheels from accidentally rolling forward and hurtling him into space.

No photographs of Whitman in Yosemite have survived, although several exist from his famous first transcontinental trip across America, undertaken three years after his up-and-back from Pasadena to the mountains. How Lester looked depended on whether he was starting a road trip or ending one. At the start he had the look of a distinguished middle-aged banker with a neatly trimmed mustache and wispy brown hair on top. By trip's end he looked more like someone who'd rather rob banks than work for them. Grimy and grizzled, swaggering about in canvas leggings with an unbuttoned leather coat, leather driving gloves that reached almost to his elbows, mud-spattered goggles perched atop his forehead, and a bandana tied rakishly around his neck, Whitman had an I-don't-give-a-damn quality about him. Sunburned from being outdoors all day long, dirt covered every inch of him.

A man who knew L. L. described him as "a jovial, adventure-seeking, strong-minded, competitive individual with considerable business acumen, a natural born craftsman and a great storyteller." He smoked cigars and loved to laugh even more than he loved to win, and the butt of his jokes was often himself. "I am always up to something I ought not to," he remarked once, and that something usually was driving an automobile a long, long way.

With side trips, detours, and coming back a different way than they had gone, Whitman and his partner had covered about one thousand miles on their two-week trip to Yosemite. The De Dion Bouton survived with only a busted spring and one punctured tire, and afterward the Pioneer Automobile Company on South Main Street in Los Angeles put it on public display. Pioneer sold Oldsmobiles and Wintons, and its owner, Leon Shettler, was always looking for ways to attract new customers. One way to do that was to sponsor attention-getting endurance runs; another was to drive cars around town so people could see them. Whitman did both jobs for Pioneer in addition to his regular duties as a mechanic.

Another mechanic at Pioneer, Eugene Hammond, became Whitman's running buddy. "My fellow autoist and cheerful companion" was how L. L. described him. With a full head of tangled blond hair, Ham was lean and wiry and strong: "He could lift any wheel of the Olds with one hand," said his admiring friend. Though nearly half Whitman's age, Eugene matched him in his knowledge and love of gasoline rigs. He lived on Delacy Street in Pasadena, not far from Whitman, and after work they'd ride the trolley home and talk about all the places they'd love to go. Both loved to push automobiles to the edge of things, and when they reached that edge, push a little harder to see what would happen. One evening on the trolley L. L. unveiled his craziest idea yet: Why not drive across America?

This was not an original idea, as Whitman knew. Almost as soon as automobiles appeared in America, people started imagining the possibility of driving across the continent. The earliest serious attempt occurred in 1899 when the husband-and-wife team of John and Louise Davis set out from New York City for San Francisco. With John driving and Louise navigating, they made it as far as Chicago before their vehicle, which had been steadily falling apart for some time, collapsed completely. Alexander Winton, an Ohio sportsman and the manufacturer of the popular brand of automobiles sold by Pioneer and many other dealers across the country, took up the cause two years later. Unlike the Davises, he began his attempt in San Francisco, figuring that he needed to tackle the Sierra first while his auto—a Winton, naturally—was still in good running order. Trying to climb the mountains after crossing the rest of the continent meant almost certain failure, he felt.

Leaving from San Francisco and taking the ferry to Oakland, Winton and Charles Shanks, the publicist who accompanied him on the trip, crossed the valley to Sacramento, which served as the gateway city for early automobilists passing into and out of the mountains. They followed current Interstate 80 and after a colossal effort made it across the Sierra, the first to do so by automobile. Their high-powered Winton soon ran aground, however, in the Nevada desert, continually getting stuck in the deep sands and quicksand. They'd dig the wheels out, drive a little, get stuck again, dig out, drive some more, get stuck, dig out, until finally they got stuck in a place that would not let them get un-stuck. With hundreds of miles of desert still stretching out ahead of them, tired and dirty and beaten, they quit. Horses pulled the vehicle out of the sand and loaded it onto a railcar, and the pair rode home to Ohio in the comfort of a Pullman car.

Since he'd been to Yosemite Whitman knew what it would take to cross the Sierra. He also had ideas on how to avoid getting bogged down in Nevada. Whatever he said that night on the trolley, it must have made sense to the good-natured Hammond. Count me in, he said, I'm good to go. What they needed, then, was a sponsor to pay for the trip, and L. L. fell to this task immediately.

Going straight to the top, he wrote a letter to Ransom E. Olds, the founder of Olds Motor Works and a big name in the burgeoning automobile capital of Detroit. Whitman proposed that he and Ham would drive an Olds across the United States, thereby earning priceless publicity for the company and showing off the durability of its vehicles. With their mechanical and driving experience, plus their knowledge of Oldsmobiles, Whitman felt confident they could handle whatever challenges the road offered. Olds loved the idea, agreeing to supply the two men with one of his cars and pay their expenses on the trip. Soon a Model R Olds runabout was shuttling across the West in a boxcar, arriving at La Grande Station in late June.

A reporter described it as "an ordinary Oldsmobile"—a low-priced, low-horsepower, one-cylinder stock model. It also weighed little, a big consideration when attempting a trip of this magnitude. "L. L. Whitman and E. Hammond of Pasadena are driving an Oldsmobile weighing 850 pounds," reads a magazine account from the time. "The two men weigh 350 pounds and they carry 300 pounds of baggage and provisions. They thought the light machine would be an advantage as they can push it along if it breaks down or the supply of gasoline fails." Scout or Li'l Scout, as they dubbed the car, had some style to it; its curved dash in front had a rounded shape almost like one of the snow sleighs Whitman built and rode when he was a boy growing up in Maine. Adapting it for the long haul, they added a luggage box behind the seat, stripped the fenders to lighten it still more, and replaced the stock radiator with a bigger one to help the engine keep its cool in the desert. After Li'l Scout checked out on its test runs around Los Angeles, they drove it down to San Pedro harbor and loaded it onto the steamer *Coronado* for the trip north. San Francisco was to be the beginning of their journey, a journey now complicated by the fact that two other automobiles had already taken off from the city in the hopes of becoming the first to cross the continent. Whitman and Hammond were already far behind, and they hadn't even started yet. Worst of all, neither was much of a seaman, and both spent the voyage up the coast sick in their bunks or heaving over the rails.

The two teams ahead of them were Dr. Horatio Nelson Jackson and Sewall Crocker, in a Winton; and E. Thomas Fetch and Marius Krarup, in a Packard. Of the two, the Jackson-Crocker pairing is easily the more famous, in part because of the perhaps apocryphal story of how Jackson got the idea for his transcontinental dash. A robust, infectiously exuberant thirty-one-year-old Vermont physician, Jackson and his wife, Bertha, were on a tour of California and the West when, one night while having drinks at the University Club in San Francisco, he happened to overhear two men discussing the harebrained idea of driving an automobile across the continent. Their loud talk included disparaging references to Alexander Winton, a man of action whom the doctor may have admired. Unable to hold his tongue any longer, Jackson spoke up forcefully, saying that not only could the impossible be done, he was just the man to do it. One of the men proposed a little sporting action to make the debate more meaningful, and they all agreed to a fifty-dollar wager to see if the good doctor could back up his words with deeds.

So encouraged, Jackson was off and running. His most inspired decision came with the hiring of Crocker, for the man of medicine would have been lost without a man of machines by his side. In his late teens or early twenties, a native of Washington, the shy, sickly Crocker worked as a mechanic in San Francisco, likely meeting Jackson when he taught him how to drive. After signing on for the trip he advised and assisted in all the preparations, including choosing the sturdy, solidly built Winton. Eager to get going, Jackson didn't want to wait for a new import to arrive from the East, so he bought a used Winton from a friend in town. Crocker bolted on a second gas tank and added more luggage space in the back. They gathered supplies, studied the terrain and distances, mapped their route, and less than two weeks after the doctor's bet they were on their way. Their first day, May 23, 1903, Jackson drove from the Palace Hotel, where he and his wife were staying, down Market to the Embarcadero. There he, Crocker, and the Vermont—Jackson's name for his car, in honor of his home state—boarded a ferry to the East Bay. Bertha, who had chosen to pass on a journey that would take months and cross over mountains, deserts, and plains, waved goodbye from the docks. She went back to the Palace, packed her bags, and rode the train back to Vermont. She was home in a week.

Called "the Mad Doctor" by some, Jackson was not as mad as all that. After disembarking in Oakland he and Crocker powered south to Hayward and cut east through Livermore over the hills to Tracy, where they spent the night. The next day they made Sacramento. But instead of turning toward Auburn and following today's Interstate 80 as Alexander Winton had done, they traveled north along modern-day Highway 99, passing through Marysville, Oroville, and points beyond. At Redding they veered northeast into the Cascade Mountains, causing a sensation in every town they passed through. Many of the people in these towns had never seen an automobile before. In Lakeview, just across the Oregon border, nearly every person in town came out to see them.

The doctor and the mechanic reached Lakeview in the first days of June, about six weeks after leaving San Francisco. Ten days later they passed into Idaho and a week after that they entered Wyoming, just as the two men from Packard were launching their version of the impossible journey. The leader was Fetch, another chauffeur in the original sense, a man who felt as comfortable working on a car as he did driving one. Just don't expect him to talk about it. At the first sight of reporters he waved them over to Krarup, an outgoing Danish immigrant who wrote articles and took photographs for the newspapers. For the rugged Western half of the trip a mechanic named N. O. Allyn shadowed the pair on the train, getting off here and there to oil and lube the Packard and tighten the nuts and bolts. Then he'd disappear back onto the train so that when Fetch and Krarup paraded into a new town, everyone could see how well the car was performing.

Before the trip started, the Packard factory in the East had sent "Old Pacific" to San Francisco. On their first day Fetch and Krarup, both Packard employees, drove it from the Packard agency on Market out along the Point Lobos toll road—now Geary Boulevard—to the rolling sand dunes of Ocean Beach on the western edge of Golden Gate Park. Poised majestically on the bluff overlooking the ocean was the castle-like Cliff House, one of San Francisco's most popular tourist attractions. Americans recognized it as the edge of the Far West, making it the perfect place for a photo op at the start of a cross-country trip.

Fetch and Krarup posed for pictures on the beach with the rear tires of Old Pacific dipping into the ocean. Or so it's said, anyhow. No one knows the truth for sure because newspaper accounts of the time differ and photographs from that day were accidentally destroyed. In any case, their ceremonial duties over, the Packardians returned down the toll road to the Ferry Building and then boated across the bay to Oakland, where the pair took a different tack than Jackson and Crocker. Instead of going south they went north through Berkeley and Richmond, where they soon got lost. After driving miles out of their way they righted themselves and made it to Port Costa by nightfall.

Day two started with a bracing morning ferry ride across the Carquinez Strait, followed by the discovery around Vacaville that they had lost their maps and compass. They backtracked until they found them, pushing hard to recover lost time and reach Sacramento by nightfall. At first Fetch and Krarup may have thought they were alone in this attempt to make history, because the two men in the lead, not being sponsored by a car company, shied away from publicity early in their trip. But along the way the press and people in the towns they passed through let Fetch and Krarup in on the news that they were second, not first. Undismayed, when the two entered cities where no one had heard of Jackson and Crocker, Packard's publicity people often claimed that their guys were number one.

Unlike Jackson and Crocker, Fetch and Krarup met the Sierra head-on, departing Sacramento for Placerville in the morning. They made a wiser tactical choice than Alexander Winton, though, climbing into the mountains via the more established Lake Tahoe Toll Road, now Highway 50. They stopped at stagecoach waystations to eat, drink, and rest, several times pulling to the side of the road to let the hard-charging horses of a Nevada stage flash by. They spent the night on the western rim of the Sierra, crossed down into Tahoe Basin in the morning, and enjoyed a fine lunch at the Lakeside Hotel in Stateline.

Pushing on, they ran into the problem that had scuttled Winton-Shanks and that Jackson-Crocker had avoided: the sands of Nevada. Their solution: place two long strips of canvas across the sand, one under each side of the car, the strips forming a bridge for Old Pacific to cross without sinking in. Sometimes this worked, many times it did not. N. O. Allyn came off train duty to help with the pushing and pulling and shoveling, and after seven miserable days and nights in "a country of nothing but sage brush, hills, sand, rattlesnakes and everlasting distances," they spent an exhausted Fourth of July in Salt Lake City.

Although well behind Jackson and Crocker at this stage of the journey, they nonetheless had a two-state lead on the two seasick Californians back in San

Francisco, who were only now staggering off the *Coronado* at Pier 10. Grateful to be back on solid ground, Whitman and Hammond watched the ship's crew lower the Scout down the side of the vessel with ropes. Then they negotiated the traffic up Market Street to the local office of Pioneer Automobile on Golden Gate Avenue for a pre-trip tune-up.

Technically, the three teams were not racing one another. But Whitman and Hammond knew about the two parties ahead of them, and if either or both of them had dropped out for any reason, they would not have been disappointed. With that in mind, they moved quickly to get out of the city and on the road.

In his advance planning Whitman had written to stores along the route, asking them to lay in extra gas and oil for when he and Hammond came through. They had also shipped tires, batteries, and parts to railroad station agents and stagecoach stops on the sure bet that Li'l Scout would be in dire need of all these things and more. Some gear and supplies they brought with them from Pasadena, the rest they bought in San Francisco. "Outfitting included a 100-foot tow rope, a shovel, hatchet, tool kit, five-gallon tin of gasoline, a gallon tin of oil, a can of grease, extra dry batteries, canteens of water, a blanket and a small valise for each man," recalled John S. Hammond II, Eugene's oldest son, who wrote articles and a book to preserve the memory of his father's and Whitman's trip. "There was a first aid kit, fishing tackle, compass, goggles and a large single rubber poncho in which two round open holes had been cut to protect all but their heads from inclement weather." They also packed four specially-made canvas tires, sewn by Sophia Whitman, L. L.'s wife, to help them get across the desert sands.

Other necessities of the road included a camera and film, which they brought out for their July 6 launch party at Ocean Beach. Like Fetch and Krarup, Whit and Ham journeyed out to the Cliff House to dip their wheels into the Pacific, but unlike the unlucky Packard team, existing photographs prove that they actually did it. They pulled a string attached to the shutter of their camera, which was mounted on a tripod, and snapped pictures of themselves sitting on Scout with the Cliff House in the background. Both were dressed nattily for the occasion in uniforms and caps. The next day they held another photo op with San Francisco Mayor Eugene Schmitz on the steps of City Hall. In a hat and double-breasted coat, Schmitz handed over a letter addressed to the mayor of New York City. The letter was to be the first piece of U.S. Mail ever delivered coast to coast by auto. On their way to the Ferry Building Whitman and Hammond stopped at a post office and had it postmarked as evidence of the time and date of their departure.

By mid-afternoon they were across the bay and heading north. While they beat Fetch and Krarup's first day progress, reaching Benicia on the other side of the Carquinez, they bedded down that night knowing their cause was virtually lost. They couldn't possibly be the first ones to drive across America; the other teams were too far in front and driving bigger rigs with stronger engines. But nothing in life or automobiles was certain, anything could still happen, and they lit out the next morning with the great Central Valley of California opening up before them. Taking turns at the tiller, they also took turns getting out to push Scout over a hill or when it got sucked into a mud hole that wouldn't let it loose. Neither Whit nor Ham complained when that happened (not much anyway), because if you were looking for an orderly, complaint-free existence, you did not go on an automobile endurance run. Screw-ups were as much a part of the job as a sore butt. Being two full-sized adults crammed into one small-sized seat that dug into their backs, they rode with their knees scrunched up and almost no room to stretch their legs. Their little roofless vehicle gave them no place to hide from the sun either; it was always there, until nightfall provided relief. Around Cordelia the wind started blowing, and without their goggles it would have been tough to see anything. As it was, the lenses got covered with dirt and mud just like everything else they were wearing. At times over the course of the trip their clothes got so greasy and smelly and dirty they just threw them away and bought a new set. They woke up dirty and went to bed dirty and were dirty all day long. On rare nights they found a place with a hot bath—which was paradise—but the next morning they'd be back on the road and eating dust same as ever.

For all the hardships, though, they loved being on the road more than anything else. Getting up early, having the empty road stretch out before them, seeing the sky dark and gray overhead but with a streak of blue in the distance, and knowing that that was where they were headed, where the blue was—there was nothing like it in the world. In the late afternoon, bands of cream-colored light streamed through the clouds as if divinely sent. Then, as the sun was lowering, the sky and clouds put on a dazzling show of oranges and reds seemingly just for them. At night the stars shone brighter than any they'd ever seen before.

Sometimes it seemed as if the road itself were pulling them along, not the engine or anything mechanical. "Without benefit of printed road maps they picked their way over the Sierras with sketchy hand-drawn maps of their own making, going by way of Sacramento, Lake Tahoe, Carson City and Reno," wrote Hammond's grandson. Wisely following the more-traveled stage route through Placerville and up the western slopes of the Sierra, they made Tahoe on their fifth day on the road. From Stateline they chugged out of the eastern side of the basin over 7,300-foot Daggett Pass. Worried about the brakes giving way, they cut down a small pine, stripped it of its branches, and tied it to Scout's rear axle. The log dragged against the ground and slowed their forward momentum as they came down the steep backside of the mountains.

From Carson City it was on to Reno, where they stopped to buy pith helmets, canteens, and other hot-weather gear. People who had never seen an automobile before crowded around them and asked for rides. When they explained that they couldn't stay, that they had to get going, some people pushed in closer and wouldn't let them leave. Finally Whitman cranked the engine, shut it off, and then quickly turned it back on again. This caused a loud backfire that made everybody jump away, giving the two a chance to escape.

Temperatures in the desert surpassed 115 degrees Fahrenheit. The sands were thick and deep but, thanks to Sophia's sand tires, passable. Her husband and his partner tied the canvas around the regular tires with rope, and they made it without a puncture. But the sand fought back hard. At times Li'l Scout got hung up on knotty ridges in the sand, and the only way to get it free was for Whitman to chop away at the underbrush with an ax while Ham pried the undercarriage loose with a crowbar. Failing this, they had to walk for miles to find someone with a team to pull Scout out of a bad spot. When they got lost, which was often, they looked for the nearest railroad tracks because the tracks always led to a depot with a telegraph operator. If they needed parts they told the operator, who relayed the message down the line, and in short order the parts were headed their way on a railcar. The railroad saved them in other ways too. Sometimes it was easier to simply go off-road and drive on the railroad ties.

Whitman and Hammond pushed as hard as they could, yet all their effort only seemed to put them farther and farther behind the leaders. Jackson and Crocker reached New York City on July 26, becoming the first to cross the United States by automobile. Their total time: 63 days, 12 hours, 30 minutes. In Idaho they had picked up a stray dog, a bull terrier named Bud, who rode with them the rest of the way and became the first dog to cross the country by car. The Packard team of Fetch and Krarup made the trip one day quicker than Jackson and Crocker had, but because they started later, they didn't make New York until August 21, still nearly a month ahead of Whitman and Hammond, who got there on September 17 after 72 days, 21 hours, 30 minutes. After delivering their postmarked letter to the mayor, they pushed on to Boston and posed for a picture with their front wheels in the Atlantic. Then they continued up the coast to Maine, where they visited Whitman's family and friends.

In total, Jackson and Crocker logged fifty-five hundred miles, about fifteen hundred more than the other teams because of their detour around the Sierra. All of them went down wrong roads, took wrong turns, experienced a raft of mechanical breakdowns, endured sun, rain, and other miserable weather conditions, got stuck countless times in mud and sand, and frequently depended on the kindness of strangers with horses to rescue them. All pushed themselves harder than they ever had before, and they and their machines passed the test. Jackson and Crocker became the first to cross the country; Fetch and Krarup, the first to cross the deserts of Nevada; and Whitman and Hammond, the first to cross the continent "in the car of the future," as historian Curt McConnell put it, "a lightweight, simple and cheap machine of the masses."

What is most fascinating about Whitman, however, is that he went on to become the foremost endurance driver of his time, a man who logged more miles behind the wheel of a car than any person of his generation. After his first transcontinental trip he came back the next year and did another. In a ten-horsepower Franklin that was bigger and more powerful than Li'l Scout, he and a new partner obliterated Fetch and Krarup's transcontinental record by going from San Francisco to New York in just 32 days, 17 hours, 20 minutes.

The speed of the crossing turned heads around the country, as did the Franklin's performance. Some cars are runners, and that Franklin with its air-cooled engine ran and ran and ran. Whitman liked it so much he used it for a June 1905 Los Angeles–to–San Francisco race against time. For that one he partnered with Ralph Hamlin, an ex–bicycle repairman turned endurance driver and salesman. Hamlin ran the

Franklin dealership in Los Angeles, where Whitman worked when he wasn't off following a trail somewhere in an automobile.

The two left Los Angeles on a Wednesday one minute after midnight, blasting out at such an early hour to avoid the horse traffic that normally clogged the roads during the day. They carried gas, oil, spare parts, and the canteen that L. L. had bought in Reno on his first cross-country trip. The canteen meant good luck to him, and he carried it on all his endurance runs. Cutting west through the San Fernando Valley with the Santa Monica Mountains on their left, they turned north up the coast with their "searchlights"—the old name for headlights—slicing through the darkness. They chugged up and over a pass and down into the farmlands of Ventura County, fording the Ventura River in thick, damp fog. It was so cold they stopped to build a fire to warm up. Beyond the river they swept around the edge of the land to the ocean, running alongside the railroad tracks in many places. After breakfast and coffee in Santa Barbara they left the water behind as they cut through Gaviota Pass into the hills around Buellton. The road curved them back to the water in Pismo Beach before they again headed inland through the rolling hills of San Luis Obispo. Up 1,500-foot Cuesta Pass, they cut down into Paso Robles, where they spent the night.

Whitman's route-finding experience came in handy throughout the trip, as he had driven these roads before on the way back from Yosemite. The next morning they launched out of Paso into the high desert and along the whitewashed hills on the eastern side of the Salinas Valley. They drove on dry riverbeds and crossed the Salinas River many times, passing over the rolling hills of Gilroy and into San Jose, where they came in sight of San Francisco Bay. Booking up the Peninsula as fast as the Franklin would carry them, they hit the finish line at Market and Third in San Francisco at 1:54 p.m. on Thursday. Their time of 37 hours, 53 minutes smashed the old mark by sixteen hours.

But they had barely gotten back home when they learned that a team of four drivers had just smashed *their* record. San Franciscan Fred Jacobs and his crew drove a Rambler from San Francisco to Los Angeles in 31 hours, 35 minutes, a full six hours faster than the Franklin. In July Whitman and Hamlin tried to recapture the record only to be hit by an unexpected summer squall on the coast. Bogged down in the mudflats around the Ventura River, they quit when they realized they couldn't beat Jacobs's record.

Despite this failure, Whitman and his road-hungry Franklin remained a hot ticket in endurance-driving circles, and he continued to do publicity and make appearances in the vehicle. Not every run was a race against time, though, and in the spring of the next year he decided to combine a little business with pleasure and take a trip to San Francisco with Sophia. They drove the familiar bad roads up the coast, going at a far more leisurely pace than what he was accustomed to, making sure to see all the sights he had gone so quickly by in the past. And not once did they stop to put on sand tires. They reached the city without a problem and had a lovely, romantic dinner at a restaurant. They parked the Franklin in a garage near their hotel, went up to their room, and snuggled in for a well-earned night of rest and quiet. The date was April 17, 1906.

FOUR

San Francisco

The city that Sophia and Lester Whitman fell asleep in and that crumbled and burned the next morning was a city of water and fog and hills. It was also a city that was tough on horseless carriages, which needed to expend every ounce of their tiny amounts of horsepower to climb its majestic hills. And when one of those horseless carriages reached the top of a hill, oh my God, look out! It may have been suicide to drive a car 60 miles per hour on a racetrack, but go down the California or Hyde Street hills relying on the brakes of this era? Now *that* was living life on the edge.

Residing on the tip of a peninsula surrounded on three sides by water, San Franciscans faced a ferry ride every time they ventured out to the East Bay or Marin. If they just wanted to pop in the car and hit the road—forget the ferry—they could go in only one direction: south. Which of course they did, traveling on El Camino Real and other dirt roads originally laid out for and at that time still mainly used by horses and wagons.

Another thing that made San Franciscans sometimes less than cheery about automobiles was the weather. With the cool winds and fog of the city, driving in a roofless car could be a miserable experience, a thing to be endured not enjoyed.

Nonetheless San Francisco, the largest city in a state of 1.5 million, remained a lively center of automobile activity. With some fourteen thousand vehicles in California as a whole, only New York, Chicago, Boston, and Philadelphia had more automobiles than either San Francisco or Los Angeles did separately, and all of these cities—east and west—had messy downtown traffic problems. But autos as yet represented only a minor nuisance compared to the horses. "The traffic consisted principally of horse-drawn wagons and buggies, with the occasional runaway horse for excitement," said one report. Police controlled the traffic by standing on the curb waving their arms or riding bicycles to cover their beats.

Traffic headaches, like chariot races, date back to the Roman Empire, when officials banned chariots and other wheeled vehicles in the center of Rome to relieve congestion. The ban worked so well that the Romans extended it to the centers of other cities in the empire. Borrowing a page from the ancients, San

Francisco and Bay Area lawmakers found that the best approach to coping with this new motorized nuisance was to get rid of it, or try to. Bans on automobiles occurred at various times in Golden Gate Park, at Stanford University, and at Mount Hamilton in San Jose. Supervisors in Marin County passed a resolution proclaiming that it was "essentially a horse-keeping and horse-loving county." Mrs. Arthur Sears of Santa Cruz circulated a similar anti-auto petition in her county, and ranchers and farmers in Hayward and San Leandro also called for a ban on automobiles in certain areas of Alameda County. "It is no longer safe [for a rancher] to venture forth with his load, for some automobile will surely whip around the corner, terrify his horses, and land him in the ditch," reported one.

The most dramatic of these bans took hold in Yosemite. After the pioneering forays of Whitman and other automobilists, more cars started coming to the mountains, and the roads, while never good, got slightly better. Improved roads in turn brought still more people, and the once-forbidding dangers of the route began to seem more like fun challenges to be overcome in the course of a spirited adventure. But some people objected to this annual summer swarm, beginning a debate on the place of automobiles in Yosemite that continues to this day. In 1906 Yosemite Reserve became Yosemite National Park, and the next year federal officials prohibited motorized vehicles from entering the park.

The opposition to automobiles focused mainly on their inability to coexist peacefully with horses. (Air pollution, one of the chief concerns today, did not factor into this debate until the 1950s, when science established a link between car exhaust and smog.) Cars were forever meddling in places where they weren't wanted and didn't belong, hogging the road and muscling aside the wagons. Central Valley farmers deliberately flooded irrigation ditches with water, waiting for an unsuspecting autoist to come by and get stuck in the mud; the only way to spring the vehicle was to pay the farmer to pull it out with his team. After the car passed on, the farmer would lay in wait for the next sucker. Most of these spider-and-fly games occurred on Sundays, the most popular day for city dwellers to rent cars or to take their own ones out of parking garages (few people kept them at home) and explore the countryside.

Like the Automobile Club of Southern California, the AAA of Northern California, Nevada, and Utah led the fight to gain wider social acceptance for the automobile. It posted road signs; published maps; sponsored rallies and races; lobbied for better roads, motorist-friendly laws, and more rigorous law enforcement; defended the rights of drivers; and battled to open up parks and other areas that had banned or severely restricted motor traffic.* In one instance, members of the AAA, who were some of San Francisco's wealthiest and most powerful citizens, successfully lobbied the city to lift its ban on driving in Golden Gate Park.

The club achieved similar success after the Santa Clara Board of Supervisors halted car traffic on Mount Hamilton. Alarmed by the bevy of automobilists driving

---

* To avoid confusion, the club's current name will be used. Its original name was the Automobile Club of San Francisco, which was later changed to the Automobile Club of California after it merged with other northern California auto clubs. For many years it was known as the CSAA—California State Automobile Association.

up to see the new Lick Observatory—Stanford University president David Starr Jordan was among the first to reach the top by car—the board decided that only horse- and mule-powered wagons could go on its steep, winding road. Enlisting the aid of former California governor James Budd, the AAA lobbied the state legislature to pass a law giving motorists the right, among other things, to drive on Mount Hamilton. The Santa Clara supervisors bowed to the pressure, and the mountain once again welcomed cars.

Livery owners, blacksmiths, and others who made money on the horse trade also griped about cars, fearing a possible loss of business due to automobiles. Even the police worried that motorcars would hurt their public image. "The policeman's most frequent opportunity to distinguish himself is afforded by runaway horses," said a 1901 newspaper article. "There is not an experienced officer on the force who has not won honorable mention at one time or another by stopping a team. More than one officer has imperiled his life in the effort to prevent a runaway from doing harm to the lives or property of others." The police won public gratitude and financial rewards for their heroism, but, as the article continued, "if horseless carriages come into general use and the runaway steed is relegated to the boneyard, what opportunities will there be to earn distinction and substantial rewards?"

Automobile drivers drove too fast—that was another complaint. Motorists came up fast, far faster than horses, and they arrived in an explosive, shotgun-like volley of smoke and sound. Innocent people got hurt and killed in these things. Over in Berkeley, another city of hills and delicate sensibilities, a spectacular accident in early April had made headlines in the *San Francisco Chronicle*. "An amateur chauffeur almost caused the death of two well-known society women of this city late this afternoon. While turning the corner of Shattuck Avenue and Center Street the light runabout in which Mrs. Paul Needham and Miss Olive Morrish were riding was enveloped in a flare of burning gasoline. The two women scrambled to their feet, one crawling over the front seat and the other escaping through the tonneau door [an open rear seat or compartment]." The chauffeur, whose name is not mentioned, brought the burning machine to a quick stop and also escaped unhurt.

Thus arose still another gripe about cars: the people who owned them. Mrs. Needham, the article was careful to note, was the wife of "the well-known stationer and clubman," while "Miss Morrish is well known in society on both sides of the bay for her talented voice and is a member of the choir of the St. Mark's Episcopal Church of this town." Only the well-to-do of Berkeley, San Francisco, and other cities across California and America could afford to buy automobiles, not to mention pay the rental for a monthly parking garage and the always hefty, all-too-frequent repair bills. And like Mrs. Needham and Miss Morrish, the rich did not even drive their own cars, hiring a man—it was always a man—to do that for them.

Many of these wealthy car owners were first-generation Americans who had migrated here from the United Kingdom, Ireland, or Europe. Often starting in poverty and hard circumstances, they had risen to achieve great prosperity in this country. Owning and driving an automobile (and letting their children do the same) represented this success; they had made it in this new land and look, here was proof. Friends smiled and commented approvingly when they drove up in their new cars. As fun as they were to ride in and drive, however, cars soon became an object of resentment for those who weren't sharing in the fun, a symbol of what divided the haves from the have-nots in society. If a car got stuck on a hill, people walking by on the street sometimes refused to help push it to get it restarted. They despised the fact that the privileged could afford cars and they could not.

One of California's and America's wealthiest men, John D. Spreckels of San Francisco, became the first person in California to license an automobile under the new state vehicle registration law, passed in 1905. He drove (or had his chauffeur drive) a White Steamer, and the registration fee cost two dollars.

These class resentments notwithstanding, Spreckels and other rich people helped this new and uncertain technology grow by spending money on it, buying cars for themselves, and investing in companies that built cars. These were the days when there was more opportunity than money in automobiles, and investing in them was as volatile as the machines themselves. Investors made money and lost it in heaping sums. But some of this money also flowed into the hands of a different class of individuals: mechanics, chauffeurs, tradesmen, dealers, and inventors. Perhaps because it had more working parts than a mule but could be just as stubborn, the automobile spawned (and is still spawning) endless innovations and inventions designed to make it perform better.

One of the most colorful and brilliant of these early innovators was Daniel Best, an Oregon native who came south in the late 1880s and formed the Daniel Best Agricultural Works in San Leandro. The white-bearded Best, who in his later years looked a little like Colonel Sanders of Kentucky Fried Chicken, pioneered the use of labor-saving steam-powered farm machinery: tractors, combines, harvesters. But like so many others, he fell head over heels for the sweet allure of the gas engine. "Well, I was smitten with the automobile fever, and accordingly set about to construct one," he told his great-grandson in his memoirs. "I tell you, that automobile was a work of art, in my opinion, with all the grace of a mud scow." Built in nine days in 1898, his mud scow was more monster truck than automobile. Possessed of giant wheels, a cloud-producing seven-horsepower engine, able to carry eight passengers at a time and reach speeds up to 20 miles per hour, it terrified every horse that came near it. In the interests of restoring peace to his farm, Best bought a horse's head at a local taxidermist and mounted it on the front of his wagon-car, figuring that if horses saw one of their own coming toward them, they wouldn't be as scared.

Best drove this vehicle for more than a decade—with or without the horse's head, it's not clear—and built a second compact model. "I constructed a second machine, a two-passenger, and later gave it to my son. He in turn traded it for a piano. I think the piano man was cheated. I have often thought that if I had stayed with automobile manufacturing, I could have out-Forded Ford. Perhaps." Best's son Clarence eventually took over his father's business and later merged with the company of another innovative farming man, Stockton's Benjamin Holt, to form Caterpillar Tractor.

Caterpillar's original home factory in San Leandro closed in the mid-1980s, but the company, now based in Illinois, remains a thriving manufacturer of bulldozers and other machinery.

The sunny and gently rolling farmlands around Best's home of San Leandro, along with Oakland to the north and Hayward to the south, became a hotbed for early automobile speed burners. This may have been another reason why some of the ranchers in the area objected to them. "A favorite stunt of the old-timers was the holding of endurance runs over the Hayward–San Leandro road," recalled one of those old-timers. "The machines would run between the two towns, a distance of seven miles, until the cars burned up or the wheels fell off, and the machine that traveled the farthest would be declared the winner." Other popular northern California touring destinations included the Del Monte Forest in Monterey, Witter Springs near Clear Lake, and Skaggs Springs in the Sonoma area. One winner of a Skaggs Springs endurance run "walked around the summer resort with his chest puffed out until the following day, when his car, for no apparent reason, took fire and burned up, despite frantic efforts to extinguish it on the part of the erstwhile proud owner."

Due to incidents like these, which were more common than not, even those not intimidated by machines regarded automobiles with distrust and fear. John Meyer, builder of the first gasoline car in California, found this out in 1897 when he arrived at the Oakland docks hoping to transport himself and his vehicle across the bay to San Francisco. But the ferry operators at the Howard Street pier would not load the car until he drained it of gasoline. They were afraid it would blow up.

This was not the first time Meyer had dealt with opposition to his car, which, evidently aware of its status in California, he named "The Pioneer." A German immigrant with a mustache and sharp, clear eyes, Meyer is a somewhat mysterious figure; men who work with machines often are. He was a family man in his thirties with a good job as a machinist for the J. L. Hicks Gas Engine Company in San Francisco. Then, in 1893, he began disappearing into the basement of his Noe Valley home in the evenings after work and on weekends. His dream: to build an automobile. But like other automobile dreamers of this era, he had little to guide him save his own smarts, instincts, and experience. As the years ticked by—1893, 1894, 1895—all his hard work and experimentation brought him only frustration and failure. His neighbors on 24th Street laughed at him and dubbed the useless mechanical thing in his basement "Meyer's Folly."

Finally, in 1896, he cut a hole in the wall of the basement and rolled his creation into the light of day for the first time. (Meyer's old house, on hilly 24th Street between Diamond and Castro, still stands, though it now has an addition in front of the basement.) Would it run? Would people laugh at him? Meyer could not know any of these things when he turned the crank on his three-speed, water-cooled engine. The work of a carmaker is not theoretical; it either runs or it doesn't, and if it doesn't, it's a failure. The Pioneer ran; it was a success. Even more, it was an improvement. On many horseless carriages the front wheels turned as a unit, but the Pioneer's front wheels worked independently of each other, which made for better steering and handling.

People take pride in their cars the way they do few other things, and Meyer was no exception in this regard. On the back of his all-black, tiller-driven single-seater—its home is now the Oakland Museum of California—a small metal plate reads, "J. A. Meyer, Maker, San Francisco, Cal." And in the middle of the next year, after tootling around Noe Valley and working out the kinks on the vehicle, its maker embarked on his groundbreaking run around San Francisco Bay.

Rattling up to 18 miles per hour in spots, he drove out of the city on Mission Street and then down the Peninsula to the South Bay, turning north at Alviso to go up the Hayward–San Leandro road to Oakland. Having come all that way, Meyer was not about to let superstition stop him, so he emptied the gas tank before boarding the ferry as required. Still, the ferry operators loaded the car last and stowed it in the back of the boat so it could be quickly pushed into the bay at the first sign of danger.

Everyone survived the crossing, and the Pioneer became the first automobile to circumnavigate the lower half of San Francisco Bay. By the next year it had become quite a lively novelty on the streets of San Francisco. At the big parade up Van Ness to celebrate America's victory in the Spanish-American War, its appearance amidst the marching bands and pageantry made such an impression on a young boy that he remembered it a half-century later. "I remember the assembling of a crowd on the north side of Van Ness Avenue between Pine and Bush Streets," said this boy, who grew up to be 1950s radio personality Budd Heyde. "And then came the cavalcade; up Van Ness Avenue, heading north, and traveling on the left-hand of the street, came the funny little mass of ingenuity that was to revolutionize our civilization. And my grandmother, who was a woman of considerable imagination, a strange co-mingling of Victorian propriety and sophistication, had tears in her eyes. And she put her hand on the top of my flat straw sailor hat and said; 'You'll never forget this day; you are seeing history made.'"

If asked, the man driving that funny little mass of ingenuity surely would not have described himself as a history-maker. His Pioneer did not form the cornerstone of a grand enterprise that employed thousands, made millions of dollars, and manufactured automobiles around the country. But he had taken a risk, a risk that was big for him and had paid off in a small but meaningful way, and one that other people—people who supposedly knew better—regarded as folly. A man could feel good about doing something like that, and Meyer did.

With the success of the Pioneer he left his old job at the gas engine company and hung out his shingle as a mechanic, promoting his business by driving in parades and other civic events. He moved his workplace out of his basement to a garage on Valencia Street, and his business cards listed his new occupation: "J. A. Meyer, Machinist and Engineer, Builder of Gasoline Engines." He had two paying customers for whom he'd built two new cars. He stored these vehicles and his beloved Pioneer at his shop, and this was where they were when the ground started shaking on April 18, 1906.

It's an overstatement to say that the earthquake changed everything for automobiles in San Francisco and California. But the calamity that destroyed one of the world's most beautiful cities was an event of global magnitude, one that people from Tokyo to Buenos Aires to Paris read and heard about. Americans especially responded to it with shock and horror, afterward seeking to learn from and absorb its painful lessons.

Immediately after the quake—an estimated 7.8 on the Richter Scale—a hell storm of fires swept through the city, burning everything in its path. Anything with wheels, anything that could move people and save lives, became precious. Horses pulling wagons performed heroically, but automobiles did not startle or bolt at noise and commotion, and they did not grow tired. All they needed to keep going was gas and oil. Suddenly these "devil wagons," as one put it, "turned into chariots of mercy."

"The machines did whatever was asked of them," said William Harvey of the Mobile Carriage Works on Golden Gate Avenue. Harvey sold Pierce-Arrows, and what he did in response to the fires was grab his motoring goggles, crank up a Great Arrow, and start carrying people to safety.

He was not alone. His dealership and others clustered around the city's emerging automobile row on Van Ness, the edge of the burn zone. Pioneer Auto, where Lester Whitman had taken Li'l Scout for a tune-up before his first transcontinental trip, had an office in the neighborhood, as did Cuyler Lee Cadillac and G. A. Boyer's Tourist dealership. The White agency, which had sold John Spreckels his history-making steamer, was building a new showroom and garage—"the finest automobile station in the world," it claimed—on Van Ness. Nearby were J. W. Leavitt Co., which sold Stoddard-Daytons and Reos, and the Middleton Motor Company, the local distributor of Columbias. Young Charles Howard of Buick also sold cars in the area, and he joined Harvey and other agents in grabbing one of the cars available to him and putting it to work. Victims of the quake, some of whom had never ridden in an automobile before, suddenly found themselves racing around the rubble-strewn streets of the city in a fancy new Buick driven by a man who decades later would become famous as the owner of the racehorse Seabiscuit.

J. C. Cunningham of San Francisco rose early that morning to take his runabout out of a downtown garage, planning to grab breakfast before catching the ferry to Oakland on the first leg of a run around the East Bay. That all changed when the earth on Larkin Street erupted. "The car moved and rocked as if some powerful man was shaking it," he remembered. "I jumped from the machine, only to be thrown to the pavement on my side. I could feel the earth pulsating under me like a living thing."

Bouncing to his feet, he jumped out of the way just as a team of panicked horses ran over the spot where he had fallen. A pile of bricks cascaded down from a building and nearly fell on top of him. Terrified people in their pajamas and bathrobes streamed into the streets from buildings that were crumbling: "Just then it seemed as if the whole of City Hall had collapsed, judging from the terrible crash of falling stone and the dust that followed. Men cried like children but such a wild howl it was. I had often heard women and children weep but never had I heard such sounds come from men."

In the chaos of smoke and fire Cunningham spotted a friend who was struggling to carry his aging mother out of harm's way. He ran back to his car, hopped in, and sped after them, stopping to load them in. As they headed down Market they saw "a great unnatural light shining over the buildings. The report went from mouth to mouth that the whole city was on fire."

People ran down the center of the street to avoid the pieces of buildings breaking apart on both sides. Cunningham steered his vehicle carefully around them and the rubble and glass in the street while almost colliding with a pair of wildly racing horses pulling a fire engine. After he dropped off the man and his mother he picked up a woman and her daughter and brought them to safety too. The injured and wounded pleaded with him for rides, and he said yes to everyone, driving them to the makeshift hospitals springing up in Golden Gate Park and other parks outside the burn zone. Gassed up and tuned for the trip he never took, the runabout ran flawlessly.

On one of Cunningham's trips to Golden Gate Park, a soldier stopped him and commandeered the use of the car for the United States Army. The soldier climbed in, and off they sped. Some soldiers did not know how to drive automobiles, relying on men like Cunningham, Howard, and Harvey to handle those duties for them.

Another who answered the call was John Meyer, whose home in Noe Valley escaped destruction. He hustled over to his shop on Valencia, grabbed his car, and started doing whatever needed to be done. It was, said a biographer, "the Pioneer's finest hour." A railroad station at 25th and Valencia served as one of the city's portals for outside aid, and Meyer in his Pioneer carried food and supplies from the station to schools in the area that were converted into emergency shelters and relief centers. The two other cars stored at his garage also saw duty as rescue vehicles.

Shaken suddenly from sleep like the rest of the city, Lester and Sophia Whitman ran out of their hotel and into the streets in panic. When they reached the Franklin, Lester drove his wife to a shelter, then came back to help. "I got out the old, faithful transcontinental car, threw away the hamper, and carried fleeing people to Golden Gate Park, where thousands slept in the open." What struck him most of all, besides the terrible devastation, was the horror on the faces he saw. "The panic of the people was terrible," he said.

Panic gradually gave way to different emotions as the last of the fires sizzled out in a few days. The flames spared no one, rich or poor; the Palace Hotel burned down the same as a Chinatown shanty. Hundreds, perhaps thousands, lost their lives, and countless more were hurt and wounded. Aid poured into the city from around the state and country, and the loved ones of the lost and missing placed personal classifieds in the newspapers hoping for information on their whereabouts. "Miss Dollie Hyland, please communicate with uncle, Michael Hyland," read one of hundreds of such ads. Dollie Hyland may have lost her life or she may have fled to Oakland or one of the other Bay Area cities that opened their doors to the survivors.

Meanwhile the automobiles and their drivers stayed on the job, assisting in the sober work of digging out from the ruins. They transported people and their belongings to ferry and railroad portals so they could leave the city. They carried soldiers, firefighters, police, physicians, nurses, and other rescue workers to where they needed to go. They took food, water, blankets, clothing, and medical supplies to shelters and hospitals. The fires destroyed the telephone poles and wires, and the army and civilian command centers communicated via messengers who usually traveled in automobiles, which also carried gas and oil to supply other rescue automobiles and machinery.

Automobiles carried dynamite too. Some buildings, though still standing, were safety threats and had to be brought down. But the drivers didn't slow down even with explosives aboard, flying around the streets to do their errands. J. C. Cunningham saw a Knox truck carrying cans of gasoline stall at the top of a hill. Instead of looking the other way, the people on the sidewalk rushed forward to push it over the hill so it could resume its mission.

In the days after the earthquake, the *Chronicle* published an article with the headline "Keep Out of the Way of the Automobiles." It read, "The people must give right of way, every consideration and all assistance possible to the machines and their drivers now engaged in most heroic messenger services. Expedience is the chief need in the gigantic task of caring for the sick, the hungry and the homeless. There is no speed limit in a time like this, and had it not been for the swiftness of the automobiles the great work now under way would have been dragging for days."

In a time of extreme crisis the work of automobiles and their drivers drew widespread praise, and many people, especially police, firefighters, and the military, began to reconsider their hostile or indifferent views toward them. This strange, unsettling machine had some practical applications after all. It was becoming useful.

Mack Sennett's Bathing Beauties usher in the era of Hollywood and the automobile.

PART TWO

TRANSFORMATION

FIVE

Suddenly Shrinking State

Lester Whitman returned to San Francisco four months later to find a dead city being slowly brought back to life. People were rebuilding their homes, going back to school and work, reopening businesses. Some downtown firms announced plans to build new "permanent" buildings made of reinforced concrete, not the temporary wood structures that had been tossed up hurriedly in the days and weeks after the quake. Whole streets were being torn up to lay in new water and sewer mains and telephone and electric trolley lines. Many of the cable car lines were also being rebuilt, and it was hard for people to get around the city. This hurt all of the businesses struggling to come back, and many did not make it.

The Sunset Automobile Company of San Francisco was like the Auto Vehicle Company of Los Angeles: a homegrown firm that made automobiles at its own plant, on Mission between Seventh and Eighth. Early in the decade it had made a popular, low-cost steam runabout that it had discontinued in favor of a pricier gasoline model whose two-cylinder, ten-horsepower motor was placed not underneath or behind the driver but in front of the vehicle under a hood. It proved to be a sales success, and two more gas Sunsets—a touring version and a four-cylinder with lots of kick—joined the line in early 1906.

Full of hope about their new cars, the men and women of the Sunset Automobile Company suddenly found themselves without jobs and a place to work. The fires had destroyed everything. Before the earthquake, an Eastern carmaker had offered to buy the company and move it to Massachusetts, but the Californians originally rejected the proposal. When the carmaker repeated its offer after April 18, Sunset, lacking the resources to make a different choice, said yes. But the company did not move east as expected. Rather, it set up shop in San Jose under a new name: the Victory Motor Car Company. There it made Victory cars for nearly two years before returning to San Francisco and reclaiming its original name. Sunset stayed in business until just before World War I, when it shuttered its doors for good.

The agencies on automobile row on Van Ness Avenue went back to the business of selling cars, lifted by the public's good feelings for their heroism. Good feelings, they had; customers, not so much. With so many San Franciscans out of work and strapped for the basic necessities, even the rich found it hard to shell out four thousand dollars for a luxury automobile considered little more than an extravagance.

Those who had cars still went on weekend getaways to places outside the city untouched by tragedy. At least for the moment, no one could view a Sunday spin around Golden Gate Park with quite the same carefree innocence as before.

Whitman did not tarry long in the city; he was just passing through en route to another transcontinental record attempt. His car was a Franklin, but not the same one he had in San Francisco during the earthquake. This one had more muscle—six cylinders, 30 horses, air-cooled engine—and it figured to need every bit of it. His goal was to break his 1904 record of crossing the United States in thirty-two days, and to do so he had recruited four other road warriors to share the driving with him. Hailing from around the country, they gathered with their leader in San Francisco to test-drive the Franklin and plot strategy, posing for a picture that appeared on the front page of the August 2 *Chronicle* sports section. They took off later that same day.

Starting from the Franklin agency on Golden Gate Avenue, Whitman and his team drove down Market to meet Mayor Eugene Schmitz at a prearranged spot. As on his first transcontinental trip, Whitman carried a letter from Schmitz to the mayor of New York, this one expressing gratitude to residents of that city for sending emergency food and medicine after the disaster. Schmitz wrote that this letter was "a particularly opportune way by which to send his greetings to a people and state that responded so quickly and nobly at the moment of San Francisco's great distress; appropriate because the automobile was the one means of travel and communication that survived the fire and earthquake and made relief work possible and effective."

Since it had been raining heavily the past few days, the team ferried past the usual jumping-off point of Oakland and traveled up the San Joaquin River to Stockton, leapfrogging over the flooded roads of the valley to save time. From Stockton they drove in teams of two and three, day and night, in continuous relays of twelve hours apiece. Those not in the car rode the train to an agreed-upon meeting point, switching places with the ones who had been driving the longest, who in turn took the train up to the next changeover point. Switching back and forth they kept themselves fresh and the Franklin surging forward, rolling into Manhattan at midnight on August 17 in a new record time of 15 days, 2 hours, 12 minutes. Nobody toasts a champion like New York City—the *New York Times* called Whitman "a man to do things, a man of obdurate, untiring will, the man to meet obstacles"—and after a few days of toasting and being toasted, the King of the Road returned home to southern California by traincar.

By now Whitman was in his mid-forties, and his career as a transcontinentalist was nearing an end. His final cross-country trip would occur a few years later, when he would reunite with his original traveling mate, Eugene Hammond, and perhaps for reasons of sentiment as much as driving, they would chug across the United States together one last time. After that, he gently eased into a Pasadena retirement. But when he came back into town after his latest record, he still had lots of miles left in him and he teamed up with yet another driving pal, Ralph Hamlin. Hamlin ran the Franklin agency on South Main where Whitman worked, and he had joined Whitman on his Los Angeles–to–San Francisco runs. Dubbed "the original speed merchants" by a writer who covered them, the pair set off for Mount Wilson in Pasadena, a 5,700-foot peak that, like Mount Hamilton in San Jose, had opened a new observatory at the summit. Whitman and Hamlin were the first to reach the top in an automobile, crawling up a horror show of a road so steep and curvy that county officials closed it to automobiles soon after.

The two Franklin men did such "stunts," as these runs were called, because they enjoyed the speed and adventure of driving, and loved setting records and making firsts. But they were also running a business, and these stunts also helped create excitement and attract attention in the hotly competitive Los Angeles car market.

A local commentator boasted, "There are probably more automobiles in southern California than in any other section of the country." While this was not quite true yet, automobile agencies were popping up all over town, trying to outsell, out-hustle, and out-excite one another. Also on South Main were the W. Cosby Company (selling Premier), A. W. Gump Auto (Jackson, "The Car That Climbed Old Baldy"), H. O. Harrison Company (Oldsmobile), Don Lee Motor Car (Cadillac), and Maxwell. The Auto Vehicle factory held down the corner of Main and Tenth. Dolson Motor Cars and P.D.Q. Auto Rentals did business on South Spring. Leon Shettler dealt Reos and KisselKars on South Grand, a short hop away from W. K. Cowan (Rambler), A. C. Steward (Dorris), and the National Auto Company. The White garage on South Broadway sold the White, Hartford, Pope, and Tribune. At various times Earle C. Anthony's Western Motor Company offered Buick, Northern, Packard, Pope-Toledo, Stevens-Duryea, Thomas, and National Electric's Edison Battery Wagon.

Clearly, Angelenos loved their cars. But why, precisely? The warm, dry weather that allowed them to drive comfortably year-round? The abundance of scenic daytrips close at hand? Some commentators, usually from the East and often unfamiliar with the city, speculated that southern Californians took to the automobile because they lacked adequate public transportation. But in fact they had a rich menu of trolley and train offerings from which to choose: Pacific Electric, Los Angeles Railway, Southern Pacific, and other lines all around the area. They preferred the automobile in part because of the sheer size of the region and the distances people needed to travel to get around it. California covered a geographical area larger than Connecticut, Delaware, New Hampshire, New Jersey, New York, Massachusetts, Maine, Rhode Island, Ohio, and Vermont combined. A trolley or train simply couldn't take folks all the places they wished to go.

Nevertheless, hot commodities as they were, automobiles did not start themselves up and drive off the showroom floor. First you had to get people's attention, draw them down to the agency, and then sell them. Just ask Leon Shettler; he'd tell you.

Shettler was Whitman's ex-boss at the Pioneer Automobile Company. When Whitman was driving Oldsmobiles and Shettler was selling them, he had supported his employee's transcontinental dreams. But now Whitman was pushing Franklins and Shettler was selling Reos and KisselKars, and they had turned into vigorous competitors.

Shettler hated to lose, just hated it. Didn't matter if it was sales or racing, he wanted to win every time. He had a thing against another of his competitors, F. C. Fenner, who sold White steamers and ran the Big Horn mine near Mount Baldy in the San Gabriels. Described in the local press as "impulsive," Fenner bragged that one of his Whites could lick one of Shettler's Reos, straight up, in a race to Mount Baldy. To back up his claim he deposited two hundred and fifty ducats—"ducats" being slang for "dollars"—at the office of the *Los Angeles Examiner* and dared Shettler to do the same. Declaring that the race wasn't about money but rather "holding up the reputation of my car," Shettler answered the challenge by raising the bet to five hundred ducats, which Fenner promptly matched.

The contest turned out to be a dud. Fenner knew the area far better than his rival and his 18-horse White easily clipped the wings of the Owl, Shettler's name for his racing Reo. In another of his impulsive gambles, Fenner challenged a Santa Fe passenger train to a forty-mile sprint across the desert. His car won that one too, although the train made a stop along the way.

Fenner and Shettler butted heads again in 1908, in the first running of what came to be known as the Cactus Derby, a rough-and-tumble road race across the forbidding stretches of desert between Los Angeles and Phoenix. Only a few automobiles had made the entire 450-mile trip into Arizona Territory, still four years away from statehood, so the Derby was part race, part survival test. Seizing the opportunity to stick a needle in his rival, Fenner entered the "steady old boat" he called Black Bess, saying his steamer would be the only car to finish the race. Shettler answered by throwing five hundred dollars into the pot to make Fenner put up or shut up. "He is sincere in his desire to make the entrance fee high," said a reporter about Shettler. "He declares that with such a price there will be 'talk' only from those who really intend to make the run." But Fenner kept right on yapping because he thumped Shettler's KisselKar and two other cars in the race. Following generally along today's Interstate 10, Fenner reached the offices of the *Arizona Republican* in Phoenix in 30 hours, 36 minutes. Two of the cars got lost in the desert, but all four made it to the finish.

Until its end in 1914, when Barney Oldfield won the last one ever held, the Cactus Derby helped spur interest in the southern route across California from the east. The Mojave Desert acted as a physical and psychological barrier that separated southern California from the rest of the country. Only the railroads could broach it before, but now automobiles were making inroads across it too.

This was not just true in the desert: it was happening all over California and the West. A onetime Michigan road surveyor turned roughriding automobilist, Harris Hanshue made one of the earliest runs from Los Angeles to San Diego, sailing through the fruit groves of Orange County before the beaches of San Juan Capistrano stopped him cold. "We hit the sand on the beach—two hundred yards of it and into the hubs," recalled Hanshue, who paid three men to help him push his Reo out. The next stretch of beach was worse: "A snake would have broken his back trying to crawl over it. I came down the hill full tilt and dived headlong into the sand again up to the axles and then some." To get out of this predicament he found some boards on the beach and slid them under the wheels for traction. They spun and sputtered and dragged the vehicle into the clear. More sand troubles followed until finally he crested a hill overlooking Oceanside. "So I coasted down into that burg. Incidentally, we located the wrong road with considerable precision." His travel time to San Diego: a hard-fought twelve hours.

Motorists needed to know the condition of the roads before starting a long-distance trip. The tales of these endurance runs in the papers provided the latest news on the roads and also argued for their improvement.

Being part of the well-traveled coastal route to San Francisco, the roads to Santa Barbara from Los Angeles were a day at the beach compared to the ones in the south. In another run in a Reo, Hanshue booked one hundred and ten miles to Santa Barbara in just under seven hours. Also competing in this run was a Rambler driver named P. A. Renton, who actually beat Hanshue's time to Santa Barbara. But speed was not the sole measure of success. Similar to the point-scoring system of the Glidden Cup runs of the East, cars left the starting line at staged intervals and did not compete directly against one another. Gas mileage, mechanical performance, and driving prowess figured into the winning criteria in addition to the time. When a spark plug wire came loose and Renton stopped to fix it, it cost him points in the overall scoring and knocked him into second despite his faster running time.

Renton also challenged the roads to San Diego, going the inland route instead of the coastal one Hanshue took. Accompanied by reporter Charles Fuller Gates, he found the roads to be "muddy and rather heavy" but in pretty good shape; the proof was that they did not need to put tire chains on for the entire route. Following the new road signs posted by the Automobile Club of Southern California, Renton and Gates saw ten other cars on the drive. One of these challenged their Great Smith roadster to a gentlemanly test of speed, but Renton smoked it with ease. The run was supposed to end at the *San Diego Union* office, but when they knocked on its front door at a little before 5 p.m., everyone had already gone home for the day. So they went over to the nearby Hotel Brewster and checked in with the manager, who recorded their official finishing time of nine hours, more than two hours faster than the old Los Angeles-to-San Diego inland record.

Renton, who later ran a successful Overland dealership in Los Angeles, belonged to the Automobile Dealers Association. So did Shettler, Hanshue, and Ralph Hamlin, its president. Fired by self-interest and honest feeling for these machines, these dealers sold cars, drove cars, talked cars, raced cars, repaired cars, promoted cars, sponsored car races, rallies, and tours, loaned cars for parades, fed car items to reporters, and advertised cars. The newspapers, anxious to encourage this growing source of revenue (which included selling space for classified ads for used cars), assigned reporters like Gates to cover automobile activities, in some cases even running their articles with bylines, unusual for the time.

Another reason why automobiling commanded space in the papers was obvious: it made for good copy. "What becomes of the men who drive and ride in the cars?" asked Bert C. Smith, another automobile writer. "Some of them become speed maniacs and meet their finish on track or road. Others graduate into the sales department of auto agencies."

Another speed-maniac car salesmen, the dashing Harry Harrison, raced from Los Angeles to the Mojave Desert and back again in a single day, enough of an achievement in 1905 to merit a lengthy article in the paper with his picture. His most sensational race occurred when he and two passengers set the Los Angeles–to–Bakersfield driving record of 5 hours, 52 minutes. After a quick stop in Bakersfield for gas and to fix a broken bolt on the Olds, Harrison and his mates continued on toward Fresno, determined to own that record as well. But south of the city they started running low on gas with no place to get any more. While Wild Harry kept the Olds surging forward, his teammates yanked the two kerosene lamps off the side of the car and poured the contents of each into the gas tank. It ran dry just as they reached a grocery store in the small town of Fowler. Buying two tins of gas, they filled up and streaked onward.

"Crowds on the streets of Fresno watched the thrilling finish, which brought the car to the center of the city at a speed far in excess of the speed limit." Nobody cared about that, though; they just wanted to see Harry set the record—and set it he did, roaring up to the four-story Hughes Hotel, Fresno's biggest building, in a triumphant 9 hours, 58 minutes, 30 seconds, shattering Renton's old mark by more than four hours and becoming the first to reach Fresno from Los Angeles in less than ten hours.

Afterward Harrison moved to San Francisco and became the Olds and Peerless agent for California and the West. Car dealerships covered wide swaths of territory, with a home office in San Francisco or Los Angeles overseeing smaller satellite agencies around the state and region. This was another reason for these runs: to showcase automobiles in the countryside.

It was also a way to make some fast ducats. Players in and out of the automobile business gambled on these races, and the size of these jackpots inspired mechanics to find ways to get their cars to go faster and drivers to whip them harder. One Los Angeles-to-San Francisco race between a Harrison-driven Olds and a Pope-Hartford featured a betting pool of ten thousand dollars.

Still more was at stake in these races than just money or sales or breaking records. Something fundamental in the lives of Americans was changing. Bakersfield and Fresno were in the same locations they always had been, but after Harry Harrison's dramatic race against time they had inched a little closer to Los Angeles. The same was true of San Diego after P. A. Renton's run, and of Santa Barbara after Harris Hanshue's. Lester Whitman, Ralph Hamlin, and many others had steadily lowered the travel time between Los Angeles and San Francisco, and Whitman especially had shrunk the distance between the two coasts. All over the state and country everybody was being pulled a little closer to everybody else, and the people at the center of this revolution in time and space were car salesmen. Fancy that.

Attitudes about nature were shifting as well. Places that had once been remote and hard to get to were no longer quite so remote. How people viewed a mountain or a hill—what it would take to get to the top of it—was changing because a car, for all its problems, almost always got there quicker and easier than a horse. And yet driving did not insulate one from nature. A trip in an automobile brought a person face to face with the elements and often required getting out to push or change a tire. It was a hardy, outdoors experience too rugged for many city slickers who would never dare venture outside of town in such a contraption.

Accounts of the exploration and settling of California and the West hardly ever mention the automobile. The stories are mainly of pathfinders in buckskin, the pioneers in wagons who came after them, the gold rush, of course, and the epic story of the building of the transcontinental railroad. But the West continued to be explored well into the automobile age. Unlike, however, the transcontinental railroad, the story of automobiles is not of one vast enterprise; it consists of countless small enterprises and individuals, all going in lots of different directions at once and making only tiny, incremental advances that are easy to overlook or ignore. But the cumulative effect of all those small steps was not small. It was monumental. It transformed society.

The most influential of these knights of the roaring road was Earle C. Anthony, owner of the Western Motor Company of Los Angeles. Nobody outsold, outhustled, or out-excited Anthony, who knew how to close a deal as well as anyone who ever hawked a car. Modern usage has dropped the "e" at the end of "Earl," but he spelled his name the old-fashioned way, and that extra "e" provides a window into his personality and what he brought to the car business. Tall and slender with a long, almost sad-looking face, E. C., as his friends called him, possessed that little something extra, the cherry on the top, that kept him one step ahead of his competitors. Described by writer Lynn Rogers as having "a visionary look in his eyes," E. C. was an optimist at heart who believed in the power of human ingenuity to fix what ailed the present and to make the future a better place. The man who would pioneer the modern service station, bring neon to America, usher in the marriage of automobiles and radio, and advocate for a bridge between San Francisco and Oakland liked big things, big things with vision, and he had ideas the way a haberdasher has hats. One of those ideas was simple and not original with him: customer service. Energetic and hardworking, he treated his customers well and dealt in quality, and people liked doing business with him.

Born in Illinois, Anthony arrived in Los Angeles with his family as a boy. A mechanically minded youngster with the smarts of Carl Breer, he decided, at age seventeen, to build a homemade electric car. "I will tell you a secret," he wrote a family friend in 1897, "but you must not write out to Los Angeles about it. I am making an Electric Horseless Carriage. It is nearly done, and I expect to have lots of fun riding about town." His Electric Horseless Carriage—the capitals are his—was a trumped-up wooden buckboard wagon with a 1.5-horsepower electric motor. It ran on bicycle tires with bicycle forks, and a broken-down wheelchair supplied the transmission. Its owner, sporting a dapper bowler hat with his pants rolled up in cuffs, steered by means of a lever bolted to the side. "To everybody's surprise but his own," remarked Rogers about the vehicle, "it actually ran," giving Anthony lots of good clean fun and one celebrated crack-up. Coming too fast down the Beaudry Street hill one day, he hit a chuckhole and crashed—the first car wreck in Los Angeles history, say some.

The very definition of an overachiever, Anthony became student body president of Los Angeles High and delivered the commencement address at graduation. At the University of California at Berkeley, his next stop, he edited his senior class yearbook and founded a campus humor magazine, the *California Pelican*, which lasted more than three quarters of a century. After receiving a degree in mechanical engineering at Berkeley and doing a year of postgraduate study at Cornell, he returned home to Los Angeles, where he formed Western Motor with the money he had earned in college writing freelance articles for newspapers.

In Western's early advertisements, Earle's father Charles and another man were listed as president and secretary-treasurer, respectively. But it was always Earle's show; he was the go-to guy, a young, rising star in a young, rising industry where there was no such thing as a Big Three and still lots of room to move and breathe and take risks. Somebody with smarts and pep and perseverance—somebody with that little extra something—could make money selling cars, and Earle C. Anthony saw no reason why that somebody couldn't be him. Plus, with his insider's knowledge of the news business, he knew how to get his name in the papers and garner publicity for what he was peddling.

The car he drove at one Riverside endurance run made a reporter do a double take: "The aurora borealis of machines, Earle C. Anthony's specialty-finished machine looks like a cat having a fit in a dish of tomatoes." Another of his rides was "finished in apple green with a maroon running gear. Anthony insists it isn't a loud finish, but something quite simple and chaste." Generally speaking, simple and chaste doesn't get you ink in the papers, which was why E. C.'s taste in automobiles, at least when he was young and on the make, tended toward cats and tomatoes.

But his cars weren't just for show; they had some brawn too, and he ran them hard. The Pasadena-Altadena Hill Climb was a mile-plus sprint around the backcountry roads of Pasadena and Altadena. Sponsored by the Auto Vehicle Company, it grew out of the early automobile adventures of Waldeman Grant Hansen and other drivers taking test runs in the Tourist. Combining elements of racing and endurance, the course ran up Santa Rosa Avenue—now the site of the famous holiday street Christmas Tree Lane—and at one point crossed some trolley tracks. When the racers hit the tracks their cars lifted off the ground, all four wheels in the air, to the uproarious delight of spectators. Not so pleased were the race organizers, who had built a temporary wooden bridge over the tracks to cut down on the flying and the wild crack-ups it caused. They also straightened out the wickedest curves and banned women from riding in the cars. "We do not care to risk women's lives in races against time," said one official. Anthony blazed around the course in just over two minutes, setting a record for the event and promoting his business in the process.

The car he drove that day was a Packard, the car he became most identified with later in life and sold in magnificent showrooms around California, including one on Van Ness Avenue in San Francisco that still stands. But in his early days as a dealer he sold lots of different makes, including the Thomas Flyer, the lone American representative in the biggest automobile endurance run ever, the 1908 New York to Paris Race.

New York to Paris was truly a big thing, a big thing with vision, and it captured the attention of people around the world, even those who opposed automobiles or showed only a meager interest in them. One reason for this was the mad audacity of the planned route: from New York to California, up through Canada and Alaska, over the frozen Bering Strait into Siberia, and across Russia and Europe to Paris. The original idea was to stay entirely on land, avoiding boats and water crossings, but the organizers soon lowered their ambitions somewhat by eliminating the trans-Canadian drive to Alaska. Under the revised plan drivers were to cross to San Francisco, go by rail to Seattle, and catch a ship to Alaska where they would resume the land race across the Bering Strait and Siberia. (Decades later Hollywood would make a comedy, *The Great Race*, based on the event.)

The race began February 12, 1908, with more than fifty thousand spectators watching in Times Square. Of the thirteen cars that signed up to participate, only six showed up at the starting line: three from France, one from Germany, one from Italy, and the Thomas Flyer from the States. Not one to let a potential sales opportunity pass him by, across the country in Los Angeles Anthony had placed ads in the local papers trumpeting his association with the car. His Olive Street salesroom also posted a large American map on the front window for those who wished to follow the progress of the race. Toy cars would be moved around the map, signifying how each team was faring.

But big snowstorms in the East crippled the race cars, causing a rash of spills, crashes, and delays. Things did not get much better in the Midwest when the snow turned to freezing rain. Even so, interest in the race remained phenomenal. Newspapers around the world carried daily reports on it and tens of thousands of Americans lined the streets of the route when the racers passed through their towns. Adding to the excitement, the Thomas Flyer surged into the lead and remained in front as the cars crossed the western deserts and set their sights on the mighty Sierra.

Here again, weather played a decisive role, as heavy snows around Lake Tahoe blocked the passes. Since none of the cars could get across the mountains, race officials decided to send them on a detour down Nevada and around the southern tip of the Sierra into the Mojave. From there they could head north into the Central Valley toward San Francisco.

When Earle C. Anthony heard about this change in the route, however, he had a different idea. Why not bring the Flyer to Los Angeles?

As luck would have it, E. L. Thomas, vice president of the Thomas Motor Car Company, was in Los Angeles visiting dealers in the area when the route change was announced. He had intended to go to San Francisco and meet the Flyer there—that is, until the top distributor of Flyers in southern California bent his ear. The car was coming south and it had already taken one big detour, right? One more little detour wouldn't slow it down that much, and look at the upside: they'd sell more Flyers, stir up excitement, make Los Angeles part of a great national and international event, and create a glorious, horn-honking spectacle. Anthony's sales job instantly hooked Thomas, who announced to the press and public that he would order the Flyer to make the detour to Los Angeles.

The ecstatic Anthony grabbed a Thomas car at his agency and, with E. L. aboard, headed east toward the desert for a rendezvous with the Flyer. In those days there was no Interstate 5 over the Grapevine, no direct route from Los Angeles to the Central Valley. Drivers had two choices, neither of them good. One, they could go north through the San Fernando Valley, climb the Newhall Grade to the Saugus area, and turn east through the Antelope Valley to Palmdale and Lancaster. From there they'd link up with what would later become Highway 99 and head north to Bakersfield. The second choice was somewhat easier but longer; it proceeded east through San Bernardino and Victorville roughly along modern Interstate 15 before making the turn north to Mojave and ultimately Bakersfield. This was how Anthony and Thomas went, driving for hours until they came to the tiny Mojave Desert mining settlement of Daggett.

Daggett was no-man's-land—and no woman's either. Freezing cold at night, blistering hot during the day, it consisted of a telegraph office and a few weather-beaten shacks at the junction of the Santa Fe and Salt Lake railroad lines. A reporter who went there to cover the race described it as "hot as a furnace, where the sun bakes the landscape a red brown, and where there is no shade." But Anthony and Thomas weren't there for the sightseeing; they had some jobs to do. One was to bring food and supplies to the Flyer's four-man crew for when they reached Daggett. Another was to order gas and oil, which arrived via the railroad. Their last and most important job was to get in touch with the Flyer's driver, Harold Brinker, and his three-man crew. They were somewhere in the deserts of Nevada, steaming south, although their exact whereabouts were unknown. So Anthony and Thomas spent lots of time in the Daggett telegraph office, firing off wires to anywhere and everywhere they thought the Flyer might stop. But they heard nothing in reply. Frustrated by the lack of response, they drove outside of town to see if they could track down the Flyer themselves. All they found was desert and more desert, sending them back to Daggett to fire off more unanswered telegrams.

"Reports that the car had been wrecked in a mudhole, that it was lost in the desert, and that the crew had given up the race began to reach Daggett soon after the arrival of Mr. Thomas," said one account. "These reports did not worry the young man who maintained his air of confidence that the car would reach Daggett right side up."

Thomas and the equally confident man at his side felt sure that despite the uncertainties, Brinker and his crew would appear in Daggett on the scheduled arrival day of Sunday, March 22. In the whole history of Daggett, nobody had ever made this much fuss about the town, and every miner within forty miles showed up to greet the Flyer that morning. After a small celebration, Anthony and Thomas planned to escort the Flyer south through Victorville and then on to San Bernardino, where it would pick up another automobile escort that included G. Allen Hancock, the wealthy and influential president of the Automobile Club of Southern California, and Los Angeles Mayor Anthony Harper and his wife.

With his flair for seizing the moment, Anthony had placed an ad in the Sunday papers proclaiming that the "Thomas Flyer, America's Winner, Will Be in Los Angeles Today." News articles had provided the details of the Flyer's expected route across southern California, and scores of automobiles and tens of thousands of people from Cucamonga to Monrovia took a cue from the miners of Daggett and came out to see America's winner. In the little town of Duarte, more than one hundred cars lined its main street. In Pasadena, "almost every auto in town was on the road with a gay party of rooters who were ready to cheer the racer." Once they arrived in downtown Los Angeles, Brinker and the crew would meet the press at the *Times* building before heading over to Western Motors for more photo opportunities. While the Flyer was getting tuned up, they'd be guests of honor at a gala banquet at the fabulous new Alexandria Hotel on Spring Street, hosted by Mayor Harper and other dignitaries. Rested and restored, America's team would return to the road and head off to San Francisco via the coastal route.

That was the plan anyhow. But it never happened.

Brinker and his men knew nothing about the proposed detour to Los Angeles. The first they learned about it was when they reached the town of Mojave and found the pile of telegrams from Anthony and Thomas asking them to come to Daggett. A quick check of the map showed that Daggett lay more than fifty miles to the south and that Los Angeles was even farther out of their way.

Race rules clearly stated that the choice of what route to take belonged to the racers and no one else. Brinker did not hesitate. He wired Thomas to tell him that he wouldn't be coming to Los Angeles after all, and he and his crew lit out for Bakersfield. Anthony and Thomas learned the news too late to inform the newspapers, and all of southern California turned out to see a sight that never appeared.

His big vision in tatters, the deeply disappointed Anthony beat an inglorious retreat back to Los Angeles. Yet Thomas was not ready to concede defeat, catching the train to Bakersfield and wiring Brinker's hotel to order the driver to wait for him there. Brinker saw the telegram in the morning and after he and his mates wolfed down a quick breakfast, they busted loose for Fresno. Thomas never did catch them, and they never went to Los Angeles.

California's biggest parades for America's winner occurred in the Bay Area. After getting lost in the swamps around Los Banos and being rescued by a group of San Jose automobilists, the Flyer received a grand welcoming celebration in Oakland and an even grander one in San Francisco when its ferry berthed at the foot of Market Street. It was, said the *Chronicle's* W. H. B. Fowler, "the hour of the automobile in San Francisco." Thousands of cheering people and a bevy of honking automobiles festooned with American flags led the Flyer through a city richly deserving of a little fun and frivolity.

After a short, champagne-soaked stay in San Francisco, the Flyer's crew loaded their vehicle onto a railcar and headed off to Seattle while the second-place car in the race, the Italian Zust, followed their tracks across the desert toward the suddenly popular Daggett. After Anthony left town, another forward-thinking automobile dealer, H. D. Ryus of White Cars, had wired the Italians to see if *they'd* like to come to Los Angeles for a celebration. The Italians thought this a wonderful idea, and Ryus met the crew of three at Daggett and escorted them into the city with Harry Harrison in an Olds and some other agents.

Although not quite the civic event everyone had expected, "thousands of people lined the streets through which the racer passed" in Arcadia, Pasadena, and other cities. Italians in Los Angeles, waving Italian and American flags, were ebullient. "At North Main Street a crowd of five hundred Italians blocked the street and at the Italian Club the car was forced to stop while the visitors were toasted." After leaving the city the Italians passed through Santa Barbara, where residents showered them with flowers and gifts of food. More gifts and celebrations followed in San Francisco before they shipped the Zust not to Seattle or Alaska but to Japan.

The two other cars still in the race, the French De Dion and German Protos, arrived in San Francisco and did the same, throwing America's car temporarily out of the lead. In Seattle the Flyer had caught a ferry to Alaska only to head back to Seattle after deciding that the scheme to cross the Bering Strait was pure madness. Race judges awarded the Flyer some extra days of travel time because of its side trip to Alaska, and penalized the Protos team for transporting their vehicle on a train part-way to San Francisco. Back in Seattle, the Flyer shipped across the Pacific to Japan, drove across that country, rode another freighter to Russia, and then set out on land again as the De Dion dropped from the race due to mechanical problems and the Zust and Protos suffered a series of setbacks in the frozen wastes of Siberia.

The German car arrived in Paris four days before the American one, but because of its partial train crossing of the United States and the time penalties levied against it, the judges knocked it down to third place. The winner was the Thomas Flyer. It reached the finish line at the Paris office of *Le Matin* on July 30, some 171 days after leaving Times Square. The Zust finished second, the only other car besides the Flyer to drive the whole way on its own power. Only one person, George Schuster, who started with the Flyer as a mechanic in New York and then took over the driving after it reached San Francisco, made the entire twenty-two-thousand-mile, three-continent trip. And when he stepped out of his car onto the streets of Paris, cheered by onlookers, dirty and bone-tired and grateful to have found journey's end, the world had suddenly become a smaller place too.

SIX

Machine Politics

The year after the Great Race, another cross-country adventurer approached California with the dream of scaling the eastern flanks of the Sierra by automobile. This adventurer had begun in New York, changed numerous flat tires, repaired the engine many times, slept in the car and on the ground, navigated by using telegraph poles in an unmapped stretch of Wyoming wilderness, crossed a river over a railroad trestle bridge, battled bugs and assorted crawling things, gone days without a bath or clean clothes, endured rainstorms and intense heat and cold, and driven on some of the worst roads this nation had to offer.

But this automobile adventurer was different than all the ones who had made this journey in the past. She was a she.

And yet something other than her gender separated Alice Ramsey, age twenty-two, from nearly all the transcontinental automobilists who had come before her. The men had buddied up in teams of two or more and usually split the driving. Not Alice. She did all the driving herself.

Her companions on this two-month journey were her friend Hermine Jahns, age sixteen, and her two sisters-in-law Nettie Powell and Margaret Atwood, both in their late forties. Not once did they take the wheel from Alice, who insisted on driving every mile.

In a trouble spot in Iowa, when her companions abandoned the Maxwell for the train, Alice refused to leave the car. Independent, good-humored, and possessed of what can best be described as pluck, she had made it that far and was not about to change. She drove to the station where she met her friends after their brief train ride. They piled back into the Maxwell and off they sallied, with Alice at the helm.

Of course, even if Alice had wanted to rest for a spell and let one of the others take the wheel, they wouldn't have been much help. They likely didn't know how to drive, which was not unusual for women in 1909. This was partly why Alice felt so determined. Being a passenger in an automobile was passive, whereas driving put one in control; Alice understood the difference, and this was why they would've had to fight her to get that steering wheel out of her hands. Her goal was to become the first woman to drive coast to coast across America.

But first she had to get over the mountain roadblock that had stymied the Great Race drivers. "There was great unspoken tenseness in this final lap of the long trek," she wrote in a book published years later about her trip. "As each passenger settled herself for the ride which would actually take us into California, I thought I could almost *hear* the sense of satisfaction silently breathed forth."

From Carson City they traveled up roads that roughly followed today's Highway 50 but of course looked nothing like today's Highway 50. "The Sierra range confronted us with sudden steepness as we started the climb to its crest. The road was heavy with sand. This was in truth no automobile highway. It was an old wagon trail over the mountains and the grades were stiff. Traffic was largely trucking wagons and powerful horses, mules or even oxen—sometimes just men in the saddle." The roads switchbacked up the steep grades, and Alice stopped and cut the motor at the end of each turn to avoid overheating the four-cylinder, 30-horsepower engine. "First a long pull; then rest and cool off at the turn—only to double back up the side of the mountain at a constantly higher altitude. Those waits at the turns brought from each of us, 'Oo-o, what a wonderful view.' What clarity in the atmosphere and how the peaks stood out against the azure sky!"

Hauling four people and their gear, the road-weary Maxwell whined and wheezed. "The carburetor was feeling the altitude but the engine kept on pulling," Ramsey wrote with obvious admiration. She decided to help it out by raising the hood as they drove up through the stands of pine and cedar. "To give the engine all the ventilation possible we raised the sides of the hood and turned them back under. It was a noisy, rattling arrangement, but the motor was grateful for the extra circulation of air and rewarded us by pulling all the harder if the grade demanded."

Being early August, snow had vacated the passes guarding Lake Tahoe and the well-ventilated Maxwell delivered the women to the top of Spooner Summit and then down into Tahoe Basin. "Majestic sugar pines, Douglas firs and redwoods lined our road on both sides," she exulted. "What a land! What mountains! What blue skies and clear, sparkling water!"

A little while later, a dull moment of prose interrupted all this poetry. They had a flat tire.

This was nothing special; it had happened at least ten times so far on the trip. The job of changing it fell to Ramsey, the team's head mechanic—its only mechanic. Shedding her "duster" or driving coat, the Vassar graduate got down on the ground in her ankle-length dress, placed the jack under the axle, and cranked the busted tire into the air. Using pliers and tire irons, she popped the rim, removed the casing, and pulled out the tube inside it. After applying rubber cement to the hole, she pumped the inner tube with air, calling on her three companions for help. They responded, enthusiastically. Ramsey then remounted the tire and in short order they were back enjoying the sights in South Lake Tahoe on their way to Meyers and the switchbacks up Echo Summit.

When Alice, a true motorhead, talked cars with Hermine, Nettie, and Margaret, they didn't have a clue what she was saying. Their minds immediately drifted off to another place as they nodded in an understanding and supportive way. Still, they took directions well and did whatever their captain asked: pump, push, pull, lift, carry. When the Maxwell's radiator dried up in the midst of a Midwest rainstorm, they all dug into their suitcases—each woman had one suitcase apiece—and pulled out the small cut-glass cups with the sterling silver tops they normally used for holding their toothbrushes and toiletries. Lacking a bucket or any other container, the women filled the cups from a flooded trench along the road and carried them over to the radiator, carefully pouring the water so as not to spill a drop. Back and forth they went, from trench to car, filling and refilling their cut-glass holders until the radiator contained enough water to start the engine and get them moving again.

The threesome also helped navigate through places like Wyoming, where there were no maps, no signs, and no one to rely on but themselves. Lucky for all, Alice really knew her stuff. When a bad plug caused the Maxwell to sputter and misfire, she didn't just replace it; she took it apart, sandpapered it clean, reassembled it, and put it back better than before.

"I was born mechanical, an inheritance from my father," she said. "As I grew up I showed great curiosity about the working of any device, and by the time I was almost out of grade school I had elected to take manual training instead of some feminine art. My father, who had magic in his fingers, understood my interests and encouraged me."

Her husband, John Ramsey, an attorney, also encouraged her interests, and it was "Bone," as she affectionately called him, who got her into automobiles in the first place. Her first love was horses; she badly wanted to own one and was forever leaning on her husband to let her take Duke out for a ride by herself. Duke was a big, headstrong animal, and Bone, fearing for his wife's safety, refused to let her. But one day when he was off at work—they lived in Hackensack, New Jersey—she hitched Duke up to the buggy and set off for town. On their way a noisy, road-hogging Pierce-Arrow nearly ran them down, and Duke bolted. Bracing her feet against the buggy floor, the diminutive Alice grabbed the forward loops of the reins and pulled hard but was unable to stop him. Only after the horse came to a hill and ran out of wind did she finally bring him under control and talk him back to the stable.

Alice's close call shocked Bone when he heard the story later in the day. Reassuring him that she was fine, she repeated her desire to get a horse. Her husband had a better idea: given her mechanical interests and abilities, why not an automobile?

Alice had to think about that one. "It wasn't exactly the same as a live animal with which one could have a certain sense of companionship. But I took to mechanics rather naturally, and the thought of getting places was most alluring." And, she had to admit, "There were drawbacks to tending live animals which an inanimate auto would not have. So, the vote was cast in favor of an automobile."

The automobile was a new red Maxwell roadster, compliments of Bone, a man who preferred to walk if he had a choice in the matter and who cared little about machines and mechanical things. That was his wife's department. He took only one nervous ride in the Maxwell to check out the brakes to make sure of his wife's safety, and then, his mind at ease, he left Alice to her fun. She took lessons, quickly got the hang of the thing, and soon started taking reliability runs around Hackensack and New York. It was on a Long Island run that a Maxwell agent spotted her and brought up the possibility of her driving across America, an idea she first regarded as daft. But with Bone's blessing she eventually warmed to the idea, recruited her three sidekicks, and in June 1909 set out for the other side of the continent.

The Maxwell ran on an internal combustion gas engine, which was steadily gaining popularity over its electric and steam competitors. If steam powered the nineteenth century, it did not appear to be the engine that would run the twentieth. Slow to start, steamers required lots of water to operate, and filling and refilling the boiler on the road was neither easy nor convenient. Even dicier were the electrics. Since their batteries only held a charge for so long, they could not stray far from home before needing to be plugged in to a power source and recharged. To solve this problem Thomas Edison and other electric car makers enlarged the size of the battery, so much so that in some electrics the batteries weighed half as much as the entire car. While the gas engine surely had its flaws, one of its drawbacks turned out to be a plus. Because it had so many working parts, the gas engine opened the door to new patents, new designs, new methods of doing things that had not been tried before. Unlike a massive locomotive, it was a machine that was human in scale. A man or a woman could work on it by the side of the road or in the yard at home. The thing ran a long way on a tank of gas too, which made it perfect for racing and for endurance runs on the open road.

The drive began on Broadway in New York at the sales office of the Maxwell-Briscoe Company, which sponsored the trip. It supplied the car and paid the expenses, provided equipment and logistical help, and assigned a public relations agent to do advance work and drum up stories for the newspapers. When Alice and her crew entered a new town a cavalcade of honking Maxwell owners, reporters, and local dignitaries frequently greeted them. This was indeed the case after they cleared the mountains and arrived at a celebration on the outskirts of Sacramento. Unable to wait until the women reached Sacramento proper, an enthusiastic group of Maxwell owners had driven out to welcome them in Folsom. There, as the *Sacramento Union* reported, "the little daughter of W. J. Mannix, the local manager of the Maxwell agency, elbowed her way through the crowd of felicitous admirers to thrust a huge bouquet of California roses and carnations into the hands of the plucky little woman at the wheel of the sturdy stock car which she had driven more than five thousand miles [actually about thirty-eight hundred] over all sorts of roads. With a suppressed exclamation of genuine delight, Mrs. Ramsey seized the flowers and pressed them in an ecstasy of happiness to her sensitive nostrils." Once her nostrils had calmed down, Ramsey spoke to the obvious issue on the minds of her supporters and detractors alike: "Women can handle an automobile just as well as men," she told a reporter. "You should have seen us get the machine out of an irrigation ditch in Wyoming. We just took our block and tackle which we carried on the rear of the machine, hooked it to a stump at the top of a ditch and although it was hard work, we got the machine out all right."

From there it was on to Stockton and more celebrations, and from Stockton across the valley. "Get a horse!" someone may have yelled at them. People yelled such things at them all across the country, as well as less-polite comments having to do with their gender. An automobile was a machine, but people regarded it as more than just a machine. It was a symbol that meant different things to different people, and it stirred intense emotions. With her dark frizzy hair poking out from under her motoring cap, the picture of Alice grinning behind the wheel of her Maxwell provoked wildly different responses among those who saw her or read about her. Some found inspiration in what she symbolized and it moved them to joy and tears. These were often women. Others didn't like what they saw; it infuriated them and they resented it. These were frequently men.

"Driving was a guy thing," said the historian Fred Zimmerman. "Men didn't think women were capable of driving these machines."

The reasons for this were many. Automobiles frequently broke down, and only a person with "magic in his fingers," almost always a man, could revive them. At times they were as hard to handle as horses, and it took raw physical strength to operate them. Power steering did not exist. Changing a flat required strength and know-how. Another challenge was the hand-crank starter. If you put your thumb over the crank and the engine backfired while you were turning the handle, the sudden jerk could break your arm. Alice and others who knew their way around machines avoided injury by keeping their thumbs close to their fingers when they turned the crank.

Over the next few years, with the introduction of the electric starter, improved steering, and other innovations, as well as the emergence in the 1920s of closed-body vehicles, more and more women took to the road. But when Ramsey was coming across the country only a few hundred women in California drove regularly, and probably only a few thousand in all of America. Women relied on men to teach them how to drive, and if they didn't have a sympathetic husband or father or brother to show them, or the money to afford lessons, they were out of luck. When a woman did finally get a chance, she invariably drove with a man seated next to her telling her what to do. Likely he also offered a critical comment or two about her efforts, adding even more pressure to what was already a pressure-packed situation. But many men never gave their wives or daughters or sisters a try at the wheel, subscribing, perhaps, to the thinking of some physicians of the time who believed that driving in automobiles was unsafe for women, that they became overly excited at high speeds and couldn't sleep at night when they did. Women, they said, experienced sinus problems from keeping their mouths open for too long in cars.

Women also faced social pressures to maintain a proper appearance, which was not easy to do in an automobile. "Danger to a woman's fair complexion is one of the chief obstacles to many a long motor trip," wrote a female travel writer who supported women motorists. "However, this can be avoided by simple methods. A thin coating of good cold cream is, naturally, the first thing to be done before starting. This protects the skin and prevents it from being dried out by the wind. Then select a red veil. It does not have to be of the intense variety of red, but one of the lighter shades of this color. The red absorbs the sun's rays and prevents tanning or burning, even in the hottest kind of weather."

Then there was the matter of clothing and accessories, and how to pull it all together with style. "The latest handbag carried by the well-dressed woman is shaped like a rustic birdhouse, the cone-shaped lid sliding over a silk cord, which forms the handle. These are very handy while motoring."

As for Ramsey and her mates, each wore a duster over her clothes, plus the mandatory goggles, gloves, and hat. "Our fair-weather hats," explained Ramsey, "were a type of large full cap with stiff visors to shield the eyes, over which crepe de chine veils were draped and came under the chin to be tied in billowing bows." Upon reaching the East Bay hills the wind nearly blew off their hats and everything else. "Near Hayward a terrific wind, gale-like in ferocity, accosted us and we feared we might actually lose our apparel. A good tight grip kept our birthday suits from showing."

They rolled on to Oakland and crossed over to San Francisco, where more horn-honking Maxwells led them up to the Maxwell agency on Van Ness. There, the history-making auto went on display and the four weary travelers checked into the St. James Hotel to freshen up for a banquet to be held that Saturday night in their honor.

They had done it. From sea to shining sea, the first woman driver and the first all-women's team. After the banquet they spent a restful Sunday in San Francisco followed by a brief sightseeing trip by train to southern California. But not having seen or talked to her two-year-old son and husband for nearly two months, Alice missed them both terribly and she rode a fast train home to Hackensack.

The next year Alice gave birth to her second child and hung up her long-distance driving gloves for a decade to raise a family. When the children got older, in the boon travel days of the 1920s, she drove them out to California to show them the sights. This reawakened her urge to roam, and from then on she started making regular driving trips to the West Coast with family and friends. Her beloved Bone died in the 1930s, and after World War II she moved to Covina in southern California. This was where she was living when the *New York Times* carried an article on the fiftieth anniversary of her history-making trip, although the reporter, apparently thinking the history-maker herself was dead, did not speak to Ramsey for the story. But the septuagenarian was indeed alive and plucky as ever. The *Times* feature revived interest in her feat, prompting the American Automobile Association to name her "Woman Motorist of the Century." Other automobile groups bestowed similar honors on her.

"I'm probably happiest when I'm holding onto a wheel," she told a reporter after driving from Covina to New York for a Vassar reunion. As much driving as she did, crossing and recrossing the country dozens of times, she only received one ticket in her life, for making an illegal U-turn in a Covina business district. "Covina was just being built up then and I didn't think of it as a business district," she said. The media periodically rang her up for comments on the old saw about women being worse drivers than men, which she dismissed as "a lot of hooey," adding, "I wish they'd teach some men to stay in their own lane."

She did concede, though, that were it not for the male pathfinders who came before her, she never would have attempted her trip. "The cross-country trip already had been made by men," she said. "I'm not pioneer enough to have attempted it if it hadn't been done."

The same might be said for Blanche Stuart Scott, another hardy young Vassar grad, who, in the spring of 1910, set out from New York to become the second woman to drive across America. As with most every other transcontinentalist except Dr. Horatio Jackson, a car company sponsored her trip. Overland supplied the vehicle (with a built-in toilet) and footed the bills, and its sales agents across the country pitched in where needed. But there was no one to help Scott and her passenger, Gertrude Phillips, on the long, hard pull up Kingsbury Grade on the eastern side of the Sierra approaching Lake Tahoe. Its engine whining like crazy and the tires spitting dirt behind them, the 25-horse Overland could not make it over a steep pitch of road and came to a forced stop. Dragging out the block and tackle as she had done so many times before on the trip, Phillips trudged to the top of the rise and began hammering a stake into the ground to secure a line to winch the car up. Then all of a sudden she let out a whoop and came running down the hill.

Breathless, her voice mixed with terror and excitement, she said, "There's an enormous wildcat up there."

Scott, who had been waiting in the car for her, shut off the idling engine and got out. "Don't be silly," she replied.

Scott may not have believed her friend, but when she went to investigate she carried a .32 caliber Colt revolver. The women had brought the gun with them on the trip for protection against predators, animal and otherwise.

When she reached the top of the rise and saw that her friend was telling the truth—that an enormous wildcat was indeed up there—she turned around and beat Phillips's time back to the car. "Without preamble I jumped in, hauled the block and tackle into a jumble in the trunk, leapfrogged into the driver's seat and yelled to Gertrude as I started the motor and poured on the petrol. 'This damn thing just has to go over that grade.'"

Sometimes desire and willpower have as much to do with operating a car as valves, plugs and carburetors. This was one of those times. The Overland did what it couldn't do before and gunned up and over the rise.

Their close encounter behind them, Scott and Phillips crossed over the Sierra and made it to the East Bay by Friday afternoon, easily within reach of San Francisco that night. But Overland's "boomer"—slang for a press agent—advised against a nighttime arrival, saying they'd receive much more publicity if they swept across the bay in the brilliant light of a Saturday afternoon. Seeing the wisdom of this advice, Scott and Phillips spent Friday night in San Leandro and ferried over to Market Street the next day. There the Presidio's United States Army Band greeted them along with the usual flag-draped, honking automobiles. Sunday papers around the country carried articles on the spectacle.

Ignoring repeated corrections by Maxwell's boomers, Overland's boomers continually portrayed Scott's sixty-eight-day drive as the first woman's automobile crossing of America. (Technically the first females to cross the country by car were the wife and daughters of the Murdock family of Pasadena, in 1908, but the father, Jacob, drove the whole way.) Scott also told this fiction to the press, revealing in her autobiography years later another trick she used to fool the public. Taking a cue from Whitman and Hammond, who had dipped the wheels of Li'l Scout in the Pacific at the start of their first transcontinental run and then in the Atlantic at the end, Scott had ceremoniously filled a bottle with Atlantic Ocean water on the East Coast. But during the trip she somehow misplaced this bottle, leaving her in a quandary. In San Francisco she asked a busboy at her hotel to fill a bottle for her, and this was what she poured into the Pacific at the Cliff House with the cameras clicking and reporters scribbling. Tap water.

Despite a weakness perhaps for self-promotion, the tiny, apple-cheeked Scott had real guts and an authentic lust for adventure, which she proved still more in the next few months. After a tour of Overland dealers around the state, she returned home to New York, where aviation pioneer Glenn Curtiss, having read about her in the papers, asked if she'd like to take flying lessons. Scott said yes, and in September 1910 she became one of the first women in America to pilot an airplane. Thus began her pioneering aviation career, a career marked by spectacular flights and some equally spectacular crashes. She broke numerous bones, some more than once.

Here was a woman who was driving a car *and* piloting a plane. Again, some people liked what this represented and others did not. But its meaning was clear: These new machines were shaking up the status quo, overhauling society from top to bottom, including women's place in it. Women were deemed second-class citizens. They could not vote in state and federal elections, and they could not hold jobs or chase opportunities that men took for granted.

In the summer of 1910, at the same time Blanche Stuart Scott was swinging through the state, California was in the midst of a political upheaval. That August, Hiram Johnson, a San Francisco attorney, had won the Republican nomination for governor in the state's first direct primary election for either party. (Before this, voters elected delegates who chose their party's candidate.) An exciting, lectern-pounding public speaker with the stern, bespectacled look of a no-nonsense schoolmaster, Johnson had gained fame as a prosecutor in the San Francisco graft trials of disgraced mayor Eugene Schmitz and political boss Abe Ruef. His election platform was simple but powerful: Kick the Southern Pacific out of politics!

The Southern Pacific ran the railroads, and it ran the men who wrote the laws. Its political and economic power touched virtually everyone in the state. Both Schmitz and Ruef had ties to it, and throwing them in prison was seen as a major victory against the "soulless Force, the iron-hearted Power, the monster, the

Colussus, the Octopus," as Frank Norris wrote in *The Octopus*, his famous 1901 novel about the Southern Pacific. Less impassioned but no less critical were R.C. Irvine, Marsden Manson, and James Maude, the three engineers who, several years earlier, conducted the first survey of California's roads for the Bureau of Highways (now Caltrans). After traveling thousands of miles around the state on horse and buckboard to see firsthand what shape the roads were in, they reported back to Sacramento with recommendations on how to improve them. While they did not have automobiles in mind when conducting this survey, their 132-page Biennial Report of the Bureau of Highways formed a blueprint for the state highway system that would follow over the next generations. One reason for the sorry state of California's roads, they said, was the railroad. The main roads of small towns tended to lead one place and one place only: the train depot. The farther you got away from the iron road, the worse the dirt roads became. Even in the big port cities the railroad was the hub of things with wagon roads and trolley lines all feeding into it. The power of rail extended even to the roads it did not directly control. With the blessing of elected officials in the pocket of the Southern Pacific, the railroad put its tracks where it saw fit, whether it needed them there or not, just to shut down potential competition.

"The [road] franchise is frequently obtained more to control a highway or to protect existing franchises from competition than to serve public interests," wrote the engineers. "In either case, the rights of the public are ruthlessly overridden."

Ruthless was an adjective often applied to the Southern Pacific, which was also the state's biggest private landowner. The railroad claimed the best lands for its lines and without fail these lines passed through company-owned property that could be sold and developed at a profit. The SP raised prices seemingly at whim and charged exorbitant fees to farmers and every other business shipping their goods to market. The same tough policy applied to passengers. The railroad dictated when they could travel, and where, and for how much. And what choice did they have in the matter? None. The Southern Pacific was the only game in town, and it stayed that way by paying bribes to the likes of Ruef and Schmitz. And if the riffraff didn't like it they could take a horse.

Into the breach charged Hiram Johnson, the leader of the reformist, or progressive, wing of the Republican Party, the state's top political party. His nomination made him the immediate frontrunner in the general election, but he took nothing for granted, conducting a campaign that those who participated in never forgot as long as they lived. "How well I remember that stirring 1910 campaign," recalled Thomas Storke, the founding editor of the *Santa Barbara News-Press* and a friend and supporter of Johnson's. "California has never seen one to equal it." He added, "In a red automobile driven by his son, the dynamic Hiram toured the highways and the backroads of the state from Crescent City to San Diego, from the maritime counties in the west to those bordering Arizona and Nevada in the east."

Johnson's ride was a shiny red 1910 Locomobile. Beginning a tradition of campaigning by car, he and his son drove from city to city around the state, keeping the top off so people could see Johnson and wave to him and the candidate could wave back. They carried a cowbell with them, and when they appeared in a town they drove down the streets clanging it. Johnson's supporters, also in automobiles, accompanied the candidate with their own bells and honking horns.

"Johnson's campaign," wrote a California historian, "was unique, colorful and literally hard-driving." Voters fully grasped its potent political symbolism. Automobiles did not represent a serious transportation threat to the railroad, nor would they for many years to come. What they represented was freedom and independence from monopoly power. Johnson, who personified and capitalized on these feelings, beat the Democratic candidate and won election in November. The next year, he pushed the state legislature to enact a series of sweeping reforms that humbled the Southern Pacific and ushered in a new era of citizen participation in the affairs of government. In October 1911 California voters approved no less than twenty-three amendments to the state constitution, including the establishment of a process in which voters themselves, independent of politicians and organized interest groups, could gather signatures and place propositions on the ballot, to be voted on by their fellow citizens. This initiative process, perhaps Johnson's most enduring legacy, remains the law today, regularly sending up twisters that rake the landscape of California politics.

One of those amendments on the 1911 ballot was women's suffrage—whether or not to grant women the right to vote in California. Taking a cue from Johnson and the suffrage campaigns of women in other states, California suffragists drove automobiles to attract attention to their cause. Unlike the new Hoover vacuum cleaner or the electric-powered washing machine, two labor-saving devices that were then coming into use, the automobile had nothing to do with a woman's traditional role as homemaker. In fact, it took her away from the house and into society at large. It gave her access to jobs and increased her independence. We can handle an automobile the same as a man, women were saying, and we can handle our business in a polling place too.

For the College Equal Suffrage League's automobile tour of the state, women drove into the center of a town with one of them playing a bugle to make sure people on the street saw and heard them. Once parked, a speaker would rise and stand in her open-air vehicle and talk to all who'd listen. Automobiles helped women take their message directly to the voters, and if the audience proved unreceptive, they also provided a quick getaway.

On Election Day, many members of the Political Equality League, the Votes for Women Club, and other suffragist committees stayed away from the polling places for fear of antagonizing male voters. Other women more boldly "swept down in automobiles, aflutter with suffragette streamers," carrying sympathetic voters to and from the polling places and doing some last-minute politicking while they were at it. Cora Foy and the four Hare sisters of Los Angeles piled into Cora's car and drove around the east side of the city singing snippets from "Everybody Votes But Mother."

"It was a new sort of machine politics," observed a reporter that day. "It was automobile politics with smiles as influence."

The smiles won. The all-male electorate narrowly approved the change, ending the all-male electorate. California became the sixth state in the nation to allow women to vote. Nine years later, in 1920, the states ratified the 19th Amendment of the Constitution, granting all American women the right of suffrage. For the national campaign, as in California, women driving automobiles became a potent symbol of freedom and its unmet promises—that when given the chance, women could do what men do and deserved the same basic rights and protections under the law.

SEVEN

Barney and Friends

When we last checked in with Barney Oldfield, in the fall of 1903, he was blowing out of Los Angeles on his way to another race and another payday. But while he has been missing from the pages of this book, the World's Fastest Human was certainly not missing from the automobile or car racing scene. He had, in fact, been dominating it, breaking records and achieving firsts and pushing the limits of what men could do in automobiles. Everybody knew about Barney. In the first decade of the twentieth century he had become an international celebrity, one of those figures whose exploits go beyond the boundaries of sports into popular culture. His name was synonymous with speed; to drive like Barney Oldfield was to be a throttle-happy daredevil.

A few years after his first, roaringly successful road trip through California, he settled permanently in Los Angeles, using it as his base of operations for his wide-ranging racing forays around the country. But the major reason for his move wasn't racing; it was a girl by the name of Bess Holland. She stole Barney's heart and vice versa. Barney had already burned through one marriage and tended not to be seen with the kind of ladies you brought home to meet Mother. But Bess, a southern Californian, was different. With her expressive brown eyes and thick brown hair, she was a deeply religious woman who believed in the power of prayer to work wonders in her life and the lives of others. "I believe in God," she said, "and I know He oversees us all, and were it not for the faith I have in prayer I would never be able to stand the strain of seeing Barney take the chances he does."

Bess admitted that prayer needed to work overtime for Barney because, as she said, "he drives like a madman." Still, she was no church mouse either; she rode in airplanes when that was a dangerous thing to do, and if the rules had permitted it, she would have ridden with Barney in his races. (Only riding mechanics could do that.) Bess did the next best thing then, traveling with Barney wherever he went and watching every race she could after they were married. Before a race she always wrote a prayer on a slip of paper that he carried in his pocket with him when he competed.

His early success at Agricultural Park notwithstanding, Barney's favorite racing venue in Los Angeles was Ascot Park, a dirt horse and auto track on the less-policed side of the city limits. When he and Bess were married, in early 1907, a horse named after him was running at Ascot. Tickled pink by this, the groom took his new bride to the track on their honeymoon and introduced her to all his friends. Meanwhile he put some money down on Barney Oldfield, the horse.

It was an odd match, Bess and the Wizard of the Track, but somehow it worked. After their honeymoon they headed off for some more romance and racing in San Diego. From Los Angeles they took the inland route, which had improved considerably from when P. A. Renton was driving it—this in part because of the efforts of three prominent and prodigiously wealthy San Diegans: A. G. Spalding, the Hall of Fame baseball player and founder of the Spalding sporting goods firm; E. W. Scripps, publisher of the national newspaper (and now media) chain and co-founder of the Scripps Institution of Oceanography; and John Spreckels, the former San Franciscan who moved to San Diego after the earthquake and built a Coronado Island mansion that remains to this day. Spreckels, who inherited millions from his father, became a tycoon in his own right, running a far-flung business empire in sugar, water, shipping, real estate, publishing, and the railroads. "Transportation determines the flow of population," he said once, and he and his two colleagues clearly believed in this principle because they supervised the construction of roads in and around San Diego. "San Diego is the only city in the world that has three multi-millionaires for assistant superintendents in streets," noted an article. "These three men assumed office for the purpose of taking personal charge of the construction of a boulevard system and have been vying with each other in an effort to construct the most and the best roads for the least cost." These boulevards, "surfaced with decomposed granite and finished in a way that makes the speed-mad automobilist gloat in joy," curled around Point Loma and in some spots ran right on the beach next to the ocean. Taking a page from the business model of the Southern Pacific, which built roads to spur development on its privately held lands, the plan was to extend and improve these boulevards and build a pricey housing subdivision in Point Loma.

Barney and Bess reached San Diego around noon, had lunch, then drove out to see the new racetrack being built at Lakeside. Owned and designed by a man named John Gay, Lakeside was the first track in California and one of the first anywhere to be devoted solely to motor racing. No four-footed nags here, only cars and motorcycles. Its name derived from the lake in the center of the track, which also drew notice for its length. "The track is two miles around, one of the largest tracks in the world and said to be the largest in America," noted a reporter. "The form is egg-shaped, and with so large a track this shape gives practically no corners." Gentle turns, long straightaways, extra banking—Gay's enlightened design sought high speeds but not at the risk of driver safety. The reporter continued: "Five racing cars could come abreast on the straightaway without any danger, a larger number than can be placed on the majority of tracks. At the turns the outside is heavily banked, so that there is no danger of the cars going wide at the corners."

With Bess and this reporter along for the ride, Barney put his 60-horse touring car through its paces, doing a lap in a little over two minutes. He pronounced himself pleased, and he and his wife said goodbye to the reporter and headed back to the coast for a little friendly street racing on those big, beautiful Point Loma boulevards. The wealthy of San Diego had a reputation for driving machines with muscle, and Barney wanted to see what he could do against them "just for fun."

Lakeside made its official debut in April, and thousands of spectators came out to watch Barney square off against local speed ace Bruno Seibel in the featured event. With Bess occupying a seat in the grandstands saying silent prayers for her husband, he drove with his arm bandaged from an injury. It hardly mattered. In the Green Dragon, a new car made especially for him by Peerless, he easily thumped Seibel in his Red Devil, setting a new world record for the mile. Then he stepped out of the Green Dragon and into a Stevens-Duryea and recorded a new fifty-mile mark.

A few weeks later at Association Park in San Bernardino, the Green Dragon again duked it out with the Red Devil with five thousand spectators looking on. This program included an old-timer's event for pre-1902 machines, a "cupid race" for couples, and lots of Barney. It could have been Barney vs. Anybody and people would have paid to see it. Love him or hate him, you couldn't take your eyes off him, and other drivers longed for nothing more than to knock him on his butt.

After Ed Apperson won the 1908 Pasadena-Altadena Hill Climb, Barney made a very public thousand-dollar wager that he could whip the defending champ in the 1909 running of the race. Apperson accepted the bet and outfitted his Jackrabbit with steel alloy axles, a first for an American gas racecar. More than twenty thousand people lined the streets of Pasadena and Altadena for Barney vs. the Jackrabbit, many of them clustering around the famous wooden bridge built over the trolley tracks where cars took flight. Knowing his car could absorb the impact, Apperson came at the bridge full speed: "I shifted into high without releasing the clutch. I kept my foot on the throttle, even when I saw the wooden bridge coming at me. When I hit it I took off like a bird." The distance from where his rear wheels left the ground to where they touched down again was eighty-eight feet.

Barney's six-cylinder Stearns couldn't touch that, and he finished behind Apperson in what turned out to be the hill climb's last hurrah. Its organizers shut it down for being too wild and crazy, leaving an opening in the California racing scene for something even wilder and crazier: the Los Angeles Motordrome.

Located between Venice and Playa del Rey, the Motordrome must've made Bess reach for the Scriptures, for nothing on heaven or earth compared to it. It was the first board track in the world and the mad-scientist inspiration for all the ones that came after. Its surface was not dirt or clay or decomposed granite but wooden two-by-fours. Three million board feet of Oregon fir went into its construction. Owner-builder Jack Prince, a former British world bicycle racing champion, designed the mile-long oval like a bicycle velodrome. The banking all around was twenty degrees, similar in steepness to the steepest grades on Hyde Street and other hill streets of San Francisco. It resembled a "pie pan" with its flat center area and upturned circular edge. From the ground to the wooden railing on top of the pie pan was twenty-five feet. A covered grandstand ran along the homestretch and offered exquisite views. Unlike with a dirt surface, no track-fed dust storms blocked the vision of spectators or drivers.

The first-ever races at Thunder 'Drome occurred in April and kicked off the 1910 spring racing season. Fittingly for a driver of his stature, Barney had brought three cars from three different countries: Knox (United States), Darracq (France), and Benz (Germany). This last, the creation of Karl Benz's global racing powerhouse, represented the ultimate in European automotive style and brawn. "The greatest motorcar ever brought to Los Angeles," said a reporter who saw it, "a roaring, plunging motor giant [that] has done the fastest straightaway miles that any car has ever made." But what's a speed burner without a nickname? Formerly called Lightning, it now campaigned under the name of the Blitzen Benz.

For Barney, new track, new car, and new rival: Ralph De Palma, an Italian kid from New York with guts and skill and dreamboat looks. Snuggled into a Fiat known as Mephistopheles, De Palma had spent the past year erasing Oldfield's name from the record books and replacing it with his. Barney didn't much like that. Nor did he appreciate the rude things Ralph said in the press about Blitzen. You don't insult a man's car and expect to hear nothing more about it, especially if that man is the Master Driver of the World. Getting the two feuding rivals together on the same track was a real coup for Fred Moskovics, Prince's partner in the Motordrome, who had arranged the deal. (Moskovics, a fine engineer, later ran the Stutz car company).

So it was Barney vs. Ralph, the headline act of sixty races spread over seven days. Records started falling even before the track's official opening. In the time trials Dutch Benny, whose real name was Ben Kerscher, showed off his chops as a driver by nearly topping 100 miles per hour in his Darracq. Caleb Bragg, a young Eastern red-hot, set a new national record for the mile in a Fiat 90. When the racing started for real, De Palma broke another of Barney's former records, this one for five miles. Swinging back hard, the Daredevil of the Roaring Road pushed Blitzen to a new world two-mile standard. Then he followed that by shattering the mile mark just set by Bragg in the trials. But the upstart Yalie earned some revenge a few days later in a two-lap match race against Barney. Despite being in a car nobody considered to be the equal of the Benz, Caleb jumped ahead of Barney at the start and beat him pole to pole.

The meet's biggest disappointment came when Mephistopheles cracked two pistons in an early outing and went on the blocks for the rest of the tourney. Ralph and Barney did go head to head in a race, but each drove one of his lesser cars and it wasn't the same thing. With Caleb Bragg and his Fiat showing so well, however, Prince and Moskovics arranged for a second duel with Barney and Blitzen. The slender Bragg was everything Barney was not—modest, thoughtful, refined, college-educated, rich. After Yale gave him his diploma his parents gave him the Fiat for a graduation present. Bragg was also an amateur racing for love of sport and glory, whereas Barney raced for love and glory plus the prize money. The press and public ate it up. The interurban trolley lines added more cars to handle the overflow, and ten thousand people journeyed to the beach for Barney vs. Caleb, round two.

This time Barney didn't let the kid jump him at the start. It was a slow, rolling start, and they both put the throttle down and hit the line at the same time, the Fiat going right and high up the bank and the Benz staying left and low along the inner rail. The Benz made the turn first, but the Fiat got through it quicker, each car slingshotting out into the backstretch. Here, the Benz broke in front once more only to have the Fiat catch it on the curve. Even in a two-lap sprint, patterns emerge. "Throughout the race," said a reporter, "Oldfield kept the lower part of the track and the Fiat had to work up to its limit of speed in order to hold its own." That was one pattern: Barney low, Caleb high. The other pattern reflected each car's relative strength. The lighter and quicker Fiat handled the curves better whereas the 200-horsepower Benz owned the straights.

The second and final lap lasted less than forty seconds. They were dead-even around the last turn until Barney, down low, slid slightly to his right. "As it rushed into the finish the Benz skidded toward the top of the track and Bragg, taking a chance, opened his throttle wide." Barney saw him but reacted too late. The Fiat shot past him on the upper rail and won by five hundredths of a second, about the length of Barney's chewed-up cigar.

Narrow or not, a win was a win, and that made it two in a row for the young amateur over the hard-bitten pro. Caleb's friends and supporters in the grandstands jumped the rails, hoisted their hero up, and carried him around the track on their shoulders "as the crowd cheered itself hoarse."

The Benz had gone 105 miles per hour at its peak, but its driver expressed disappointment in it afterward, saying that in the future he'd run it on tracks with longer straights than the Motordrome. It wasn't long, however, before Barney was running into a different sort of problem, one that had less to do with racing and more to do with his judgment.

In the fall of that year he agreed to take on yet another automotive challenger, Jack Johnson, the heavyweight boxing champion of the world, who loved cars and had done some motor racing. A few months earlier Johnson, who was black, had beaten Jim Jeffries, the "Great White Hope," as he was labeled, in one of the most celebrated boxing matches ever. Jeffries also happened to be Barney's close friend and drinking buddy, so Barney, eager to avenge his friend's loss, accepted a promoter's offer for a Barney vs. Jack showdown at a dirt track in New York. This was when the American Automobile Association, the official governing body of motor racing in the United States—a position it held until the 1950s—stepped in. Deriding the event as nothing more than a publicity stunt for money, the AAA threatened to suspend Barney if he went ahead with it. Barney being Barney, he ignored the warning and bested Johnson in their two races.

But the stunt backfired. Following through on its threat, the AAA suspended him from organized racing. Ornery as ever, Barney responded to this ban the way he responded to anyone who tried to tell him what to do: with his thumb and nose.

Nobody was bigger than the Speed King of the World, nobody could sell tickets like him. That was Barney's opinion anyhow, and to prove his point he took his act on the road in defiance of the pooh-bahs of the AAA.

He had always made money on the county fair circuit, going back to the days of his record-setting spree in California years before, but many of those races had received the official imprint of the AAA, which oversaw the timekeeping and other rules of competition. Now, with the organization banishing him from its races, he turned to the "outlaw" circuit, where the rules were more lax but the betting just as fierce. No county fair was too small or out of the way for Barney as long as it met his price and the checks didn't bounce. For these events he sent his racecar ahead of him on a special train car. Arriving two or three days before the race, it was put on display at the rail depot or some other prominent place where people could come by to ogle it and buy tickets. Then, the night before the big day, the star attraction rolled into town escorted by marching bands, reporters and the like. And in case anyone missed the show, the hotel where he was staying posted a large banner in front that read "Oldfield Sleeps Here."

Meantime Dutch Benny, a less-known but no less vital member of the troupe, slipped into town. Dutch Benny was a Motordrome veteran and a legitimate driver when he had to be, but he didn't have to be when out with Barney on the outlaw circuit. All he had to do was follow the script, which called for him to lead the entire race only to have Barney pass him on the final turn. He always finished second in these races because his contract required it.

Chomping that famous unlit cigar, handsome and charismatic, Barney always put on a show because that's what he did. But these races more resembled choreography than sport, which made people ridicule him and call him a joke.

Barney Oldfield, the World's Fastest Clown.

This was a mournful period in Barney's life in which he thought seriously about quitting motor racing. He had thought about it before, many times, and yet there had never been a more perfect time for it than now. Bess loved him, he knew, and would stick by him no matter what. He had broken every record in the book, achieved all the glory a man could ever hope for. Thousands upon thousands had cheered themselves hoarse for him, and now these same people were laughing at him.

He had a little money—he hadn't blown all of it on good times—and he'd sunk some of it into a saloon in downtown Los Angeles on Spring Street between Fifth and Sixth on the west side. People from motorcars, the fight game, gambling, the trotters, baseball, the newspapers—they all hung out there, lured by the star power of its owner. Oldfield's featured a long, glistening mahogany bar with brass rails, spittoons on the floor, a player piano in one corner. Photographs of Barney and other sports legends hung on the walls. They served sandwiches and pickled sausages. Beer cost a nickel a mug, and two shots of whiskey set you back two bits.

Lots of nights Barney would hold down center stage at the saloon, telling stories about old Henry Ford and the days when a mile a minute was a big deal in an automobile. In other, more downbeat moods, perhaps after closing time, with stale tobacco smoke in the air and empty mugs on the table around him, he'd talk about the drivers he'd known, friends of his, who'd been hurt badly in crashes. Then there were the ones who weren't as lucky as that. All those fellows taken away too soon, and all those loved ones they'd left behind. Just the thought of it made him miserable, and at times like these, in moods like this, he'd talk about never stepping into a racecar again.

Nah, no chance. Not Barney Oldfield, World Champion Automobilist. He wasn't done, not by a long shot.

In early 1912 the AAA lifted its one-year suspension of Barney, partially conceding his point. Motor racing simply wasn't as interesting without him. Free to run with the big boys again, in races that weren't hokum but really mattered, Barney announced his comeback event: the Santa Monica Road Race. Begun three years earlier as a way to boost tourism in the tiny beach community of Santa Monica, the race had grown into California's answer to the prestigious Vanderbilt Cup: a test of bravery, skill, and mechanical ferocity with some of America's best drivers in some of the world's most powerful machines. It promised to be the fastest road race in the world.

The practice runs for the three-hundred-mile race occurred in late April and the first days of May, with the main event set for Saturday, May 5. Its cash prize was three thousand dollars—70 percent of which was to be awarded to the winner and the rest divided between second and third places. Those who finished fourth or lower were out of the money. Seven cars entered. Though every one was considered to have a reasonable chance at the money, some clear favorites had emerged: the supremely prepared and methodical Earl Cooper in a Stutz; Barney's old nemesis at the Motordrome, Caleb Bragg, still running a Fiat; another Eastern millionaire speedboy, David Bruce Brown, in a Benz; and past champion Teddy Tetzlaff. The quietly intense Tetzlaff had won the 1910 Santa Monica Road Race in a Lozier and was back again this year in a Fiat.

But, as always, nearly all the pre-race excitement and speculation centered on Barney. Could he do it? Could he come back after being away from top-flight racing for so long?

No longer a fresh-faced pup in his twenties, the man who embodied so much of early racing history was now in his middle thirties, grizzled and worn and beaten down a little by life. Cheating death on a regular basis will do that to you. He'd broken bones in accidents, been knocked unconscious, woken up in a hospital bed. His critics, of whom there were many, claimed his spirit was broken too, that he was finished as a professional driver. Famously cocky and full of bluster, Barney was strangely thoughtful in practice, conceding that his critics might have a point. "Bert," he told *Los Angeles Times* automobile columnist Bert Smith after his Fiat struggled on some test laps around the 8.4-mile course, "if it was like you knew me three years ago, I'd walk away with this race." But it wasn't three years ago, and Barney knew it. His walking-away days were over.

Even Smith, a longtime admirer and friend, admitted that Barney was "out of training as a racer" and possibly out of his element in this race. Barney had become

Barney by going fast around enclosed circular tracks; Santa Monica was neither enclosed nor a track. On its longest straightaway, a three-mile sprint down Wilshire Boulevard, speeds eclipsed 115 miles per hour. Barney had gone that fast before but not in a road race and not for a while and not against racers of this quality who were all younger and hungrier than him and gunning to take him down. This led to another of the questions swirling around him: Did he still have it? Did he still have the guts and desire and will to be a champion?

Crowd estimates on race day ranged from one hundred and fifty to two hundred thousand. So many people came out that the Automobile Club of Southern California published a map in its monthly magazine to show Los Angeles residents how to get to Santa Monica by car. From downtown they traveled Washington Boulevard to the beach or took Wilshire part of the way. In recent years Wilshire had been extended all the way to the ocean, and Santa Monica civic boosters wished to encourage its use. But on race day, officials had blocked the western section of the street because it formed part of the course.

The course, sections of which can be traveled today, began on Ocean Front Boulevard (now Ocean Avenue) north of Wilshire. This was where the judges and timers were located, as well as the grandstands. From Ocean the cars made a sharp left onto Wilshire—"Dead Man's Curve," it was called—followed by a long, straight blast leading up to a milder turn known as Soldier's Home Curve. Then came mostly straight stretches down the Palisades and San Vicente Boulevard. A left at the end of San Vicente brought the cars back to the start/finish line on Ocean.

The Ancient Arabic Order of the Mystic Shrine had planned its annual convention around the race, and thousands of Shriners from around the world helped fill the grandstands. The grandstands and box seats on Ocean ranged from fifty cents to a dollar; everywhere else, the race was free. Throngs of people from all walks of life—"the farmer in the country, the clerk from many a downtown store, and the mechanic from the shop," as one account put it—stood along the streets, in some places four and five deep, craning their necks to see the cars, stepping at times dangerously into the roadway before being shooed back by race monitors and police on foot and horseback.

The morning schedule consisted of light- and medium-powered cars competing in shorter races. The preliminaries over, the big dogs rolled in: three Fiats, two Stutzes, a Benz, and a Simplex. Each boasted a power plant with more than 300-cubic-inch displacement, each roaring and blowing smoke like a dragon. The crowd cheered the loudest when Barney appeared with his cigar perched between his lips. He waved and grinned widely. But his lined and weary face grew solemn when he set his goggles into place and squeezed his body into the Fiat with the number 22 painted on its long red snout. Folded neatly in his pocket was Bess's prayer for him.

Joining him was his "mechanician." In longer races every man drove with a mechanic in the car with him. Almost as vital to success as the driver himself, he performed quick repairs, changed tires, served as another pair of eyes, and put his life at risk too. Many a crash had claimed both driver and mechanic.

Fourteen mortal men, seven impersonal machines. Men, women, and children in the stands nervously watching and waiting. The clock said one. The starter raised his pistol. The shot rang out. Suddenly the scene broke into a million different moving parts.

"Never was a more spectacular start seen on any race course than was witnessed at Santa Monica," marveled Bert Smith. "Mighty motors spat out clouds of smoke and flame."

First out of the smoke came Dave Lewis in his Stutz. He took Dead Man's Curve wide open and jumped down Wilshire, an oiled dirt corridor lined by open lots, low-slung buildings, and tens of thousands of faces. Next through this human corridor came Earl Cooper, also in a Stutz, thundering down Wilshire with Barney cutting up the space behind him. A battle for second rapidly developed between the two. If Barney was too old and out of shape for racing, it would've been tough to convince Cooper of this fact. By the end of lap one Barney had passed him and had a bead on the Stutz. He let 'er rip on Ocean and, with his flair for the dramatic, headed Lewis just before Dead Man's Curve. When he flared again onto Wilshire he saw nothing but empty road ahead of him, and the lead was his.

But not for long. Coming up fast behind him was David Bruce Brown in his Benz. A reporter wrote, "Brown on the Benz came down the stretch like a whirlwind. It was nerve-thrilling to see the big boy as he raced through the lines of spectators." Then came Teddy Tetzlaff in his huge Fiat. Starting in fourth position, the former champ had knocked off Cooper, Lewis, and now Brown in succession and was looping around Soldier's Home Curve, rumbling down the Palisades going close to 100 and demanding more. Barney's mechanician saw him first. He yelled and pointed, and Barney looked over with an empty feeling. "He realized in a second that Tetzlaff had his great monster wide open and was planning to have it out with Oldfield on the long straightaway. Oldfield accepted the dare and leaped away with his throttle held down. The two long red machines split the air with their cannon-like discharge."

It was Barney vs. Teddy, Fiat vs. Fiat. Teddy took him on San Vicente and never looked back, averaging 78.5 miles per hour for more than three hundred miles, a new national record for road racing, to win his second Santa Monica title. Caleb Bragg and David Bruce Brown took second and third respectively. After its opening charge Barney's Fiat suffered from mechanical problems and he dropped out. He never really figured in the race, finishing out of the money and delivering a good news-bad news message to the critics who thought his career was done.

The good news: He lost. The bad news: He was back.

EIGHT
The Original Hollywood Fast-Car Guy

Santa Monica represented a return for Barney Oldfield to the life he loved—throwing back cold ones with friends, smoking good cigars, racing hot cars in fast company. There was nobody like Barney and everyone knew it, including the people from the new motion picture business springing up in town. Show people liked to come around Barney's place and drink and socialize too. One of them was Mack Sennett, an actor, director, and producer for his Keystone Company. Sennett's thick black hair, rakish mustache, and matinee-idol looks hid the heart of a clown. He was funny and bright and women adored him, which made him great company in a bar. He lived at the Alexandria Hotel on Spring Street, a dice throw away from Oldfield's saloon, and in late 1912 he dropped in to see Barney after work one evening. He had an idea for a picture, and he wanted to see what the Speed King of the World thought of it.

In his early thirties and just coming into his own as a filmmaker, the Canadian-born Sennett worked hard but also enjoyed many pleasures in life, one of which was driving fine automobiles. "An occasional ride to the beaches or into the hills in his racing Fiat is the limit of his recreation," said a gossip item. His recreation also included watching motor racing. He was a big fan, and this was why he was pitching Barney. He wanted to make a racing movie with him, and not just any old racing movie but a spectacular one, something that nobody had ever seen on screen before.

Bad Boy Barney would naturally be the star, the name above the title. Heck, he'd be the name *in* the title: *Barney Oldfield's Race for a Life*. That's what they'd call it because, well, that was the storyline: Barney going all out to save the life of a beautiful young woman in peril. What else, right? This was the moving pictures business, after all. You gotta have a damsel in distress, and Sennett had the perfect gal for the part. Nobody played innocent like Mabel Normand; she'd been doing it for years.

Also perfect as the mustache-twirling villain was Ford Sterling, another member of the Keystone troupe. After Mabel's character rejects his advances, the evil Sterling ties her to the railroad tracks and then—get this—climbs into the cab of a locomotive, knocks the conductor dizzy, and takes over the train. The train starts bearing down on Mabel, who'll be killed unless Mack Sennett, her true love (also romantically involved with her in real life), finds a way to save her. He spots Barney Oldfield, who's nearby, and they hop into his famous Blitzen Benz and tear off to rescue Mabel from the oncoming locomotive.

So whaddya think, wanna be in a movie?

Barney being Barney, it all sounded pretty nifty to him, especially the title. The big problem was scheduling. Barney was busy with his revived racing career and Mack—well, nobody worked harder at being funny than Mack Sennett. Keystone had only been in business a year, and Sennett had already acted in and directed dozens of movies. A motion picture was soundless, black-and-white, and lasted only ten to fifteen minutes, so it was a snap to do, right? Not hardly. Mack and Mabel and the gang worked morning till night churning out pictures to fill the viewing public's seemingly insatiable demand for new, new, new. "That sweater-swaddled figure that may be seen any morning running over the Edendale hills is not an aspirant for a championship title, only Mack Sennett, taking his daily five miles of road work before beginning work at 8 a.m.," said another column. "He leaves the studio at anywhere from 5 to 8 at night. Quiet, lazy sort of life, what?"

On the eastern edge of downtown Los Angeles, Edendale was the capital of show business in the days before Hollywood, when people called the movies "the pictures" and the men and women who appeared in them "picture players" or "showplayers." Proper society, the type that wouldn't be caught dead in Barney's saloon, regarded showplayers and the work they did as somewhat unseemly, playing as these pictures did in cheap nickelodeons and frequented by the lower classes easily entertained by the comedic farces that Sennett specialized in. Live theater performed by actors on stage—that was the only true theater, not this shadow-play of images beamed onto a screen accompanied by the tinny sounds of a mechanical player piano, another garish modern invention that brought frowns from refined society. Though many disapproved of the trend, the pictures were growing, and Edendale was growing to keep up with them.

Located on Alessandro Street (now Glendale Boulevard), Keystone consisted of a few small offices and a large barn-like building with "Mack Sennett Studios" painted in white letters on the roof. Selig-Polyscope and the New York Motion Picture Company also had studios in the neighborhood. Then there were D. W. Griffith's Biograph on Pico Boulevard in Los Angeles and Thomas Ince's company out in the San Fernando Valley, to name but two of the new picture companies in the area. Griffith made serious-minded dramas and Ince made Westerns, but all the picture players pretty much fell into the same category: refugee New Yorkers from the worlds of theater and vaudeville come out West to explore this new medium for telling stories and making money. They spent the winter in the land of oranges and sunshine, then when the weather warmed up back East they returned to New York and New Jersey. Gradually, though, more and more players stopped going back East for the summer and stayed in California year-round to make pictures.

It is no coincidence that the picture business started to grow at the same time that the automobile was shaking up American society. "Of the machines that changed American life in the first half of the twentieth century," write historians James J. Rawls and Walton Bean, "the movie camera was as important as the internal combustion engine....The history of the movies and the history of the automobile were especially interwined." And this intertwining began very early on, in part because it was so darned hard to make movies using public transportation.

Actor and director Charles K. French was one of the first filmmakers to shoot a movie on the West Coast. His forty-year motion picture career began with a bit role in the 1909 drama *The Cord of Life*, which was filmed at a studio in Los Angeles. This was typical, as movies were nearly always shot in a studio, not on location. "When I came to the Pacific Coast six years ago," he recalled in 1915, "the auto had not begun to take a part in the making of pictures. On the few trips that were taken, we were forced to rely on the public conveyances. Long delays had to be put up with, as there was no other way."

The public conveyances provided mainly frustration for French and his fellow showplayers, who needed to arrive at a location shoot in full costume and makeup. There were no dressing rooms or trailers on site, not even for big stars like Sennett and Normand. And if the big stars didn't have dressing rooms, there certainly weren't any for the supporting actors. They did their preparations at the studio, rode the trolley looking like the character they were playing in the movie, and arrived on set ready to go. Then at day's end they rode the trolley back to the studio, undressed, and went home.

The production crew faced equally daunting challenges. They had to carry all the props, extra costumes, supplies, camera, and film on the trolley as well. Because a location shoot was so hard for everybody involved, moviemakers mostly avoided it—that is, until the arrival of the automobile. "Take the auto away from the picture producers and the enterprise would go back to where it was six years ago," said French. "The companies would have to content themselves with taking the scenes in the close vicinity of the studios. With the motor car, it is now possible to travel many miles from the studio and take pictures at a number of different places in one day. The other day I took the entire company into the mountains, thirty miles from Los Angeles, finished twenty-seven scenes and was back in town by six o'clock that evening. Without a machine, it would have been necessary to ship the stuff up there the day before and I am sure the one-day's work would have taken at least three days."

The varied geography of southern California proved a boon to filmmakers now that they could drive to these outlying areas. They could get off the beaten track and shoot in visually arresting settings, improving the look of their movies. "Comparatively little of the work is now done at the studios," said French, who, like other directors, suddenly had the means to tell stories on a grander scale. He wasn't tied to a studio anymore. His stories could involve more characters, be wider in scope, take place outdoors in nature or in cities.

Life got better for actors and actresses too. Whenever possible they ditched the trolley and rode in automobiles to location shoots; tourists from the rest of the country knew they were in Pictureland because they'd see actors in Los Angeles driving together in a car all in full makeup and costumes. The crew liked these new vehicles as well. Just throw the gear into a car or motor truck and off they went.

Location shooting gave the movies a competitive leg up over live theater, which took place on a stage, indoors. Then as today, filmmakers faced intense pressure to come up with new ideas and new stories told in fresh, never-before-seen ways. They also faced business pressure to get their products into the marketplace ahead of their competitors. Automobiles helped them on both counts by making the filmmaking process faster, easier, and more efficient.

Many studios in the early days rented vehicles, which sometimes caused problems. For *The Elopement*, starring Phillips Smalley and Lois Weber and produced by the Rex Company for Universal Pictures, the location shoot took place in the southern California desert. In the story, Smalley and Weber, who play newlyweds, get lost while eloping in their car, which the Rex Company had rented for the day. That night, after shooting wrapped, an employee from the rental company picked up the vehicle without telling anyone and returned to Los Angeles with it because another movie company needed it the next day. When the outraged crew of *The Elopement* found out what happened, they demanded the car back, and the rental company quickly sent another to replace the one it had taken. But this obviously would not do because Smalley and Weber had gotten stranded in a certain vehicle, and how would it look to have them suddenly driving, for no apparent reason, a different car?

Taking matters into his own hands, Smalley rushed back to Los Angeles, made some investigations, and found the car in question at a local garage where it was being repaired after it had smashed into a streetcar. "A squad of auto repair experts worked overtime until the car was in condition to rejoin the photoplayers in the heart of the desert," a movie writer concluded happily.

Automobiles helped change the look of a picture even if the picture was shot at the studio. Members of the crew drove around and found things—palm tree branches, old diner stools, baskets, whatever the story called for—that were added to the set to create authenticity. Cars also made a location scout's job far easier and more productive. The Automobile Club of Southern California assigned an employee to work with location scouts and others from the studios to help them find what they were looking for. "'Where's a bridge that's been washed out in the center?' is one of the latest queries to the Auto Club from a big moving picture concern in Hollywood," said a newspaper account. Other requests were for "a perfectly good mountain with one side burned off [or] a hot little landslide fresh from the peaks, or a spring (of water) that steams on demand." The studios needed unusual and scenic places to shoot, and the club happily provided tips on where to find them. The southern California vistas that appeared in these pictures boosted tourism and encouraged drivers to take to the road to see the country for themselves—messages that agreed with the goals of the club.

For similar reasons of boosterism and advertising, auto dealers and manufacturers loaned vehicles to the studios for use in their pictures. "One day last week L. F. Gottschalk of the Oz Studio called on the Bekins-Speers company for a demonstration of a Haynes Light Six car, and it so happened that a one-act comedy entitled *The Magic Bon Bon* was to be filmed in the afternoon," wrote a movie reporter. "During the progress of the play a motor car is used and [so] the Light Six was pressed into service." This exchange, reported as a coincidence although it almost certainly wasn't, ended with the Light Six making a cameo in the movie and studio head Gottschalk buying a new one from Bekins-Speers, probably at a discount. All this back-scratching also produced publicity for the car and the picture. The next week a photograph of *The Magic Bon Bon's* star, Violet MacMillan, riding in a flashy new Light Six, appeared in the newspaper.

The actress Lillian Gish, whose sterling career spanned both the silents and talkies, recalled that when she was starting out in pictures, the supporting actors rode the trolley to location shoots while the stars and directors always came in hired cars. "Four o'clock rising was not unusual during location trips," she said. "While it was still dark we would board the trolley car that would take us to the country. When we had leading parts we came by car, which the company hired. Mr. [D. W.] Griffith was driven by car too."

Thus began one of the enduring perks of celebrity culture: Stars do not drive; they are driven. But this status symbol originated largely from necessity. Many leading ladies and men did not know how to drive a car, or drive one safely. Being from the East and unfamiliar with southern California, they often got lost on Los Angeles roads, a not unfamiliar story today. The studios hired drivers to make sure the stars got to where they needed to go on time and in one piece.

Movies and cars had the best sort of business arrangement, one in which everybody benefited. Off screen, owning a luxury automobile became a hallmark of what it meant to be a star. Conversely, stars sold cars. Dealers couldn't buy the kind of advertising they got when a Mary Pickford or Douglas Fairbanks appeared in one of their cars, on screen or off. And so the rise of the Hollywood star system further intertwined the movies with automobiles.

As star salaries rose, so did the cost of making pictures. But cars helped keep these costs down. In trolley time, it took weeks to shoot a picture; in automobile time, only a few days. The machines worked at night when the high-priced stars partied and slept. The crew drove the film that had been shot that day to the processing labs, rounded up props and supplies, and ran errands so that everything could start promptly the next morning when the stars rose from their beauty sleep.

The motion picture industry was among the earliest industries in America to put the automobile fully to work. "Not only touring cars for the people," said one report from this time, "but large trucks for scenery and properties are used. The Selig Company keeps an immense Alco truck plying constantly between its East Side and Edendale studios; and when large scenes are planned at, say, San Pedro or Balboa or up in the San Fernando Valley, the truck is dispatched with the wardrobes, scenery, properties, etc., and everything is made ready before the touring cars deliver their human freight." Selig's motor fleet included Alco and Buick trucks and Pierce Arrow, Stearns, and Studebaker roadsters. In a given week shoots at Universal Studios used more than three hundred cars, owned and rented. The Balboa Feature Film Company owned and operated a garage to hold its one-hundred-thousand-dollar stable of cars and trucks. The American Film Company owned twenty-five cars, a trifle compared to Lasky Company's one hundred and the New York Motion Picture Company's two hundred. D. W. Griffith called on more than one hundred machines to move actors and equipment for a single scene in one of his epics.

"The motion picture people could not exist without the auto now," said French, mirroring the sentiments of the industry as a whole, "and it has made the game what it is today."

Nobody understood this better than Mack Sennett, who had the fastest and most expensive cars of any moviemaker in town. His drivers parked them in a row along Alessandro in front of the Keystone lot, with their snouts pointing out toward the street ready to go whenever they heard their boss shout, "We got us a spectacle, kids!" at which point actors and crew would run for the vehicles, clamber in, and speed off to whatever piece of lunacy, scripted or not, Sennett had in mind for them.

Whenever anything out of the ordinary was going on—parade, street fair, outdoor concert, air show, auto race—Sennett and his players created a story around it and filmed it. (Or they went out and shot the event first and then made up the story.) Spectators at the Santa Monica Road Race one year reacted in shock to a body being pulled behind a car on the course. The police saw it too, and set out after the car. Keystone's photographers captured the chase on film—real cops chasing a dummy being dragged around the streets—and it may have wound up in one of their comedies. (Many of Keystone's films have been lost; even the ones that survive are grainy and jumpy and hard to watch by modern standards.)

Sennett, said a film historian, was "the man whose work first presented us with the three noblest inventions of movie comedy: the pie, the banana peel, and the car." Sennett saw what filmmakers ever since have realized: Cars create action on the screen. Keystone's cars hurtled through walls and crashed into things, and in films such as *Love, Loot and Crash*, his chases featured the Keystone Cops, one of Sennett's—and film's—most original comic creations. Consisting of a handful of comic actors dressed in police uniforms, hats askew, with big furry mustaches, they pinballed crazily around the streets, climbing all over one another and hanging off the back of their out-of-control vehicle. Nobody was safe with the Cops on the loose, including the Cops, none of whom used doubles. During one chase sequence the Cops accidentally hit a gardener who was riding a motorcycle, knocking him to the ground. They stopped filming, loaded the man into their car, and started off for the hospital, smashing into another car on the way.

The climactic scenes of *Barney Oldfield's Race for a Life*, shot in Inglewood in February 1913, involved the use of a locomotive, baggage car, and passenger coach as well as an unused section of railroad track. Keystone's people had arranged with the

Redondo Railway to use its trains, equipment, and track. Local authorities also permitted Barney to break the speed laws in the Blitzen Benz, which was a nice treat for him because usually he did it without permission. A report filed afterward tells the story of the shoot: "Mack Sennett, the Keystone director, finished a picture yesterday in which speed is shown to an exaggerated degree. Barney Oldfield races his Benz at 90 miles an hour against a Santa Fe train traveling at the rate of 65 miles an hour, and rescues Mabel Normand, who is tied to the tracks. The villain, Ford Sterling, ties Miss Normand to the tracks, climbs into the cab of the locomotive and, with a blow on the head, renders Engineer McNeil of the Santa Fe unconscious and, with the throttle wide open, dashes down the track. Mack Sennett, the lover, discovers Barney's car. He calls the speed king and asks him to help him save the girl. Oldfield jumps into the car and, pulling Sennett into the seat beside him, dashes down the road in pursuit."

Keystone photographer Walter Wright filmed Oldfield and Sennett in the Benz, and Lee Bartholomew stood on the running board of the locomotive shooting Ford Sterling in the train. It was Barney vs. the Train, and Barney won the day. "The climax comes when Barney rounds a curve at 50 miles an hour and stops the car and Sennett jumps out and rescues Miss Normand from the shadow of the approaching train." With Mabel and Mack safely reunited, Barney in the Benz kept chasing Ford Sterling, who started throwing things at him from the cab of the locomotive. The film came out in June, and moviegoers around the country thrilled to see the great Barney Oldfield in what was surely the most exciting car sequence ever put on film up to that time.

Things worked out so well that Sennett invited Barney to do another picture later in the year. *The Speed Kings* starred Barney, fellow race drivers Teddy Tetzlaff and Earl Cooper, and Mabel Normand and Ford Sterling doing their usual schtick. Keystone Pictures continued to use autos and auto racing whenever possible, and in early 1914 it shot a picture at a children's car race in Venice, California. This one starred the young Charlie Chaplin. Donning a fake mustache, a too-small derby hat, and pants and shoes that were too big for him, Chaplin, in only his second movie, performs some humorous bits in front of the camera with the race in the background. *Kid Auto Races in Venice* marks the debut of the Tramp, one of the greatest comic characters to ever appear on film.

NINE

Shows of Wonder

After teaming up in the movies Barney Oldfield and Mack Sennett went their separate ways, though their paths crossed again at two of the biggest events in America in 1915: the Panama-California Exposition in San Diego and the Panama-Pacific International Exposition in San Francisco.

The San Diego fair began at the stroke of midnight on December 31 with a click of a Western Union telegraph key by President Woodrow Wilson in the White House. The click set off lights and fireworks in Balboa Park, the home of the fair. Expecting fireworks of a different sort, fifty thousand people lined the boulevards of Point Loma a week later to watch a road race featuring Oldfield and a top field of drivers that included the young Eddie Rickenbacker. One of the best in the world, Rickenbacker raced many times in California, enough to also become chums with Mack Sennett and visit him at his Edendale studio. The fun-loving Sennett once planted a story in the Los Angeles papers about a "Baron von Richenbacher," a Prussian nobleman cut out of the family will by his tyrannical father who had come to America to compete in the Santa Monica Road Race. At the starting line, the Baron was revealed, to the surprise of the other drivers, to be Eddie, who was not Prussian at all but a likable Midwesterner. In southern California for another year's race in Santa Monica, Rickenbacker took his first-ever airplane ride, a significant event for him personally and for the future of aviation. A pioneering and adventurous pilot, he won the Medal of Honor for air combat in World War I and later founded and ran Eastern Airlines.

But neither Rickenbacker nor Oldfield did much at Point Loma. Steady-as-she-goes Earl Cooper won the three-hundred-mile race with ease, averaging 65.3 miles per hour in his Stutz. Afterward he accepted his trophy at a Plaza de Panama ceremony in Balboa Park.

Much smaller than San Francisco or Los Angeles, San Diego (pop. 40,000) did not lack for ambition, and its fair—the largest such fair to be put on by a city of its size—sought to advertise its charms to the world. It had a beautiful, bustling port—the first American port of call for ships steaming up from the newly opened Panama Canal—and Balboa Park, its new civic park, offered such attractions as the Spreckels

Organ, donated by John Spreckels. More than one hundred and eighty thousand visitors came to the city in the first month of the fair; three of them were Sennett and his two Keystone stars, Mabel Normand and Roscoe "Fatty" Arbuckle, a young, rotund comedian with a gift, like Mabel, for slapstick. They were as ever a whirlwind of activity, shooting *Fatty and Mabel at the San Diego Exposition* and releasing it in January to capitalize on the fair's nationally publicized opening.

Fatty and Mabel play a married couple in the film. They watch a parade and do some slapstick bits in front of the expo fountain at Balboa Park. Even here Sennett managed to get his characters into moving vehicles, Fatty and Mabel jumping into a sightseeing cart and speeding off. The cart they drove may have been an Electriquette, an electric vehicle owned and designed by Clyde Osborn, a local attorney who ran the Fritchie electric car dealership in town and dabbled in electronics. Realizing that fair visitors would need wheels to get around spacious Balboa Park, he designed the two-passenger, battery-run vehicle with a body made entirely of wicker. It looked like a lounge chair on wheels. Rides cost a dollar apiece, and the battery ran eight hours before needing a boost. The two hundred or so Electriquettes at the fair apparently ran well enough, although Osborn abandoned electric car manufacturing after the fair and returned to his regular line of work.

Having finished their film, Sennett and Fatty Arbuckle almost surely drove back to Los Angeles rather than take the train. The Santa Ana–raised Arbuckle, who honed his comic skills by appearing in vaudeville houses around California, enjoyed fine automobiles with a gusto to match Sennett's. And as his fame in movies grew along with his bank account, so did his ability to indulge in all sorts of pleasures, automotive and otherwise. It's not as certain how Mabel would've gotten back home—by train or car—but she was a gamer, so it's easy to see her joining her friends for a frolicsome ride up the coast in something fast and expensive.

One place they surely would have stopped was the ritzy enclave of Del Mar, a popular tourist destination between the two cities. Despite the improvements over the years, the highway between San Diego and Los Angeles was still awful, a rough and treacherous dirt road with steep grades and sinking sands. Save for Del Mar and some other stops along the way, few places sold gas or snacks because there wasn't enough business to support them—no cars on the road. The Automobile Club of Southern California held in April what it claimed to be the longest motor rally ever, a string of some two hundred and fifty cars winding their way south from Los Angeles to the fair. A designated "scout car," bedecked with pennants so other drivers could easily spot it, blazed the trail. Its main job was to go ahead of the others to make sure the roads were passable and safe. "With a single stop, and that for luncheon at Riverside," said the club's bulletin, "the cars continued on to their destination through falling rain, over slippery roads with the determination to show the world that it could be done." Equally determined was the club's vow to improve these roads. "Although southern California, at this writing, is without doubt the most active territory in the world so far as road building is concerned; although there are more, longer and better boulevards in southern California than in any other part of

America, the 1915 Motor Tour of the Automobile Club has shown that not for a minute can this activity be allowed to lag, that it must continue until there are no dirt roads at all, which can be washed by the rains or buried by the dust, until San Diego is connected with Los Angeles by a solid ribbon of concrete looping along the coast and flattened out through the mountains."

The Auto Club drivers that day followed blue and white steel signs put up by other members of the club, whose work could be seen on roads all around southern California. In preparation for the San Diego fair, D. C. Smith, Perry Howard, and Judson Smith spent more than a year driving thousands of miles around California and the West in a three-ton truck putting up directional and mileage signs. They dynamited holes in the rock in some spots to mount the signs solidly in the ground. They and other club employees posted some four thousand signs along the National Old Trails Road, the precursor to Route 66 that began in Kansas City, Missouri, and crossed the Southwest until the road ran out of land in Santa Monica.

The year before the signs, only a couple of hundred hardy souls drove the Old Trails Road, which was, as its name suggests, little more than an old wagon trail. The signs perked up traffic on the trail considerably, although the number of cars on it was small compared to the more popular northern route across America, the Lincoln Highway. The Lincoln Highway was, along with Route 66, the other great east-west highway in the early years of automobiling. It was originally the idea of Carl Fisher, who had another grand idea that helped to shape automobile racing: the Indianapolis Motor Speedway, home of the Indianapolis 500. Fisher and the Lincoln Highway Association—an organization that still exists today, to keep alive the memory of the old road—saw the highway as a kind of Main Street of America, a decent, well-maintained set of roads that would, like the man it was named after, unite the country. Female driving pioneer Alice Ramsey covered portions of the Lincoln Highway before it had the name, crossing the Sierra along the path of today's Highway 50. The Lincoln Highway claimed both road crossings, Highway 50 and Interstate 80, reuniting in Sacramento after the split over the mountains. From Sacramento it carried south to Stockton, then cut across the Central Valley to the East Bay and the end of the line in San Francisco. (The highway could not go today's more direct route from Sacramento to San Francisco on I-80 because the Sacramento River spilled over its banks frequently, flooding the farmlands around Davis and making driving impossible. The construction of the Yolo Causeway in 1916 finally solved this problem.) Rough as they were, the roads in California were judged to be some of the best on the Lincoln Highway.

"In 1913 practically the only pavement on the Lincoln Way between the two coasts was in the cities," according to a highway guide. "About 655 miles of good macadam or stone road existed. The rest of the road, 2,480 miles, was natural dirt, gravel and sand." Just as the auto clubs installed road signs to help travelers, the energy, impetus, and financing for road construction largely came from private sources. Only a handful of states had highway departments like California's, and even California's, though growing, lacked resources and punch. Washington pitched in little as well, leaving the

Lincoln Highway Association to come up with creative ideas to pay for new roads. One of the association's ideas was the "seedling mile." Typically built in farm areas of the Midwest, a seedling mile consisted of a short stretch of concrete highway a few miles outside of town, far enough that people would have to get in their cars and drive over the usual rotten dirt roads to get there. Once they saw the difference between a smooth ride and a bumpy one, and one that turned to mud in winter versus one that functioned year-round, the hope was they'd be willing to pay more in taxes to let this seedling grow and multiply. And sure enough, people along the route mostly said yes, dipping into their pocketbooks for better roads and faster travel.

From these beginnings emerged "the first modern transcontinental highway," further shrinking the distances between communities and boosting communication and commerce. An early milestone was reached in 1912, when a team of drivers set out on the Lincoln Highway from New York City carrying three tons of Parrot soap in a flatbed Alco truck. People across the United States stood by the side of the road and cheered as it passed through their town. When it reached San Francisco it rode the ferry to Marin and drove up to the Carlson Currier Company in Petaluma, its final stop. There it dropped off the soap and completed the first coast-to-coast truck delivery of goods in American history.

The Lincoln Highway and the National Old Trails Road formed new immigrant trails for westward-bound travelers. Before the Panama-Pacific International Exposition in San Francisco, the Reo Motor Company predicted that a thousand Reos would travel from the East to San Francisco for the fair. The American Automobile Association estimated some six thousand vehicles would make the trip. Said one observer, "The Panama-Pacific International Exposition became a prime reason that more people were becoming adventuresome in their motorcars and exploring their nation."

One adventuresome family was Arthur Ryus, his wife, and their two children. They left New York in January and drove the Lincoln Highway to Chicago before turning south on the National Old Trails Road, accompanied every step of the way by rain, snow, and hail. "What we lacked in white-flaked blizzards," joked Ryus, "we made up for in good old black and sticky mud. In some places the thick adobe mud seemed as though it had been purposefully laid in front of us." Seven weeks after they started, they straggled into Los Angeles. Still, they and their Model K Hupmobile had enough fight left in them to turn north and reach the Panama-Pacific in time for its spectacular opening-day festivities.

Another who drove to the fair—or tried to, anyhow—was Emily Post. Post would later become famous for her bestselling book on manners and etiquette, but she began her career as a novelist and magazine freelancer with a lively wit and keen appetite for adventure. In April her editor at *Collier's* assigned her to do what so many other New Yorkers were doing that year: driving west to see the expo. (A popular song was "Hello Frisco.") Post thought this was a swell idea except for one thing: She didn't drive. So she called on her son Ned, who agreed to take a break from his studies at Harvard to handle this chore for his mother.

Starting later in the year than the Ryuses, the Posts still encountered bad weather and muddy roads. Another problem was the dearth of highway signs. And when one did appear it was often incorrect and sent them in the wrong direction. Which led to this conversation in Ohio when they pulled to the side of the road to ask a man for directions:

"Can you tell me which is the best road to California?" said Emily.

"The Union Pacific," came the reply.

While the Posts were floundering about, Henry B. Joy of Detroit was embarking on *his* transcontinental trip west. Joy drove a 12-cyclinder Packard—fitting, because he ran the Packard Motor Company. He also followed the Lincoln Highway, another apt choice because he was president of the Lincoln Highway Association. Meeting with far fewer problems than either the Posts or the Ryuses, he said hello to Frisco after only a few weeks on the road. As might be expected for someone with his connections, Joy found a prime parking spot at the exposition, driving his Packard Twin Six onto the fairgrounds and into the Palace of Transportation, where it went on display at the Packard exhibit.

Joy reached San Francisco ahead of the Posts, who had veered south on the National Old Trails Road, where they ran into more miseries, an experience Emily later recounted in her book *By Motor to the Golden Gate*. But, to be precise, they did not reach the Golden Gate by motor, at least not automobile motor. Figuring they'd had enough fun for one trip, the Posts shipped their car home from the Grand Canyon and caught the train the rest of the way. Progress was all well and good, but on the whole, they'd rather take a Pullman.

The Posts trained to the fair in San Diego and then went north to the one in San Francisco, which opened a month later. At noon on February 20, President Wilson, reprising his bit from San Diego, pressed a button in the White House sending a radio wave transmission to a New Jersey telegraph station, which beamed a signal across the country to antenna wires atop the four-hundred-foot-high Tower of Jewels, the center of the exposition. Its signal bounced simultaneously over to Machinery Hall, whose main doors opened automatically, and the Fountain of Energy, which burst into song. Fireworks shot into the sky, and a show of technological wonders never before seen in human history had begun.

More than 425,000 people, the largest gathering ever on the West Coast to that date, crowded into the Tower of Jewels area next to the Court of the Universe, roaring their approval at these theatrics. After the standard opening speeches by dignitaries and fair officials, more theatrics followed with the dazzling aerial acrobatics of Lincoln Beachey. The young native San Franciscan, America's most famous daredevil pilot, had for the past year toured the country in a series of Airplane vs. Automobile races with Barney Oldfield. Sweeping across the sky in his biplane—which, like all planes in 1915, had an open cockpit—he performed the loop-the-loop, his nerve-wracking perpendicular drop and other stunts. Also craning their heads to watch were those on boats scattered around the bay. Another memorable part of opening festivities was the parade of the battleship USS *Oregon* and other American naval ships entering the Golden Gate after crossing from the Atlantic Ocean through the Panama Canal.

Staged along bayfront land in what is now the Marina District of San Francisco, the expo contained more sights and amusements than anyone could see in a day, or a week: eighty thousand exhibits in dozens of pavilions sponsored by foreign countries and states. The eleven main palaces—Agriculture, Education, Food Products, Horticulture, Liberal Arts, Transportation, Machinery, Manufacturers, Mines and Metallurgy, Social Economy, and Varied Industries—formed "the most comprehensive collection of the activities and industries of the world ever assembled at a universal exposition." Festival Hall seated three thousand concertgoers, and Machinery Hall boasted the world's largest frame building under one roof. (Only one building from the exposition site, the elegant Palace of Fine Arts, survives today.)

Easily the loudest, wildest, and most exciting events at the fair were the American Grand Prix and Vanderbilt Cup road races. Both followed a scary four-mile course that ran through the streets of the exposition and looped around an old dirt and board track in the Presidio. "There probably never was a worse course thrown open to a set of speed men," remarked one writer who saw it. Cars needed to slow to 30 miles per hour just to make the short, sharp corners in the Presidio. Then the rains came and things turned ugly. Sloshing through dirt chuckholes filled with pools of water, their tires unable to grip the slick paved surfaces, racecars slid off the streets into areas thick with spectators. Even so, the fastest machines cracked 100 miles per hour on the Avenue of the Palms and, after throttling down to negotiate some hairpin turns, revved it back up to 85 on the backstretch past the Court of the Universe. England's Dario Resta in a Peugeot won the four-hundred-mile Grand Prix in late February, besting Oldfield, Rickenbacker, Earl Cooper, and other drivers who uniformly cursed the layout and the risks it obligated them to take. A week later the Englishman beat all the Americans again in a three-hundred-mile Vanderbilt Cup marred by close calls and crashes, though none apparently involved spectators. The worst crash involved Bob Burman in a Case speedster that "turned turtle at the right-angle turn near the Palace of Machinery. Burman and his mechanician, Joe Cleary, were thrown out. Both men were unconscious and were rushed to the hospital. Burman, it was found later, was only slightly injured, but Cleary's legs, shoulder and two ribs were broken."

Despite its dangers, or perhaps because of them, the Vanderbilt Cup drew one hundred thousand spectators astonished by these huge machines traveling at such high speeds over the rain-polished streets of the city. "This is a scene of indefinable beauty and fascination," wrote Jeanne Redman in a piece entitled "A Girl's Impressions of the Vanderbilt Cup Race." Redman, on assignment for the *Los Angeles Times*, covered other automobile activities for the paper, another sign of the growing appeal of cars among women. "I am on the ground standing waiting for the Vanderbilt Cup race. A clear blue sky above us, the bay spread out before us, the green hills of Marin County in the distance and Mt. Tamalpais towering over all. As for the fascination, I did not dream that an automobile race could hold so much of excitement and rapturous interest."

Also surely enraptured by these goings-on: Mack Sennett. Like other Keystone players he had come to San Francisco to see the spectacles and shoot film. *Wished on Mabel*, also starring Normand and Arbuckle, a comedic pairing that represented box office gold, opened in nickelodeons in March after being shot in Golden Gate Park.

But the biggest show at the expo, bar none, was at the Palace of Transportation on the north side of the Court of the Universe. America's last great world's fair had occurred a decade earlier in St. Louis; it featured fewer than two hundred automobiles and highlighted the latest in horse-drawn transportation. In San Francisco, noted one commentator wryly, "an exhibit of horse-drawn vehicles would have looked like a hangover from the days of Rip Van Winkle." In another sign of changing times, railroad exhibits occupied only a quarter of the one-hundred-thousand-square-foot building; cars, trucks, and motorcycles took up the rest of the space.

The still-young automobile industry was "the fastest growing industry in history," and looking around the palace one would have been hard pressed to dispute this fact. More than sixty of America's top car companies—Atterbury, Chalmers, Chesterfield, Dodge Brothers, Hudson, KisselKar, Locomobile, Maxwell, Metz, Mitchell, Oldsmobile, Paige, Pathfinder, Pierce-Arrow, Oakland, Ohio Electric, Overland, Reo, Saxon, Smith, Stearns-Knight, Sternburg, White, Willys-Overland, Winton, and many more—were showcasing their latest models, all of which were available for sale to the public. "No doubt the largest and costliest mechanical display ever under a single roof," marveled one. "The greatest automobile show in the history of motordom," said another. Everywhere you turned, some shiny, tricked-out dream-mobile was vying for your attention.

Arthur Ryus and his family surely stopped in at the Hupmobile exhibit at Location 783 in Block 11 of the palace. The popular Hup had recently been shown in New York and Detroit, but its manufacturer was making a special promotional push in San Francisco, an effort shared by other manufacturers as well. White's large exhibit included a twelve-passenger bus and ten touring models. Buick nearly matched that with a truck and seven pleasure cars. Maxwell brought a touring car that converted into a sleeper for camping trips. All three KisselKar brands—Kissel, Briscoe, and Federal trucks—presented floor models. Because the internal workings of automobiles were still a mystery to many, lots of companies displayed engines and chassis. Chalmers exhibited "a specially made polished steel chassis with baked enamel cylinders and casings." An Overland chassis alone cost $15,000.

Henry B. Joy's company impressed with "a very beautiful Packard in a glass case. It was painted in cream white with gold leaf trimmings, on a black chassis, and it had white wheels and black upholstering and was altogether a sumptuous and handsome object, illustrative of the luxury of modern life." And when Joy parked his dirtied-up cross-country Twin Six next to this beauty, it made a sales pitch to prospective buyers without having to say a word: Packards were beautiful *and* tough.

The war in Europe, begun the previous summer, stopped many foreign companies from coming to California, but a few still displayed their wares: England's Rolls

Royce and Italy's Isotta-Fraschini and Italia-Bianchi. The dark times overseas made the Jeffery Company's exhibit of particular note. It included "three trucks on display, including one of the four-wheel-drive 'Quad' trucks which have become so popular in the European war zone as an armored car." Jeffery's off-road armored car featured a Colt machine gun mounted on the roof.

The Automatic Transportation Company was showing off its electric trucks powered by Edison batteries. Other truck makers at the show were Bessemer, General, Sterling, and two California brands: Baker of San Francisco and Moreland of Burbank. Walt Moreland, the owner of Moreland Trucks, designed an early version of the Tourist automobile for the Auto Vehicle Company of Los Angeles. While there he met Carl Breer, who was working part time for the company while going to college. After Breer fulfilled his engineering requirements at Caltech, Stanford admitted him and he went off to study in Palo Alto. In the summer he returned home to Los Angeles to work for Moreland, who had left Auto Vehicle to create the Duro, a sporty new car. Breer helped design the Duro and liked it so much he drove one back to Palo Alto when he resumed school in the fall.

The Duro later fizzled out but the two engineers remained friends. When Moreland founded his truck company, he hired Breer to work for him there as well.

Studebaker, another car builder with California ties, had a booth at the fair too. John Studebaker, one of five brothers, came to California during the gold rush and earned a reputation among miners for building sturdy, well-made wheelbarrows. Returning to his native Indiana with the money he made out West, he went into the farm vehicle business with his brothers. Steadily they left horses behind and began manufacturing the Studebaker Auto Delivery Vehicle and other cars with a reputation for durability and quality.

One of those milling amidst the crowds at the exposition was a thirteen-year-old San Francisco boy whose parents had given him a yearlong pass to the fair, so he could see as much of it as he wished, and as often. "The exposition was large, complex and astounding: a confusion of multitudes of people, more than I had ever encountered, with conversations at excitement levels and innumerable things to see," recalled Ansel Adams years later in his autobiography. "In some respects it was a tawdry place, a glorious and obviously temporary stage set, a symbolic fantasy and a dream world of color and style."

The year before, Adams had experienced his first-ever automobile ride compliments of a family friend. As he wrote, "One day Mr. Born drove me into town and back in his two-cylinder Reo automobile. Proceeding home out Lake Street at 18 m.p.h. with hands white-knuckled grasping the jiggling steering wheel and the engine coughing and clattering under the seat, he yelled, 'If a front wheel should come off, we would be crushed to jelly!'"

The wheel did not come off and Mr. Born and his passenger arrived safely home, and a good thing too. For in the summer of his fourteenth year the boy would achieve another lifetime first: going to Yosemite. In the park his parents would give him another gift, that of a Kodak Box Brownie, and he would begin taking pictures.

When the young Adams, whose interests centered more on music and art than cars, entered the automobile section of the palace, he would have seen huge electrified relief maps showing the routes for the Lincoln Highway, National Old Trails Road, and state highways such as El Camino Real (roughly Highway 101 today), which was becoming a popular way for motorists to explore California's missions. The remarkable Plank Road, built of wooden planks, stretched across the Sand Hills desert and connected San Diego drivers with the Imperial Valley and Arizona. Even more remarkable was the Ridge Route, the precursor to Interstate 5 along the Grapevine and one of the biggest highway-building projects in the United States. Beginning north of the Santa Clarita Valley around Castaic Junction, the Ridge Route cut a trail through the Tehachapi mountains where none had existed before, cresting at 5,300 feet and scaring the hell out of every driver who braved its windy, narrow roads and dizzying cliffs. "It skirts thousand-feet precipices," said one, "and disappears within cuts that are tunnel-like in their depth." The biggest cut, Swede's Cut, went one hundred feet into the mountainside, and over the course of the project 1 million cubic yards of earth got picked up and moved from where nature had originally put it. The road contained nearly seven hundred curves and sprouted a forest of blue and white signs warning drivers to go slow, take it easy. Many travelers got sick to their stomachs because the drive was so curvy.

Still, the benefits of the Ridge Route outweighed its magnificent flaws. It cut more than 60 miles off the drive between Los Angeles and Bakersfield and linked southern and northern California in a new, more direct way. No longer did drivers or truckers have to make the long detour through the Mojave to go between Los Angeles and the San Joaquin Valley. "[It is] one of the most remarkable engineering feats by the State Highway Commission," wrote the *San Francisco Chronicle.* "It is Southern California's magnum opus in mountain highway construction." Over the years, though, the road caused too many accidents and claimed too many lives, leading to the construction of a safer alternate route in the early 1930s. Interstate 5 over the Tejon Pass opened in 1970.

Road building in California had been helped by the passage of an $18 million highway bond measure in the same election that brought Hiram Johnson to power. Over the decade California voters would approve three more highway bond measures, each bigger than the last: $15 million in 1915, $18 million in 1917, $40 million in 1919. California trailed only New York, a far more populous state, in car registrations. To keep up with this ever-rising tide, the state formed a new agency, the Department of Motor Vehicles, to oversee registration and licensing. All those who wished to operate a car or truck now needed a license to do so, and these fees brought millions into the state treasury. The first California license plates had a brick red background with white characters; the registration tag was originally affixed not to the plate but inside the cab, usually on the dash. (A metal registration tag did not appear on license plates until 1916.) State registration cost three dollars, with an additional fee based on the size of the vehicle's engine. But this "horsepower tax," as critics called it, proved highly unpopular, and the state later dropped it in favor of a new method of raising revenue that applied to all motorists regardless of the beast they were driving: a gasoline tax. California's first gasoline tax, in 1923, was two cents per gallon.

The 1916 federal Highway Aid Act boosted road building still more. It provided matching funds to the states for road construction on the condition they form a highway department. California was already ahead of the game in this regard, having created its bureau of highways many years before, and it received millions in federal aid.

All this activity represented a shift in the public's attitudes toward automobiles. One more sign of this shift: Ansel Adams's future stomping grounds of Yosemite National Park ended its ban on cars, as did Sequoia National Park in the southern Sierra. The lifting of these bans came about due to lobbying by the auto clubs and industry advocates, but the small towns and businesses on the roads in and out of the mountains also supported the change. Cars brought tourists to these out-of-the-way places, and the tourists spent money on gas, souvenirs, groceries, restaurant meals, and the like, boosting the local economy.

The automobile was showing itself to be a remarkably resilient organism with an almost evolutionary ability to adapt to its environment. It found ways to fit into people's lives, whatever they were doing, wherever they were. And nowhere did it find people more welcoming, and the environment more conducive to growth, than in California.

"I think the reason for the rapid growth of the use of automobiles on the Pacific Coast is found in the eagerness of the Californian to adopt new ideas," wrote one observer from this time. "The motor-driven vehicle was a new idea, and where the conservative East waited, the impetuous West seized at it and made it its own."

Appropriately, considering how he had ridden into office, Governor Hiram Johnson arrived at the Panama-Pacific Exposition in a car, forsaking his old Locomobile steamer for a gasoline-powered Cadillac. This Cad, one of six purchased by the state of California for use by the governor and fair commissioners, boasted a new type of engine: "the new model, eight-cylinder V-type motor [that] is proving of great interest to motor enthusiasts," as indeed it would for the next century or so. Cadillac was the first American company to build a V-8, and it had brought it to San Francisco for its West Coast debut. (A few years later the engine would go out of production.) The Cadillac Eight also served as the official ambulance for the expo.

Except for special cases such as the governor, private vehicles could not enter the exposition grounds, a rule that created an opening for Volney Beardsley, an enterprising automobile man from Los Angeles. Another graduate of the Auto Vehicle Company, he had formed the Beardsley Electric Company to make electric coupes and roadsters and like the Electriquettes in San Diego, his cars supplied rides for leg-weary fairgoers in San Francisco. But electric cars were not as novel as they once were, and so Beardsley needed to do something to make them stand out from the crowd.

What he did was stage an endurance run, but not with Lester Whitman or some hoary old guy but rather his wife, Minnie. Accompanied by a woman observer appointed by the press, Minnie drove a Beardsley Brougham fifteen hundred miles around California on fourteen consecutive days in July. Each day she covered a little over one hundred miles on a single battery charge, demonstrating her husband's claim that the Brougham needed only one charge to run all day long. The observer riding with her stipulated that yes, this was indeed the case, and when Minnie arrived in San Francisco her husband's car got far more attention than it would've ordinarily received.

Other electric manufacturers showed their stuff in San Francisco, as did parts and accessories manufacturers for steam and gas engines. The W. C. Hendrie Rubber Company of Torrance staked a claim as the first manufacturer of tires in California. Then there were the scads of motorcycles—Davis, Dayton, Harley-Davidson, Indian—on display from all over the country. Also drawing interest was the Standard Oil of California exhibit—a life-sized replica of a filling station, a novelty for many people who'd never seen one before. Standard Oil and other oil companies in the state were developing filling stations as a means of solving one of their biggest problems: how to get gasoline easily and conveniently into the thirsty tanks of automobiles. Supply was not a worry then. Rich lodes of crude oil were discovered in southern California as early as the 1850s, and more strikes continued in the decades after that. Nor was price a problem either. Since oil was abundant and locally grown, gas was cheap. And with the growing popularity of automobiles, refineries around the state were rapidly turning their processing power away from kerosene—formerly the most valuable crude oil product—to gasoline, the new coin of the realm. Still all of this did nothing to solve the vexing problem of delivery.

Motorists had grown tired of the old method of buying gasoline in tins in hardware and grocery stores. Even less popular were the wholesale outfits known as "bulk depots." Bulk depots stored gasoline in big steel drums stacked onto wooden scaffolding in an outdoor lot. Each drum had a control spout, and you placed your empty gas can under the spout, filled it up, then poured the contents into your tank with a funnel. This was unfiltered gas, so you had to put a chamois cloth over the tank's opening to stop sediment from getting in. Since early automobiles lacked fuel gauges, a refilling tube similar to an oil dipstick showed how much fuel was in the tank. If a refilling tube was curved, however, you needed to put your ear to the end of the line and listen to the sound of the sloshing inside to get an accurate reading on it. Sometimes an air bubble formed and shot liquid back out the tube, giving you an earful of gas.

Even if you avoided this indignity, gasoline inevitably spilled onto the ground and formed puddles when you were filling up. Fires and accidents at bulk depots occurred all too often, which was why they were usually located far outside of town. Truckers started bringing gasoline from these depots to stores in town that were abandoning the old over-the-counter sales method and installing pumps outside in front. But these curbside pumps raised safety worries and created messes of their own. By zoning and other methods, city planners restricted where and how gasoline could be sold, eventually giving birth to the modern filling station.

One of California's pioneers in this regard was a young Stanford graduate named Earl Gilmore. His father, Arthur Gilmore, owned a dairy farm in the Rancho La Brea district, around the area of Third and Fairfax, now the site of the Farmer's Market. In the early 1900s, while looking for a water supply for his cattle, Arthur sunk a drill into the ground and found something even better: California crude. His dairy farm quickly became an oil farm, creating the sort of dizzying wealth that, among other things, allowed Arthur to send his son to Stanford. But the money wasn't wasted on the industrious Earl, who, after receiving his diploma in Palo Alto, came back home to the Gilmore oil fields, borrowed an old farm wagon, painted it red and yellow, mounted a gas tank onto the rear bed, parked it on a busy stretch of nearby Wilshire Boulevard, and sold gasoline to all comers for ten cents a gallon. His idea took off from there, and in the years to come a string of brightly painted red and yellow Red Lion gas stations opened up around California and the West. (Mobil Oil later bought the stations.) Earl also built Gilmore Stadium, which became the center for midget automobile racing in this country in the 1930s, and Gilmore Oil sponsored the Gilmore Red Lion Special cars that won racing championships up and down the coast.

Unhappy about buying gas in tins at the store or at those ugly and dangerous bulk depots, Earle C. Anthony can also claim some gas station pioneering. His employees erected a pump outside his Packard dealership on Olive Street in Los Angeles and painted it red and white to match Packard's colors. Like Earl Gilmore's, Earle Anthony's concept took off and he came to own some two hundred and fifty Red and White Filling Stations before selling out to Standard Oil the year before the exposition. The logo for Standard Oil, now Chevron, is one of the world's best-known corporate trademarks. It derives from Anthony's original logo design for his Red and Whites, a chevron with diagonal stripes.

Filling stations were another example of how automobiles were fitting into people's lives, and how their lives were changing because of them. The pace of modern society was quickening, and the cause was as simple as the difference in speed between a horse and a car. Visitors to the Palace of Transportation could see, with their very own eyes, how much faster life was becoming at the one, absolute, must-attend exhibit of the entire fair. The Ford Motor Company exhibit wasn't just an exhibit; it was an event. Every person mentioned in this chapter who came to San Francisco surely visited it, for no one could leave the fair without saying he or she saw it. But it wasn't just for car buffs. Nobody in California or the West had ever seen anything like it. For that matter, few people in the world had ever witnessed anything so spellbinding.

Two years earlier Henry Ford had introduced the moving assembly line at his Highland Park, Michigan, factory, the first in automobile history, and he and his company had built a smaller version of it in San Francisco. Frank Morton Todd saw this working demonstration of the future and explained how it worked: "This plant was one of the main show places of the Exposition. Every afternoon hundreds of visitors lined up along the guard rail and watched the process as though life depended on it. They saw a chassis start down a long pair of skids, moving at the rate of fifteen inches a minute and, under the skilled hands of operatives that worked deliberately but never made a waste motion, accumulate springs, wheels, transmission shafts, a tonneau, the requisite cushions, an engine, a top, a windshield, a gasoline tank with a little gasoline, and everything else it needed, and then, under its own power, glide out into the court where the big Neptune's Daughter was standing on a fish."

Instead of one or two men building a car by hand over a period of months, as had been the custom in automobiles since the beginning, the crowds jostling against the rail in the northeast corner of the palace saw groups of workers standing at stations alongside a moving belt, attaching parts, only parts, to the machine they were building. They used standardized parts—another Ford innovation for automobiles—and astonishingly, unbelievably, built a complete, fully functioning, fully drivable automobile *in minutes*. Todd continued, "Within four minutes after the Exposition opened, this plant sent out the first car. After that it assembled eighteen cars a working day throughout the season, practically speaking. It may have missed a few, or assembled a few less cars sometimes, but it turned out a total of 4,338, all of which were taken immediately by the distributors. They were spoken for, weeks in advance. Some went directly to China on the steamers from San Francisco. There were from forty to forty-five men in attendance. The material came into the grounds in trucks after eleven o'clock at night, and the work began at 1:40 in the afternoon, and continued until 4:40."

The car they were ordering in China, the car gliding one after another into the courtyard of Neptune's Daughter, was the Model T.

The Model Ts being built in San Francisco were fundamentally the same ones being sold around the world. With the same basic color (black), same basic features, and the same ridiculously low price—as little as $675 per vehicle—this explained why Ford dealers were finding it impossible to keep them in stock. Most everybody could afford a Model T, and most everybody wanted one.

Ford's advertising for the Model T claimed "High-Priced Quality in a Low-Priced Car." Remarkably, and this was only one of the many wonders of the car, it actually delivered on this promise. Offering great gas mileage, built high off the ground (to miss the bumps and rocks on the bad roads of the time), innovative (it introduced left-hand steering so drivers could see oncoming traffic better, a feature copied by other manufacturers), with excellent steering, a simple three-pedal system, and its parts all fitted to a T, it ran better than cars that sold for thousands of dollars more. When it was introduced in 1908 it became an instant hit, and by the time of the fair it had passed 1 million in sales. It thrived in the city or on the farm, hauling like a champ wherever it went. You could chop its top off and turn it into a flatbed truck or mount steel wheels or harrows in the rear and use it as a tractor. It was also easy to drive and it did anything you asked it to without complaint. Well, it complained. Every car does, from time to time. But with an inspired use of boot leather or bailing wire, even a nonmechanical person could put a quick fix on a T and be back on the road again in no time. Striking another blow for independent women, magazine writer Helen Gaut became the first female to drive solo across the desert from Pasadena to Arizona on "one of the roughest and worst [roads] in the world." The car she did it in was a Model T Torpedo Runabout.

Yet for all its astonishing success, and here was another wonder of the car, Henry Ford did not raise its sales price; he *lowered* it, figuring that with the efficiencies he was achieving through mass production he could make money by selling in volume. The average price of a T dropped to less than $400 and its already sky-high sales shot to the moon. By 1920 half of all the new cars in the world were Model Ts. Ford ultimately sold 15 million of them, the most ever for a car until, decades later, the Volkswagen Beetle surpassed it.

But even the Beetle cannot match the social impact of the Model T. Its low-cost excellence was only one part of the revolution it caused, a revolution that included higher wages for those skilled Ford operatives on the assembly line. The company paid its employees the unheard-of wage of five dollars a day, higher than any other manufacturer of cars or other mass-produced products, based on the premise that motivated, well-compensated employees would produce inspired work. (Ford's benefits package was a model, too.)

Henry Ford, a non-Californian, changed the lives of millions of Californians and Americans by putting car ownership within their grasp, making it an achievable part of the American dream. The rich would continue to seek status by buying expensive automobiles that others could not afford, but Ford exposed this class of buyers as only one piece of the marketplace, and a narrow one at that. The biggest class was ordinary Americans, the people who were buying the Model T in record numbers and watching them spring to life at the Palace of Transportation.

With the coming of the Model T, motor vehicles reached—to use a contemporary term—critical mass. The tipping point was tipped. To the pleasure principle of automobiles, together with the freedom, youthful desire, and worldly success they embodied, Henry Ford had added ingredients solidly in the American grain: practicality, reliability, durability, and simplicity, all at a bargain price. Cars were no longer a trend or a fancy; they were *here.* America was on wheels.

Hopped up about hop-ups at a 1956 southern California drag race.

PART THREE

Birth of the Modern

TEN

Wheelboys

Henry Ford's moving assembly line later got installed on a more permanent basis in Ford factories in Long Beach and Richmond. The Long Beach Assembly Plant on Henry Ford Avenue in Long Beach opened in 1929, producing hundreds of thousands of cars and trucks until it closed in the late 1950s. During World War II it retooled to build tanks and military vehicles, as did its counterpart in the north. The Richmond Assembly Plant opened the year after Long Beach and became known during the war as the Richmond Tank Depot, another of the factories that worked 'round the clock for the Arsenal of Democracy. Its car building plant shut down in the fifties as well. But the old Ford building, innovative for its use of windows and natural light in a factory setting, is now part of the Rosie the Riveter/World War II Home Front National Historical Park in Richmond.

When the factories in Long Beach and Richmond opened, the United States dominated world automobile production. It manufactured 5 million new cars a year compared to No. 2 Great Britain with 240,000. French, German, and Italian carmakers trailed the British, and Japan made only five hundred cars annually. The United States manufactured more automobiles than the rest of the world combined, and this astounding productivity came mainly from three companies: Ford, General Motors, and Chrysler. The Big Three established manufacturing plants in California, which ranked second behind Michigan in the assembly and production of cars, a standing that has of course changed dramatically in recent years. With the death knell sounding in 2009 for the last car factory in the state, the joint GM-Toyota plant in Fremont, California no longer is a home for major automobile manufacturing.

But in 1915, the year of the world fairs in San Diego and San Francisco, this new Machine Age was only beginning to kick into gear, and excitement about it was everywhere. One could see it in the awestruck expressions of the faces crowding into the Palace of Transportation and indeed in faces all around the exposition. One could hear it, too, in the proud comments of San Diego and San Francisco civic and business leaders, showing off their cities to international acclaim. Every American felt similar pride over the completion of the Panama Canal, an engineering and construction triumph that ranked with the greatest anywhere, at any time, by any country. France couldn't build it but America could, and did, ushering in a new global era of trade and transportation.

But amidst this excitement, amidst these feelings of hope and optimism for what the future might bring, a sober realism tempered the joy. While the assembly line brought jobs, rising incomes, and staggering productivity, it also struck at the heart of individual creativity, the traditional and honored role of the craftsman making one piece by hand and feeling pride of ownership in his work. A person on the line assembling a machine was like a cog in a machine himself, and although many line workers felt pride in what they did—a pride to match any craftsman—it was not the same thing, and people understood this. They also realized that some of the machines they were admiring in San Diego and San Francisco—crawler-type tractor-tanks, four-wheel-drive vehicles mounted with guns, airplanes capable of dropping bombs from the air—were doing duty in the killing fields overseas.

Again, in San Francisco, people saw, with their very own eyes, a spectacular display of the destructive potential of these new machines. A month after he had wowed the crowds with his aerial stunts on the Panama-Pacific's opening day, Lincoln Beachey went up in a new monoplane to perform one of his signature tricks, the perpendicular drop. For the drop, which he had done many times before, he shut the engine off and fell straight down hundreds of feet in the air before restarting the motor and pulling out of it. But this time, with thousands watching from the waterfront, including his brother, the engine did not restart and his plane plummeted out of control into the bay, disintegrating on impact. The USS *Oregon* and other ships immediately launched a search and rescue mission and recovered his body a few hours later.

The death of the famous young daredevil, not yet thirty years old, made headlines around the country, and surely knocked at least a temporary hole in the business of the flying concession at the exposition. This loss of business may have caused the concessionaire to pack up and leave. In any event, late in the year, a new flying service took over the job of providing airplane rides to fair visitors. Given Beachey's fate and the fact that airplanes were an even more dangerous and exotic proposition than automobiles, you'd have to be an optimist of the most extreme sort to think you could make a business like that succeed. Actually, in this case, there wasn't just one extreme optimist; there were two. Their names were Malcolm and Allan Loughead.

The Loughead brothers—later they changed the spelling of their name to Lockheed—ran the Meyer-Loughead Flying Service of San Francisco. Their jobs with the company matched their respective personalities: Malcolm, late twenties, quiet and inwardly drawn, the chief mechanic; his younger brother Allan, the pilot, sociable, outgoing, "the hail-fellow-well-met type," as a friend and partner of theirs, Jack Northrop, put it later. Allan doubled as the salesman for the service, sweet-talking the tourists out of ten dollars apiece for the chance to see Alcatraz Island from the rear seat of their canvas and wood Model G seaplane with its top speed of 60 miles per hour. But for all their differences, the brothers had plenty in common.

Both had blade-sharp engineering minds although neither had ever set foot in a college classroom or taken a formal engineering course. What they knew about engines their hands and eyes and ears had taught them through endless hours of tinkering on both planes and automobiles.

The Lockheeds loved driving almost as much as they loved flying. Born in the East Bay town of Niles, they were living with their parents on a farm in the Santa Clara Valley when Malcolm left for San Francisco in the early 1900s to make his way in the big city. The White Steamer agency on Market and Franklin hired the teenager as a mechanic, and his duties included road testing the cars after they were repaired. Malcolm drove those cars hard, demonstrating a family trait. "Speed," said a biographer, "had a visceral appeal for the Lockheed boys."

It was as a thrill-riding teenager that Malcolm first started thinking about a better way to bring automobiles to a stop. Car brakes then worked much like bicycle brakes: you stepped on a pedal that connected to a line leading to the brake assembly, which put pressure on a drum to slow or stop the turning of the wheels. But the brake often applied uneven pressure on the drum, causing the car to jerk haphazardly or pull to the left or right as it came to a stop. You also had to stomp hard on the pedal, and even then you couldn't be sure it would engage properly.

Following his big brother's lead Allan came to San Francisco a couple of years after Malcolm. He too found work as a mechanic and acted as a "demonstrator" for Corbin automobiles, driving them in races and exhibitions around the city. His racing in a Full Jewel Corbin earned him a local reputation as a heavy-footed daredevil.

Allan made six dollars a week as a mechanic, which kept him going while he nurtured his dreams of flying. Those dreams started catching up to reality when his stepbrother Victor asked him to join him in a new airplane venture he was working on in Chicago. Like Malcolm and Allan, Victor grew dreamy at an early age about the possibilities of planes and cars. He repaired cars and wrote about them and helped found the national Society of Automotive Engineers before pursuing an even stronger interest in aircraft design and engineering. In Chicago he had formed an airplane company with a wealthy car dealer in the area. Needing a mechanic for their planes, they contacted Allan, who quit his car job to pursue the calling he would follow the rest of his life.

Allan took his first flight in Chicago in the company's plane; it was hard to control, even harder to turn, and nearly impossible to land in one piece. But "none of this bothered Allan Lockheed, who was certain that his automobile racing aptitude would be transferred to flying." The instincts of this kid—he was twenty-one—were spot-on. His plane took off from a racetrack, flew a few wobbly circles in the air, bumped back down on the ground and skidded to a stop. "It was partly nerve, partly confidence and partly damn foolishness," Allan recalled years later. "I was now an aviator."

An aviator, yes. And an automobilist too. When things turned sour in Chicago—both Allan and Malcolm fought with Victor and broke off relations with him—Allan sold his motorcycle to buy two train tickets to San Francisco for his wife and himself. Back on his home turf, he caught on again as an automobile mechanic, probably at the

White agency where Malcolm had become a supervisor. This was a consistent pattern for the brothers. Whenever one of their flying projects crashed and burned and they went broke—"not a new experience," Allan joked once—they found paying gigs in automobiles to lift themselves out of the mess they were in. One of Malcolm's most colorful adventures occurred during the Mexican Revolution when he briefly served as a mechanical advisor for the rebel forces in Mexico, staying just long enough to acquire a Paige roadster driven by a commander in the field. It's not known if the commander gave it to Malcolm in gratitude for his work on behalf of the cause or if Malcolm bought it from him. In any case, Malcolm's roadster caused comment in San Francisco because it was the only one in town with bullet holes in it.

Reunited with his brother, Malcolm found their flying business in its customary state of upheaval in 1915. An angry investor had locked their experimental Model G seaplane in a warehouse and refused to hand over the key until the Lockheeds paid him the money they owed him for financing the plane's construction. Here, San Francisco restaurateur Paul Meyer rode to the rescue, fronting them the cash to get the Model G out of hock. The brothers restored it to tip-top shape and it was then that they formed the Loughead-Meyer Flying Service to deliver thrills to visitors at the Panama-Pacific Exposition, many of whom had never flown before.

The flying service represented a turnaround in luck for the luck-starved Lockheed brothers. They earned six thousand dollars in two months, enough to buy out Meyer and take full control of the Model G. The next year they moved to Santa Barbara, where their mother was living and where they had family ties. The Model G made the trip with them to Santa Barbara, becoming the biggest and virtually only material asset of their new company, the Lockheed Aircraft Manufacturing Company. Like early automobiles, airplanes were the ideal investment for those who wished to never see their money again. But the Lockheeds attracted some seed capital from investors and set up shop in the back of a garage on the 400 block of State Street, where they aroused the curiosity of a recent Santa Barbara High graduate, John Northrop.

Like the Lockheeds, the shy and serious Northrop learned about engines by tinkering on automobiles. But, also like the Lockheeds, he wasn't just interested in making engines get up and go, he wanted them to get up and go off the ground. Skinny and blond and from a poor family (he lived in a boardinghouse and tent when growing up, with floorboards over the dirt), he had started as a car mechanic before landing a job as an architectural draftsman. The office where he worked was near the Lockheeds' garage, so every day he'd poke his head inside to see what the brothers were up to. Northrop, who had been to San Francisco and seen the Model G in action, felt confident he could contribute to the operation. "Entirely self-taught, having no formal college education in engineering sciences, Northrop was a natural genius at the then little-known science of stress analysis," said one who knew and admired him. Finally the youngster screwed up his courage to ask for a job, citing his drafting, design, and mechanical skills. The brothers hired him to be their "chief engineer," and the Lockheed Aircraft Manufacturing Corporation, strong on optimism but light on cash, had a new partner.

This was 1917. The war in Europe was in its third year and the United States was about to join the fight. The war consisted primarily of long infantry and artillery battles, but American-built planes piloted by the likes of Eddie Rickenbacker served a useful role, engaging in spying and reconnaissance, bombing runs, and aerial dogfights with the German air force. When the Lockheed brothers tried, and failed, to obtain contracts to build fighter aircraft for the United States government, it forced them to scramble to make ends meet any way they could, flying at carnivals and air shows, ferrying tourists between Santa Barbara and the Channel Islands, and doing stunt work for the motion picture industry.

Meantime Malcolm Lockheed returned to the problem that had perplexed him since he was a teenager: how to get a car to stop better. He felt that an all-wheel hydraulic braking system would be a vast improvement in safety and efficiency over traditional mechanical braking methods. You didn't have to push as hard on the pedal with hydraulics, and yet you gained more control because the car responded quicker and more reliably. To test his theories he called on his old Paige roadster from the Mexican Revolution, driving it around Santa Barbara in a frenzy of stopping and starting. He bragged at one point that he could "stop the car on a dime and have a nickel change left over." And to prove it he drove headlong into a garage and stopped the Paige within inches of the rear wall.

Malcolm was still working out the kinks on his system when the Lockheed Aircraft Manufacturing Corporation collapsed. One of Allan Lockheed's and John Northrop's big ideas was to create a flying equivalent to the Model T—"an everyman's plane," durable, cheap, easy to operate. Their prototype was a failure and busted them once more. Needing work, Northrop left for Los Angeles (there to join another young man with flying dreams, Donald Douglas), and Allan went back to his familiar standby of car repair until he could cobble together some more money or find a new financial angel.

This latest failure brought an end to Malcolm's aviation career and began a new one for him in automobiles. He left California for Detroit and founded the Lockheed Hydraulic Brake Company, which landed its biggest client in the early 1920s when the Maxwell-Chalmers Company agreed to install hydraulic brakes on its Chalmers automobiles. The head of Maxwell-Chalmers was Walter Chrysler, who became the founder and president of the Chrysler Corporation. One of Chrysler's best hires as a chief executive was Carl Breer, who, after getting his education in California, also left for greater automobile opportunities in the heartland. He and two other Chrysler engineers, Owen Skelton and Fred Zeder, became known in the industry as the Three Musketeers because they always worked together as a team. Walter Chrysler described the trio as "wizards," assigning them the task of perfecting Malcolm Lockheed's innovative but as yet imperfect braking system. Breer and his fellow musketeers improved and refined hydraulic brakes to make them suitable for production cars. In the years to come all-wheel hydraulic brakes would become the industry standard, preventing accidents, injuries, and saving lives. Most cars today use hydraulic braking systems.

Malcolm Lockheed later sold his brake company for $1 million. Ever the lover of risky schemes he plunged his fortune into a gold-mining venture in the Sierra foothills, destroying both his fortune and his spirit. He died in Mokelumne Hill in the late 1950s, old enough to see the twin passions of his youth, cars and planes, grow into maturity and industrial might. After the collapse of their Santa Barbara company, Allan Lockheed and Jack Northrop reunited later in the decade to form the Lockheed Aircraft Corporation of Burbank. There they designed and built one of the most famous airplanes of all time, the Lockheed Vega, which carried Amelia Earhart across the Atlantic in 1932, the first solo transatlantic flight by a woman. Allan ultimately lost control of the company bearing his name to another ownership group, which grew Lockheed into one of the world's most formidable aircraft concerns. Jack Northrop went off and founded his own company that, along with Lockheed and other southern California aviation factories, helped to make the planes that won the air war of World War II. Lockheed Martin and Northrop Grumman, as these companies are now called after mergers, have since evolved into major aeronautics and aerospace firms.

It's been pointed out many times that Los Angeles was unique in that it grew up as a city at the same time that automobiles were coming of age, and this was why it became such a home for them. But Los Angeles also grew up in the formative era of airplanes, and this mattered a lot too. The automobile, airplane, and motion picture camera transformed the twentieth century, and southern California was a petri dish of experimentation for all three. Automobiles influenced airplanes and vice versa, and because their engines and mechanical workings were similar, especially early on, ideas moved freely back and forth between the two. So, too, did the men who worked on them. Flyboys were almost always wheelboys too, and this tradition carried well into the age of hot rods and beyond. Many machinists, welders, and metalworkers, having learned their trade in the aircraft factories of southern California, unleashed their home-built hot rods on the streets of Los Angeles after the war. These same craftsmen souped up the engines and fabricated the chassis for the California-built racecars that dominated the Indianapolis 500 in the 1950s and early '60s. Car designers also often borrowed ideas from airplanes. The twin tail fins of the Lockheed P-38 Lightning, one of the fighter planes most feared by the German Luftwaffe, inspired one of the defining automobile design touches of the 1950s, Cadillac tail fins. Hot rodders even sometimes installed actual airplane parts on their cars, such as the streamlined belly tank of an old P-38. The first hydraulic systems used by low-riders to make their vehicles "hop" came from surplus aircraft stores.

The father of the southern California flying scene was Glenn L. Martin, whose first jobs naturally were in automobiles. Raised in farm-country Kansas, Martin sold Queen automobiles as a young man, driving from town to town so that people who'd never seen a motorcar before could take a ride and perhaps buy one. His interest in cars flourished when he and his family moved to an apricot ranch in Santa Ana. Martin, in his mid-twenties, found work as a car mechanic, but he wasn't your typical grease monkey; slender, shy, and on the gawky side, he dressed with a sense of style away from the garage. A bank officer, suitably impressed, floated him an eight-hundred-dollar loan to start his own car agency, and the polished Martin began selling Maxwells and Fords. It never hurts to have a bit of show business razzamatazz when selling cars, and Martin once drove a Ford up the steps of the Santa Ana Courthouse to advertise its climbing power. The business did well enough for him to hire his father and another man to run it, leaving him free to pursue another business interest of his, that of airplanes.

Flying, like racing fast cars, was a near-suicidal calling marked by supercharged blasts of adrenaline. Practically any time an airplane lifted off the ground it put at risk those inside it. Nobody needed a pilot's license; most everyone who flew had a screw loose anyway and they could just take their chances. Martin's experiments in flying began a year or so after the opening of his car dealership, allowing him to sink his automobile profits into airplanes and convert them into losses. To help spread his costs around, the mechanics at his agency also repaired his planes. A stripped-down Ford engine powered a Martin biplane, which barely cleared the tops of trees after takeoff and set down hard in the unplowed fields of Santa Ana, sometimes splintering into pieces. Like the Lockheeds, Martin helped pay the bills by stunt flying, performing barrel rolls and loop-the-loops at carnivals and air shows, the chance of a fiery fatal crash giving the festivities that little extra spark of interest. After one crash Martin put his broken arm in a sling and went right back up in the air, still maintaining the sartorial style—dark leather jacket, riding breeches—that earned him the nickname of "the Flying Dude."

When pioneering aviator Blanche Stuart Scott passed through southern California on her 1910 cross-country trip, she stopped in to see Martin, who was selling Overlands, the car she was driving. Scott did not apparently fly with Martin at that time, but after she returned to New York and took her first solo flights, she came back to Santa Ana two years later and flew in planes built and designed by the Glenn L. Martin Company. It was also Martin who piloted Eddie Rickenbacker on his first airplane ride. (Martin later moved his company to Maryland; it too became a successful aerospace firm and merged to form Lockheed Martin.)

Airplanes were so new that many in the auto industry worried that they were going to hurt the sale of cars. No serious person in the early years of automobiles and airplanes believed they would replace horses and the railroad as the dominant forms of transportation; the question was, what would people choose as an alternative after horses and the train? Harry Harrison, the endurance driver and Peerless dealer, felt certain that planes and cars could coexist without a problem. "There is an ever-increasing field for the motor car, according to Harrison, in spite of the sudden great access of the airship," reported the press. "There is room for both, Harrison says, and the aircraft will never entirely replace the motor car."

Airplanes and automobiles represented the modern. You were stodgy and old-fashioned—a horse and buggy person—if you didn't drive an automobile and at least consider the possibility of going up in a flying machine. Those who did these things were trendy and hip, and the hippest and trendiest of all were movie stars.

Martin appeared with Mary Pickford in a 1916 film, *The Girl of Yesterday*, one of the earliest pictures to romanticize flying. Not everyone shared these enthusiasms, though. One theater critic worried that the "motion picture, the phonograph [and the] player piano" were destroying the traditional stage. "These, with the increased interest in the automobile and aeroplane, have created a condition, so serious, that the men who cater to the public entertainment in the older fashion are less inclined to assume risks."

All these new influences and trends—the speed and thrills of driving and flying, the scandal and romance of motion pictures, the promise of technology, the appeal of the modern—were coming together in booming, sun-splashed, youth-happy, oil-rich southern California. For his early airplanes Glenn Martin contracted out the fuselage work to one of the leading automobile coachbuilders in Los Angeles, Earl Coach and Automotive Works. Its proprietor, Jacob W. Earl, was a transplanted Michigander who had ridden a prairie schooner west during the land boom of the 1880s. Originally a blacksmith, Earl started a coachbuilding business in the decade that followed. Coachbuilding was as venerable a tradition as blacksmithing, an age-old trade that the influx of automobiles in the 1900s swiftly turned on its head. Along with the usual horse-and-buggy staples, Earl Carriage and Automobile Works—the name changed to reflect the changing nature of the business—made custom automobile bodies and parts such as windshields. "Have you seen our oval glass fronts?" read one 1907 ad. "A folding glass front of brass and glass plate can be raised or lowered with one hand while the car is going full speed." It required no bolts or screws to put on, protected the driver and passengers from cold and wind, and was "guaranteed not to rattle."

With his business, especially in automobiles, growing rapidly, Jacob moved his shop to a bigger site on South Main Street, not far from Louis Breer's blacksmith shop on South San Pedro. The coming of automobiles did not immediately finish off blacksmiths and harness makers, as one might think. They existed side by side with car garages and agencies because many people owned both horses and autos. Among the automobile trade, however, Jacob Earl's shop was gaining a reputation for excellence, and risk-takers such as Martin became customers. When using ground transportation the Flying Dude loved beautiful cars, and two of his rides were a green Stoddard-Dayton with "nickel trim and a mohair top" and a Stutz Biarritz with snakeskin trim upholstery.

When Martin started coming around the shop, Jacob's second-oldest son, Harley Earl, was eighteen years old, and if the flier happened to be there at the same time as the boy, it is impossible to believe Martin did not notice him, for Harley was strikingly tall. An accomplished track athlete who long jumped and high jumped competitively in high school and college, it's easy to spot Harley in his team pictures at Hollywood High and the University of Southern California because he's the one who stands a full head higher than anybody else. "A young man of considerable altitude," as one observer put it, he stood six foot, four inches with a solid, sizable frame attached to it, a giant by the standards of the day. For his entire life Harley physically looked down on virtually every person he met. But unusual perhaps for a youngster of his size, he was not self-conscious about his body or looks. On the contrary, with a hawkish nose and dark, slicked-back hair parted in the middle, he appeared quite comfortable in his own skin, a person who dressed well and carried himself with style. Martin and the Hollywood showplayers who stopped by the South Main plant to check on their cars would have surely noticed this about him as well.

A photograph of Harley as a young man shows him at the wheel of a flashy new Mercer raceabout. Wearing goggles and with his motoring cap turned around backward, he's in a bowtie and crisp white shirt, its long sleeves gathered up above his elbows. With one large hand on the oversized steering wheel and the other on the gearshift, he looks like he knows what he's doing in an automobile, and clearly he did. Cars formed an everyday part of his life. It was nothing for him to see headlights, taillights, mirrors, door handles, hood hinges, and horns sitting on shelves or lying on workplace floors around his father's building. He saw seats, tops, and windshields being put on and taken off. He saw doors, fenders, body shells, and hoods being painted, repainted, smoothed, and shaped by his father's employees, all craftsmen of the first rank who, like Jacob Earl, had learned their trade in the East and brought it with them to California. Young Harley saw a chassis come into the shop and leave as a fully formed and stylish automobile. And as he grew older and more confident he began to make design suggestions about the coaches being built around him.

After USC he attended Stanford to study art, architecture, and engineering, and after Stanford he came home to Los Angeles to join his father's business. By then "Carriage" had fallen from its name and it was simply Earl Automobile Works. Having apprenticed in his father's trade, Harley had decided that this was how he wanted to make his living too: by building and designing automobiles. But the son was about to do more than just surpass his father's accomplishments. He was about to change the art and design of American automobiles for all time.

ELEVEN

Long and Low

The man who designed the Corvette and invented tail fins for automobiles made his formal design debut in January 1919 at the Los Angeles Auto Show, three months after the end of the Great War. Some in the industry worried that it was too soon to hold a car show—that "the public interest, long taken away from motor cars by the great war, had not yet returned to normal channels to warrant the holding of a big motor salon." Their worries proved groundless. The first big postwar auto show in either the United States or Europe attracted keen interest with a thousand car buffs lining up on Grand Avenue waiting to get in as soon as the doors opened Friday afternoon.

Sponsored by the Los Angeles Motor Car Dealers' Association, the eighth annual Los Angeles Auto Show featured two hundred passenger cars and fifty trucks displayed in three large white tents in Prager Park at Washington and Grand. Each vehicle was drained of gasoline and inspected by a city firefighter before being allowed to enter; once it was deemed safe, show employees and salesmen pushed it from the street, over a curb, and through the tent opening to its exhibit. For too long the fighting in Europe had sunk Americans and the American car scene in gloom, driving up prices, depressing production, and causing parts and material shortages. Motor racing had gone on during the war, but it provided only a minor relief from the grim drama unfolding overseas. Now, people just wanted to have a little fun. Go to a show and look at some nice cars and imagine driving around in one. The dealers' association did its best to accommodate these desires, "bossing"—Jazz Era slang for making something look cool—the tents with an exotic Hong Kong motif. Dozens of Chinese lanterns and chandeliers hung from the ceilings, and the canvas walls held elaborate and expensive Asian tapestries and fine art paintings. At night the electric lanterns cast a warm romantic glow over the polished and gleaming machines arrayed across the floor.

Anyone who loved boss cars and boss people had a gay time. "Beautifully gowned women with their escorts" chatted with "oily-tongued salesmen with hair slicked back." Four solemn United States Army soldiers with revolvers stood guard over a 400-horsepower, 12-cylinder Liberty aviation engine used in the war. In another section "a distinguished-appearing young man just back from the front [was] telling all about other types of motors, comparing automobile power plants with those of airplanes." More slick salesmen talked up the virtues of two mammoth Mack trucks that had performed admirably in Europe. War had been good news for the advancement of the motor truck, especially the four-wheel quads. They could not be built fast enough to keep up with demand, and truck sales of all types had soared into the hundreds of thousands. Cadillac, Dodge Brothers, International, Moreland, Paige, and other truck and military vehicle manufacturers also brought models to the show.

An impressive fleet of automobiles was under the lights too: Apperson, Autocar, Dort, Essex, Hudson, Nash, Olds, Packard, Reo, Studebaker, Winton, and more. Some of these cars boasted custom bodies made by Fleetwood Metal Body of Pennsylvania, regarded by many as the finest automobile coachbuilder in America. (Later purchased by Fisher and absorbed by General Motors, it is best known today for its Cadillac Fleetwood lines.) But what was striking to William Henry of the *Los Angeles Times* was that custom designs from California were not only holding their own with Fleetwood and the best of the East, they were surpassing them. "Homegrown talent is occupying the limelight at the Auto Show, despite the wonderful attractions from the East," he wrote. "It's a good, safe bet that half the crowds you see at any exhibit are grouped around something that was made in Los Angeles." These Los Angeles "motor fashion designers" were making "complete cars of striking style quite unknown to the custom-built bodies of the East."

Aware, perhaps, of being charged with hometown favoritism, Henry pointed out that Californians had already created many innovations "now in universal use" across the automobile industry, such as new styles of tops and windshields. Further, he noted a trend in which more and more Los Angeles dealers were ordering chassis from the East and then turning them over to local specialty shops such as George Bentel's, on Grand Avenue not far from the show.

An edgy, innovative Los Angeles car man since the days of one-cylinder putt-putts, Bentel sold Mercedes and Mercer before moving into custom design. A 1918 *Motor Age* credited him with having "introduced wire wheels to the Pacific Coast, [along with being the] first to build Victoria tops, first to put disks on wheels, first to make tonneau windshields, first to make a roller curtain top." The Mercers he modified became known as "California Mercers," and swashbuckling film star Douglas Fairbanks was among those who bopped around town in them. Ralph DePalma and other thoroughbred drivers raced them.

Bentel's "sporting and rakish" designs turned humdrum vehicles into rides that were trendy and fine. Nor was he afraid to put his own spin on some tired idea sent west from Detroit. His exhibit at the auto show included an Oakland Six that looked nothing like it did when it left the factory: it sported a new body and a roller curtain top of Bentel's devising. Side curtains were generally stored under the rear seat, where they stayed until the first drops of rain or a cool breeze came up. To put them on, people had to stop the car, get out, pull them from under the seat, and attach them to the top. But this was always a struggle and the curtains seldom behaved properly once they were on. Bentel's new side curtains, by contrast, were as simple as window shades: roll them up and out of sight when you didn't need them, or pull them down and easily fasten them when you did. And you could put them on without stopping the car.

Pleasing as these style touches were, the big buzz at the show centered on another Los Angeles designer. Wrote Henry, "Perhaps the most startling local models at the show are those built by the Earl Automobile Works, whose sensational Chandlers and Marmons are attracting huge crowds. These cars are designed by Harley J. Earl, a local man who only three or four years ago was broad jumping and high jumping for the University of Southern California, and who has sprung into prominence as a maker of motor fashions almost overnight."

This maker of motor fashions had concocted a gray four-passenger Marmon built for seven thousand dollars for a New York banker. This banker could have easily hired Fleetwood or some other Eastern shop; instead he chose a coachbuilder on the opposite coast. After the show the Marmon was to be shipped by rail to its new home, where it "would make the most blasé New Yorker stop and blink his eyes if taken for a jaunt down Riverside Drive."

Even more eye-catching was another Harley J. Earl creation, a blue Chandler town car. "About the classiest thing of its kind ever shown on the coast, it is surely distinctive, being a low-hung creation, so low that a good-sized man can stand alongside it and look right over the top, yet there is sufficient room inside to keep one from being cramped." To illustrate this point the designer himself sat in the car, showing six inches of clearance between his head and the top. And if the super-sized Earl had that much clearance, everybody else could count on a great deal more.

William Henry, whose detailed and descriptive accounts suggest that a new style was evolving not just in automobiles but in automobile writing, noted that the Chandler and Marmon had not been gussied up just for the show, nor had they taken a year or more to finish. Employees at the Earl Automobile Works—many of them ex-Fleetwood workmen—had fabricated the Chandler body in about a month.

Some fifty thousand people paraded through the eight-day show, some of them hailing from the motion picture colony that had migrated from Edendale to the hills of Hollywood. The show hosted a special Saturday night ceremony for picture stars, and almost certainly the designer of the Chandler and Marmon showed off their headroom that night too. Over the years Harley Earl came to know many Hollywood stars as friends and clients. Director and producer Cecil B. DeMille lived next door to him, and Al Jolson, star of the first-ever talking picture, *The Jazz Singer*, was a close friend. Jolson, DeMille, and other Hollywood friends gave Harley tips on how to grab an audience's attention, and he admitted that "some of their showmanship may have rubbed off on me."

But the hot young designer's next big client came not from Hollywood but from one of the richest and most prominent families in California. The most storied oil discovery in state history occurred in 1892 when Edward Doheny and another man plunged a pick and shovel into some land on West State Street in Los Angeles and brought up lots of water but some oil too. They then brought in a boring rig that drilled a seven-inch hole to a depth of 150 feet, then 225 feet, and up came more of that bubbling crude. Their success led to more digging, more wells—and extraordinary wealth for, among others, Doheny. He became the head of a far-flung oil empire, a mover and shaker in Los Angeles civic and social circles, and the father of Edward Doheny, Jr. Ned, as he was known—probably to get him out from under the long shadow cast by his father—went to school with Harley at USC. He joined the Navy for the war and after returning to civilian life contacted his old friend about designing a new automobile as a gift for his socially prominent wife. In his auto-show articles Henry had discussed a Los Angeles man who had paid three thousand dollars for a chassis to be shipped from Detroit and then another ten thousand for it to be customized by a local coachbuilder. This unidentified man almost certainly was Ned, and the coachbuilder was Harley. The chassis was a Pierce-Arrow.

In the months after the show Harley talked frequently with his client to find out exactly what he wanted in the car. This was typical of his style. "He had lots of interaction with his clients," said Richard Earl, Harley's grandson and an expert on his career. "Look at it like an architectural project and how an architect deals with a client. Harley found out what the client wanted in terms of color and the interior and the look and style."

Ned Doheny came down to South Main Street and Harley escorted him around the three-story, flat-topped brick building that housed Earl Automobile Works. A flag bearing the company name flew from the roof in front as smoke billowed out of chimneys in back. They walked up and down the stairs of the building and through the various workrooms that Harley had run around in as a tall, gangly boy. Still tall but no longer gangly, with a young man's rising confidence in his creative powers, Harley showed Ned how automobile coaches sprang to life, forming a beautiful new skin over a skeleton-like chassis. Earl Automobile Works billed itself as "builders and designers of automobile bodies, automobile tops, automobile wheels, and Earl wind shields." ("Wind shield" was originally two words.) If someone needed an engine repaired, sorry, they couldn't help you. But if you wanted the best coachwork in town—"remodeling, painting, upholstery or repairing"—come right in. You had found the right place.

Harley once described the business on South Main as "a little hole in the wall with about four hundred to five hundred men." From this little hole in the wall came ideas and techniques that would transform American car design. Whereas Fleetwood Metal Body crafted its coach designs out of metal, not so with Harley, who borrowed from his father's coachbuilding methods and updated them for automobiles. His process began with a drawing, followed perhaps by some client interaction, then more refinements. Next came wood modelers who built a three-dimensional wooden armature of the car to be made. Then Harley and his team formed a clay model over this structure, shaping the engine compartment, hood, seats, windows, doors, side panels, and other parts. Easier to work with and softer and more forgiving than metal, clay gave Harley a feel for how to make everything fit together just so. "Since childhood," writes an automobile historian, "Earl had been fascinated by the visual/tactile process of sculpting fluid forms in clay....He found that clay forms could be manipulated and adjusted until the proportions were just right." If something wasn't right, he and his staff changed it, molding the clay with tools and deft fingers and hands. "This made it possible to produce more unified, sculpted, less stiff designs than resulted from hammering them out of metal, as was the usual custom."

None of the Detroit automakers used full-sized clay modeling, and it would be years (after Harley went to General Motors) before any of them adopted it. Nowadays, every car manufacturer in the world uses it. "What was most important about it was that every single element of the car, from roof to running boards and from headlights to taillights, was consciously styled to be in harmony with every other element," writes another historian.

What was also important about it was that clients such as Doheny could see how much care was being put into their automobiles before their actual construction. "Harley would do a clay model of the car to see if it was going in the right direction," said Richard Earl. "This was one of the reasons these movie stars and millionaires were so impressed with him, because he went to the trouble of doing these clay models."

Another reason they responded to him was that he was clearly a creative thinker, a person who lived and worked and was guided by a certain set of aesthetic principles. He believed an automobile was something more than an appliance on wheels. It was an object of breathe-deep and feel-prosperous luxury, both real and symbolic, and at its best a work of art. A fine automobile could move a person emotionally in ways that had nothing to do with transportation. It had the capacity to delight the mind and senses and raise the spirit to joy just like the finest works of art in the greatest museums of the world. The carmakers of Britain and Europe all understood this, and for years they had produced stylish and fast marques that Harley admired intensely. He also admired Duesenberg, Mercer, and other top American designs because they, too, represented a different vision for the automobile than Henry Ford's utilitarian Model T.

In some ways Harley was the anti-Ford. Raised in the craftsman tradition, he saw the usefulness of beauty, believing that a car was more than just the sum of its parts, more than just a mobile black box. As such he became "America's first professional car stylist" who helped create "the perception that cars should be tailored to the individual consumer's needs," producing islands of color amidst a sea of black.

But there was one thing Harley never changed, no matter what his clients said. Every car he designed in his long and illustrious career conformed to one basic principle: long and low. "My primary purpose for twenty-eight years has been to lengthen and lower the American automobile," he said in the early 1950s.

Ned Doheny flipped when he first laid eyes on the long and low lines of his new purchase. He had seen it as a two-dimensional drawing on a piece of paper and then a sculpted three-dimensional form in clay, but none of this prepared him for the beauty of the finished product. He couldn't stop smiling. Nor could his wife and children when they saw it. They were so happy that somebody—perhaps Harley's people, perhaps Ned's people—called the *Times* to get Bill Henry to come over and take a look. Henry and a photographer saw it, and they flipped too. The *Times* ran a four-column photo of it across the top of the page with a caption saying, "If you wouldn't like to own this car, you can't be satisfied." Calling it "the classiest creation of the year" and "an automobile body that seems to surpass even the wonderful creations of the recent Automobile Show," Henry used the word "special" three times in his opening two paragraphs, filing this report:

> It is a special four-passenger body, ordered by Mr. Doheny as a present for his wife, and is mounted on a Pierce Arrow chassis with special English 32x5 wire wheels, with one spare wheel mounted on each side of the hood. The different points that make this car attractive are bicycle fenders, aluminum steps, double spotlights, and a windshield with deflectors on each side. A silver engraved monogram inlaid in red enamel is mounted on each door. The panel between the doors over the little extra fender [has] special designed coach lamps. These lamps were designed and constructed by the Tiffany Company of New York. These lamps give the car a very foreign touch.

Further, "the car is upholstered in bright, long-grain red leather, which forms a great contrast with the body and wheels, which are painted Wiley's battleship gray, with satin finish."

The photograph is in black and white, so the car's vivid colors are lost in the paper. But one can still see the proud new owner sitting behind the wheel with Harley next to him in the passenger seat. In the rear seat, with its stylish Burbank Victoria top folded down out of view, are Doheny's two young children and his wife, the person who is actually receiving the car. This is clearly a big moment for her too—although Henry neglected to identify her by name—and Mrs. Doheny is wearing a lovely hat with flowers on it. (Of course, she may not have been as happy as all that. Ned hired a driver for her when he bought her the car. She and the chauffeur later had an affair that caused a local scandal.)

All this good press did not fail to escape the notice of Don Lee, a hustling, go-get-'em Los Angeles Cadillac dealer, the biggest purveyor of Cadillacs in the city, state, and probably the nation. Lee was to Cadillac what Earle C. Anthony, his top competitor, was to Packard. He oversaw a network of dealers around the state, selling Cadillacs, driving Cadillacs, promoting Cadillacs, and sponsoring Cadillacs in attention-getting endurance races. In one such race a Cadillac Thirty went from Lee's agency in Los Angeles to Bakersfield, Fresno, and San Francisco in record time. Then after a quick turnaround it headed south down the coast and pulled into the place where it started thirty-nine hours after it had left, setting a new record for the fastest inland and coastal loop between Los Angeles and San Francisco. Lee, who had a casual, easygoing business style but knew a few things about showmanship too, immediately put the Thirty on display at his showroom, the mud of the roads still clinging to its fenders and tires.

This record-setter occurred not coincidentally in the same year that Lee became the Cadillac distributor for all of California. The next year, 1912, Cadillac introduced the electric self-starter, ending the hand crank era and making automobiles appeal to a wider audience. "The electric self-starter and electric-lighting system introduced by the Cadillac company has placed the gasoline car where any woman can drive it with the greatest of ease," said one report of the time. "The motor can be started and the lights lighted without leaving the seat." Cadillac sales spiked with these improvements (rapidly copied by other carmakers), and Lee moved into fancy new digs on 12th and Main, the better to serve his growing list of high-profile customers. Governor Johnson's new Cadillac V-8 at the Panama-Pacific Exposition in San Francisco came from Lee's dealership.

Balding and with glasses, Lee "had a personal habit of doing everything in grand style," a trait that surely appealed to Harley Earl and his father. Lee's first showroom on South Main was a block away from the Earl Automobile Works, which had done repair and custom jobs for him. Lee knew the Earls and the Earls knew him and respected the Cadillac brand. It was a good fit for all. In July 1919, seven months after Harley's debut at the auto show, Lee bought Earl Automobile Works—"the largest business of its kind west of Detroit"—and folded it into his Cadillac operation.

"We will create as well as build," Lee said when he announced the purchase. "We aim to have the largest plant for the building of high-grade bodies in the United States." Jacob Earl, who was in his early fifties, became manager of the new Don Lee Coach and Body Works, though he gradually eased into retirement and handed the reins over to the next generation. Two of his sons, Carl and Arthur, became assistant managers at the plant, while Harley remained in charge of coach and body design. No question Harley was a key part of the deal. "With an idea of learning the trend in enclosed cars for the fall and winter season, Earl will leave for a tour of the Eastern factories today [the day the deal was announced], and when production is resumed abroad, will be sent to Europe."

This merger of talents—creative and artistic with sales and marketing—formed a business powerhouse that tapped into a local automobile scene unlike any other in the world. The Don Lee Coach and Body Works certainly sold its custom-made wares to rich New York bankers looking to impress their friends. But it didn't need to look that far afield for customers because, right in its own backyard, lots of glamorous and suddenly rich young people, some in oil, some in transportation, some in real estate, but mostly in the movies—"the new-rich Westerns," as Emily Post called them—simply *had* to have unique luxury automobiles that made a statement to the world about who they were.

The same year Harley and Don Lee linked up, Mary Pickford and Douglas Fairbanks moved into Pickfair, the stupendous Beverly Hills mansion that Fairbanks bought for his new bride as a wedding present. Pickfair featured a swimming pool and a host of other amenities, such as living quarters for the couple's two chauffeurs, one of whom doubled as projectionist for the home movie theater. Both Pickford and Fairbanks owned cars customized by Harley Earl at Don Lee's. Mary's favorite was said to be a Pierce Arrow, which had a speaking tube from the back to front seat so she could talk to her chauffeur (a standard feature in Pierce Arrows). Mary's brother Jack Pickford also drove a Harley custom, as did Wallace Reid, Viola Dana, and other screen stars.

In working with screen star Ann May on her automobile, Harley heard something her fans across the country never did: her voice. She rode to premieres in a Harley-built six-fender touring sedan with a California top. *Madame X* star Pauline Frederick lived on Sunset Boulevard next to the Beverly Hills estate of Edward Doheny Sr. A referral from the Dohenys may have been how she met Harley, who set her up with a customized town car crafted on a Cadillac chassis. Not to be left out of the fun was Lee himself. He drove a Cadillac touring sedan with side-mounted coach lamps fitted out in the grand style.

For Cecil B. DeMille's car, as for all the customs he designed, Harley signed his initials, HJE, on the drawings, signifying his personal connection to his work.

The biggest Western star of the day was Tom Mix, who was pulling down seventeen thousand dollars a week as the "King of the Cowboys." On the screen, the handsome, upright, plain-talking Mix spun his six-shooters, twirled a lariat, and chased down the bad guys on his black stallion Tony. (An authentic horseman, Mix did all his own stunts.) Off the screen he was another of the original Hollywood fast-car guys. Drive fast, live hard—that was their unofficial motto, and nobody did it with more exuberant country charm than Mix. Married five times but never settling down once, he wore white suits, diamond-studded belt buckles, ten-gallon hats, and rhinestone buttons on his embroidered shirts. A purple tuxedo hung in his closet and on the shelves were more than six hundred pairs of cowboy boots. His house had a fountain in front (later lit by neon), stained-glass windows inside, antique French furniture, a handmade rock fireplace, and seven cars in the garage. Mix's brand—TM with a bar underneath—appeared on the gates of the mansion, the front door, his saddles, shirts, Western gear, and the tread of the tires on his Rolls Royce. Driving the Rolls on dirt he always left his mark behind him.

So what sort of car did Earl build for Mix? Well, it had a leather saddle mounted on the roof and showcased the TM bar as a hood ornament. His client loved it all.

Fatty Arbuckle became another satisfied Harley client. After he started making real money in the pictures Fatty rewarded himself with a new car, an Alco. For his development deal at Paramount the studio gave him a Rolls Royce as a signing bonus. The garage in Fatty's house in Silver Lake held six luxury cars, including that Rolls and a shiny white Caddy from the Don Lee Coach and Body Works. Fatty drove all his cars too fast and collected handfuls of speeding tickets. Whenever he appeared at the courthouse for a traffic offense, mobs of reporters and fans came out to see him. Afterward he signed autographs and posed for pictures with the judge, promising to obey all the traffic laws from then on, a vow he forgot as soon as he drove away.

Harley built four cars for Fatty—every one of them long, low, and luxurious. One twenty-five-thousand-dollar custom on a Pierce-Arrow chassis contained a cocktail bar and a toilet. The car was such a joy to drive that Fatty usually took the wheel and let his chauffeur ride in back, chatting with him through the speaking tube. Like the other stars who drove them, when Fatty took ownership of a new Harley Earl custom, he posed for pictures with it. One photograph shows him seated on the running board of the car, his head resting on his hand in a pose that somehow mixes humor and sadness, suggesting his great gifts as a comedian. But what is most interesting is where the eye travels when looking at the photograph. It does not fix on Fatty but rather on the automobile. The car had become the star.

TWELVE

The Go-Fast Kid

During the same summer that Don Lee was buying Earl Automotive Works and acquiring the services of its chief design talent, Ascot Park in Los Angeles was hosting a gala fundraising event to benefit older actors and actresses who had fallen on hard times. "The Fashion Parade and Beauty Show," as it was called, featured movie starlets such as Pauline Frederick, Juanita Hansen, Lila Lee, and Gloria Swanson, all clad in their summer hats and finery, while cowboy stars Hoot Gibson and Pete Morrison also appeared. The fundraiser was both fun and lucrative, raising thousands of dollars for its cause and combining in a single event two of Hollywood's favorite pastimes: automobiles and airplanes.

Donald Crisp directed and played villains in the pictures, but for the day at Ascot he became a madcap automobile racer, spinning out in one race and crashing in another. "In the fifteen-mile race he took a turn too fast," wrote a reporter. "He spun around three times, held the car upright even if he did go off the track, backed on again, and finished second. In [another] race he went through the fence, sending planks flying as he spun around and around and came up smiling."

Tom Mix rode away with the featured twenty-five-mile event, lapping the field and setting hearts aflutter in the grandstands. "The handkerchief waving was at its high tide during this event, all the girls simply fluttering their arms sore and yelling, 'Oh Tom, you darling.'" After taking the checkered flag Mix "motored past the girls in the bleachers with a smile and walked down through the grandstand with his trophy. Nobody could mistake him, for his straw hat was built like a sombrero and his sport coat was dazzling."

More highlights included a three-lap race between Cecil DeMille and professional race driver Eddie Hearne—Hearne in a car, DeMille in his plane. "Cecil de Mille [sic] proved that he is a real he-airplane driver when he skimmed Eddie Hearne's head for three laps, stood on end on the curves and ran away from the automobile. A man who can handle a plane like that master director has a right to get peeved if anybody calls him an amateur driver."

Certainly nobody in Hollywood had a right to call him an amateur driver because DeMille could handle both automobiles and airplanes with aplomb. He flew a Curtiss

Jenny biplane, raced against Hearne and other drivers in it, and owned an airfield in the oil district around Fairfax and Wilshire in Los Angeles, near the Miracle Mile before anyone had ever conceived of a Miracle Mile. He also drove luxury automobiles such as his Harley Earl Cadillac custom, and he and MGM studio boss Louis B. Mayer threw some money into the kitty to help pay for the Los Angeles Speedway in Beverly Hills, another of the southern California meeting spots for the car and plane set. The Los Angeles Speedway combined the best of both worlds because it was big enough to host a car race and aviation meet at the same time. Planes took off and landed on a runway that ran parallel with the backstretch, and on race days the director of *The Ten Commandments* and other screen epics flew there in his Curtiss Jenny.

Though the track was in Beverly Hills, at the junction of Wilshire Boulevard and Beverly Drive, they called it the Los Angeles Speedway because nobody in the rest of the country and not that many in California would have known where Beverly Hills was, much less how to get there. It wasn't much of a town to speak of, mainly farms and lonesome dirt roads leading to more farms. The arms of oil derricks pumped alongside graceful rows of eucalyptus. Precious little about the place could be described as swanky, except for the dreamy new digs of Mary Pickford and Douglas Fairbanks up in the hills. Pickfair looked down across the open lands at the new speedway.

This must have made the man of the house happy, because he was mad for racing. He made the scene on opening day in February 1920, and so did his wife. Beverly was the most gorgeous and glamorous racetrack in the world, and a lovely way to spend an afternoon. "It was beautiful, and we spared no expense," said one of its builders. "We had roofed grandstands with large boxes, each holding ten hand-built chairs that were contoured for real comfort. Everything was deluxe and so was our clientele." That A-list clientele—Fairbanks, Pickford, Mayer, DeMille, all the dazzling stars and starlets at the Tom Mix bash, Fatty Arbuckle, Charlie Chaplin and so many more—sipped drinks and smoked cigarettes in their casual yet elegant rags, chatting and laughing, a sort of motorized version of the Kentucky Derby come west.

Beverly—the shorthand name for the speedway—was a board track but not just any old board track; it was the Pickfair of board tracks, "the most elegant wooden speedway of all." Two immense grandstands holding thirty thousand spectators apiece faced each other on opposite sides of an expansive one-and-a-quarter-mile banked wooden oval. The grandstand to the north was covered; the one to the south, open to the rays of a benevolent sun. Both were painted to blend in with the setting's country charm. "An entirely new color scheme to blend with the green of the hills and purplish haze of the distance has been worked out. Instead of brazen colors of country barn hues, there has been an attractive blending of subdued terra cotta and blues."

Even more appealing, perhaps, was the abundance of parking. "What probably will be more than welcome news to those who have attended former race meets in Los Angeles is the announcement that more than five miles of parking space has been provided in the infield." Tunnels had been built underneath the track so that people could drive their cars onto the infield and watch the festivities from there.

Built in a little over a month, the Los Angeles Speedway bore some resemblances to the old Los Angeles Motordrome, which made sense because Jack Prince designed them both. Having gone from awesome breakthrough to nightmare death trap in a few short years, the Playa del Rey track no longer existed and not a soul alive missed it, not even its creator. Its splintered and cracked wooden boards had blown out tires and sent cars and drivers flying, killing some of them. Boys were known to sneak underneath the track, wiggle the boards loose, and poke their heads up to watch the cars speeding around. The Motordrome went down in flames in 1914—"to a great savings of lives," in the sarcastic words of Ring Lardner—but only after it had inspired the creation of similar wooden saucers around the world. In Beverly Hills, with a more lavish budget to work with, Prince had expanded his vision of what a wooden track could be, using up to four million board feet of lumber, divided into two-by-fours, meticulously cut and fitted end to end in the shape of a bowl. His more advanced design widened the straights, reduced the steepness of the banks, and created smoother transitions between the straights and turns. Cars could take the bends at 80 and get up to 110 and beyond on the straights. It was in fact stipulated in Prince's contract that contestants must be able to exceed 110 miles per hour to make them eligible for world records. Based on the times clocked in practice, the transplanted Brit surpassed this goal. Nearly twenty drivers averaged above 100 miles per hour in the warm-ups, raising anticipation for the inaugural 250-mile main event. "The competition," noted one sharp-penned scribe, "will be warm enough to bring perspiration to the brow of an undertaker."

Before moving onto the race, though, it is worth pausing a moment to spotlight another face in the crowd, one who was yukking it up and sharing stories with Mix, DeMille, and the other celebrities in their box seats. He surely had a cigar going, although unlike when he was racing, this one was lit. Still the biggest name in motor racing, Barney Oldfield had at long last quit the game for good, for he was not at Beverly Hills as a race driver but in his new capacity as businessman. With the backing of Firestone he had formed the Oldfield Tire and Rubber Company in Ohio. As a man whose cars had burned up hundreds of tires over the years, he had real knowledge to impart on this subject, but probably his biggest contribution to the venture was the use of his name and the publicity he brought to it. Barney also acted as a promotional spokesperson for Firestone, although in the middle of the decade they parted ways and he started a new company to manufacture cars in Los Angeles.

The Oldfield Motor Corporation built a prototype and opened a downtown showroom to attract investors, but spectacular, can't-miss automobile ideas have a habit of blowing away with the wind, and this was one of those cases. The Wall Street crash broke him financially, and at the end of the Depression he was running a country club in Van Nuys—his name on the sign out front, of course. But the Barney Oldfield Country Club attracted mainly an older clientele, and then there were all the young people who came in who had no idea that the fellow behind the bar was once the World's Fastest Man on Wheels. Barney died of a heart attack in 1946 at the age of sixty-eight, surprising people all the way to the end. One surprise was that for a man who had cheated death so many times on racetracks, he died in his home, in Beverly Hills.

Another surprise was the person by his side in the last year of his life. Bess Oldfield had stuck by Barney all through his racing years, tending to him spiritually and nursing him back to physical health after his injuries, but after he retired they split up and he married another woman. That match did not turn out nearly as well. The two fought bitterly, and they divorced. Shortly after the divorce became final, Barney and Bess remarried after having been separated for more than two decades. A man and a woman who should have never been together in the first place, and yet who never should have been apart, felt happy and grateful they had found each other again before it was too late. Who would have thought it? Barney and Bess, a love story.

Also at Beverly Hills that day was a friend of Barney Oldfield's named Harry A. Miller, though he wasn't up in the grandstands but down in the pits. The pits were a noisy, smelly, grimy, hot place, and this was where Miller belonged and felt most comfortable. A short, stocky, and slightly rumpled figure in overalls, with probing blue eyes, a thin mustache, and coarse wire-brush hair, he huddled with other men in overalls, readying their machines for the race that was to come. Engines were started, shut off, restarted. Once one was deemed suitable for action it was pushed forward toward the track or it was started up and the driver inside steered it slowly through the area, on its own power, rumbling and popping. The heat of this machine, the heat of all these machines, added to the heat of the sun and the heat of the paved surfaces, and sweat poured off the faces of these men, who were completely absorbed in the business at hand. They hardly noticed, or simply took for granted, the smoke that spurted from a tailpipe upon ignition. The sounds these engines made were like bees, a hive of angry bees buzzing around the track, and the noise they made was almost palpable, a thing that could be heard *and* touched.

"I walked down under the stand into one of the underground tunnels," wrote a reporter, Harry Williams, wishing to hear and touch these sounds for himself. "Overhead there was a deafening crash as each car rounded the turn into the stretch. It sounded like tons of steel being thrown against the structure, and that's what it was. In making the turn or going from them into the stretches the cars literally smashed themselves into the track."

At home amidst these smashing cars, Harry A. Miller would've been at the eye of the storm in the pits, speaking patiently and with complete assurance to drivers and mechanics in the urgent and desperate minutes before the start of the race. Many decisions had to be made in these final minutes, decisions that could make the difference between winning and losing, and no one was better qualified to make them than Miller, "quite simply the greatest creative figure in the history of the American racing car." His middle initial stood for Arminius, but he never much used it in public. Professionally he was always Harry A. Miller, possibly to distinguish him from all the other Harry Millers in the world who didn't know the difference between a carburetor and a crankcase and wouldn't know what to do with them even if they did. This Miller, Harry A. Miller, knew the difference all right. He designed and built carburetors, crankcases, crankshafts, pistons, valves, headers, superchargers, and gearboxes all with one goal in mind: to make his racecars take off as if shot from the barrel of a gun.

Why did the internal combustion gas engine outperform the other types of engines? Why did it keep improving, keep getting better and faster? One big reason was Harry A. Miller and men like him who expressed their creativity through it. He lay in bed at night unable to sleep, his mind spinning on a new design for an engine part or a new way to fit the parts together to create a new effect. He was "volcanic... [an] inventor-engineer with a wizard's touch for motors," another of those individuals whose eloquence derived not from his words but the things he made with his hands.

Growing up in the timber country of Menomonie, Wisconsin, Miller gained his knowledge of tools and machines the way most boys of his generation did: in a blacksmith shop. But even as a boy it was clear that for him the life of a smithy was not to be. In his late teens he fled the piney woods to tramp around California and the West, finally returning home to work as a foreman at an iron foundry. But he didn't stay for long. Fascinated by automobiles, his interests acquired a more specific focus: automobile racing. Leaving Wisconsin behind once more, he became a mechanic for an Ohio-based Vanderbilt Cup racing team. But something about southern California had gotten under his skin—maybe the dry winters, or the developing speed scene—and when the Vanderbilt job sputtered out, he and his wife came to Los Angeles at about the same time Barney Oldfield was chomping his first cigar at old Agricultural Park.

In his first engine shop, which was "just a backyard lean-to which he managed to equip with an old lathe and drill press," Miller devised a carburetor that made car engines start quicker, idle better, run faster. The Harry A. Miller Manufacturing Company, which at the start was really just him working alone in his backyard lean-to, also patented new types of spark plugs, pistons, and fuel pumps. Despite being located way out West, far away from the big cities of the East and Midwest, orders from around the country poured in. An Indianapolis firm bought the carburetor side of his business, supplying him with the cash to finance more of his restless nighttime ideas. He soon dreamed up an even better version of a carburetor and manufactured it using a unique lightweight aluminum alloy he created. These high-performance carburetors and pistons put zip into racing machines, and pretty soon anyone with a yen for life in the fast lane was pulling up in front of Miller's brick-walled factory in Los Angeles.

"I was headquartered at Miller's," said Tommy Milton, who twice won the Indianapolis 500 in Miller-built engines. So was most every other driver in the country who wished to duplicate Milton's feat. There were in fact only two places to be in the United States if you were serious about winning major motor races in the 1920s—Fred and Augie Duesenberg's speed shop in Indianapolis and Harry A. Miller's in Los Angeles. Miller came to work in a tie and white long-sleeve shirt, but as soon as he walked through the door he was rolling up his sleeves and diving into something greasy and oily. His thick arms and tree stump of an upper body came not from pushing around weights in a gymnasium but from pushing around engine blocks in the dark and dingy spaces of his factory floor. Piles of metal shavings, tools, and spare parts lay around his machine department. A web of cables hung from the ceiling. Large, ancient machines whined and thumped and made godawful noises. The dozen or so men who worked there wore heavy boots, grease-stained overalls, bow ties, and motoring caps. The machines they operated drew their power from a pulley and wheel system on the ceiling. A cable ran from a wheel on the ceiling to a machine on the floor, and this cable turned the turbines on the vertical mills and giant Monarch lathe that cut and shaped the engine parts.

The machine department occupied half of the 12,000-square-foot main work floor; the other half was for assembly. There were also rooms in the plant for sheet metal and bodywork, supplies, testing, and the coal foundry that powered the pulleys, wheels, and machines. A flight of wooden stairs at the back of the machine department led up to a drafting room and the offices where Miller met with his clients.

The Harry A. Miller Manufacturing Company built passenger car engines, marine engines, and airplane engines, including the engine for the last plane Lincoln Beachey ever flew in. But racing engines were Miller's stock in trade, what built his reputation and fortune. Before World War I Eddie Rickenbacker made a pilgrimage to Los Angeles to ask for his help. The engine of his Peugeot had died in a race and he needed Miller to breathe life back into it. This he did, with the able assistance of machinist Fred Offenhauser, a bespectacled, practical-minded former machinist and toolmaker with the Pacific Electric Railway in Los Angeles. Soon after this Wild Bob Burman's Peugeot blew up and he came to Miller to ask him to do what he had done for Rickenbacker. Miller and Offenhauser built a new engine from scratch and virtually a whole new car for Wild Bob, who drove it for about a year, winning lots of money in it, before being killed.

Burman's death occurred at the Corona Road Race, one of the most unusual stops on the national racing calendar. At the base of the Santa Ana Mountains in Riverside County, Corona was a small, picture-postcard farming community best known for growing oranges and lemons. What made the town so picturesque was its layout, for all the streets of the Circle City were encircled by the three-mile-long Grand Boulevard. Originally made of dirt, the boulevard had received a fresh coat of asphalt, which made it the perfect venue—or so the town's boosters thought—for a ripsnorting, fireballing road race. The premiere event, held in 1913, attracted a crowd of one hundred thousand and the best drivers in the country, including Wild Bob. Three years later Wild Bob's wife had a dream in which she saw her husband killed in a crash, and frightened by this vision, she begged him not to run at Corona. An old hand at taking and surviving impossible risks, Wild Bob told her no, he was a professional driver and he was making the race. His decision made her a widow.

When a tire popped at high speed it turned his Peugeot into an out-of-control missile. It rolled over and over and bounced high into the air, flying over the boulevard barriers and ramming into a parked car and telephone poles. A half-dozen fans suffered major injuries. Three people—a security guard, Wild Bob's riding mechanic, and Wild Bob himself, a few days shy of his thirty-second birthday—died.

The accident shocked the racing world, which thought itself immune to such shocks, and ended Corona's efforts to promote her charms through car racing. But out of Wild Bob's death came another vision: the most daring and original racecar of its time, the Golden Submarine. Its creators were Harry A. Miller and Barney Oldfield. Like all racers of his day, Wild Bob had driven an open cockpit car with no roof to protect him, and seeking to change that, Miller and Oldfield devised the world's first aerodynamic racing vehicle with an enclosed teardrop-shaped body. Writers now describe it as "fantastically advanced for its day," "the most fully streamlined vehicle ever seen in the United States," but back then they were skeptical. One reporter said its submarine-style body looked like "a nightmare version of a U-boat"; another likened it to an egg on wheels. Barney sat inside the egg staring out through narrow slits covered with steel netting to keep out the dirt and flying rocks. After the metallic gold car flunked its first test, dropping out of a race in Chicago in 1917, the wags in the press dubbed it "the Golden Lemon."

Things improved a little from there. In typical Barney fashion he took the car out to the people, campaigning it at tracks around the country and setting some records. But at a race in the Midwest the Golden Sub crashed, flipped, and burst into flames with Barney inside it. For one terrifying instant he fought with the door and could not get the handle to work. Finally it opened, and he sprung out of the burning car and into the life-giving air.

Although Barney raced some more after that, this was the event that pretty much finished him as a professional driver, convincing him to move into publicity and sales. But Harry A. Miller's experiments with avant-garde racing vehicles did not end here; if anything, they were just beginning, thanks in part to the contributions of Fred Offenhauser and another gifted Miller employee, Leo Goossen, a Dutch immigrant who had been warned by a doctor that he was going to die if he didn't move to a dry climate to improve his lung condition. Goossen took the advice and found a creative home in the drab second-story drafting room of Miller's factory on Long Beach Avenue. An exceptional draftsman, Goossen oversaw four other draftsmen who wore eyeshades and sat at wooden drafting tables pushed up against the windows. On bright days they put butcher paper over the windows to reduce the glare. With Goosen and his team of designers preparing the layout drawings, and Offenhauser and his team crafting the parts and engine, and both Goossen and Offenhauser contributing original ideas of their own, Harry A. Miller now had a racing operation in place that could beat the best in the world.

Goossen came aboard in mid-1919, and the next year the fabulousness that was the Los Angeles Speedway at Beverly Hills unveiled itself. The opening races drew a world-class field, but in a surprise to many, a twenty-five-year-old unknown named

Jimmy Murphy pushed his Duesenberg to first place in the trials, claiming the pole. Before his qualifying run Murphy was all grimness and seriousness of purpose; nothing could pull a smile out of that long, narrow face and those sad puppy-dog eyes of his. But afterward, after the pressure had lifted, he could open up and relax a little, his tough determination melting into boyish laughter and smiles. His goggles casually draped around his neck and his leather driving cap pulled from his head, his dirty and sweaty face beamed with joy. This was the Jimmy Murphy other drivers knew and recognized and why, even though they were competing hard against him, they adored him almost to a man.

Another reason they liked Jimmy was because he had supported them in the past, riding with many of them as a mechanic. Quiet and awkward around people and constitutionally unable to brag on himself, a shy bachelor married only to the temptress of speed, Murphy was a kid from the neighborhood—specifically, South of the Slot on Mission Street in San Francisco. Growing up in a tough neighborhood, the son of immigrants, he had been "a frail, slight Irish youth who, when called 'a mick,' smiled ingenuously," and walked away from the hurt he felt. Then came a hurt he couldn't walk away from—his mother, killed, in the '06 earthquake. This was followed swiftly by another loss: his father, unable to find work and support his son, abandoned the ruined city and, in what was not an unheard-of practice for the time, left the boy with some relatives to raise. The twelve-year-old stayed with them a year until his mother's brother, Judge Martin O'Donnell, brought him to Los Angeles to live with him and his wife in the Boyle Heights section of the city.

The boy attended Huntington Park High and soon discovered the joys of motorcycle riding, which pretty much ended his formal schooling. His informal education consisted of taking engines apart and putting them back together again so they ran faster, and in this he excelled. His talents and instincts led him into racing, and he caught his first ride as a mechanic at the scary-fast Vanderbilt Cup at the Panama-Pacific International Exposition in San Francisco. The Duesenberg he was riding in with Eddie O'Donnell (no relation to his aunt and uncle) "turtled" or turned over on the street, but neither man was hurt. Then the next year he and O'Donnell entered the Corona Road Race, the one that killed Wild Bob Burman, and Jimmy again saw firsthand the terrible risks associated with this mad thing he craved. Still, with Jimmy riding lookout, Eddie O'Donnell had won Corona, so the youngster was also getting a firsthand look at success and the perks that came with it. Danger, the thing that frightened so many about the sport, did not turn him away from it. It was what drew him to it.

But for the longest time Murphy didn't steer his own ship. He was always the sidekick, never the hero. He and Eddie Rickenbacker served together during the war and it's said that Eddie was the one who convinced him to make the jump from mechanic to driver. Tommy Milton, his teammate at Duesenberg, probably put in a good word for him too. In any case, when finally entrusted with wheels of his own, Murphy ripped it up, setting track records at a race in New York. His next big race was the coming-home party at Beverly.

The newspapers were all over the local-boy-makes-good angle, but most of the sharp-dressers in the stands didn't give him much of a chance against Milton, Cliff Durant, the high-flying son of the founder of General Motors, and other big names in the eighteen-car field. The wise guys felt smart at first because Murphy got passed almost as soon as the green flag dropped, clearing the way for Milton. Milton was blind in one eye and couldn't see all that well out of the other, but that didn't stop him from holding first place until lap 36 when Art Klein in a coal-black Peugeot snuck past him. But only barely, and just for one lap, after which Milton sent him back in line. Just as quickly Klein jumped back in front of Milton, and the two jockeyed back and forth for the lead until the Peugeot skidded out helplessly and Milton's Duesenberg reasserted command.

Up came Ira Vail in a Philbrin. Vail was a dashing, mustachioed East Coast driver who relished the Hollywood scene, particularly the ladies in it. He had flipped for Rudolph Valentino's ex-lover and the couple was married at St. Francis Hotel in San Francisco, Earl Cooper stepping in as best man after a last-minute scheduling conflict forced Eddie Rickenbacker to take a pass on the ceremony. Vail stole the lead from Milton and then Joe Boyer in a Frontenac stole it from him. Boyer stayed first for the next forty-four laps until—aha!—the go-fast kid rode up behind him. Jimmy Murphy on your tail was like a dog with a bone; he wouldn't let you go until you switched positions with him and you were on *his* tail. Dropping down at the start but not knuckling under, he had threaded his way through the field until Boyer and Boyer alone appeared in his sights. Jimmy hauled him down and that was it. He beat Boyer by four laps and everyone else by a lot more than that, averaging 103 miles per hour over 225 thundering miles. It was like something they dreamed up in Hollywood: The underdog mechanic-turned-driver steps in and wins, with seventy-five thousand spectators on their feet cheering him on. A star was born.

In the fall, at the debut of the new Jack Prince-designed board track at the Fresno County fairgrounds, Jimmy did it again. With seventy-five thousand watching, he started at the pole, fell back, regained the lead, then fell back again after being forced to pit because his tire was burning up from the friction of the wood. With a new tire he climbed back into the thick of things and won first-place money.

Returning to Beverly Hills on Thanksgiving Day Jimmy got a reminder of how fragile success was in motor racing. His old friend and mentor Eddie O'Donnell was leading the field in a Duesenberg. On lap 160 Gaston Chevrolet in a Frontenac bounded up hard on his rear, clipping the Duesenberg. Both cars spun out of control. The Duesenberg turtled and rolled, killing O'Donnell and his mechanic. The Frontenac rolled over and over again and smashed through a section of fence. The Swiss-born Chevrolet, the youngest of the racing Chevrolet brothers—his brother Louis founded the car company of the same name—died as well.

No one was immune, they all knew it. Everyone who raced seriously for a living understood that what happened to Gaston and Eddie and Wild Bob and nearly happened to Barney could happen to any one of them, at any moment, and on some deep level they all accepted it. They accepted it though they seldom talked about it, and if, like Barney, one of them decided to throw in his cards and end this poker game with death, they all knew the vacant seat at the table would not stay vacant for long, that it would be snapped up in an instant by some full-of-himself youngblood who believed himself immortal.

Still driving better with one eye than most people with two, Tommy Milton set the world land speed record in a 16-cylinder Duesenberg and won the national racing championship in 1920. The next year, Jimmy Murphy took the French Grand Prix at Le Mans, also in a Duesenberg, becoming the first American to win a European Grand Prix race in an American-made car. His victory brought international acclaim to the marque, and this may have been when "duesey" or, as the word is more commonly spelled, "doozy," entered the popular lexicon, meaning something or somebody that was special in some way. Special or not, Murphy demanded more guts than what the Duesey presently offered him, so back in California after his triumph in Europe he asked Harry A. Miller to switch out the engine that had won Le Mans and replace it with a Miller-built 183-cubic-inch engine. As they did for all of Miller's engines Leo Goossen and his eyeshade-wearing peers made engineering drawings for the parts. Then Fred Offenhauser's men machined these parts into being. Their hands and overalls may have been dirty but the work they produced was spotless: "a combined jewelry and race car factory" was how one writer described the Miller plant.

Murphy first tested out the 183 at Beverly Hills and at two fast board tracks in the Bay Area, San Carlos and Cotati. Thus satisfied, he shipped the car east for its national premiere at the Indianapolis 500. After cracking two ribs in practice he won the pole with a 100.5-m.p.h. clocking. The doubters had all faded away by now; Murphy in a Miller 183 was as close as it got to a sure thing. Breaking into the lead at the front he pushed the pace and kept pushing it, seeing only empty track ahead of him until he started to lap cars. His pole-to-pole 1922 triumph averaged a record-setting 94.8 miles per hour. Even better was his payday—twenty thousand dollars for first place, plus the money they awarded to drivers for each lap they led during the race. Since Jimmy led all the laps, he collected all the loot.

But, characteristically, he said he deserved only partial credit for the win. "It has to be a Miller-Murphy affair, for I refuse to take a bit of credit away from Harry Miller and his wonderful ability," he told a reporter. Not to slight the other important player in his win, he added, "I truly believe the place of honor should be given the car, and not to either Miller or me."

The Murphy Special's triumph brought still more attention to its creator, who admired Jimmy and regarded him like a son. No ego, no phony bravado, "unassuming, unpretentious," "a sweet, clean, lovable character" who always dealt with people on the square. But the kid was no pushover. That was another thing Miller liked about him. He didn't just participate, he competed. There's a certain kind of person who, with the right machine around him, just has to see how fast it will go. James Anthony Murphy was that kind of person.

The folks back in Los Angeles threw a victory party for Murphy after Indianapolis, and then he was off to the races again, picking up paychecks in Cotati and other places. In Tacoma, Washington, he set a new 250-mile speed mark, a record he broke at Beverly Hills in a canary yellow Durant with a cat-quick Miller 183 purring inside. All this racing and winning earned him national honors as the year's best driver.

It also turned the Miller 183 into "the hottest thing in wheels," a lean, mean driving machine that balanced lightness with strength and boasted an array of technical advances. Miller 183s won every big-money race they competed in and did so in ridiculously decisive fashion, blowing other cars away and rewriting the record books. Known for the clean simplicity of their designs, using fewer working parts than other comparable motors, Team Miller had lifted engine craftsmanship to a level nobody else in the world could touch.

Due to the speed of the 183 and other racing machines, and the dangers they were creating, Indianapolis 500 officials changed the rules of the sport, requiring the use of smaller engines. So Team Miller revolutionized American racing—again—with a new 122-cubic-inch engine that was smaller, lighter, and narrower than the 183 but almost as fast. From the days of the Golden Submarine and before, Miller had always been interested in the design of the entire car, not just the engine, and his Miller 122 became the highest expression of what he had been building toward all these years—fully designed and engineered, inside and out, by his team, a light, stylish compact racing machine with only a slim seat for the driver and no space for a riding mechanic. What's more, in a move similar to what Harley Earl was doing with passenger cars at Don Lee Coach and Body Works, Miller dropped its body low to the ground—three feet, to be exact, from the soles of his shoes to the top of the radiator. It looked like "a fat clubhouse cigar" to writer Paul Lowry, who dubbed it "the new baby go-fast machine."

This new baby go-fast machine made its inventor "the originator, in the United States, of the racing car as an art object." It also "moved American racing vehicles from the square, upright era of the 1910s into a low, rakish look that precisely fit the era." In 1923 the Miller 122 dominated Indianapolis as thoroughly as the Miller 183 did the previous year. It breathed under the hood of half the cars in the race. It claimed first place—Tommy Milton, in his second 500 win—and made the most advanced racecars of Europe and America "look like tamale carts in comparison." Jimmy Murphy finished third but might have done better were it not for having to change his sparkplugs eighteen times. Then there was that crazy-sweet moment when he stopped on the backstretch and got out of his car to help his teammate Cliff Durant, who had pulled to the side with ignition problems. Jimmy asked if there was anything he could do for him. Durant waved him on, and Murphy ran back to his car and resumed the race.

In September Murphy went to Europe to race in the Italian Grand Prix, training across the continent and riding an ocean liner over the Atlantic with the Murphy Special below deck in the cargo hold. He finished third at Monza and then returned to the United States for more competition. Later in the fall, back on his home turf at Beverly Hills, he lost a close contest to Eddie Hearne, who also nosed him out for the national title because Murphy had gone to Europe with his friend and missed two stateside races that would have earned him enough points to win. Determined to regain the title, Jimmy went on a rampage in 1924, winning three races and piling up nearly twice as many points as the second-place driver in the standings. Barring a disaster, he was a lock to win honors as America's best driver for the second time.

A disaster occurred. At a race on a dirt track in Syracuse Murphy tried to take the car in front of him on a turn. That was always his style: push on the turns. But on this one he cut the steering wheel too sharp and his rear wheels couldn't hold the speed. His Miller-built car slid off the track and smashed into a four-foot-high concrete fence post that "forced its way through the hood of the car and cut a wide gaping hole in Jimmy's chest." Those who saw it turned away in horror. Medics, mechanics in the pits, and race officials sprinted to the scene. The caution flag came out, slowing the other cars in the race. No one else was hurt.

The medics found Jimmy in a "crumpled mass" inside a tangle of steel and aluminum. "His back and neck were broken and his legs were twisted almost off his body," said an eyewitness. But he was still breathing. Rescuers carefully freed him from the wreckage and loaded his body by stretcher into an ambulance. Before the ambulance reached the hospital his breathing quit.

The death of the best racecar driver in America shocked the country, but especially his home state and city. The *Los Angeles Times* alone carried ten articles about it. One wire service photo showed Jimmy rounding a curve in the race; another, taken moments later, showed his busted-up vehicle. Writers in Los Angeles naturally sought out the shaken Harry A. Miller, who had called New York as soon as he heard the news. He talked to Tommy Milton, who was in the race, and heard what happened from him. Milton and the other drivers had done their job and finished the event but without enthusiasm or heart. Afterward some of them met at a bar and shared their mutual disbelief about the fate of their friend, who would never see thirty.

It fell to Milton, Earl Cooper, and some other drivers to ship Jimmy's body from Syracuse on Tuesday at 12:15 a.m.—"the midnight train," as one reporter poetically called it. Milton and Cooper stayed behind in New York to clean up Murphy's affairs, while Riley Brett, his mechanic, accompanied the casket on the train. Just as he had ridden with him many times as a mechanic, Brett rode with Murphy on his final trip across the country. Judge Martin O'Donnell and Harry Miller met the train in San Bernardino and rode it into Los Angeles.

A few hundred people—Jimmy's racing buddies as well as racing fans who had only seen him drive and never met him in person—were waiting in the harsh sunlight at Santa Fe station when the train pulled in, blowing clouds of smoke and steam. The smoke rose into the sky and melted away, a mute commentary on the fleeting nature of human life and achievement. As one who was there wrote, "All that is mortal of Jimmy Murphy, the racing world's greatest star, came home to his friends in Los Angeles yesterday. Gathered at the Santa Fe station when the long train bearing Murphy's body from the East rolled in were hundreds who stood with heads bared and sobbed as six former racing champions carried the copper casket from the train to the waiting hearse. Strong men and courageous women broke down and wept. Steel-nerved race drivers, hardened by constant brushes with death, were unable to control themselves."

Every man there took off his hat and all the men and women lowered their heads in respect as the casket passed by them. A few reached out to touch it.

The open rear compartment of the hearse slid open and just before it closed someone placed a floral wreath on the casket—a wreath in the form of a checkered flag, white with black squares. The doors shut, and the long black car drove away.

The Cunningham and Cunningham funeral parlor received the body. A private Sunday night memorial service was held at the Knights of Columbus hall. An honor guard of Knights and Elk's Lodge members stood by the casket during the viewing. The next afternoon a funeral mass, open to the public, took place at St. Vincent's Church at Grand and Washington. Mourners filled every seat in the pews, and hundreds more stood on the sidewalks outside by the stone statues of the saints. Since Jimmy's roots reached back to San Francisco and his driving had won him fans across the state, people from around California were in attendance.

"Jimmy Murphy, before God and Man, is worthy of respect," said Father Martin Hanley in his eulogy. "He knew the chances against him, and he was prepared to meet them. There is happiness for those who knew Jimmy Murphy best." The reverend went on to say that success never spoiled Jimmy Murphy and that he always treated everyone fair and straight. Such was a person's life sometimes. Not every happy story ends happily.

A single floral tribute, a bouquet of American Beauty roses, lay on his casket. A local soprano sang "Ave Maria." Two of the pallbearers were his two surrogate fathers, Martin O'Donnell and Harry A. Miller, and they helped carry Jimmy's casket out of the church into a hearse. Eight motorcycle police led the funeral procession to Calvary Cemetery. The lead car displayed a banner posthumously awarding Murphy the title of 1924 United States racing champion. After this car came the hearse and a long string of automobiles following behind. At the cemetery the pallbearers did their job once more and put the casket into a hole in the ground. The priest said some more words and then they covered him with dirt.

THIRTEEN

Something Happening Here

Jimmy Murphy's death sparked strong comment among those who disapproved of motor racing and automobiles in general. In his Sunday sermon Edgar F. Daugherty, minister of the First Christian Church of Los Angeles, argued that Murphy's pursuit of speed at all costs reflected a larger social sickness, one that placed haste above other, more important values.

"There is nothing so marking the alienation of our times from God as our applause for haste," Daugherty told his congregation. He said the fallen race driver was one of society's "sacrifices on haste's altar, part of the price we continue to pay for speed records. Granted that the pursuit of a speed record puts zest in our life. [But] is that the big thing in human experience?"

Some inventions make a big impact when they first appear, yet their novelty quickly wears off or they become obsolete and are replaced by still newer inventions. But automobiles stubbornly refused to follow this pattern. Rather than diminish over time, their influence kept growing, reaching into every aspect of American life, churches being no exception. The Interchurch World Movement conducted a study to determine whether the pleasures and freedoms of driving encouraged people to go to church or led them away from it. On the one hand, yes, a nice sunny day and a nice set of wheels with the top down tended to make one less inclined to spend Sunday morning in church. On the other hand, the study found that automobiles made it easier to get to service and come from farther away. Call it a toss-up.

But there was no dispute that cars were changing people's lives, and that not all of these changes were good. "We now have a thousand roads reeking with national neurosis of hurry and burnt gasoline," wrote *The Catholic World*. "The horse and buggy have vanished from our roads, and all happy days seem to have gone also. For who can be constantly in a hurry and ever really enjoy himself?"

Indeed, with all this hurrying to and fro, people were walking a lot less than they used to, and driving practically everywhere they went. "Everybody who is anybody at all has his own car—and a goodly number of others who are not anybody," a California guidebook author wrote during this time. "They not only have them, but they use them to the extent that the easterner does not dream of. Your Californian thinks nothing of running out from Los Angeles to take luncheon at Pomona, cutting back to drive in Hollywood, and spending the evening at Long Beach." A joint state and federal traffic study confirmed this impression. "In California," it stated, "all traffic except motor vehicle traffic is negligible."

More than a million Californians owned automobiles in 1924, one of every three adults in the state. This compared to 15 million automobiles in the United States and 18 million in the world. By the end of the decade the number of cars would double in the state and California would claim one of every twelve cars in the nation, trailing only New York. Most of these cars were used, although dealers, in an effort to attract new customers, had begun accepting trade-ins in exchange for reduced prices on new vehicles. Another innovation that spurred sales was buying on time. In the old days people paid cash for a new car—one reason why only the rich could afford them. But as installment plans were introduced, with buyers coming up with a down payment and agreeing to finance the remainder of the purchase price, more bodies were put into cars and more cars put on the road.

The surge in the automobile population of California coincided with a surge in the human one. As they had since gold rush days, outsiders were flocking here from all over, and California was growing twice as fast as the rest of the nation. Nearly 3.5 million people called the state home in 1920—more than double the number in 1900 but 2.5 million fewer than there would be in 1930. The economy suffered its usual ups and downs but the general trend for everything—spending money, stocks and bonds, real estate, jobs, farming, mining, manufacturing, movies, the arts, education—was up, up, up. These were good times and getting better every year, and for many there was no question why this was so. "From whatever angle you may view southern California's striking progress," observed one writer, "you will be compelled to acknowledge that the automobile is responsible more than any other half dozen factors, for its phenomenal advancement." Said another, "The significance of the automobile in California to all the inhabitants there really needs no discussion. It is too obvious."

Pastor Daugherty and other critics of the automobile were a tiny, eccentric minority, out of step with the mass of the population who saw motorcars as modern, as the way of the future, as the vehicle of economic and social progress. "We are a fast-moving nation," said one San Franciscan. "We must have speed in our travel, and efficiency in our business. And any device that reduces time is eagerly sought for by Americans." Those who waxed sentimental about the old, simple pleasures of rural life almost certainly did not work on a farm, for mechanized, gas-powered agriculture—trucks, tractors, combines, spreaders, balers, loaders, harvesters—had evolved into "one of the greatest labor-saving devices invented." Farmers who once flooded dirt roads to trap automobilists and scare them away from their land were using these machines to increase their acreage with fewer hands on deck. Then on their day of rest they'd drive into town in their Model T for church and a picnic after.

Some car businesses sprung from old horse-and-buggy businesses. Not every family owned a horse or a horse and buggy, but livery stables rented saddle horses for a couple bucks a day and a horse and buggy for a dollar more. These stables either moved into renting cars or they went out of business.

Early horseless carriage drivers did not understand car insurance at first or why anyone would ever need such a thing. (Nor did the law require it.) So Fireman's Fund of San Francisco and other insurance companies marketed their services by sponsoring informational booths at car shows and organizing endurance runs and races. The auto clubs also began to offer car insurance. Studies by the Farmers Automobile Inter-Insurance Exchange of Los Angeles found that with less traffic in the country, farmers got into fewer wrecks than city residents and therefore deserved to pay lower premiums. This became the founding principle of what is today the Farmers Insurance Group.

The 1920s saw a new and bigger round of oil strikes in Kern County and elsewhere, bringing more flush times to the oil industry. Californians drove automobiles fueled by oil and gas from California oil fields and refined by California refineries, and there was enough left over to sell to other states and countries. Oil companies both big and small—Gilmore Oil, Seaside Oil, Standard Oil, Union Oil (now Unocal), Richfield Oil (now ARCO)—thrived in the state and distributed their products through filling stations. Richfield Oil's new twelve-story black and gold building rising in downtown Los Angeles became a visible symbol of the company's prosperity, and indeed the prosperity of the city and region in general.

For all this automobile-fueled prosperity, though, there were lots of automobile-fueled growing pains, and not even the most ardent Chamber of Commerce booster could deny it. "It is almost unbelievable only twenty years ago automobiles were little seen on the streets of Los Angeles," said one 1920s-era driver. "Today one has to be careful in crossing the streets, out of the central traffic zone, because of the traffic." Traffic in Los Angeles was so bad that the City Council entertained a proposal to ban parking downtown as a means of restricting the "auto-hogs," as streetcar riders called them. This triggered an intense debate about the place of automobiles in the city. Whereas many trolley riders, walkers, and bicyclists wanted them gone, merchants most definitely did not. "The day when the automobile was a 'pleasure car'...is long since past," argued one opponent of the ban. "The motor car is just as much a necessity to business as the street car." The proposal kicked up such a fuss that the City Council eventually backed away from it, but the controversy inadvertently showed how closely linked society and cars were becoming. "There is no longer any argument as to the necessity of the motor car," said one observer. "It is as much a part of modern life as shoes."

To ease the mess downtown, the Automobile Club of Southern California—which now boasted the largest membership of any auto club in the nation, with the San Francisco–based AAA of Northern California, Nevada, and Utah not far behind it—advocated the construction of a network of boulevards that would sweep around the crowded Spring Street area where the red Pacific Electric cars and the yellow Los Angeles Railway cars converged. Signaling that "the future would be tied to the car, not the trolley," Los Angeles voters approved a bond measure to finance the boulevards, and the city took another step toward what it is today: a metropolitan area not with one central downtown hub but several regional hubs connected by highways.

One result of the rise of automobiles was a decline in train and trolley passengers, a decline that would only accelerate in the years to come. "Trains are becoming as obsolete in our family as the horse," said one woman who, like most Californians of her day, traveled on narrow-gauge railroad lines all around the state and shipped packages on them. But with trucks steadily taking over the job of hauling goods, and cars hauling the people, local steam trains gradually chugged off into extinction. (Some remain alive for tourism and sightseeing, such as the Skunk Train between Fort Bragg and Willits and the Niles Canyon Railway in the Bay Area.)

Meanwhile automobiles were undergoing the greatest leap in comfort and ease of use since the introduction of the electric starter: the closed body. Before the Great War, open cars were the rule. Then closed models took over the market—nine out of every ten new cars by the end of the 1920s. The rise of closed models coincided with an increase in women drivers; California in 1920 boasted more female motorists—eighty thousand—than any other state in the nation. Not only that, women were showing increasing skill and independence behind the wheel. "It is a perpetual surprise to see the remarkable competence with which the American woman manages her own car," remarked an Englishman on a tour of the state. "When we visited a woman's college in California my companions and I were taken out for a drive one afternoon by a group of the senior students in three enormous throbbing monsters driven by three small college girls whose little feet could hardly reach the pedals. It was magnificent."

Those throbbing monsters, despite the traffic tie-ups they caused, made life in the city more sublime. One could zip around town to see friends, the theater, art shows, sporting events, and for a thousand other purposes. The wealthy and privileged of the city tended to live in the hills, and the less well-to-do in the flats. But automobiles carried people up and down hills more easily, opening these areas to greater development and giving flatlanders the chance to enjoy views and real estate values once the exclusive preserve of the rich.

For those who did not wish to live in the city, or could not afford to, automobiles provided a way out. In the days of the horse and buggy, only doctors, attorneys, and the like could afford to live in the country and maintain an office in the city. But now, a new class of workers known as "commuters"—more middle class than upper—was starting to emerge. They lived in outlying communities, drove to their jobs downtown, then returned home at the end of the day. "The working man, and the man of moderate means, [can] live a considerable distance from work, thereby enabling him to own his own home, and to have lawns, flowers and shrubbery." As a result homes and families were sprouting in all sorts of formerly out-of-the-way places, and cities were growing up around them where only tiny settlements had been before.

The coming of Pickfair, for instance, triggered a real estate boom in Beverly Hills, which became suddenly a trendy spot to live. Farmland was bought and subdivided, roads paved, and expensive new homes built. With the cost of land getting so high, it no longer made sense to devote two hundred acres to occasional car racing meets, and the Los Angeles Speedway closed a few months after Jimmy Murphy's death.

Beverly Hills remained a separate entity from Los Angeles, but the automobile—and those community-spanning commuters—brought the two cities closer together, just as it brought Los Angeles closer to Pasadena, Burbank, and Santa Monica. Over time cities would blend into one another, and the distinctions between them would in many cases disappear entirely. No longer tethered to development along rail lines, cities pushed their boundaries outward into areas that once would have been considered off the beaten track. Near Cecil DeMille's airfield and along the edge of the northwest oil district of Los Angeles, plans were afoot for a new shopping district on Wilshire Boulevard. This "Miracle Mile," a term first coined by shopkeepers and the developer and later adopted by the press and public, was based on the then-unique retail concept of attracting people in their cars and then taking care of them once they got there. Shoppers could escape the crowds of downtown, find row upon row of parking spaces, wander leisurely around the shops, and return home the same way they came: by automobile. Still drawing shoppers to this day, the Miracle Mile influenced shopping center design around the country.

Similarly, drive-in markets began to pop up at corner locations all around Los Angeles. Also offering easy in-and-out for drivers and ample parking, Ralph's Grocery on Wilshire Boulevard featured long, wide aisles in keeping with the tastes of its customers, who had arrived there on long, wide boulevards. Taking advantage of the southern California climate, Frank Lloyd Wright designed the Yucca Vine Market with its fruits and vegetables displayed outdoors in a canopied, open-air setting. "Los Angeles in particular became known for its large market buildings, which had distinctive open-air fronts made practical by the warm, sunny climate of southern California," writes Chester H. Liebs, an architectural historian. "Free parking was often provided either in front or at the side of the store—a harbinger of changes that would eventually take place in food-market design nationwide."

While some of these motor trends were occurring elsewhere around the state and nation, they found the most fertile soil in southern California, "where the use of the automobile was spreading more rapidly than in any other time or place in history." A given trend may not have started there (though most of them did), but it hardly matters because invariably that was where it grew into its most splendid and wacky flowering. One example of this was the roadside restaurants built in whimsically creative ways or with big, easily identifiable objects out front. Opened in Rosemead in 1927 and moved the next year to South Gate, Hoot-Hoot I Scream became the place to go if you wanted to eat in a restaurant shaped like a giant owl with a moving head and blinking eyes. The Toad Inn in Santa Monica served ice cream and soda pop through the legs of a large toad. The Mother Goose Pantry in Pasadena served lunch and dinner in a building that looked like a shoe, while the more sophisticated Brown Derby in Hollywood resembled a hat.

All these places operated on the same premise: draw the eyes of passing motorists. In the era of the horse and buggy, signs did not have to be that large or colorful because nobody was passing by that fast. But with people now speeding by in their cars, roadside merchants needed to grab their attention with bigger and flashier signs, a trend that inevitably led to garish excess. "Hot dog stands and unsightly shacks" were nearly as common as trees on some busy roads. On Foothill Boulevard between Pasadena and San Bernardino one driver saw "324 billboards, 74 filling stations, nine garages, 117 roadside markets, inns and food stands, and one junkyard," and this didn't even count all the roadside litter he saw.

Also popping up on the highways to accommodate the millions of Americans now taking to the road were inns, auto courts, and tourist camps. "The trend of American tourist traffic has been largely westward during the past six or eight years," wrote a Lincoln Highway Association executive in 1923, and it's safe to say that a good deal of that western traffic ended up in California. In the 1920s hundreds of thousands of people came by automobile to the state every year—some to live but some just for sightseeing. An architect named Arthur Heineman was the first to coin the term "motel," joining the words motor and hotel, for the new Milestone Motels in San Luis Obispo.

Not only were the outsides of buildings changing because of cars, so were the insides. Bedrooms in new homes were being built smaller because people were spending less time in them due to the hours spent on the road either commuting or on weekend road trips. Garages began to be built as part of the house rather than detached from it, as in the days of the horse. "When a man buys an automobile, the question of housing it becomes a very pertinent matter. Sooner or later every man feels the need of having a place to store his car on his premises." Advertising in the early 1920s prominently listed the built-in garage as a selling point for new homes, although it took decades for this trend to become commonplace. Many ranch-style homes built in the 1950s still featured two-car garages detached from the main house. Gradually garages moved from the back of the lot to the front until they finally became a common part of the house itself, functioning as they do today in many homes as a second front door.

Garages became places to store automobiles as well as the tools needed to work on them. "Men who know very little about machinery can, after a time, with their own garage to work in and some necessary tools, keep their car in good conditions and learn to do most of their own repair work on a small scale." But garages became more than just at-home repair shops. They were part of the house but not part of the house, indoors but not precisely indoors either. Their large front doors opened out into the world, letting in sunlight and breezes and sometimes the scruffy neighbor boys from down the street. Garages became a refuge especially for men, who hung out in them and chewed the fat with other men. They were also places to be alone, to tinker with things, and not just automobile things but mechanical and electrical devices of all kinds. People with creative ideas and a wish to develop them didn't have to pay rent or anything extra for the space in their garage, so they could work there at night and on weekends in their free time away from their regular jobs, testing their inventions and theories without worrying about making money from them right away. They could think, create, and discover. The garage, usually with one or both of the cars parked on the street to free up space, evolved into one of the central places of creativity in American life, where experiments were tried, new inventions first tested, and companies born. Some great California and American industries, such as high technology, trace their roots to the garage.

Automobiles, an engine of economic and social change, were changing personal morals too, which was a problem for Pastor Daugherty and other critics. Cars fostered independence and rebellion among teenagers seeking escape from their disapproving parents. "The automobile is the undoing of many a boy," said one study. "With the automobile at his command, the boy early speeds up beyond home control." Some of these boys were underage, and some stole cars and went "joy-riding"—a term that first appeared in the 1920s—to impress girls and take them on dates. "I fear that the automobile is encouraging all sorts of night excursions on the part of the young...[and] is not for the best interests of society."

Another problem: Couples were making whoopee in automobiles, and not just teens either. Here, again, technology in the form of the closed car body helped to create this trend. While it was certainly possible for two people with the urge to come together in an open-air automobile, it was generally warmer, more comfortable, and more private to do so in a car with a roof and the windows rolled up but cracked just a little to let some air in. Although clearly some showed more discretion than others. "The practice of making love on highways is becoming alarmingly prevalent," reported one Los Angeles paper. "In many cases it is flagrant, open." To escape prying eyes, couples drove out into the country on lonesome dirt roads or up into the hills overlooking the lights of the city.

And while indulging in activities of this sort, what else might they be doing? Drinking and driving. Never a good combination at any time, drinking and driving contributed to the high teen death and accident rates, as they do today. But in 1924, with Prohibition fully on, drinking alcohol anywhere at any time was forbidden by law. Still people did it anyhow, drinking and driving too fast on their way to speakeasies where they sipped Bacardi cocktails and smoked Jaguar cigarettes and swung their bodies to the sounds of Gershwin into the late hours of the night. Dr. French Oliver of the Los Angeles Bible Institute called the automobile, the dance hall, and the movies "the triumvirate of hell" for their harmful influence on the young. Rich movie stars who led dissolute lives and paraded around in their fancy cars came in for censure as well.

The automobile became the machine of choice for bootleggers transporting illegal alcohol, guns, and narcotics across state lines or the Mexican border. Other sensational car-related crimes captured headlines: holdups with the robbers driving away in a getaway vehicle, kidnaps with the victim being shoved into a car, murdered bodies found in automobiles. Worst of all was the mayhem—there is no other word for it—that was occurring every day on the nation's streets and highways. "Never before in human history except in time of war had so many people been exposed in the course of their daily lives to the risk of violent death," writes author and historian Ashleigh Brilliant, illustrating his point with a grim accumulation of statistics. Fewer than seven hundred people—drivers, passengers, pedestrians—died in auto accidents in California in 1919. Each year in the 1920s the number grew larger than the previous year, so that by 1929 the annual death toll in the state had risen to twenty-one hundred.

Awful as these tragedies were, the public generally came to accept them as one of the costs of modern living, just as they came to accept that a greater and greater share of the machinery of government—taxes, fees, and bonds for road building and maintenance, licensing, regulation, laws, stoplights, signs, traffic control, traffic courts, law enforcement, and jails—would center on this creative-destructive force. "Every American soon took it for granted that a large fraction of any city's police force would be assigned to traffic duty, that state troopers, officers or rangers would patrol the highways by motorcycle [and] that state and local governments would spend more for highway construction and maintenance." The state legislature formed the California Highway Patrol in 1929 to enforce the State Vehicle Act on county roads and state highways, and in its first year the CHP consisted of 280 officers driving 80 patrol vehicles and 225 motorcycles. Communications were primitive; a patrolman on the road checked in with the dispatch office by calling in from a public pay phone. Later the CHP worked out a system in which certain businesses would post a red flag on the outside of their building to signal to officers that they needed to call headquarters. As radio networks improved over the decade, so did the communication methods of CHP officers, although their ability to prevent accidents and stop speeders would always be limited.

And this was the essence of what Pastor Daugherty was saying: Why can't we slow down? A soul needs stillness and time for contemplation—and speeding around in an automobile took one away from that. Spending so much time in a car was isolating, it removed one from other people, and that meant less time for family and friends. Another concern was the gross materialism that seemed to go hand in hand with owning an automobile. People flaunted their new Packards or Buicks, and their neighbors, not wishing to be outdone, overspent on their cars to keep up with them. Going into debt for a car only increased the pressure to work more, earn more, rush around more. This preoccupation with worldly pleasures and material goods, of which enough was never enough, made people miss the truly big things in life and contributed to this disease of haste. Go too fast in your life and you will crash. And if you doubt it, just look at Jimmy Murphy.

It's unlikely Harry A. Miller heard about the pastor's remarks, and he surely would not have cared for them if he had; he was not the sermonizing sort. He had lost a good friend who was close enough to him to be his son, and his feelings were not easily packaged into tidy moralistic lectures. Why did Jimmy, of all people, have to die? And why did he, Harry A. Miller, get to go on with his life whereas Jimmy did not? If Miller thought about such questions, and surely he did, he did not let them overwhelm him. He did what he had to do after Jimmy died, what Jimmy would have wanted him to do. He went back to work.

The second half of the decade became even more successful for Miller than the first. Famous and wealthy, his work admired around America and Europe, he kept creating racing machines that kept cracking through speed barriers. His speedboats with Miller marine engines won top races and set international records. Earlier he had served as vice president of Leach Motor Company in Los Angeles, crafting the engines for the stylish and expensive Leach Power Plus Six, which became a fad with Hollywood stars. But the fad passed on and the company failed, and Miller returned to his specialty of grooming go-fast racing engines.

Many of the ideas he developed for racecars showed up in passenger cars. The most dramatic of these was front-wheel drive, which car builders had experimented with for years. It is now the most popular steering mechanism in automobiles, and the first one to really nail it was Miller, whose Miller 122, unveiled in 1925, became the finest racing car in the world to be so equipped. "The world never had seen such a low, sleek and purposeful racing machine," said one admirer.

After more rule changes that required still smaller engines, he created a new go-fast baby machine: the Miller 91 with a 91-cubic-inch engine and either rear- or front-wheel drive. More superlatives followed: "If Harry Miller had done nothing more than give the world front-wheel drive as a practical reality, his significant place in history would be assured. There was something about [the Miller 91] that was close to being sublime," said a biographer. Designed inside and out by Team Miller, it looked sharp, had a rakishly low profile, handled the corners like a dream, and blew the competition away the same as his past cars.

With the success of these California-based cars, even the most ardent European or East Coast racing fan would have been hard pressed to dismiss what was going on in the westernmost strip of the United States. A Californian, Frank Lockhart, driving a car designed and built in California, won the 1926 Indianapolis 500. Another Californian, Harry Hartz, finished second behind him, and in 1928 another Californian, Louis Meyer (born in New York, raised in Los Angeles) claimed the first of three Indy 500 wins in his career. These trips to the winner's circle at the Greatest Spectacle in Racing came on top of previous trips by Murphy, a born-and-raised Californian, and by Midwesterner Tommy Milton, who spent so much time at Miller's hop shop on Long Beach Avenue that the state might rightly claim him too.

The force behind all this winning was, of course, Miller, whose cars won eleven times at Indianapolis and dominated in every other way too, each year placing at least six cars in the top ten during the twenties. In 1923, nearly half the entries ran on his engines; by 1925, it was three-quarters of the field; and by 1929, all but six of the thirty-three cars in the starting lineup came from Miller, including the one that finished first. Miller cars claimed as many speed records as they did checkered flags. Lockhart in a Miller 91 later set a world record for its class of 164.84 miles per hour and also set a new one-lap record at a track in Atlantic City, a championship car record that wasn't broken until 1960.

Beyond racing, however, it was impossible to miss what was occurring in California as a whole in terms of automobiles. Backwater it was no more. Something was happening out there, and what was happening was not exactly like anywhere else. California seemed to have more of everything than other states—more cars per capita, more population (actually still behind New York, but nipping at its heels), more racetracks, more filling stations, more funny-shaped hot dog stands, more open-air markets, more commuters, more women drivers, more, more, more—and yet it was also different and screwier than the norm. Some saw this screwiness, if screwiness it was, as being out of touch with the rest of the country, and maybe it was. But being different and out of touch also meant it wasn't copying what others were doing nor looking to be ratified by them, at least to some degree.

The California car scene was going its own way and following its own lead, which might explain its trendmaking tendencies. More, different, and frequently first—that was it in a nutshell. Certainly those in the automobile industry had begun to recognize this fact, particularly a shipping clerk at the Cadillac factory in Detroit who noticed that an astounding number of Cadillac chassis were being sent to the same address: Don Lee Coach and Body Works, Los Angeles, California. Hundreds of chassis—not complete cars, just chassis—were going out West every month, and it boggled the mind as to why. It boggled this shipping clerk's mind anyhow, and he asked a fellow clerk about it. The answer he received could be summed up in two words: Harley Earl. Earl was converting all these platforms into custom cars for Hollywood stars. Everybody who was anybody in the picture business could be seen cruising down Sunset in a Harley Earl–designed status bomb.

This story, which was told as part of a modern-day General Motors advertising campaign, smacks a little of legend-making, but there's enough truth to it to ground it in reality. Earl and Don Lee were in fact doing a land office business at their Cadillac custom shop, and the quality and quantity of their work was a secret perhaps only to that unsuspecting shipping clerk. Since his debut at the 1919 Los Angeles Automobile Show, when his Chandler and Marmon made the other cars "look like something the cat dragged in," people in the know recognized the size of his talent. Two of them were Alfred P. Sloan, the president of General Motors Corporation, and Lawrence Fisher, the head of GM's Cadillac division. Both were smart, seasoned automobile men who had succeeded in a tough business and knew the car industry as well as anyone. Having just become the president of Cadillac, Fisher, with his boss's blessing, embarked on a tour of Cadillac dealers around the country to introduce himself and get to know them. One of his stops, and by far his most important, was at 12th and Main in Los Angeles, where he went to personally inspect the Don Lee Coach and Body Works and meet its creative guru.

The first thing Fisher noticed was how tall, how terribly tall, Earl was. Another thing he noticed was how well he dressed and the style and command he showed as he walked his visitor through the process of building a custom automobile. Fisher was one of the famous Fisher brothers whose company had been making top-tier automobile bodies for decades and was now making most of the bodies on GM cars. But, as Sloan wrote in a memoir years later, "He [Earl] was doing things in a way that Mr. Fisher had never seen before." After seeing Earl and his employees use modeling clay to shape the parts instead of hammering them out of metal and then blending the entire automobile into "a good-looking whole," Fisher walked away feeling "impressed," as Sloan put it in his elegantly understated way. In a somewhat less understated way, the head of GM explained what this meeting meant to automobile history: "It was an important meeting, for Mr. Fisher's interest in this young man's talent was to result in actively influencing the appearance of more than 50 million automobiles from the late 1920s to 1960."

This meeting, followed by the usual wining and dining—Earl and Fisher both loved the finer pleasures of life and became fast friends—led to more meetings, until Fisher made his offer to Harley to come to Detroit to design a new car for General Motors, to be called the LaSalle.

As Fisher and Sloan saw it, the LaSalle would be "a companion car to the Cadillac," occupying a price niche just below Cadillac and just above Buick. In the GM auto hierarchy, Cadillac occupied the top tier, followed in pricing by Buick, Oldsmobile, Pontiac, and Chevrolet, in that order. Founded in 1908, the same year as the introduction of the Model T, General Motors was the No. 2 carmaker in the world, trailing only Ford. But it had set its sights on the top spot, and under Sloan, who became president in the early twenties, the company believed it had the resources and strategy to do it. The new LaSalle was to be one leg in this strategy, a strategy that emphasized style over Henry Ford's utilitarian one-size-fits-all philosophy.

For General Motors, style was no longer a luxury; it was a necessity. Car performance had improved greatly over the years, and the basic mechanical and engineering problems of the internal combustion engine had been solved or were being solved. People always thought about performance and reliability when buying a car, but with these engineering advances they could also think about something else—the look and color and comfort of their ride. People naturally wished to impress their bosses, colleagues, and friends with what they were driving, but they also wished for their car to reflect something else about themselves, what they believed to be their true identity, the one hidden from society or ignored by it. Maybe in real life they cleaned carpets or delivered the mail or sold insurance, but inside an automobile, the right automobile that is, they could be hardy outdoorsmen or sleek urban hipsters or elegant tycoons—whatever they wished or imagined themselves to be.

For all these reasons and more, Fisher and Sloan needed Earl, and for an equal number of reasons Earl could see the advantage of throwing in with them. It was an opportunity to broaden his career, make more money, join a growing, aggressive company with superb leadership and a plan for the future, and work in the capital city of American autodom. It was also an opportunity to grow as a designer and, as Harley put it, "execute something distinctively different."

And so, in January 1926, he traded the warmth and sun of California for the snow and cold of a Michigan winter to begin work on "the first American mass-produced automobile to be designed not by an engineer, but by a stylist."

Earl, whose first official title with GM was "consulting engineer," did not set out with grandiose dreams of making history; if he had, he surely would have uncorked a dud. Instead his idea was to create a car he himself would enjoy, something stylishly long and low that he could slip into and drive with confidence and pleasure. "When you are a designer," he said, "you kind of think, 'Well, if I were building one for myself, what would I do?'" What he did was base his designs on a French-Spanish bombshell, the Hispano-Suiza, one of the most gorgeous cars of the era. Wisely, considering his designs would ultimately be implemented by mechanical and production engineers who would likely resist him at first, "I didn't want to take too big of a chance and do something that didn't look like anything," he said.

"The self-confident young Californian" passed his first test with flying colors, meeting with Sloan, Fisher, and other department heads to show them his sketches and preliminary mock-ups. "Mr. Sloan brought in the heads of the departments and asked if they saw anything that would be a problem," Harley recalled. "They went over it very thoroughly and said they would make some little dies and stretch metals. They didn't have any trouble." They didn't have any trouble although, like Fisher in Los Angeles, some of what they would do and see over the next year would be entirely new to them. The methods by which Earl created his designs revolutionized the automobile industry, and he used all of these techniques to fashion his introductory statement at General Motors, the breakthrough LaSalle.

It debuted in March 1927, the same year Lindbergh flew solo across the Atlantic, Babe Ruth hit sixty home runs in a single season, and Harley's neighbor, Al Jolson, appeared in *The Jazz Singer,* the first talking motion picture. The LaSalle marked yet another expression of a nation on the upswing, one that could unite technological know-how with artistic achievement, and the public adored it. One auto critic of the time called it "the most beautiful of cars." The LaSalle came in several different styles and two different lengths, and every inch of it looked long and low and regal. It featured deep Flying Wing fenders, reapportioned side windows, soft, rounded corners, and a hundred other design touches that delivered on Alfred Sloan's wish to have "a production automobile that was as beautiful as the custom cars of the period."

All that, and power too: a 303-cubic-inch, 75-horsepower V-8 engine that surpassed 100 miles per hour on speed tests. Though priced high at twenty-six hundred dollars, it seemed worth every penny. More than seventy-five thousand LaSalles sold in its first year, a figure that surely delighted Sloan as much as the critical praise.

Eighty-five years later, the praise continues. The 1927 LaSalle had that "intangible essence that sets some automobiles apart from their contemporaries the moment they appear," writes historian James Bell. "There was never any doubt that the LaSalle had it—and deserved it." Vincent Curcio agrees: "The original LaSalle was a watershed in U.S. automotive design. Being the first production car to really have been thoroughly styled, it symbolized the growing maturity of the American automotive market. No longer were Americans content with basic transportation. The automobile had become an expression of one's good taste and lifestyle, and the owner of a LaSalle was recognized as a person of discriminating judgment in the choice of his automobile."

A month after the LaSalle's debut, Sloan, having seen enough, offered Earl a permanent job—forget the consultant tag—as the head of a new automobile styling department at General Motors. The Art and Color Section, as it was called, was the first design department of any mass-production American car company. Harley would organize and lead the section, which had fifty employees to start, all working under him to fashion the bodies, running boards, lamps, fenders, radiators, grills, windows, hoods, doors, door handles, and other appearance parts for every model and line made by General Motors.

Accepting Sloan's offer, Harley returned home in May to take a six-week vacation and prepare, with his wife and family, for the move to the Midwest. Now identified in the press as "the man who designed the LaSalle," he spoke in Los Angeles to a gathering of local Cadillac and LaSalle dealers at the office of his old boss, Don Lee. Lee and the other dealers, some of whom knew his father Jacob and had known Harley since he was a boy, greeted him with thunderous applause.

"We designed and planned the LaSalle for the coming generation," he told the dealers, whose job it would be to sell the LaSalles and other cars that Harley designed. "We dreamed of it as a fine, flexible, powerful American car—distinctively American in its lines, appearance and atmosphere. We leaned toward the demands of youth in that we reached out into the field of racing, and adopted some of the streamline effects that have been used in a somewhat different manner in racing cars."

He explained that the LaSalle had been designed with women as well as men in mind. "With woman's ever increasing importance in the automobile marketplace, we designed every possible feature for m'lady," he said. These features included a smaller-than-normal steering wheel and easy-to-operate clutch. Harley closed with some remarks about the new Art and Color Section and his role in it, and the dealers sent him off on vacation with another round of applause.

In early summer Earl and his family left for Detroit, and not long after that Earl and his good buddy Lawrence Fisher took an ocean liner across the Atlantic to the Paris Auto Show to meet and recruit European car designers. The Art and Color Section needed staff after all, and Europe had more designers than America. Generally the Europeans, less under the Henry Ford influence, placed more emphasis on automotive style and encouraged creativity in design. Over the years this would become one of Earl's greatest contributions to American automobiles: the discovery and cultivation of young American design talent, including women. The so-called

"Damsels of Design" hired by Earl in the 1950s became the first female automobile stylists in the male-dominated car industry.

Returning from Europe to Detroit, Earl received his next big assignment from Sloan: overhaul the 1929 Buick, from stem to stern. Redesign it to make it a new, better, and more stylish automobile. This was to be the first automobile fully designed by the Art and Color Section, and Earl and his staff went to it.

FOURTEEN
The Big Three

While Harley Earl and his team at Art and Color began work on what they hoped would be the next big thing in automobiles, the top Buick salesman in the country looked forward to seeing what they could produce. Charles Howard knew Earl and admired his work—who, after all, had not fallen in love with the LaSalle?—and he relished the idea of the hottest car designer in America revitalizing the Buick brand. The head of the "largest automobile distributing organization in the world," Howard could sell Buicks like no man alive, and he had sold lots of them in his lifetime. He oversaw all the Buick dealerships in California and the West, which meant that even if he didn't sell the car personally, a percentage of every Buick sold in these states found its way back to the coffers of the Howard Automobile Company on Van Ness Avenue in San Francisco.

In his early fifties, tall and lean and rangy with a craggy Western look about him, Howard had the vigor and force of a much younger man. Although life had treated him roughly in recent years (he lost a teenage son in a fatal car accident), he still burned with the ambition of the twenty-something New York bicycle mechanic who had arrived in San Francisco in 1903 with only pennies in his pocket. Handy with tools, he got a job as a bike repairman and eventually opened his own shop on Golden Gate Avenue. But with so many new auto agencies popping up in the neighborhood, his fancy soon turned to these strange contraptions that lacked the power to even make it up Nob Hill or Telegraph Hill or over the rolling hills of Nineteenth Avenue out by Golden Gate Park.

Convinced nonetheless that automobiles were destined to be the next big thing, and a very big thing at that, he raided what little savings he had and bought a train ticket to Detroit. There he met with Billy Durant, the president of Buick Motor Company, who was looking for people to run Buick distributorships around the country. Howard knew how to sell and he believed in what he was selling, and this made all the difference. Durant named him the Buick sales manager for the West, and when Howard returned home to San Francisco, three new shiny Buicks rode along with him on the train.

The new Buick general agent of California's most populous city brought three cars back with him because that was all that would fit into his tiny salesroom. These were the days when the Howard Automobile Company and other dealers placed what they called "demonstration coupons" in the local papers to prospect for new customers. Those who were interested filled out the coupon with their name and address and a convenient time and date they'd like to come in and talk, and sent it in to the agent. Some people were so intimidated about walking into a car dealership on their own that they hired mechanics to do it for them. The dealers did not mind this, though; they encouraged it, inviting inspection of their cars before purchase. "If you are not qualified to judge [a car] for yourself," one dealer advertised, "employ a high-class disinterested mechanical engineer to visit our shop and examine every part of our car. Pay him for his time as you would a lawyer or doctor, and if he fails to confirm every claim we make, you will not be asked to purchase." Still, it did not seem to matter how many coupons Howard put in the papers or how many high-class mechanical engineers came down to see him. His Buicks sat...and sat...and sat—some lookers now and then, but no takers.

Then the land shook on that day in 1906 and those Buicks being ignored in his salesroom suddenly found a higher purpose. Like other agents who did the same with their cars, Howard jumped into one of his two-cylinder Buicks and hurried people to safety as the fires swallowed his office. Fortunately, though, the insurance settlement checks he received afterward helped him reopen the Howard Automobile Company in a temporary building. Gradually his company moved into a permanent home on Van Ness Avenue, profiting from the good fortune that can sometimes follow misfortune.

Because of their Johnny-on-the-spot usefulness during the earthquake, automobiles underwent an image reversal in San Francisco, as did the people who sold them. Residents noticed, with approval, how Howard and other agents did not cut and run afterward; they stuck it out, showed true pioneer grit, and contributed to the rebirth of hope. Dealers employed people at a time when jobs were nowhere to be found, and they and their employees spent money in the city, buying groceries, hardware, stationery, furniture, and goods of all kinds from their neighbors who ran shops of their own and who were starting from scratch again too. Used to be automobiles were for rich folks only; not anymore. Most everyone in every line of work could see how, once they got their finances in order, they could use one. And when it came time to buy, many of them looked up that pleasant Howard fella.

In this new era of good feelings, sales of new Buicks started to climb. But it would be a mistake to think this alone did it for him—that Howard rode these good feelings to the kind of wealth that allowed him to eventually buy a 163-foot yacht, live in a Burlingame mansion, own a thoroughbred racing stable and a sprawling horse ranch in Willits in redwood country, belong to the most exclusive clubs, establish a foundation for children with tuberculosis and get it going with an initial gift of $150,000, and then, after his son's death in 1926, build a hospital in Frank's memory, also with his own money. (The Frank R. Howard Memorial Hospital of Willits is serving patients to this day.) These good feelings surely helped. So did Howard's understanding of the American Dream and what it meant for many Americans to own an automobile. He knew this dream because he had lived it. He had started with nothing and had made it, then he'd lost everything and come back and made it again. He knew there were lots of other folks just like him, and that they were not going to drive something inferior. They were going to drive a car that made them feel good about themselves and what they had done in their lives.

Howard also believed strongly, as he said, that "the day of the horse is past and the people in San Francisco want automobiles. I wouldn't give five dollars for the best horse in this country." Maybe he wouldn't give five dollars for a horse, but he *would* accept one as a trade-in on the purchase of a new Buick White Streak. And he and his handpicked sales team gave automobile driving lessons to any customer whose only previous driving experience was in a buggy. Two years after the quake the Howard Automobile Company grossed eighty-five thousand dollars on the sale of eighty-five White Streaks, and for him the future had arrived. Creative, energetic, and almost messianic when talking up the virtues of a new Buick, Howard, said a writer, "had the feel of a giant onrushing machine."

Anything having to do with automobiles in San Francisco, this two-legged machine was there, a major presence, asserting influence. "Donning a gridiron helmet, a white scarf and goggles," Howard drove Buicks with the same passion with which he sold them, competing in local endurance climbs that attacked the steepest, ruggedest, gnarliest hills in the Bay Area. "He could climb anything that grew rocks," joked one reporter. His dashing five-hour run from San Francisco to Oakland (via the ferry) and then by land to San Jose set an early speed record. Howard's brother Frank also raced Buicks, and later Frank—the uncle and namesake of Charles's son who died—became the general manager of the Los Angeles office of the Howard Automobile Company.

The racing Howard brothers battled Leon Shettler, Harry Harrison, Ralph Hamlin—all those crazy car dealers who competed against one another for publicity, records, cash, and sales. When the Howards needed more office space in Los Angeles, they bought Hamlin's garage and salesroom from him. Besides the racing, they knew Ralph from seeing him at auto shows around the state.

What distinguished Buick from other makes was Howard's sales moxie, his zest for publicity, and his creative ideas on how to get it. The art of sales was not in strong-arming people or coercing them, as he knew; it was in getting them to buy what they longed for in their heart even if their head told them something different. To get the buying public excited, to get their hearts pounding, Howard staged a series of colossal, attention-getting stunts that may have never been matched in the entire history of colossal, attention-getting car stunts. In May 1910 he shipped one hundred and thirty Buicks worth close to two hundred thousand dollars by train from Detroit to the Bay Area—the biggest shipment of automobiles by rail to a single destination until two years later, when fifty double-decked carloads of Buicks made the trek. Six models of Buicks, two hundred and thirty cars in all, "fully equipped with tops, glass fronts and Prestolite tanks," to be exact. The charismatic, highly quotable Howard promoted and advertised the crossings heavily, and the newspapers returned the favor with generous coverage. "Trainload Howard," reporters started calling him, especially after he did it again the next year, only bigger: 88 double-decked freight cars packing 415 Buicks to the tune of five hundred thousand dollars. Sightseers all along the Southern Pacific line in the West came out to see this amazing string of cars pass through their town.

When Buick introduced an electric starter, something other car companies were doing as well, Howard promoted it in the press as a breakthrough for women. "There is no question that the necessity of cranking a car has been one of the chief drawbacks to women driving," he said, predicting grandly that "the near future will find as many women as men at the wheel of a new Buick."

Whatever the trend in automobiles—endurance runs, women drivers, recreational travel, the surge in car ownership before and after the Great War—Trainload Howard could be found at the center of it or on its leading edge. Unhappy with the ban on automobiles in Yosemite, he led a squadron of Buicks into the park in defiance of the law. Lucky for Howard, park officials decided not to charge him; if they had, they could have thrown him in jail. In the end, he and his fellow protesters left after getting a ton of free ink for their cause, and ultimately they won their case as the park lifted the ban.

By 1915 the Howard Automobile Company was selling one of every ten new Buicks bought in the United States. Its four-story headquarters on Van Ness had become one of the biggest automobile dealerships in the country, featuring high ceilings, grand, curving staircases, and ballroom-sized display spaces. Howard was doing so well that when Billy Durant, the head of General Motors who had given him his first big break in the car business, ran into money problems, Howard bailed him out with a hefty loan. How hefty is a matter of dispute; estimates range from $190,000 to $3 million. Probably the former is closer to the truth. Anyhow, Howard wisely asked Durant to pay back the loan in the form of GM stock, and when the company's fortunes soared in the 1920s and beyond, Howard's wealth soared with it.

Even so, he kept pushing, kept doing what he loved: putting people inside their motorized dreams. Getting too old to climb rocks himself, he hired others to do it for him. In 1921 a Howard-sponsored Buick coupe went 750 miles from San Francisco to Portland in a little over twenty-nine hours, setting a speed record for cars *and* trains. (Train supporters conceded that yes, the Shasta Limited's fastest time between the two cities was forty-four minutes slower, but only because it stopped to load and unload passengers along the way.) The man at the wheel for this record run was likely C. L. Franklin, better known as "Outdoor" Franklin, who achieved a number of driving firsts for Buick. In July of that same year, starting from the eastern side of the Sierra, he steered a Buick Six through deep snowdrifts and washed-out roads to become the first person to pass over the Tioga Road that summer and reach Yosemite Valley. Earlier in the season, Outdoor was the first to make the valley via the Wawona Road.

A sign on Outdoor's rig read, in large print, "Buick Information Car," and this was one of the jobs Charles Howard paid him to do: gather information on the roads for Buick drivers looking to make summer pleasure trips in the mountains. Another duty of his was to gather publicity. The next December, when the road to the new Lake Arrowhead Reservoir in San Bernardino County opened for the first time in winter, the first car over the Cajon Pass was a Buick Six, and the man at the controls was Outdoor. That year he also repeated his stunts of being first across the Tioga and Wawona Roads into Yosemite after the winter.

In 1924, Charles and Frank Howard opened a glitzy new five-hundred-thousand-dollar Buick showroom on Figueroa Street in Los Angeles, the city's "Gasoline Alley." They were selling so many automobiles in Los Angeles they could no longer fit into their old digs on South Flower Street; thus, the move into this block-long, four-story-high building. And if anyone was confused about the building's name, all he or she had to do was look up at the gargantuan electric rooftop "BUICK" sign cutting a hole into the sky. Located near the headquarters of the Automobile Club of Southern California, which had also outgrown its old offices and built a new site at Figueroa and Adams (where it is today), the Buick Building consisted of 150,000 square feet of showroom space, offices, parts rooms, service garage, blacksmith shop, movie theater, and employee game and exercise lounge. Its week-long grand opening party attracted movie stars and thousands of visitors who enjoyed the Art Hickman Orchestra, dined "a la king" (in the words of a reporter who also partook of the free food), and received guided tours of the building led by Howard employees. The opening generated great press buzz and the public loved the sheer, out-there display of Hollywood-style automobile showmanship. But industry gossips saw more at stake than just a new car dealership opening up in a neighborhood already thick with them. Charles Howard, the heavyweight champion of San Francisco car dealers, was stepping into the ring against Earle C. Anthony, the heavyweight champion of Los Angeles car dealers. Frisco vs. LA, north vs. south, General Motors vs. Packard. Lace up the gloves, and let 'er rip. The fight was on.

One can easily argue that the Big Three California auto dealers of this time—Charles Howard, Don Lee, and Earle C. Anthony—did more than just move cars, they moved history: Howard, as the owner of the great racehorse Seabiscuit, who lifted the country's spirits during the Depression with his remarkable comeback saga; Lee, for his support of Harley Earl, arguably the most influential American car designer ever, and for his pioneering ventures in radio and television; and Anthony, who helped shape not just California car culture but American popular culture. One of Anthony's achievements, perhaps the biggest one, involved radio.

"Radio," observed one historian, "came to the state virtually as an automobile accessory," and the man primarily responsible for this was Anthony, who, besides having a gift for sales, had a lively mind that was interested in how things worked and how they could be made to work better. His love affair with radio began after he read an article in the *Saturday Evening Post* about the experiments in broadcasting taking place in the east. His curiosity sparked, he decided to see if he could build a radio transmitter of his own. Being a mechanical engineering graduate of the University of California at Berkeley, he knew a thing or two about electrical systems, and he gathered the necessary tubes, parts, and wires on the kitchen table of his home, then assembled them into a transmitter probably no more sophisticated than the homemade electric horseless carriage he had devised as a teenager. But like his electric car, the transmitter crackled to life; it worked. Anthony was to Packard in the West what Howard was to Buick, and originally he imagined that a radio network would let him communicate with all his Packard dealers spread around California and the western states. Phones, telegrams, and letters worked well enough in this regard but nothing like a wireless system in which Anthony could relay messages to everyone in the company at the same time. That was his hope.

Encouraged by his modest kitchen table experiments, Anthony built a larger radio transmitter and wired it to an antenna that his employees erected on the roof of his Packard building at Olympic and Hope Streets. On April 6, 1922, KFI Radio went on the air for the first time. Of course, since the signal was weak and only a few radio techies in all of southern California owned the proper receiving equipment, its maiden broadcast made only a limited impact. But, as was his lifelong pattern, Anthony quickly saw in this device the makings of something bigger, much bigger. Radio could do more than just talk to Packard dealers, he realized. It could ultimately broadcast to all of Los Angeles and southern California.

The next month the new radio division of Earle C. Anthony Inc. advertised in the want-ads for a radio salesman: "Man of stability and aggressiveness to sell complete radio equipment in Los Angeles." A radio station is nothing without listeners, but before people can become listeners they need equipment on the receiving end. Radio was becoming a national phenomenon but in southern California it was Anthony and his stable but aggressive sales team that took the lead in demonstrating its virtues. This tribute to the new medium, likely written by Anthony or one of his employees, appeared in a KFI advertisement in July:

> Last night at home
> I heard a guitar
> in El Monte.
> I listened
> to Catalina gossip.
> I heard an orchestra
> in a theatre.
> And I heard the
> audience applaud.
> I heard a fox trot
> from Pasadena, and a
> Los Angeles quartette

sing an old hymn.
It's weird and fascinating,
this new magic of Radio.

That is the way it was written, with the "R" capitalized, because Radio was not a small-letter sort of thing. It was big, it was new, it was magical. People did indeed wish to hear the strumming of that guitar in El Monte and what the gossips were saying in Catalina, and those old, powerful hymns. Equipment sales took off, listenership blossomed, and then the magician of Hope Street pulled another rabbit out of his hat that nobody had ever seen before, not just in Los Angeles and California but in all of America. Neon, it was called.

Anthony did not invent neon signs; that distinction belongs to a French scientist named Georges Claude, who discovered a commercial method of lighting tubes of neon gas to produce radiantly glowing reds and blues and greens. Claude formed a company to make and sell these signs, and in that glorious summer of 1922, when all this radio excitement was kicking up, Anthony traveled to France on a two-month vacation with his wife. In Paris he saw Claude's signs lighting up cafes and shops and thought how wonderful they would look at his dealerships. He placed an order for two custom-made signs, both of which spelled out "PACKARD" in large, vibrantly electric letters. When they were finished and shipped overseas, one sign ended up at Anthony's Van Ness agency in San Francisco and the other at the corner of Hope and Olympic. The next year, when the Hope and Olympic sign with its radiant blue borders was unveiled, Angelenos just flipped. "That very first night, passing cars jammed the boulevard to get a glimpse of the word 'Packard' written out in searing orange tubing," wrote one. "No one—including the advertising men who worked at the downtown agencies—had seen anything like it before. The bold colors sent a shock wave through the industry as the days of the bulb-lit billboard and externally illuminated advertising sign were out of juice."

A flashy display of neon, luxury cars, swinging musical sounds—no one knew at the time, but a piece of modern Las Vegas had just been invented on a street corner in Los Angeles. (The first neon sign in Las Vegas would not appear for another five years.) Neon was like visual radio; people just had to have it once they got onto it. Car dealers and businesses of all kinds quickly followed Packard's lead and lit up the night skies with neon, as did cowboy star Tom Mix outside his Hollywood mansion.

Not long after, Anthony announced plans to make KFI "one of the most powerful broadcast stations in the United States," more than twenty times larger than its current size and comparable to the most powerful stations in New York. A new 5,000-watt antenna would replace the old 500-watt one, although federal law at the time prohibited antennas larger than 1,000 watts; the extra wattage was to be held in reserve for special situations or if the law was ever changed. (Today's radio stations are limited to 50,000 watts.) The roof of Anthony's building eventually carried two flat-topped antennas lit by neon signs that said "KFI PACKARD."

A formal, dignified man whose employees always referred to him as Mr. Anthony, KFI's owner nevertheless was the same public relations whiz who offered out-of-town celebrities free use of a Packard to take them to their hotel after they arrived at La Grande Station. Then he'd tip off a photographer so that a picture of the celebrity in a Packard would appear in the newspaper. "Never at a loss to sell a Packard automobile," Anthony used KFI to push Packards, and vice versa. Early radio stations sent special stamps in the mail to listeners as a way to confirm that they were receiving the signal. The orange KFI stamp contained a drawing of a farm scene, the station's call letters, and Anthony's signature, which functioned much like a company trademark, his personal guarantee of quality. A plaque with his signature and the KFI call letters was mounted on the dashboard of every Packard sold at his dealerships.

"This is KFI," a voice intoned at the top of every hour, "the radio central superstation of Earle C. Anthony, Incorporated, California Packard distributors." The station broadcast only during the evening hours at first, and it would be decades before radios would become a standard automobile accessory. But the ability of this new medium to reach people—and sell stuff—continually amazed. Once KFI held a promotion offering a free crate of oranges to every person who wrote in. Listeners bombarded the station with letters, surprising the staff and forcing their boss to reconsider his offer since it would've cost a small fortune to ship all those oranges around southern California. But Earle C. Anthony did not get to be Earle C. Anthony, Incorporated by making a promise and then reneging on it, so he simply redefined what a "crate" was. Each letter-writer received three oranges in a little box.

In 1927, the year of LaSalle, Anthony did to Charles Howard what Howard had done to him three years earlier: open a big, new, showy palace of automobile excess in his competitor's backyard. Able to afford the best, Anthony hired the best: architect Bernard Maybeck, who designed, among many other notable buildings, the First Church of Christ, Scientist in Berkeley and the Palace of Fine Arts in San Francisco. Telling his construction crew to imagine themselves "working in the gloom of a cathedral of the Middle Ages," Maybeck combined a variety of styles and materials—red North African marble, black Belgian marble, Corinthian columns, Spanish and Gothic doorways, high wooden ceilings, sculpted marble friezes—to create Anthony's Packard showroom, "the queen of the Van Ness Avenue automobile palaces." Normally a hard-minded businessman, Anthony himself fell under the queen's spell, calling it "an Aladdin's palace in which the gorgeous panoply of the Arabian Nights vies with the luxury of the Middle Ages." As if the Middle Ages and Arabian Nights weren't enough, Anthony tossed in a dash of Tinseltown too, installing dazzling multicolored lights in the showroom. The grand opening party created a commotion on Van Ness with appearances by movie stars, politicians, car industry people, Chamber of Commerce types, Anthony's customers both past and potential, and throngs of the curious. Add in all that neon, those long, gorgeous, and beautifully lit new Packards, and a live radio broadcast transmitted via the twin towers mounted on the roof. Anthony loved the new building so much he hired Maybeck to design another Packard showplace in

Oakland, redesign his Olympic and Hope offices, and design a mansion for him in the Los Feliz section of Los Angeles.

The Packard Building in San Francisco sat near the bottom of Van Ness, anchoring automobile row. Virtually from the inception of the car business in the city—John Meyer had paraded his Pioneer on the avenue in the heady days after the Spanish-American War—auto agencies had clustered on and around Van Ness, the city's widest street. Going north on Van Ness toward the bay you'll hit the Marina District, the site of the Panama-Pacific International Exposition. Here, Lombard Street intersects Van Ness, and a few blocks up Lombard is the tourist-friendly "crookedest street in the world," as it bills itself, built in the 1920s in a switchback pattern so that cars could more easily get up and down its steep hill.

The original term for the street or streets occupied by car agencies and garages was "Gasoline Row." Over the years the industry upgraded its image and it became "Automobile Row." (Now the favored term is Auto Mall.) During the boom years of the Roaring Twenties auto rows popped up all around California and America, but few of them anywhere could match Van Ness Avenue for its mishmash of elements, both grand and grandly tacky. A few blocks down from the queenly Packard Building was the majestic San Francisco City Hall. (The War Memorial Opera House was built later.) Nearby was a Keaton tire and rubber shop and a Hudson/Essex dealer. Continuing up Van Ness from the Packard Building were two more agencies—Reo and Kissel—and another major automobile shrine, Don Lee Cadillac. The front of this 1921 ten-story building features two large Greek-style pillars on both sides of a giant arched doorway with "Cadillac" carved in stone above it. Two naked male figures recline above the archway, each holding a wheel, the symbol of transportation. Bears sit atop two other pillars along the facade. More pillars, but without bears or naked men on them, are inside in the grand showroom, along with an elaborate curving wooden staircase with blue tile steps leading up to offices. Anthony and Maybeck no doubt studied Lee's building and resolved to outdo it with a grander statement of their own.*

But Lee also closely watched what Anthony did and, "not to be outdone by his rival," he too entered the world of broadcasting by buying KFRC Radio in San Francisco. In 1927 he cut the ribbon on new studios in the mezzanine of his Cadillac building and erected a 1,000-watt Western Electric transmitter with an antenna on the roof. Then he did much the same in Los Angeles, buying KHJ Radio and converting his Seventh and Bixel building into a combined radio station and Cadillac dealership. Suddenly the two old-time car rivals were the owners of the biggest radio stations in California. A few years later Anthony began another radio station, KECA, and Lee founded the first television station west of the Mississippi, W6XAO of Los Angeles, now known as KCBS.

When Anthony introduced neon to Van Ness Avenue, Lee quickly did the same at his building, and it's a near certainty that on the next block up, the F. J. Linz Motor

---

* Van Ness remains the city's automobile row today, but the dealerships mentioned here are mostly long gone, as are their buildings. The Packard and Lee buildings still exist and have been recognized as San Francisco historical landmarks. The Anthony building is a car dealership; Lee's is a movie theater.

Company and California Stutz lit their showrooms with neon too. The Sutter block of Van Ness must have been a forest of neon as well: Studebaker, Stephens, Winton, Dodge, and Federal Cord Tires all had shops there in the 1920s.

At Van Ness and California there were more salesrooms—Nash, Jordan, Mercer, Studebaker—and more neon forests. But the dominant building at this intersection belonged to the Howard Automobile Company (it's now a Ford dealership). This was where Charles Howard ran his Buick empire and where the new 1929 Buick would go on sale, as soon as General Motors released it to the public. Much was riding on this car. Packard was whipping Cadillac in sales, and GM boss Sloan, alarmed by this trend, had taken steps to stop Cadillac's slide. Among them was assigning Harley Earl to add some style touches to the Cadillac, which he did, but also to take on the much bigger project of redesigning the Buick. A hipper and trendier Buick would surely lure buyers away from the more expensive Packard.

Released in July 1928, Earl's design met with an instantaneous public reaction similar to the LaSalle's, only in this case the reaction was all bad. People thought it looked puffy and bloated rather than long and low. Years later Earl explained what happened: "I designed the 1929 Buick with a slight roundness both ways from the beltline highlight, and it went into production. Unfortunately the factory, for operational reasons, pulled the side panels in at the bottom more than the design called for. In addition, five inches were added in vertical height, with the result that the arc I had plotted was pulled out of shape in two directions. The highlight was unpleasantly located, and the effect was bulgy."

In plain words, it stunk. According to Earl, operations did not keep him abreast of what it was doing because Art and Color was new and did not yet have any clout in the company. The Buick may have also been a victim of a classic organizational struggle between more established interests and "an advocate for change," in Alfred Sloan's words. Production and operations engineers had always had the first and last say at GM in the past, and they may have resented this "automobile stylist," whatever the heck that was—and one from Hollywood to boot—moving in on their territory. The sales staff also worried that too much power was being handed over to one man and one department, and that GM's cars might all look alike in the future. Whatever the reason for the lack of communication, Earl said he was "unaware of what had happened until I later saw the completed cars. Of course, I roared like a Ventura sea lion, but it was too late to keep car buyers from having a lot of fun naming the poor *enceinte* Buick."

Enceinte, in English, means pregnant, and that was what people called it: "the pregnant Buick." If General Motors was going to clip the wings of Packard, it would have to find another way to do it because even Charles Howard, who could sell a boat to a man stranded in the desert, could not get people to buy the Buick. The car flopped.

FIFTEEN
The Curious Case of Doble Steam Motors

The failure of the pregnant Buick inadvertently worked in Harley Earl's favor because it showed that style had in fact become a chief consideration for the American car buyer. The Buick ran well but looked out of whack somehow, and this ruined it for the public. Style mattered. It mattered as much in buying a car as it did for a watch or suit or fedora. Rather than weaken his influence at General Motors, as one might expect, the incident strengthened Earl's position at the company and bolstered Alfred Sloan's desire for him to succeed. With GM now making annual style changes in its cars, the Art and Color department took on a more direct name—Styling—and its new director moved ahead with his plan to design production cars that provided mini-vacations for drivers. "You can design a car so that every time you get in it, it's a relief," Earl said. "You have a little vacation for a while."

The changing habits of car buyers also forced changes at Ford Motor. Citing declining sales, it stopped production in 1927 of the Model T and temporarily closed the Highland Park factory that had built so many of them. Some 15 million Tin Lizzys—built to take a pounding and keep on going, and affordable on any budget—had rattled off the line since their beginning and, in a testament to their enduring quality, most of them were still rattling around the roads. But America had changed, and so had its taste in cars. Later that same year Ford released a more stylish successor, the Model A, which became a popular hit too. One of its first customers was Douglas Fairbanks, who gave one to Mary Pickford as a Christmas present. Ford manufactured the Model A at its Rogue River, Michigan factory and in factories around the country including its Richmond and Long Beach assembly plants, which opened in the late twenties.

These years were also when the Big Three started to become the Big Three, churning out more automobiles than most countries and dwarfing Packard and the rest of the competition in sales. Despite the misstep of the pregnant Buick, in the early 1930s General Motors became the world's largest automaker, a title it retained for the rest of the century. There is no question that Harley Earl's presence at the company, and the decision to elevate style in the design and building of its cars so that engineering flowed from it rather than the other way around, contributed greatly to GM's rise. In going from the T to the A, Ford admitted that style had indeed become king. Under the design leadership of the brilliant Edsel Ford, Henry's son, it hired automobile stylists groomed by Earl at GM. So did Chrysler, which nevertheless had some strong competitive attributes of its own: outstanding leadership by Walter Chrysler and one of the industry's top engineering teams, the Three Musketeers of Owen Skelton, Fred Zeder, and Carl Breer. Like his fellow expatriate Californian Earl at GM, Breer rose to great influence and prestige within his company yet not without a stumble now and then. He designed the 1934 Chrysler Airflow, perhaps the most advanced streamlined mass-production vehicle of its time. But car buyers hated the way it looked, and it flopped as badly as the pregnant Buick.

By the end of the 1920s GM, Ford, and Chrysler built three of every four new cars sold in America, a figure that would grow even higher in the decades to come. Some 20 million Americans owned cars, including 2 million of them in California. The desire to drive and own an automobile cut across all classes, all races and ethnic groups, all geographic boundaries, all ages from teens on up. Automobile use had become an ordinary fact of life for Americans even as auto manufacturing power had become concentrated in fewer and fewer hands. Gone were the days when hundreds of small-time backyard operators were hammering out prototypes with dreams of putting them into production and forming real automobile companies. The efficiencies of the moving assembly line, the massive quantities it produced, and the vast sums of money required to design, build, test, sell, market, and distribute automobiles killed off these dreams. Fewer than fifty companies in all of America built production cars, and most of these, like the Big Three, clustered in or around Detroit.

But there were holdouts here and there, and one of the most fascinating of these alternative car companies—a term that would have never been used then—was the Doble Steam Motors Corporation of San Francisco, California. Its founder and president, Abner Doble, was alternative by choice, not necessity, for he had as sharp an engineering mind as could be found in Detroit or Europe. "Intellectually he was the equal of many a scientist," writes one automobile historian. "In practical engineering he was at least the peer of the best gasoline designer of his day." But Doble chose to apply his intelligence not to gas or electric machines but to steam. That, he believed fervently, was the best operating system for an automobile.

Born in 1890 in San Francisco, Doble had two things going for him right off the bat: brains and parents with money. His grandfather came to California during the gold rush but, no fool, he didn't try to get rich by mining for gold. He owned a forge that made tools, and he sold these tools to gold-happy miners. Abner's father co-invented a waterwheel that was also used in mining and for other purposes. His business later merged with the Pelton Water Wheel Company, and in pre-earthquake San Francisco the Dobles were one of the families who could be seen taking a Sunday spin around Golden Gate Park in their privately owned Locomobile.

But being who they were, the Dobles also liked to pop open the engine box and see what was going on inside. Abner's parents made him take piano lessons, but what he really loved to do was hang out in the afternoons at his father's factory and bang around with the tools and machines. He built a steam car from scratch as a sixteen-year-old student at Lick High (now Lick-Wilmerding) with his kid brother John helping him out. They worked in the basement of their parents' house, lifting a boiler from an old White steamer and salvaging parts from other junkers. Whatever parts they couldn't find themselves they machined in their father's shop. Abner designed the engine.

Carl Breer did some consulting for White Cars after he built his homemade steamer in Los Angeles, but he eventually left steam for gasoline cars. Not so Abner, who never strayed from his first love. Beginning with that basement special, which barely made it out of the basement because it ran so poorly, Abner—and John too; indeed all four of the Doble brothers—became certain that conventional wisdom was wrong, that the internal combustion gas engine had had its day, that steam provided a superior form of engine thrust, and that steam could do for automobiles what it was doing for the locomotives that rolled across the nation every day and every night trailing great plumes of smoke behind them.

In 1910, a twenty-year-old on a mission, Abner enrolled in the Massachusetts Institute of Technology. But "impatient of academic education, always itching for practical work," he dropped out of MIT to start a machine shop in Waltham, near Cambridge. Doble described himself as "high-strung and sensitive," "impulsive," and impatient "with what I believe to be hypocrisy or shallow reasoning." With a high forehead and short wavy hair, hands jammed sullenly into his pockets, and his narrow, handsome face wearing a brooding expression, Abner resembled a college intellectual impatient with the hypocrisies of society. He had the air of a deep thinker, which he was, but his thoughts, unlike those of most every other serious automobile person in the country, centered on the pluses and minuses of steam engines, and how to turn those minuses into pluses. One drawback of steamers was the need to light a pilot light in order to heat the burner and boiler, which propelled the car forward. When the engine was cold, lighting the pilot sometimes required an acetylene torch. Another drawback was the clouds of steam—similar, though on a much smaller scale, to what blows out of a steam locomotive—released by the car into the air. Being around all that smoke and fire scared people and made them think the vehicle was going to explode.

Abner had lots of ideas on how to fix these problems, and one day he journeyed to nearby Newton to see the Stanley twins, Francis and Freelan, makers of the most famous steam car in the world, the Stanley Steamer. The Stanley Motor Carriage Company was not only the most successful steam car company in America, it was one of the few still hanging on to life. White had stopped making steamers and switched over to gas, as had Locomobile, the car that took the first auto adventurers to Yosemite Park. In the early 1900s a Stanley Steamer broke the world's speed record with a run of 127 miles per hour, faster than any gas car up to that time. The brothers Stanley knew steam and had fought for it against indifference and opposition, and

Abner eagerly looked forward to discussing his latest ideas with them—how to get steamers up and running faster, how a new type of condenser could get rid of those fear-inducing clouds, and so much more.

Their meeting went badly for both parties. "It was," said a writer, "an encounter between nineteenth-century conservatism and complacency and twentieth-century technology, vision and youthful ambition." The Stanleys, who were in their sixties, listened as this sensitive, high-strung college dropout told them all the things they were doing wrong and how to do all the things they had not yet figured out in more than a decade of building and racing steam automobiles. Predictably, the nineteenth century told the twentieth century to take a hike.

Returning to his workshop determined to prove the merit of his ideas, Abner made a good first step in this direction: calling John to join him from the West Coast. His brother came to Waltham and together they built their second steamer, the Model A. The Model A—no relation to Ford's; Doble designated his models with letters from the alphabet—was a big step up in quality from their basement special because, for one, they could actually drive it places. And one of the first places they drove it—no surprise here—was back over to Newton to see the Stanleys. Abner, at the wheel, did not bother to come inside this time, instead driving back and forth in front of the factory until the twins quit ignoring him and came outside to take a look. What they saw—or didn't see—astounded them. No steam clouds curled from the engine. A steamless steam car? What the heck was up with that? Suddenly full of more questions than answers, the Stanleys yelled "Stop! Stop!" until Abner, who must have cherished this moment, pulled over to give them a little look-see. Score one for the brooding young intellectual. Three years later, in 1915, the Stanleys brought out a steamer that had a condenser similar to the Dobles'.

By that time, though, the Stanleys were old news; the hottest name in steam was now Doble. Abner and John's latest creation, the Model B, pushed the technology farther than it had ever been pushed before. The brothers "rethought, and in most cases, reconfigured" every aspect of a steam automobile, questioning everything they had done before and coming up with new and better answers. Another traditional steam car drawback was its thirst for water; the tank quickly ran dry, forcing people to make frequent stops on the road to fill it up, and if no water could be found, they were stuck. But with the steam that was formerly released into the air now being converted into water through a more efficient Doble-invented condenser, the Model B could travel fifteen hundred miles on one twenty-four-gallon tank.

But the car was only a prototype, and to produce it on a mass scale Abner needed capital and lots of it. With this in mind he moved to Detroit, driving there in the B. Nothing much happened for him for two years, but he kept knocking on doors and finally rounded up some investors to form the General Engineering Company. Despite its name the know-how for General Engineering was really quite specific: it was Abner and John, working together, tackling perhaps the biggest problem of all associated with steam—its slow start-up time. It took up to twenty minutes to start a steamer on a cold morning, far slower than a gasoline model. Nonetheless, some steam die-hards felt an intense rivalry with their gas machine peers, refusing to use any of their techniques even if what the gassers were doing was better. The Dobles had no such qualms; if a thing worked they'd apply it to what they were doing, usually improving it in the process. That was what John did to lick the starting problem, converting an electrical ignition system then being used on internal combustion engines and applying it to steam. Their flash boiler stoked up in less than ninety seconds, comparable with the starting speed of gas cars. With this and other improvements the next-generation Model C—also known as the Doble-Detroit or the GEC Doble—was ready for the big time.

"Big time" in early 1917 was the National Automobile Show in New York, the biggest auto show in the country, displaying scores of gas models, a handful of electrics, and one steamer. But that lonely Model C stole the spotlight from the other cars, drawing crowds of excited onlookers and raves in the papers. All this interest snowballed into a flurry of national attention and "within two and a half days the mail from all parts of the country was of such great volume that the post office refused to deliver it," said one account. "More than fifty thousand letters were received in a few days. Seven hundred telegrams arrived from dealers and from people interested in the car or the company." Happily for General Engineering, this interest translated into money in the bank. It received more than five thousand orders, many with checks attached. One San Francisco dealer placed an order for one thousand cars. Riding this wave of enthusiasm, the company signed a lease for a 52,000-square-foot plant in Detroit and ramped up to start building cars.

It never happened. The quiet, dependable, quick-starting, smooth-gliding, fast-accelerating, non–steam emitting Model C never went into production, and General Engineering collapsed. Accounts differ as to why. Abner Doble blamed wartime steel shortages. Only a few months after the New York show the United States entered World War I, and the National War Emergency Board restricted the use of steel by companies judged as not vital to the war effort. General Engineering fell into this category, and without steel to build its cars it was lost. Another explanation cites not the war abroad but one at home. In the years before New York, John Doble had filed patents on some of his steam car innovations, and when these innovations appeared on the Model C without his permission and without compensation, he sued Abner for patent infringement. Their father sided with John in the fight, and the Model C became tangled in a family feud and a mess of legal claims and counterclaims.

With his latest big idea coming to naught, Abner returned home to San Francisco to begin work on a Model D prototype, a project that also went nowhere. For the first time since he was a boy he was building a new car without his brother. Then, after years of family tension, in February 1921, at age twenty-eight, John died of lymphatic cancer. His death ripped up Abner and the family more profoundly than a haggle over money and patent claims, and they healed their rift. Not long after the funeral the two other Doble brothers, Warren and William Jr., who also possessed blade-sharp engineering minds, joined Abner to form Doble Steam Motors in a two-story building on Harrison Street in San Francisco.

Doble Steam Motors may not have been the last steam automobile company in America, but it was the best and most ambitious. Against all evidence to the contrary, it still believed in the future of steam. The Stanleys were done; they had sold their company and were out of the business. Their former firm still made steamers, but its sales were nosediving and by the middle of the decade they'd be finished. But if Abner and his brothers were going to succeed where so many others, including Abner himself, had failed, they knew they couldn't just make a good steam machine; they had to make one that was better than any other gas machine on the market. Otherwise how could they attract investors and, ultimately, customers? They had to remove all doubts from people's minds, and the only way they could do that was to create the perfect steam car.

This, then, became Abner's quest, a quest he'd been on in one form or another since his car-building days in his parents' basement. Convince the naysayers, do what no one else believed possible. Take on the big boys in Detroit and achieve perfection.

In so many ways he was the perfect man for the job. Though still shy and intellectual, he no longer resembled a brooding college student. At the wheel of one of his cars, dressed in a suit and tie and with his wavy hair combed into place, he had a refined look about him. He looked like money and he looked like he belonged with people who had money. He got along well with his employees at his plant too, at least until he saw one of them doing work that was not up to his standards. Then his impatience got the better of his self-control. "We don't have that kind of work in this establishment," he'd say sharply, telling the person to stay on the job until the job was done right. But if the opposite occurred, if he saw examples of fine craftsmanship, he was quick to praise.

After two years of praise and cajoling, first in San Francisco and then in a larger plant across the bay in Emeryville, where the company moved after it outgrew Harrison Street, Abner released the prototype for the Doble Series E, "the ultimate steam car," as it was advertised. Everything about it was top-shelf; Abner, who supervised every detail of its design and manufacture, would have it no other way. The prestigious Walter M. Murphy Coach Works of Pasadena crafted its body styles. Its Bosch electrical system, Ferodo brake linings, and Rudge-Whitworth wire wheels all came from Europe. In statements grand and small the Model E with its ebony steering wheel ranked with the best of the best: Packard, Pierce-Arrow, Cadillac, Rolls Royce, the very best luxury cars on the planet. Even what might be considered a flaw, its weight of more than fifty-five hundred pounds, turned into a source of admiration once people drove the car. "There was a mysterious majesty about them," said one driver, "which derived from their combination of massiveness and the ability to go like the wind without scarcely a trace of sound." Driving a Doble Series E was like riding a magic carpet, they said.

To raise money for mass production, his perpetual bugaboo, Abner took an early prototype of the E on the road to show it off to the public and potential investors. One such demonstration took place in late 1922 in Los Angeles, where, as the newspaper reported, "promptly at 2:25 Saturday afternoon, Abner Doble turned the switch on his master motor car creation, advanced the throttle, and in less than twenty seconds rolled silently and smoothly out from the Doble Showroom at 952 South Broadway." From there he headed south, gunning up and over hills that struck fear in the hearts of many a gas driver. "Grand Avenue hill with its 27 percent grade has provided the Waterloo of many a proud demonstrator," observed another paper, "but it was a victorious field for the Doble. At the steepest point of the incline the car was stopped and then given the gun. It continued its way without a quiver and the speedometer registering 25 mph at the summit." The sponsor of the event was the financial agent handling the stock sales for the company. "Doble spells opportunity," said one of its advertisements. "Come to the Doble Showroom at the earliest possible moment—and come prepared to buy Doble stock at $12.50 a share."

After southern California the Model E traveled to an auto show in Modesto and then on to San Francisco early the next year, when it caused a huge stir. Then back it came to Los Angeles for another demonstration outside Tally's Broadway Theatre. Those who came to see the car—with Doble, who loved to drive, doing the demonstrating—could also stay for an international newsreel and a showing of the movie *The Dangerous Age.*

The most spectacular demonstration of the E's prowess came in New York, the financial capital of America, where car manufacturing dreams lived or died. After being parked overnight in a garage, the Model E was rolled out onto the street where it sat for more than an hour and a half on a cold winter's morning. When the time came to flip the ignition switch, "the boiler roared to life," said one. Then the countdown began: twenty-three seconds for the boiler to reach operating heat—forty-one seconds for the car to take off—and twelve and a half seconds for it to go from 0 to 40 with four people aboard. Its performance astonished the testing engineers but hardly ruffled Abner Doble, who'd seen it do better. In tests it had gone 0 to 75 in ten seconds, and it easily crested 90 miles per hour.

Although major financing continued to elude it, Doble Steam Motors got priceless publicity in New York and made sales to customers who could afford the E's hefty nine-thousand-dollar price tag. The husband of silent screen star Norma Talmadge bought one for her. The Maharajah of Bharatpur ordered one with taps for water and beer to be used on his tiger hunts in India. Howard Hughes, then a young, ambitious Texas oil heir, bought a Doble shortly before coming to Hollywood to get into producing motion pictures. Hughes left his Mercedes, Cadillac, Packard, and Rolls stabled in Texas; his prized Doble he brought with him to California.

The E had an exalted reputation among those who owned it; trouble was, there weren't enough of those. The Emeryville factory produced only two dozen or so cars. One reason for this was lack of money. Despite his best efforts Abner could not raise enough manufacturing capital—partly because his troubled track record made investors fidget, partly because it was a steam car, and partly because of geography. "The Model E was essentially a West Coast undertaking," said historian Stephen Fox, "far removed in every sense from the centers of automotive financing in New York and of automotive design and manufacturing in Detroit." Being a made-in-California car, mostly California money supported it, and when the whole thing went bad, mostly Californians got stung.

Abner and his company had come under investigation by the State of California during his road show. Doble Steam Motors had received permission to sell $1 million in stock, which it did. But it evidently did not stop there, selling more of those $12.50 shares to raise another $770,000. All this it did without permission. When the company applied for a permit to sell more shares, the state refused to let it do so because it had not built enough cars to justify further sales to the public. Nevertheless the financial agents for Doble kept taking people's money, and in 1924 a San Francisco court issued indictments against Abner, his brother William, and three other company employees.

The two Dobles and their employees remained free on bail while a Superior Court judge set the date for their trial. The employees, who had handled the company's stock sales and finances, pled guilty and provided evidence against Abner in the 1926 trial. A jury found him guilty on all five counts of violating the state Corporate Securities Act. "It was revealed that the firm had constructed only one automobile and had been active principally in the promotion of stock sales," said a report on the case. An angry state commissioner labeled Abner and his associates "unscrupulous," accusing them of bilking investors for nearly $2 million. William Doble was found not guilty, but his brother received a one- to five-year sentence in San Quentin. Remaining free on bail, however, Abner appealed the decision to the California Supreme Court, which ruled in his favor. The justices decided that the company books had been improperly admitted as evidence during the trial, and there was no proof that Abner actually knew what was going on with the stock sales. The district attorney who prosecuted the case reacted with disgust, saying the ruling undermined the jury's will and that as a result another trial was pointless. Charges against Abner were dropped, and he walked out of a San Francisco courtroom a free man and into a long-running historical dispute.

What, if anything, did he know about the illegal shenanigans of his company? The answer, say some, lies in his character. Doble was a man for whom perfect was never perfect enough. Nothing on the Series E was ever done, not completely anyhow. Doble believed it could always be made better, even if, by most people's standards, it was already perfect. He revamped his designs so much that no two Model Es were ever alike. So absorbed was he in this pursuit of a thing that cannot be achieved that he had no time for company finances and even less interest in them. He knew nothing about the specifics of the stock sales, just that he was raising badly needed money for the company. He trusted his financial agents to handle that side of the business for him, and those agents—the same ones who turned evidence against him—betrayed him. That is one view. Another, less charitable opinion says that Abner showed a "lifelong tendency to shade the truth," and that this finally did him in.

The controversy killed any lingering dreams he may have had about mass producing the Model E. Stubbornly he began work on a successor car, the Model F, but hard work and a determined will were no longer enough. After the Wall Street crash, what little investment capital there was dried up and blew away. In 1931 Doble Steam Motors dissolved and the factory in Emeryville shut its doors.

Today, automobile collectors and historians regard the Doble Series E as "a state of the art engineering masterpiece" and "the last and finest flowering of an obsolete technology." The latter remark would have no doubt rankled Doble, who insisted till his last breath in the superiority of steam automobiles over internal combustion. "The present pre-eminence in internal combustion in road transport is due to an aggressive policy [by the auto industry], and is not the result of any fundamental superiority in an engineering sense," he said once. He believed that Detroit automakers, specifically General Motors, had conspired against him, using their leverage with parts and material suppliers to drive up his prices and make it impossible to produce the Model E efficiently. In his later years Doble became a steam consultant, advising companies around the world on steam engines for ships, rail, and other uses. So expert was he that England, the land where steam technology was invented, brought him over to do some consulting. In the 1950s he advised a southern California firm that was building a steam car prototype called the "Paxton Phoenix." But nothing much came of this effort, and a man who went his own way and paid a price for it passed on, in relative anonymity, in Santa Rosa in 1961.

Doble's story contrasts sharply with that of another automotive genius who fell on hard times after the stock market collapse, Harry A. Miller. Before the collapse, Miller engines dominated racing on land and water, and his earnings reached close to $1 million. But, like Doble, "he was not remotely a businessman." Sometimes he sunk the payroll money into his latest great idea, a trait that did not endear him to his employees. But they stuck with him because they believed in him and the bigness of his vision. They got paid eventually, just not always on time. Harry's free-spending ways also troubled his wife, Edna, who wished they would put more away for the future. Yet she knew her husband too well to expect that. Back when they first came to Los Angeles, back when Harry was building his first-ever automobile engine in his adamant refusal to go into a career his father approved of, she asked him what they were going to do if they ran out of money. "Oh, I'll make more," he told her, and he always had.

In October 1929, mere weeks before the market meltdown, Harry's company merged with a Los Angeles engineering firm, Schofield, Inc. According to a report published at the time of the merger, Miller-Schofield planned to become "one of the world's major manufacturing organizations of its kind," mass-producing auto, marine, and aircraft engines, carburetors, superchargers, and other Miller-engineered products. Under the agreement Harry was to receive one hundred thousand dollars and a cushy seat on the board of directors. While the old Long Beach Avenue plant would remain in operation, Miller-Schofield looked to break ground on a new building on a nine-acre site elsewhere in town.

Everything rapidly fell apart, and Miller-Schofield died shortly after birth. No building was built, no world manufacturing titan formed. If Harry received any of the money promised him, it wasn't much and it didn't last long. By 1930 Edna's fears had finally come to pass. One year after making the deal that Harry thought would set them up for life, they were broke.

But Miller still had his talent and guts and brains, and fortunately he still had Fred Offenhauser and Leo Goossen too. The two had gone to work for Miller-Schofield but their jobs vanished with the company, and they rejoined the Old Man at a small machine shop he had started to keep money coming in. After all the years that had gone by, after all that had happened, the old gang of three—the bold visionary, the practical machinist, the elegant designer—were back together again, resuming their pioneering experiments with front-wheel drive and building the go-fast machines that had competed and won so many times at Indianapolis.

It was like old times, only it wasn't. The country had sunk into the Depression, a term that had dual meaning for Miller. He started drinking heavily, never a good play for a diabetic, and he ignored the advice of Edna and everybody else on how he might set his company aright. But that was the Old Man for you. He had been doing things his way for so long he wasn't about to change, even if his way of doing things no longer worked. The shop was bleeding money but, unlike in the old days, he couldn't figure out how to make it stop. Bankruptcy came in July 1933, and the creditors divvied up and sold what was left of his business, his house, and his ranch in Malibu. Miller was so discouraged that he even gave away his beloved parrot, a pet bird that flew free around the drafting room on Long Beach Avenue.

Miller hated the Detroit scene and the kinds of machines they built there—"Detroit iron," he called them with disdain. But for a motor man down on his luck, where else to turn but Motor City? He left the state where he'd had his greatest triumphs and sorrows and went to Detroit to pursue new automobile and airplane engine projects, and it's said that in his last years he worked on an early prototype of the jeep. He died in 1943 in Grace Hospital in Detroit, rightly praised in his obituary as a "mechanical genius [who] left an indelible mark on the modern automobile." Every year the Milwaukee Mile in his native Wisconsin holds a racing meet in his honor.

But even though their mentor had left, Goossen, Offenhauser, and the parrot—Harry had given it to Goossen—hung on. Goossen had gone to Detroit to work with Miller, but after only a few months he returned to Los Angeles and reunited with Offenhauser, who had started a new company to build racing engines. With so many people out of work and barely scraping by, it was a risky time to start a business, let alone a racing business, but Offenhauser had a few advantages to get him started on the right foot. One was his own integrity and character. When as a Pacific Electric Railway employee he first applied to work at Miller's company in the years before World War I, he interviewed Miller for the job as much as Miller interviewed him. "I went down and talked with Miller and told him that I wasn't interested in making a change if I had to be somebody's relative to get ahead," he recalled. "I wanted to get ahead on my own ability. He seemed to like that and he hired me." But Offenhauser would only take the job if granted the independence and power to run the factory the way he thought it should be run. Miller agreed, and the plant became a squeaky-clean model of workmanship and efficiency.

Another advantage Offenhauser had was that he had bought some of Miller's patents, drawings, machine patterns, even some of his old tools. Another was that he rehired some of Miller's ex-employees to work for him. Best of all, there was Goossen, "the original Miller engineer," as a fellow engineer put it, who embodied "an amazing measure of the substance of American racing history." The big-vision guy was gone, but the other members of the team—Offenhauser, Goossen, the guys in the greasy overalls, and that parrot—had reformed and were ready to get the thing moving forward again.

It wasn't the end, then; in some ways, it was the start. What Harry A. Miller had created wasn't dying, it was only taking new forms. And so the elegant Leo Goossen sat down on his stool in the drafting room of the new Offenhauser Engineering Company. His drafting board was the same one he had used to draw the Miller 183 and all the dream machines that had come after it. His paper, ruler, T square, compass, and triangles lay spread across the board in front of him. He picked up a pencil and began to draw one of his most daring and imaginative creations yet.

SIXTEEN

Blood on the Tracks

Some of the first designs to come off the Goossen drawing board and be machined to life by Offenhauser and crew centered on a new class of racecars known today as "midgets" but known more colorfully during the Depression as "pee-wees." Actually, sportswriters had a field day describing these cars, calling them "pint-sized petrol burners," "go-buggies," "hot roller skates," and "bantam buzz wagons." The full-sized boys and men who drove these tiny cars had equally colorful handles: Happy Woodman, Speedy Lockwood, and Curly Mills, to name a few. Nearly all of them lived in southern California, where the sport originated.

The first midget races in the world occurred in the summer of 1933 at the Loyola Speedway, a scrawny little dirt oval at a Jesuit high school in Los Angeles. Nineteen-year-old Billy Betteridge, another of the sport's originals, competed there. His roller skate of a ride stood half as high as a normal racecar and had twice the fun. Everything about it was runty: its weight (less than one thousand pounds), length (seven feet), wheelbase (sixty-five inches), tires (forty inches). Betteridge made the body out of aluminum and lifted the engine from an outboard motorboat. He spent a few hundred bucks and was good to go.

Maybe it's recorded somewhere who won those first midget races at Loyola, but no matter who did, he didn't see a nickel from it. Money wasn't the point; getting kicks, that was the point. Ken Brenneman, an anomaly among the early midgeteers because he hailed from Alameda in the faraway Bay Area, fitted out his machine with a Henderson motorcycle motor and airplane wheels. Others used little Overland or Austin car engines. People could use rubber bands and clothespins if they wanted—it didn't matter as long as the engine displacement size did not exceed one hundred cubic inches. Even with this limitation, or because of it, the tinies put on one heckuva show, eight of them digging around the dirt at the same time, spinning and swirling around the curves and revving up to a 50-mile-an-hour whine on the short straights.

Only a handful of family and friends graced the weathered wooden stands at Loyola. Word got around, though, and it wasn't long before the gatherings grew from small and curious to big and enthusiastic, and the mainstream media had to scramble to catch up with what was going on.

"Midget racing," wrote Bill Henry the next summer. "I never heard of it until about a year ago, and neither did you. So I investigated this business of racing vest-pocket automobiles on hat-sized tracks." What the automotive writer of the *Times* found was that "the whole bughouse idea started with a few fellows who thought it would be fun to build miniature racing cars to drive around town." But in a year the core group of Happy, Speedy, Curly, Billy, and the rest had grown to about one hundred strong with a racing circuit blossoming at Loyola High, Gilmore Stadium in Los Angeles, the Los Angeles County fairgrounds in Pomona, Moto Speedway in Long Beach, and hat-sized tracks in the Bay Area and Central Valley. Already the sport showed signs of spilling outside California's borders with promoters in Chicago and other eastern cities expressing interest.

One of the joys of midgets was that almost any promoter could put on a race, almost anywhere. You didn't need a big layout like with the Class A Indianapolis-style cars; a quarter- or one-fifth-mile high school or county fairgrounds track would do just fine. And because expenses were low, the track didn't have to charge an arm and a leg for tickets, which was an advantage at a time when many people would have rather stashed their money under their mattresses than in a bank. The first car race lots of kids and grownups ever saw was a midget race, and they laughed like crazy at the whiz-bang spectacle of it all.

A three-lap race on a fifth-of-a-mile track could be over in a minute. Stand up to go to the bathroom and you'd miss it. Bill Henry's report described what type of fuel the buzz wagons ran on: a mixture of gasoline and alcohol. But, as Henry noted, "you can't drink the stuff, so it isn't any extra fun."

Curly Mills, known as the "mad man of the short tracks" and whose real name was Jack Ozark Mills, was the top money-winner on the circuit. This meant that in a good week he netted a few hundred dollars in prize money, split between him and his mechanic. The two trailered their midget and drove all around the state to the various races. Since Curly drove at the track during the day, it was only right that the mechanic did the driving at night while Curly slept. The biggest one-night payday Curly ever received was $118 at Gilmore. Some of the tracks awarded lap money—one dollar for every lap led in a race. So even if Curly didn't win he could walk away with a little something if they held the lead for a lap or two, and this gave him and his mechanic enough for a beer and some eats before they moved on down the road to their next stop.

After it opened in early 1934 Gilmore Stadium became the hottest midget track in America. Even at that time, the former oil field was an island of open space surrounded on all sides by the fast-growing metropolis of Los Angeles. Built in the shape of a horseshoe on a corner piece of the property, Gilmore Stadium hosted football games, rodeos, community rallies, the circus, and motorcycle and bicycle racing. But the top ticket during the season was the weekly pee-wees held under the lights. The evening air was warm and lovely, the doings on the track were unfailingly a blast, and up to fourteen thousand people, many of them families, clicked through the turnstiles for the biggest events. From their seats they could see the bug-eyed faces of the drivers as they roared around the track, and they cheered and booed with lusty vigor. After Curly Mills bested Happy Woodman in a three-lap duel but then peevishly refused to shake hands with his rival afterward, boos rained down on Curly's curly mane. After a similar display of non-sportsmanship Pee Wee Distarce responded to the boos by speeding along the rail and spinning his tires so that plumes of dirt sprayed onto the fans in the stands.

Midget races became so popular that promoters began offering more prize money for them than to the American Automobile Association-sanctioned big-car events. Another sign of the sport's rising appeal was the bombshell announcement in September 1934 that Fred Offenhauser and Leo Goossen, "formerly engineers for the famed Harry A. Miller," as a newspaper described them, had built a Miller-style 98-cubic-inch engine specifically for the midgets. Nothing about Offenhauser and Goossen was small-time, as everyone in racing knew, and the Gilmore Stadium debut of their little-big machines represented "the most important development in the small car racing game since its inception a year and a half ago."

The Offenhauser-Goossen midgets—dubbed "the Mighty Midgets" by the wordsmiths in the press—combined speed, lightness, and acceleration in an engine that was larger than what had run at the Indianapolis 500 just a few years earlier. Two Mighty Midgets wowed the fans and Gilmore officials placed a rush order to buy twelve more to race at the stadium as soon as they could be built. Suddenly the future at Offenhauser Engineering Company looked brighter, just as the days of innocence in midget racing came to an abrupt end.

In less than a week the two Mighties, driven by Curly Mills and another man, had erased all the track records previously held by the outboard motor guys. Having seen the future, Billy Betteridge said he was dumping his old pee-wee for an Offenhauser. Art Scovell, another early outboarder, did not react to this passing of an era quite as gracefully, calling the Mighty Midgets a "menace" and accusing Fred Offenhauser of being a Johnny-come-lately who was taking money out of the pockets of the originators of the sport. Scovell proposed lowering the piston displacement rules from one hundred to eighty-six cubic inches, which would keep the outboard motors in the game but oust the Mighties. The quiet Offenhauser, who liked to stay behind the scenes, refused comment.

But a protest led by Scovell quickly fizzled out, coming as it did on the heels of a far more serious event: the death of driver Chet Mortemore in a midget race at Gilmore, the track's first fatality. "Mortemore's passing was a terrific shock," said a reporter, "because it was assumed the Gilmore track was foolproof." Mortemore was not driving a Mighty Midget but rather a conventional one that he had handled safely in many races before. So the post-race investigation did not center on the car; it blamed the death on a fact impossible to ignore: he was not wearing a crash helmet. In fact, none of the drivers at Gilmore wore crash helmets, for many reasons.

One of the charms of the sport was its intimacy. If drivers wore helmets their fans in the seats could not see their faces as easily. The drivers themselves also balked at helmets because they regarded them as uncomfortable, unnecessary, and cowardly. Midgets were considered far safer than the big cars, and serious crashes were rare. Another argument against helmets was simple economics. The drivers couldn't afford them.

"Why don't all the drivers wear crash helmets?" asked one press account. "The answer is simple: Most of the kids cannot afford the luxury of such protection. A good crash helmet costs $15. Sounds like a small sum to prevent a loss of life, but scores of the drivers in midget auto races in southern California go out night after night and never win a dime." Gilmore Stadium officials distributed a questionnaire to the racers asking how much they made in an average week. A few responded, "From fifteen to forty dollars," but most said, "Nothing at all." Nearly all the drivers were teenagers in or just out of high school whose only job, if you want to call it a job, was the midgets. They were lucky to earn enough to keep them in gas and oil. Due to the low upkeep of their cars, though, they could hang in there from week to week in the hopes of getting a luck-changing payday. After the death of Mortemore, however, Gilmore Stadium officials bought a dozen helmets for the drivers who couldn't afford them, and helmet use became standard at the track.

This was not the case in Class A big-car racing, which was reeling from a string of grisly deaths and injuries that had left a trail of blood around the state. In March 1934, five thousand spectators turned out for a race at the El Centro Speedway in the Imperial Valley near the Mexican border. During the fifteen-mile main event, engine trouble forced a car to stop in the middle of the track. Dust swirled around it and obscured the view of Swede Smith and his riding mechanic Hap Happerly as they came suddenly up on it. As they passed by they accidentally sideswiped the car and hooked one of its wheels. This threw their car into a wild spin and it flipped over, trapping Smith underneath and throwing Happerly out of his seat. Coming around the curve at this moment were two of the best drivers on the West Coast, Ernie Triplett and Al Gordon, running side by side against each other in a battle for first. As the wire service account reads, "Gordon and Triplett, running close together and leading the race, were immediately behind Smith. As they swerved to go around the wrecked machine, one on each side, a dozen mechanics rushed on the track to pull Smith from the wreckage of his machine. Happerly was struck by Triplett's machine, which then swerved into the fence, rebounded and grazed Gordon's machine and plunged ten feet into the air with the pilot skidding along the track. Triplett was picked up unconscious and his machine was a total wreck. Gordon lost control of his machine and crashed into a fence near the judges' stand."

Gordon was the lucky one amidst this mayhem; he walked away unhurt. The driver and mechanic of the stalled car also escaped without injury. Smith, Happerly and Triplett all lost their lives. It was revealed later that Triplett, a popular, well-liked figure among both fans and drivers, had talked recently about quitting racing because of all the injuries he had suffered over the years. Upon hearing the news of his death, some friends expressed surprise that he was even racing at El Centro that day.

None of these men wore crash helmets and, judging by how Happerly was thrown from his car, almost certainly none used safety belts either. Most racecars of this period did not come with seat belts and definitely not shoulder harnesses, and the drivers would not have worn them even if they did. The speed of these racing machines had progressed mightily since the days of Barney Oldfield, but the safety standards had not kept pace. Nor had the thinking about safety. It was still considered akin to suicide to be belted into a car in a crash. Nor did these cars have roll bars, a safety feature that might have saved Al Reinke's life the next month at Legion Ascot Speedway in Los Angeles. Tall and good-looking, until recently a student at Manual Arts High School, Reinke was taking an "easy practice spin" around Legion Ascot—a reference to the local American Legion Post that managed the track—when his borrowed car spun in the gravel and soft dirt of a turn and rolled on top of him, crushing his chest. He died of internal injuries at the hospital.

The site of the next tragedy was the Oakland Speedway, the center of northern California racing. Built in 1931 on East 14th Street in San Leandro—the spot is now a shopping center—the mile-long dirt oval hosted racing of all kinds in a splendidly sunny farm setting. The track also briefly served as a testing ground for the newest cars made at the nearby Durant Motor Company. Billy Durant, the ex-president of General Motors, and his son Cliff, a long-time racer and co-investor in the Los Angeles Motor Speedway in Beverly Hills, owned Durant Motors. It's said that the two of them had pushed for a track to be built in the East Bay to have a place to test their latest models. But the company folded in the early 1930s, another victim of hard times.

The Oakland Speedway stayed alive, though, and Indianapolis 500 winners Louie Meyer, Fred Frame, Billy Arnold, and Wild Bill Cummings all raced there. Rajo Jack never won Indy, but he did claim victories at Oakland, Silvergate Speedway in San Diego, and Mines Field in Los Angeles. A southern Californian who had lived in the state since his teen years, Jack was one of the few black race-car drivers in the nation. He drove stock cars, so it's conceivable he was in the field for the championship 250-mile stock car race held at the speedway in early May. For this event the track's management had changed the layout of the course, adding a V-shaped left-right-left series of turns to the backstretch. The results were disastrous. On Thursday's practice run Pinky Richardson and his riding mechanic Jim McBride made the hard right turn at the bottom of the V, but the car's steering mechanism broke and they crashed. Behind them came another driver and mechanic who crashed in nearly the same spot. Those two survived, as did Richardson. But McBride did not, and his death caused a public outcry.

Friday's *Oakland Tribune* carried vivid photos of the victim, the wreckage of his car, and diagrams of the curve that killed him. "Death Curve," the paper called it. On Saturday Alameda County District Attorney Earl Warren ordered track officials to stop the racing until they eliminated Death Curve. "Failure to comply immediately will result in their arrest on misdemeanor charges and in filing of injunction proceedings designed to close the track permanently," it was reported. The aggressive, forty-three-year-old DA, who would go on to become Governor of California and an influential Chief Justice of the United States Supreme Court, accused the promoters of "deliberately introducing hazards to life that they might reap a financial profit." Deputy sheriffs appeared at the speedway to serve the order and make sure the track returned to its normal circular shape. Chastened track officials did as they were told, and on Sunday Louie Meyer snared the checkered flag in front of seventeen thousand fans.

Possibly due to the fallout from this controversy, the Oakland Speedway did not hold another race for the rest of the year. But the problems at the track and elsewhere in racing mirrored a wider social issue, one that would not go away: the lethal nature of automobiles. The issue affected everyone, even racecar drivers when they weren't racing. Sam Palmer, who finished second behind Meyer in the Oakland 250-miler, earned the nickname of "the Miracle Man" for the many times he escaped death on the tracks. One particularly bad crash trapped him inside his car while it burst into flames. He continued driving for a half-mile with the car on fire before managing to get out. His injuries took nearly a year to heal before he could return to racing. On his way home to Los Angeles from the race in Oakland that day, though, Palmer crashed his car in a ditch south of Bakersfield and died. The Miracle Man could survive Death Curve but not the blood alleys of California's highways.

In June 1934, following these highly publicized racing deaths, the California Highway Patrol released a four-year study of motor accidents in the state. From 1929 to 1933, the last year of the study, 325,000 car-related casualties—both injuries and deaths—had occurred in the state. One person had died in every thirteen accidents, and in almost all the bad accidents, fatal or not, the culprit was the same: too much speed. "At high speeds practically everyone in the car may be killed," said E. Raymond Cato, chief of the CHP, adding that excessive speed was "the dominant influence in California motor vehicle fatalities."

Cato defined excessive speed as being 45 miles per hour and up, although he conceded that many people drove far faster than that. While comprising only 4 percent of the state's total driving population, "habitual speeders usually on pleasure bent" caused most of the accidents. Because novices tended to be slower and safer, these habitual speeders were usually experienced drivers, and it was precisely this experience that led them to believe—foolishly, in Cato's judgment—that they could handle the higher speeds. "Thus it is seen that the man who says he can drive 80 miles an hour in safety does not state a fact. He really does so only at great risk."

One habit closely associated with speeding was drinking alcohol. Many of the more serious accidents involved drunk drivers, and the rate of drunk driving accidents had climbed in each year of the study. "No man or woman who has been drinking is a safe driver," said Cato.

In the early twenties, there were slightly more than 2 million registered drivers in California. Los Angeles County led the state with 845,000 vehicles registered, compared to 152,000 in San Francisco and 147,000 in Alameda County, the second- and third-ranked counties in terms of registrations. Given the higher number of cars on its roads, Los Angeles County also led in traffic accidents by a wide margin, with more than half of the state's 31,000 accidents in 1933 occurring there.

The CHP's jurisdiction covered fourteen thousand miles of state highways and sixty-six thousand miles of rural and county roads. Rural roads tended to be both safer and more dangerous than city streets, according to the report. Fewer accidents occurred in rural areas, but when they did, they tended to be deadlier because people drove at higher speeds and the conditions of the roads were generally poorer. More fatal accidents occurred on unpaved roads than paved.

In all, an average of two hundred people a month—also not wearing seat belts, which would not come into widespread use for decades—were being killed on the roads and highways of trend-setting California, an annual death toll unmatched by any state in the nation. "California still has the country's major traffic problem," the report concluded gloomily, although Cato felt that adding more officers in patrol cars and motorcycles would improve the situation. He identified the "Bay Shore Highway" on the Peninsula from San Francisco through San Mateo County as "one of the most dangerous speedways in the state," even though a recent CHP crackdown on speeders in the area had greatly reduced the number of accidents, none of which was fatal.

Elected officials, city, county, and state government agencies, police and sheriff's departments, business and community groups, insurance and automobile industry associations, car clubs, newspaper editorial writers, and concerned citizens around the state joined Cato and the CHP in its campaign against speeders. They called for tougher law enforcement, more cooperation among police agencies, more uniform traffic laws, stiffer penalties for offenders (such as more jail time or revoking their licenses), and more education, especially at high schools, about the dangers of drinking and driving. Palo Alto, one of the cities on the Bay Shore Highway, adopted a novel plan to stop the practice of speeders who immediately slowed down when they saw a black-and-white patrol car. The officer would pull the car over and hand the driver a card that read: "The officer who hands you this card has just observed a violation of the speed laws by you, but was unable to clock your speed before you slowed down. Your name and address will be filed, and an increased penalty will be imposed if you are hereafter convicted in this city of any violation of the traffic laws."

Later in the year Los Angeles County launched an aggressive campaign against speeders, hauling down fourteen thousand offenders in a month. Despite these efforts, accidents and traffic-related injuries there fell only slightly compared to the same period the year before, and the number of deaths actually rose. The problem with automobiles seemed to be one without solution, or one with only partial solutions—that the accident rate could be improved over time, but the dangers of driving would never go away. Progress could occur but only slowly and never without horrible sacrifice.

So it was with racing too. Wilbur Shaw is regarded as the first California racer to wear a crash helmet, but when he showed up in one for a 1932 race at Legion Ascot, fans booed him, and his fellow drivers scoffed. Only after he survived a potentially life-threatening crash did a few of his colleagues take a second look at his headgear. Helmets remained an optional accessory and most drivers did not bother with them until the spring of 1935, when the American Automobile

Association made them mandatory for all drivers and riding mechanics competing in its races. The helmets, said the AAA, must be "made of light, comfortable and unbreakable materials and lined with shock absorbing rubber headpieces." They were similar to miners' hard hats and the helmets worn by the race drivers who challenged the world land speed records.

But still, the deaths did not stop. In late January 1936, in a race at Legion Ascot, Al Gordon and his riding mechanic Spider Matlock drove hard into the south turn and, as reporter Bob Ray writes, "as he was coming high off the curve his car hit a slick spot on the track, spun around crazily and went backwards through the loose dirt that separates the oval from the guard rail. As a scream, half of excitement and half of fear, went up from the throng, Gordon's car smashed through the fence and hurtled down the twelve-foot graded embankment outside the track. The car disappeared from view and it went down the embankment and the spectators were spared the grewsome [sic] sight that greeted track attendants who pulled the twisted human forms from the wreckage."

Gordon, who had escaped with his life after the close call at El Centro, was not so lucky this time. His car spun completely around once, then halfway around again, then catapulted backward through the rail down the embankment. Among the ten thousand people in the stands that day were teenager Maurice Holladay and a girlfriend he had met on a blind date on New Year's Eve. He didn't know exactly what happened to Gordon and Matlock because they disappeared from his view. "I remember that the announcer never reported the condition of the two," he recalled years later. "While on our way home to Long Beach we were in a drive-in for refreshments when my parents came by, saw our car and stopped to tell us the sad news they heard on the car radio."

The news that two more lives had been sacrificed on the altar of haste did more than shock people; it forced change. For years the *Los Angeles Herald Examiner* had waged a campaign against Legion Ascot, using graphic photos and sensational headlines—"Widow Weeps as Mate Dies," "Legalized Murder"—to lobby for its closure. These latest deaths brought the paper plenty of company. "A rising crescendo of protest arose from citizens and public officials," went one report, "demanding that something be done to curtail the useless slaughter of humans." Twenty-five drivers and mechanics had died at Legion Ascot in the twelve years since it had opened in 1924. Adding to the horror surrounding Gordon's death was the fact that his wife and one of his young sons were at the track that day.

Why did these men keep driving when they knew the risks? Money, to be sure. There was a bit of that. But almost all the drivers still had to work regular jobs to support themselves and their families; the little they won at the track couldn't do that alone. The greater lure was the glory and adventure of it all. In any pursuit—even the most dangerous ones—certain individuals will always want to be first, win championships, be recognized as the best. And yet most of those who risked their lives never won championships; they were just middle-of-the-pack guys who got a charge from the competition and the brotherhood of racing. In this last respect they resembled soldiers in combat, a comparison that is not all that farfetched considering the alarmingly high casualty count in some of these spectacles. These men raced because they found honor in it. And they wished for their fellow drivers and mechanics to hold them in honor too. When one of their brothers-in-arms died, they came out to support his widow and her fatherless children.

Services for Spider Matlock were held at a Los Angeles chapel a few days after his death. The ceremony for Al Gordon took place in the same chapel a day later. In his early thirties, married, and with two children under the age of ten, Gordon lived in Long Beach but grew up in Redlands. The son of a chauffeur, he became a mail carrier in rural San Bernardino County, but this was not a job that was going to satisfy him for long. He started racing as a teenager, on the streets and on the track, and drove for the first time at Legion Ascot in its inaugural year, later going on to become a Pacific Coast champion. After the service, friends and family drove his body out to Redlands, where it was laid to rest at Hillside Cemetery next to the gravesite of his half-brother Ernest Scammell, an ex–restaurant owner in town who had been killed in a highway traffic accident a few months earlier.

The next month the AAA's national office demanded improvements at Legion Ascot. The AAA's list of safety measures included strengthening the guardrails, reconditioning the track surface, eliminating drops in the roadway and, most especially, revamping the south curve where Gordon and Matlock had met their end. These changes were never made. In April a fire burned down a section of its grandstands and Legion Ascot Speedway, the proving ground for some of the best racecar drivers ever, closed, never to hold another race.

Later in the decade some drivers and mechanics began to experiment with roll bars by installing heavy arched steel tubing both in front of the car above the radiator and directly behind the driver's seat. But the widespread use of these lifesaving devices was still many years away. As for the AAA, it had seen enough. It withdrew its stamp of approval from racing on the West Coast and did not sanction another big-car race in California until after the end of World War II.

SEVENTEEN

Hopped Up

Fred Offenhauser did not like dealing with the press, but after the deaths of Al Gordon and Spider Matlock he spoke in defense of his profession and his calling. "From the block down to the tiniest lock washer, every part of the motor is made to specification," he told a reporter, explaining how his engines were made. "We can't use a single stock part. But some day the parts we are designing will be regular stock parts. This is because every major improvement in the American automobile industry has first been tested on the race track."

From major innovations such as front-wheel drive to minor ones such as sturdier lock washers, racetracks acted as laboratories for the passenger cars of tomorrow. This was Offenhauser's view, and it carried weight in the industry because he had helped develop many of those innovations, first with Harry A. Miller and now as the head of his own successful company. In only a few years Offenhauser had gone from being out of work to being proclaimed "America's No. 1 builder and designer of fast automobile engines." Those fast automobile engines included the ones for the Mighty Midgets and bigger and faster cars at the laboratory of speed in Indianapolis, Indiana.

Early in 1935 a California dirt track driver named Kelly Petillo came to see Offenhauser and Leo Goossen about how to climb out of also-ran status at Indianapolis. A short, dark-haired Italian American from Huntington Park, Kelly's first name was actually Calvino. But when he was growing up, the guys in the neighborhood "couldn't or wouldn't pronounce Calvino," as one writer put it, so he adopted Kelly instead. One of his first jobs as a teenager was trucking fruit over the Tehachapi Mountains via the Ridge Route. The windy and mountainous Ridge Route was so dangerous that drivers from Los Angeles had to stop at Castaic Junction to get what was called a "check ticket" before they could pass on. If they didn't stop for their ticket, authorities phoned ahead on the road and blocked them from proceeding farther. But driving a truck wasn't what Petillo had in mind for himself, so he started racing at Legion Ascot, Silvergate, and the Oakland Speedway. He tried his hand at the Indy 500 but never cracked the top ten in three starts. Feeling frustrated, knowing he could do better if only he had the right mount, he paid Offenhauser Manufacturing twenty-five hundred dollars to build an engine for him.

This was a risk for Petillo, because he basically drained his savings to hire Offenhauser, an unknown save for his association with Miller. "Miller was well known," observed a reporter. "He had a dependable reputation for building fine motors. But who was Offenhauser? Could his motors be trusted?" In his late forties, balding, stocky, a machinist since he was a boy, the soft-spoken ex–Pacific Electric superintendent had labored in Miller's shadow for two decades. In all that time he'd never driven a racecar, riding as a mechanic around a track only once, and that for a practice lap. But he had been one of the creative lights behind the Golden Submarine and some of the most dependably fast racing machines of his time, and that was enough to persuade Petillo and two other California drivers, Wilbur Shaw and Rex Mays, to go with "Offys"—the shorthand term for Offenhauser-made engines—at Indianapolis that year.

The gamble paid off. "Driving like a wild man," in the words of an observer, the Huntington Park Italian brought down the checkered flag averaging 106 miles per hour over five hundred miles. Behind him in second place came Shaw. Only a broken bolt in Mays's Offy prevented a possible one-two-three sweep. That year three Offys ran at Indy; the next year, thirteen did, and another Californian repeated as champion: Louie Meyer, who drove an Offenhauser that was a Miller, or a Miller that was an Offenhauser, depending on your point of view. Meyer firmly believed that "there never was an Offenhauser engine. No matter what name you call it, it's still Harry Miller's design." Filling out his entry form before the race he listed his car as a Miller. But Wilbur Shaw showed no such divided loyalties; he listed his engine as an Offenhauser, and in 1937 it carried him to the first of three victories at the Brickyard.

"The fifty-year reign of the immortal Offy," in one writer's phrase, had begun. Offenhauser engines, built originally by Offenhauser Engineering of Los Angeles and then later by another Los Angeles company co-founded by Louie Meyer after he retired from driving, won at Indianapolis twenty-four times, an achievement without peer in motor racing. But Offenhauser's influence—and that of Goossen and Miller—spread well beyond the track. It's a complicated chronology but worth telling: In the late 1920s, after Miller had sold his business to form Miller-Schofield, the new company began to make cylinder heads for Ford Model A engines. These heads, which put pep into a sluggish stock product, proved to be a success but not enough of one to save Miller-Schofield, which went bust. After the bankruptcy a man named Crane Gartz and another person bought the patents, patterns, and tools for the cylinder heads and formed a company in Hollywood to manufacture them. They renamed these heads "Cragars" and soon went bankrupt themselves.* Enter a colorful ex–animal trapper and cannery worker named George Wight, who bought Cragar's old patterns, finessed their design, and started selling these speed-generating heads at his auto parts store on Gage Avenue in the little suburban town of Bell near Los Angeles.

---

* The name was formed by joining Gartz's first and last name: Cra-gar. Cragar today is a well-known maker of custom wheels.

Bell Auto Parts sold new and old parts, the old parts coming from the wrecking yard behind Wight's brick building. The wrecked cars and parts of wrecked cars that lay in glorious shambles around the yard served as a magnet for teenagers in the area who were looking for dirt-cheap cast-off automobile treasures to fix up and install in their cars—or, as they called them, their "hop-ups."

"'Hopping up' light stock cars for amateur racing is the major avocation of a group of Southland young men who would rather compare cylinder heads and carburetors than dunk doughnuts," reported an article in the *Times* on this new trend. "The Rattlers of Burbank is a typical aggregation of hopper-uppers. Similar clubs exist in many Southland cities. The prerequisite for membership is an underslung vehicle with a protruding exhaust pipe, an open-air top and a minimum speed of 80 miles per hour. The Rattlers recently acquired a deluxe chicken house which they transformed into clubrooms, with cooperative tool and floor space for a half-dozen cars. Members gather there weekly to take their cars to pieces, discuss the comparative virtues of various types of gaskets, and to swap accessories. The original stock car ancestry is hardly recognizable after a Rattler has finished combining parts from several makes, plus gadgets of his own devising, into a beetle-like racer."

Drivers of these beetle-like racers looked a lot like the original midget drivers—young, with pimples but not much facial hair, mostly white, suburban, killing time in high school or trade school or no school, living at home with Mom and Dad although desperately wanting out, possibly holding down a job but probably not, broke nearly all the time and, if they had any money at all, invariably pouring it into their cars. Cars had been around since they were born—they grew up with them so it felt natural and right to drive one. These hopper-uppers—the term hot-rodder had not yet come into use—went out with girls, of course, in their hop-ups. You could no more go on a date with a girl on the trolley than you could drive a car without wheels. You could take your parents' car (that is, if your parents let you), but a much better look, indeed the very best look, was pulling up in front of the girl's house in your very own underslung open-air vehicle that made low, grumbling sounds like a lion in heat. Then again, considering that her parents would probably be around and wanting to check you and your car out, it might make more sense to meet her down at the corner. Wherever it was, after she got in and admired the shine you'd put on the outside and the fact that, for a change, there were no gum wrappers and crumpled cigarette packs on the floorboards, the two of you would rumble down to Simon's or Carpenter's or Robert's or Van de Kamp's with the big windmill on top, or any of the other neon-lit drive-in palaces that were turning up on every other intersection these days. Or maybe you'd head down to the Giant Tamale or the Tail o' the Pup, the hot dog stand shaped like two buns with a hot dog sticking out of it.

But to really impress the girls (and the other guys too, for that matter) your hop-up needed hop, and to get it you probably needed to spend a little time at George Wight's store in Bell or at Lee Chapel's on San Fernando Road in Los Angeles. Chapel, like Wight, ran a junkyard along with selling the new Cragar heads and other parts of his own devising. Ed Winfield, a miracle worker with carburetors and engine design, ran a similar shop on Treadwell Street. These shops—the modern term for them is "speed shop"—were places where the hopper-uppers could find speed equipment but also hang with guys who were like them and who understood them and their values. Automobile dealers did not sell much racing equipment, nor did they generally approve of hopper-uppers and what they were up to. Some places in the Midwest and East sold speed equipment by mail order, although their gear was mainly intended for sprint car racing around a track. What these southern California boys were doing—and this was happening nowhere else in the country to this degree—was converting this speed equipment for illegal racing on the streets.

Bill Harrah got his first car, a 1926 Chevrolet, when he was a freshman at Hollywood High in the late twenties. It was a gift from his father, and over the next six months, using money from his part-time job parking cars at a movie theater, he added eleven horns and twenty-six lights to it, including strings of tiny lights along the running boards. The car had a top speed of 55 miles an hour and naturally, "I drove it 55 miles an hour all the time," he said. After the Chevy he moved into a Ford, which was without question the hop-up of choice. There were seemingly endless numbers of Ford Model Ts around, as well as the Model A and the stylish and smart Model B and Model C that came after. You could pick up an old Model T for practically nothing, which fit into the typical hop-up's budget, and you could find lots of good, cheap parts for them at the wrecking yard. Some manufacturers also provided speed equipment for Fords. Ruckstell Manufacturing of Berkeley built a rear axle that helped the Model T go faster and handle better. Of course, another method of obtaining parts was "midnight auto supply." Whippet radiators became a must-have item for many hopper-uppers, which made it tough on owners of Whippet automobiles. One might go to bed at night with his car fully intact but when he went to start it up in the morning the radiator was missing.

Bill Harrah's Ford was a '29 Model A Cabriolet, painted cream and brown. He lowered its roofline a couple of inches to streamline its profile—"chopping," this practice would come to be known—and installed Chrysler wire wheels and a Miller-Schofield (or Cragar) head. The Cabriolet could do 65 when it first came out of the factory; after Harrah got done with it, it could hit 80. And naturally he drove it 80 all the time and "spent a considerable amount of time in juvenile court."

Despite the consolidation of the American automobile industry and the concentration of manufacturing power in fewer and fewer companies, the backyard, do-it-yourself car-building tradition in this country had not died, and Harrah and the hopper-uppers were among those keeping it alive. They turned something old into something new, something tired into something fresh, and something sluggish into something loud and fast that shook windows and scared parents and put the law onto them. By hook or by crook, and after long hours of hard work and tender loving care in their backyards and garages, they rebuilt, reconditioned, remodeled, repainted, and re-imagined these old Fords until they became something more than just Fords, far different from the uniform products that rolled off the line at the factory. They became unique, individual, *personal* statements: Yam Okamura's Ford or

Stu Hilborn's Ford or Mel Leighton's Ford or Manuel Ayulo's Ford or Bill Harrah's Ford—and not stock. Anything but stock.

Harrah went to the University of California at Los Angeles and just as he did when he was at Hollywood High, he worked part-time while going to school. This job was at his father's gambling parlor in Venice. Bill enjoyed the gambling business and gamblers—not crooks or evil sinners as they were often portrayed, but just plain folks in many cases—and his customers in turn enjoyed the "prodigiously charming" young man who made them feel at ease. But the police raided the joint with depressing regularity and Bill quarreled with his father, finally buying him out and taking over the parlor on his own. Harrah's gambling philosophy was simple and effective: "Get rid of the shills, make the customer as comfortable as possible, and display an honesty and integrity so that even losing customers would want to come back."

Nevertheless, since gambling was against the law in California, the police kept coming back too, which made Harrah eventually decide to set up shop in Reno, where gambling was legal. This was the start of his Nevada casino and hotel empire, where he achieved such wealth that he could, in his later years, pursue a love for collecting cars. He amassed probably the greatest personal collection of automobiles in the world. Some of his most distinctive cars were sold at auction after his death in 1978, but many notable classics remain. Known as the Bill Harrah Collection, it is housed in the National Automobile Museum in Reno and features historic automobiles such as the Thomas Flyer that won the 1908 New York to Paris Race.

When, in his twenties, Harrah was just getting his gambling business started in Nevada, he commuted back and forth between Los Angeles and Reno, usually traveling Highway 395 on the eastern side of the Sierra. This lonesome country road, like all lonesome country roads of the time, operated on the widely understood and legal "ROP" principle—meaning that drivers could travel at a "reasonable or proper" rate of speed. Trouble was, the highway patrol defined ROP as 65 miles per hour whereas Harrah, having traded in his Cabriolet for a new 1936 Lincoln Zephyr coupe, defined it as around 90. This disagreement meant that even as a grown-up Harrah logged some time in traffic court.

Harrah confessed to ignoring the speed limit on occasion—well, on many occasions—but he swore he never once got into an accident, the kind of statement that Judge Cecil Holland of the Beverly Hills Municipal Court would have regarded with a patient sigh. Justice Holland may have even dealt with Harrah in Harrah's running-around days, and even if he did not, loads of other hop-up guys appeared in front of him offering creative reasons as to why they'd been doing 50 on a street posted at 25. By 1936, when a newspaper reporter dropped by his court to do a feature on him, Holland felt that he had heard every excuse in the book for speeding and other traffic violations. There was this one: "Your Honor, I have just bought a new car. I was washing it and wanted the water to dry evenly on it. That's why I was speeding."

Then there was the man arrested for drunken driving: "My dentist gave me novocaine for an extraction. The pain was so strong that I drank just one glass of beer to offset the pain."

One person cited for parking in a red zone said he thought "the merchant had painted the curb so that his customers would park there." A motorcyclist explained he had just installed a new windshield on his bike and that his usual way of judging how fast he was going—by the "strength of the wind"—was thrown off and this had caused him to ignore the posted limits. One man arrested for speeding swore the judge had the wrong guy—that "it must have been another man with the same name who was speeding." A young man cited for "one-arm driving" said that he had just come out of a cold church and that he had put his arm around his girlfriend to warm it up.

Justice Holland, who wore a mustache, glasses, and a generally solemn expression on the bench, tended to look more favorably on imaginative excuses, ones he had not heard before, and to judge more harshly those alibis "reeking of antiquity." Some in this category were:

"I was late to work and didn't want to lose my job."

"I didn't know it was against the law."

"I only took one little drink, Your Honor."

"I didn't know how fast I was going."

"I've been a taxpayer here fifteen years," said a person apparently thinking this somehow excused him from obeying the traffic laws. The judge responded to this man the same way he did to those who begged for leniency for reasons of "unemployment, sick wife, sick children, children to support, on relief and no money." If it was so important to you, said Holland, "Why didn't you think of it before you did this?"

While he had an appreciation for the lighter side of his work, the justice recognized, as did others in law enforcement, the seriousness of the problem they faced. Los Angeles had become the national center for outlaw street racing. Hop-ups dueled each other in nighttime races on Glenoaks Boulevard west of the Burbank city limits, Peck Road in El Monte, Foothill Boulevard in Arcadia near the Santa Anita racetrack, Sepulveda Boulevard south of San Fernando Road next to the Van Norman Reservoir, and Lincoln Boulevard next to Mines Field (then the site of a racetrack and now Los Angeles International Airport). Plenty of other places hosted impromptu races, from streetlight to streetlight, starting when the light turned green. Guys raced for pride, money, and pink slips, never white slips. A white slip meant the car was still being financed, and you'd have to be a fool to take on someone else's car payments as the prize for beating him in a race. A pink slip meant the guy owned his car and if you shut him down you drove away with his car, free and clear.

The best street races occurred on flat, paved, straight roadways with few or no side streets. Night races were best because there were fewer cars out (of course, in general, there were far, far fewer cars on the roads than there are today). Going 80 miles an hour and up, these hop-ups needed time to stop, so the streets beyond the agreed-upon finish had to be watched and guarded too. Another reason for forming a car club like the Rattlers was to have enough people and cars to watch the side streets for cross traffic during races.

Two cafés, the Frying Pan and the Twin Barrels, served as neutral territory for the different clubs to get together, have a piece of pecan pie and ice cream, and plan that evening's racing schedule. Glenoaks Boulevard was a prime locale for duels because the Burbank police did not patrol it, and the Los Angeles police had to travel all the way from the Van Nuys station to get there. You could do the deed and make your getaway before the cops even reached the scene of the crime.

But the cops were never far away, and that was the problem. They were always around somewhere, if no place else than lurking in the back of your mind. You couldn't get away from them, or the thought of them, and it was the same with parents and teachers and probation officers and judges and all the rest of them. If they busted you for speeding you got cited and had to pay a fine. But not before they made you show up at muni court and listen to some stone-faced judge mock the reason you were there or deliver some sermon about the dangers of speeding. The dangers of speeding? Of course it was dangerous. That's why you did it, that's what was so fun about it. But a judge wasn't going to sit still for that kind of backtalk, so all you could do was stand there like an idiot and take your lumps and hope he didn't throw you in the clink. Going to juvey would just mean more tears from Mom and more screaming from Dad and all those boring old folks who just didn't get what an incredible rush it was to be at the controls of your own machine, a thing you built with your own hands and tools, you and a couple of your buddies in your backyard, late at night, and basically for peanuts, and how many things in the world can you say you really own, and that you really love, and that are yours and yours alone and no one else's?

Old folks didn't get it, and they never would. But there was a place for hopped-up boys and girls to go, a place they could truly be themselves without a cop or teacher or parent around to judge them. The highway patrol didn't keep stats on it; in fact, the highway patrol and every other law enforcement agency stayed far away from it, and that suited everybody just fine. There were no traffic laws there and nobody to enforce them, no stop signs or speed limit signs or traffic lights or side streets. There were no streets at all, no paved ones anyhow. It was basically a patch of dirt in the middle of nowhere, and it was almost paradise. The name of the place was Muroc Dry Lake.

Hop-up paradise lay about two and a half hours east of Los Angeles in the Antelope Valley region of the Mojave Desert. The first recorded instance of people racing automobiles at Muroc Dry Lake occurred in 1906 when Dana Burk, the mayor of Ventura and a southern California businessman, journeyed there with a party of four including a reporter. The car they drove was said to be the original 999 car, built years earlier by Henry Ford and driven by Ford when he set the land speed record for the mile. Barney Oldfield also raced the 999 and set records in it. Eventually, though, it fell into disuse and became the property of the railroad company, which sold it to Burk. He reconditioned it, renamed it the 30, and on a Sunday in September decided to find out what it could do in a straight, flat, wide-open, push-the-throttle-down-and-don't-let-up setting.

Beginning early that morning, the group drove from Los Angeles up the stiff Newhall Grade, turned east at Saugus, and followed the Mint Canyon Road up and down two passes into the Antelope Valley. They reached the Mojave by noon. At a town near the Hamilton mine they stopped for water and gas, then continued east past the town of Rosamond until reaching the shores of Muroc Dry Lake (now Rogers Dry Lake on Edwards Air Force Base). There they found the wreckage of a sort-of sailboat on wheels—described by the reporter as "a strange ship of the desert"—that had apparently raced at Muroc until it fell apart under the heat and winds of the desert. Antelope Valley ranchers had raced horses at the dry lakes for years, which may have been how the Burk party and other pioneering automobilists found out about Muroc in the first place. The railroad also passed through the area, and this was another way in which word about it spread.

One of the men who raced the 30 was named, appropriately enough, Jim Speed. Speed, the 30, and Muroc all performed with distinction that day. "Once on the glassy, smooth, cement-like surface of the lake, the car ran like a cannonball, with almost no effort," wrote the reporter. "At the highest speed there was no skidding, nor slipping, nor even a jar. It was found to be perfect—an automobile paradise."

Bruno Seibel, a professional driver who later dueled Barney Oldfield at Lakeside track in San Diego and other tracks around California, had traveled up with the party as well. He also took a test drive in the 30 and came away impressed with Muroc, predicting speeds of 130 miles per hour in the future. The reporter, equally caught up in the moment, thought the dry lakes might even replace the oceanside course at Daytona Beach as the premiere spot in America for world land speed record attempts. "California has all the rest of the earth beaten when it comes to natural race courses," he wrote. "The big dry lakes will soon be the mecca of the automobile racers."

It took nearly twenty years for his prediction to come true. While many informal speed tests by cars, motorcycles, and possibly sailing ships on wheels undoubtedly took place there in the intervening period, the first serious attempt at the world land speed record at Muroc occurred in 1924 with Tommy Milton in the cockpit of not one but two Miller Specials: 122 and 183. This was Milton in his hard-driving prime, and the team of Miller-Offenhauser-Goossen in theirs. In early April they pulled the two flame-red speedsters on trailers out to the site, following the same roads as the Burk party. The passage of years had brought at least one improvement: road signs, posted by the Automobile Club of Southern California.

A horde of spectators, auto industry reps, reporters, photographers, and newsreel cameramen came out to see and record the event, overwhelming the general store in the tiny town of Muroc about two miles from the lakebed. Having run out of just about all his supplies, the shopkeeper sent Indianapolis 500 winner Jimmy Murphy over to nearby Lancaster to pick up some food and drinks. Murphy did as he was asked, but instead of coming back to the store he drove straight to the lakebed and distributed the bread, crackers, cheese, cold drinks, and beer to the people there.

As before, Muroc excited awe among those seeing it for the first time. "Certainly never in the history of automobile racing has there been a setting like this for speed trials," wrote a reporter, Frank Howe, who was covering the Milton attempts. "Dry lake is a flat bowl in the desert, approximately six miles in diameter. The surface is like hardened lava, snow-white and flat and smooth as a hardwood dance floor." In addition to Muroc there were (and are) three other dry lakes in the area: Rosamond, Harper, and El Mirage. All have been home, at one time or another, to racing. People to this day confuse them with Utah's famous Bonneville Salt Flats, but they are made of dried mud, not salt. Located 2,800 feet above sea level, the lakes occupy large lowland areas, into which water settles and then evaporates, leaving a smooth, hard-packed finish that is dead-flat and, like Bonneville, a prime locale for thinking about speed and nothing but.

The Milton-Miller party set up camp on the lakebed, testing the cars during the day to get them ready to run. At night they stored them in the stable behind the Muroc general store.

One reason for taking a shot at the record in April was to avoid the intense heat of summer. Mojave heat was a painful heat, a hurtful heat, the kind of heat that can kill you if you're stuck out in it too long. At night the temperatures dropped below freezing and during the day they soared above 110 degrees Fahrenheit, with the wind sweeping across the dry, softly rounded hill forms of the landscape. Sagebrush, coyote brush, and Joshua trees shaped like desert coral seemed the only plant life able to survive in this environment. Another characteristic of the desert was mirages, which make people think they're seeing water when they're not. Frank Howe said that Milton's car appeared to be speeding through water on one of its runs: "From the finish line, Milton's car appeared to be hurtling through a shallow lake, with water splashing high on either side. As he approached at his 150-mile gait, the red car alternately became wide and low; then narrow and high. Disappearing in the distance, the phenomenon was reversed."

Milton in the Miller 122 and Milton in the Miller 183 both set new world records for their class: 141.71 miles per hour for the former and 151.26 for the latter. Each car took what was called a "flying start," gradually building up speed for two miles before hitting the starting line. The course itself ran a mile, followed by another two-mile section for stopping. This was a necessity; braking parachutes did not exist then. Milton wore a dark hood and goggles, no helmet. Officials from the American Automobile Association supervised the arrangements and did the timing.

Three years later the Long Beach Avenue gang again made the journey out to Muroc, this time with a new speedster on the trailer—the Miller 91—and a new driver, Frank Lockhart. But Lockhart had more on his mind than just beating Milton's old numbers. Two months before, Malcolm Campbell had gone 174 miles per hour to set a new world land speed record. Campbell, who was English, drove an English car on a beach course in England. Then, in March, another Englishman, Major Henry Seagrave, smashed his countryman's record with a run of 203 miles per hour in a 24-cylinder, 2,760-cubic-inch monster. It was Lockhart's and Miller's desire to bring the land speed record back to America.

And if anyone could do it, it was little Frankie, a man who was born for the driver's seat, a total natural, "one of the true geniuses of American sport," as one writer put it. A fast machine is one thing, but it needs a person inside it to make it go, and Lockhart was that type of person. He was born in Ohio, but when his father died, his mother, Carrie, brought him and his brother to Los Angeles for a fresh start. They didn't have much money, and she supported her sons as a seamstress. Little, skinny, blond-haired Frankie was a troublemaker in school who loved mathematics and building things, especially automobile things. His first racecar was a wooden soapbox derby car. When he turned sixteen a man offered him a real car, a Model T, as long as Frank got it out of the man's Boyle Heights yard. But Frank didn't have any way to tow the car, so he and his brother took it apart in the man's yard, then carried it piece-by-piece back to their house in Inglewood, where they reassembled it, better than ever. Another friendly person gave him a Model T engine. Frank rebuilt the engine, installed it hop up-style in his T, and had a set of wheels a poor kid could feel proud of.

When he started racing at Legion Ascot, Frankie's mother could only stand back and shake her head at how her son poured himself, all of himself, into that homebuilt T. "What little money he made just fed the car," said Carrie. "He'd come home with burned feet and so tired that he couldn't get his shoes off. But that was what he had to do. He lived on grease and iron."

The California Institute of Technology in Pasadena, recognizing Lockhart's math and engineering talents, invited him to take its entrance exams. He took the tests and scored at genius levels, according to his biographers, but declined the university's offer to attend because he felt he needed to make money for his family. Besides, school didn't interest him all that much; *nothing* interested him like being in the cockpit of a racecar ravaged by the sin of haste. "No one ever sat in a race car like Frank. On a mile dirt track he seemed to begin his slide in the middle of the straightaway," said an awestruck Ernie Olson, a riding mechanic who worked at the Miller shop. Frank himself summed up his driving style this way: "All I think of from one second to the next is how to drive to win."

"Because of his youth, fighting heart and chance-taking proclivities," the boy with burned feet became an instant fan favorite at Ascot. The track's press agent hung the tag of "boy wonder" on him, and the press picked up on it, even though, as one curmudgeon noted, Little Frank "has to have his whiskers scraped every day." Whiskers or not, the twenty-one-year-old wonder grabbed the attention of Miller, who pulled him out of that homemade T and installed him in a sleek and purposeful Miller-built dirt track car. He ran on the oiled dirt of Legion Ascot and this turned out to be the surface Lockhart thrived on. He won dirt track races all around the city, state, and country.

In May 1926 he showed up at the Indianapolis Motor Speedway not supposed to race in the 500, probably because of his reputation as a dirt track specialist. But Ernie Olson arranged for him to try out another driver's car, and on that run Lockhart set a one-lap speed record, which was what convinced Team Miller to let him take the place of a sick driver and go in the 500. Go, he did. Lockhart's abilities derived not only from his bravery and skills on the track but also the innovative mechanical ideas he applied to every engine he raced, including Miller's. In this case, though, he was driving a Miller 91 that was unfamiliar to him. Nonetheless, the dirt-track wizard won a rain-shortened Indianapolis 500 on his first race there.

The next year was when Lockhart went to Muroc not only to bring the land speed record back to America but to disprove conventional thinking. Judging by the size of Campbell's and Seagrave's vehicles, bigger in the world of racing clearly meant faster, and that was what made Lockhart's attempt so compelling. Not only was his Miller 91 much smaller than the other two vehicles, it was smaller than the cars that would be described six years later as "midgets."

The run took place on April 11, 1927, and Art Pillsbury, a race track builder and designer who had already witnessed many land speed record attempts and who would witness many more at Bonneville, was there. "The most spectacular mile I ever saw in my life was that one of Lockhart's," he recalled. "The dry lake was small and to get that record with his little 91 he went in a huge arc on two wheels and came sliding onto the straightaway. He was a race driver. He could drive anything, anywhere."

On his first run Lockhart went 171.02, nearly reaching Campbell's mark. For land speed record attempts, drivers make two runs—the average of the two being their recorded mark—and coming back in the opposite direction, Lockhart on his second run made 157.85 for an average of 164.85. Nobody had ever driven that fast in that small of a car, but such was the nature of the man that his accomplishment only left him hungry for more. The next year, Lockhart, no longer affiliated with the Miller team, went to Daytona with the goal of yanking the land speed record away from the Brits. The new record holder was Campbell, who broke Seagrave's record with a clocking of 206 miles per hour in February. All this meant to the Californian was that he was going to have to push his 181-cubic-inch twin-supercharged Stutz Black Hawk that much harder. And he did. Experts on the scene said the Black Hawk was going 225 miles per hour when it hit a soft spot on the sand, flipped end-over-end into the ocean, skipped across the waves, landed upright in the water, and began to sink. People watching from the stands and from parked cars along the beach rushed into the surf to pull him from the wreckage before he drowned.

Remarkably, Lockhart survived. Even more remarkably, perhaps, after the Stutz factory in Indianapolis rebuilt the mangled Black Hawk and restored it to running order, he decided to shoot for the record again the next month. This time, no one could save him. On his fourth and final run down the beach his right rear tire blew and the car flipped and rolled and crushed him. One of the horrified onlookers was his wife. His mother, still a seamstress in Los Angeles, was deeply hurt when she heard the news, although she could not have been wholly surprised. A boy who had lived on grease and iron had died by it too. The acclaimed King of the Dirt Tracks, "one of the greatest race drivers the world had ever seen," in the judgment of virtually everyone in the sport, was gone. He was twenty-five.

Lockhart's death and the demise of the Miller speed factory ended the world land speed record attempts at Muroc. The traditional American center for these attempts, Daytona Beach, also fell from its ascendancy in the mid-1930s, when Malcolm Campbell became the first to go faster than 300 miles per hour in an automobile. He did this on the long, broad salt flats of Bonneville, which took over as the global meeting place for those who wished to test the boundaries of how fast humans could travel on land.

Muroc remained a center of speed activity, however, and record attempts took place for different classes of cars.* In 1930 Shorty Cantlon, another California dirt track vet, went 144 miles per hour in a Miller, setting a record for four-cylinder cars. Car companies also conducted tests at the dry lakes to create the aura of speed around their new models. One such test, conducted by Chrysler for its DeSoto Six, attracted none other than Outdoor Franklin, the famous Buick endurance driver, who had come to Muroc as an observer. Outdoor had long since hung up his endurance driving gloves and become a representative of Richfield Oil, which supplied the gas and oil for the DeSoto runs. Gilmore Oil also sponsored cars at the dry lakes, and when Stubby Stubblefield in a Gilmore Special broke Cantlon's mark for "four-bangers"—the delightful modern term for cars with four-cylinder engines—company president Earl Gilmore, who attended the run, made sure the press noted the fact that the car used Gilmore Blu-Green gasoline and Lion Head Motor Oil.

Not all runs at Muroc were straight shots; many took place on a circular one- or five-mile course set up on the lakebed. In 1928 a Ford Model A sedan known as "the Phoenix Flyer" circled the five-mile course one hundred times, averaging 62 miles per hour. Three years later the same car, now with 64,000 miles on it, returned to do another 500-mile circuit at a slightly faster clip. This was, however, a mere tune-up for what was to come. In a tribute of sorts to the old Cactus Derby, the Flyer drove from Los Angeles to Phoenix and back again in fourteen hours, eclipsing by a full two hours the previous fastest round-trip between the cities. Ford Motor claimed that except for a new set of piston rings and a valve job at forty thousand miles, the car was the same as the day it had left the factory. Even the tires were original.

Besides the sponsored events, plenty of un-sponsored events went off at Muroc—far more of those in fact. Guys showed up in whatever they had and took on whoever else was there, gunfighter style. The first attempt to turn these unruly shootouts into something more organized came in 1932 with the formation of the Muroc Racing Association. The association assigned cars to different categories based on their speed: 70 to 80 miles per hour; 80 to 90; 90 to 100; and above 100—remarkable speeds all, given the homebuilt nature of these vehicles and the wrecking-yard parts they used. Most of the cars were four-banger Fords with some Chevys and Dodges in the mix, and many were altered to produce more speed, with rules governing such modifications as the size of the driver's seat (no less

---

* Pismo Beach also hosted speed runs during this era. In 1931 Ernie Triplett went nearly 131 miles per hour on the beach to set a new American record for his class of cars. Pismo's motorized heritage remains alive today, as cars and motorcycles can still drive on certain areas of the beach.

than thirty inches wide) and windshields and tops (strictly forbidden). Still, things remained pretty wild. To know what category your car belonged to, you first made a timed run through a quarter-mile course. Then organizers put you in a race against other cars of your class. Sometimes as many as five cars rolled across the start at the same time, bumping, sliding, spinning, skidding, and crashing around the course. Drivers and occasionally spectators got hurt when a crosswind flared and pushed cars into one another or out of bounds. A strong crosswind could make a driver lose control, so if the cars were poised to go and a large, Dust Bowl-size cloud came rolling across the lakebed, the starter held them off until the cloud passed and the wind calmed. Once the cars took off they stirred up waves of dust of their own. The faster they went, the larger the plumes that trailed behind them. The guys in second through fifth place struggled to see as they steered through the dust kicked up by the cars in front of them.

When the hop-up clubs began to form around southern California, they all started coming to Muroc. What they found there disappointed them. The Muroc Racing Association was a skeletal group with no planned meets, no trophies for the winners, no efficient timing system, no real oversight. Some of the clubs worried that match racing and multi-car racing was going to blow the good deal they all had at the dry lakes. If things got too out of hand maybe the authorities might pay more attention to them. Nobody wanted that.

In late 1937 representatives from a half-dozen southern California clubs—Throttlers, Sidewinders, Idlers, Ramblers, Road Runners, 90 MPH—formed the Southern California Timing Association to take over from the Muroc group. The Southern California Timing Association—which exists today, holds racing meets at El Mirage, and remains the most famous organization of its kind in the world—tamed the wildness somewhat by banning match races, sticking to a regular schedule, establishing points standings, championships, and other competitive criteria, and making technical rules to govern the cars, engine sizes, and classes. By its second meeting a dozen more clubs had signed on, and the SCTA held its first-ever meet at Muroc in the spring of the following year.

Mostly at the dry lakes, people had used handheld stopwatches to do the timing—one person recording the time at the start, another at the finish. To improve upon this, the SCTA developed and refined an electronic system that used trip wires a few inches off the ground that were set off when a car's tires rolled across the line. Safety also improved. Members of the various clubs took turns patrolling the sidelines and keeping things under better control.

At the close of the 1938 racing season the SCTA crowned its first individual points champion: Ernie McAffee of the Road Runners. Two more Road Runners, Wally Parks and Eldon Snapp, put out the first issue of the SCTA *Racing News,* a four-page mimeographed monthly newsletter that was free to members but cost everyone else a nickel. It listed the upcoming race schedule, gave the latest news, and contributed to a sense of belonging for young men who often did not fit in at school or in other social settings approved by their elders. In their clubs, and at the dry lakes under the umbrella of the SCTA, the hop-ups had found other brothers to hang with, goals to shoot for, and places to go besides the street.

Of course, many of the fellows who raced at Muroc still loved to drag on the streets, despite the danger and the unyielding disapproval of authorities. One of them was a jaunty twenty-year-old named Bob Estes, who had developed a pretty good reputation as an outlaw street racer. He worked at a Union gas station at the corner of Pico and Sepulveda in West Los Angeles, and he let it be known to all comers that the station closed at 10 p.m. if anyone ever wanted to take him on. The police knew about Estes and sometimes tailed him after he got off work just in case something was brewing. But no cops were around on the evening a man in a black Packard pulled into the station a few minutes before quitting time.

The man had black hair, a mustache, and a solid chest and shoulders. He dressed nice and looked nice in the seat of his sleekly luxurious convertible. Now, it's possible this man did not know about Estes and his reputation, but it's more probable he knew exactly who he was. The man in the Packard had raced at the dry lakes and on the street, and he enjoyed both, so perhaps he was playing it coy. But while Estes was filling his tank, the man started asking him questions about his car.

Estes's ride, a rakish black 1925 Model T roadster with white trim, sat in a visible spot in the station lot. Its speed features included an Ed Winfield-designed carburetor and one of those Ruckstell rear axles from Berkeley. It had gone 107 miles per hour at Muroc and punished street challengers around the city. Being his pride and joy, Estes kept it shiny and clean and ready to rumble at all times.

"I see we both like black cars," said the man in the Packard admiringly.

By this time Estes may have realized who the man in the Packard was, but he may have decided to play it coy himself and pretend he didn't recognize Clark Gable.

"Yeah," said Estes. "Too bad your Packard won't go like my T."

Estes finished filling the Packard, and Gable paid him. "You really think it's faster than my Packard?" Gable said, intrigued.

As if in reply, Estes walked across the lot and started the engine. It emitted a deep guttural growl. The T didn't need to move a muscle; it just *sounded* fast.

Estes repeated his claim and proposed a little match race to prove it. First one to Santa Monica Boulevard wins five bucks. Gable thought he could handle those stakes and agreed. After all, his 12-cylinder Packard, one of the most expensive Packards built in the 1930s, had a little hop in it too.

While Estes went to turn off the lights and lock the doors, Gable drove out of the station and waited in the street, his engine purring in the sweet warmth of a southern California night.

Two views of early 1900s driving: Above, motorists in Yosemite Valley. Below, sporting goods manufacturer Albert Spalding and his wife on a spin around La Jolla.

An automobile repair garage, circa 1908.

Two pioneers of cross-country automobile travel: Lester Whitman, left, and Eugene Hammond.

Out for a Sunday drive amid the cypresses of Monterey.

CAR RACING,
SPORT OF DAREDEVILS

Left: Earl Cooper, in an advertisement for a Sacramento paper.

Below: Driver and riding mechanic in a southern California race.

Opposite page: The one and only Barney Oldfield, cigar and all.

Two scenes of Barney Oldfield in action: Above, in a Christie racecar leading a Curtiss biplane at Ascot track in Los Angeles. Below, closing in on Eddie Pullen in No. 4 at Corona in 1916.

MY ONLY LIFE INSURANCE
Firestone
TIRES

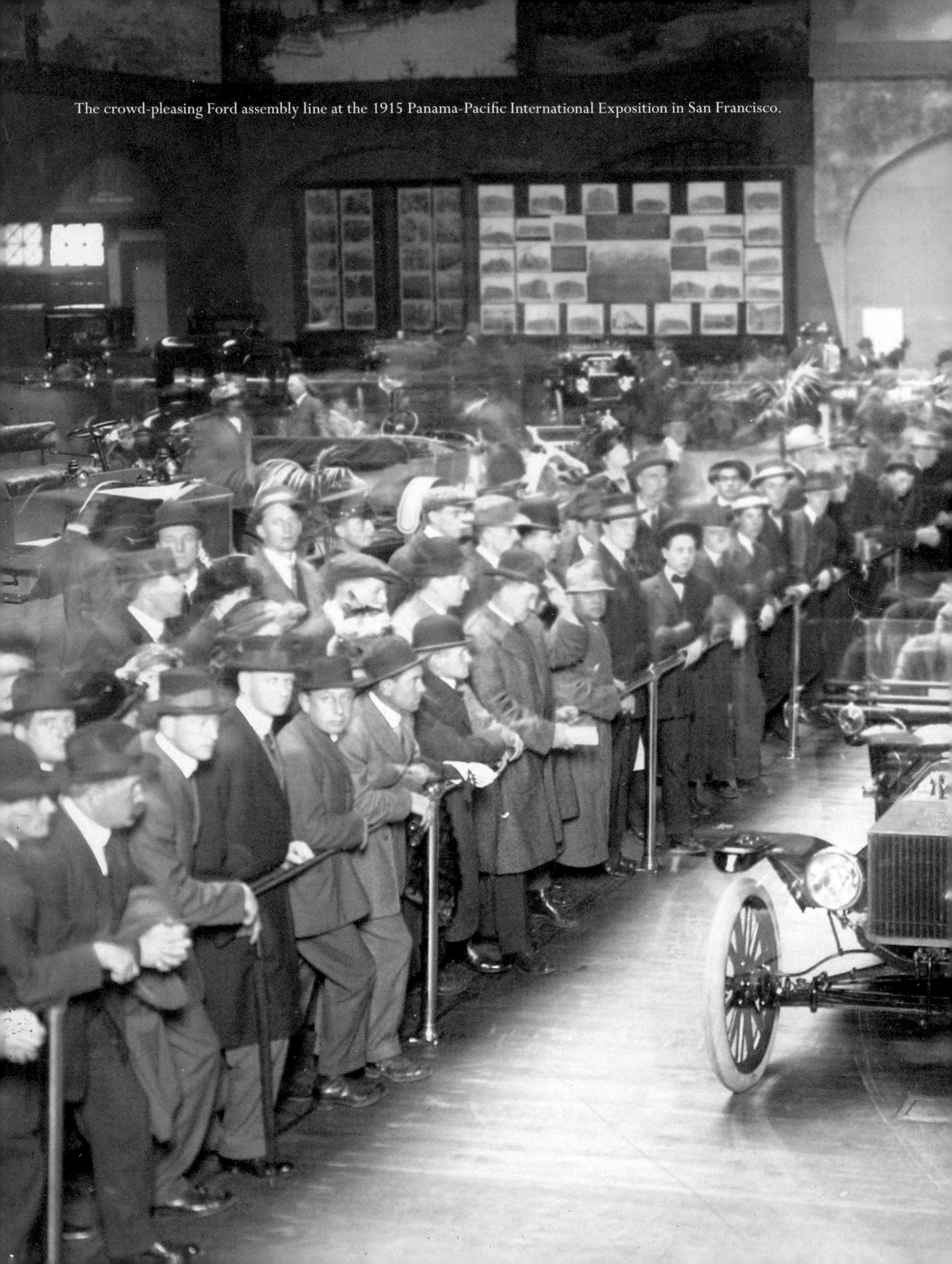

The crowd-pleasing Ford assembly line at the 1915 Panama-Pacific International Exposition in San Francisco.

Motor Company

The glamorous Mary Pickford and chauffeur, in her custom Pierce-Arrow.

Food and automobiles begin their ongoing romance: Carpenter's Drive-In, Los Angeles, 1932.

Mack Sennett's slapstick Keystone Cops pioneered chase scenes in the movies.

A gallon of gas sold for less than the tax on it at a 1930s Hollywood service station.

Clark Gable, the King of Hollywood, poses next to one of his many regal rides, a Packard Twin Six.

San Francisco Buick distributor Charles Howard and his prize racehorse, Seabiscuit.

Gary Cooper, Gable's screen rival in the 1930s, also loved beautiful women and fast, beautiful cars.

On sunny days in the 1930s people flocked to San Francisco's Ocean Beach—and created traffic jams while they were at it.

Harley Earl stands next to the experimental Firebird prototype he designed in the 1950s. Earl began designing customs in Hollywood in the 1920s, went to work for General Motors, and became the most influential American car designer of the 20th century.

Two of Harley Earl's automobile visions: Above, the Corvette, America's first sports car. Below, tail fins on a Cadillac.

Hot rods racing at the Pomona drags, circa 1954.

EIGHTEEN

Gable and Lombard

Bob Estes's Model T handled Clark Gable's Packard, and Gable could not believe it. He asked for and got a double-or-nothing rematch. They turned around and went back the other way, and the T spanked him again. Estes drove away ten bucks richer, and Gable drove away muttering to himself.

The Packard cost close to eight thousand dollars, new. And what did the T go for originally? Five hundred? A thousand? Whatever it was it wasn't much, and Estes hadn't driven it new off the showroom floor either. It was probably a hand-me-down from his dad or maybe he picked it up for a few bucks from an aunt who only drove it to church and on ladies-who-lunch outings. How he got it didn't matter. What mattered was what he did with it, and what he did with it blew Gable away. With new parts from Ed Winfield's shop and old refurbished parts from the junkyard, plus his own knowledge and experience and desire, Estes had home-engineered a machine that could go as fast as —no, faster than— one of America's most expensive factory cars, driven by one of its richest and most glamorous men.

Was this a freak event? Something that could never happen again? Not at all. Estes, who later raced at Indianapolis and became a car dealer in Los Angeles, "was but one of hundreds of enthusiasts wheeling cars around the city with performance that positively stunned owners of expensive, seemingly unbeatable machinery like Gable's Packard," said automotive writer Brock Yates. Speed had been democratized, and the King of Hollywood talked about it for days afterward. Finally, who should appear at the Union station at Pico and Sepulveda where Estes worked? None other than Carole Lombard, one of America's most beautiful and glamorous movie stars, and Gable's girlfriend.

"Clark has talked about nothing but that car for two days," she told Estes, and offered to buy it from him. When he refused she upped her offer. But the answer was the same and she left empty-handed.

This disappointed Lombard immensely because she knew how much Clark would've enjoyed that car. Not only because it went so fast but because it was a hopped-up version of the car he had driven as a boy. Born in Ohio in the early 1900s at the beginning of the automobile age, Gable had driven and worked on cars all his life. His father bought a Model T for the family and showed him how to take apart and reassemble an engine. Father and son worked on the T together. It gave them something in common, something to talk about that interested them both, and it strengthened a sometimes troubled relationship.

The youngster's mechanical skills also served him well as he grew older. After dropping out of high school and leaving home he found a job at Firestone Tire and Rubber in Akron. But eventually a different sort of work called him, and Gable came to Hollywood in the early 1920s hoping to make it as an actor. He struggled at first to get noticed, working as a gas station mechanic to help pay the rent, but even during the lean times he loved nice cars, as nice as he could afford. "We used to bum around together," said Paul Fix, a friend and fellow struggling actor. "Clark had an old automobile that he was real proud of—an open-top roamer. It was designed after the Rolls Royce. He'd drive us out to Griffith Park, where they'd put in a public golf course. I owned a putter and Clark had an iron. We'd look around the roughs for stray balls, then play all day with two clubs."

Gable moved from bit parts to leading man roles in the early thirties, and his rugged if unconventional good looks (his ears were rather large) turned him into a movie heartthrob. He steamed up the screen with the likes of Jean Harlow and won an Oscar for his performance in *It Happened One Night*. The 1934 film includes a wonderful sequence in which Gable and Claudette Colbert, who also won an Oscar for the movie, are doing something that came into vogue in the nineteen teens with the widespread use of automobiles: hitchhiking. "Vogue" is not the right term, actually, because even back then hitchhiking was potentially dangerous and had a slightly unseemly reputation. While most of the young men who did it merely wanted to catch a ride in an automobile rather than hop a train, a few of them preferred to conk the driver on the head and steal his wallet. Such was the fear anyhow. Others regarded hitchhikers as freeloaders. "What is a hitchhiker?" asked one newspaper editorial. "He is what many California motorists call a ride-moocher—a person who asks for a lift in almost any car that happens to come along." Women hitchhiked too, although not as much as men and almost never alone, and a young woman who did it was courting scandal. This was what made the scene between Colbert and Gable so much fun and highly provocative for its time. Gable's character begins by bragging about his knowledge of hitchhiking and showing Colbert how to do it. But no one stops for him and he gets more and more ticked off as cars whizz past them. Colbert, supposedly the innocent one, hikes her skirt up, shows off her leg, and stops the next car that appears. Gable's brash he-man attitude became a touchstone for the battle of the sexes in Depression America; if a man became too forward on a date, a woman might say to him as a way to back him off and get him to act more properly, "Who do you think you are? Clark Gable?"

Gable loved expensively tailored clothes, loved to dress well, and kept himself immaculately groomed. "He was so clean," said a female admirer, "you could eat off him." It was the same with his automobiles. When the money started pouring in he rewarded himself with a garage full of clean, shiny, and fast cars. His dad could barely afford a Model T, but here he was, a high school dropout from farm-country Ohio who could write a check for a custom-made 1935 Duesenberg SSJ, a car so beautiful, so fast, and so unique that only one of them existed on the entire planet. Unfortunately for Gable, that one SSJ belonged to his acting rival in Hollywood, Gary Cooper.

"There was a competition in Duesenberg ownership between Clark Gable and Gary Cooper," said auto historian Fred Kern. The fact that Cooper owned the SSJ and Gable did not irritated the latter and pleased the former. Like Gable, the star of *The Virginian* and *A Farewell to Arms* was a man's man on screen and off. He hunted, fished, courted fabulously beautiful women, and drove fast, fabulously beautiful cars.

"Cars, cars, cars—Cooper loved cars," recalled his daughter Maria. "They were a lifelong passion." This passion made him feel protective too. His daughter tells a story about him in his later years when he and Anthony Quinn had popped the hood of Cooper's new Jaguar and were admiring it on the driveway of his Brentwood estate. Fellow actor Peter Lawford appeared and began to fiddle with something in the engine. "Peter," said Cooper, stopping him. "You can fiddle with me, you can fiddle with my wife, but you can't fiddle with my car." Probably the word he used was some other f-word, not "fiddle."

Well before this, well before his daughter was even a twinkle in his eye, Coop could choose from his own private stable of Duesenbergs—a yellow one with green fenders perhaps, or if that didn't suit his mood, one painted canary yellow and robin's egg blue. Whatever it happened to be, said his daughter, he "would take his favorite car of the moment to the Muroc dry lake bed, where drivers could test their 'babies.'"

Cooper nearly competed in the most famous celebrity race ever held at Muroc, a match race between the automobile babies of Hollywood agent Phil Berg and Zeppo Marx, the fourth Marx brother. Zeppo appeared in *Monkey Business*, *Duck Soup,* and other comedies before his brothers decided to downsize their act and he lost his spot. On all things automotive, however, Chico, Groucho, and Harpo all deferred to Zeppo, who really knew a camshaft from a crankshaft. He drove a new Mercedes SSK roadster, and one night in 1932 he and Chico cruised over to Al Jolson's place on Sunset to play some cards. Being a connoisseur of fine automobiles, Zeppo observed with some interest a sharp-looking Model J Duesenberg parked outside. The J belonged to Berg, who represented a stable of A-list stars including Gable and Cooper, and during the evening the conversation inevitably turned to the cars out front and whose had more zip: Phil's or Zeppo's? Zeppo said he'd put down ten thousand dollars to find the answer. Phil called him and raised him, and when they were done one-upping each other the wager had climbed to twenty-five thousand, not counting side bets. Both agreed to settle things right then and there with a trip to a street-racing spot in Santa Monica until someone proposed a better venue for a showdown: Muroc Dry Lake.

Preparations began the next day. To drive the Mercedes, Zeppo hired Joe Reindl, a mechanic at Hollywood Spring and Axle on Sunset. Zeppo knew him from the repair work he'd done on his Mercedes, and Reindl also raced cars. To find someone to drive for him, Phil Berg called his neighbor in Beverly Hills, E. L. Cord, who knew Duesenbergs because he owned the company that built them. He also owned the companies that built two other fine cars, the Auburn and the Cord, as well as engine and aircraft firms that later evolved into Checker Cabs and American Airlines. The original creators of the Duesenberg marque, the Duesenberg brothers of Indiana, had focused their talents on the engineering and racing side of their automobiles. But after Cord took over the company, he introduced the style and elegance that made Dueseys appeal to the likes of Berg, Cooper, Gable, and the Hollywood set. Coming to California from his native Midwest, the patrician Cord fit right into the upper tier of Los Angeles society. His mansion, known as "Cordhaven," looked like a little piece of Colonial America dropped into Beverly Hills. Actually, a big piece: thirty-two thousand square feet with sixteen bedrooms and nearly two dozen bathrooms, every one of them outfitted with 14-carat gold and silver fixtures. The unveiling of Cordhaven helped launch the career of its architect, Paul Revere Williams. Williams, an African American, went on to design many star homes and notable buildings in the Los Angeles area, including the Beverly Hills Hotel and Saks Fifth Avenue. He also participated in the design of the flying saucer-like Theme Building at Los Angeles International Airport.

Cord gave Berg the name of a driver, Eddie Miller, who participated in the testing program for new Auburn automobiles at Muroc. He also ran a repair shop in Hollywood a block away from Paramount Studios and had worked on the Duesenbergs of Hoot Gibson, Cecil B. DeMille, and others.

So it was set: Miller vs. Reindl, Berg vs. Marx, Duesenberg vs. Mercedes. Word about the throwdown spread quickly around Hollywood, and Gary Cooper briefly thought about entering his Duesenberg phaeton. But Zeppo's Mercedes was "lower, lighter, smaller [and] supercharged," and Cooper's slower and heavier tourer didn't stand a chance against it. Even Berg's 265-horsepower Duesenberg, which was quicker than Cooper's, was considered a poor bet against the German sprinter.

In early October four busloads of Hollywood celebrities took the bumpy ride out to Muroc to put the bragging to rest and let the cars have the final say. Cooper, Gable, and Lombard were there. So were Zeppo and his brothers, Mae West, Al Jolson, whose card game had started it all, and Bebe Daniels. Daniels, a musical star who appeared in Busby Berkeley's *42nd Street* that year, loved cars as much as any man and drove them just as hard, a habit that earned her a slew of speeding tickets. After one such ticket, a Santa Ana traffic judge, unconvinced that she was ever going to lighten up on the pedal, sent her to jail for ten days, causing a national sensation. Being a movie star, Bebe received celebrity treatment in jail, dining on catered restaurant meals delivered to her by a uniformed waiter, and lounging on furniture brought into her cell to make her feel more at home. Visitors gave her chocolates and flowers. Photographers snapped her picture, and she granted numerous jailhouse interviews, although even she finally tired of all the attention. After a guard informed her that yet another reporter had come to interview her, she responded, "Oh, I can't see him. Tell him I'm out."

Skipping the long bus ride, Wallace Beery flew out to Muroc in his private plane, landing on the lakebed along with other star planes. It's not clear how E. L. Cord got there—by plane, bus, or car—but he too came out to watch. Harry A. Miller, who in another year would return to the Midwest and leave such earnestly silly hijinks behind him, served as the starter. Ben Lyon, star of *Hell's Angels* with Jean Harlow, drove the pace car. In a Lincoln he guided the Duesenberg and the Mercedes to a rolling start of 35 miles per hour, after which he got out of the way and let Miller and Reindl have at it.

They ran the five-mile circuit, Reindl bursting ahead at the start and Miller steadily hauling him back in. The first time around, the two went back and forth, nip and tuck, a virtual dead heat. Over the next two laps Miller poured on the coal and won easily with a 102-miles-per-hour average over fifteen miles. On a grand scale one could see the Duesenberg's win as a triumph for American technology over German, but it was probably more just a case of Phil's car beating Zeppo's. Everybody had lots of laughs, and Phil shared a cut of his $25,000 payday with his driver.

With so many Americans struggling to earn a living, Hollywood stars knew they had to be careful about showy displays of wealth or else their public image and box office drawing power would be hurt. But because the Duesey was an American car, built in America by American workers, the public tended to view it with a little more tolerance. This may partly explain why Cooper, who in 1935 earned more than three hundred thousand dollars while most American families were lucky to make one or two thousand dollars that year, could order his one-of-a-kind Duesenberg SSJ, and why Gable would want to have one just like it.

Cooper's SSJ was smaller, faster, and sportier than the Duesenberg touring car he had almost entered in the Berg-Marx race. It featured "a short 125-inch wheelbase chassis and a supercharged engine with two carburetors, making it the most powerful and fastest car Duesenberg ever produced." Gable evidently saw it and had to have one for himself, and so E. L. Cord's factory built one for him too. Cord's son Charlie delivered it to Gable on the MGM studio lot. Only two Duesenberg SSJs were ever made; Gable liked to joke that his was a foot longer than Cooper's.

Like Cooper, Gable owned more than one Duesey, and the Duesenberg SSJ was different than the Duesenberg JN he drove on the night of the Mayfair Ball. The Mayfair Ball remains one of the most storied evenings in old Hollywood lore, for this was when Gable's romance with Lombard began in earnest. Hosted by the Mayfair Club, a private Hollywood social club, it took place in January 1936 at the Victor Hugo Restaurant in Beverly Hills. It was a formal dress affair with a theme of white: The women all dressed in white gowns, the men in white tie and tails. Bouquets of white roses and gardenias graced every table. Attendants in white jackets served drinks and hors d'oeuvres to Humphrey Bogart, Claudette Colbert, Henry Fonda, Barbara Stanwyck, Jimmy Stewart, Gloria Swanson, Spencer Tracy, Loretta Young ,and hundreds of other beautiful and famous glitterati, all clad in white. Cab Calloway, in white tie and tails, conducted his swing orchestra playing dance tunes.

Wearing something flimsy and clingy, Lombard was herself a vision of white with her blond hair and pale complexion. She served as honorary hostess for the evening, a tribute to her status as one of Hollywood's most beloved stars. Despite her beauty-queen looks, Lombard, in her late twenties, never took herself too seriously; she was the kind of actress who would take a pie in the face if the scene called for it. Indeed, earlier in her career she had worked for the pie-throwing king, Mack Sennett, who had spotted her talent and cast her in several of his pictures. With him she developed a daffy comedic style that brought her to the attention of Paramount, which signed her to a five-year contract around the same time that Metro Goldwyn Mayer was signing Gable. The two appeared together in a 1932 film called *No Man of Her Own,* and this may have been when they first started dating. They went as a couple to the match race at Muroc that year, and they were still an item when Gable pulled into Bob Estes's gas station a year or two later. But at some point they broke up, and they had not seen each other for quite some time until Gable, looking about as good as a man can look in formal evening wear, strode into the Mayfair Ball that night. Lombard, as hostess, stood up from her table near the door and said hello.

Whether it was an old flame rekindled or a new one sparking to life, both felt the exchange of heat. Gable was legally separated from his wife; Lombard's husband had died a few years before. Both were, as they say, available. Both had come to the ball with dates but when Cab Calloway's band started in on "Cheek to Cheek" and the two of them stepped onto the dance floor together, everyone else in the world just melted away. After the music stopped Lombard suggested they step outside for some fresh air. To which Gable replied, How about we take a spin in my new Duesey?

Lombard could not resist, and the two slipped out of the ball and into his beautiful and luxurious Duesenberg JN (an automobile that resides today, among other beautiful and luxurious Duesenbergs, at the Blackhawk Automotive Museum in Danville.) In a short while their drive brought them to the Beverly Wilshire Hotel, where Gable lived.

He suggested they go up and see his apartment.

She looked at him and said, "Who do you think you are? Clark Gable?"

Stung by her sarcasm (evidently he did not hear no from women very often), Gable sped back to the ball in a huff. The night ended with cool goodbyes. The next day, after reconsidering her position, Lombard sent Gable a gift to soothe his hurt feelings. He called her as soon as he received it, and the two started seeing each other in a more serious way.

Well, not so serious sometimes. Lombard, an independent spirit who played sports when she was a girl and had older brothers, felt comfortable around men, comfortable enough to play jokes on the biggest hunk in Hollywood. With Valentine's Day coming up, she ventured over to a local junkyard and paid twenty-five dollars for a rusted-out Model T that barely ran. She then had it towed to a body shop where they painted it white with red hearts.

On February 14 the car was delivered to the MGM lot where Gable was beginning rehearsals for *San Francisco*, his movie about the 1906 quake. A note on the steering wheel said "You're driving me crazy," with no other identifying message. Gable, delighted by the gag, gave his *San Francisco* costar Spencer Tracy a ride around the lot in the T. When it broke down, some extras helped them push it back to their set.

Gable got his revenge on Lombard on their next date: an evening of dinner and dancing at the Trocadero Ballroom in Hollywood. Slipping into one of those clingy numbers that made men's knees buckle, she expected him to pick her up in style in the Duesenberg JN. Little did she know that Clark had been doing some engine work on the T, and this was the car he arrived in. Not altogether pleased by the surprise, she climbed into the tattered passenger seat with the springs sticking out, and they clattered off on their date.

Lombard had a more troubled view of machines than Gable, arising from a bad car accident she was in as a teenager that had gashed her face. Her surgeon told her that if she used anesthetic during the operation, it would relax her facial muscles and possibly disfigure her. With dreams of becoming an actress, she could ill afford that, so she endured more than a dozen stitches in her face without anesthetic. Over time, and with some plastic surgery, she was left with a small scar that all but faded. But the memories lingered, and she did not like it when Gable put a hopped-up new engine in the old T. He drove so fast it scared her, and she refused to ride in it again.

She much preferred the Duesenberg JN roadster, their Mayfair Ball car. Not long after the ball Gable decided to revamp it too. There were only ten Duesenberg JNs in existence, all with bodies crafted by a New York coachbuilder, but Gable wanted a more distinctive, one-of-a-kind look, and so he turned to the Pasadena firm of Bohman and Schwartz.

Bohman and Schwartz were among the best coachbuilders in America, the latest in a distinguished line of California automobile stylists that included George Bentel, Harley Earl, and Walter M. Murphy. Murphy in the mid-twenties ran another highly esteemed Pasadena design shop that had crafted the exquisite styling of the Doble Series E cars for Abner Doble. His company foundered during the Depression and Christian Bohman and Maurice Schwartz, two of his employees, went off to form their own coachbuilding firm. Both Bohman and Schwartz had emigrated from Europe (Sweden and Austria, respectively), and their designs blended Old World styling with that razzle-dazzle Hollywood thing. They earned a reputation for building "interesting cars for interesting people," some of whom included a Russian prince, the evangelist Father Divine, and Ethel Mars of the Mars candy fortune.

Clark Gable definitely fit into the "interesting people" category, and for his Duesenberg JN roadster Bohman and Schwarz called on their top designer, a forward-looking young stylist named W. Everett Miller. Miller's job was to free the JN of its NY look and give it one that said LA. He did this by lowering the car, extending and restyling the hood, flaring the fenders, and adding dual rear-mounted spare tires. Gable himself participated in the design process and worked with Miller to get the car just the way he wanted it, and it paid off. Carole Lombard loved it.

Already their favorite car, the remodeled Duesenberg JN became still more special to them, and they took it to Victor Hugo's and the Trocadero and on drives out to the seaside and mountains. They did not drive it, however, when they eloped, figuring it to be a tad too conspicuous for a secret getaway. Instead they opted for Otto Winkler's somewhat less attention-getting DeSoto.

Winkler was their press agent. It was March 1939. Given a couple of days off from shooting *Gone with the Wind,* Gable called Lombard at her house in Bel Air early in the morning. They had been talking about it forever and now, he said, the time was ripe. Let's get married. She was a doozy, that one, always up for a grand adventure. Lombard said yes, and after they rang off, Gable called Winkler to tell him to get ready because he was about to go on a road trip. Everything was last minute and tossed together. "Packing their wedding clothes in a suitcase," wrote one biographer, "they made the trip in their shabbiest shirts and dungarees, with Lombard wearing no makeup and her hair tied in pigtails." The two stars arrived incognito at Winkler's house. His wife, who was staying home, made sandwiches and thermoses of coffee for them. The three of them piled into the blue DeSoto and headed east from Los Angeles on the highway that was originally called the National Old Trails Road. In the late twenties the federal government had stopped calling highways by proper names and replaced them with numbers; the Old Trails Road was now Route 66.

Gable drove, Winkler rode shotgun, and Lombard sat in back so as not to be spotted sitting next to the King of Hollywood. Gable, who won this title after balloting by more than 20 million movie fans in a newspaper poll, switched places with Lombard and hid in the backseat whenever they stopped at a gas station. Without makeup and dressed in shabby dungarees, Lombard could get in and out of places without being spotted. But Gable—well, people *noticed* him. At the Arizona border they bought flowers to wear during the ceremony—lilies of the valley for her, a carnation boutonniere for him—and then pushed across the Colorado River to reach the old mining town of Kingman by four in the afternoon.

After filling out the paperwork at the town hall, they drove over to St. John's Methodist Church where a minister was waiting for them. Winkler had called ahead to ask him to conduct the ceremony without identifying the bride and groom. The bride disappeared into a separate room, put on some makeup and brushed her hair, and emerged wearing a lovely yet modest light-gray designer ensemble. The groom, in a blue suit, nervously fingered a platinum wedding band he had bought four months earlier with this day in mind. After the vows he slipped the ring on her finger and she cried. It was his third marriage and her second, and the first one they got right.

After the ceremony Lombard called her mother, and Gable giddily came on the line to talk to her too. Outside Kingman they sent telegrams to the studios and the gossip columnists to let the world in on the news as well. They had done it. They had had a quiet, dignified ceremony without anyone in the business except their friend Winkler being the wiser. Now they didn't care who knew. Passing back into California they stopped at a Harvey House, probably in Needles, and ate jumbo steak dinners. Everyone there recognized the two stars, and they happily signed autographs for anyone who asked. Then they got back on the highway and headed west across the desert. Winkler took the wheel and the two newlyweds sat in back holding hands as the tiny headlamps of the DeSoto cut through the darkness that lay ahead.

Tach it up, tach it up: The Beach Boys and a '63 Corvette Stingray.

PART FOUR

Wheels of Change

NINETEEN

1942

Beginning in 1939, a time of calamitous events on the world stage, a series of tragedies struck the California car community and the nation.

The first of them was Rust Heinz, whose dreams took the form of an automobile called the "Phantom Corsair," and like many automobile dreams of this period, it owed a measure of its inspiration to Buckminster Fuller. In the early 1930s Fuller, influenced by airplanes and aeronautical principles, designed a three-wheel, pod-shaped car known as the Dymaxion, whose purpose was to show that an automobile could get good gas mileage, carry a number of passengers, and still travel at decent speeds. Beset by mechanical and other problems the car performed better in theory than in real life, but the inventor's vision of the future inspired other dreamers around the country, including Heinz.

Rust's grandfather had founded the H. J. Heinz "57 Varieties" Company, and his father built it into a national food products empire. But Rust's interests centered less on the family business and more on automobiles. *Esquire* called his designs for the Phantom Corsair a "conception of the car of tomorrow" and prominently featured them in the magazine. For the next step, turning his paper flights of fancy into iron, steel, and sheet aluminum, Heinz turned to Bohman and Schwartz, coachbuilders for Clark Gable's Duesenberg JN and other fine automobiles. The Pasadena firm crafted the Phantom's "wildly voluptuous," impossible-not-to-stop-and-stare-at body, which looked even better in real life than it did on the pages of a magazine. Everything about its shape was extreme. Looking out of narrow, curving windows, the driver and three others sat in the front seat while two more in the back faced to the rear. The Phantom Corsair appeared in all its glory on the cover of *Motor Age* and in a 1938 movie, *The Young in Heart*, where they referred to it as "The Flying Wombat." Inspired by the car's warm reception, Heinz planned to put it into limited production and sell it to the public. But a fatal car accident in July 1939 killed those ambitions and his family's ambitions for him. He was twenty-five.

The chassis used for the Phantom Corsair was that of an 810 Cord, one of the cars manufactured by E. L. Cord, the prominent Beverly Hills industrialist. An employee of Cord's and the top designer at his company was Gordon Buehrig, who, early in his career, apprenticed under Harley Earl at the Art and Color Section of General Motors. Entering an in-house design contest at GM, Buehrig submitted drawings for an automobile that looked very much like what the Cord 810 eventually became. But the judges saw little merit in his design, and it finished in last place.

Some years later Buehrig left GM and went to work for Cord, who was looking to develop a car with a price point between his high-end Duesenberg and the more moderately priced Auburn. Buehrig dusted off his old drawings, made some improvements, and designed a car that E. L. liked so much he named it after himself. In 1936 the Cord 810 made its sensational debut, and the celebrity set fell in love with its strikingly beautiful appearance. (So did the Museum of Modern Art in New York, which later praised it as an automotive work of art.) Olympic ice skating queen Sonja Henjie was said to have owned two Cords. Whenever she needed to get around on land, Amelia Earhart drove one. So did Johnny Weissmuller, the Olympic gold-medal swimmer who played Tarzan in the movies, and Tom Mix, who breathed his last breaths in the plush interior of a Cord 812.

One story of Mix's death begins with him on a bar stool in Tucson, chatting with a fellow who was about to fly his private plane to Phoenix. Mix starred in a traveling Wild West circus named after him, and this was why he was in Tucson. The other performers in the circus went from town to town in trailer-pulling trucks and their own vehicles, but not Tom. He drove in style in his cream-colored Cord, the kind of car that, when it glides up to a movie premiere or luxury hotel, people just have to stop to look at because they know somebody important is about to get out. The cowboy hero of hundreds of Westerns knew what his fans expected of him and never wished to let them down. Plus, he liked cool things. This was why, on the day he died, he was wearing TM bar–brand cowboy boots, an embroidered cowboy shirt, a diamond-studded belt buckle, and a ten-gallon white Stetson. One account says he was also carrying six grand in cash, close to two grand in traveler's checks, and a bag of jewels.

Why would somebody want to carry so much cash and a bag of jewels around with him? Well, if you were Tom Mix, you'd know the answer to that.

It was the way he lived. Like it or not, that was the King of the Cowboys for you, the same man who put a leather saddle on the roof of his car and neon outside his Hollywood mansion. His Cord had similar flair, with a top made of black mohair and red piping along the edges. Its supercharged engine could also explore the upper regions of speed, which was where Mix liked to travel. Estimates of how fast he was going when he was killed range from 50 to 80 miles an hour, but it was probably closer to the latter figure because you have to drive pretty fast to beat an airplane. That was Mix's bar bet: him on wheels versus the other guy on wings. First one to Phoenix wins. No one can say who would have won the bet, however, because Mix, age sixty, never finished. Screaming across the desert near Florence he came up too fast on a highway construction crew, swerved to avoid them, and collided with a road barrier. His car flipped. A reinforced metal suitcase, perhaps carrying all those jewels, hurtled forward from the backseat and struck him from behind. It broke his neck and killed him instantly.

Mix's death, in October 1940, occurred a month before the election, for the third time, of Franklin Roosevelt as president of the United States. It was a time when national and international events forced themselves into the lives of ordinary people all across the world. The German Army had overrun Europe, the Luftwaffe was bombing Britain. Through the election and into the following year, Americans debated what their response should be to yet another war on European soil: Stay out or get involved? Although neutral in name, the United States had already chosen sides, supplying Britain with fighter planes and ships on generous financial terms and slapping embargos on another hostile foreign power, Japan, which had invaded China and Indochina and formed an alliance with the German-Italian Axis. Then came the December 7 attack on Pearl Harbor, shattering the peace along with the illusion of neutrality.

Americans reacted with shock and horror to these events, and they responded to FDR's radio address to Congress asking for a declaration of war with actions of their own. Defeating the Nazis and Imperial Japan was going to require lots of things, not the least of which was money. The government began issuing defense bonds and stamps to finance the war effort, and this was how Carole Lombard felt she could help. A month after Pearl Harbor she left Los Angeles on a bond tour across the West and Midwest. She rode the train with her friend and business agent Otto Winkler, and her star power helped sell bonds and attract big crowds in Salt Lake City and other towns. In Indianapolis, not far from her birthplace of Fort Wayne, she headlined a rally that drew a crowd of three thousand. Military bands played "The Star Spangled Banner" and a church choir sang "The Lord's Prayer." In her brief speech Lombard encouraged people to dig into their wallets and purses for Uncle Sam, and they did, buying $2 million in bonds that day. After the rally Lombard decided to take a break from the tour and fly home to Los Angeles with her mother and Winkler. All three of them died when their plane crashed outside Las Vegas. The pilot, crew, and other passengers on the flight died as well.

The news of Lombard's death added to the grief already felt by so many. Because she was on a bond tour serving her country, her death was considered a casualty of war. President Roosevelt sent a telegram of condolence to her husband, who flew to Las Vegas to assist in the search and recovery at the crash site in the Potosi Mountains. Otherwise Clark Gable stayed out of public view, disappearing into the Oregon woods to fish and clear his head. The car he drove to Oregon was a Dodge station wagon, the same one he and Lombard had taken on their hunting and fishing trips together. The station wagon, Gable could live with; the Duesenberg JN, he could not. The car he drove on the night of the Mayfair Ball had too much of her in it, too many memories. He sent it off to Canada and never had anything more to do with it.

The surprise attack on Pearl Harbor killed twenty-four hundred United States servicemen, sunk the USS *Arizona* and other American ships, destroyed war planes on the ground, and scared people up and down the West Coast, who worried that the Japanese Zeros might target them next. Beginning on December 9, nighttime blackouts brought traffic and normal life to a temporary halt in Los Angeles. "Blackouts became more than fiction here," said reporter Maury Godchaux, who found out personally how real they could be. "Pitched in inky blackness, the nation's fifth largest city groped around in a quiet terror, guardedly afraid, comforted and dismayed by those new characters, the air raid wardens."

Other California cities experienced much the same thing in the coming days: air raid sirens followed by the lights of buildings and homes going dark, then popping back on after the all-clear signal. In many coastal cities, military officials established "dimout areas"—areas where building lights needed to be out at night for defense reasons. The dimout rules applied to driving too. Cars under these regulations could only drive with their parking lights on and headlights off.

More drastic events followed. At Christmas, with hundreds of thousands of young American men spending their last holiday at home before going into training for combat, Japanese forces continued their advance across Asia, driving through the jungles of the Malay Peninsula and parachuting onto the island of Sumatra in the Dutch East Indies. Their mission: seize control of the world's rubber supply and cripple the ability of the United States to fight back.

"Rubber," said one analyst at the time, "is indispensable in modern warfare," for it was used in everything from cars, trucks, airplanes, and ships to antiaircraft barrage balloons and gas masks. Despite warnings, as this analyst said, that "the dependence of this country upon a single, concentrated area for any basic raw material was economically unsound," and a threat to the national defense, the United States relied heavily on rubber imports from Malaysia and the East Indies, which produced three-quarters of the world's natural rubber. This reliance became a weakness when Japan captured Singapore and cut off all rubber exports to the United States and its allies.

Fearing a possible war with Japan, the United States had stockpiled rubber for the past two years, but these reserves came nowhere close to supplying the seven hundred thousand tons of rubber used by Americans every year. The country had to produce more rubber and preserve what it had, and it needed to do both things very quickly. Four days after Pearl Harbor the government banned the sale of new tires and rubber products to anyone who did not meet strict eligibility requirements. On January 4, after the end of the holiday season, it ordered a nationwide rationing of auto and truck tires. "For the time being," said Leon Henderson, director of the federal Office of Price Management, "production of new passenger tires will be almost entirely eliminated and production of new truck tires will be curtailed." All new tires would be made for military purposes only. New cars currently in production would still have four tires, but no spares would be issued unless they were made of reclaimed rubber. Production of nonessential rubber items such as tennis balls and bathing suits would stop immediately.

Henderson, whose name is largely forgotten now but who appeared on the cover of *Time* magazine during these months and became a prominent domestic wartime figure, announced the formation of civilian tire rationing boards around the nation. Almost immediately a black market for tires sprung up. Tire plants around California and the United States—Firestone, Goodrich, United States Rubber, Goodyear—had already gone on twenty-four-hour production schedules, manufacturing tires around the clock. Synthetic rubber, a solution to the crisis suggested by some, offered only a limited fix. Synthetic rubber factories were being rapidly developed and rushed into operation, but at best, said the government, they could produce only three hundred thousand tons of synthetic rubber by the next year, 1943, although that was still not nearly enough to supply what was needed for an all-out global war. Further, even if the United States met these ambitious production targets, synthetic rubber could not fully replace the natural kind. Synthetics worked well enough for treads and sidewalls, but not for the body of a tire. And even synthetic rubber products contained some natural rubber.

The grim news continued from overseas. The Philippines came under siege, and American soldiers under General Douglas MacArthur retreated into the jungles and mountains of the Bataan Peninsula. There they fought hard against a determined enemy that forced their retreat to the tiny island of Corregidor. More tough fighting ensued even as the government was issuing the first of many pleas for Americans to search "from attic to cellar" for scrap to contribute to the national defense. The first scrap drives began in January and continued virtually until war's end. Although many people were struggling to make ends meet and didn't have much to give, they found things they could live without: "old stoves, pieces of plumbing, crank handles, tools, lawn mowers, tire chains, bedsteads, flatirons, garden implements, bed springs, all kinds of metal, rubber, rags, Manila rope and burlap bags." All these throwaway items found a second life in warfare. Silk scarves and nylon hosiery could be turned into parachutes. Even waste fats and cooking grease had potential military value, serving in the creation of glycerin, a component of gunpowder.

So much of the scrap was vital in so many ways, including as the raw material for reclaimed steel, iron, tin, copper, lead, and other badly needed metals. But rubber remained an urgent and overriding concern. Thus the emergency call for any and all rubber items, especially old car tires. Households and businesses everywhere turned in mountains of tires, big enough for the Boy Scouts who were helping collect them to climb around and play in them.

In early March, Price Administrator Henderson reappeared on front pages across the country with his startling testimony to the United States Senate that the government might "requisition" the tires of millions of passenger cars around the country. The Associated Press wrote, "The public tonight was told frankly and grimly that no rubber is available for new or recapped tires, that the speed limit may be cut to 40 miles an hour, that gasoline rationing may be invoked, and that the government may soon requisition tires from private owners." Of the 27 million passenger cars in the United States, 1 million of them could be "immobilized" by July so the government could take their tires. Even more drastic, 12 million more cars could be immobilized in 1943 for the same reason. "There is no sense fooling ourselves," said Henderson. "We face the possibility of requisitioning all rubber stocks."

But no matter what, he continued, the nation's 17 million war workers had to get to their jobs. They would receive priority if hard choices had to be made about who got to keep the tires on their cars.

Hard choices were being made all over—by men going off to war, by women going to work in jobs vacated by the men, by children learning to climb under their desks at school in case enemy bombers appeared in the skies overhead. Other people had no choice at all.

In February the president had issued an executive order calling for the roundup of Japanese immigrants and their families along the West Coast, and their detention in internment camps away from the strategic coastal zones. Most of the 120,000 Japanese affected by this order were American citizens, and the ones who were not could not become citizens because of rules against their naturalization. The deadline for compliance was May, at which point they had to be out of their homes and in the camps or detention centers they had been assigned. Despite the unfairness of the order and the fear and prejudice that had inspired it, about one thousand Japanese American men in southern California decided to go to their camp in Manzanar in late March, ahead of deadline, to help set it up for their wives and children and the thousands of others who would follow them. Some rode the train from Los Angeles; others drove. This latter group packed their cars with their belongings and tied chairs and luggage boxes to the outsides. They met at dawn at the Rose Bowl in Pasadena, forming a string of vehicles that stretched about four miles long on the highway. The caravan consisted of ten groups, with an army jeep at the head of each group leading the trip across the Mojave Desert into the Owens Valley. Army maintenance trucks formed part of the caravan to do repairs and provide gasoline if needed. At the end of the road, "in good humor but still holding in their hearts the knowledge of the serious situation which faces the nation now at war with the country of their ancestry," said a writer who went on the trip, "the Japanese got their first glimpse of Manzanar." Then they disappeared inside the gates not knowing how long they'd have to stay there because the news from overseas remained awful.

Corregidor fell in May, and those on the homefront expressed dismay at another American defeat. "The morning when Bataan fell, and then Corregidor—do you recall that weak feeling in the pit of your solar plexus?" wrote Godchaux. But people could do more than just feel "weak feelings"; they could buy and sell bonds, volunteer at their local defense councils, help out at the USO, become air raid wardens, learn first aid in case of emergencies. And they could keep collecting and contributing scrap. More pleas went out, and more scrap came in. People jacked their cars up, put them on blocks, and stripped the tires. Neighborhood gas stations served as collection points for tires, paying a penny a pound for them. Old, formerly unwanted cars were troves of vital war materials, shifting public attention to a place beloved by the young hopper-uppers, many of whom were shipping out to go to war: the automobile junkyard. One report on the rubber emergency described Los Angeles as the "automobile junk capital of America" and said that California's "automobile graveyards are storing more potential scrap in the form of unwrecked cars than those of any other state."

Junk cars moved from the scrap dealer to the wrecker's yard and then to the steel mill for their rendezvous with the blast furnace. Owners of the cars to be junked received compensation at prices set by the government. "If the owner of the junked automobile refuses the offer, government investigators will determine if it is fair," said one account. "If the owner then refuses a fair price, the government will requisition the old automobile." Grumbling or not, most vehicle owners went along with the government's offer because they had little choice in the matter and because that was what people did. The times required it.

In the last days of May and early June 1942 every radio in California fell silent for five days on the orders of the Western Defense Command. A huge Japanese armada was amassing to take on a smaller fleet of American ships near Midway Island in the Pacific, and radio silence needed to be observed for military reasons. Because the radios in their homes went dead, Californians "had a feeling of a proud participation in a gigantic conflict," said one, and an even greater feeling of elation when they heard that America had finally won one, and a big one at that. Combined U.S. air and sea power had sunk a flotilla of enemy aircraft carriers and ships, knocking the stuffing out of Japanese claims of military invincibility and gaining a key strategic advantage for the Allies. With this loss, Japanese submarines could no longer threaten Hawaii and the West Coast (not easily anyhow), and Californians slept a little easier in their beds that night.

That summer began "the first summer in modern American history with large areas of the country almost without gasoline for pleasure purposes," as one reporter noted. Those areas centered mainly in the East, which had begun gas rationing in the spring. California had thus far avoided gas rationing, and most drivers in the state flatly opposed it. A national poll conducted by George Gallup (he had formed his New Jersey polling institute a few years earlier) found that nearly 60 percent of the population in "non-rationed areas" of the country felt that rationing was unnecessary. The head of the California Chamber of Commerce, Preston Hotchkiss of San Francisco, agreed, sending a telegram to FDR to make sure the president understood the views of business on the matter. "In view of the fact that California is more dependent on the private automobile for transportation than any other state in the Union and because our whole industrial and agricultural economy is so vitally interwoven with motor transportation," he said, "we respectfully urge that no gasoline rationing be imposed on our state."

The oil industry in the state opposed rationing too because, as one oilman correctly stated, there was "a super-abundance of motor fuel" available for both civilian and military purposes, and simply no need for regulation. Oil and gas were plentiful; it was rubber that was scarce. And that was the kicker: Gas rationing had nothing to do with saving gas and everything to do with saving rubber. Declaring that he was "not trying to save rubber or gasoline but the nation," President Roosevelt initiated a "Drive for Victory" campaign over the summer, asking drivers not to exceed 40 miles per hour. But the voluntary campaign confused some people, who thought it was okay to drive 40 even if the speed limit sign said 25. Those who disregarded the president and drove over 40 risked being branded as unpatriotic. "It is an unpatriotic act to waste rubber deliberately," said one Safety Council member. "It constitutes a deliberate act of help to our foes."

In September Bernard Baruch, a special advisor to the president and the head of the national rubber committee, visited California and other Western states to talk about the issue. In interviews with the press he agreed that the West had a "unique transportation problem" because its population was spread over large distances, unlike the more concentrated East. Californians relied on their cars to get around, and this had to be considered because of the state's large role in defense production; one of every four U.S. planes and ships came from factories in Oregon, Washington, and California. Additionally California farmers produced 30 million tons of vital produce and livestock a year, all of which got moved by trucks at some point along the line. In Los Angeles alone, almost all of the 475,000 war workers drove automobiles to work, in part because they lived in areas not served by streetcars. The streetcars themselves were already overflowing with riders, and more trolleys could not be built nor the lines extended because of materials shortages. "In the West, were the automobile wheels of all but 'essential motorists' to stop," said Baruch, "chaos would ensue."

Despite the pleas of Californians, after leaving the West and returning to Washington Baruch recommended nationwide gas rationing, mandatory speed limits of 35 miles per hour, and reduced driving by everyone in the country. Americans drove an average of sixty-seven hundred miles per year; Baruch urged a decrease to five thousand per year, but only if these miles were for "necessary driving"—that is, for work or war purposes. Pleasure drivers must drop their mileage well below five thousand, he said. The president immediately accepted these recommendations and issued an executive order to put them into effect.

The tire rationing boards that had been set up in January, and had since been used to ration sugar and other commodities, oversaw the distribution of gas rationing coupons. An "A" coupon book entitled people to buy four gallons of gas for any purpose they chose. This included pleasure driving, although that generally met with disapproval. "B" and "C" coupons entitled people to buy gas for driving to and from work.

The start date for mandatory gas rationing was set for December 1. On that date more than 20 million motorists in thirty-one Western and Midwestern states would join the 7 million drivers in the East whose gas was already being rationed. On the weekend before, knowing they wouldn't have the pleasure again for a long time to come, Californians went on drives to the coast and mountains. Public officials worried how people would respond when the order actually went into effect. "There either will be a complete breakdown in local transportation which will paralyze the life of the community," said Los Angeles Mayor Fletcher Bowron, "or we will pull through."

They pulled through. People shared rides to get to work, eliminated unnecessary car trips, drove less. They took the bus and walked. They found seats or stood on the crowded interurban trains. Businesses cooperated with the transit agencies, staggering the times they asked their employees to report to work to free up space on the trains. Municipal workers went in a half hour later than usual. Junior high and high school students changed their schedules to start class at 9:30 a.m. and get out at 4:15 p.m. Retail and department stores opened slightly later to adjust to the changed workday schedules of their customers.

One San Fernando man even came up with his own unique answer to the crisis: an electric car. An electric car? What an idea! But C. W. Henderson (no relation to Leon), who was retired, thought it made great sense. “It’s like a submarine,” he told a reporter, explaining how his 1912 Detroit Electric coupe worked. “All you got to do is keep the battery charged.” And if the battery stayed charged, it could go about seventy miles before it needed another charge.

Henderson had bought the car in the 1930s from the daughter of Confederate Army general Robert E. Lee, who was then in her nineties. The original body was covered with patent leather. He had stored it in his garage all this time never imagining it would be anything more than a novel conversation piece. But the war had changed his thinking, and he decided to bring it out for short trips into town and to the store. The car still ran on rubber tires, which was a problem, but he’d figure that one out a little bit later on down the road.

TWENTY

Abner of California

Before the war Dean Batchelor didn't have a care in the world save for his '39 Merc. True car guys never call a Mercury by its full name, and Batchelor was nothing if not a true car guy. He came from Kansas as a boy and, after inhaling the sweet smells of gas and oil and seeing and hearing those really loud, really fast hop-ups on the streets of California, he went over, a complete goner, lost in San Fernando Valley automobile heaven. Batchelor went to Burbank High and one time he and Ed Le Tourneau drove Ed's Model A roadster through the open gates of the football field and onto the dirt track around it. Ordinarily they held running races on the track, not automobile tests of speed, but the two friends, who may have been drinking a little, wanted to see what the car could do on it. Ed drove, Dean sat in back. They were sliding out on the turns having a good ol' time when an athletic coach appeared and started yelling at them to stop. They did not. They sped over the track, across the football field, and back through the open gate onto the street to make their getaway.

The next day, Dean and Ed got hauled into detention at school, although their antics did lead to educational reform. From then on the gates to the football field remained locked when school was not in session.

But Batchelor had an itch, and a little detention wasn't going to stop him from scratching it. Another time he and another buddy, Bill Farris, were sitting in his Merc at a stoplight on Olive Street in Burbank when who should pull up beside them but Cal Evans and Lloyd Wade in Wade's smoking-fast three-window Ford coupe. It was, said Batchelor, a "slick-looking car: black, with Buick rear fender skirts and whitewall tires, twin foglamps down front, and two spotlights mounted on the windshield posts." Not only was it slick to look at, it ran like the wind. Wade in his coupe was the king of valley street racing.

Its engine rumbled menacingly, and Batchelor looked uneasily at his pal.

"They're gonna wanta race, aren't they?" he said.

"Sure they are," said Farris enthusiastically. "Let's do it."

That was easy for Farris to say because it wasn't his reputation at stake. It was embarrassing to lose a street race, for both driver and car, and Batchelor wasn't sure his Merc had the guts to handle Wade's black beauty. Nevertheless, when the light turned green, he went for it, popping off the line and pushing hard through the gears down Olive until he noticed—well, actually, he noticed it right away—that Wade and his whitewalls were nowhere to be seen. Batchelor didn't know if something was wrong with the coupe or what. All he knew was that a peaceful transfer of power had just taken place. His Merc had deposed Wade's Ford as the fastest wheels in town, although it turned out to be a mixed blessing for the new king of the valley.

"The following week every owner of a supposedly hot car in Burbank wanted to race me," he said. "I knew how the gunslingers of the old West felt."

Though he had obvious street cred, Batchelor didn't do much of anything in the early days of the Southern California Timing Association because he was only a high school kid and hadn't yet fixed up his Merc so it could run with the best cars at the dry lakes. Shortly after the first SCTA meet at Muroc Dry Lake (now Rogers Dry Lake) in the spring of 1938, the United States Army kicked the group out and told it to go find someplace else to race. In the early thirties the Army Air Corps had established Muroc Army Air Base (known today as Edwards Air Force Base), and within a few years it began holding bomber training exercises in the region. Fortunately for the hopper-uppers, the army backed off a little and let them hold meets now and again over the next couple of years at Muroc. They could also go to the other dry lakes in the area—Harper, Rosamond, and El Mirage. That these joyriding teenagers no longer had a place to call their own hardly concerned the general public, which largely regarded them as troublemakers who drank and used foul language and spun doughnuts on football fields and engaged in reckless and illegal street races. But a few of the adults felt these boys deserved more respect than that.

"Instead of cussing out boys who hop up flivvers and can't resist the desire to race them, " wrote the columnist Lee Shippey in words that would prove prophetic, "we should feel that they are our coming inventive geniuses, developing the nerve and technical know-how that will make them mighty useful if they are called on to defend their country. The fact that nearly every American youth can build a flivver out of junk may be of tremendous importance in time of emergency."

In the summer before Pearl Harbor, Batchelor, who was nineteen, was working the swing shift at Lockheed in Burbank. The Lockheed and Vega plants there formed the core of the southern California aviation industry, along with Douglas Aircraft in Santa Monica, El Segundo, and Long Beach; North American Aviation in Inglewood; Consolidated Aircraft and Vultee in Downey; and Northrop in Hawthorne. Lockheed's factory was near the Burbank airport, which was known as Lockheed Air Terminal (now Bob Hope Airport). Batchelor lived nearby, and his usual Sunday routine went like this: At 12:30 a.m. he'd punch out after his Saturday shift, speed home, change into fresh clothes, hop back into the Merc, and bop over to a buddy's house. The buddy could have been Bill Farris or Bill's brother Charlie or Ray Charbonneau or Clark Stone or Gene Savant. All of them lived in Burbank, but they all couldn't go with Batchelor to the dry lakes at the same time because they couldn't all fit into his car. Batchelor worked the line at Lockheed with two other car guys, Will Donovan and Tiger

Baymiller, both of whom belonged to car clubs (Bungholers and Centuries, respectively) and both of whom stayed plugged into the dry lakes scene. They knew about the races there and tipped off Batchelor, who told his buddies, and that was why Bill or Charlie or one of them would be up and ready to go when Dean in his gassed-up Merc came hauling up to their house in the dead of the night.

From there they'd bomb up from the valley to Highway 6 (now Highway 14), cross through Mint Canyon and the Antelope Valley, and reach Palmdale or Lancaster at two or three in the morning, where they'd scarf down breakfast and drink coffee at an all-night diner. They'd hit the dry lakes with the sun on the rise, and for the rest of the morning and into the afternoon they'd happily think and talk about nothing else but motors, motors, motors. All right, maybe they'd talk about girls too, but mostly it was motors and racing. They could listen all day long to the terrible, beautiful racket one of those motors made when it peeled off the line in a pure test of speed. In their ears it was like a symphony, a symphony of V-8s. But by mid-afternoon the music ended and Batchelor and whoever had ridden up with him climbed back into the Merc and they headed home. On the way back they sometimes stopped at the Saugus Café in Saugus, which opened early and closed late to serve the dry lakes crowd. "Beer up before and after the races," said one of its advertisements.

Back in Burbank Batchelor dropped his friend off, or maybe his friend stuck with him for the next round of pleasure-seeking. This consisted of Batchelor roaring back to his house, washing and shining the Merc to make it look pretty, another quick change into some fancy nighttime wear, then off again to the Hollywood Palladium on Sunset. The great white bands—Tommy and Jimmy Dorsey, Harry James, Glenn Miller, Woody Herman—all played the Palladium, and Batchelor, who loved to swing, really dug those hepcats. But he also dug the black bands that couldn't play the Palladium in those days, so sometimes he'd cruise over to the Trianon or out to Ocean Park Pier in Santa Monica to hear Duke Ellington or Count Basie rip it up.

Batchelor only had one day off at the plant—Sunday—so he had to make the most of it. Dry lakes by day, big bands by night. Late Sunday night or early Monday morning found him at last curled up inside his sheets, snoozing away until he had to get up and go to work again.

It was, in historian Stephen E. Ambrose's words, "the dream life of an American teenager," and it all came to an end for Batchelor and millions of other American teenagers when the news came over the radio that the nation had been attacked and was now at war. The last meet at Muroc or any other dry lake occurred in July 1942. A few months earlier the Indianapolis 500 held its last race, the next one to be held no one knew when. Motor tracks in California and around the nation went dark too. The national emergency was too great, and the tire-burning sport of motor racing had to shut it down.

By the fall of 1943, after Allied successes in the Pacific and North Africa, an easing of the dimout rules occurred along the Pacific Coast. The Western Defense Command eliminated some of the zones altogether and allowed some cities still in them to keep their lights on longer at night. Restrictions on driving with headlights also eased. The scrap drives continued, though, as did the rationing of gasoline and many other commodities. It was almost impossible for an ordinary person to buy a new car or a set of tires. The demand for rubber and other materials of war pushed civilian goods and needs to the back burner.

Even more urgent, the nation needed manpower. More than 15 million Americans served in the war. Dean Batchelor went away to fight. So did Ed Le Tourneau, Cal Evans, Lloyd Wade, Bill Farris, Charlie Farris, Ray Charbonneau, Clark Stone, Will Donovan, Tiger Baymiller, and lots of other guys who left behind their girlfriends, wives, and families. Clark Gable, another California hot-shoe guy ("hot shoe" being slang for hot car), joined the Army Air Corps and flew bombing runs over Germany. So many men went away that it created opportunities for women, albeit opportunities they would have happily done without because it would have meant their husbands and boyfriends and fathers and sons and brothers would have been safe at home with them. But that was not to be, and so they stepped forward to do jobs they had never done before.

When the editors of the SCTA's monthly *Racing News* went into the service, Veda Orr took over for them. Without any races to report, Veda, whose husband, Frank, also shipped out, printed the letters of drag racers who wrote about what they were doing in the war and the good times they used to have on the dry lakes. And these newsletters, mailed around the world, raised the morale of the men on the battlefront who received them.

Millions of Veda Orrs around the country did whatever was asked of them, filling in wherever there was an empty slot, and there were plenty. Casualty lists began appearing in the papers. Nearly every home in every neighborhood in every town and city in the country hung a blue star banner in the front window, signifying that a member of their family was away at war. Women went to work at aircraft plants, shipyards, and other defense factories. First they took more traditional female jobs such as typist or secretary, but the old arrangements could not hold in the face of such times, and women rapidly took their places on the assembly line, handling rivet guns, spot welding machines, and welding torches. They then moved into positions of greater responsibility as "final inspectors, group leaders and expert installers. By dozens, hundreds, and now thousands, they took up vital work that men had dropped," said one report of the time. "At first it was daring but now it is commonplace. Experience has dispelled the notion that aircraft factories are strange and fearsome places for women."

The war demystified machines for many women and dispelled lots of stereotypical male notions about females. "Back in peacetime, it was one of the American male's favorite jokes to deride women automobile drivers," remarked one woman writer. But WAACs—members of the Women's Army Auxiliary Corps, one of several newly formed female branches of the armed forces—were driving jeeps at Allied Headquarters in liberated North Africa while women civilians were commanding the heavy-duty "deuce and a half" (two-and-a-half-ton) trucks at Fort MacArthur at the Los Angeles Harbor Defense Post.

"When the boy husbands left for war to become men," wrote Stephen E. Ambrose, "the girl wives became women. They traveled alone—or with their infants—to distant places on hot and stuffy or cold and overcrowded trains, became proficient cooks and housekeepers, managed the finances, learned to fix the car, worked in a defense plant, and wrote letters to their soldier husbands that were consistently upbeat."

Women went to work at the defense plants along with high school students who were too young for war and retirees who were too old. Blacks and Hispanics who might normally have been shut out of these jobs because of their skin color got hired and took their spots on the line too. Out-of-work whites in Plains states and the South flocked to California and found jobs as well. Sometimes you need a job more than you need a house, and many of these out-of-state workers lived temporarily in their cars—"auto trailers," they were called—until they could find someplace more permanent. Together, they worked at unprecedented rates of speed and productivity. United States wartime production surpassed that of the British less than seven months after Pearl Harbor: in a year American workers built 257,000 tanks, jeeps, and other vehicles, 40,000 big guns, 25 million rounds of big gun ammunition, millions of small arms, and 2 billion rounds of small-arm ammunition. At their peak, aircraft factories in southern California and elsewhere manufactured 8,000 planes a month.

The American car industry produced three-quarters of the world's automobiles in 1941. Despite losing lots of men to the armed forces, General Motors, Ford, Chrysler, Packard, Nash, Hudson, and other car companies converted rapidly from peacetime to wartime purposes, using the same mass production techniques they had developed for passenger cars. Willys-Overland Motors mainly produced the most famous vehicle to emerge from the war: the jeep. The roofless, door-less, pint-sized jeep went everywhere and did everything on the battlefield, conducting reconnaissance, engaging in firefights, carrying troops and ammo, transporting medical supplies, pulling out other vehicles stuck in the mud, and more. Stateside, the brass rolled out jeeps and other military hardware to the bond rallies and parades to show civilians what their money was buying. The jeep—its name seems to derive from "general purpose car," or GP—even briefly inspired a teen dance, popular among the swingers on the assembly lines. "Hepcats and alligators are reported taking to this war jig," said one newspaper, "which is really a sort of madhouse-style leapfrog."

The jeep became a popular symbol of America's army on wheels, and in this case the symbol had substance to it. In World War I, the United States Armed Forces had one motor vehicle for every ninety men; in World War II, it had one for every nine men. A WWI infantry division had a mechanical capacity of 3,200 horsepower; a WWII infantry division had 400,000 horsepower. The quality of the machinery had improved as well. The quick and maneuverable four-wheel-drive jeeps far outperformed the Volkswagen car used by Hitler's troops. Despite the frightening technological firepower of the Blitzkrieg, the Germans relied a great deal on horses to transport artillery and other equipment across Europe. The Americans, in contrast, used mechanical locomotion, and this gave them immense advantages in battlefield mobility and speed despite having to first transport mountains of vehicles, equipment, and supplies across the oceans and land them in the midst of withering enemy fire on beaches without ports.

John Steinbeck discovered another advantage enjoyed by the Americans when he met "Abner of California" on Steinbeck's wartime tour of army training bases and flying fields. Abner of California served as an aerial engineer on a bomber crew, and two years after the publication of *The Grapes of Wrath,* Steinbeck interviewed him for a nonfiction book he was writing on the Army Air Corps. Steinbeck was the perfect man to write this book not only because of his prestige and skills as a journalist and writer but also because he knew and understood machines and felt great affection toward the men who work with them. Born and raised in Salinas at the turn of the century, Steinbeck grew up at a time when owning a car in horse country was considered close to an act of treason. "The first car I remember," he recalled, "was, I think, a Reo....It was owned by a veterinary who got himself a bad name in Salinas for owning it. He seemed disloyal to horses." Steinbeck himself loved cars—he once wrote an article for *Holiday* magazine entitled "Jalopies I Cursed and Loved"—and he recognized that cars, like families, had genealogies. In *Cannery Row*, his novel about life on the Monterey waterfront published in the last year of the war, Steinbeck lovingly records how the Model T truck owned by grocer Lee Chong was first a passenger car owned by Dr. W. T. Waters, who "used it for five years and sold it to an insurance man named Rattle." But Mr. Rattle "was not a careful man," as Steinbeck writes, and he drank too much and leaned hard on the T and beat it up, so much so that the next man who owned it "cut it in two and added a little truck bed." Then this man sold it to a squid salesman named Francis Almones who took off the windshield because he liked to have the breeze blow directly in his face. But Francis got into money troubles and to pay off a grocery debt he sold it to Lee Chong, who then began his own history with the car.

The Model T was especially dear to Steinbeck, for it was the car that carried so many of those Oklahoma and Kansas refugees to California during the Dust Bowl. (A Model T is a centerpiece of the Steinbeck exhibit at the National Steinbeck Center in Salinas.) It was also the car that helped create the sons and daughters of those refugees. "Most of the babies of this period were conceived in Model T Fords and not a few of them were born in them," noted Steinbeck.

Bombs Away, his wartime book published in 1942 to publicize the U.S. Army Air Forces and raise money for an Air Force trust fund for the families of men killed in the line of duty, was "the story of a bomber team"—pilot, copilot, navigator, bombardier, gunner, radio operator, aerial engineer. For security reasons Steinbeck could not reveal the last names of the men he spoke to nor the bases he visited, but the photographs in the book clearly reveal that he went to Muroc Army Air Base and other military sites in the Mojave Desert. In addition to bombing practice, the Mojave and the western deserts of Arizona and Nevada hosted extensive tank training maneuvers led by General George Patton (a born-and-bred Californian, by the way). Patton's men endured oppressive desert conditions—the heat inside a tank reached as high as 185 degrees—to prepare for battle against German Panzer divisions in Africa and Europe. The tanks could stay on the move because of the maintenance battalions that kept them up and running. Army mechanics could get a stalled tank or jeep back in gear in a few hours or less, working in mobile machine shops that advanced in synch with the attacking forces they supported.

Abner of California did not work on tank engines, although he probably could have figured them out with a little sweat and elbow grease because, as Steinbeck wrote, "he talked to motors, questioned them. He started the motors and listened and he could tell a great deal about a motor by listening to it." Abner had a "long chin, muscular body, gray eyes [and] straight blond hair," but what fascinated the man observing him were his delicate hands and his marvelously deft fingers. "He had a way of caressing an engine lightly with his fingers. He had a way of cocking his head and rubbing his chin while he listened to an engine."

Steinbeck does not identify Abner's hometown, saying only that the people there weren't happy when he decided to join the fight. "When Abner enlisted in the Army, a month after war was declared, his little community in California was upset. Who would repair bicycles? To whom could you take a car and know it would get the best treatment?" Abner was the best car mechanic in town, a distinction he earned after salvaging a couple of broken-down Model Ts when he was a high school sophomore. Combining the frame of one T with the engine block of the other, plus two good wheels from each, he fashioned one drivable car. Then he chopped the fenders off, smoothed out the dents, applied some paint, and did some engine work. Around the streets of his little town his custom-built T made heads turn and went very, very fast, which was how Abner liked all his vehicles, whether they were cars or B-17 Flying Fortresses with 2,000-horsepower engines.

"People trusted Abner to do anything," said Steinbeck, "he was a wizard with an automobile."

Another person who trusted him was the bomber pilot, who counted on Abner to tell him about the condition of the engines. Abner also trained as a gunner, navigator, and co-pilot, and he could take over any of these positions if called upon to do so. Flying a bomber required teamwork, and everybody on the crew counted on everybody else to do his job because everybody shared the same goal: do the mission and come back alive. Abner was single but he wanted to get married and he figured he would, someday, if...

Abner did not consider himself special, and Steinbeck agreed: "In nearly every small town in America there is a garage run by a natural mechanic. He has usually graduated from high school, and even while he was in school he has repaired automobiles." Abners of California—and Abners of Nevada and Georgia and Maine and every state in the Union—could be found all over the armed forces. They served in a multitude of positions, and they were helping to win the war. Writes Steinbeck:

> Two generations of young men have couped up their cut-down Fords, have kept them going with spit and wire long after they should have gone on the junk heap, have torn them down and rebuilt them. Keeping their crazy cars going, they have learned motors more

> completely than they could have any other way. Experimenting to get every last ounce of speed out of their aging motors, tinkering their carburetors to get every last possible mile out of their gasoline, these boys in high schools and on the farms know motors as few people in the world know them; and Army instructors say that these young men make the best possible flyers.

More than sixty years later historians still agree with this assessment. "For the Allied Air Forces," writes Eric M. Bergerud, "it was a priceless advantage that Western economies were firmly in the era of the internal combustion engine." "Japan, by contrast," says James Bradley, "was much less mechanized, exposing many fewer of its young men to machinery." Adds Stephen E. Ambrose, referring to the European battleground but making the same point: "No army in the world had such a capability....Kids who had been working at gas stations and body shops two years earlier had brought their mechanical skills to Normandy, where they replaced damaged tank tracks, welded patches on the armor, and repaired engines. Even the tanks beyond repair were dragged back to the maintenance depot by the Americans and stripped for parts. The Germans just left theirs where they were."

In the first year of the war a change in language indicated a change in heart for Americans. Instead of "defense," the emphasis turned to "victory," because defense alone could not end the suffering and destruction. The only way to do that was to go on the offensive, and so they did. Allied tank corps retook North Africa from the Axis and crossed into Sicily and Italy to take back those areas as well. After incurring many losses early on, Air Force bombers punished German cities, and fighter planes eventually shredded the Luftwaffe. By June 6, 1944, the Allies largely controlled the skies, enabling them to stockpile fleets of vehicles and 6 million tons of equipment and supplies in England before D-Day. Meantime the Americans engaged in ferocious naval and air battles with the Japanese across the Pacific, retaking Guadalcanal, Saipan, the Philippines, Iwo Jima and Okinawa, island by bloody island, on their way to an anticipated and highly dreaded invasion of the Japanese mainland.

The invasion never took place. Other events transpired instead.

Zeppo Marx, the Marx brother who loved cars and raced at the dry lakes, played a small part in those events. Creative and mechanical, he founded a company, Marman Products of Inglewood, California, which manufactured clamps and straps to hold cargo in place while it was being transported. One of his company's products, the heavy-duty steel Marman clamp, secured the atomic bomb in a rack carried by the *Enola Gay* as it approached the skies over Hiroshima.

The bomb hit Hiroshima on August 6, 1945. Three days later, another atomic bomb, also secured by Zeppo Marx's invention, fell on Nagasaki. Japan surrendered unconditionally on August 14, and parties and dancing broke out in the streets of the free world.

TWENTY-ONE

The Great American Road Trip

Bobby Troup was sitting with his wife Cynthia in a Howard Johnson hotel on the Pennsylvania Turnpike having a bite to eat and looking for the best road to take to California. They had a map spread out on the table in front of them, and they could see how Route 40 ran west across the country to San Francisco.

In a lighthearted tone Cynthia said to her husband, "Why don't you write a song about Route 40?"

This question didn't come entirely out of the blue, for her husband wrote songs for pay. A Pennsylvania boy, he came from a musical family; his father played the piano and tried hard to teach his son the instrument. "But I was not a very good pupil," Bobby recalled, "and he gave up on me. He died when I was in high school never knowing that I had taught myself to play."

Not only did his father never learn about his piano playing, he never knew that Bobby wrote a song, "Daddy," recorded by Sammy Kaye, which hit No. 1 on the pop charts and stayed there for eight weeks in 1941. Troup graduated from the Wharton School at the University of Pennsylvania but his real love was music. He was getting seventy-five dollars a week as a songwriter and arranger for Tommy Dorsey's band when Pearl Harbor interrupted his musical career. Troup enlisted in the Marines, did his part to defeat Tojo in the Pacific, then mustered out in late 1945 with the rank of Captain. But after he returned to the Lancaster area of Pennsylvania, where his family owned a couple of music stores, he realized the place could no longer hold him. "I told my mother I had to find out if I had any talent and there were only two places for a songwriter to go to—New York or Los Angeles. I picked L.A.," he said.

Bobby and Cynthia, who were in their twenties, had two young daughters whom they decided to leave with Troup's mom while they drove across country. They'd call for them later, after they were there and settled. They threw their suitcases in the trunk of an old green Buick convertible and headed off down the turnpike, pulling over at the Howard Johnson's to plot strategy on the map.

Nah, said Bobby. Writing a song about Route 40—in an earlier day, the Lincoln Highway—didn't make any sense because they weren't driving that way to the coast. They were going Route 66.

That pretty much ended the discussion for the moment. They paid their tab, stoked up the Buick, and pointed its nose west. Once they reached Chicago they turned south on Route 66 and somewhere along the line they stopped at another coffee shop and Cynthia had another flash of inspiration, leaning across the table and saying with a smile, "Get your kicks on Route 66."

Now, Troup liked *that*. "What a marvelous idea for a song," he told her. "What a great title."

And so it went—the two of them winding across the west on Route 66 and Bobby "putting the song together in the car."

What the Troups had embarked upon—the Great American Road Trip—was hardly invented in the postwar era. Adventurers had been coming west since the days of Lewis and Clark and before. They came on foot, horseback, wagon, boat, stagecoach, and train. The arrival of the automobile on the front edge of the twentieth century kicked this westward migration into a new phase, one that held promise not just for male adventurers but for women and families as well.

The first couple to attempt to drive across America, John and Louise Davis of New York, made it to Chicago before their 1899 Duryea broke down and they abandoned the trip. Two men, Dr. Horatio Nelson Jackson and Sewall Crocker, followed with the first successful crossing a few years later, but it was not until 1908 that a family—the Murdocks of Pasadena—made a serious effort to cross the country by automobile. The Murdocks consisted of Jacob, Anna, and their three children, Florence, 16, Alice, 14, and Jacob Jr., 10. They summered in Pennsylvania, where Jacob Sr. ran a lucrative lumber and railroad business, and during the winter resided on South Madison Avenue in Pasadena. Inspired by the New York to Paris Race, Jacob hatched the idea for the trip while crossing the country on the rail "looking out of the car windows and dreaming dreams." He figured he had the machine for it, a sturdy and sizable Packard Thirty, and he hired mechanic Phillip DeMay to ride with them and see to it that it performed. For his guide he chose Lester Whitman, the famous endurance driver who also lived in Pasadena. Although he knew every bump and sinkhole between San Francisco and New York, Whitman had never taken the southern route across the States before, and he agreed to accompany the party on its history-making attempt.

They left Pasadena the morning of Friday, April 24, 1908, their Packard groaning with the weight of great expectations plus seven people and all their luggage, gear, tools, food, and water. Outside Daggett in the Mojave Desert the roads went from good to awful to nonexistent. When they got stuck in the expanses of drift sand they tried Whitman's old technique of putting down canvas strips to provide traction for the wheels, a trick that only succeeded in sinking their wheels deeper. They camped their first night in Death Valley—or "California's Sahara," as one magazine called it, "terra incognito"—feeling as if they were the only people in the entire universe. No lights except the stars overhead were visible anywhere. To Jacob it felt like "a vast lack of everything but sand."

They attacked the sands again in the morning. Their maps proved worthless because "the latest United States survey maps show a blank space in the Death Valley district," and their compass guided them only from blank space to blank space. "As noontime drew near," wrote Anna in a diary, "the sun got so hot it almost burnt the seat covers." The sands blew in every direction. The adults raised the top and side curtains of the car to protect the children. Despite the canvas strips and the ropes they tied around the wheels to stop them from slipping, the Packard stalled constantly. Out came the shovels and they dug the car out, freeing it to go a few hundred yards more until it stalled again. Worst of all was the realization that they were lost.

Wrote Anna, "By this time we knew absolutely nothing of where we were. We had been pushing ahead in the hopes of coming to something or some place. As to how we could get out of the terrible valley, we had no idea." They had enough food to last a week and a limited supply of clean drinking water in their canteens. They stopped at a spring that could provide more drinking water after boiling, and they looked around in despair. She continued, "When we got out our field glasses and scanned the horizon and could find no trace of anything behind us except miles of terrible, threatening sand, which we had labored through and which it would have been folly to attack again, and which separated us from the living world, we realized our danger."

At this point two of the men, probably Whitman and DeMay, set off on foot to look for help, stumbling onto the Tonopah and Tidewater Railroad line. The men reunited with the Murdocks, got the Packard going, and hooked back up with the rail, following it across Death Valley to a mining camp. The trip, while never easy, became somewhat more routine from there, and the party crossed into Arizona and Utah. In Ogden, feeling as if the worse was over and the family could make it the rest of the way without him, Whitman trained home to Pasadena. The Murdocks, DeMay, and another man, who had joined the party in Utah, reached New York City on May 26—32 days, 3 hours, and 7 minutes after departing Pasadena—thereby becoming the first family to drive across America and survive.

In 1909 Alice Ramsey showed that a woman could drive the distance, and a half dozen years later the San Diego and San Francisco world fairs stirred thousands of others to see the country by automobile. A Hollywood starlet named Anita King ran contrary to the popular trend that year by motoring from west to east. She left Los Angeles at 5:50 on the evening of August 25 and drove all night to San Francisco, arriving the next day at close to noon. This set a new women's solo record for the coastal route and garnered fabulous publicity for her studio, Paramount Pictures, and her six-cylinder KisselKar. Both Paramount and KisselKar were footing her bills, and her horn-honking, flag-waving arrival at the exposition drew large, adoring crowds. Explaining why she was next planning to drive to New York, King said that a Hollywood producer had told her that "if I had pluck enough to make the trip through to New York I could be known hereafter as 'the Paramount girl,' and that I could have a picture all my own. What more inducement could a girl want?"

King had the pluck, all right. Her time of forty-eight days to New York City clipped Ramsey's former women's record by five days, and the next year Paramount rewarded her with a starring role in *The Race,* a picture based on her journey.

After reading about King's exploits in the paper, Amanda Preuss, a petite, bespectacled twenty-five-year-old law stenographer from Sacramento, thought to herself, "Gracious. I can beat that and never half try." A member of the Young Women's Christian Association, Preuss loved the outdoors, fired a rifle like a sharpshooter, and handled motorcars with skill and pride. When she came up with the idea to drive solo across the country, she asked Oldsmobile to back her with an automobile, which it did, and then she approached the YWCA for moral support. "I was going to prove that a capable, self-respecting, well-behaved young woman could go alone from one end of this country to another without molestation or trouble of any sort," she said, "for I do hate girls who are always whining about the persecutions of men and the dangers of solitary adventurings." The YWCA came on as a sponsor too. So did the Lincoln Highway Association, which always liked it when people drove its roads and generated good PR for its cause.

One morning before the trip Preuss went to start the car she was training on. The crank jumped and broke her arm. Nonetheless, two weeks later, she saddled up her Oldsmobile V-8 with her arm in a cast and set off with speed marks on her mind. Leaving Oakland on August 8, 1916, she passed up and over the Donner Pass that same day, faster than any female driver, and most males, had ever gone before. A reporter noted with admiration her swashbuckling getup of "khaki riding breeches, a Norfolk khaki coat, heavy tan walking shoes with puttees [leggings], and a leather cap and goggles." But Preuss never hung her cap for long in any one place, maintaining her record pace across the West. Seemingly nothing could stop her until something did: a horse. In Nebraska a horse appeared out of nowhere on the road and her car hit it. One of its legs was broken, and it had to be shot. While the Olds survived intact, the accident sent Preuss into a deep funk. "Had I not been steeled by a determination to go through with my venture at all costs," she said later, "I would not have had the nerve to continue." Her parents met her in Indiana to cheer her up, and she ignored her exhaustion and drove some stretches for twenty-four hours straight. When she rolled into Times Square at 2:45 p.m. on August 19, she had obliterated King's previous record for the 3,250-mile distance. Her time: eleven days.

Admirable as these trips were, Preuss and other endurance drivers cannot be classified as "average motorists." They weren't simply people setting off in their cars and letting the road take them, not like when Evangeline Lindbergh and her son Charles drove to California from Minnesota in the months after Preuss's record run. Charles, who was fourteen, did all the driving because his mother did not know how. A slim, bright, mechanically minded youngster, he had learned to drive automobiles in his family's Model T, squiring his father around the backroads of Minnesota during his failed bid for the United States Senate in 1916. For the campaign Charles drove a Saxon Light Six, the same car he and his mother took to California. Because of his road time in Minnesota, Charles thought the way west would be a breeze—not so. They checked into the Hotel Armondale in Los Angeles after forty days of harsh weather and miserable road conditions.

The Lindberghs came to Los Angeles to visit an ailing family member who lived in the area, and once in California, they decided to stay awhile. Charles enrolled in the eleventh grade at Redondo Union High School in Redondo Beach, and on the weekends drove the Saxon up and down the coast to see the missions. One night while coming back from exploring a beach, the car's headlamps would not turn on, forcing him to steer through the darkness with only a windshield light as his guide. A highway patrolman stopped and ticketed him, summoning him to appear in court. The next day the traffic judge noticed that the boy was two years under the legal driving age and ordered him off the roads.

Charles and his mother thought this was ridiculous, seeing that the boy had driven halfway across the country and around the state with nary a problem of his own making. But this ruling was not the reason they decided to leave the state. They needed to get back home for family reasons, and in late winter Evangeline and Charles and another family member returned to Minnesota. Ignoring the judge's order, Charles drove every mile. California would not see him again until 1927 when he came west—via train, this time—to Ryan Aircraft of San Diego to oversee the creation of the *Spirit of St. Louis*, the plane that would carry him on the first nonstop flight across the Atlantic.

While the Lindberghs were visiting California, a family from Michigan—Edith and Dr. Frederic Loomis and their two daughters—were coming out to stay. One Loomis girl was five years old, the other was an infant, and Edith was pregnant with their third child. But Frederic, anxious to set up a new obstetric and gynecological practice in the Bay Area, did not wish to waste a minute, and so the family lit out for parts west. Years later Dr. Loomis would write a memoir that included a chapter about their 1916 cross-country road trip. This chapter, written by Edith, contains a wealth of practical advice to anyone else who might have been considering such a drive. "Transcontinental touring is no longer the exclusive sport of millionaires," she wrote. "My husband is so far from being a millionaire that a hundred dollars is a matter of gravest importance to us."

Driving cost less than rail and it made sense for families, "especially for those who are planning to move west permanently." Edith and Frederic chose their modern prairie schooner—a black seven-passenger model, its make not identified—with the trip in mind, finding one with roomy rear seats to let the girls wiggle around and sleep during the drive. They bought car insurance and thoroughly road tested the vehicle and had a mechanic check it over before leaving. These precautions proved prudent because, while on the trip, "we saw party after party held up in strange places, waiting days and even weeks to have a broken spring or some other part replaced." Spare parts often needed to be ordered from places hundreds of miles away, and it took time for the railroads to deliver them.

Friends said that Edith's gentle, practical nature—she was a former Episcopalian missionary—softened her somewhat starchier but well-meaning husband, and this side of her shines through in her writing. She recalled how "we shall never forget a family, including children, which we found in the dark, in an isolated spot on the windswept Arizona desert, their car broken down, their lights useless and without food or water." The Loomises always carried extra food and water with them on the road, and they shared both with this family. They also never drove without a spare canister of gasoline in case they ran out on the long deserted stretches of western highway.

Edith, Frederic, and the two girls slept in their car almost every night, folding over the front seats and using an old couch mattress they had brought with them. Usually they parked their car at night in a field or orchard, first asking permission from the farmer who owned the land. The farmer invariably said yes because he could then sell them eggs, milk, and vegetables. The Loomises carried an oil stove but also burned a wood fire in the open areas where they spent the night, sizzling up ham, bacon, and pancake breakfasts on the griddle in the morning. Like travelers for generations to come, Edith and Frederic never drove off in the morning without their extra-large container of coffee filled to the brim. Usually they skipped lunch, preferring to power through and rack up the miles as long as the children would let them. Fred drove while Edith made sandwiches on her lap, using the bacon from the morning.

The Loomises arrived in late December in Pàsadena, where a friend urged them to settle permanently. Dr. Loomis had his sights set on more northern climes, however, and they pushed on to Oakland, renting a house near Fabiola Hospital on Broadway (now the site of Kaiser Permanente Medical Center). There Frederic established the city's first obstetrics practice, delivering more than three thousand babies in his career but not, sadly, the one he most would have wished to. After setting up their new home in their new state, Edith contracted influenza and pneumonia. Both she and the unborn child she was carrying died in the catastrophic 1918 influenza epidemic that killed millions around the world.

Another catastrophic global event, World War I, brought a temporary halt to cross-country road trips, but after it ended, Americans revved up their engines and sailed off down the highway again. One of the most unusual transcontinental trips took place in the summer of 1919, when Dwight Eisenhower, then a twenty-eight-year-old lieutenant colonel, led a convoy of slow-moving army vehicles from Washington, D.C., to San Francisco. One purpose of the trip was to test the roadworthiness of the army's motorized fleet. The results were not good. "There were moments," joked Eisenhower, "when I thought neither the automobile, the bus, nor the truck had any future whatsoever." Many of the vehicles broke down over the two-month trip. This was due in part to mechanical issues and in part to America's roads, which were almost as bad as the army's vehicles. But in this regard California compared favorably with the rest of the nation. Eisenhower described the state's highways as "the best" they encountered during the crossing.

No one better personifies the go-go nature of the motorized 1920s than Erwin G. "Cannon Ball" Baker, so named because of his cannonball-like speed driving exploits.

An Indiana native and ex-vaudeville acrobat, Cannon Ball won the first race ever held at the Indianapolis Speedway, in 1909. But if anyone was born for the open road it was Cannon Ball, who crisscrossed the country on motorcycles, trucks, and cars. No driver of this period went in and out of California more times than Cannon Ball, and none did it faster. In 1915 he drove a Stutz Bearcat from San Diego to New York in 11 days, 7 hours, and 15 minutes. Amanda Preuss eclipsed that time a year later, but by then Cannon Ball had zipped between the coasts in a Cadillac Eight in seven days, thus ensuring the cross-country record stayed in his name.

Cannon Ball told the car companies that sponsored him that if he didn't deliver a record, they didn't have to pay him. They ended up paying him a lot because he set a ton of records, piling up more than 5 million miles in a hard-driving career that surpassed even Lester Whitman's. The same year Charles Lindbergh soloed the Atlantic in a plane, Cannon Ball drove a General Motors two-ton truck from New York to San Francisco in 5 days, 17 hours, and 30 minutes, a record for trucks as well as most passenger cars. At journey's end he poured a vial of Atlantic Ocean water that he had brought with him into the Pacific, a tribute to the endurance drivers of the past who had done the same. Five years later, in 1933, his all-out New York–to–Los Angeles sprint of 53 hours and 30 minutes set a cross-country record that stood for more than forty years. In the early 1970s the writer Brock Yates organized a famous coast-to-coast automobile race that was known officially as "The Cannonball Baker Sea-to-Shining-Sea Memorial Trophy Dash," a tribute to the man and his exploits. The Cannonball Run inspired books, and a movie of the same name starring Burt Reynolds.

For drivers in the 1920s and '30s, including those like Cannon Ball who tended to disregard the speed limits, it was impossible to miss the forests of signs, billboards, motels, service stations, and restaurants that had sprouted up along the roadways of America. In the early 1930s, as a way to attract tourists during the Depression, the small town of Leggett in northern California opened one of the nation's more unusual roadside attractions: a redwood tree with a hole cut in the base wide enough for an automobile to pass through. The Chandelier Tree, as it is known, still attracts tourists, as do two other drive-through trees—one in Myers Flat and another near Klamath.

Separating themselves from the clutter of signs along the highway were the Burma-Shave advertising signs, which broke up the monotony of the road by telling a lightly humorous joke through a sequence of short messages, such as:

Does Your Husband
Misbehave
Grunt and Grumble
Rant and Rave
Shoot the Brute Some
Burma-Shave

And:

SAID JULIET
TO ROMEO
IF YOU WON'T SHAVE
GO HOMEO
BURMA-SHAVE

The signs first appeared in the mid-1920s outside Minneapolis, the home of the Burma-Vita Company, makers of the shaving cream. They spread from there around the country, reaching Pacific Coast highways by the end of the decade. The format changed somewhat in California, where, instead of a sequence of six red-and-white signs as in other parts of the country, the message was often conveyed in two, such as:

COVERS A MULTITUDE OF CHINS
BURMA-SHAVE

Or:

PAYS DIVIDENDS IN LADY FRIENDS
BURMA-SHAVE

Different signs, not nearly as humorous, popped up in California in 1935 and 1936 when poor farm families fled the parched wheat fields of the Plains for the fruit-and-vegetable cornucopia of the Golden State. One sign outside a Central Valley store said, "Okies and Dogs Not Allowed Inside."

These Dust Bowl migrants—an estimated 221,000 came west in these years—tended to hang on to their cars despite their lack of means, a fact that was generally true of Americans during the Depression. People needed their cars to get to work, and to find work, and they would have been worse off without them. The Okies and Arkies stuffed their belongings into the backseats and trunks and tied onto the roof whatever wouldn't fit elsewhere. The cars they drove were usually dirty, beat-down, still-kicking Model Ts, which they also slept in. Route 66—"the mother road," as Steinbeck called it—led them across the California border, after which they turned north to the tent camps of Tulare and the Central Valley, following the harvest and catching on as day laborers in the fields.

But not everyone struggled during the Depression; this was the same time Gary Cooper and Clark Gable were sporting around Hollywood in Duesenbergs. This was also when Gertrude Stein and her partner Alice Toklas made a road trip of their own around California. The two lived in Paris, and Stein's writing had made her a celebrity in avant-garde artistic and literary circles. On a speaking tour of the United States Stein and Toklas came to Los Angeles to lecture and hobnob with writers and movie stars. Soon, though, they tired of the social scene and rented what Stein called "a drive yourself car," heading off for Yosemite Valley.

Both Stein, in her early sixties, and Toklas, who was a little younger, had connections to California. Stein spent part of her childhood in Oakland and San Francisco; Toklas was born in San Francisco and had family roots in the San Joaquin Valley. Alice had been to Yosemite many times, but not Gertrude, and the two looked forward to it eagerly. But when they reached Merced, Gertrude began to worry about the steep mountain roads. "I am always afraid of precipices," she confessed, "and I could not believe that in going into the Yosemite there would not be lots of them."

Worried but not without resources, Stein paid a Merced teen to drive them into the valley. There, the women spent the night in an unnamed hotel, likely the Ahwanee. The next day, Stein drove out of the Sierra across the Central Valley to Monterey. After a short stay on the coast they journeyed up to Oakland and San Francisco, where Stein had to again confront her fear of precipices. "It was frightening quite frightening driving there," she said, summarizing neatly what drivers over the years have felt while negotiating San Francisco's hills.

Another expatriate American writer, Henry Miller, spent much of 1941 road-tripping across America, although he didn't have nearly as much fun as Stein and Toklas. "There's one thing I'd like to advise anyone thinking of making a transcontinental journey," Miller wrote in "Automotive Passacaglia." "See that you have a jack, a monkey wrench and a jimmy. You'll probably find that the wrench won't fit the nuts but that doesn't matter; while you're pretending to fiddle around with it someone will stop and lend you a helping hand."

A born-and-bred Brooklyner who had just come from living in Paris, where he didn't own a car and got around mainly on foot, the author of *Tropic of Cancer* found himself looking for help all too often. In Louisiana he searched a half hour trying to find his jack and tools only to discover them under the front seat. A drunk nearly drove him off the road in Oklahoma, and in New Mexico the Buick petered out and he needed a tow to reach Albuquerque. These and other misfortunes gave Miller the time to work on a book and observe, up close, a breed of man well-known to all stranded motorists: the roadside mechanic. "They all have something of the surgeon about them, these entrepreneurs of the automobile industry," remarked Miller. "The bill is always indisputably correct and of a figure no less than formidable." He found that if you're stuck in a town long enough you will inevitably hear about a mechanic who would've done a much better and cheaper job than the guy to whom you just paid a small fortune. No matter who does the work, though, "take it for granted that nobody, not even a genius, can guarantee that your car won't fall apart five minutes after he's examined it."

Escaping Albuquerque, Miller reached the end of his "nightmare trip around America" in Beverly Glen. He stayed there with friends after the war broke out and then moved to Big Sur, where he lived and wrote for many more years.

The road Miller drove from Albuquerque was, of course, Route 66, the same one that carried Gable and Lombard home after their nuptials in Kingman. At some point the happy couple veered off to Beverly Hills, although Route 66 kept going all the way to the junction of Santa Monica Boulevard and Ocean Avenue in Santa Monica.

The end of the old road is marked today by a plaque honoring Will Rogers, the beloved humorist and cowboy movie star who died in a plane crash in 1935. Rogers, who grew up in Claremore, Oklahoma, one of the towns that Route 66 passed through, lived and owned land in Pacific Palisades. "This Main Street of America, Highway 66, was the first road he traveled in a career that led him straight to the hearts of his countrymen," reads the plaque. At a ceremony in the early 1950s Route 66 was christened "The Will Rogers Highway."

"Route 66. The name is still magic," writes contemporary historian Michael Wallis. "It will always mean going somewhere."

But roads don't become magic on their own—they need poems and songs to help people see their magic. Landing in Los Angeles after his cross-country trip with his wife, Bobby Troup spent the next week trying to arrange a meeting with Nat King Cole. Troup idolized Cole, whose voice had magic in it too. But like everyone in the music business, Nat Cole lived on hits, and he always had his ear out for a possible hit record. When Bobby at last got in to see him, he played a few of his songs that Nat thought were okay, nothing special. So Bobby mentioned how he was working on this other song that "wasn't quite finished" yet. Nat said all right, let's hear it anyway.

Bobby played and sang,"Get your kicks on Route 66," and Nat positively flipped. He said he wanted to record it right away, which he did. The Nat Cole Trio produced a swinging song featuring Nat's buttery smooth vocals, his usual fine work on piano, and clean, spare guitar lines by Oscar Moore. Capitol Records released the song in March 1946 and it immediately flew to the top of the pop charts.

"I never realized when I was putting it together that I was writing about the most famous highway in the world," said Troup. "I just thought I was writing about a road." He didn't know it at the time but he had just written the road song that would set the standard for all the road songs to come and, some would argue, one that has yet to be surpassed. Something about it captured something of what it meant to be on the road—the joys of setting off, the satisfactions in coming home, and all the victories and indignities in between. Over the years artists from Chuck Berry to the Cheetah Girls have gotten hip to that California trip and recorded covers of the song, which also inspired a television series, *Route 66,* in the early 1960s.

In the long run "Get Your Kicks on Route 66" granted Troup a little piece of songwriting immortality. In the short run it helped him and Cynthia throw enough scratch together to get settled and later buy a house. They called Mom to tell her to bring the kids because they weren't going anywhere. They were staying in California.

TWENTY-TWO
Outlaws of Speed

Lots of people were coming to California in these years, and lots of people were staying because there was no place like it on earth, especially if you loved cars. "It was a grand time for car nuts," said Dean Batchelor. "The streets of southern California, particularly in Los Angeles County, were thick with interesting cars—hot rods, custom cars, and the occasional imported sports car."

Batchelor, the former king of San Fernando Valley street racing, loved all three types of cars—hot rods, customs, and sports cars. Given this, it's no surprise that he later became a distinguished car writer and editor of *Road and Track* and other car magazines. He also worked as a technical advisor for Bill Harrah and Harrah's sports car–heavy collection, although Batchelor, who set speed records at Bonneville and the dry lakes, remained, to the end, a hot-rodder. His book *The American Hot Rod*, which was published after his death in 1994, is as authentically real as the hot rods he used to drive—one of the best hot rod books ever written.

In looking back on his life, Batchelor described the years after World War II as "the greatest years of the hot-rodding hobby. Although rodding was starting to lose its amateur status to the entrepreneurs, it hadn't quite done it yet. Those were the days when competitors on the dry lakes, at Bonneville, and on the drag strips were running more for the fun and excitement of competition than for money. Sponsorship hadn't taken over, and the atmosphere was more friendly than frantic. There was an intense rivalry between Chevy and Ford guys, coupe and roadster, four-cylinder and V-8, and club versus club, but it was competition among friends, not enemies. I wish you could have been there. It was great."

What also made it great was that the war was over and life could get back to normal. Normal had never seemed so exciting. Batchelor had served as a radio operator on a B-17 that was shot down on a bombing run over Germany, but he made it out in one piece and in July 1945, two months after V-E Day, he was back home in Burbank on an RRR—Rest, Recovery, and Rehabilitation. He had some time and a little cash on his hands so he went shopping for a new roadster—a new *old* roadster, to be exact. He paid four hundred dollars for a '32 Ford—a "Deuce" in hot-rod slang—that didn't run. Opening the hood and peering inside, he identified the problem:

crossed spark plug wires. After he took them out and put them in the right way, the Deuce's engine ignited with a pop. Cracking 100 in it was going to take a miracle, "but by God I had a roadster and I was a happy GI." In another month the war in the Pacific would be over, making GIs happy everywhere, and a month after that he'd be out of the army and back in civilian life with a fire-breathing Deuce in his garage. "Life couldn't have been better," he said.

The same was true for his pal Ray Charbonneau, who mustered out at the same time and found himself at the helm of a '29 Model A Ford roadster that looked like "a junkyard fugitive," as Batchelor said, but had never been beaten in a street race. One night Charbonneau and another Burbank guy returned from the war, Charlie Farris, were sitting in Ray's roadster at Larry and Carl's in Pasadena when a V-8-powered Deuce—not Batchelor's—pulled up alongside them.

Ray and Charlie were having burgers and fries. The two guys in the Deuce ordered coffee from the carhop. After everybody finished, the guy in the passenger seat of the Deuce leaned out his window with a big smile and said, "Wanna try it out?"

"You bet," said Ray. "Let's go."

They flipped on their headlights to get the attention of the carhop, who came outside to take their trays. Then they headed off to Washington Boulevard in East Los Angeles where, after a slow rolling start, they went at it. The '29 jumped out in front but the Deuce caught it in second gear, the two of them going 80, 90, 100 miles an hour side by side down the street. Their outing ended in a tie, however, and they repeated the run back the other way on Washington. This one did not turn out so well for Ray, who felt his transmission go out on him when he shifted into second. He lost the use of all but his highest gear, and he and Charlie limped back to Burbank in his wounded car, avoiding any streets with stop signs or with lots of other cars. But things turned out fine for them after all. A few days later, back at Larry and Carl's, they met the driver of the victorious Deuce, Randy Shinn, who turned out to be a cool cat and a fellow dry lakes racer. Shinn invited them to join his club, the Road Runners, and they accepted. Dean Batchelor joined the Road Runners too.

Other dry lakes guys who'd been away were getting themselves back into vehicles, joining clubs, readjusting to being a civilian. The racing Spalding brothers, Bill and Tom, maybe got the biggest shock of all when they came home. Before they left they had run a "streamliner"—a type of dry lakes racer—homemade with junkyard iron that had gone nearly 130 miles per hour at Muroc. When they returned from the service they learned that their parents had junked it for a scrap drive.

The Spaldings belonged to the Mobilers Club of Azusa, one of nearly forty car clubs that belonged to the reassembling Southern California Timing Association. These clubs ranged south to the San Diego Roadster Club, north to the Whistlers of Ventura–Santa Barbara, east to the San Bernardino Roadster Club, and west to the Low Flyers of Santa Monica. After nearly a four-year hiatus the first official postwar SCTA meet took place April 28, 1946, at El Mirage. Other signs of normalcy were reappearing as well. The midgets again started making fans happy at Gilmore Stadium, and motor tracks in big towns and small around California announced new racing seasons. On the national scene, the Indianapolis 500 roared back to life. Auto shows also reappeared, and car dealers looked forward to having something in their showrooms they hadn't seen much of lately: new models.

The end of the war meant the end of tire and gasoline rationing. Driving for pleasure was okay, speed limits went up, and Americans could buy new passenger cars and trucks again. Trouble was, at least in the immediate aftermath of the war, there weren't enough new cars to go around. Bobby and Cynthia Troup had come west in a '41 Buick. That was typical; a person's chance of buying a new 1946 automobile in early 1946 was about as good as finding someone whose life had not been changed by the war. In 1942 there were an estimated 27 million passenger cars in the United States; by war's end there were about 24 million. Where did those three million cars go? Nearly all of them met the fate of the Spalding streamliner: scrapped for the war effort.

Of the 24 million cars still around, nearly all of them were used—and highly so. In 1940 three of every ten cars in America were at least ten years old. Considering the scarcity of new civilian automobiles during the war, that meant that by 1946 three of every ten cars were at least sixteen years old. Nearly 10 million cars in the country had a resale value of one hundred dollars or less. Predictably, consumer surveys indicated that 12 million Americans wanted to buy a new car, and another five million wanted a better used car than they had. The global leader in automobile production before the war, the United States emerged even stronger as carmakers rapidly switched their assembly lines back to civilian purposes to meet the overwhelming pent-up public demand for driving machines.

Complaints about traffic, which never really went away even during wartime, grew louder and more insistent with the coming of peace. More cars on the road meant only one thing: more traffic. Many people also expressed rising concern about air pollution, particularly in the Los Angeles Basin, but most of the criticism at this point focused on factories and industry, not automobiles. Without doubt, the biggest public outcry about cars in 1946 had to do with the thirty-eight thousand Americans who died on the nation's streets and highways that year, up significantly from the twenty-eight thousand fatalities in 1941. While inconvenient and disregarded by many, the lower speed limits and restricted driving during wartime had produced at least one big plus: fewer traffic accidents and deaths. But with these problems now back on the rise, public concern centered once again on teen speeders who were converting their old jalopies into "hot-rods" and racing on the streets.

This new term entered the public lexicon the year after the war ended, usually put in quotes and hyphenated. It replaced the old term of "hop-up," which gradually faded. Many young people didn't even like to have their cars called hot rods because of the term's negative associations; instead they preferred "roadsters." Hot rods, wrote *Times* columnist Al Wolf in 1948, were "poor man's rockets. They're mostly Model T bodies—trimmed with bailing wire instead of chrome. And under the hoods you'll find almost anything, up to and including bird's nests. Some of the motors are homemade conglomerations, a little of this and a little of that, like an alley mutt. Others hide sleek power plants under their homely exteriors."

A less colorful but more succinct definition from this time describes hot rods as vintage automobiles that have been "stripped down on the outside and souped up on the inside," often with special parts supplied by shops such as the So-Cal Speed Shop in Burbank. Alex Xydias, a good friend and racing partner of Batchelor's, opened So-Cal the same day of his formal discharge from the Army Air Corps in 1946. Karl Orr came home from the war and started a speed shop too, in Culver City. (His wife, Veda, who had edited the SCTA newsletter while the boys were away, became the first woman to compete at the dry lakes, clocking 121 miles per hour in a Merc in 1947.) Parts builder Vic Edelbrock ran a gas station in Hollywood that sold speed equipment, and the racing Miller brothers—Ak, Larry, and Zeke, from a family of Danish immigrants—owned a garage that did the same in Whittier. Lee Chapel had closed his pioneering Los Angeles speed shop and opened a new one in the emerging street rod capital of the Bay Area, East 14th Street in Oakland. Another early southern California speed shop, Bell Auto Parts, had a new owner, Roy Richter, who sold speed parts over the counter and also distributed a mail-order catalog of flywheels, cams, manifolds, and equipment devised by Ed Iskenderian and other creative parts builders.

These speed shops were the incubators of hot-rodding, which began on the streets and dry lakes of southern California. As in the old hop-up days, what the teenagers couldn't afford at the speed shops they found for much cheaper at the auto graveyards. Army and Air Force surplus stores were another rich source for used engine and body parts. Jim Woods's '29 Ford roadster, to name only one among thousands, ran with home-built exhaust headers and a surplus gas tank from an old military vehicle. Many of the hot-rodders were good engine builders because they had punched a clock on the assembly lines of southern California's aircraft factories. At these factories, as Brock Yates says, "thousands of young men were trained in every phase of high-tech manufacturing, welding, tool-and-die making, machining, and metalworking. They formed a core of skilled enthusiasts who, on their off-hours, built automobiles and accessories for the street and the dry lakes."

They did it mostly for fun and for little or no money, although some of them started businesses that prospered in later years. They built cars that ran faster and looked better than many production models, and they did it without any support from the car companies. Their parents often opposed them. The police chased after them and when they caught them, sent them to judges who slapped them with fines and suspended their licenses or threw them in jail. Skip Hudson of Riverside had to sell his '29 roadster to pay off all his unpaid speeding tickets, otherwise the courts would have impounded it.

Hot-rodders faced the same predicament everyone else in postwar America did: not enough new cars. But they turned this predicament in their favor. As one observer noted, "Rebuilding of standard V-8 motors and revamping of old model cars into 'hop-ups'...has developed to major proportions due to the lack of new cars." The car companies weren't delivering what these kids needed or wanted, so they created their own, using the materials available to them locally and what they could get on the cheap (or on the sly), continuing a tradition of teen automobile do-it-yourselfers that reached back to the horseless carriage days of Waldeman Hansen and Carl Breer.

But who were these hot rodders anyhow—the people behind this new trend? This was another thing Al Wolf needed to explain: "Most are mechanically inclined youngsters who like to patronize junkyards and auto cemeteries, cart away a mess of wreckage and build themselves cars." These junkyard dogs were nearly always male, but plenty of females were around too—watching the races and helping out, hanging at the drive-ins, going on drives with the clubs, riding and partying with the guys, and sometimes driving cool cars of their own. Female or male, the hot-rodders were nearly always young.

With so many older teenagers and young men overseas during the war, the state allowed boys and girls under the age of sixteen to drive legally if their parents or guardians signed consent statements permitting them to do so. Farm areas in California had lobbied for such an exemption earlier, arguing that they needed those youngsters still at home to drive vehicles to help bring in the crops. Once the farm kids got this sweet deal, "that let down the bars, and thousands of city kids wanted licenses to drive too," said one observer.

City kids, suburban kids, farm kids—all licensed, underage, and on the loose. According to one public official, an estimated "three hundred thousand kids of fourteen or fifteen years in the communities of southern California" had these emergency licenses, and many of them were dating—and mating—in their cars, adding to the public safety problem. One proposed California State Assembly bill struck at the heart of hot-rodding by banning speed equipment on car engines. All engines had to remain as they were when they left the factory; no Eddie Meyer heads or George Riley carburetors to boost performance. Another bill in 1945 sought to stop hot-rodders from pulling the fenders off their rigs to lighten the load and produce more speed: "Every motor vehicle shall be equipped with four fenders or mudguards," it read. Both these bills failed, but the problems on the streets continued and the authorities kept looking for ways to crack down. In late 1946 the state legislature enacted a change in the Motor Vehicle Code that made it illegal for "any person or persons to engage in speed contests on highways." This law, which *did* pass, took dead aim at the capital of outlaw street racing in the state and nation: Los Angeles County.

Hot-rodders swarmed the drive-ins of southern California on warm Friday and Saturday nights, arriving in waves of sound and color and smoke. For all teens, even the non-racers, the appearance of these machines put a charge into an otherwise routine night out. "We'd all be at the Piccadilly or some place, and guys would start challenging each other," recalled the custom car builder George Barris, then a teenager and a new arrival to the southern California car scene. "Well, as soon as a few guys had challenged each other, everybody would ride out onto this stretch of Sepulveda Boulevard or the old divided highway, in Compton, and the guys would start dragging, one car on one side of the center line, the other car on the other. Go a quarter of a mile. It was wild. Some nights there'd be a thousand kids lining the road to watch, boys and girls, all sitting on the sides of their cars with the lights shining across the highway."

After dragging one way down Sepulveda, the two cars usually turned around and raced back the direction they had come, in just enough time for the cops to show up. "Then you really saw something," Barris said. "Everybody jumped in their cars and took off, in every direction. Some guys would head right across a field. Of course, all our cars were so hopped up, the cops would never catch anybody." Not right away, perhaps, but the men in blue proved to be a persistent lot. One night after a big street race they swept through Piccadilly and hauled hundreds of hot-rodders away to jail. "That pretty well ended the Piccadilly," said Barris.

Besides drive-ins, speed shops, and high school parking lots, the largest numbers of hot rods could naturally be found on the roads and highways leading to the dry lakes: Rosamond, Harper, and most popularly, El Mirage, the new home for Southern California Timing Association meets. Riverside and San Bernardino car clubs traveled Route 66 over the Cajon Pass to Victorville, turned north on Highway 395 to Kramer Junction or "Four Corners," then west to the dry lakes. Los Angeles and San Fernando Valley clubs tended to go the traditional, not-as-steep Highway 6–Mint Canyon route through the Antelope Valley. For those who needed a break from the drive, the Solemint store at the junction of Mint Canyon and Soledad Canyon Roads sold tall frosted mugs of root beer for a dime. For those who liked their beer without the root, the Saugus Café was also popular. It being so hot in the Mojave, most everybody brought liquid refreshments of their own. Some showed up with tanks of water on a trailer, and one person hauled in an ice machine to make sno-cones. Joe Goss liked to flavor his sno-cone with Manischewitz wine.

Hundreds of racers and spectators came to the SCTA meets. The sheer number of hot rods on the highways, the fact they often traveled in groups, the distinctive look of these topless, windshield-less, fender-less, bumper-less, running board–less black-and-red machines, the tranquility-shattering roar of their engines, the fear—grounded often in reality—that the drivers were drinking, and of course, the speeds they sometimes traveled, alarmed Palmdale, Lancaster, and other high desert towns. (To be street legal, most hot-rodders drove with their windshields, bumpers, and mufflers on, taking them off only when they reached the dry lakes, but some openly flouted the conventional rules of the road, infuriating the authorities.) Along with the highway patrol and sheriff's deputies, the Lancaster police instituted a crackdown on "the problem of local schoolboys who have caught the 'hot-rod' contagion," positioning more ticket-writing patrolmen at strategic spots between Los Angeles and the dry lakes. The meets at El Mirage, Harper, and Rosamond were generally safe because they were wide-open areas, and the SCTA supervised what went on there. The SCTA also banned street racing by its members and suspended anyone caught doing it. All this still meant little to an aroused public who pressured the police to stop what some referred to as "killer cars."

Just as the dangers of hot rods were real, so were the passions and excitement they stirred. These new machines and the young people driving them were creating so much interest that the SCTA decided to do something nobody had ever done before: put on a hot rod show. About fifty hot rods, fresh from the streets and dry lakes, would be shown at the first annual Automotive Equipment Display and Hot Rod Exposition at the National Guard Armory in Exposition Park in Los Angeles. Lone hot rods had appeared here and there at car shows, but never before had so many of them come together in an exhibition hall. It promised to be something to see.

TWENTY-THREE

Hot Rod Nation

The world's first hot rod show took place at Exposition Park, the same site where the first horseless carriages raced in Los Angeles a half-century before, back in 1903, when people called it Agricultural Park and horses did most of the racing at the mile-long fairgrounds oval. Barney Oldfield went a mile a minute in his famed Bullet there, astounding spectators with his daredevil speed and bravery. In 1910 the park received its current name and a new purpose—that of becoming an urban center for museums and cultural activities as well as athletics. By the late forties the Natural History Museum and the Los Angeles Memorial Coliseum held down places at the park, but the Sports Arena and some of the other attractions there today had yet to be built.

Barney Oldfield's most famous racecar, the Golden Submarine, bore many similarities to the hot rod show's featured car, a belly-tank streamliner designed by longtime custom car builder Bill Burke. Using a Model T frame with an inverted Mercury engine in the tail, Burke fashioned a distinctive aerodynamic shape out of the belly tank of a Lockheed P-38 Lightning fighter plane. Advertisements described Burke's design as "part airplane and part automobile, the car of tomorrow," reminiscent of how people had once viewed the wildly futuristic Golden Submarine. Oldfield's car, though, completely enclosed him in it, which was not the case with the streamliner. The young Colleen Townshend, named "Miss Safety First" by the Southern California Timing Association, posed for a publicity photo inside the car, and her smiling features and curly black hair poked up well above its body.

Another comparison: Barney cracked 100 miles per hour in the Golden Sub; the transmission-free streamliner had topped 142 in timed tests on the dry lakes.

Held in the tenth anniversary year of the first Southern California Timing Association meet at Muroc Dry Lake, the hot rod show represented a public coming-out party for the group—"taking the veil of semi-secrecy off their operations," as an article in a new magazine put it. This new magazine was called *Hot Rod*—no quotes, no hyphen—and its publishing debut coincided with the three-day January 1948 show. The twenty-four-page newsletter-type publication with black-and-white photos sold for twenty-five cents. But if a person were interested in buying a copy, he couldn't do it inside the National Guard Armory where crowds of onlookers engulfed the belly tank special and forty-nine other spruced-up rods. He had to go outside and track down the guy who was selling them, a good-looking, dark-haired twenty-one-year-old with bounce in his step named Robert Petersen.

Robert was his given name but his friends called him "Pete." He was more of a Pete than a Robert anyhow: informal, relaxed, eager to talk to anyone and everyone about his new publication.

Volume 1, Number 1 of *Hot Rod* featured the picture of hot-rodder Eddie Hulse on the cover, "who a few moments after this picture was taken"—as the cover copy explained—drove his Class C roadster to a new dry lakes record, bettering the old mark of Road Runner and valley racer Randy Shinn. Perched in the cockpit of his roadster, Hulse is wearing a leather cap, goggles on his forehead, and a big grin. No photo credit is given, but it's a good bet that the guy who took the picture was the same one who was digging into his pocket for change on a dollar bill after someone bought a copy of his little magazine. Petersen may have also had a camera hanging from a strap around his neck so that when he went back inside the armory he could take pictures of hot rods for upcoming issues, assuming, of course, there would be upcoming issues.

But there would be, Pete knew it, based not only on the reaction he was getting—"Right from the beginning, people just went crazy for *Hot Rod,*" he said—but on the fact that he believed so strongly in it. He knew the magazine had an audience, even if many of the people in that audience—hot rodders themselves—had serious doubts about its chances for success.

A few months earlier at the last SCTA meet of the season, Petersen had appeared at El Mirage full of enthusiasm for his new project. Enthusiasm was about all he and *Hot Rod's* co-founder, Robert Lindsay, had at that point; they had no magazine yet, nothing on paper to show people what they had in mind. But in order to take that next step into publishing, they needed money, which they had little of, and to get more they needed advertisers such as Alex Xydias of the So-Cal Speed Shop. Xydias was up at the dry lakes with Dean Batchelor, testing out the V-8 they had recently installed in Batchelor's Deuce. Petersen approached them in the pits and introduced himself. Neither Xydias or Batchelor had met him before, but that didn't stop the talkative newcomer from pitching Xydias on the benefits of advertising in this new magazine that had barely advanced beyond the pipe-dream stage but was certain to be a huge hit. Xydias told Petersen to come by the shop or call next week and they'd talk about it then, more or less to get rid of him. Xydias had no intention of buying an ad.

After Petersen left, Xydias turned to his friend for his reaction. "What do you think? Will it work?"

Batchelor, one of the most adroit observers of the car scene in the country, said maybe in southern California, given its bustling hot rod scene, "but I can't see much success in other parts of the country."

The aspiring publisher did not hear this conversation, and even if he had he surely would have ignored it because there were so many other people to talk to, other potential advertisers to pitch. And although Xydias didn't bite on that first issue, others did: Regg Schlemmer, who had a speed shop in South Gate and who owned the Hulse-driven car featured on the cover; George Riley, who made racing carburetors; Ed Winfield, the engine builder and parts designer; Roy Richter at Bell Auto Parts; Paul Johnson at the 100 M.P.H. Garage; and Sam and George Barris at their custom shop in Compton. Other advertisers in that first issue included Cannon Engineering, Carson Tops, Drake Brothers Machine Shop, Elmer's Muffler, Navarro Racing Equipment, Russell Tire, Smithy Muffler, and Weber Tool. Hollywood Trophy bought a one-column ad because although the dry lakes racers did not win prize money, they still liked to take home a plaque or trophy with their name and time on it to prove to the folks back home that they really did go as fast as they claimed. Puritan's Homemade Candies also advertised, perhaps on the thinking that Valentine's Day was just around the corner and the boys might wish to buy some chocolates for their girlfriends or moms.

The center spread of the magazine consisted of two full pages of hot rod pictures, and on page 15, in a feature entitled "Parts With Appeal," nineteen-year-old bathing beauty Jane Norred posed with a fuel pump in her hands. Petersen likely took all these photos, or most of them anyhow, and wrote the copy for them as well. While Bob Lindsay handled the office side of things, Petersen did just about everything else: shooting photos, sweet-talking advertisers, thinking of ideas, punching out copy on the typewriter, overseeing editorial and proofreading, arranging it so that advertisers could also write articles, giving them a little more play than just the space they paid for, and signing off on every page before the issue went to press. Then he and Lindsay drove the final pages to the printer, did press checks to avoid any last-minute screwups, picked up the bundles after printing, and delivered them to speed shops where they could be sold. With mountains of unsold magazines still sitting around the office, Petersen—"the doorknocker" type, as his friend Wally Parks put it—loaded stacks of them into his car and went off in search of hot rodders.

"At first, I'd go up to the dry lakes and I'd go from guy to guy and I'd just sell 'em, for a quarter apiece," recalled Petersen. "I'd say, 'Hey, get your *Hot Rod Magazine.* And I used to go to the racetracks at night, circle tracks like Ascot. Gilmore Stadium was the big deal then. 'Hot Rods at Gilmore.' I'd go down and shoot pictures during the race. During the breaks I'd sell magazines. We had a deal with the stadiums: We'd pay them a nickel a copy and we'd keep twenty cents."

Petersen hustled around to these and other tracks in the area: Bonelli Stadium in Saugus, Culver City Speedway, Huntington Beach Speedway. On Sunday afternoons the Throttlers car club met at Porter Ranch in the bare hills of the San Fernando Valley, picnicking and racing on a dirt track oval used by the movies to shoot horse racing scenes. Petersen showed up at places like that too, or maybe he popped over to the Triangle, where the Outriders liked to go, or the Piccadilly before the cops raided it and it fell out of favor. "That's how we got enough money to eat some nights," said Petersen. "We'd be at a drive-in or a race and we'd say, 'Let's go sell some subs.' We'd sell 'em, then we'd have enough money for supper."

Petersen liked to eat, so he kept selling. Long hours didn't bother him; growing up in Barstow in the desert, he had learned the value of hard work from his father, a Danish immigrant. His mother died when he was young, and his father, a mechanic, raised him from boyhood and introduced him to engines. After graduating from Barstow High he went off to Los Angeles, where he worked as a mechanic and became a gofer at MGM Studios, over time moving up to its publicity department. His nonstop energy and enthusiasm made him a natural for publicity; he never took a rejection personally and never stopped at one rejection, staying on the phones and pitching until he found an angle that worked. A wartime stint in the Army Air Corps followed, after which he returned to pumping up the reputations of Hollywood stars. In the service, he had learned to wield a camera, and that skill went into his toolbox too. Soon he left MGM to help form Hollywood Publicity Associates, the company that was handling the publicity for the hot rod show and the same one that had stopped him from selling his magazine inside the armory next to the businesses that had paid for their booth spaces. Undaunted, Petersen flagged down hot rodders as they were coming in and out of the armory and made sales to them.

Personally involved in the organization of the show, Petersen promoted it heavily in *Hot Rod*. An article on page 10, "First Annual Hot Rod Exposition," explains why the exposition was being held: "Long regarded as a screwball diversion for a lot of reckless kids with more nerve than brains, the building and racing of hot rods has finally come to be recognized as a major sport in this area. Realizing that there is more to the sport than just an outlet for a bunch of young buckos to blow off steam, the public has finally accepted this activity."

Petersen and *Hot Rod* were engaged in a little wishful thinking here, because the public had far from accepted hot rods and the young buckos who drove them. But this was another of the show's motives: to present a different side of hot rodding than the gruesomely sensational stories about it that appeared in the press. All or nearly all of the fifty hot-rodders with cars on display at the show posed for a group picture that ran with *Hot Rod's* article. The photographer, probably Petersen, stood on a ladder or the bed of a truck to get all six rows of cars, seven and eight cars to a row, in the shot. Every car has a driver in it, and every driver is smiling and waving for the camera. Not a one of them looks like a hoodlum.

These same friendly faces appeared at the armory, standing or sitting next to their colorful machines, chatting with the public, answering their questions, and posing for pictures with them. On Sunday, the show's final night, a group of them demonstrated custom car building by transforming an ordinary Ford roadster into "a dazzling, chrome-plated hot rod"—or so said the advertisement, possibly written by Petersen too—while the public looked on and KMPC Radio broadcast live from the hall.

Over the three days of the Automotive Equipment Display and Hot Rod Exposition, a visitor could have walked around and seen Robert Petersen, Bob Lindsay, Dean Batchelor, Alex Xydias, Ed Winfield, George Riley, George and Sam Barris, Roy Richter, and many other hot rodders unknown to the general public. But to an enthusiast of the hobby they were like the delegates to the First Continental

Congress, the Founding Daddyos of Hot Rod Nation. Another of the founding Daddyos was a tall, lean native Oklahoman by the name of Wally Parks, who could be seen around the hall too, chatting up everybody and checking out the cars. He was the general manager of the SCTA and a good friend of Petersen's who had helped him conceive of and put on the show.

Nobody knew the emerging hot rod scene better than Parks, who had been modifying cars since his teens after his family moved to southern California when he was a boy. "Modify" is a term often used to describe what hot-rodders do to their cars; what it actually means is to "maximize," not modify, its capacity for speed. Parks saw his first races at Muroc in 1932; a year later he maximized a '27 Chevy coupe and drove it 82.19 miles per hour at the lakes—again, hardly fast by today's standards, but remarkable considering what the hopper-uppers of this era had to work with in terms of money, equipment, and support. "A tall man with a deep voice and a statesmanlike presence," Parks ran organizations as well as he drove cars. In 1937, when the southern California car clubs pooled their resources to form the SCTA, he became one of its leaders, editing the newsletter with another man and making a lasting contribution to the dictionary of speed.

It was Parks who first used the phrase "drag race" in print, in a March 1939 article in the newsletter. He used the term again in the next month's issue, but it did not catch on until after the war. On December 7, 1941, Parks was working the line at the Los Angeles GM assembly plant, and for the scary, unsettling months after. When the plant switched over from producing cars to tanks, he test-drove tanks to find and fix any mechanical flaws. Called to active duty in the South Pacific, his hitch for the 754 Tank Battalion on Bouganville included the building of a V-8 jeep with open exhaust pipes, what one writer has called "the world's first jeep rod." After the war Parks returned home to reclaim his old GM job, only to lose interest in it with the explosion of hot rods on the streets. But Parks was no joyriding party animal; quite the opposite. Increasingly disturbed by the lawless and violent reputation of this thing he loved, the SCTA's first paid staffer argued for greater controls and an end to street racing.

As he saw it, the show at the armory was the first step in reversing public opinion about hot-rodding. "We weren't planning or marketing geniuses or anything like that," said Parks. "Things happened and we went with our instincts."

One thing their instincts told them was that they needed to turn enemies into friends, and Parks and others at the SCTA reached out to form alliances with the police and highway patrol. A few months after the show three hundred members of the SCTA participated in a public ceremony in downtown Los Angeles vowing never to speed on city streets. As police and CHP captains looked on approvingly, a municipal court judge administered the oath, the purpose of which, said the judge, was "not only to prevent injuries and deaths but also to keep people out of the courts by educating them in respect to traffic laws." Each hot-rodder received a Green Cross safety sticker from the National Safety Council. In his remarks the judge said that it was "unfortunate" that the cars driven by these young men were called "hot rods," considering the term's bad reputation. Though not offering any alternatives himself, he recommended that a new name be adopted for these cars, a suggestion that met with little support from the safety-sticker winners.

Asked once why he called his magazine *Hot Rod*, Petersen said, "That's what they were called. Anything else wouldn't have been believable." His single-copy and subscription sales went well enough for him to put out Vol. 1, No. 2 in February and Vol. 1, No. 3 in March, and to keep on publishing. These issues and the ones that followed contained safety and how-to articles, hot rod photos, race results, news and humor, and more of those popular "Parts With Appeal" features with pictures of bathing beauties caressing fuel pumps, brake rotors, and air filters. Alex Xydias overcame his initial reluctance and bought a display ad in the magazine. He and other shop owners realized, to their surprise, that there was a market outside California for their products and that *Hot Rod* could help them reach it. "If it weren't for *Hot Rod*," said Xydias, "how else would a guy in Ohio who wanted to buy a Winfield cam know where to buy it?"

Hot Rod's first issue contained a footnote to the editor's column inviting readers "throughout the world" to send news items and photos to the magazine at its Los Angeles address. Considering that its readership at that point barely extended beyond the steps of the National Guard Armory, this request might have seemed a bit of a stretch. But Petersen's instincts and judgment, like those of his friend Parks, turned out to be extraordinarily sound. Hot-rodding, it turned out, could be exported just like movies, oranges, and oil. Not just the machinery of it, but the ducktail and flat-top coolness of it all. Here an Oregon teen recalls what it was like to first set eyes on a genuine, honest-to-God, too-cool-for-school California hot-rodder: "A guy named Johnny Johnson came up from California, and he was what we expected a real hot-shot, hot-shoe So-Cal hot-rodder to be: red hair slicked back, a tough expression, a weight lifter given to wearing tight T-shirts." But what really blew this teen's mind was Johnson's blown car: "A red '32 Ford five window, channeled, top-chopped and a dropped axle that gave the coupe a wicked rake." Hot-rodders didn't just act cool, they talked cool in a language that uncool grownups did not savvy. Hot-rodders sounded like Martians to adults, and that was the wickedest thing of all.

In the words of one observer, *Hot Rod* delivered "gasoline-powered dreams" to mailboxes across America, but it also delivered practical advice on how to make those dreams come true. Petersen Publishing, the name of Petersen's new company, tapped into a new audience for auto magazines—not the moneyed elite traditionally associated with luxury cars but the young car nuts who, after reading George Riley's article on the correct gear ratios and fuel mixtures for racing engines, applied what they learned to their own machines. These how-to articles on engine repair, engine building, and customizing helped to spread the gospel of hot-rodding, and in time the rest of the country gradually upped its coolness quotient and created speed equipment and hot rods to challenge California's.

By the second annual Automotive Equipment Display and Hot Rod Exposition, in January 1949 and also held in the armory at Exposition Park, the hot rod scene had changed dramatically. One sign of this was the greater respect shown by the mainstream press, which was now making distinctions between authentic hot-rodders and those driving "squirrel cages" in "the helter skelter jalopy class." The Southern California Timing Association and its companion organization, the Russetta Timing Association, were no longer the problem; they were part of the solution. "Their biggest fight," said one writer, referring to the authentic hot-rodders, "is against kids who create traffic hazards with unsafe jalopies." The Los Angeles Police Department sponsored a booth on safe driving at the show, as it did the first year. And almost certainly Pete Petersen moved his sales off the steps of the armory and inside to a booth in the hall.

Some seventy-six thousand people attended the show, admiring dozens of hot rods such as Bob Tattersfield's P-38 belly tank streamliner that had clocked 158 miles per hour in a speed trial. The star car of the first show, Bill Burke's streamliner, returned, boasting a higher speed than it had achieved the year before: 153 miles per hour on a run at the dry lakes, driven by Wally Parks.

Parks again played a leading role in the exposition, as did Petersen. Joined by mutual admiration and interests, the two became major influences in a hot rod industry they were helping to create. Young, single, and on the upswing, Petersen rented a garage apartment in West Los Angeles, scooting across town on a beat-up old Harley motorcycle. He worked late lots of nights and some nights didn't go home, bunking on an old Army cot in the magazine's tiny office. Parks was in his mid-thirties, more than a decade older than Petersen, and acted like a big brother and mentor to him, dropping by his office to boost his spirits. "He never lost confidence," said Parks about Petersen, "even when things looked bad."

Sometimes things did look bad, and not just things in publishing or business. In the spring of 1949 Rulon McGregor had just finished up a run at El Mirage in his custom Merc. Moments later Robert Fadave picked up two of his friends, Jackson Pendleton and John Cuthbert, in his Ford coupe and drove onto the course where McGregor had made his run. A member of the Gents car club, the twenty-two-year-old Fadave was driving patrol to stop cars from going onto the course while contestants were racing. Unfortunately, no one stopped him. Unaware that McGregor had turned around and was coming back the other way, Fadave was taking his friends to the other side of the course when McGregor, focusing dead-ahead and not expecting anything to appear in his path, smashed into the driver's side of the Ford. McGregor and Jackson Pendleton were killed on impact. Fadave died in the ambulance on the way to San Bernardino County Hospital. The teenaged Cuthbert received treatment in San Bernardino before being transferred to Queen of the Angels Hospital, and survived.

A well-liked member of the SCTA, Rulon McGregor, age twenty-one, belonged to the same club as Parks—the Road Runners—and had participated in the 1949 hot rod show. As in the first year, a bunch of the guys built a custom roadster on site for the public to see, and McGregor was one of those guys. A few months later his buddies were attending his funeral.

Parks became editor of *Hot Rod* that year while continuing to lead the SCTA, which adopted stricter safety controls at the dry lakes. 1949 also marked the launch of Pete Petersen's second magazine, *Motor Trend* ("the magazine for a motoring world" as it dubbed itself), which was aimed at a broader, more mainstream audience than *Hot Rod*. Parks's influence and reach were growing as well. He spoke at a Tulsa conference of the prestigious Society of Automotive Engineers, bringing a hot rod with him to show the group. "The once roundly condemned 'hot rod' automobile has reached respectability," said a wire service report on the meeting.

Meantime southern California was giving birth to a new motorized activity: *legal* off-street drag racing. The Goleta airport north of Santa Barbara hosted the first of these races, starting in the spring of 1949. Sponsored by the Santa Barbara Acceleration Association with the cooperation of the California Highway Patrol, the hot rods raced down a road at the airfield that was no longer in use. The races were loose, casual, and conducted without timing equipment, unlike those held a year later in Santa Ana. These latter races, widely regarded as the first *organized* legal drag races, occurred July 2, 1950, on a vacated asphalt runway strip of the Santa Ana Airport, now John Wayne Airport. They timed the cars, and an ambulance waited nearby in case of an accident.

Many dry lakes hot-rodders competed in the drags, although differences quickly emerged in the two types of racing. Unlike early dry lakes cars, which used a rolling or moving start, dragsters took off from a standing start. Drag racing in many respects resembled street racing, the major difference being, of course, that it was safely away from city streets. Two cars nosed up to the starting line, their engines knocking and pounding. The starter stood between and slightly ahead of them in the center of the runway, holding a flag. (The starter has since been replaced by a sequence of lights, similar to traffic lights, with green signaling for the cars to go.) With a flourish the starter jumped up and waved the flag, sending the two cars down a flat, straight, quarter-mile strip of asphalt blowing smoke, burning rubber, fishtailing, and racing side by side. Engines erupted into flames, transmissions dropped, clutches and brakes went haywire. It was wild. Spectators stood behind ropes or guardrails along the sides of the runway, breathtakingly close to the action.

Relying on his friends and supporters in law enforcement, Wally Parks worked with Gordon Browning of the Los Angeles Police Department, Sergeant Bud Coons and Chief of Police Ralph Parker of the Pomona police, and many others in authority who saw the need for socially approved methods for young men to blow off steam in cars. You couldn't just tell these kids no and expect them to meekly obey; they were going to race their cars no matter what their elders said or did, so a better approach was to try to get them to do it in a controlled setting. Fortunately, many of the airstrips built during the war had fallen into disuse, and these places could easily serve as drag strips without endangering the public or requiring large outlays of public funds.

In 1951 Parks formed the National Hot Rod Association, now the governing body for drag racing in the United States and Canada. "That was always Wally's dream," said Petersen, who helped his friend get the organization off the ground. The LAPD's Gordon Browning joined the original board of directors, and the NHRA established rules, promoted safety, sanctioned races, and grew its membership rolls around the country. Of course the kids still dragged on the streets, as kids will do, but the NHRA became a strong voice against this activity and provided a home for those kids who wished to do it legally, in safer settings.

From these origins, drag strips sprouted around the country in the 1950s—more than one hundred of them in forty states holding races that drew close to 3 million spectators by the end of the decade. Notable California strips included the Fremont Drag Strip in the Bay Area, Paradise Mesa in Chula Vista, and Lions Drag Strip in Wilmington next to Long Beach. All of these have since closed, the victims of high California real estate values; as with the long-ago Beverly Hills speedway, the cost of land became too expensive to support a track, and developers chopped up the land for other uses.

But the Pomona Speedway, the Yankee Stadium of drag racing, remains in business today. Formerly a section of parking lot at the Los Angeles County Fairgrounds, it hosts the first and last races of the annual NHRA season. The Pomona fairgrounds is also the home of the Wally Parks NHRA Motorsports Museum, dedicated to the history of drag racing. A statue of Parks stands outside it. With its headquarters in Glendora, east of Los Angeles, the NHRA now sponsors nationally televised races around the country, featuring ground-shaking, ear-assaulting dragsters with millions at stake in prize money and revenue. Wally Parks's passion has grown into one of the biggest motor sports in America.

Parks died, at the age of ninety-four, in September 2007, seven months after the passing of Robert Petersen, at age eighty. Both men achieved the truest success: long, wonderful marriages, families who loved them, deep enduring friendships. And both lived to see their onetime disrespectable hot rod hobby turn into a merchandising and nostalgia phenomenon with reunions, rallies, museum exhibits, websites, books, magazines, movies, documentaries, model kits, toy cars, art, postage stamps, and on and on. After founding *Hot Rod* and *Motor Trend,* Petersen became a kind of phenomenon himself, creating a stable of car and specialty magazines. Petersen Publishing evolved into one of the most successful publishing companies in the United States, boasting a total circulation of 43 million and yearly profits of up to $40 million. The Hearst Corporation bought the company for $450 million in the mid-1990s, ending Petersen's association with it.

Petersen was an avid collector of cars. Asked by a reporter what car he drove, he responded, "When?" A generous benefactor of charities, his most generous gift went, fittingly, to automobiles. His $30 million endowment established the Petersen Automotive Museum in Los Angeles. Located on the Miracle Mile at Wilshire and Fairfax, it is the biggest and most prestigious automobile museum in the country.

TWENTY-FOUR

Enchanted Kingdom

The week before the Orange County Airport hosted the first organized legal drag races in 1950, the nearby Santa Ana Naval Air Station welcomed a different group of race car drivers. These drivers were as American as any hot-rodder—many of them, in fact, *were* hot-rodders—but the cars they drove mainly came from foreign countries: MGs, Jaguars, and Allards from England; Alfa-Romeos from Italy; and Mercedes-Benzes from Germany. The arrival of these cars in the United States was another sign of the changed political map of the world; war-ravaged Europe was being rebuilt with the aid of the Marshall Plan, and ex-GIs were driving sports cars made by their former enemies in Italy and Germany.

Detroit did not make a sports car at that time, so these imports were truly rare and exotic sights on the streets of California and America. When they were overseas the GIs saw and drove Triumphs, Austin-Healeys, and Jaguars, and when they came home they wanted to drive them too. These British and European marques had definite curb appeal, and when a person tucked in behind the wheel of one and started to takc it through its paces, "the construction gives the driver the feeling that the machine actually is a projection of himself," as one driver put it. Not just GIs but many other Californians also adored them, and the state rapidly became the No. 1 American market for imported cars, a position it maintains to this day.

The Santa Ana Road Races took place in late June on what was then still an operational Strategic Air Command base in Tustin. (It later became a Marine base and is now under civilian control.) The cars raced on a two-and-a-half-mile layout around aircraft hangars and on the paved runways and roads of the base. Spectators stood behind guardrails along the course, which was marked off by traffic cones. Hay bales positioned along the bends and straights protected the fans while blocking the drivers from going off the pavement. Their cars knocked against the hay bales, righted themselves, and got back into the race.

America's first postwar sports car road races occurred in Watkins Glen, New York, attracting one hundred thousand spectators in 1949 and showing the crowd-pleasing potential of these new exotics. Palm Beach, Florida, held a big race after

Watkins Glen, and California got into the game soon after that with an event at the Palm Springs airport in the spring of 1950. Next came Santa Ana.

The favorite for the twenty-five-lap main event at Santa Ana was Sterling Edwards, who had won at Palm Springs and figured to dominate the other fifteen cars in the field. A well-known "Beverly Hills sportsman and construction financier," according to the papers, Edwards paid sixteen thousand dollars for his custom speedster built by Eddie Meyer, a longtime southern California hot-rodder. In 1940 Meyer drove 121.95 miles per hour at the dry lakes, then the fastest time ever for a roadster at the lakes. Over the years, he had gained a reputation as a top car builder, and this was why Edwards hired him.

Unlike most of the cars in the race, the Meyer-Edwards custom was all-American—sculpted white Ford body on the outside, growling V-8 on the inside. Some driver-builders used the body of the import but dropped in an American-made Mercury or Cadillac engine for their power plant. Sports car purists generally mocked these homebuilt cars as "backyard specials," dismissing them as inferior to the classic European motors and designs. The men who built these backyard specials in turn ridiculed the sports car people as "tea-sippers," regarding them as elitists who were more impressed by image and foreign brand names than actual performance. It was "an us-versus-them attitude," said Dean Batchelor, who loved both hot rods and the European imports. "On one side were the rich, or nearly so, types who favored exotics from overseas. On the other side were the specials builders—hot-rodders mostly."

One side favored American, the other European. One side built cars to go straight and fast through the timing traps, the other liked speed in combination with deft handling on the turns. The two camps also disagreed on engine preferences, which translated into different sounds on the street and track: "the huffing and chuffing of a big American V-8" versus "the howling screech" of a foreign model, as Batchelor said. The huffers and chuffers liked nothing better than to beat the howling screechers and vice versa, and the fourteen thousand fans who came out to Santa Ana knew about this rivalry and rooted accordingly. All of it added up to big fun.

Confounding the handicappers, Sterling Edwards and his sixteen-thousand-dollar bomb barely figured in the main race, dropping out on the fifth lap due to a misbehaving clutch. But even without this problem he likely wouldn't have done much, not with Roy Richter in the field. Richter, the owner of the Bell Auto Parts speed shop and a hot-rodder to the core, drove a Mercury-powered Allard—British exterior, American interior. It was a backyard special with nothing second-rate about the car or Richter's ability to handle it. Starting on the pole, he grabbed the lead and refused to yield it to anyone, opening up large swaths of pavement between his rear end and the rest of the field.

But a pattern quickly emerged in the race, one that disturbed Richter despite his car's dominance. No matter what he did, he could not shake a Jaguar XK-120 tagging along after him. Each time they hit a straightaway, the more powerful Allard pulled away with ease. But as soon as they entered an S-shaped series of turns in the twisty air station layout, the second-place Jaguar swallowed up the distance between them. This scenario—the Allard drawing away in the straights, the Jaguar closing in the "S" section—played out again and again over the fifty-plus-mile race. Clearly the Jaguar didn't have enough for the Allard on this track, unless the Allard suffered some mechanical failure that knocked it from the race. But equally clear, the man in the Jag had some mad driving skills. His name was Phil Hill, and he was twenty-three years old.

It's an accepted fact," writes the automobile historian Richard Lamm, "that many of the men who established America's road racing powers, influenced Indy cars, and designed and engineered many of America's production cars had their beginnings in the hot rod movement of southern California." Although he's not commonly associated with it, Phil Hill, one of the finest Grand Prix drivers of all time and the first American to win the Formula One world driving championship, had his roots in hot rods too. Born in Miami in 1927, Hill came to California as a baby. His family took up residence on 20th Street in Santa Monica, where he spent his boyhood and lived for many years as an adult. His father, a former navy lieutenant and manager of a Mack Trucks office, became Santa Monica's postmaster. His mother loved music and wrote and produced songs—from pop ("Down at Miami's Beaches") to religious ("Jesus Is the Sweetest Name I Know"). She taught her young son the piano but, as he recalled years later, "I was far more interested in my mother's shiny new Marmon speedster than I was in learning to play the piano. It had been one of a pair of New York show cars. Barney Oldfield bought one, Mom bought the other, and even at four I knew it was a beautiful thing."

Hill grew up with an appreciation for and knowledge of beautiful things—beautiful music, beautiful art, beautiful automobiles. He explored the strange new world hidden under the hood of the Marmon and showed still more curiosity when his aunt, Helen Grasseli, visited them from her home in the San Fernando Valley. Aunt Helen's love for fine things extended to automobiles, the same as her nephew. She drove an elegant World War I–vintage Packard, which she had designed herself in association with the Fleetwood Body company in Pennsylvania. Her other car was a grand and stylish 1931 Pierce-Arrow Le Baron; she bought it new during the Depression—a good clue to the wealth possessed by Aunt Helen and the Hill family, and to the sort of upbringing young Phil had.

Here was another: Every day, Aunt Helen's chauffeur drove Phil and his brother to Franklin Grammar School in Santa Monica in the Packard, and some mornings she rode along with them to make sure they showed the proper decorum. "This was during the Depression period, and we felt just awful being taken to school like a couple of royal princes," recalled Phil. "We'd try to hide on the floor, but my aunt would pull us back up on the seat, and we'd squirm there miserably while all our schoolmates gawked at us."

Aunt Helen had her ways, but she doted on Phil and fostered his development. And she did what Phil's father and mother would not do: show him how to drive a car. Ordering her chauffeur into the back of the Packard—Aunt Helen did her fair share of ordering in her time—she slid into the driver's seat while Phil climbed into her lap. She turned the key and they were off, Phil whipping around the big wooden steering wheel, his aunt operating the clutch and brake pedals, the chauffeur watching anxiously from the back. Phil eventually learned to shift the gears himself, although he could not do it in the beginning because his legs were too short to reach the floor pedals. He was nine years old.

Even at that age, the boy had a knack. Aunt Helen could see that, and the boy saw it too, his enthusiasm and confidence growing each time they went out together in the car. Finally, he felt ready to give it a go without her. When a family friend visited the Hills in Santa Monica in his Oldsmobile, the cheeky nine-year-old asked if he could drive it around the block. By himself. The friend, amused by this request, said yes; his not-so-amused mother and father said no. But the friend reassured them that he'd be in the passenger seat himself and would quickly take over if anything happened. With his parents' grudging consent, the boy eagerly plunged ahead. To make up for his lack of size he stuck pillows behind his back and sat forward in the seat to see over the long, long Oldsmobile hood. His forward perch also allowed his feet to reach the floor pedals. "So off we went, with a kind of lurch as I shifted into second. At the first corner I almost nailed the curb, but got around okay. Then, to my great embarrassment, I stalled the engine twice at San Vicente and 19th Street," said Hill.

The big boat of a car lurched to a stop on a section of the old Santa Monica Road Race, which was originally run in the days when Wilshire Boulevard was called Nevada Avenue and when Santa Monica itself was a tiny, isolated town flanked by the ocean on one side and farms and pasturelands on the other. The ocean hadn't changed much since then but most everything else had. By the middle 1930s automobile traffic traveled briskly up and down San Vicente, and parked cars occupied spaces along either side of the street. But the boy did not panic; he restarted the engine and finished the rest of the trip without incident, returning home with a story to tell his parents and "foolishly happy in the knowledge that I could now drive without assistance."

Hill attended a military academy in Hollywood with other children of privilege, but as ever the boy's interests strayed elsewhere, to subjects not taught in class. If his parents disapproved of this fixation of his, Aunt Helen never did. On Sunday afternoons when Phil and his brother and sister came to visit her in the valley, "I'd begin pestering Aunt Helen to take me out in the car," he recalled. "She understood me better than my parents did, and we grew very close. I could tell her how I really felt about things and knew she'd listen." They went on long drives around the valley together, not with Phil on her knee but in the driver's seat, in control of the machine. Phil's brother and sister came along on these trips too, and no one breathed a word about them to their parents. It was their secret—theirs and Aunt Helen's.

One day in 1939 Aunt Helen and her favorite nephew were walking in downtown Los Angeles when they stopped to admire a Model T in the window of a showroom on Figueroa. Though more than a decade old, the T looked totally cherry—"in absolutely amazing condition. The seats were perfect, the tires were not worn, the top was like new," remembered Phil. Insisting on a closer look, he hurried inside only to be knocked back when he learned the car's price: forty dollars, far above the usual going rate for a used Tin Lizzy. Even after he became a professional driver Hill could never hide his emotions. If he felt something during a race—gloom, frustration, joy—his soft, expressive face showed it plainly, and he let people know what he was feeling with a rich, colorful vocabulary. But in this case Phil did not need to utter a word because his face said it all. He realized he'd never be able to buy the Model T on his own, and he was crushed. This was not a situation Aunt Helen could tolerate for long. She paid cash for the car on the spot, and the salesman delivered it to her home that evening. Watching from an upstairs window and seeing the car appear on the street, Phil raced downstairs to meet it at the front door with his aunt. The salesman offered the boy a quick lesson on the T's three-pedal planetary transmission, and Phil, impatient as he was motivated, got the hang of it in a breath, operating it on his own almost instantly. Too excited to sleep that night, he skipped school the next day with his aunt's permission and spent every waking minute getting acquainted with his new companion.

Phil's father did not approve of Aunt Helen's gift, feeling strongly that a twelve-year-old boy was too young to own his own car. But he did not take it away from his son, only making him promise not to go on public streets in it. Phil readily agreed, probably because he and George Hearst, a friend from the military academy who owned a car too, had already figured out a plan to stay off the streets and avoid being cited for underage driving. George was one of *the* Hearsts; his grandfather, the publishing czar William Randolph Hearst, owned a Texas-sized spread in Santa Monica Canyon where the backcountry dirt roads were even better than in the valley. Phil and George raced their cars in the canyon as hard and fast as they dared, without any adults nagging at them to slow down.

This began Phil's hot rod period, which, not coincidentally, also began a period of rebellion against his parents and elite upbringing. Owning his own car and being able to fix it when it threw a rod made him feel independent and strong, and he expressed this independence by rebelling against the uniform-style clothing they made him wear at the military academy. The holey, grungy, dirty T-shirts and jeans he adopted were, he admitted, "an unconscious effort to annoy my parents," an effort that surely succeeded given the heavy helpings of arrogant teen attitude that went along with his new look. At Santa Monica High, the first public school he attended, he met other guys who dressed in wrecked jeans and T-shirts and drove raked Model Ts. Running with these guys, he began to "swagger and smoke and raise hell," meanwhile dating girls who got a charge out of bad boys like him.

Not being into baseball or football or conventional school activities, Phil's thing was cars. "I'd wander through junkyards, looking at all the old rusted cars," he remembered fondly. The first auto race he ever saw was the midgets at Gilmore Stadium, but this occurred in late 1940, and it wasn't long before Gilmore and every other track in the area was shutting down for the duration.

While other boys his age were fighting overseas, Hill, prevented from joining the military by a chronic sinus condition, remained at home, working part-time at gas stations and later on the Douglas Aircraft assembly line. Over time he traded in the T for a Chevy, the Chevy for a Packard, and the Packard for a Plymouth. All these he bought used, and all these he tricked up to indulge a passion for illegal street racing—"dragging away from stop lights," as he put it.

After high school he enrolled at the University of Southern California, doing his best to put his teen rebellion phase behind him and become, in his words, the "good citizen and solid businessman" his parents always wished him to be. This didn't last long. He bailed out of USC in June 1947 to work as a mechanic for a Hollywood midget racing team, competing at Gilmore, Memorial Coliseum, the Rose Bowl in Pasadena, the Carrell Speedway in Gardena, and other tracks. Not driving, just being a mechanic, getting greasy and grimy by taking apart the guts of machines, Hill found his identity as a man—not his parents' conception of who he should be, but who he was, truly. "I had an identity," he said. "I had a real label which I could hang onto at last."

From there things happened fast. Raised on born-in-the-USA automobiles, Hill grew fond of the British and European exotics that started appearing on the streets of Los Angeles with war's end. He'd seen pictures of MGs but never in person until he drove past one parked on Wilshire. He immediately swung his '46 Ford around and just like with Aunt Helen and the Model T, swooped in for a closer look. He felt like an ancient sea voyager discovering a new continent—awestruck and humbled. A few days earlier George Hearst had told him about some MGs on display at International Motors in Beverly Hills. Phil decided then and there to book over to International to see for himself. After a test drive in one he was, as he said, "hooked."

He sold the Ford, borrowed two hundred from Aunt Helen to cover the shortfall, and bought a new MG roadster with red leather seats, carpets on the floor, and "the dash with the big round tach. Everything was so neat and different," he said excitedly. Hill took his infatuation one step further by quitting his mechanic's job at the Packard agency in town and going to work in the garage at International. On and off the job he worked on and drove MGs, and in January 1948, almost as a lark, a fun thing to do on the weekend, he entered a road rally in Palos Verdes and finished second. This was a rally, not a race, and was similar to an old-time reliability run where drivers earned points based on time and automotive skills. The next month he competed in another rally in Chatsworth, earning top points. A rally in Santa Barbara followed, and it was about then that Hill sold his MG for a faster one and decided to get serious about racing.

His first competitive auto races, on a July evening in 1949 at Carrell Speedway, pitted his MG against a fleet of other MGs, BMWs, Talbots, Jaguars, Renaults, Fiats, and Morris Minors on a half-mile oval with eight thousand people in the stands. Hill entered three races—a Class B contest for his category of cars, a trophy run for all comers, and an all-MG sprint—and won all three. Nevertheless, he wasn't entirely pleased by the results, concluding that the MG didn't have enough zip to suit him. With the support and financial assistance of International Motors and probably Aunt Helen, he then went to England to personally pick out a new Jaguar XK-120, "generally acknowledged the fastest stock car in the business," as the press said. While there, he took mechanical courses on foreign cars and toured the factories of Jaguar, MG, and Rolls Royce. Staying in the UK into the spring of 1950, he returned to California in June eager to test out his new purchase on home soil. His first outing was the Santa Ana Road Races, where he started on the outside with Roy Richter on the pole.

The race bunched most of its action into the first three laps when Hill's black XK-120 went after Richter's hopped-up Allard. "Into the first tricky S-turn Hill did a complete spin trying to pass Richter. He stalled and the other fourteen cars went sweeping by. Hill restarted and in two laps regained his second spot," said an eyewitness account. From then on the race fell into its pattern of Hill gaining on the curves and dropping back on the straights with Richter unable to put him away. "I was always aware of Phil in my rearview mirror," Richter said afterward.

Unknown on the local racing scene up to that point, Hill's name circulated quickly after Santa Ana. One reason for his rush to prominence was "the most theatrical style of any driver I believe I have ever seen," writes Joe Scalzo, "all flailing arms, screaming engine revs, and with his face wracked by grimaces." Pouring his nervous energy into his racing and using every bit of his muscular five-foot-ten, 160-pound frame to lean into the curves, Hill drove with a kind of controlled desperation that race fans loved.

Likely because of his sudden celebrity, International Motors transferred Hill from the repair shop to the showroom floor, which he just hated. He liked driving and working on cars, not selling them. But he had enough clout at International to persuade the dealership to hire Richie Ginther as a mechanic. Ginther, who would become a superb Grand Prix driver in his own right, grew up a few blocks away from Hill in Santa Monica. They met at a party, found they shared some mutual interests—cars, mainly—and sometime after that Ginther, who was a few years younger, wandered over to Phil's house to see what he was up to. As usual Phil was up to his ears in cars. "The next thing I knew I was helping him prepare his MG," said Ginther, who acted as Hill's chief mechanic for his next race at Pebble Beach.

Sponsored by the northern California chapter of the Sports Car Club of America, the first annual Pebble Beach Road Races were set for November 5, 1950. Nobody had ever raced automobiles at Pebble Beach before, and nobody knew exactly what to expect. One thing was certain, though: It was an impossibly spectacular setting. Santa Ana was a military base, Palm Springs an airport. But this course weaved through the magical Del Monte Forest of the Monterey Peninsula on the two-lane asphalt roads driven by tourists and residents of the community. A segment of the course ran along the famous Seventeen Mile Drive.

The 2.4-mile layout resembled an elegant woman's boot, twisting through columns of Monterey cypress and beginning and ending on Portola Road near the Pebble Beach Riding Stables (or Equestrian Center, as it's known today). Spectators could bring picnic lunches, lay out checkered tablecloths and blankets on the pine needles, drink wine, eat bread and cheese, and watch from various points around the course. Even when they couldn't see the cars they could hear their engines roaring through the forest—or, as one poetically minded observer put it, "the reverberations of nude exhausts bounding from massive tree trunks."

The race included sports car guys and hot rod guys from around the state, all of them dependent on one another to not take stupid risks. Their safety also hinged on the performance of their machines, which put Hill at an early disadvantage. In a trial run the clutch lining on his Jaguar shredded, dropping the clutch pedal to the floor and rendering it useless. But the thing went haywire too soon before the start of the race, and neither he nor Ginther had time to fix it. Hill had to run the fifty miles essentially clutch-free, practicing the "hazardous and difficult art of shifting without disengaging the clutch."

The green flag dropped, and more things went wrong for him. While the other cars flew past him down Portola, the Jaguar stayed put, earthbound and immobile. The only thing moving on the car was its driver's arm, frantically waving for help from Ginther and his crewmates. They ran out and pushed it to get it rolling. Hill popped it into gear and he was off, scrambling to catch up, which he did, quickly. At the end of lap one he saw the leader, Arnold Stubbs in an MG Special, turning onto the long straightaway down Stevenson Drive. Stubbs held the lead until the ninth lap, when he pitted and Mike Graham in his Cadillac-powered Allard took over first. Behind him came Bill Breeze and Hill, both in Jaguar XK-120s and both gunning for Graham. First Breeze got him, then Hill right after that, making the Jaguars one-two in the race. Trailing behind, Hill noticed how Breeze slowed on the corners, which suggested that his brakes were fading. Hill was right. He slipped by Breeze on lap eleven and on lap twelve Breeze had to quit, done in by bad brakes.

Now Hill had the lead all to himself—or did he? He wasn't sure even after Ginther held up a sign in the pits that said, "Long Lead." Did that mean he had a long lead, or that a driver named "Long" had the lead? Hill mistakenly thought the latter, and put the pedal down on his Jag even as "his own brakes were rapidly failing. He skidded into bales, dragged the rear wheels and roared up escape roads when his speed was too great to negotiate a turn."

On the next lap Ginther held up another sign, perhaps to clarify the previous misunderstanding. This sign read "One." This only created more confusion, however, because Hill thought it meant "One more lap to go." In fact, there were seven more laps. Hill realized this when he came skidding and dragging around Portola and instead of a checkered flag saw another Jaguar XK-120 pop into his rearview mirror.

Its driver was Don Parkinson, a close friend of Hill's who later became his brother-in-law. In second but eyeing first, Parkinson was making up ground fast on the wildly careening Hill, who could not afford to ignore the sudden appearance of yet another challenger in his rearview mirror—Mike Graham in his revived Allard. Lacking brakes and a clutch Hill outraced them both to win the biggest race of his career so far in 44 minutes, 8 seconds. Runner-up Parkinson finished forty-five seconds behind him, and James Seeley, in a backyard special built by hot-rodder Ted Cannon, came out of nowhere to steal third away from Graham, who finished fourth.

Ten thousand fans exulted in this mad dash through the pines, which attracted attention around California and the nation. Almost instantly Pebble Beach became *it*—"the glamour track and sports car event of any season," the most important road race in the West and the most important in the country save for Watkins Glen.

That first year also saw the start of the Concours d'Elegance, a car show of the most elegant kind. The rarest and most exotic automobiles in the world went on display at the Del Monte Lodge and along the Pebble Beach Golf Links, as well as being driven around the streets in a parade. The grandest and most influential of these now-common exhibitions, the Concours quickly became an in-crowd event for the beautiful and famous, unequalled in this country for the "color, pageantry, showmanship" of the automobiles as well as the lavish parties thrown by the wealthy of Pebble Beach at their Seventeen Mile Drive mansions. The usual weekend schedule consisted of racing trials and practice on Saturday morning, followed by the Concours at 11 a.m. and for the rest of the afternoon. Sunday was all-day racing, climaxing with the Del Monte Trophy race for the cars in the biggest and most powerful class.

Just as the Crosby Clambake on the Monterey Peninsula was more than just a golf tournament, the Pebble Beach Road Races and Concours d'Elegance became more than just an auto race and show. They were the premiere events of a racing circuit filled with distinctive stops—the sunny desert oasis of Palm Springs, the Mediterranean splendor of Santa Barbara and its 2.2-mile "pretzel circuit" at the Goleta Airport (where the early drag races were also held), and the more mundane but still exciting tracks at Santa Ana Naval Station and other airfields. Additionally there were two other coastal road races, Golden Gate Park in San Francisco and Torrey Pines in San Diego. Like Pebble Beach, Golden Gate Park and Torrey Pines took place on actual roads driven by members of the public. Fast, dangerous, and strikingly dramatic, these courses made California one of the global hot spots for sports car racing, an enchanted kingdom, said one who was there, of "romance, splendor, elegance, Ferraris and race drivers who are gentlemen."

More than ninety thousand people saw the May 31, 1952, race in Golden Gate Park, a place that had once banned horseless carriages as a public nuisance. City officials suspended the park's normal speed limits for the day, and on timed practice runs the cars reached 125 miles per hour on the straights of the 3.1-mile course. When the real thing got under way Bill Pollock in an Allard broke away at the start and kept right on going, at one point leading the pack by twenty-five seconds. Then the pack started coming back on him, or at least one prominent member of it: Phil Hill, in his fastest, smoothest-handling machine yet. After his win at Pebble Beach, Hill went through his customary merciless machine evaluation, found his Jag wanting, and cut it loose. In quest of ever-faster wheels he went through an Alfa Romeo, an Aston Martin, and a Chrysler-powered Briggs Cunningham before phoning Luigi Chinetti in New York. Chinetti was the North American distributor of Ferrari and a scout for its factory racing team. Like Aunt Helen, Chinetti had a sharp eye for talent, and he'd been watching the young Californian's progress for some time. For all his intellectualism Hill drove with passion, a quality Chinetti and the Italians admired. Beginning what would become a long and fruitful relationship between Hill and the quintessential Italian racing machine, Chinetti offered to sell him a 12-liter Ferrari at a steep discount. Hill grabbed the deal, and this was the car he was chasing Pollock in, desperately driving the turns and clocking speeds a whisker shy of 120 miles per hour in his effort to catch up. Closing to within four seconds of the lead, he was passing a slower car on the inside when an engine coil in the Ferrari sprung loose and ruined its ability to accelerate. Pollock won the shortened race—thick fog caused its original distance of one hundred miles to be reduced to eighty-six—but most fans went away talking about Hill's second-place comeback. That and Mike Graham. In a sprint to the finish line Graham lost control of his car and smacked into a tree, walking away unhurt.

Hill got his revenge over Pollock in July at Torrey Pines, the rugged 2.8-mile asphalt track on the graceful ocean bluffs of San Diego just west of the Pacific Coast Highway (it's now the site of the Torrey Pines Golf Course). The races drew twenty-eight thousand fans and 120 cars, but Hill and the Ferrari drained the drama out of the featured event by seizing the lead in the first mile and breezing through the next seventy-nine to win easily. The only excitement occurred when a race driver blew a tire and veered off course toward a San Diego TV cameraman. The cameraman jumped out of the way to escape injury but could not save his equipment, which was crushed.

TWENTY-FIVE

The Car of Tomorrow

The European sports car invasion of America caused a revolution. They were beautiful, they were sleek, they were fast, and America had nothing that could touch them. Consequently car manufacturers and designers from coast to coast scrambled to build an American sports car that could hold its own with the best from Britain and the continent. One of the designers involved in this effort was a stylish southern Californian named Howard "Dutch" Darrin, whose latest creation, a sports car prototype, was previewed at the Los Angeles Motorama a few months after Phil Hill's win at Torrey Pines. The night before the Motorama's Saturday opening at the Pan-Pacific Auditorium, Darrin hosted a swank party at his Benedict Drive home in Beverly Hills to give his friends and clients a sneak peek at the car, which was made from a revolutionary new lightweight plastic called fiberglass.

Of all the sports car models shown at the Motorama—a General Motors–sponsored auto show—the Darrin prototype created the most buzz, partly because of its rakish, low-slung innovative design and partly because of the man who designed it. A handsome, silver-haired gent in his mid-fifties, Darrin dressed with country club elegance and had a debonair Gallic charm, though he was American born and raised. The press referred to him as "one of the world's most famous custom designers" and "the internationally known Paris and Hollywood custom car designer." An advertisement called him "Paris' brilliant Howard Darrin." His Sunset Strip custom shop was "Darrin of Paris." Many of his customers did indeed think he was French, a mistake Darrin did not labor to correct. "In Hollywood," he said about his European reputation, "that was better than all the work I had ever done."

But Dutch Darrin was no poseur; he was the real deal. His automobile lineage included consulting and designing for General Motors and Stutz in the United States, Citroen and Renault in France, Rolls Royce in England, and Daimler-Benz in Germany. This work he did in the 1920s and '30s while living in Paris and jointly heading up a firm with Tom Hibbard, another top American automobile designer who'd achieved fame overseas. "We had one thing in our favor," Darrin said about his association with Hibbard. "We thought ideas should be young, and numerous old customs disregarded." Many wealthy European royals thought the same, and Hibbard and Darrin became one of the hottest design shops on the continent until first Hibbard, and then Darrin, migrated back across the Atlantic out from underneath the darkening political clouds of the Third Reich. But rather than follow his former partner to Detroit, Darrin came to Hollywood, where he found clients galore and an active polo scene to boot.

"The three things I most enjoy in the world," he wrote once, "[are] building cars, flying airplanes and playing polo." Polo was how he first met Darryl Zanuck, who served as his entrée into the movie colony after Darrin moved to Beverly Hills. When Zanuck, the head of Warner Brothers, showed up at the Paris Polo Club in the early thirties he knew hardly anyone and felt out of place. Enter Darrin, who spoke French, got seated at good tables in the best restaurants, and knew everyone worth knowing at the club. He invited Zanuck to play polo with him, and their team won a tournament. The grateful producer asked what he could do to return the favor and Darrin, who owned a theater in Paris, said that if Warner Brothers had any pictures it was willing to show there, he'd be happy to accept. Zanuck released to him the hit musical *Forty-Second Street*, and throngs of tap-happy Parisians packed the theater for a solid year. The two became friends and when Darrin announced plans to move to California, Zanuck said come on, he'd save a spot for him on his polo team.

The arrival of the former American in Paris caused an immediate splash in Hollywood. The Countess Dorothy Di Frasso, a rich socialite rumored to have had affairs with several of Hollywood's leading men, became one of Darrin's first clients, bringing a Rolls Royce to him with only one request. "She specified only that it had to outshine the Rolls of Constance Bennett, her great social rival," Darrin said. "The general contention is that it did."

As did the elite of Europe, the elite of Hollywood came to Darrin not because he created just beautiful luxury cars, but beautiful *unique* luxury cars. Cars that no one else had, cars that signified prestige and glamour and money, cars that tweaked the beaks of social and box office rivals. His hottest prewar setup was a Super 8 Victoria Packard convertible roadster that combined elegance and flash, much like Darrin himself. Its unique styling became so associated with him that the car came to be known as the Darrin-Packard. "He was like an early George Barris," said Fred Zimmerman, the auto historian. "He cut the top off a Packard and made it into a convertible." Bohman and Schwartz of Pasadena crafted its aluminum body, and "it was the car to have in Hollywood before the Big War."

After the war Darrin formed a partnership with a man who figures large in the history of California and the West but who is not typically associated with automobiles, Henry J. Kaiser. A balding, portly man with a taste for the grand and the monumental, Kaiser ran companies that built ships, dams, tunnels, pipelines, and houses, and manufactured steel, aluminum, and concrete. But his first success in business came from cars—that is, the roads that cars drive on. Leaving New York during the First World War, Kaiser settled with his wife and son in British Columbia, forming a paving company that quickly developed a reputation for low bids and fast, quality work. In 1916, when the federal highway bill started pouring public funds into road construction, his contracting business migrated southward into Washington, Oregon, and California. In 1921, a one-hundred-thousand-dollar paving job between Redding and Red Bluff led to more highway jobs in the north of the state. That same year, seeing the extraordinary opportunities in fast-growing California, he relocated his company to Oakland, the home of the many far-flung Kaiser enterprises that would follow and the headquarters today for Kaiser Permanente, the largest managed health care organization in the country and its founder's most enduring achievement.

Kaiser Paving blacktopped its first Bay Area roads around Livermore in the early 1920s. When its business sagged, the head man lobbied Sacramento for the passage of the 1923 state gasoline tax to ensure a steady stream of financing for highway building. The first federal gas tax came early the next decade; it was one cent a gallon on top of the state gas levy. By this time, though, Kaiser was virtually out of the paving and road business and onto bigger, more ambitious projects such as dam building. His company helped build the monumental Hoover Dam on the Colorado River.

Hoover Dam opened in 1936. The year before, an article about an experimental three-wheeled, one-cylinder automobile appeared in the trade paper *Automotive Daily News.* The paper carried few details about the car except for its creator's last name: Kaiser—as in Henry J. Kaiser, who apparently did not have enough things on his plate building the Hoover Dam and needed to fiddle around with designing an experimental car. But Kaiser had long enjoyed cars, especially big ones that went vroom. "The boss," as every employee in the home office knew, "enjoyed driving his own big cars at hair-raising speeds."

In 1945 he took this enjoyment to an extreme, forming his own automobile company with Joe Frazer, a car industry executive. Although General Motors, Ford, and Chrysler controlled 90 percent of the American car market, Kaiser, whose shipbuilding during the war had won him and his company wide praise, felt he could compete against them with a dependable, low-cost car modeled on Ford's old Model T. At a kickoff press conference in New York in early 1946 he and Frazer introduced two prototypes warmly welcomed by the public. In the next months the company received hundreds of thousands of orders, its stock price hit a high on Wall Street, and it began building a new factory in Willow Run outside of Detroit. Regarded as a maverick by some for his unconventional business practices (such as offering low-cost group health insurance to his workers, the model for his medical plan), Kaiser at first envisioned a West Coast challenge to the Midwest auto industry. "But," said a biographer, "logistical and other problems persuaded him to center operations in Detroit." Wherever its cars were made, however, Kaiser-Frazer would always have a strong westward tilt because that was Henry Kaiser's base of operations and the region he knew best.

The Kaiser-Frazer Corporation manufactured nearly 12,000 cars in its first year. Things got even better in year two when it produced nearly 150,000 autos, captured 3 percent of the American market, and made a profit of $17 million before taxes. This was an exciting moment for the company in an exciting time for independent carmakers. The pent-up postwar demand for new automobiles created opportunities for Packard, Nash, Studebaker, and other established independents, as well as start-ups such as the Tucker Automobile Corporation and Kaiser-Frazer.

But this early excitement faded fast as Kaiser-Frazer started running into problems—some of its own making, some perhaps not. Many of its top managers came from shipbuilding and construction, Henry Kaiser's bread-and-butter industries, and were learning the car business on the fly. Then, like Abner Doble before them, they ran into the wall that was General Motors. When steel shortages hampered production, Kaiser-Frazer executives charged GM and the steel companies with conspiring to run them out of business. While this may have hurt the company, it did not kill it. For that, Kaiser-Frazer had itself to blame. Its new models were dowdy and plain, and potential car buyers reacted in the worst possible way: with yawns. To move its cars the company had to slash prices. Reluctant to push an unpopular product, dealers fled Kaiser-Frazer in droves. Needing close to $20 million to prop itself up, the company released more shares of its stock for sale. Problems with the handling of these sales arose, and lawsuits followed. Relations at the top between Henry Kaiser and Joe Frazer crumbled as well.

By 1949 the company faced losses of $30 million and the damning public sentiment that its cars were "overpriced and out of date"—a fatal condition for any consumer product but especially automobiles. To reverse this image and upgrade the style and quality of its cars, Kaiser-Frazer turned to Darrin of Paris, the Frenchman of Sunset Boulevard. "So I signed a contract, came up with a car, and the engineers proceeded to botch it up anyway," said Darrin in his urbane, witty style. "It was unrecognizable." Known as the Henry J, the car was the sort of low-cost, no-frills compact that its namesake had wished to create when he'd originally formed the company. But after enduring the deprivations of the war, the public for the most part did not want an update of the Model T. What they wanted, said one analyst, was "pizzazz." So with the problems mounting higher and the red ink flowing more freely, Kaiser-Frazer turned once more to Darrin, and this time the engineers stayed away and he designed a sports car with the style and pizzazz of the European imports: the buzz-creating Kaiser-Darrin 161 prototype on display at the Motorama.

It's not known if Henry Kaiser attended the show, but Darrin certainly did. He drove over from Beverly Hills the day after his Friday night preview party, possibly sunk in thought over the heavy expectations placed on his little car. One sports car to save a company? That was quite a load to carry, especially considering the fact that one of America's top designers, Harley Earl, was at that moment engaged in a sports car project of his own.

This project, code-named "Project Opel," was a closely held secret within General Motors, so Darrin likely did not know about it. But given his knowledge of car industry trends and of Earl himself, it would not have surprised him to learn what his rival was up to. Every other American car designer was busily sketching ideas for new sports cars, why not Harley too?

Earl had been out to California in September, but not to push sports cars. Rather, he was at the Beverly Hills Hotel talking up his latest dream vehicle, Le Sabre, the

1952 version of "the motorcar of the future" and "the car of tomorrow," as the press dubbed it. Among the features drawing raves were a powerful 335-horsepower V-8 engine and a swooping, streamlined design. Harley liked the car so much he drove it himself, and he posed for a picture in it that appeared in the newspapers.

Impressive as Le Sabre was, it was no more so than the man presenting it—the man of today selling the car of tomorrow. Some of the locals remembered Earl from his days as a custom designer for his father Jacob and Don Lee Coach and Body Works. (Both his father and Don Lee died in the 1930s.) The boy—well, he wasn't a boy when he left California; he was in his thirties—had gone off to the Midwest and made his hometown proud. Now he was the grand elder statesman of American car design—and a vice president of the world's largest car company.* Tall and commanding in person, he was welcoming, gracious, professional and, for some, intimidating as hell. What intimidated people was not just his size or his impressive storehouse of automobile knowledge, it was the whole package, the confidence and ease with which he carried himself. The man had style as a teenager, sporting around Los Angeles in a Mercer with a motoring cap, goggles, and bow tie, and that same sense of how things *ought* to be, in a more gracious world, had not deserted him now that he was in his fifties, married, and the father of two boys. When celebrities and dignitaries came to see him at his office at General Motors, they sat in Mies van der Rohe chairs and relaxed in an ultramodern space designed by Eero Saarinen's firm. A closet in his office held extra suits of light blue, his favorite color, in case the one he was wearing became wrinkled in the heat or if he needed to slip into an ensemble more appropriate for a cocktail party. He wore handmade English shoes. On his twentieth anniversary with GM, his employees gave him a museum-quality Patek Phillipe pocket watch with a platinum pocketknife and a watch fob chain.

Dutch Darrin, another man with an elevated sense of how life should be lived, had known Harley a long time, dating back to Dutch's Paris salon days. They'd had lunch together at the Paris Auto Show in the summer of 1927, after Harley's success with the LaSalle. Harley and Lawrence Fisher had gone to France to see the latest styles and to scout designers who might be tempted to join the new Art and Color Section at General Motors. Darrin's colleague Tom Hibbard did indeed leave Paris to sign on with GM several years later, and Darrin himself did some consulting for Art and Color before departing for California before the war.

Some mistakenly thought it was Darrin who had coined the term "pregnant Buick," referring to the big flop early in Earl's tenure, but this wasn't true, said Darrin. Earl's boss Alfred Sloan and many other people called it by that name. As Darrin well knew, great success defined Earl's work at GM, not the reverse. In 1938, the year after Art and Color became Styling, Earl introduced the Buick Y-Job, GM's first experimental or "concept" car. That year's car of tomorrow, the long and low

---

* Before retiring to Florida in the late fifties, Harley advised Bill France Sr. on the founding of his new racing circuit, NASCAR, and France credits Earl's influence and guidance with helping him get it off the ground. The winner of the annual Daytona 500, NASCAR's greatest race, receives the Harley J. Earl Trophy, which Harley designed himself.

Y-Job—always with Harley, long and low—featured disappearing headlamps and other novel features that later showed up on Buicks and Cadillacs. Also that year Cadillac released the first American mass-produced automobile without a running board, one more Harley Earl design hit in a string of hits. Two years later Sloan made him a vice president of GM, the first designer to attain such heights at a major American car company.

Little in the way of new passenger car design occurred during World War II. Nor did this change in the euphoria that followed V-E and V-J Days. The public wanted new cars and they wanted them now, and GM and everybody else just had to pump them out, style be damned. Within a few years, however, people's tastes shifted once more, and they were looking for power, automatic transmission, comfort, extras, and style. As it happened, Harley and his team of designers had just the ticket for them.

During the war Earl was taking a tour of a Michigan air base when a P-38 Lightning parked on a runway caught his eye. Besides being a terrific fighter, the P-38 boasted a striking design with "twin Allison engines, twin fuselages and twin tail fins." Ah, those tail fins. They intrigued Harley most of all and "when I saw those two rudders sticking up," as he recalled, "it gave me a postwar idea." He asked his tour guide, a friend of his, if he could send some members of his staff over to do some sketches of the plane. His friend said sure, the designers did their sketches, and when Harley revealed to others at GM what he had in mind, "we almost started a war in the corporation." But Earl won the in-fighting and in 1948, for the first time ever, Cadillacs appeared with tail fins. The original tail fins were mild, gently rounded shapes with an almost "Pardon me" quality about them, perhaps owing to the battle within GM about whether they should exist at all. Over the next ten years they would grow into tall, angular, shark-fin shapes with nothing apologetic about them—what future generations would come to see, for better or worse, as a symbol of 1950s America.

Lockheed Aircraft of Burbank designed and built the P-38, the inspiration for tail fins. The man who first imagined tail fins on automobiles came from Los Angeles, lived for years in Beverly Hills, designed customs for Hollywood stars, and hobnobbed with some of them. These are no accidents of history. Throughout his years in Detroit Harley had always stayed in close touch with his home state, maintaining a membership, for instance, in the Los Angeles Country Club although he lived two thousand miles away. He traveled many times to California to visit friends and family and to keep an eye on what was growing in the fertile automotive garden out West. "There is a touch of Oldfield and DePalma in most Americans," he wrote once, "and frankly I wonder sometimes if there isn't a trace of the old Santa Monica racetrack in every car I've ever designed." The road races he saw as a young man in Santa Monica drew top drivers and cars from around Europe and America, and forty years and two world wars later, European and American cars and drivers were at it again in sports car races on the coasts. Earl watched the races at Watkins Glen and undoubtedly in California as well, admiring the Ferraris, Porsches, and Jaguars the same as everyone else. It was during this period that he assigned a designer on his staff, Bob McLean, to create the preliminary sketches for a new sports car to rival the Europeans.

Beginning with fifty staffers in the 1920s, the Styling Department had by this time swollen into a massive bureaucracy of fourteen hundred people. But for Project Opel, Earl kept things small and simple and hush-hush, closing the door to all but a select handful of top assistants to work with him. Each step of the way Harley guided the process, first showing a full-sized model of the car to Chevrolet's engineers in the summer of 1952, a few months before his September press conference in Beverly Hills to promote Le Sabre. But on that trip Harley breathed not a word to reporters about the true car of tomorrow being built at that very moment in Detroit. Its time had not yet arrived, but it was coming soon. This prototype went on display for the first time at the January 1953 Motorama in New York City, and its name was Corvette.

"Harley Earl is the father of the Corvette," says the national museum dedicated to the car. "The Corvette was his idea, pure and simple." The public and automotive press greeted his idea with pure and simple delight. Though the car was considered to be underpowered in its early years, no one doubted the achievement of Earl, his team of designers, Chevrolet, and General Motors. They had answered the call. They had built a kick-ass American sports car.

New Corvettes began rolling off the line in September 1953, and the first Californian and one of the first Americans to take delivery on one was actor John Wayne. He had seen one at a car show earlier in the year and had to have it. Unfortunately though, his six-foot-five-inch frame could not fit comfortably into the little two-seater. So, without so much as taking it for a spin around the block, he gave it to his friend Ward Bond, a fellow actor and car buff. Bond was also a big man, and the car cramped his legs too, and he later sold it.

Dutch Darrin's sports car, the Kaiser-Darrin 161, suffered a far less glorious fate than the 'Vette, although at the Los Angeles Motorama and elsewhere, critics sung its praises too. Its four-panel fiberglass body looked splendid, and in a novel touch its two doors slid forward into the front of the car rather than opening out in the conventional manner. But it was not nearly enough to save Henry Kaiser's faltering automobile venture, and fewer than five hundred of them were ever built. In 1954 Kaiser-Frazer lost $35 million and ended its Henry J car line, ceasing operations altogether the next year. In a life of epic sweep and achievement, Henry Kaiser could not solve the automobile business. He was not alone in this regard, however; in the years to come more independent carmakers—Studebaker, Nash, Willys, Packard—would also fade away, leaving the American market under the near-total control of General Motors, Ford, and Chrysler. (Them, and those pesky imports.) Preston Tucker's Tucker Corporation, the subject of a popular film decades later by Francis Ford Coppola, failed during this period as well.

TWENTY-SIX

Bob Hirohata's Wild Ride

The vanquishing of the independents by the powerful Big Three could not conceal the fact that things had shifted in the world of automobiles. Things were not the same as they were before.

In the global shakeup that occurred after World War II the center of the fine art world moved from its traditional home of Paris to New York City, just as the capital of the political world relocated from London or Paris to Washington, D.C. A similar shift occurred in automobiles. Detroit remained the headquarters city of the Big Three and the top manufacturer of automobiles in this country, which led the world in car production. But for so many other things having to do with automobiles—the trends, the turmoil, the creative ferment—the center was not Detroit. The center was Los Angeles.

Beginning with the arrival of horseless carriages at the turn of the century, this trend had gathered force over the decades with the streams of people, money, jobs, and opportunity pouring into the state. Mid-century Los Angeles had become a sprawling metropolis of 2 million, and the tastes and habits of southern Californians had emerged as a major influence on American society at large.

"I am a very happy man," wrote one of those tastemakers, Raymond Chandler, in 1948. "I haven't got a brain in my head, an idea in my mind, or a longing in my soul, except for a convertible." At that point the author of *The Big Sleep* and *Farewell, My Lovely* was living in La Jolla, prime convertible country. He had become a big-money screenwriter sought after by Hollywood producers for his ability to capture in words the dark underbelly of sun-washed Los Angeles, a city he came to know the only way one can: by automobile. Earlier in his life Chandler had worked as an executive for several independent oil companies in the state, and after he left the oil business to take a stab at writing he drove around the city and along the coast, stopping to browse at filling station newsstands when he gassed up. These newsstands carried *Black Mask*, *Dime Detective,* and other magazines with lurid stories about killers and the private eyes and cops who brought them to justice. Stories of this ilk were not quite respectable reading for adults and were off-limits to youngsters, but Chandler, a naturalized English citizen schooled in Europe, felt strongly drawn to them. "Wandering up and down the Pacific Coast in an automobile, I began to read pulp magazines, because they were cheap enough to throw away and because I never had a taste for the kind of thing which is known as women's magazines," he wrote.

Chandler began to sell stories to these magazines, eventually graduating to novels and screenplays, and he and another California writer of an earlier vintage, Dashiell Hammett, helped lift crime fiction out of the gas station and into literary salons, libraries, and the university.

In this way and in so many other ways, Californians were remaking American culture. Harry and Esther Snyder were a young married couple with an interest in automobiles and food. They wondered if their customers would be willing to drive up to their Baldwin Park hamburger stand and, unlike at a traditional drive-in, order without getting out of their cars or being served by a carhop. The Snyders rigged up a two-way speaker system that let drivers talk to a clerk inside, pick up their order, pay, and drive through—all without getting out of their vehicle. They thought of the perfect name for this new concept, and the first In-N-Out Burger opened in Baldwin Park in 1948, perhaps the first drive-through restaurant in California (it had no table service) and one of the first anywhere.

The McDonald brothers, Maurice and Dick, also had ideas on how to best serve the teens and families who frequented their hot dog stand in Arcadia. They opened for business in the late 1930s and relocated to San Bernardino in 1940. They muddled through the war years selling mainly barbecue ribs and sandwiches, serving customers by carhops. But when the bad times finally ended, Dick McDonald took a closer look at the business to see what their customers actually liked to eat. To his surprise he found that the bulk of their orders came not from ribs or dogs but burgers. An overhaul of their menu swiftly followed, sweeping out the unpopular items and putting hamburgers front and center. The brothers also dumped the carhops but not the young employees, dressing them in white pants, white shirts, and white paper hats, and training them in the "Speedee Service System" they had developed for preparing and delivering those hamburgers in quick-time. The world's first McDonald's restaurant premiered December 12, 1948, at 14th and E Streets in the small but growing Route 66 city of San Bernardino. The McDonalds served what they called the "All American meal"—fries (ten cents), hamburger (fifteen cents), shake or malt (twenty cents)—at prices and speeds that made people hungry for more. Dinner for a family of five cost $2.25 and they could sit down to eat it less than a minute after ordering. A hot-rodder on a date with a girl could buy two All American meals for a buck and get a little change back. They could eat there, or they could take their meals with them and get back to cruising the boulevard where all the action was.

The same year the McDonald brothers began drawing crowds in San Bernardino, Bob's Big Boy on Riverside Drive in Burbank lit up the night for the first time. A hamburger impresario named Bob Wian founded the Bob's Big Boy chain, and his story bears similarities to those of the Snyders and McDonalds. In the down days of the Depression he sold his De Soto for three hundred dollars and borrowed any money he could get his hands on to buy a ramshackle hamburger joint in Glendale.

Creative in the kitchen, he invented a deluxe Dagwood-style cheeseburger sandwich with two patties and buns, and pretty soon "Bob's Pantry" became better known around the valley as the home of the "Big Boy Burger, the original Double Deck Cheeseburger." The name of the place segued into Bob's Big Boy with an assist from a local cartoonist who, basing his sketches on a hamburger-loving customer of Bob's, drew up a chubby black-haired boy in checkered overalls as the symbol of the eaterie. A statue of Big Boy stood outside the Bob's of Burbank on opening night (as it does today), although that was not what motorists first saw when they drove down Riverside Drive. That would have been the colossal seventy-foot-high neon Bob's sign—what the architecture critic Alan Hess would describe, decades later, as "the billboard raised to an art form."

The billboard as an art form? A hamburger drive-in as an architectural masterpiece? Such preposterous, category-defying notions (preposterous to some, anyhow) find expression in this Bob's Big Boy, the oldest existing Bob's in the United States and now designated by the state as a point of historical interest. Designed by San Diego's Wayne McAllister—"one of the most significant architects of the twentieth century in terms of creativity of form and influence," said a historian—it is a still-thriving example of another widely copied California cultural influence, the architectural style known as "Googie."

The phrase derives from Googie's Restaurant, a John Lautner–designed coffee shop on Sunset Boulevard in Los Angeles that once resided next to Schwab's. (Both are gone now.) But Schwab's, the famous drugstore where a movie talent scout discovered the teenaged Lana Turner, was built in the late 1920s, and Googie's was pure postwar 1949 optimism, starting off, as it did, "on the level like any other building. But suddenly it breaks from the sky. The bright red roof of cellular steel decking suddenly tilts upward as if swung on a hinge, and the whole building goes up with it like a rocket ramp." This space-agey rocket ramp of a coffee shop made Douglas Haskell's head snap around the first time he saw it. "This is Googie architecture," said Haskell, a prominent New York architecture critic, and the tag stuck because it had a certain derisive tone to it. Though Haskell took Googie architecture seriously, many other cultural observers did not. They viewed it with contempt. To call a thing "Googie" was a put-down—appropriate, in their view.

Googie invited scorn for many reasons. For one, it did not originate in New York City, the home of the nation's leading architecture editors and critics and many top architects. It also showed less deference to the architectural conventions and traditions of Europe that held such sway on the eastern seaboard. Googie buildings did not go straight up and down like skyscrapers or the storefront façades of railroad-era Main Street shops, but rather carved up the sky using playful, nontraditional forms such as boomerangs, dingbats, and diagonals—"a lot of upward hard-driving diagonal lines," as another New York writer, Tom Wolfe, put it. Googie architects viewed billboards as a potential marriage of commerce and art, and gussied up their buildings with Earle C. Anthony's gift to America, neon. Instead of blending anonymously into the landscape, Googie coffee shops and drive-ins—Bob's Big Boy of Burbank,

Coffee Dan's, Dimy's, Googie's, Goody's, Harvey's Broiler, Norm's, Pann's, Romeo's Times Square (later Johnnie's), Tiny Naylor's, Ship's, and the Wich Stand, to name a few—slapped sleepy suburban intersections awake, turning them into alive, happening, gotta-go-there meeting places.* The public flipped over Bob's Big Boy in Burbank—and it still does, particularly on Friday nights when eyeball-friendly, eardrum-attacking custom cars and motorcycles take over the place—because Wayne McAllister designed it not with the idea that people would come there on foot, like the Main Street shop of yore, but that they would arrive in cars. With its bright windows in front and the drive-in area in back, Bob's made a complete design statement, merging beauty and usefulness by attracting, welcoming, and catering to the needs of drivers. As McAllister himself said, his designs were "influenced by the automobile, not the architect."

These were some of the reasons that opinion-shapers on both coasts disapproved of Googie. Here was another: Googie architects did not, for the most part, earn their fees by designing towering urban expressions of money and power or large civic edifices of consequence (although sometimes they did: Dodger Stadium, built in 1962, is pure Googie). The patrons of Googie were generally men and women merchants who ran small businesses in suburbia: coffee shops, drive-ins, drive-in theaters, gas stations, car washes, car dealerships, skating rinks, bowling alleys, laundries, motels, supermarkets, apartment houses, and hamburger palaces such as the McDonald's on Lakewood Boulevard in Downey that opened in August 1953, the year after the Googie style got its name.

The McDonald brothers were clearly onto something, and they had begun to sell franchises on the model of the national Howard Johnson's restaurant chain. The Downey McDonald's was the third in history—and the oldest one still in business—and it, too, had a big sign out front: golden arches, sixty-four feet high. Near the top of the arches is "Speedee," a colorful little cartoon character on the order of Big Boy who cavorts on a long, diving board–like platform that says "Hamburgers." At night Speedee in his white chef's hat and green bowtie lights up, and his legs churn as if to symbolize the super-fast McDonald's system. But even more eye-catching than the sign is the restaurant itself, designed by Stanley Meston. Two more golden arches curve over each side of the building, but these are not signs or logos on a sign—these are real arches, each extending from the ground in front of the restaurant through the roof to a high point in the air and then gracefully back down through the roof to the rear. The arches form part of the building, and because of this they create a sense of discovery when seen for the first time. They make a person smile.

The year after the Downey McDonald's opened, a business genius masquerading as a malt-mixer machine salesman arrived on the scene. His name was Ray Kroc. He bought the franchise rights from the McDonald brothers, adopted their system but

* The years have been tough on Googie, as many of its classic coffee shops and buildings have been destroyed or badly altered. Bob's Big Boy in Burbank and McDonald's in Downey still exist, in part because of the efforts of the Modern Committee of the Los Angeles Conservancy, which recognizes the architectural and historical value of these old Googie masterpieces and seeks to preserve them.

made improvements of his own, moved the company headquarters to Illinois, junked the Speedee logo, kept hiring young people, and built the worldwide restaurant chain that has since become synonymous with the concept of fast food.

But McDonald's, In-N-Out, and Bob's Big Boy are not the only fast food chains with a southern California birthplace; others emerged from there during this period as well. Among them were:

- Carl's Jr., founded by Carl Karcher and his wife, Margaret, who borrowed $325 against their 1941 Plymouth, added some money from their savings, and bought a hot dog cart in downtown Los Angeles. This hot dog cart eventually grew into Carl's Jr. hamburger restaurants, based in Anaheim;
- Jack in the Box, another drive-through service innovator, founded by Robert Peterson. The first Jack in the Box opened in 1951 in San Diego, where the company is now headquartered;
- Denny's, begun by Harold Butler as "Danny's Donuts" in Lakewood in 1953. It changed its name and widened its menu at the end of the decade and took off from there;
- International House of Pancakes (or IHOP), founded in 1958 by Al Lapin in Toluca Lake;
- Taco Bell, originated by Marine Corps veteran Glen Bell, who ran a hamburger drive-in in drive-in-rich San Bernardino after the war but later switched to Mexican food, put his own name in the title, and established the first Taco Bell in Downey in 1962; and
- Wienerschnitzel, originally "Der Wienerschnitzel," the creation of an ex-employee of Glenn Bell's, John Galardi, who set up his first restaurant in Wilmington.

These restaurants grew in popularity because they catered to automobiles and fit in with the busy, full, faster-paced lives that people were leading after the war. California's population grew by 3 million in the 1940s, with the majority of these new residents—two hundred and fifty thousand a year—settling in Los Angeles and environs. Come the 1950s the pace of growth increased still more, with housing subdivisions and paved roads springing up on what had once been farmland or open space. Joining the rush to the suburbs were more small businesses: grocery stores, hardware stores, jewelry stores, toy stores, clothing stores, bookstores, and more. Thus, the advent of another postwar California creation: the outdoor suburban strip mall.

Like Googie, the term "strip mall" carries a negative, dismissive tone to it—well-earned in many places. But at its best, said Alan Hess, "the commercial strip generated a fresh, appropriate architecture that spoke the common design language of the public streets, understood by a wide cross-section of the population." People liked shopping centers because they delivered easy automobile access with one-story shops set back from the street and arranged conveniently (and sometimes attractively and cleverly) around ample parking. McDonald's and other drive-ins flourished in these settings, luring patrons who spent money at the other shops too.

It's not just that the automobile was changing California and America, it's that Californians and Americans were thinking in terms of automobiles, and their ideas were producing change. Most people look at a parking lot and see a parking lot, but hot-rodder Art Ingles saw a potential race track. So inspired, he devised a "little car"—that was what he called it—with a lawn mower engine. He attached four wheels to a metal frame, put on a seat and steering wheel, and ran a chain between the engine and rear wheels. The contraption was so small that Ingles, a normal-sized man, had to bend his knees and hunch his body just to sit in it. Nevertheless it scooted along pretty well, so he went down to the parking lot of the Rose Bowl and started racing his little car around, to the amusement of his friends who came to watch. Well, it was more of a cart than a car, and that was what his invention came to be called: a Go-Kart. All his buddies got turned on by it and built their own Go-Karts, a manufacturing company shortly followed, and an enduring children's and adult pastime (and now, the international motor sport of karting) was born.

The genesis of Wallace Byam's idea occurred in the late 1920s when Byam, a magazine publisher, ran a do-it-yourself article in one of his magazines on how to build a travel trailer. When his readers tried to do it themselves and complained that the plans did not work, he decided to give it a go himself. He failed too (the plans were badly flawed), but the attempt inspired him to create his own trailer design—one that lowered the floor and raised the height of its ceiling, allowing people to do something they had never done in a vacation trailer before: stand up. Readers responded enthusiastically to his article and design, prompting him to get out of publishing and start selling trailer-building plans and kits for five dollars each from his Los Angeles home. His designs gradually evolved into a "teardrop-shaped, thirteen-foot canvas and Masonite marvel" that he sold through his company, Airstream.

During these years another southern Californian, William Hawley Bowlus, was pondering his own ideas on travel trailer construction. Bowlus, a former Ryan Aircraft employee who had worked on Lindbergh's *Spirit of St. Louis*, applied aerodynamic principles and tubular steel construction to his invention. Innovative though it was, the design had one fatal flaw, the trailers sold poorly, and he went out of business. Seeing the potential, Byam bought Bowlus's patterns and leftover models and fixed that fatal flaw. Instead of having the door in front of the trailer above the hitch where Bowlus had put it, Byam moved it to the side, making it easier for people to get in and out. Indeed, ease and comfort fairly defined Byam's new Airstream trailer, introduced in 1936. Sleeping four, with the seats and dinette set folding into beds, it featured a sink with water, electric lights, excellent heating and ventilation, and an interior cooling method using dry ice. And, of course, you could stand up in it.

Achieving some success before the war, the Airstream Clipper came into its own during the vacation-happy years of the late 1940s and '50s. It became a leader and symbol of the emerging new motor home industry, centered in southern California, and its lovely silver teardrop shape attracted admiration even among those who have never set foot in one. Airstream built its early models in Santa Fe Springs, California, expanding in August 1952 into a second manufacturing plant in Ohio. The company has since moved its headquarters there and continues to build Airstreams and other motor homes.

In 1946, with all those vacationers on the road, California motel owner M. K. Guertin figured they had to spend the night somewhere. He opened the first Best Western in the state and fifty more of them across the West by year's end. By 1963 the number had climbed to nearly seven hundred nationally, and it's in the thousands now. Two construction men from Santa Barbara, Paul Greene and William Becker, founded the Motel 6 chain in the early 1960s on a seemingly simple premise—charge six dollars a night, every night, for every room. Not so simple, as it turned out. They encountered intense opposition from rival motel owners who feared they'd lose customers to Motel 6's cheap prices. The appearance of a new Motel 6 in town (the first was in Santa Barbara) often met, as one report said, with "power lines cut, signs spattered with paint and windows smashed in" during the chain's early years.

George Urich, an independent service station operator in Los Angeles, also faced hostility to his idea at first. His competitors feared his prices were going to undercut theirs, and workers worried they were going to lose jobs. After the war California and the United States enjoyed a surplus of oil and gasoline, giving rise to independent service stations that competed against the chain stations operated in association with the major oil companies. Every gas station in the country employed attendants to pump the gas, check the oil, and clean the windows of their customers' cars, but Urich thought he could sell more gas at lower prices if his customers did the pumping themselves, and so he began the nation's first self-serve station. Pretty soon a *Newsweek* correspondent was dropping by to note the station's distinctively southern California spin: "Five or six pretty girls in sweaters and slacks roller-skate from island to island making change and collecting. A supervisor in a glass booth directs them by loudspeaker and keeps an eye out for customers violating the no-smoking regulations." *Business Week* dismissed self-serve as "a strictly local phenomenon," a sentiment shared by many drivers who liked to be waited on when they pulled up to the pumps. But over time the "Gas-A-Teria"—*Life* magazine's term for this strange new hybrid of roller-skating girls and gasoline—became "California's newest contribution to the drive-in way of life." After Urich, the second self-serve in California was a Rotten Robbie in San Jose.

Many gas stations around the state exhibited Googie-esque flamboyance in their construction, and some of them—such as the one in Los Angeles where the wings of an airplane served as the canopy over the pumps—had a style all their own. This was also true of drive-in movie theaters, another big California contribution to the drive-in way of life, although credit for its invention belongs to a New Jersey businessman, Richard Hollingshead. Hollingshead and his partners rigged up a large outdoor movie screen on a lot near a busy highway in Camden, New Jersey, and history welcomed the first drive-in in June 1933. Some skeptics doubted whether moviegoers wished to trade the comforts of indoor theater seating for an automobile, but these skeptics forgot about California. Hollingshead licensed his patent rights to a California firm, and America's second drive-in theater, boasting the biggest screen in the world, began showing pictures at Pico and Westwood Boulevards in Los Angeles in 1934. Once again a correspondent from an Eastern magazine, *Collier's*, made a safari out to the western provinces to see what was up with the natives: "Out on Pico Boulevard we located drive-in service as it neared its peak. We drove in through a tollgate, a girl seated in a booth took money for tickets, and we entered the Drive-in Theater. An usher bearing the badge of his office—a flashlight—jumped on the running board and guided the car to a space marked out with white chalk lines. We leaned back and watched the picture shown on the open-air screen."

This usher told the correspondent why the drive-in appealed to so many teenage boys and girls: "You see, an auto's a lot more comfortable than a theater seat.... We get an awful lot of couples. They like the privacy."

Into this amped-up, throbbing caropolis—of convertibles and pulp fiction, of Googie glamour and excess, of prodigious youthful appetites for hamburgers, speed, and sex, of change and resistance to change, of wartime deprivation turned to postwar prosperity, of Asian, tropical, and Mexican influences as well as Southern, Midwestern, and Eastern, of a population spilling out everywhere and constantly rewriting its borders, and with all sorts of stray, restless, lonely, mixed-up, searching souls pouring in from all over—into this ferment came George Barris, who had some creative architectural ideas of his own. Only his ideas about architecture had to do with cars, not buildings. Free, single, and eighteen, he arrived in a custom '36 Ford that, in his words, "was chopped, had an alligator jaw hood, push-button doors, the front fenders swept back into the rear fenders, and the headlights were flush with the fenders."

Chopped, in custom car lingo, means "lowering the top of the car, bringing it nearer to the hood line." "Channeling," another favorite customizing term and something Barris also probably did to his Ford, is to lower the body of the car closer to the ground—*a lot* closer to the ground, maybe two or three inches above it. An alligator jaw hood tapers to the front much like an alligator snout. All these features and more made Barris's hot rod stand out in a town already brimming with dazzling, stand-out rods.

For a hipster with such slick wheels, Barris hailed from a pretty unlikely place: Roseville, in the heart of Sacramento farm country, where he and his brother, Sam, grew up. Their parents died when they were infants, and in the late 1920s their aunt and uncle brought them west from their native Illinois. Both boys showed a keen interest in cars—as a ten-year-old, George carved car models out of balsa wood with a penknife. When he and big brother Sam got a little older their aunt and uncle gave them a beat-down old Buick that acted as a guinea pig for their early customizing experiments. With no money to speak of and only the crudest tools, they hammered pot lids onto the wheels and called them hubcaps. George liked the look of the knobs and handles on the kitchen cabinets at home, and liked them even better on the grill of the Buick. He recalled that when his aunt came home at night, "she'd go to open up her cabinets and there were no knobs or handles."

His aunt and uncle ran a hotel and restaurant in Roseville and hoped George would follow them into the business. "They wanted me to be a restaurant man," he said, "like every other typical Greek, I guess." But the short, solidly built youngster had other ideas for himself and "as a kid, instead of delivering papers for pin money, I did little things to customize the cars of my friends."

Customizing as we know it today was just starting up in the late 1930s when Barris was a boy. Its origins are less clear than those of hot rodding, and more geographically diverse. Early choppers and channelers worked in southern California but also the Bay Area and Central Valley. In fact, the man described as "the father of customizing," Harry Westergard, was a Sacramento garage man who taught the tricks of the trade to Barris and other aspiring, quick-to-learn teens such as Dick Bertolucci.

"He did all his work in his garage," remembered Bertolucci. "Matter of fact, it was a chicken coop. It was on Fulton Avenue near where I lived. He used to do custom work for all the kids in town. I used to go over and see him myself, and talk to him." So did George Barris who "saw the things Westergard used to do and so, like all the rest of us, he'd go home and try to duplicate them," said Bertolucci, who later opened a Sacramento body shop that's still in business. Barris graduated from cabinet knobs and pot lids to more sophisticated materials and methods, getting oily and greasy at a small body shop in an alley near 19th and G Streets. Bruce Brown owned this shop and also nursed the talented youngster along, loaning him his spray gun for painting. Here the apprentice came to outshine his teachers. George had an artist's eye for color and line and form, matched only by his brother's expertise at shaping and crafting metals.

After war broke out, Sam joined the navy and left his little brother at home. Near the end of the hostilities, George, done with high school and uninterested in a career in restaurants, headed south on Highway 99 for Hot Rod City. His '36 Ford functioned like a business card on wheels; guys at the drive-ins and street races saw it and admired it and asked him to make them a boss gator snout like the one he had or to "french" their headlights (remove the chrome around them and recess the lamps). He did ordinary repair jobs to make ends meet when he first came to Los Angeles, but his heart was in customizing. It was both what he did and who he was, and the style of his cars made heads turn; teenagers with an eye for such things could spot a George Barris custom rolling by on the street or parked in a school parking lot. When the war ended and Sam joined his brother in Los Angeles, that was when things really started to click for them. Sam on metals and George on paint and talking things up—now *that* was one helluva team.

They did not just customize cars, they reinvented them. To appreciate this fully it's best to see the stock version of the car they started with, and then how completely they transformed it—from frog to prince. Tom Wolfe saw this process in action and wrote about it in his 1965 *Esquire* piece on George Barris and the California custom scene, *Kandy Kolored Tangerine Flake Streamline Baby*. Of Barris he wrote, "He is a good example of a kid who grew up completely absorbed in this teen-age world of cars, who pursued the pure flame and its forms with such devotion that he emerged as an artist." He wasn't just "building cars, he's creating forms....In effect, they're sculpture." True to his ideals, Barris, like other artistic-minded customizers, felt no need or desire to leave Los Angeles to seek the establishment's stamp of approval in Detroit. Why would he want to do that? The custom scene was all happening in California, so what did he care what they thought of him in the East? The only opinions that truly mattered were those of kids like him, fellow travelers in "the teenage netherworld," as Wolfe put it some twenty years later.

Word of mouth in the teen netherworld spread quickly after the 1948 hot rod show at Exposition Park, when George and Sam Barris displayed a refashioned 1941 Buick convertible that looked only vaguely like a 1941 Buick convertible. It was probably the only true custom machine at the show; the rest were fire-breathing hot rods. In general, hot rodders cared less about appearance and more about speed whereas customizers went the opposite way—more show, less go. But the Barrises lived *la vida* hot rod too, as did all custom guys in the beginning, and an advertisement for their shop appeared in the premiere issue of *Hot Rod*. George and Sam called their shop "Barris Custom," as they had yet to adopt the handle that would later become George's trademark. (Sam died of cancer in 1967.) Perhaps the first customizer to substitute the "c" for a "k," George gained fame for building "krazy kustoms" at his "Kustom City" or "Kustom Industries" plant on Riverside Drive in North Hollywood, which still makes kustoms today.

The hot rod show gave the brothers a nice bounce on the street, and the postwar shortage of new cars also helped their business. Folks may have been stuck with their old wheels a while longer but that didn't mean they couldn't spruce them up a little, and the Barrises could do that and more. Leaving a car the way Detroit made it was like accepting what your parents said as gospel and obediently doing it. The Barrises weren't into that, at least not when it came to customs. They mainly did makeovers of Fords, Chevrolets, and Mercurys with an occasional import thrown in. Their first show-business customer was the bandleader Lionel Hampton, who drove a new 1949 Jaguar sedan. Imports were unusual sights in those days, and the Jag didn't need all that much spiffing up, but the Barrises added some flair to it, and word about their work started getting around in music and show-business circles too.

Nick Matranga wasn't famous or in show business. He was just a car guy looking to deluxe up his ride, and this was another sweet thing about customizing, and one of the many sweet things that separated it from what the Big Three and European carmakers were doing. The Barrises did not produce vehicles for the masses; they only had to please their clients and themselves, and not necessarily in that order. They made cars for individuals, and the best ones they and others did became identified by the name of that individual, the fellow footing the bill. Hence, Nick Matranga's princely '40 Merc came to be known simply as the Matranga Merc, one of the most influential of these early customs.

As the Barrises made a name for themselves in the teen underground, the powers that be were following their work more closely than they thought. "I was amazed," George said, referring to conversations he had with Detroit car designers in later years. "They could tell me about cars I built in 1945. They knew all about the four-door '48 Studebaker I restyled. I chopped the top and dropped the hood and it ended up a pretty good-looking car. And the bubbletop I built in 1954—they knew all about it. And all this time we thought they frowned on us." As with Googie architecture, industry leaders were turning thumbs down with one hand and taking notes with the other. Tom Wolfe said that Detroit "lifted some twenty designs from [Barris] alone....Barris says 'lifted' because some are exact down to the most minute details."

The January 1950 National Roadster Show in Oakland became a pivot point in early custom history, the first major juried display of customs in the West and probably the United States. At other car shows the crowds filed in, ogled the machines, and filed out again. Now at the Exposition Building in Oakland, for the first time ever, judges mingled with the nearly thirty thousand people who packed the hall over the course of the exhibit, evaluating and scoring the one hundred cars on display in a variety of categories. "If there was any one marked trend to be noted at the National Roadster Show," said the writer Griffith Borgeson, who was at the hall noting the trends, "it was that hot roddery is coming of age."

One proof of this was the geographic diversity of the entries; cars came from all over—or all over California anyhow. Bill Carash of Oakland won the originality prize for street roadsters for his flaming-red V-16 Cadillac. Other prize-winning Oaklanders were Al George, Larry Neves, and Lee Chapel, the ex–Los Angeles speed shop owner who had moved his operation to East 14th Street. The Oakland Roadster Club and Satan's Angels of Hayward were two of the clubs sponsoring the show. Finishing close to the top in roadster design were two brothers, Jim and Paul Nelson, who were from Sanger in the San Joaquin Valley. More valley men earned kudos: Dick Bertolucci and Harry Westergard, two of the customizers from Barris's old neighborhood in Sacramento.

The Barris Kustom Shop of Los Angeles picked up awards in "Greatest Contribution to Auto Industry," "Construction—Street," "Originality—Street," and "Most Magnificent Custom Convertible." But the top overall prize for "America's Most Beautiful Roadster" went to Bill NieKamp of Long Beach. It took NieKamp, an auto painter by trade, more than a year to build his sky-blue '29 roadster, and Griffith Borgeson cited him as one more sign of the growing reach of hot rods and customs beyond their core audience of teenagers. NieKamp was middle-aged.

Yet another example of the wide appeal of customizing was another brother team, Gil and Al Ayala of Los Angeles—East Los Angeles, to be exact, behind the House of Chrome on Olympic Boulevard. The Ayalas were kind of like the Barrises—Al the back-shop metal man, the painterly Gil upfront and sociable—and their work commanded equal respect. Like Joaquin Arnett and the self-styled "Bean Bandits" racing team that ran fast cars at the dry lakes and drag strips, the Ayalas came out of the East Los Angeles hot rod tradition. Once Gil got busted for street racing, but rather than face a judge he decided to take a vacation in Mexico. The authorities frowned on this, caught him before he crossed the border, and threw him in jail for three months. After he got out he went back to making cars with his brother, and their customs held their own against those from the suburbs.

More juried shows around the state followed Oakland's, and these contests gradually changed the custom scene. The Ayalas, Barrises, Joe Bailon, Dick Bertolucci—when they entered cars in a show they obviously wanted them to look cherry. That meant more and more people were driving these customs on the street less and less, which was what made Bob Hirohata's haul-ass, three-days-and-three-nights dash across America so remarkable, even by the standards of 1953.

For as long as he could remember, Bob Hirohata longed to own a real custom car. When he was in the navy he and his buddy Azzie Nishi used to talk cars all the time. After returning to civilian life, in the months before the end of the Korean War, he decided to act on these dreams, wheeling his '51 Merc into the driveway of the Barris shop.

In his early twenties, with black combed-back hair, white slacks, a thin white belt, and black short-sleeved shirt showing off a formidable pair of upper arms, as if he'd been pumping iron in the navy as well as sitting around talking cars, Hirohata projected an air of extreme youthful cool. But Barris would not have cared about that, instead fixing his gaze on the car—"a bathtub Merc," he might've called it. Customizers like Barris loved the plump and bulky Mercurys because they offered such a large canvas upon which to work, and some of the best customs ever done were on bathtub Mercs.

"When I took the car to the shop, Barris and I discussed a few minor changes," Hirohata wrote later in an article for *Rod and Custom*, one of the southern California car magazines that arose in the wake of *Hot Rod* (and like *Hot Rod*, it's still publishing). Hirohata emphasized that he thought the changes to be done were minor. But Barris clearly had something else in mind, for three months passed before he phoned Hirohata to tell him that his car was done. Hirohata lived in Arcadia and caught a fast ride over to Barris's shop in Los Angeles. What he saw when he got there rocked his soul.

Fifty years before the advent of reality TV, Hirohata had a *Pimp My Ride* moment: "When I picked up the car, I would have sworn it wasn't the same one that I left there originally." After recovering from his initial shock, he started to hone in on the details: "The top was chopped four inches in front and seven in back, the upper door posts had been eliminated so that the car looked like a hardtop convertible [and] the whole car was so close to the ground that you could hardly see under it." The body had been raised in front and lowered in back, so much so that with the fender skirts in place he could glimpse only a sliver of white on the rear whitewall tires. Barris had also frenched the headlights and narrowed the front windshield so it "looked like a couple of narrow, slitty little eyes." As for the factory-issue chrome, it was mostly gone ("dechromed," in the argot). If Detroit was making a statement with all the chrome on its cars, Barris was making the reverse statement: Get rid of it. And that seafoam green color! It knocked Hirohata back just looking at it, with black panels on the sides that started above the front tire and swooped wickedly down to the back.

Connoisseurs of the art of customizing generally agree that no custom has ever had the national impact of the Hirohata Merc. This was because of the pathfinding adventurousness of Barris's design, which influenced so many of the customs that came after it. But it was also because of what Bob Hirohata did next.

Memorial Day was approaching, which gave him an idea. He had the car of his dreams, why not do the other thing he'd always dreamed of? Along with owning a custom, he'd always wanted to see the Indianapolis 500. Held in conjunction with the 500, the Indianapolis Custom Show was hosting one of the biggest and most important custom shows in the country. Hirohata could enter the Merc in the show and see the race while he was there. He quickly sent off an entry application, which got accepted. Then he called his old navy sidekick Azzie Nishi, who said yes, he'd go with him. They both arranged to get some time off work and started preparations.

With less than two weeks to go before the show, there was a lot to do, especially when Hirohata decided to switch out the stock engine for a new Cadillac power plant. Lyon Engineering took the car in on Monday and finished the job on Friday night, at which time Hirohata drove it straight over to Nate's Mufflers. Nate's installed the headers on Saturday morning, and by the afternoon Hirohata was winging back home in his Mercury-Cadillac hybrid—"the Mercillac," he dubbed it—and just about ready to hit the road.

From an article he'd read about driving in the Southwest, Hirohata knew to bring an extra can of gasoline in the event the Merc ran dry with no filling stations in sight. Gaylord's Kustom Shop rigged up a nifty leatherette sack so the gas can wouldn't topple over in the trunk, and George Barris painted the can seafoam green to match the car. Then Hirohata greased and tuned the engine and applied masking tape to all the exposed parts of the exterior to prevent the paint from being chipped by loose gravel kicking up from the roadway. Feeling like he was starting to run out of time, he got on the horn to tell Azzie to get his butt over there because they were good to go.

After Azzie arrived they both realized they didn't have a clue how to get to Indianapolis. They made some calls, scrambled around for a map, and realized that fortune was smiling on them. Bobby Troup's highway, Route 66, ran right through Arcadia, and all they needed was to get on it and point east. They did some more last-minute running around—buying film for the camera, tanking up—and said their goodbyes "to what seemed like the whole town," as Hirohata said. Finally, no kidding around this time, they were ready to load up and hit the road.

But first, they had to get out of the driveway.

Said Hirohata, "We loaded the luggage, spare tools and equipment into the trunk—the car settled down about two inches from the weight. I got in—the car went down another inch. Then Azzie got in and the car looked as though we had forgotten to put wheels under it." Once worried about making it across Arizona, "I couldn't even get out of my own driveway." They did get out but only "after scraping the bottom of the Mercillac from front bumper to rear" as they backed into the street.

The original plan called for a Tuesday afternoon getaway. They finally blasted out of Arcadia in the predawn darkness of Wednesday morning. Indianapolis was a good twenty-five hundred miles away, and they had to be there in three days.

Instantly they made a decision: Power out, all the way. No stopping except for food, gas, and bathroom breaks. No overnights in a motel. There wasn't enough time, not if they wanted to make the Saturday noon deadline. Whichever guy wasn't behind the wheel, he could catnap in the car if needed.

That first morning after crossing the desert they stopped in Prescott for gas and ran into a nightmare they would encounter all across the country: careless filling station attendants. If Hirohata and Nishi didn't keep an eye on them they'd slam the hood or trunk lid down (the car gassed up through the trunk) and chip the paint. Moving on to Gallup, they made a big mistake by leaving the Mercillac by itself for a few minutes with its electric doors unlocked; "Not only did people look at it," said Hirohata, "they crawled all over it, under it and through it." This was another constant: attention everywhere. Town or country, drive-ins, stores, filling stations, roadside stops, every time they paused at a traffic light—people responded to the Mercillac as if they'd never seen an automobile before, and they hadn't, not like this one anyhow.

Driving straight through, night and day, flipping around the dial to find something to listen to, dozing off from time to time, talking about nothing and everything, eating whatever and whenever they could, but always moving, moving, moving down the road, they made it to Indianapolis on Saturday, May 23, 1953, with hours to spare. Two drivers, one Mercillac. They cleaned it up inside and out, waxed and polished it, peeled the protective tape off its lower extremities. A little before noon they reached the exposition grounds, stopping to take a picture before they entered.

They had been doing this throughout the trip, Bob and Azzie trading the camera back and forth to take photographs of each other but mainly of the Mercillac: pulling out of a parking spot onto a main street, gassing up, bombing across the desert, being surrounded at a stop by curious schoolkids, speeding alongside a huge trailer truck, getting pulled over by an Oklahoma state trooper who just wanted to look at their car, crossing a Mississippi River bridge, and the sweetest image of all, cruising onto the grounds of the famed Indianapolis Custom Car Show.

After dropping off the Mercillac at the exhibition hall, they caught a ride over to where they were staying, collapsed on mattresses, and slept like the dead. They hadn't been in bed in one hundred hours.

When they woke they went back over to the hall and fielded question after question about their wild ride and their even wilder car. Did they ship it or drive it from California? What happens if it gets stuck in the mud, or it has to go off the pavement into the dirt? And how did they see out of that slitty little windshield? Indianapolis showed the same curiosity as every other town they had been in over the past three days.

Those who attended the show did the judging. People picked up a form when they entered the hall, filled it out while reviewing the customs on display, then dropped it in a box on their way out. Hirohata could not predict how this would go. He loved his car, no doubt. It made a statement about who he was and what his values were and his sense of personal style. Somehow a piece of himself, his identity, found expression in that car. But what would others think of it? He had no idea.

They liked it. The Hirohata Merc won first-place honors. When they announced his name at the awards ceremony, Hirohata thought they were kidding at first. Then they handed him the trophy, a feeling of elation swept over him and, he said, "I almost fell over in a dead faint."

TWENTY-SEVEN

Indianapolis Takeover

After his triumph at the 1953 Indianapolis Custom Show, Bob Hirohata fulfilled the other half of his dream, driving the Merc over to the Indianapolis Motor Speedway to see the last day of qualifying for that year's Indianapolis 500. Hirohata and Azzie Nishi reported being "astounded at the speeds of the cars."

Thirty-three cars race in the Indianapolis 500, and they earn their starting spots by qualifying in preliminary trials. The faster they go, the closer they are to the front of the lineup. But a driver and car can qualify early in the trials only to be bumped out later by a driver and car that go faster, and that's what Bill Holland, the 1949 Indy champion, found out early Sunday morning, losing his spot in the starting lineup to Bob Sweikert. Sweikert had gotten into the Dean Van Lines Special when its previous driver, Allan Heath, had resigned from the car because he "didn't feel quite right." Sweikert felt exceedingly right in it, averaging 136.82 miles per hour in his ten-mile qualifying run—four laps around the two-and-a-half-mile track—which earned him a berth in the field of thirty-three and knocked Holland out of it.

Knocked him out, that is, if he chose to accept such a thing, which he did not. Realizing that if he didn't do something fast he'd be watching the 500, not racing in it, Holland hopped aboard a car owned by Ray Crawford and galloped over those ten miles in 137.86 miles per hour, fast enough to return him to the starting lineup next to the man who had nearly bumped him out. Holland and Sweikert occupied the inside and middle of the tenth row, far back in the field in the next-to-last row. But at least they were in the race, and that was what mattered.

Watching the action from the stands, Hirohata and Nishi may have felt as if they had nothing in common with the cars and drivers pounding around the storied brick-yard course. After all, the Hirohata Merc was more of a look-cool car than a go-fast one. Then again, the two Californians may have felt very connected to what they were seeing because practically everywhere a person looked at the speedway, somebody from California was doing something of note.

Bob Sweikert was from Hayward, Allan Heath from Northridge, and Ray Crawford from El Monte—these were only three of the Golden Staters making the scene at Indy. Even Holland, who lived in Indiana, drove a car designed, built, and owned by Californians. Ditto for Tony Bettenhausen, an Illinois wheelman who qualified sixth—second row, outside—in a car owned by J. C. Agajanian of San Pedro. Agajanian was about as Californian—and American—as a person could be, and if Hirohata and Nishi knew what he looked like, they may have spotted him down in the pits or shaking hands in the grandstands or press box. J. C. (or "Aggie," as everyone called him) was as decked-out and brightly colored as his No. 98 racecar. "Dressed in a manner which would make Bing Crosby envious, so far as color schemes go," he loved richly tailored, gaudily colored sportswear ensembles that coordinated perfectly with his ten-gallon hats, cowboy boots, and the chartreuse Cadillac convertible he drove. "The Armenian Beau Brummell," the press called him, although Beau Brummell never owned a stable of racing machines the way Aggie did.

It takes money, and considerable sums of it, to sponsor racecars at Indianapolis, and Aggie piled up his sums through ranching and agriculture. His parents had come to the United States from Armenia in 1913, just months before he was born. Settling in the harbor town of San Pedro, "Pappa" Agajanian supported his growing family first as a dishwasher and then worked his way up to garbage man, forming his own garbage collection business. Eventually he bought some land and moved into hog farming. Each step up the economic ladder represented greater opportunity and freedom for him, and he became a wealthy man, the old-world patriarch of a new-world family. Some of the customs of his adopted country he approved of, others not so much. When his teenaged son drove up to the house one day in a hopped-up roadster, just like what other teenaged American boys were driving, Pappa said no, absolutely not, not in a million years. "You can own it," he told his son, "but you can't drive it."

This began Aggie's interest in owning and promoting racecars, rather than driving them. "It's a saga of an American family," said the auto writer Jack Curnow. "Pappa to pigs to pistons to a papa himself." As Aggie took on a wife, fathered three boys and a girl, and took over the family hog business after Pappa passed on, he never let go of his teenaged love for hopped-up cars, entering one in the 1948 Indianapolis 500. Johnny Mantz of Long Beach drove it to a twelfth-place finish. Unsatisfied, Aggie turned the car over to Eddie Kuzma, also known as Eddie "Kazoom" for his ability to make turtle-like racing machines go like cheetahs. A Los Angeles car builder and designer, Kuzma reworked the J. C. Agajanian Special and the next year Freddie Agabashian drove it to first place in the national one-hundred-mile big-car championships at the state fairgrounds track in Sacramento. Another improving driver with big-race dreams, Agabashian hailed from the East Bay town of Albany, and like Agajanian, Freddie came from an Armenian immigrant family. Ever alert to such things, the wags in the press dubbed the two of them "the shish-kebab kids."

Agajanian, Agabashian, Mantz, Kuzma—all listed California addresses on their business cards and all were at Indianapolis on that final Sunday of qualifying in 1953. The Agajanian Special with Bettenhausen was in. So was the Crawford Special with Holland; nobody was pushing him out now. A hot driver in a hot car, Agabashian in the Gracor-Elgin Piston Pin Special had qualified on the first day with the second fastest time. He was first row middle, and some of the serious gambling action picked him to win it all.

Not so fortunate was Mantz, the former Pacific Coast big-car champion who had been flinging the Pat Clancy Special around the track for days unable to break into the starting lineup. Finally he gave up and turned the car over to Jimmy Davies, a twenty-something red-hot who had just gotten out of the army after a hitch in Korea. The Van Nuys resident averaged 135.30 miles per hour and grabbed a spot in the last row, shoving out Cal Niday of Culver City.

Niday then hastily pulled a Bill Holland, climbing into his Miracle Power Special and taking another charge at getting back into the field with time slipping away. His average speed of 136.09 miles per hour, recorded fifteen minutes before the 7 p.m. qualifying deadline, put him on the outside of the tenth row next to Sweikert and Holland.

With the close of qualifying that Sunday, Hirohata and Nishi left Indianapolis to go to a car show in Michigan, eventually returning home to Arcadia. While on the road they kept up with the latest goings-on at Indy via the newspaper and radio, learning how speedway officials had shut the track down on Wednesday morning to prepare for Saturday's race and the 175,000 spectators expected to attend. No race-cars were permitted on the track during this time. All fuel and carburetion tests and other mechanical procedures had to be done in the garage areas of Gasoline Alley, which shifted pre-race attention to the mechanics and drivers making last-minute adjustments to their cars.

The dominant figure in Gasoline Alley was another Californian, Frank Kurtis. His Kurtis-Kraft plant on West Colorado Street in Glendale had built no fewer than twenty-four of the thirty-three cars in the final field. A Harry A. Miller–esque figure of volcanic energy and inventiveness, always looking to do things different and better than the way he did them before, the tall, brawny Kurtis was the son of Croatian immigrants, having learned metalwork in the mines of Colorado before being drawn in the 1920s to the budding automobile metropolis on the coast. The Don Lee Coach and Body Works hired him as a teenager and quickly rising to shop foreman, he hammered Harley Earl's custom visions into metal and steel while playing around in his spare time with his own mechanical visions. The jalopies he rescued from the junkyard evolved under his care into raked and streamlined racing machines. In the mid-1930s he moved into midgets and from there, into the big leagues of racing at Indianapolis.

With Bud Winfield, a La Canada mechanic and engine designer, Kurtis devised a breakthrough racecar known as the Novi Governor Special, a sleek, technologically advanced runner that clicked around the Brickyard like nobody's business when it debuted there in 1946. Veteran Los Angeles driver Ralph Hepburn set a new Indianapolis Motor Speedway record in it with an average of 133.94 miles per hour in qualifying. After leading part of the way in the 500, Hepburn and the Novi Governor sputtered out before the finish. Indianapolis had nevertheless seen racing's future, and Frank Kurtis was building it.

The Offy, the gold standard in Indianapolis racing engines, served as the Novi Governor's basic power plant. In 1946 Fred Offenhauser sold his company to three-time Indy champ Lou Meyer and his friend Dale Drake. The Meyer-Drake Corporation of Los Angeles carried the Offenhauser tradition forward, manufacturing these engines with the guidance of designer Leo Goosen, the former Offenhauser and Miller man who joined Meyer-Drake as its chief engineer.

Beginning in 1947 and for every year through the forties, fifties, and into the early sixties, Offenhauser engines powered most of the cars that competed at Indianapolis and all of the winners. Pop the hood of a car in the winner's circle at Indy during this time and you'd see an Offy. The Offenhauser heritage, car builders and designers like Kurtis, Winfield, and Kuzma, money men such as Agajanian and North Hollywood's Lou Moore—all these elements help to explain why every other guy in greasy overalls walking around Gasoline Alley seemed to live in Long Beach or Glendale or Bakersfield. But there was another, perhaps more important reason for California's takeover at Indy: the midgets, the chief proving ground for car racing in the state.

California drivers won nine of ten Indianapolis 500s during the 1950s and, writes Brock Yates, all of them "honed their skills in southern California roadster and midget competition in the late 1940s and rose to dominance in American championship competition." Walt Faulkner—"the little dynamo," as a reporter called him—belongs in that group. Before taking on Indianapolis, the Texas-born Faulkner had to prove himself first in the midgets because he was a bit of a midget himself, small and sleight of build and hard-pressed to get the needle past 120 pounds when he stepped on a scale. Midget cars were smaller and easier to handle than the Indianapolis bruisers, and race-car owners of the latter group doubted his ability to withstand a grueling five-hundred-mile endurance test. No one doubted his toughness; Faulkner had shown that many times in the midgets, including the night at Gilmore in 1948 when his car "flip-flopped all the way down the backstretch" with him inside it. After it stopped flip-flopping they pulled his body from the wreckage and rushed him to the hospital where doctors set several of his broken bones. It took him five months to fully mend.

Just as Indianapolis car owners shied away from him, Faulkner did not show much interest in the 500 until Rex Mays, a Pacific Coast champion and longtime Indy challenger who lived in Glendale, talked him into taking another look at it. "Just drive it like you've been handling that No. 16 miggie," said Mays, whose death at age thirty-six in a 1949 crash at Del Mar Speedway shocked Faulkner and many other younger California drivers, who had looked up to him and regarded him as a friend and mentor.

Johnny Mantz had run the Agajanian Special at Indianapolis in 1948 and 1949, but in 1950, no longer feeling right in the car, he recommended that Faulkner take over for him. But Aggie didn't think Faulkner was up to it. There was this little matter of his size, plus he'd never raced at Indy before. Finally, though, he relented, and Faulkner proved he could run with the big dogs with his record-setting qualifying run of 134.34 miles per hour, snapping the mark set previously by Ralph Hepburn.

Despite his qualifying mark, Faulkner did not win Indianapolis that year; that honor belonged to Johnnie Parsons of Sherman Oaks. As talented as he was good-looking, Parsons drove a Kurtis-Offy to a rain-shortened 500 triumph in only his second race there. The actress Barbara Stanwyck greeted him in the winner's circle with a "smackeroo"—fifties slang for a kiss. Led by Parsons and the seventh-place Faulkner, eighteen California drivers raked in one hundred thousand dollars as a group that year at Indy, half the total purse, and every last one of them had traded paint in the midgets.

The midgets groomed so many top drivers because California offered so many places to race and so many testosterone-charged young males anxious for the chance to do so. And the purses weren't bad sometimes: ten thousand dollars for a night. Big paydays like that occurred at Gilmore or Memorial Coliseum in Los Angeles, where crowds of fifty-five thousand came out to watch the little beasts go bump in the night. But the midgets raced all over the map: Rose Bowl in Pasadena, Lincoln Park Stadium in Lincoln Heights, Carrell Speedway in Gardena, speedways in Saugus, Huntington Beach, and Culver City, Del Mar Speedway and Balboa Stadium in San Diego, the Bakersfield Raceway and at county fairground tracks wherever they put on county fairs. Hughes Stadium in Sacramento sponsored purse-paying midget races as far back as the early 1930s. The new Oakland Stadium, which was built in 1946 to replace the old Oakland Speedway torn down on the eve of World War II, hosted jalopies, Indy cars, motorcycles, and the midgets. Other Bay Area racing venues included Pacheco, Vallejo, and the impossibly narrow and crowded track at the Cow Palace in Daly City. "The Cow Palace was dangerous," said one driver's wife. "If something happened, there was no way to get out of the way."

This was the way it was with the midgets: It was hard for cars to get out of the way of other cars, and sometimes they didn't—on purpose. For these and so many more reasons, spectators loved to "sit forward in our seats and grunt and groan and oh and ah as a daredevil driver sprints through a field of racing automobiles and nudges a rival to the outside of the track." The young Phil Hill got into midgets but quickly got out of them because they were too scary. "I felt sure I'd crash sooner or later," he said. "I am honestly afraid of those little bombs."

Before leaving those little bombs, though, the future star of the Ferrari international racing team ran at San Bernardino and Carrell Speedway against no fewer than five future Indianapolis 500 champions: Troy Ruttman (1952), Billy Vukovich (1953–1954), Sam Hanks (1957), Jimmy Bryan (1958), and Rodger Ward (1962). Also in those midget scrambles were drivers who never won at Indy but backed down to no one: Walt Faulkner, Manny Ayulo, and Jack McGrath, to name but three. Except for Hill, every one of these drivers nailed down a spot in the starting lineup of the 1953 Indianapolis 500, and all of them lived in California or had strong ties to the state. In all, nineteen Golden Staters were in the field, including the three fastest qualifiers. Outside front: Jack McGrath of South Pasadena. Center front: Freddie Agabashian, the Shish-Kebab Kid. And the man on the pole, inside front, the fastest qualifier: thirty-four-year-old Billy Vukovich, who had a nickname too. The press called him "the Mad Russian" although he was not, alas, Russian. His parents were Yugoslavian-born, and Billy's son-of-immigrants, growing-up-in-America story is as rich as anyone's.

When they arrived in the United States from Yugoslavia, John and Mildred Vukurovich shortened their name to Vukovich. They had eight children, including Billy born in 1918 in Alameda. When he was very young the family left the Bay Area for the Fresno area, where John found work as a carpenter and came to own a farm. Billy's first race, it is said, was in a "two-seated buggy with his father's Shetland pony for power." But when the boy was thirteen or fourteen his father committed suicide, and the family fell into an emotional and financial hole. They lost their farm. Money was something other people had, and they struggled to put food on the table. Billy and his older brother Eli quit high school and worked to support their mother and brothers and sisters, who also did everything they could to help the family get by.

Billy turned to competitive racing as a teenager partly because it was a job that paid cash money. Not much, but a little, and it sure beat picking cotton. Racecar owner Fred Gearhart saw Billy drive and asked him if he wanted to run Gearhart's hopped-up Chevrolet in a dirt track race. Billy said sure, and drove it to a second-place finish. It wasn't long before other jalopy owners in the valley hated to see that Chevy pull up to a race because it meant Billy was in it and they were going to have a scrap on their hands and probably lose at the end of it. For some, motor racing was sport. For Billy, who surely loved to go fast, it was too serious to be called sport. By whipping the other farmboys in the dirt track races around the valley, he could make fifteen dollars in a good week. And with the interest and money flowing into midgets in the 1930s, Billy flowed that direction as well. In his first midget race his car lit on fire and he broke a collarbone, some ribs, and burned his hand in the crash. Less than two months later he was back on the job, occasionally teaming up with Eli, who had joined the racing fraternity too. The brothers drove all over the state in search of purse-paying races, and at night they slept in their truck.

Both Billy and Eli knew how to handle an automobile at speed. Both took risks and faced the dangers of their sport bravely. But they were different in that one of them always pushed it, always had to win no matter what. "Don't tangle with me," Billy told his brother once. "Out on that track you're just another driver."

Billy could be that way—direct and blunt, too much so at times, sounding arrogant without necessarily meaning to be. Those who knew and loved him enjoyed his sense of humor, and everyone agreed he was lucky to have met Esther. He and Esther married in 1941 when Billy was recovering from a racing injury that was bad enough to keep him out of the military. During the war he repaired jeeps and other army vehicles, adding to his knowledge of machines, another quality that made him such a good driver. He contributed ideas and made fixes that boosted the performance of the cars he was in.

Vukovich won the Pacific Coast midget championships in 1946 and 1947 driving a pint-sized red mini-battleship called "Old Ironsides." This was when the press hung the "Mad Russian" tag on him which, except for the Russian part, fit him fairly well.

In a sport filled with car-passing, car-banging, go-for-broke drivers, the farmboy in Old Ironsides was the fastest and car-bangingest of them all. Fit and muscular, he saw himself as an athlete and trained as such, running and bicycling to stay in shape, and avoiding cigarettes and booze. Taking on all comers, he never willingly conceded an inch to any of them. "One of the toughest, most nerve-less throttle mashers in the game," was how Jack Curnow described him. "He could do anything with a midget except make it talk." His fiercest duels in the midgets, and there were plenty to choose from, came against another driver who could almost make them talk, a "hot dog kid" from Ontario named Troy Ruttman. In 1952 the two Californians shifted their rivalry to Indianapolis and put on one of the finest shows ever seen there.

Both drivers appeared at Indianapolis as rookies in 1949, but Ruttman only did so-so and Vukovich never got in the race. By 1952 that had all changed. Replacing Walt Faulkner, Ruttman had taken over the Eddie Kuzma–designed J. C. Agajanian Special, whose owner was still looking for his first win at Indy after four years of trying. Meanwhile Vukovich showed up in some mad wheels of his own: the Howard Keck Special built by Frank Kurtis and designed by two bright young engineers, Jim Travers and Frank Coon. The car's owner, Howard Keck, also owned Superior Oil, an independent California oil company (later acquired by Mobil). With such deep pockets to draw from, Keck let Travers and Coon create without budget worries, and so they did. Some called them "the Rich Kids," a reference to Keck's money, and some called them "the Whiz Kids," a nod to their youth and brains. Sometimes whiz kids with money can waste their money and talent, but Travers and Coon did not, and the fuel-injected machine they brought to Indianapolis revolutionized the 500, ushering in what racing historians refer to as "the roadster era." This roadster surprised people at Indianapolis because it was "unusually low-slung," lower to the ground than any other car there. "This is accomplished by tilting the engine 36 degrees, shifting the drive shaft to the left. This arrangement permits the driver to sit low in the car, beside the drive shaft rather than astride it as in conventional racers," wrote a reporter.

The man sitting beside that drive shaft was Billy Vukovich, and that made all the difference. He qualified eighth—third row, middle—but once the race began he quickly reshuffled the deck. On lap seven he blew past Jack McGrath who had led the first six. Enter Troy Ruttman, who slipped past Vukovich on lap twelve. Vukovich answered by passing him on the next lap, and suddenly the greatest spectacle in racing resembled a Thursday night shoot-out under the lights at Beverly and Fairfax. "Between Ruttman and Vukovich, the 'mad Russian' from Fresno, speed marks fell lap after lap. It looked like a couple of midget kids going around Gilmore Stadium," wrote Jack Curnow, who'd seen plenty of those duels. Vukie led until lap 60 when he pitted. On came Ruttman "with his foot through the floorboard." But when Rutttman pitted on lap 83 Vukovich stormed back, gaining the lead and holding it until lap 135 when another pit stop returned it to Ruttman. When Ruttman pitted thirteen laps later, guess who came back into first, stretching the distance between his rival to fifty-five seconds while pushing the Kurtis-Coons-Travers-Keck special past 200 miles per hour on the straights.

Both men had pitted for the last time. If Ruttman was going to catch Vukovich he was going to have to do it without the benefit of a Vukovich stop. Steadily, relentlessly, he started pulling Vukovich back toward him. By lap 184 he had closed the margin to twenty-six seconds; lap 187, twenty-five seconds; lap 188, twenty-four seconds. By lap 191 Ruttman had closed to within ten seconds. He was making up ground fast, but was it fast enough? With nine laps to go, did he have enough time to catch Vukovich? These questions suddenly became moot when Vukovich skidded into the wall on the northeast turn, shocking those who saw it. So close to the checkered flag—and yet there he was jumping out of his crippled revolution on wheels and scrambling over the wall as Ruttman, possibly as stunned as everyone else, ka-zoomed past him. With his chief competitor out of the way, Ruttman cruised to an easy three-lap win, becoming, at age twenty-two, the youngest ever to win at Indianapolis. A beaming J. C. Agajanian joined him in the victory circle and doffed his cowboy hat to the cheers of the crowd.

One hot-rodder and two midget guys, all Californians—Jim Rathmann, Sam Hanks, Duane Carter—took the next three places. Based on Vukovich's time and how many miles he completed, race officials awarded him seventeenth place, hardly the result he was hoping for.

Not knowing what had happened in the moment, Jack Curnow attributed Vukovich's run-in with the wall to luck—good for Troy, bad for Billy. In reality, the culprit was a broken steering column pin, which made it hard for Vukovich to steer, explaining why he kept losing ground over the final laps and ultimately why he lost control of the car. "The hard-luck loser" of the race, as Curnow described him, Vukovich nevertheless had better luck after it than Ruttman, who later suffered a bad wreck that knocked him out of competition for a time and prevented him from defending his title in 1953 at Indianapolis.

Not that Ruttman's presence, or lack of same, mattered to Vukovich. Returning to the speedway in the Whiz Kids' fuel-injection special, he had a score to settle, a job left undone. On the first day of qualifying he averaged 138.39 miles per hour, putting him on the pole, where he wished to be and where he felt he belonged.

As predicted, a full house of 175,000 people turned out on Memorial Day, their cars jamming the roads leading to the speedway. Temperatures and humidity rose above 90 degrees, and the radio commentators—there was national radio coverage, no television—said it was maybe the hottest Indianapolis 500 ever held. Some of today's Indianapolis 500 traditions, such as the pre-race festival parade, had yet to begin, but others were firmly established. The gentlemen in their racecars started their engines on command, moving slowly forward as a group behind the pace car. The Brickyard track was no longer made of bricks as in the early days; its surface was largely asphalt. The pace car went once around the track at about 45 miles per hour and then turned off into the pit lane, igniting an explosion of noise and smoke as the cars behind it burst forward.

On the inside front, Vukovich, in No. 14, surged into the lead around the first turn with hot-rodder Manny Ayulo, in No. 88, jumping from the second row to about a car's length behind him. But that was about as close as he got because Vukovich led every lap of the first forty-eight. Stopping briefly in the pits for gas and maintenance, he graciously allowed a few of his fellow Californians to earn a little lap money: Freddie Agabashian, lap 49; Jim Rathmann, lap 50; Sam Hanks, laps 51, 52, 53. After that Billy retook the lead and never had to retake it again, averaging a near-record 128.74 miles per hour to seal a victory made especially sweet by his disappointment of the year before. His payday, including lap money, was $89,496.96, and Tommy Milton thought he deserved every penny of it. The grand old-time Indy champion called Vukovich "the finest I've ever seen at any time. He is the greatest driver ever to compete at the Speedway."

Only the horrible heat detracted from his achievement. One driver died from heat stroke, and heat exhaustion put at least two others out of the race. Some drivers in the starting lineup used relief drivers because they needed a break from the intense temperatures. In the winner's circle Vukovich looked pale and exhausted; he had sweated so much his black hair looked like it had been rained on, and his undershirt was soaked through. Still, no relief driver spelled him; he drove every inch of the five hundred miles. Asked about the sweltering conditions, he said, "If they think this is hot, they've never been on a tractor in Fresno in July."

Back home in Fresno the folks were ecstatic. "We were so happy we cried," Billy's youngest sister, Florence Bieden, said. "We were glued to the radio from start to finish. . . . It was nerve-wracking." Brother Eli was so nervous he couldn't sit still at home by the radio, so while Billy was racing in Indianapolis he was bumping around in an Oakland Stadium midget race. Another sister, Ann Gusse, was so distracted she couldn't concentrate on a thing. "I'm afraid I didn't get much work done this morning," she said. "I was so excited I almost emptied the garbage in the garage."

After the race's happy conclusion the family started planning Billy's homecoming celebration in earnest. The phone rang nonstop and friends and family dropped by the house to share in the excitement. It was a day filled with such joy and promise that both Florence and Ann allowed themselves a small hope—that their brother would now quit motor racing "as he has promised."

If Billy promised his sisters he'd quit, he didn't do it. He came back to Fresno, bought a gas station in town with his winnings, kept raising his family with Esther, continued to race (though not quite as much as before), and returned to Indianapolis in 1954. Despite starting well back in the field he won his second straight 500 and affirmed his reputation not just as a great midget driver but as one of the greatest drivers anywhere, anytime, in any sort of vehicle with an engine and driveshaft. But because of that broken steering pin in the '52 race, something still nagged at him. The job was as yet undone. Nobody in the long, storied history of the Indianapolis 500 had ever won three in a row, and Billy Vukovich wished to be the first. So it wasn't long before the clock started ticking again and he resumed preparations, once more, to chase his destiny.

TWENTY-EIGHT

Twelve Months

On the set of *Rebel Without a Cause*, the hottest young actor in Hollywood was hoping that the shooting of the film would end in time for him to go to Indianapolis to see Billy Vukovich defend his title. Growing up in the Indiana countryside a few hours' drive from Indianapolis, James Dean had listened to the Indianapolis 500 on the radio as a youngster and knew all about the race and loved it. He also drove racecars himself, and this may have been another reason why he was eager for shooting to wrap—so he could get back out on the circuit and do some more racing in his Porsche.

It was a cool thing to be young and alive in 1955, and it was an even cooler thing to be young and alive and James Dean. He was in his early twenties, single, so good-looking people couldn't take their eyes off him, a magnet for beautiful women. He had begun filming *Rebel Without a Cause*, his second film, in April, only a month after his first, *East of Eden,* had turned him into a major star. Actually, this transformation had begun a few months earlier, when the *Los Angeles Times* sent a photographer over to the Warner Brothers lot in Burbank for a feature the paper was running on the final days of shooting *East of Eden,* the picture based on the Steinbeck novel of the same name.

The young Julie Harris, Jo Ann Fleet, and Raymond Massey were also appearing in the movie, although they held the photographer's interest in only a limited way. The person who fascinated him, the reason he was there, the point of the assignment in the first place—that was James Dean. And there certainly was no disputing one thing: The camera loved him. There he was, in a heated exchange with Massey, who plays his father. Click! With Jo Ann Fleet, his movie mother, and other cast members in a dramatic confrontation. Click, click! The film critic for the *Times*, Phillip K. Scheuer, who was writing the feature, could not turn his eyes away from Dean. "At once a roughneck and an introvert, the unloved one, he is inevitably being compared with Marlon Brando, another Kazan favorite," he wrote.

Kazan was Elia Kazan, the director of *East of Eden* who had previously directed Marlon Brando in *On the Waterfront* and *A Streetcar Named Desire.* He had also directed Montgomery Clift, another beautiful, brooding actor who had become a giant

Above: When the men went off to war in World War II, the women pitched in and did unfamiliar jobs at home. *Below, another war scene:* Men from all around the country came to California to work in the shipyards and aircraft factories, sleeping in their cars until they could find more permanent housing.

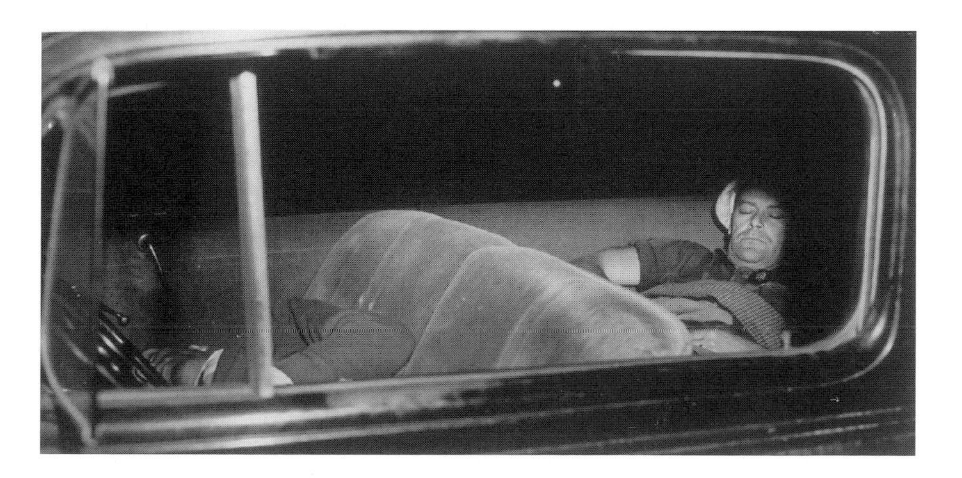

Two teen hangouts in the 1940s and '50s: drive-in movie theaters and diners such as Bob's Big Boy in Burbank.

The young Wally Parks, founder of the National Hot Rod Association.

Sam Barris stands proudly next to the Hirohata Merc, a famous custom car built by Sam and his brother George. George Barris, one of the most creative custom car designers in a dazzlingly creative California custom scene, built many TV and movie vehicles, such as the original Batmobile (opposite page).

Original Batmobile

The hot rods in the world's first hot rod show, the 1948 Hot Rod Exposition at the National Guard Armory in Exposition Park in Los Angeles.

Above: Girls didn't just go for rides in hot rods, they drove and worked on them too. Below: Everyone, girls and boys, liked to park their cars in secluded places and enjoy the view, among other pleasures.

Ferrari

Two dashing stars of the California racing scene: Carroll Shelby, opposite page, and Dan Gurney, in the center above.

The Concours d'Elegance at Pebble Beach.

Church service at a North Hollywood drive-in movie theater.

American kids embraced—and squeezed into—the Volkswagen bug in record numbers in the 1960s.

Protesting discrimination at a car dealership on Van Ness in San Francisco.

75

IN THE TIMES OF THEIR LIVES,
THEY TRULY LIVED

Left: James Dean, at a race in Palm Springs.

Above: Fresno's Billy Vukovich waving to his fans at the Indianapolis 500.

Next page: Steve McQueen, the coolest (and fastest) movie star of his generation.

Craig Breedlove and the Spirit of America, the fastest car on wheels in the 1960s.

Hollywood star seemingly in the blink of an eye. But neither Clift nor Brando had generated the kind of buzz Dean had even before his first movie was released.

A few weeks after the *Times'* photo spread appeared, Hedda Hopper called Dean "the most exciting young actor to hit the screen in years." That Dean had yet to actually hit the screen mattered not a whit to Hopper, whose excitement only increased after the movie reached theaters in March. "I can't remember when any screen newcomer generated as much excitement in Hollywood," she wrote in a follow-up piece after *East of Eden*'s release. Hopper, who was approaching seventy but retained the same youthful enthusiasm for movies and celebrities she had always had, didn't like Dean at first. "I'd seen Dean only once," she confessed. "Slumped, surly looking and carelessly dressed, in the studio commissary. He was not impressive." Then she saw him in *East of Eden*—saw that scene when he hops off a moving train with effortless grace, saw his torment when he shoved those blocks of ice down the barn chute to get his father's attention—and her eyes opened to everything he was bringing, and could potentially bring, to movies. You couldn't not watch him when he was on screen. Yet his performance wasn't showy or actor-ly but real and raw and straight to the heart.

Being one of the best-read gossip columnists in a gossip-hungry business, Hopper invited the hottest young actor in America over to her house for an interview. "He arrived on the dot," she observed, "wearing a charcoal-colored suit, black shirt and tie, and on his feet heavy riding boots." She said nothing more about those boots, and why should she? Dean was wearing motorcycle boots and had ridden to her house on a motorcycle, details she would have cared little about because she, like the rest of the country, knew precious little about him at this point. They did not yet know about his interest in, and love for, fast-moving bikes and cars.

Being more interested in people than machines, Hopper naturally inquired about Dean's background. "My family came to California and before it was over my mother had me tap-dancing," he said, being flip and casual. But how else was he supposed to act, talking to one of the grand dames of show business? Six months earlier Hopper would have called the cops on him if he had showed up at her house on a motorcycle in those big heavy riding boots. Now she was giggling at his jokes and scribbling down his every word for the paper.

Explaining how he was anemic as a boy, Dean paused, broke into that shy, endearing smile of his, and asked Hedda to put on some background music for him. You know, like violins for a sob story. Laughing, she slid a record onto the turntable and switched it on.

They were having a merry time of it, the new star and the old columnist. But for her article, Hedda filled in a few more of the biographical details she knew her readers would like to see. Born in Indiana, Dean had moved to Santa Monica when he was very young. His father, a dental technician, had brought the family west to take a job in the Veterans Affairs Hospital in Westwood. His mother contracted cancer and died when he was eight, and struggling over money and believing it best for his son, his father sent him back to Indiana to be raised by his aunt and uncle there. Anemic and a little sickly as a boy, James took to farm life and grew into a gifted athlete, competing in baseball and track at Fairmount High. During these years an interest in drama also developed and he joined the theater club at school. His rendition of a Charles Dickens poem won an Indiana state drama contest.

"My whole life has been spent in a dramatic display of expression," he told Hedda. He wasn't joking when he said this. Nor did she laugh.

After high school Dean returned to Santa Monica to be with his father, who had remarried but still worked at the VA hospital. He took acting classes at Santa Monica City College and the University of California at Los Angeles before leaving for New York, where he appeared in plays and television programs and won a promising newcomer award. This stirred the interest of Kazan, who gambled on an unknown and cast him in *East of Eden*. Although the picture had been out less than a month, Warner Brothers had already signed Dean to a nine-picture deal over the next six years. His next film was to be *Rebel Without a Cause*.

On the day Hopper's article came out in the *Times*, Dean might have been excused if he had decided to grab the paper and have breakfast with some of his actor-friends at his favorite coffee shop, Googie's, on Sunset and Crescent Heights. But he didn't go to Googie's that morning; instead he was in Palm Springs, getting a charge out of life in one of the best ways he knew how: racing automobiles.

The eighth annual Palm Springs Road Races, held at the airport on a 2.3-mile track, attracted twenty thousand fans and hundreds of sports cars, including Dean's white Porsche 356. Like Dean in Hollywood, the Porsche 356 had gained a rapid and enthusiastic following after its introduction to this country the year before. This was his first race in it, his first sports car race in California—a one-hour, twenty-seven-lap feature event for stock and modified cars with engine sizes under 1500 cc. His competitors included the British-born driving ace Ken Miles, a newcomer on the American sports car scene who was beating the stuffing out of just about everyone he faced in his MG Special. Miles won this race with ease too, followed by a driver from Los Angeles. But Dean came in third, serving notice that he was not just some Hollywood pretty boy but a driver with talent. "James Dean, Hollywood actor, drove his Porsche Speedster with veteran aplomb," said one reporter.

Dean collected two trophies for his showing at Palm Springs, and a photograph of him holding these awards reveals none of the on-screen torment and conflict for which he was known as an actor. In a jacket and white T-shirt, with that great puffed-up dirty blond hair of his, he's smiling and happy.

Dean raced again in Bakersfield before beginning work on *Rebel,* which, fittingly, had a lot to do with cars. By early April two other promising young actors, Natalie Wood and Sal Mineo, had signed to star with Dean, and the director, Nicholas Ray, announced more cast additions at the end of the month. (Playing a gang member in a bit part was Dennis Hopper, who years later would make another story of youthful rebellion, *Easy Rider,* about an ill-fated motorcycle trip across country.)

After *Rebel* wrapped, Dean had hoped to visit his aunt and uncle in Fairmount while taking in the annual Indiana state celebration known as the Indy 500. But shooting ran long and he couldn't make it back East so he missed the race, although he certainly followed the sorrowful events that occurred there.

California hot rodder Manny Ayulo was nearing the end of a May 17 qualifying run at the Brickyard. His was the last practice lap of the day; officials planned to shut the track down after he finished. Then Ayulo "came down the main straightaway and smashed into the concrete wall without turning even slightly into the curve," in the words of a shocked onlooker. His Peter Schmidt Special hit with a tremendous impact and he was killed. Leaving behind a wife and four-year-old daughter, Ayulo, age thirty-three, was a dry lakes veteran who had displayed a car at the world's first hot rod show in 1948. Skilled in all forms of racing, he knew how to avoid danger in an automobile, which made the circumstances of his death puzzling. "There were no skid marks on the track," investigators found, which appeared to indicate he did not brake before hitting the wall. "Witnesses said Ayulo appeared to be tugging at the steering wheel as he headed into the turn," suggesting a steering malfunction of some kind, a malfunction that rendered him helpless as he met his end.

Ayulo was the forty-fifth fatality at the Indianapolis 500 since the race began in 1911. The forty-sixth, Billy Vukovich, occurred on the day of the race.

The Vukovich family was gathered around the radio at home in Fresno, their usual practice when Billy raced at Indianapolis. The only ones who weren't there were his wife Esther and brother Mike, who had gone to see it in person. Most everyone else had an ear to the radio: sisters Florence and Ann and their husbands, Eli Vukovich and his wife, Marlene, Billy's thirteen-year-old daughter, and Billy Jr., his eleven-year-old son.

It was a nerve-wracking and exciting time, made even more so when Billy swept past the other cars into first. First place! For a while it seemed as if he really was going to do what no one else had ever done before and win Indy three times in a row. But on the fifty-seventh lap, several cars skidded and got tangled up on the track. None of the men in these machines was hurt seriously; that unlucky fate befell the one who was not involved, who tried to get out of their way. Coming up at high speed Billy saw the mess of cars and, said one observer, "chose to take the wall rather than smash into other cars scattered around the track." While seeking to avoid the pileup, "Vukovich's sleek dark blue racer leaped the two-foot wood-and-metal barrier. It tumbled end to end five times then caught fire. The car landed upside down, Vukovich trapped underneath."

With No. 14 flipping over the wall and the chaotic pileup on the track, the radio announcers could not tell exactly what had happened to Billy, or why. Thus, the people listening at home did not know either. But Eli Vukovich, an accomplished driver himself, instantly sensed that something was wrong and he "raced into the backyard, pounding his fist."

Other family members and people all around Fresno reacted with shock and horror. "Many residents who had been listening to the Memorial Day classic on the radio at first were unable to believe that Wild Bill had cracked up," said a wire service report. "Others were visibly affected by the news and snapped their radios into silence."

Billy's racecar had flipped over the wall and landed upside down trapping him underneath. A wire service photograph taken a moment later shows the car riddled with flames with smoke pouring out of it. Its original caption reads "The badly burned Hopkins Special in which ace driver Bill Vukovich was burned to death smolders at Indianapolis Speedway with its driver pinned underneath." Another photograph, taken after the unsuccessful rescue efforts had begun, shows two uniformed men and another in a hat and coat standing by the smoking wreckage, looking on "helplessly," as the wire service put it.

The Vukovich family strongly disputed any suggestion that Billy died from immolation. "Billy didn't burn to death," said Eli. "He was killed when the car went over the wall and smashed down on two cars parked outside the wall." The speedway's medical chief of staff later agreed that Billy was "probably dead" before the car caught on fire.

Eli spoke to his brother Mike on the phone after the crash, but it was days before he could talk to the press about it. "The shock was almost too much," said his wife. "We were all stunned." This was true of people across the country. Many Americans of this era only followed one motor race a year, that being the Indianapolis 500. Stock car racing was nothing like it is today, and of the major sports, only professional baseball held the interest of fans across America. Football and basketball were mainly college games, and their professional leagues were small and of little consequence. There was widespread attention on the 500 and consequently even non-racing fans had kept up with Billy's story, and his death triggered headlines and radio reports around the country.

The Speedway Christian Church in Indianapolis held funeral rites for him the day after the 500. From there his body was flown to Los Angeles, where a hearse took it to Fresno for services and burial.

Unfortunately, though, the bad news kept coming. Less than two weeks after Indianapolis, a burning, out-of-control Mercedes racecar somersaulted over a wall and flew into a crowd of spectators hugging the roadway at the Le Mans endurance race in France. The driver of the Mercedes and seventy-six other people died, and dozens more suffered injuries in the worst racing calamity ever. With some 250,000 spectators in attendance, the 24 Hours of Le Mans was (and is) one of racing's greatest events, winding around the French countryside on an eight-mile course over public roads. It drew many of the world's best drivers, including Santa Monica's Phil Hill, whose Ferrari escaped trouble amidst all the mayhem.

After Le Mans, Hill returned home to California to race at the July 10 road races at Torrey Pines, where still more tragedy followed. In the fourth race of the day, the "Ladies Race," as it was called, Margaret Pritchard of Phoenix jumped out to the lead on the first turn but, as a report said, "her Morgensen Special swerved to the right of the course, hit a clump of dirt, spun back across the course and turned over." She became, at age thirty-four, the first female fatality in a sanctioned Sports Car Club of America event. Originally scheduled for six laps, the race was shortened to four after her death.

During this year, this awful year, the National Safety Council embarked on a public education campaign on highway safety. Its slogan was "The life you save may be your own." Businesses, community organizations, and government agencies around the country cooperated with this campaign. One of the companies to do so was Warner Brothers, which was then starting to promote its upcoming fall release, *Rebel Without a Cause,* starring James Dean. That summer Warner made a series of short promotional programs called "Behind the Cameras," hosted by actor Gig Young, the purpose being to provide an inside glimpse of the movie business while promoting Warner's pictures. For one "Behind the Cameras" program, Young interviewed Dean, whose fast-car habits were now quite well known around Hollywood.

Looking debonair in a suit and tie, with a smart tie clip and groomed black hair, Young starts the segment by introducing a scene from *Rebel*—the turning-point scene in which Dean and a rival boy prepare to drag their cars on a bluff overlooking the Pacific. It's nighttime. Dean, smoking a cigarette, is at the wheel of a car that customizers and hot-rodders would have recognized in a blink: a black '51 Merc.

"This is a drag race, otherwise known as a chicken run," Young says in voiceover. "But it has nothing to do with chickens. It has to do with kids, nice kids." One of those nice kids, played by Natalie Wood, runs out to a point in front of the two cars. She's the starter. In two rows on both sides of her are the cars of the other teens who have come to watch the race. When she yells "Hit your lights!" their headlights pop on. Dean and his rival will race between these cars with the ocean dead ahead. The one who bails out first is the "chicken." Looking vibrant and beautiful and every inch the young movie star, Wood raises her hands above her head and flings them down dramatically. The cars are off.

Cut to Gig Young, who then introduces "the star of our picture. Ladies and gentlemen, James Dean."

In comes the slouching, smiling figure of Dean, dressed in a cowboy hat and getup. He has a rope in one hand. A cigarette hangs from his lips.

"Hiya, Jim," says Gig.

"Hiya, Gig," says Jim.

The program was shot in an office on the Warner lot. There are two chairs against the wall. Dean sits in one and Young occupies the other, explaining that Dean is currently on the set of his newest picture, *Giant.* He's playing a Texan in the movie, and that's why he's dressed this way. Referring to the "chicken run" clip, Young says that Dean is "a real racer, not a crazy one."

"Speaking of racing," he continues, "have you ever been in a drag race?"

The young cowboy smiles, pulls the cigarette from his mouth, leans back, and says, "What, are you kidding me?"

Young, who could do both comedy and drama as an actor and later won an Oscar, handles the moment easily. "I just thought I'd ask," he says with a smile.

He asks how fast Dean's car will go in a race and Dean mumbles, "Oh, 106, 107."

"You've won a few races haven't you?"

"Oh, one or two. I showed pretty good at Palm Springs. I ran at Bakersfield."

Perhaps because the result was not what he had wished for, Dean does not mention a Santa Barbara race he ran on Memorial Day weekend, the day before Billy Vukovich was killed. There, his Porsche blew a piston and did not finish.

Dean is slumped and looking away. He appears bored.

"Jimmy," says Young, getting to the point of why they are there, "we probably have a lot of young people watching tonight and I'd like your opinion on fast driving on the highway. Do you think it's a good idea?"

"Good point," Dean responds. "I used to fly around quite a bit and took a lot of unnecessary chances on the highways. And then I started racing. Now I drive on the highways and I'm extra cautious. Because no one knows what they're doing half the time. You don't know what this guy is going to do, or that one. On a track there are a lot of men who've spent a lot of time developing rules and ways of safety, and I find myself being very cautious on the highway. I don't have the urge to speed on the highway. People say racing is dangerous, but I'll take my chances any day on a track than on a highway."

Having delivered the message he was supposed to, he stands up to go. He's got to get back to the set, he says.

Rising to his feet with him, Young feels the need to underline the point. "One more question," he says. "Do you have any special advice for the young people who drive?"

Dean is at the door of the office, on his way out. He looks directly into the camera that so adored him and says, "Take your time driving. The life you save might be mine."

Young laughs. Dean exits.

In early September Dean attended a sneak preview of *Rebel* with Ursula Andress at the Village Theater in Westwood, while he finished up shooting *Giant*. So worried was Warner Brothers about Dean's racing that his contract stipulated that he could not race during the making of the film. After *Giant* wrapped, he was a free man again. "Motor racing," said a biographer, "had become for him as much of a passion as acting." Equally to the point, Dean now had plenty of freshly minted movie cash to pursue that passion. A friend had tipped him off about the new Porsches on display at Competition Motors in Hollywood, and Dean went over to take a look. He was not a tough sell. On September 21 he traded in his old Porsche, covered the rest of the ticket with three thousand dollars, and drove away in a new, silver 1955 Porsche Spyder—"a tiny vehicle with a topless aluminum body as fragile as an eggshell," as one writer described it.

Tickled by his new acquisition, Dean spun over to the Warner lot and gave a wild ride in it to *Giant* director George Stevens. The car scared Ursula Andress, however, and she refused to get in it. When Alec Guinness saw Dean in it at the Villa Capri, he begged him to get rid of it. He felt sure it would kill him.

The Spyder, though street legal, was intended for racing, and in order to enter it in a competition it needed a number. Dean brought it over to Dean Jeffries, a much in-demand Hollywood car customizer, who painted "130" in stylized black script on the doors and hood. He also painted the words "Little Bastard"—Dean's name for the car, a private joke with a friend—above the rear license plate.

When he was on location for *East of Eden* Dean had gotten to know the town of Salinas, which was holding a sports car race the first weekend of October. So it seemed a natural place to give Little Bastard its first competitive test. Originally Dean, a member of the California Sports Car Club, planned to tow the Porsche on a trailer behind his Ford Country Squire station wagon, but he changed his mind—"at the last minute," says one account—and decided to drive it instead. A photographer, Sanford Roth, who was shooting a magazine photo essay on Dean, and another man took the Ford, while Dean and his mechanic Rolf Weutherich went ahead of them in the Spyder. Blasting out of Los Angeles late Friday morning Dean reached the Bakersfield area at 3:30 p.m. The time is known precisely because that was when California Highway Patrolman Oscar Hunter pulled him over on the highway for a speeding ticket—65 in a 55 m.p.h. zone. Dean signed the citation and after pledging to appear in municipal court in two weeks he drove off, stopping for gas at a filling station a little while later.

By this time Roth in the station wagon had caught up with his subject. He brought out his camera and snapped a picture of Dean—the last photo of him alive—in the gas station. Behind Dean in the photograph are the station wagon and the empty trailer that originally was supposed to carry the Little Bastard to the race. The shiny silver sports car with the black 130 on the front was already gassed up. Dean is standing next to it by the driver's door. He's got a cigarette in his mouth, sunglasses, white V-neck T-shirt, light blue casual pants. He's pulling a racing glove onto his right hand. He's ready to rock.

Heading east on Highway 46 (then Highway 466), Dean was traveling at an estimated rate of speed of 85 miles per hour when his Porsche collided with a car driven by a man named Donald Turnipseed (also spelled, in some accounts, as Turnupseed). Dean's speed comes from figuring the amount of time it would take for a car to go from the spot where the CHP had stopped him to the site of the accident—the intersection of Highways 46 and 41 in the postage stamp-sized town of Cholame in central California, about a half hour east of Paso Robles. Turnipseed, a student at Cal Poly San Luis Obispo, was going home from school for the weekend, traveling west on 41. A news account said that Dean's eggshell Porsche met the Ford "almost head-on" at 5:59 p.m. on September 30, killing Dean instantly. Turnipseed suffered minor injuries and Weutherich was hurt more seriously, but both got away with their lives. Dean was declared dead on arrival at the War Memorial Hospital in Paso Robles. He was twenty-four.

From his first mention in Hedda Hopper's column in January 1955 to the day of his death, Dean was famous for nine months while he was alive. His fame, in death, may never die, and this posthumous acclaim began the next morning with dramatic radio bulletins and banner headlines in newspapers around the world. Bearing his own private grief, Dean's father, Winton, took the long ride to Paso Robles to see his son and make arrangements for his body to be sent back to Indiana. The family held services in Fairmount and the onetime farmboy who had learned to drive on a tractor was laid to rest in Marion, where he was born. A San Luis Obispo coroner's jury appointed to investigate the cause of the crash declared it to be accidental, concluding, however, that "neither man had his safety belt fastened."

Praise and sadness accompanied the arrival of *Rebel Without a Cause* in theaters at the end of the month. Film reviewers noted the irony of how Dean had survived the chicken run in the movie but could not survive a highway crash in real life. Most felt, as did critic Phil Scheuer, "the sense of real loss Hollywood has suffered in the abrupt cutting off of a young life and a major talent."

The racing community shared this sense of loss, the unfairness of a young life being cut off too short. But almost unbelievably, the losses were not over yet. Jack McGrath died in a November race in Phoenix when his car flipped on the eighty-fourth lap and crushed his skull. The thirty-five-year-old Californian, who wore a metal plate in his head due to an earlier racing accident, raced hot rods, midgets, sprint cars, Indy cars, and anything with four wheels. In 1951 he spelled Manny Ayulo as a relief driver at the Indianapolis 500, and they took third. He and Ayulo were best friends, hot rod buddies, and now both were gone.

The old year passed, a new one came in, the calendar flipped to April, and still more calamities followed. Walt Faulkner and Ernie McAfee died on the same day, Sunday, April 23, in separate races in northern California. In a modified stock car at the West Coast Speedway, a dirt oval near Vallejo, Faulkner's car blew a tire at 70 miles per hour, spun out of control, and flipped over five times. The Little Dynamo—whose shoulder strap broke although his waist strap held, throwing him partly out of the car as it rolled over—understood full well the risks of his profession. "Listen," he said, "when you mash the button on a racecar you can see a little guy with a harp right up there over the left front wheel. And the faster you go, the bigger he gets." He added, "Whether you slip on a banana peel or get it on the race track, when your time comes, brother, that's it."

Ernie McAfee's time came on the thirty-third lap of the main event of the Pebble Beach Road Races. A Beverly Hills import car dealer who had recently moved with his wife and six-month old daughter to a new home in Pacific Palisades, McAfee had earned a reputation as a man who could not only sell sports cars but drive them too. On a hairpin curve between turns five and six, the brakes on his Ferrari gave out and the car slid across the two-lane asphalt road and smacked broadside into a pine tree in Del Monte Forest. The tree crushed the side of the car where the thirty-seven-year-old was sitting. A newspaper reported, "The car was buckled against the tree and it took crowbars to free McAfee's body." Those crowbars reached his body well after he had stopped breathing.

Services for McAfee were held Tuesday at St. Mark's Episcopal Church in Glendale. Faulkner's rites followed two days later at the First Methodist Church in Long Beach. Most of the men who carried Faulkner's casket were race drivers. His family named twenty-two honorary pallbearers, all racers as well.

Another solemn ceremony took place in Fresno one month later, on Memorial Day 1956. From one Memorial Day to the next, twelve months had passed, and in that time so much hurt, so many losses. An irreplaceable piece of their lives had been forever taken from them, yet the Vukoviches didn't want to leave it at that. They felt Billy should be remembered for what he had done when he was alive, how he lived his life. He was a son, brother, husband, father, friend, and one helluva racecar driver, and they loved him.

With the townspeople of Fresno chipping in the money to pay for it, the city erected a monument to Billy on the lawn of the Fresno Memorial Auditorium. Some three hundred people, many of whom knew him personally, came out for the unveiling. His wife, Esther, was there. So were his children, Marlene and Billy Jr. Some drapery covered the statue, and they gave Billy Jr. the honor of pulling the drawstring to release it. Billy Jr. did his job, and the crowd reacted to the sight of the eleven-foot-high monument with tears and applause. It showed Billy with his No. 14 racecar and two crossed checkered flags, the symbol of victory in motor racing. The words on the plaque called him "a true champion" and saluted "his accomplishments, his courage, his sportsmanship and his will to win."

It must be noted that in 1990, Billy's grandson, Billy Vukovich III, died in a crash during a sprint car race at Mesa Marin Raceway in Bakersfield. Like his grandfather, Billy III started racing as a teenager, loved to drive, and although he never won at Indianapolis, he competed there with distinction. He was twenty-seven.

TWENTY-NINE

Comeback

On the day in 1956 Fresno was honoring the memory of Billy Vukovich, thirty-three of his colleagues stared down the little guy with the harp over the front wheel, punched the starter button on these wonderful, frightening machines of vast consequence, and lived life on the edge for the next few hours. Eight Californians finished in the first eight places at Indy that year. In order of finish they were: Pat Flaherty, Sam Hanks, Don Freeland, Johnnie Parsons, Dick Rathmann, Bob Sweikert, Rodger Ward, and Bob Veith.

The happiest among them was, of course, Flaherty, and the most disappointed, by far, was Hanks, who wanted nothing more in life than to win at Indianapolis but had never done it. Eleven times he had raced in the 500, eleven times he had watched some other guy get a smackeroo from a Hollywood star in Victory Circle. This last loss was the most galling of all, a lousy twenty-two seconds—*twenty-two seconds!*—behind first place.

But Hanks's disappointment, and Flaherty's joy, again had to be viewed with perspective. Hayward's Bob Sweikert, who won the Indianapolis 500 in which Billy Vukovich and Manny Ayulo were killed, had been running near the lead in the 1956 race when his car brushed against the wall. He did not crash, but after the incident his vehicle wasn't quite right, and he fell back into the pack to finish a frustrating sixth. A few weeks later in a race in Salem, Indiana, another brush with a wall did not end so benignly. His car jumped over a guardrail and crashed, exploding into flames. "Rangy, curly-haired" Sweikert, a thirty-year-old father of three, died of head injuries.

Although born in Los Angeles, Sweikert represented a northern California response to the Southland's racing dominance. He lived as a teenager in the East Bay city of Hayward, where he later ran an auto repair shop while sharpening his driving skills at the Oakland Stadium. But he was not just a local hero; pretty soon he was challenging the big blasters on the national scene. In those days motor racing had a kind of Triple Crown—the Indianapolis 500, the Midwest Sprint Car Championships, and the national big-car championships. In 1955 Sweikert became the only man to win all three in the same year. After watching him at Indianapolis, then Salem, his wife Dolores became another of the widows who returned to California with her husband in the belly compartment of an airplane. She and her children laid him to rest in Lone Pine Cemetery in the hills of Hayward.

When Sweikert won his national big-car championship, the American Automobile Association, which had governed competitive auto racing since the earliest days of the sport, acted as the sanctioning organization. But in late 1956 the AAA formally ended its relationship with racing "because it was no longer in accordance with the association's objective of promoting safe driving," in the words of a newspaper report. The last race in the West sanctioned by the AAA was the Phoenix dirt track race that killed Jack McGrath.

Other groups were also reevaluating their attitude toward the sport. In July the organizers of the Torrey Pines sports car races announced that the races were no more—at least not at Torrey Pines, not after the oceanside course had claimed the life of a female driver. That summer the races shifted to Montgomery Air Field in San Diego on a layout similar to the relatively safe airport courses of Santa Barbara and Palm Springs, which continued to hold their meets.

Pebble Beach announced that it was dropping out of motor racing as well. "Certain things are apparent," wrote a reporter about the road course through the trees of Del Monte Forest. "The serpentine black-top circuit is too dangerous for the fast cars. Pine trees are unyielding. At Pebble they are huge and virtually crowd upon the road." Many others shared this sentiment, and the race that killed Ernie McAffee was the last one held there.

Even so, many people felt strongly that racing still belonged on Monterey Peninsula—not in the foggy, forested lowlands perhaps, but somewhere. The races had brought national and international attention to the area, drawn huge numbers of visitors, and everyone agreed that nothing on this side of the Atlantic could match the automotive splendor that was the Concours d'Elegance. Late in 1956 the Chamber of Commerce, Cannery Row merchants, residents, and sports car devotees came together with the idea of creating a permanent home for racing in Monterey. To this end they formed an organization, the Sports Car Racing Association of the Monterey Peninsula—or SCRAMP, which still oversees racing in the area—and entered into negotiations with the United States Army to lease some of its hillside acreage at Fort Ord to build a racetrack there.

The next year the new Laguna Seca Raceway opened for business in the hills of Monterey. Originally 1.9 miles long, the course consisted of nine turns, the trickiest being the aptly named Corkscrew, the now famous double turn on the hilly backside of the track that comes up out of nowhere and drops like a rollercoaster. Pete Lovely in a Ferrari won Laguna Seca's first race during a party-filled opening weekend, enlivened on Saturday by the Concours d'Elegance. This, then, began Pebble's current setup—the Concours being held annually at the Del Monte Lodge (now the Pebble Beach Lodge) in conjunction with vintage automobile races at Laguna Seca. Now regarded as one of the best road courses in the United States, Laguna Seca holds a variety of championship automobile and motorcycle events throughout the year, along with the vintage races.

The move from Pebble Beach to Laguna Seca reflected the general trend of motor racing in California: eastward away from the ocean (Golden Gate Park halted its racing too), and into the less populated inland areas where land was cheaper and more readily available for low-density uses such as a racetrack. Clearly, motor racing had its problems, but it also retained widespread fan and community support and the backing of business, media, police, public safety officials, and the automobile industry. On top of its popular and commercial appeal, racing remained an effective, high-stakes method for testing and refining mechanical, design, and safety innovations for their eventual use in passenger automobiles and trucks.

One of those safety innovations came about after another of the tragedies that marked this period: the death of a Bay Area sports car driver, Pete Snell, whose Triumph TR2 roadster rolled at a 1956 race at the Arcata airport in Humboldt County. Coming to his aid that day was a Sacramento physician named George G. Snively, a director of medicine at Sacramento County Hospital who also raced sports cars. Snell's death affected the doctor deeply and puzzled him as well. Snell had been doing the right thing, wearing an English-made leather helmet that was considered state-of-the-art protective headgear. And yet it had not saved him. Working independently, Snively had been conducting crash tests on helmets for some time, comparing the manufacturer's claims of safety against how well they actually performed. After Arcata, he redoubled his efforts to find out why Snell's helmet had survived the crash in such good shape whereas the head inside it had received a fatal blow.

Also stung by the death of one of their own, members of the San Francisco chapter of the Sports Car Club of America decided to assist Dr. Snively in his testing program and to form, with him, the nonprofit Pete Snell Memorial Foundation. Its mission was to raise money to expand the scope of the tests and conduct them in a laboratory setting for a full scientific analysis of the issues involved. This it did. Representatives from government and racing organizations observed the tests, and the results shocked all involved. Of the sixteen helmets sold commercially and used by both pro drivers and the public, nearly all were "virtually worthless with respect to head protection," concluded a report. A major reason for this was the helmet liner, which basically did the opposite of what it was designed to do. Rather than absorb the blow to the head, it *focused* it—in scientific argot, it directed the "force vectors at a single point on the skull," thereby increasing the impact. When published in the July 1957 issue of *Sports Car Illustrated* (now *Car and Driver*), Dr. Snively's findings forced a reevaluation of helmet use and manufacturing methods.

One of those who immediately changed the way he did business was Roy Richter, the hot-rodder and race driver who ran Bell Auto Parts, the pioneering speed shop. Through retail and mail order, Richter sold crash helmets he thought kept people safe, including himself, but the Snively article jolted him out of his complacency. He stopped selling his old brands, started using the liner of former competitor Toptex—whose liner actually did the job it was supposed to do, absorbing the shock of a hard hit to the skull—and made the first helmet to be approved by the Snell Memorial Foundation. His company, Bell, has since become a national leader in making helmets. Today the Snell Foundation, based in North Highlands near Sacramento, researches, tests, and evaluates helmets for cars, motorcycles, bicycles, and other activities. "No one can calculate the number of lives worldwide that have been saved because of the pioneering and ongoing work of the Snell Memorial Foundation," said one observer, "but it must be huge."

Another hot-rodder, Ray Brown, who ran a speed shop on Western Avenue in Los Angeles and raced at the dry lakes and Bonneville, also helped to improve driver safety. Starting early in the decade, his company made seat belts for passenger cars—"Impact Auto Saf-Tee Belts," they were called—and it grew into the first supplier of safety belts for federal government vehicles.

But the problem with seat belts and crash helmets was the same as it had always been: people had to use them in order for them to work. And in the general population, as well as among race drivers, many questioned the value of these and other safety measures. In a late 1950s Los Angeles newspaper poll of one hundred race drivers, half of those surveyed favored shoulder harness straps and roll bars on their vehicles, twenty-five drivers had no opinion on the subject, and another twenty-five—"the hairy-eyed tempters of fate," as one writer referred to them—opposed these devices and said they would not use them. These drivers generally relished their desperado image and regarded themselves as risk-takers and daredevils. For them, danger and death were part of the game. If you feared either, the answer was simple: Get out of the game.

Around the same time that Laguna Seca Raceway was forming, a similar effort to build a track in Riverside County was moving forward. The reasons for it, like that of Laguna Seca, were to host and promote big-time racing of all types, bring dollars into the community, and create a bigger, more contained, more wide-open setting for these ever-evolving machines. The new Riverside International Motor Raceway debuted in late summer 1957, providing easy access for fans at a site five miles east of Riverside near Highway 60. With a capacity of at least sixty-four thousand spectators, it included a challenging 3.5-mile loop for sports cars that made turns and straight asphalt strips for dragsters that did not. In one of its first events, a local sports car race, Richie Ginther put his foot down on the mile-long back straight and crested 150 miles per hour in a Ferrari. But the raceway's first big test came in December when it welcomed the best stock car drivers in the country for a national championship stock car race, sanctioned by NASCAR. With the departure of the AAA from the sport, NASCAR and other organizations—notably the United States Auto Club and the Sports Car Club of America—stepped in to oversee their respective forms of racing.

The big field at Riverside starred Indianapolis veteran and local favorite Sam Hanks, who supplied a feel-good story for a sport in desperate need of one. Tall and skinny with a brainy sort of appeal—he looked, said one person who knew him, "more like a chemical engineer than a reckless race driver"—Hanks had been ready to pack it in after his razor-thin loss at the 1956 Indianapolis 500. Yet another of the superb California drivers of this period, he had been racing cars since his early teens, parking them (at various times he owned more than one) along Hellman Avenue in Alhambra, where he grew up. Everybody in the neighborhood knew when Sam revved up one of his hop-ups ready to go on a ride. "There's Sam," one mother told her children at a nearby house. "Get the baby off the porch." From scaring babies on porches to racing midgets back in the days when guys drove outboard motors and stock engines chopped in half and goosed-up washing machine motors, Hanks could make anything go fast, including airplanes. After learning to fly at age fourteen, Lieutenant Hanks of the Army Air Corps helped develop a method to increase aircraft engine horsepower that enabled bombers to fly higher during the war and avoid enemy fire on land. When he was done with that he went back to the midgets in the golden postwar years, when you could actually make a little money racing them. Life had treated him well, no complaints there. He had a beautiful wife, Alice, who loved him. They lived in gracious style near the ocean in Pacific Palisades, and trophies and awards from his illustrious career filled the den of their house from floor to ceiling.

But the one piece of hardware he really wanted—the Borg-Warner trophy, the sterling silver beaut they gave to the winner at Indy—wasn't there. And the forty-two-year-old Hanks had just about resigned himself to the fact that it never, ever was going to be there until George Salih invited him and Alice over to his house one evening for dinner.

Salih lived in Whittier with his wife Freda and worked as an engineer and plant manager at the Meyer and Drake factory in Los Angeles, manufacturers of Offenhauser-style engines. Like Hanks, Salih had a good family, a good job, a fine reputation in the industry. But this wasn't enough for him, not entirely, because pretty pictures danced in his head, pictures of a radical new form of racing engine. "I began doodling on napkins and so forth," he said, "and I kept coming up with basically the same shape." The engine shape he saw in his mind and that he kept drawing pictures of was smaller than normal and mounted "in a nearly flat position instead of the customary upright position." The idea was so extreme that even for someone with his credentials—Salih was chief wrenchman for the winning car at the 1951 Indianapolis 500, among other achievements—he couldn't find any money men to back him. They thought his napkin doodling only added up to ruined napkins. But Salih and Howard Gilbert, a buddy of his who also didn't like to take no for an answer, poured their own money into it and went ahead and built the thing anyway, the two of them cursing and getting dirty and banging away till all hours of the night in Salih's garage. Finally they figured they had something good enough to show somebody—that somebody being Sam Hanks, when he came over for dinner that night.

A middle-aged hot-rod hipster, Salih called everyone he met "Dad," and most everyone in turn called him "Dad." So it was Dad and Freda and Alice and the Thin Man, that being Hanks's nickname in the press. And at some point in the evening the Thin Man stepped away with Dad into the warm comfort and privacy of the garage to check out his flattened vision of a racing machine. Originally feeling pretty low about his prospects, Hanks perked up as the conversation went on. What inspired him even more than the details, although the details were absolutely vital, was the sheer radical audaciousness of Dad's scheme. Sam abandoned all thoughts of quitting, which may not have been that serious anyway, and agreed to drive the car at Indianapolis.

Sandy Belond, another grown-up hot-rodder and owner of the Southern California Muffler Corporation, joined the Salih-Hanks-Gilbert conspiracy. Belond had dough, and he threw enough of it into the project to get it named after him—the Belond Exhaust Special. Los Angeles designer-builder Quinn Epperly also came in. Along with Frank Kurtis, Eddie Kuzma, A. J. Watson, and Lujie Lesovsky, Epperly was another of the reasons why the Indianapolis 500 could have been renamed the California 500 during these years. From 1953 to 1963 these five men, working out of shops in Glendale and Los Angeles located a few miles from one another, built nine of every ten cars that raced in the 500 and nearly all of the winners. Epperly fabricated a lightweight, streamlined body for the Belond Special whose least original aspect was the most fundamental: the four-cylinder Offenhauser, engine of champions.

But the car drew scoffers when it appeared at Indianapolis in May and qualified thirteenth—inside, fifth row. Not a bad showing, but still no big shakes. Once the engines started blowing and the smoke started pouring and things got shaking for real, though, attitudes changed swiftly. Hanks passed five cars in the first lap, three more in the next three laps. He was in fifth and suddenly living a dream. "I felt this car could do anything," he said. "I knew I could dust anything on the track."

None of the cars he was passing could match the Belond Special's speed around the turns nor its extreme low profile. "It looked strange," said one eyewitness, but the capacity crowd of 175,000 was beginning to warm to the sight of it, largely because of who was handling it. Fans in Indianapolis liked Hanks and knew his story, and they started pulling for him.

The radio announcers couldn't hide their enthusiasm either. That was the Thin Man out there, and he was moving into first place!

Somewhere Alice Hanks was in the crowd too, but she knew it was far too early to give in to hope. One lap was a lifetime at Indianapolis, and there were fifty of them left to go. Her husband led by nearly a lap, but he was pulling into the pits and Jim Rathmann in second was coming on.

Rathmann was another Californian, also from Alhambra. You could get in an argument over who was the better driver, him or his older brother Dick, who had run fifth at Indy the year before. Both of the Rathmann boys competed at the highest levels and earned lots of shiny trophies themselves, and neither was particularly sentimental about who they had to beat to get them. As far as Jim was concerned, Alice Hanks's husband could take the doughnut at Indy—twelve races, twelve losses. He was in it to win.

In the Chiropractic Special (its sponsor was a chiropractor), Rathmann gained ground on the straights but lost it on the curves. But now with Hanks in the pits he had a chance to slip past him. The Belond Special received gas, oil, water, and three new tires. Thirty-four seconds after it entered the pits it roared out again, and Rathmann was only six seconds behind.

That was as close as he ever got. Averaging a record 135.60 miles per hour for five hundred miles, Hanks held off Rathmann and even stretched the lead a tad, winning by an even narrower margin than he had lost the year before: seventeen seconds. When the old man of Indy took the flag, fans went a little batty. It was, said a writer, "the most popular win in the history of the event." On his victory lap Hanks "blipped," or revved his engine in a salute to the fans, peeled off his goggles, and twirled them on a finger, and waved to the crowd. They loved every minute of it. When he reached Victory Circle he started to cry. A mob of well-wishers surged around him and his car. When Alice reached him she was crying too. Somebody put a bouquet of flowers in her hands. She took it and watched as her husband felt the light caress of Cyd Charisse's lips on his cheeks, a caress he had been waiting for all his life. Then it was Alice's turn. She hugged her husband and it was no light caress she gave him. They were both a mess.

Later Alice received a congratulatory telegram from Lois McGrath, Jack's widow. Jack had always wanted to win Indy and never did, and Lois knew what it was like to live with a man who felt such disappointment for so long. Now Sam could do what Jack had not—get out of racing alive.

Before the race the graying Hanks said that, win, lose or draw, this was to be his last Indy 500. "This is the only ambition I have left in racing," he told *Time*. "When I win the 500, I'll hang up my goggles so fast it'll make their heads swim." Well, not quite. Hanks was a race driver after all, and race drivers, like boxers, always seem to feel as if they have one more in them, and maybe one more after that. In December 1957 he agreed to help break in the new track at Riverside International Motor Raceway. Eighteen thousand fans cheered him on to third place.

Hanks returned to the Indianapolis 500 the next year but only drove the pace car, an honor that would be bestowed on him several more times. George Salih also came back again to race his and Howard Gilbert's garage special, now acclaimed for its brilliance and vision. With Hanks out of the picture, Jimmy Bryan took over as driver. Aware of Bryan's Barney Oldfield–like habit of chewing cigars while he drove, Salih had stitched three loops on the upholstery of the seat to hold three cigars to keep him happy during the race. "Dad," Bryan told him. "You think of everything." Bryan took over from there and brought the low-riding special into Victory Circle for the second straight year.

"It seems hard to comprehend now," says the automotive writer Donald Davidson, "but the fact remains that a car that won the Indianapolis 500 two years in a row was built by two men in their spare time in a backyard garage."

Sam and Alice Hanks lived all of this, and when it was over they came back to their house by the ocean with that sterling silver trophy in the den.

THIRTY

McQueen

Sam Hanks's win at Indianapolis was only one of many inspiring stories being written by California drivers, engine builders, designers, and owners in the late 1950s and early '60s. After Hanks and Jimmy Bryan came Rodger Ward's title in 1959. Ward, the son of the owner of a Los Angeles car-wrecking yard, had come up through the midgets like every other California driver of his generation, and had a record of futility at Indianapolis that could almost match Hanks's: eight tries, eight losses. But he refused to knuckle under and took the flag on his ninth try, in 1959. Then he came back the next year and, in one of the closest Indy races ever, lost to the man who had lost to Sam Hanks in 1957, Jim Rathmann. Rathmann beat Ward by less than thirteen seconds. But Ward shook it off and in 1962 repeated his title, joining fellow Californians Billy Vukovich, Lou Meyer, and Wilbur Shaw in a select group of drivers to visit Victory Circle at Indianapolis more than once.

The year after Ward's second championship, Parnelli Jones won his first and only Indianapolis 500. "I don't want to sound like I'm bragging," Parnelli told a reporter once, "but I always felt the other drivers were there just to be beaten." And with Jones in the field, that happened a lot: The other drivers just got beat. Born in rural Arkansas, he moved as a teenager to Torrance where he began entering the fiercely competitive jalopy races at Gardena Stadium. "The competition was so stiff," he recalled, "that when I got to midgets—and even Indy cars—they didn't seem too tough." "Tough" was an adjective that people applied frequently to Parnelli who, in 1962, became the first to average 150 miles per hour at Indianapolis. His win at the Brickyard the next year was only one of the many championships—in stock cars, sprint cars, endurance runs, and other forms of racing—that he achieved in his decorated career.

One of Parnelli's chief rivals in these years was an equally versatile and talented driver, Dan Gurney. "If you were in a race with Parnelli, you knew you were going to have to deal with him," said Gurney. "And if you beat him, you knew you'd really accomplished something." The same could be said for Gurney, who never took Indianapolis (two runner-up finishes there) but won just about everything else here and abroad, including Le Mans and a clutch of Formula One titles. Born and raised in New York, the son of Metropolitan Opera singer John Gurney, he moved with his family after high school to Riverside, hot-footing cars around the dirt roads of orange groves. His first sports car race, the 1955 Torrey Pines Road Race, was the last one ever held there; and the first sports car race he won was the race that replaced it at Montgomery Field. In that Torrey Pines race he drove against Phil Hill and another driver who, like Gurney and Jones, came from another state but was deeply involved with California racing and American automotive history, Carroll Shelby.

Shelby is best known as the creator of the Shelby Mustang GT and the Shelby AC Cobra, "the most formidable sports car of the 1960s," in the judgment of one writer. Both were manufactured at the Shelby American factory on a twelve-acre site south of the Los Angeles International Airport. Ford financed the venture, and early in the decade it sent an analyst from Detroit to check on the operation and drive a prototype of the Cobra. "He [the analyst] slipped behind the wheel of the refined two-seater," goes one account of this first test drive, "and almost drove it into a telephone pole. It was the fastest car he had ever been in." Buoyed by the success of the Cobra in world racing competition, Ford handed the keys of its breakthrough 1964 sports car, the Mustang, over to Carroll Shelby to boost its performance. Boost it, he surely did. The high-powered Mustang GT-350 and the even more high-powered Mustang GT-500 became two of the first and foremost muscle cars ever made. Today, rare Shelby Mustangs can command prices at auction of $750,000 or more. In 2007 at the Barrett-Jackson auction in Scottsdale, a 1966 Cobra 427 driven by Shelby himself went for $5.5 million.

Born and raised in Texas, the tall, skinny Shelby hot-rodded around hardscrabble Southwest dirt tracks before turning in his early twenties to the loftier and more glamorous realms of the California sports car circuit. The newspapers identified him as "a thirty-two-year-old Texas oilman," although in reality his business background involved chicken ranching more than oil. But really, the man was a race driver, as gifted and colorful as they come, and his victories in California and around the country made him two-time "Sports Car Driver of the Year" in the mid-fifties. He beat Phil Hill and the novice Dan Gurney in that last-ever Torrey Pines race, nipping Hill by a few car lengths in the forty-lap main event. This win sparked the interest of Los Angeles racecar owner Tony Paravano, who asked Shelby if he'd be interested in campaigning his new 12-cylinder Ferrari around California and the globe. The ex-chicken rancher said yes, and this launched his European Grand Prix racing career. (Shelby later won the 24 Hours of Le Mans—as did Hill, three times.)

Shelby won the last Pebble Beach Road Race in 1956, again denying the second-place Hill. Both drove Ferraris. Then he reappeared on the Monterey Peninsula a year later for the opening of Laguna Seca, although Pete Lovely won that one and Shelby had to settle for second in a Maserati. Then, in 1958, he entered the biggest and most important road race ever held in California up to that time: the United States Grand Prix at the Riverside International Motor Raceway.

Its organizers described it as "the world's greatest sports car racing event." Sponsored by the United States Auto Club and the Federation Internationale de l'Automobile, the governing body for motor racing in the world, the Grand Prix featured, among many other top drivers, Shelby and his rival Phil Hill, who had just won for the first time at Le Mans. "The toast of Europe," as the hometown press called Hill, had also become the toast of California's racing community, and when his TWA flight from London set down in mid-September in Los Angeles, hundreds of California Sports Car Club members greeted him at the airport. The Ferrari he was driving at Riverside was being brought from New York by his friend Richie Ginther, who was also competing in a Ferrari. After Riverside, Hill planned to fly back to Europe for the Monaco Grand Prix.

France's Jean Behra and England's Roy Salvadori led the European contingent in the fifty-car field. As for the American contingent—well, just about every driver who mattered was there. Sam Hanks was not in the field—his retirement appeared to be holding firm—but two other Indianapolis champions were: Troy Ruttman and Johnnie Parsons. More names to be reckoned with were: Ray Crawford, Indy veteran and 1954 champion of the Carrera Panamericana, a grueling road race through Mexico; Jerry Unser, a recent California transplant and brother of stock car marvel Bobby Unser, who was also suiting up at Riverside; sports car veterans Bill Pollock, Bob Oker, and Johnny Von Neumann; and a hot rod–dry lakes–Bonneville–Carrera Panamericana jack of all trades, Ak Miller. Still largely unknown outside local racing circles, Dan Gurney received scant pre-race notice in the press; one newspaper article misspelled his name as "Guerney."

Fan favorite Max Balchowsky and his even more popular Old Yeller were in the starting lineup too. Balchowsky ran the Hollywood Garage on Hollywood Boulevard in Hollywood and worked on movie star cars, both foreign and domestic. Not just Max worked on these cars, by the way—so did his wife Ina who, said her husband, "can do everything a guy can except lift out the transmission." Max was curly-haired, good-looking, fun, and lively, and Ina was dark-haired, good-looking, and equally fun and lively. Together they made a novel team in a sport filled with novel personalities. Ina's mechanical skills and aptitude derived from her father, the owner of a southern California auto repair shop. Max, a native West Virginian and ex–machine gunner on B-24 Liberators, had come west after the war to work at his brother's filling station and garage in South Gate. Being a car guy he was naturally into hot rods, a scene that drew Ina's interest too. They first met when he rumbled past her high school one day in his annoyingly loud and fast rod. Annoying to some, but not Ina. They married in 1949, the same year they opened Hollywood Motors.

An early motto of Hollywood Motors was "We can replace anything with anything." So the shop developed a reputation as a quality place to go for switching out an anemic stock engine for a new Buick power plant high in red blood cells. Another company motto was "Free Advice With Purchases Only," which visitors could plainly see on a hand-painted sign on a wall of the shop. But the sign was mostly a joke, and Max and Ina did lots of discount jobs for the lean and hungry boys who had blank spaces in their wallet where there should have been bills.

Along with helping others with their racing machines, the Balchowskys raced machines of their own. Being practitioners of the hot rod school of car cookery, Max and Ina took a little of this and a dab of that and mixed it all together with a Buick engine to create perhaps the most special of all the backyard specials, Old Yeller. One writer of the time described Old Yeller's composition as "a tossed salad of component parts." Even Dean Batchelor, who was adept at building cars with a variety of secondhand parts culled from a variety of sources, marveled at its "amazing amalgam of parts." Max likened it to a mongrel dog—hence its name, Old Yeller, from the 1957 Disney movie of the same name in which a homely yellow mutt befriends a boy on a ranch and has adventures with him. Old Yeller the automobile was also yellow, also a mutt, and one of the homeliest-looking sports cars you'd ever want to see.

Sportswriters had a grand time with the car, describing it at various times as the "brutish yellow special," "horrible old yellow Buick special," "double-ugly Old Yeller," "battered, dog-eared Buick special," "world's ugliest sports car," and more. But Old Yeller was as fast as it was ugly, and it delivered nothing but heartache to the owners of the purebred Ferraris and Maseratis it lined up against.

Hot rod lovers rooted for Old Yeller in its underdog battles with the high-priced factory-made machines from Europe, while sports car purists disliked most everything about the car. Self-professed sports car snob Joe Scalzo saw the car in action and simply could not stomach it: "Like its canine namesake, Ol' Yeller was indubitably a mongrel. Its square body had been fabricated out of a Coke sign, its steering had been liberated from a Ford pickup rusting in a field, its white sidewall tires were dubious recaps, and its bellowing Buick motor had come from wherever Max or Ina chose to tell you at a given moment, both Balchowskys being devoted to the enhancement of Ol' Yeller's legend. Ol' Yeller wasn't backyard, it was junkyard." Knowing what Scalzo and the purists thought of him and his car, Max never missed a chance to tweak their beaks. He wore garage overalls when he raced, and licensed the car to drive legally on the street. Whereas the pampered imports arrived at a race on the bed of a trailer, Max drove Old Yeller on the highway with Ina riding beside him in the passenger seat. They also went grocery shopping in the car.

In the 1958 Labor Day races at Santa Barbara, Max and Old Yeller had one of their best weekends ever, winning Saturday's featured event ahead of second-place Richie Ginther in a Testa Rossa Ferrari and third-place Bob Oker in an Aston Martin. Another shocker followed on Sunday when he again thumped Ginther in that well-beaten Testa Rossa with Johnny Von Neumann and Ken Miles, also in Ferraris, filling out third and fourth. Meantime he set a track record and delighted all twenty thousand of the spectators—well, most of them anyhow. "I observed Ol' Yeller not with admiration but rather fear and dread, inwardly wishing for it to break so that the Ferraris could continue winning as usual," said Scalzo. "But the damned yellow thing seemed as reliable as it was fast. It possessed torque plus wicked, tire-peeling acceleration perfectly suited to the hairpin corners of California tracks."

The next month at the Riverside Grand Prix, Balchowsky and Old Yeller qualified seventh, two spots behind the up-and-coming Dan Gurney in fifth. Phil Hill in that Ferrari from New York qualified second, in between two Scarabs driven by Chuck Daigh of Los Angeles and the owner-driver of the Scarab team, Lance Reventlow. The Scarabs, named after a beetle held sacred by ancient Egyptians, were nearly as exotic as the young visionary behind them. The twenty-two-year-old Reventlow was the only child of Barbara Hutton, the beleaguered heiress mocked by the press as the "Poor Little Rich Girl." The granddaughter of the man who founded the Woolworth department store chain and the daughter of the co-founder of the E. F. Hutton brokerage company, Hutton inherited $50 million as a young woman. Her only child was Reventlow, who became interested in motor racing after his mother married a Grand Prix driver. Another of Barbara's husbands (she was married seven times) was Cary Grant, and so Lance spent lots of time in Hollywood soaking up the sun and sports car scene there. Reventlow knew James Dean and saw him on the last day of his life at that gas station outside Bakersfield where Dean filled up his Porsche Spyder. Reventlow happened to be there too, heading for Salinas like Dean. They chatted amiably and agreed to get together for dinner that evening before each went his own way.

With enough money to buy a flotilla of European imports, or do whatever he wished really, Reventlow decided to create his own sports car brand, the blue and white Scarab. Its designers were Jim Travers and Frank Coon, the Whiz Kids who had built Billy Vukovich's winning rides at Indianapolis. They packed into the car a hotted-up 350-cubic-inch Chevrolet engine and a fuel injection system created by dry lakes speedster and engineer Stuart Hillborn. Three Scarabs entered the United States Grand Prix at Riverside, and two of them, driven by Daigh and Bruce Kessler, qualified first and third. Reventlow cracked up his Scarab in practice and failed to make the final field, but nothing in heaven or earth was going to stop Barbara Hutton's son from driving in the greatest sports car race in America that year. He bumped out Kessler and took over his Scarab, lining up in the third slot behind Daigh and Hill.

For all his behind-the-scenes maneuvering, though, Reventlow showed poorly on race day, October 12. His Scarab got tangled up with Johnny Von Neumann's Ferrari on the first lap, and neither finished.

The commotion at the start affected neither Daigh nor Hill, who quickly turned the race into a contest between just the two of them. Observed a sportswriter, "Daigh got off the mark in front. Hill headed him in the first lap, kept the lead for five laps, and dropped it to Daigh again for two more trips around the circuit. Then Hill recovered and led for four laps more." The two of them exchanged the lead twice during a single lap, both reaching 200 miles per hour on that long aircraft runway of a back straight. But on the twelfth lap Daigh headed Hill a final time and the Scarab took control. The thirty-four-year-old Daigh averaged 88.8 miles per hour over two hundred miles, winning the biggest race of his career and the biggest ever for Team Scarab.

A leaky fuel pump had sabotaged Hill after those opening laps. He pitted many times to correct the problem, never did, and finally dropped out. That Sunday in Riverside temperatures climbed to above 100 degrees, and many cited the hot weather for the high burnout rate of the cars. Others who joined Hill, Reventlow, and Von Neumann on the Did Not Finish list were Carroll Shelby, Troy Ruttman, Johnnie Parsons, and Jerry and Bobby Unser.

In a sign of brighter days to come, Dan Gurney, "a hometown Riverside boy who has driven in the big-time less than a year," took second, far ahead of Max Balchowsky in seventh. But at least Old Yeller made it all the way to the finish line, and race organizers and the seventy thousand spectators went away happy because "not a single person, driver, or spectator was injured in the entire three-race program."

This, then, was the California sports car scene circa 1959: all these beautiful, and beautifully ugly, machines, every one of them fast and with distinctive qualities of its own, driven by some of the best drivers in the world, some with money, some not, some glamorous, some not, nearly all with big, incorrigible personalities as loud and distinctive as their machines, the sun pouring down on everyone and everything, the parties and women and champagne and high times, and throughout it all, underlying it all, not pretend risk or make-believe danger but real risk, real danger, real violence. No wonder Steve McQueen fell for it.

In the fall of 1958, weeks before the United States Grand Prix at Riverside, a new television series, *Wanted: Dead or Alive,* debuted on Saturday nights on CBS. Billed as "an adult Western," its lead character, a bounty hunter named Josh Randall, was a new sort of Western hero—"a hero but also a cold-blooded killer." Lest there be any doubt about this, Randall went after the bad guys with a long, sawed-off Winchester rifle that he carried on his right hip. The actor playing Josh Randall was Steve McQueen.

"His restless manner makes one think of a boy much younger in years," wrote a reporter about the twenty-eight-year-old McQueen. "But his cold blue eyes reflect a sureness of character—they show a man who has learned from life." These life lessons included a boyhood spent on a Missouri farm and leaving home at a young age for a series of rough adventures and jobs. McQueen, said the reporter, had "worked on a tanker as an able-bodied seaman, labored in the oil fields of Texas, traveled with a carnival as a huckster, toiled in a lumber camp in Canada and drove a tank for the U.S. Marines. A man without a high school diploma who became a star." The reporter failed to mention another colorful item in the star's bio: During his troubled teen years he had left the Midwest to come to Los Angeles to live with his mother, but his mother, unable to control him, sent him to the California Junior Boys Republic, a youth reformatory in Chino Hills. (After becoming famous, McQueen visited the Boys Republic many times, setting up a scholarship fund there and giving generously to it. Its recreation center is named after him.)

Other colorful aspects of his bio, noted by the reporter, touched on his hobbies: "Off the set his loves, besides actress Neile Adams, are sports car and motorcycle racing, hi-fi, classical music and reading." In the wake of James Dean, news of a star with an interest in fast machines set off alarm bells in Hollywood, but at this stage of his career McQueen was generating nothing close to the heat that Dean had in his brief time in the spotlight. He was an unknown actor in an unproven TV Western and had appeared in only a smattering of B movies and television programs.

McQueen's first movie role had occurred several years earlier; he was an extra. His next film role was an uncredited bit part in *Somebody Up There Likes Me*, the 1956 boxing movie that would have been James Dean's next picture after *Giant* if he had lived. With Dean gone, the producers cast the title role with another young actor in the same mold—handsome, talented, with a rebellious look that appealed to younger moviegoers. Paul Newman's star turn in *Somebody Up There Likes Me* drew critical hosannas and launched him in the picture business. Newman went on to play Billy the Kid in *The Left-Handed Gun,* another movie that had been slotted for Dean, and later in his great career he became avid about motor sports as well, driving at Le Mans, owning a piece of a race team, and making an Indianapolis 500-themed movie, *Winning*. He also voiced the character of Doc Hudson in the 2006 animated movie *Cars,* whose hero is named Lightning McQueen, a tribute to Steve.

By comparison, McQueen's *Somebody Up There Likes Me* performance made such a splash he didn't work again in movies for two years. Meantime he found jobs in television, which led to the science fiction movie *The Blob* and another picture, and these roles in turn helped get him the Josh Randall part in *Wanted: Dead or Alive*. The show rapidly became a hit, and in January a show-business column called him one of the "new faces" to watch for 1959. Later in the spring, in a meeting of Hollywood fast-car guys past and present, he and Clark Gable served as judges at a Concours d'Elegance automobile show at Steer's Restaurant in Beverly Hills. But he did not approach anything close to Gable's star power, and when he showed up at the Santa Barbara Road Races on Memorial Day weekend, no one in the press made a fuss over him. Nor, for that matter, did any of his fellow competitors.

If they recognized who he was, and some of them surely must have, they treated him much like any other race driver. This was one of the reasons the sport appealed to him. "Around the studios everybody waits on me," said McQueen. "They powder my nose and tell me what they think I want to hear. And after a while you're convinced you are superhuman. But when you're racing a motorcycle, the guy on the next bike doesn't care who you are. And if he beats you in the race, well, it means he's a better man than you are. And he's not afraid to tell you that you're lousy. Racing keeps my equilibrium intact. It makes it difficult to believe I'm God's gift to humanity."

The weekend races, held on the track at Goleta airport north of Santa Barbara, attracted nearly three hundred entries, the sports car season's biggest event so far in California. Organized by the California Sports Car Club, the field included "forty of the hard-to-beat German Porsches, some twelve specials, a dozen Lotuses, twenty Corvettes and at least five Ferraris," according to the *Times*. One of those hard-to-beat Porsches belonged to McQueen who was scheduled to compete in the opening race on Saturday in the Novice Production category, for drivers who had never entered a California sports car race before.

Although a newcomer to the sport, McQueen had friends at the races he could turn to, people who did not regard him as God's gift to humanity but who knew how to boost the horsepower of a Porsche Speedster. One of them was Max Balchowsky, who worked on his cars at Hollywood Motors and gave him racing advice. So McQueen enjoyed the camaraderie and appreciated the fact that this was definitely not a Hollywood scene. But then a terrible thing happened to him at those Santa Barbara races, something that sealed his fate for good.

He won. In his first-ever sports car race, eight laps around the 2.2-mile course, he averaged 63.9 miles per hour and nosed out an Austin Healey and an Alfa-Romeo to walk away with the first-place trophy. "That was the worst thing that could have happened," McQueen joked. "I was really hooked after that."

So hooked was he that he sold his Porsche and bought a pricey British-made Lotus, which he brought back to Santa Barbara a few months later for the Labor Day Races. By then his hit show *Wanted: Dead or Alive* was about to start its second season, and he could no longer slip in and out of a race without the press noticing. The *Times* ran a picture of him in his new Lotus.

His bosses in Hollywood were also beginning to notice—and stoke up the pressure on him to find a new hobby. As McQueen said, "The studio kept putting out memos that McQueen had better stop racing. The insurance company and the sponsor were getting pretty difficult." But he raced at Santa Barbara anyhow, losing in a near dead heat to another Lotus. The time separating the two cars: one second.

During the summer hiatus from his TV series he shot a movie with Frank Sinatra and Gina Lollobrigida, *Never So Few,* and his performance increased the chatter about him. "Steve McQueen's hotter than the pistols he handles in TV's *Wanted: Dead or Alive,*" wrote Hedda Hopper, who still knew a star when she saw one. She added that "he's so busy acting he no longer has time for racing, which is a blessing."

Well, perhaps not. His next film was *The Magnificent Seven,* and despite the pressure from producers and insurers and the whispers around town that he was a thrill-seeker with a secret death wish, he kept racing. "I never have gotten a thrill from racing," he said in answer to his critics. "When you're riding that close to death there's no thrill involved. Racing is something I feel very deeply about. So is acting, and in some ways the two are similar. Both require unique concentration, and in both, you have to be able to function creatively within a chaotic situation." McQueen mentioned his daughter and his wife Neile, saying that because of them, "I don't want to go out and 'prang' myself up."

In late 1961 McQueen went to England to shoot *The War Lover,* leaving a couple of months before production started so he could race with his friend Stirling Moss. The two had met in Santa Barbara during McQueen's first summer of racing when Moss had come to California to check out the scene for himself. The great English driver was one of McQueen's racing heroes, and Moss gave him driving lessons on a track in England, probably Brands Hatch. "I would follow Stirling around the course," McQueen recalled. "He'd signal with one hand, indicating with his fingers which gear to use. He was driving with one hand and there I was, hanging on for dear life." McQueen went on to race Formula One cars in Europe while competing at Santa Barbara, Palm Springs, and two other tracks in the state, Del Mar in the south and Cotati in the north.

After leaving television (*Wanted: Dead or Alive* ended after three seasons), McQueen brought his rebellious, anti-hero screen persona to the movies full-time. Two of his best films made use of his considerable skills on two wheels and four. One was the World War II prisoner-of-war movie, *The Great Escape*. His motorcycle riding, while trying to escape the Germans, is one of the film's highlights, although it was a friend of his, expert motorcyclist Bud Elkins, who actually did the famous jump over the barbed-wire fences. (His costar in that film, James Garner, also became intrigued by car racing and starred in *Grand Prix,* which contains sensational footage of Grand Prix racing in Europe. One reason these sequences are so good is because Phil Hill drove the MGM camera car.)

In 1968 McQueen starred in *Bullitt,* a crime drama set in San Francisco. Its chase sequence over the streets of the city remains the greatest automobile chase scene ever filmed. It features a black Dodge Charger and a dark green Mustang GT blowing smoke, screeching around corners, and getting air as they fly down San Francisco's steepest hills, those same hills that terrified Gertrude Stein and so many other drivers over the years. The bespectacled Bill Hickman drove the Charger, and Bud Elkins also participated. McQueen drove the Mustang, and this is partly what gives the sequence its drama and power. That is no stunt double; that really is one of the world's biggest movie stars behind the wheel of that sliding, fishtailing, tire-burning Mustang. Another satisfying element is the engine sounds made by the Mustang and Charger as they chase after each other. The mechanic for the two cars, the man who made those engines growl and kept them in tip-top racing shape, was Max Balchowsky.

THIRTY-ONE

Heroes and Anti-Heroes

During the filming of *Bullitt,* the *San Francisco Chronicle* critic John Wasserman journeyed over to the corner of Vallejo and Divisadero to watch a scene being shot and to interview McQueen. Afterwards, in his piece for the paper, Wasserman described him as "one of the new folk heroes. He vigorously defends youth in rebellion, has professionally raced cars and motorcycles, spent time as a youth in a correctional facility, exudes a magnetic field that is tough but inherently warm, and has been immortalized, along with Bogart and James Dean, on the enormous posters that have become the art collections for a million young people."

McQueen had by then become one of the kings of Hollywood, but his appeal was not all that much different from when he was starting out as an actor playing the gun-toting Josh Randall in *Wanted: Dead or Alive.* McQueen himself summed up his character in the show this way: "Randall is associated with violence and that's why he uses such a violent gun. He doesn't go for this jazz, 'OK—draw.' He shoots first and makes certain that he has killed."

A survivor in a violent world, a person who plays by his own rules and adheres to his own moral code, distrustful of authority and intolerant of the hypocrisies of conventional society, tough but warm—these are the characteristics of many of the leading characters we see today in movies, television, and books. But in the late 1950s and early 1960s this sort of reverse hero, or anti-hero, was just beginning to emerge in popular culture. Steve McQueen, Paul Newman, and Marlon Brando* were playing versions of this anti-hero in the movies and on television, while in books Jack Kerouac was introducing another famous anti-hero, Dean Moriarty, in *On the Road,* published in 1957.

---

* One of Marlon Brando's most famous movie moments occurred on the back of a Triumph motorcycle in 1953's *The Wild One.* When Brando leads his biker gang into a small town, a townsperson asks him what he's rebelling against. "What have ya got?" says Brando. The movie was based on events that took place in Hollister, California, when a group of unruly motorcycle riders went on a drunken rampage in town. This riot, said *USA Today,* "gave birth to bike culture" in this country, a culture with its own pantheon of heroes and anti-heroes. Every year motorcyclists meet in Hollister to commemorate the event.

The novel mainly follows the real-life adventures of two people—Kerouac, in the form of narrator Sal Paradise, and Neal Cassady, fictionalized as Dean Moriarty. Cassady/Moriarty takes drugs, drinks heavily, abandons his wives and children at times to go on the road, sleeps with whores, can't hold a job for long, and steals cars. And yet...*and yet*...he is also spontaneous and vital, dialed into the wild, beatific heart of life, and thus in many ways a figure to be admired and emulated. Living life as he sees it and feels it, he does not buy into the conventional American orthodoxy "with its millions and millions hustling forever for a buck among themselves, the mad dream—grabbing, taking, giving, sighing, dying," as Kerouac puts it. Cassady/Moriarty and Kerouac/Paradise may not hustle for a buck, but they are constantly hustling, constantly on the move, bopping from the East Coast to Denver and out to California; to San Francisco and Los Angeles and around the Central Valley; back to the east but back again to San Francisco; then back to Denver and into Mexico. And the way they do all this hustling, all this moving, is by car.

There's not a plane or train to be found in the book; except for some bus rides by Kerouac, they get around by automobile. Dean, Sal, and Carlo Marx (the poet Allen Ginsberg, in real life) go to midget auto races when they're in Denver. For their long-distance trips Sal and Dean occasionally use "a travel bureau car," a hired car for which people paid a fee and rode with others going to the same destination. On one freewheeling night in San Francisco they ride in what Kerouac describes as "a Frisco taxi-jitney, which was an ordinary taxi that ran a regular route and you could hail it from any corner and ride to any corner you want for about fifteen cents, cramped in with other passengers like on a bus, but talking and telling jokes like in a private car." Kerouac disliked driving and drove timidly, unlike Cassady who sped around crazily in a wrecked '37 Ford. Comfortable around machines, Cassady worked in a Firestone tire shop when he lived in San Francisco.

On the Road captured the spirit of its times—a spirit of youthful rebelliousness, restlessness, the American love for movement. More than ever, automobiles revealed a person's place in American life and his or her view of it. Even in protest, one could not get away from them. Hero or anti-hero? Establishment or counterculture? Young or old, upper or lower, in or out? Look at the car a person drove. That gave you the answer, or a good start on it anyhow. And if the person didn't drive a car and hitch-hiked or took the bus, well, that told you something too.

By 1960 1.5 million teenagers owned a car, a figure that would grow even larger over the decade. The first Baby Boomers, the generation of children born between 1946 and 1964, the largest generation in American history, started turning sixteen and getting their driver's licenses in 1962. These legions of mobile young people often drove their parents' cars, of course. But, influenced by European style, they also liked jaunty little things with panache—the Thunderbird, for instance, which debuted in 1955. Not surprisingly, a product of California's convertible culture helped create the T-bird: Frank Hershey (also sometimes spelled Hersey), who designed automobiles for Walter M. Murphy, the esteemed Pasadena coachbuilder of the 1920s. Harley Earl admired Hershey's work and when Earl moved to Detroit,

Hershey became one of his first hires at the new Art and Color Section at General Motors. Later Hershey moved over to Ford and co-designed the T-bird, which quickly became a sales rival of Earl's baby, the Corvette.

Rock 'n' roll music was born during these years, and teens from coast to coast listened to rock and pop songs on Top 40 AM stations playing on the radios of their cars. One of the bands whose music came to dominate the airwaves was led by Brian Wilson of Hawthorne, California. Brian and his brothers Carl and Dennis, along with their cousin Mike Love and buddy Al Jardine, liked to play music and harmonize together. At age nineteen Brian wrote a song called "Surfin'," which became, in 1961, their first hit record. The next year the song appeared on their first album, *Surfin' Safari,* which also became a hit. The album contained more surfing songs as well as a hot-rod song, "409." More hits followed, and the Beach Boys became known for Brian's beautiful, melodic compositions, their harmonies, and the things they sang about—the beach and surfing and girls and summer and woodies and hot cars. For many people around America and the world, this *was* California, and still is. In 1964 the Beach Boys released one of their most memorable songs, "Fun, Fun, Fun," about a teen girl having the time of her life until her Daddy takes her T-bird away.

The Beach Boys' album cover art from this time provides a snapshot of California youth culture—*Summer Days and Summer Nights* (the boys on a sailboat in the ocean), *The Beach Boys Today* (in sweaters, by a swimming pool), *Shut Down Volume 2* (in blue jackets, with a Corvette Sting Ray), *Little Deuce Coupe* (with a blue custom hot rod), *Surfin' USA* (somebody, not one of the boys, riding a monster wave), and *Surfin' Safari* (on a woodie with a surfboard, checking out the surf). Woodies, one more pure-California car creation, were originally station wagons used by farmers and ranchers around the West in the 1930s and '40s. But the wood paneling on the sides—made of real hardwoods, not plastic—required regular upkeep, and many owners did not bother with it. Thus, these "termite traps" fell into disfavor except among California surfers, who loved them because they were cheap, looked cool, and they could fit their ten-foot-long surfboards in the back.

Another car, with a somewhat less sleek profile than the T-bird and not a surf vehicle, was also capturing the fancy of young people, much to the surprise and dismay of the automobile establishment. There were those who could not understand its appeal, frankly, for it lacked seemingly all of the features the typical American preferred in an automobile. It was small, slow, homely in appearance. It was a two-door. The back seat was cramped. The motor was in the rear. It was also German-made, a fact that veterans of D-Day and the Battle of the Bulge resented. But West Germany was now an ally of this country, the children of those vets had not fought in the war, and they liked that the car ran forever on a tank of gas and that even the most non–mechanically minded person could learn to work on the engine and at least change its oil. In 1963 1.6 million Volkswagen Beetles were tootling around America, on their way to surpassing the Model T as the best-selling car of all time, ultimately reaching 19 million before their production ceased in the early seventies.

The popularity of Volkswagens represented another form of rebellion, one that Californian and American hot-rodders had been engaged in for years.* Although they generally disliked the imports and bought domestic, they, too, found Detroit iron lacking in many respects, especially in the area of design. George Barris was becoming almost as famous as the people he was building cars for. He reupholstered Liberace's Cadillac convertible in black and white to make the seats look like piano keys, with a candelabra in the back. For Elvis Presley, the King of Kustomizers installed gold records on the ceiling of his 1962 Cadillac, along with a refrigerator and a wall-shaking stereo system, a much-requested item by celebrities. Barris also designed cars for movies and television, and these creations included Dean Martin's swingin' station wagon in the Matt Helm movie *The Silencers,* Jethro's hot rod in *The Beverly Hillbillies,* and the original Batmobile for *Batman and Robin.* The growing interest in Barris's work brought him attention from New York (Tom Wolfe was dropping in around this time to write his famous *Esquire* piece), as well as from Detroit designers who copied many of his innovations for their cars.

But the Big Three did not need to lift from Barris alone; they had a whole convoy of original and iconoclastic California car customizers from which to choose. Among them were:

- Joe Bailon of Hayward. Said to be the inventor of the color "candy apple red," he once transformed a car so completely no one could determine its original manufacturer. People dubbed it "The Mystery Car."
- Dean Jeffries of Hollywood. Another wildly inventive customizer, he designed the moon buggy in James Bond's *Diamonds Are Forever* and the red Monkeemobile for the *Monkees* television series. It was Jeffries, not George Barris as is often reported, who painted "Little Bastard" and "130" on James Dean's Porsche Spyder.
- Ed "Big Daddy" Roth of Maywood. Described by Tom Wolfe as the Salvador Dali of customizing, Roth earned his nickname because he stood six-foot-four and weighed 270 pounds—"the size of a good NFL linebacker," as one reporter put it. But he also had a puckish sense of humor; his sweating, eyeball-popping "Rat Fink" cartoon character was a cult hero among the young who sported its picture on their T-shirts and bought Rat Fink car model kits. Roth's customs, such as the bubble-topped Outlaw and Beatnik Bandit, expressed his vision of automobiles not merely as utilitarian vehicles but as objects of fancy and fun. Roth frequently appeared at car shows dressed in a top hat and tails and sporting a monocle.
- Von Dutch of Los Angeles. Born as Kenneth Howard, Von Dutch reinvented himself as a bohemian-style artist whose canvas was the automobile. An early and expert pinstriper, which consists of painting freehand lines of different colors on the insides and outsides of cars, he also excelled at another favorite of customizers, flames. One of his most famous flame jobs, on a Mercedes sports car, shocked those who revered

* At this time the Japanese had only begun to export cars to the United States. They were known mainly for their cheap but fun motorbikes, commemorated by the Beach Boys in one of their songs, "Little Honda."

the German marque. "People couldn't accept a flamed 300 SL Gull Wing back then," he said with a laugh. "They thought it was desecrating a shrine."

- Larry Watson of Long Beach. At his shop on Artesia Boulevard he created a wild palette of colors and combined them with illustrations, flames, pinstripes, scallop shapes, "S" and "Z" patterns, and swirling lines. Watson patterned his seaweed-style flames on the seaweed dripping off the Gill Man in *Creature from the Black Lagoon*.

These and other customizers—Pete Chapouris, Norm Grabowski, Tommy the Greek Hrones, Ed Iskenderian, Russ Meeks, Gene Winfield, to name only a few—showed how cool cars can look when designed and painted with imagination and flair. Ron Aguirre was another top customizer; his '59 Corvette had been channeled so close to the ground he could barely get it out of his garage before some cop was pulling him over to write him up. It was illegal to drive a car whose body was lower than the wheel rims. Then one day Aguirre was at a body shop watching them repair a bumper with hydraulic lifts, and an idea hit him. "I wondered if I could stick that in my car," he thought. So he went to an aircraft surplus store and bought a hydraulic system that had been used on a fighter plane. Returning home and enlisting the help of his father, Louie, he "began jury-rigging a simple system that would raise the car with a hidden hand pump." With the pump Aguirre, stationed in the driver's seat, could make the body of the 'Vette go up and down—up when the police were around, down when they were not.

This magical up-and-down car was named the X-Sonic, and it made its public debut at a car show in Long Beach. Imagine the looks on people's faces when they saw the X-Sonic lift itself up and over a barrier, with the smiling Aguirre inside. His invention was a mindblower but it also had practical implications: No more scraping the rear of your custom on the ground when you drove it on the street. It was thought that the police might even lighten up too. (A vain hope, as it turned out; the cops didn't like hydraulics any more than channeling.)

The paint-and-flame man Larry Watson, who also ran into troubles with the law whenever he went cruising in his channeled '59 Cad, loved what Aguirre did. He, too, installed lifts into his Cad and did a metalflake paint job on the X-Sonic as well. Over the years Watson painted the X-Sonic a half-dozen times because Aguirre, a true perfectionist, kept fiddling around with its design.

Vividly painted customs with hydraulic lifts suddenly became a happening deal. Aguirre belonged to the Krankers, and after everyone in the club saw the X-Sonic they all wanted lifts for their cars too. So did the Pharaohs of Rialto, and pretty soon car guys and gals around southern California were dropping into Earl's surplus aircraft store in Lawndale or Palley's in Los Nietos to see if they had any used fighter plane hydraulics in stock.

Beginning in the 1960s, the spiritual and geographic center of this latest southern California trend to sweep the nation was East Los Angeles. Bill "DeCarr" Ortega, Jesse Lopez, and many others put hydraulics on all four wheels of their customs, boosting them up to make them hop. They held hopping contests on the street, lifting two wheels on one side, or two wheels in the front or back, or all four of them at once to see how high they could get off the ground. The art on their cars also steadily grew more elaborate, featuring murals, Catholic icons, references to their Pachuco zoot-suit heritage, and other expressions of the Mexican American experience. Like Steve McQueen and Neal Cassady and Big Daddy Roth, these low-riders became heroes and anti-heroes too, expressing themselves and their views through their automobiles.

From 7 million residents before World War II, California grew to 10.5 million in 1950 and almost 16 million in 1960. Four years later the word came down from the Census Bureau that California had officially passed New York as the nation's most populous state. Meantime the state's motor vehicle population was nearly doubling every ten years—2.7 million in 1940, 4.5 million in 1950, nearly 8 million in 1960. As always, Los Angeles led the way in this regard, with more cars per capita than any other city on earth.

Naturally, with so many people using so many autos so much of the time, the old familiar headache of traffic became a major problem for millions of drivers, especially in their weekday commutes. This was not a new trend; this was rather a worsening of a pattern that had begun well before the cataclysm of World War II. A 1937 traffic study conducted by the Automobile Club of Southern California noted how "the automobile is used by all classes in going to and from place of residence to place of business or employment." Even though they could choose from two major interurban lines, the Los Angeles Railway and the Pacific Electric trolley, Depression-era southern Californians still drove their automobiles most of the time. During the 1920s traffic jams mainly plagued the downtown, but after that "the problem has not only grown in intensity in the city proper but has spread far into contiguous territory where in many sections street congestion, traffic delays and hazard to life and property are as great as in the central traffic district," said the study.

In the early years of the automobile its speed and relative ease of travel had shortened the distances between communities, states, and the entire country, bringing everyone a little closer together. But the report warned that the traffic snarls were starting to create the opposite effect: "The growing street and highway congestion is slowly but surely pushing the various communities farther and farther apart."

Adding to the aggravation, according to the report, was the "chaotic intermingling" of land uses throughout the region—highways that ran through commercial and industrial areas as well as stop lights, signs, and cross streets that impeded the orderly flow of traffic. In an attempt to solve these problems, a new idea arose: the freeway, a non-toll road with limited access that allowed cars to travel at unfettered rates of speed. In 1938, the year after the auto club's report, construction began on the first freeway in California: the nine-mile Arroyo Seco Parkway between Los Angeles and Pasadena. The road, which represented the beginnings of the Los Angeles metropolitan area freeway system, attracted heated opposition during its planning and approval phases because its route went through several public parks. In the end, this more scenic approach helped sell it to the commuting public—thus the "parkway" tag. The first stretch of the $4.5 million Arroyo Seco Parkway (now the Pasadena Freeway and a National Historic Civil Engineering Landmark) opened in December 1940. Hailed as "a marvel of innovation [with] new types of signs, safety systems and specially banked curves," it was also a marvel for what it lacked: cross traffic, left turns, overhead wires, neon lights, billboards, and other roadside clutter. The smooth-flowing six-lane divided highway could carry forty-five hundred cars an hour in each direction, shortening the commute between the two cities to a mere twenty minutes.

Twenty minutes, that is, when there was no traffic. After World War II, when Los Angeles began to jump big-time and made the 1930s seem like an automobile-free paradise, clogged roadways became a constant during the morning and evening commutes. Something clearly had to be done. In 1947 Governor Earl Warren signed the Collier-Burns Highway Act, a landmark piece of legislation that raised the state gasoline tax by one and a half cents a gallon. This bitterly opposed tax hike passed the legislature only because of the promises contained in the bill—that this new revenue would go toward building "a modern state highway system" that would be the envy of the nation.

People were noticing California's highways all right, although not always with envy and admiration. A 1949 article in *Life* described Los Angeles as having "the world's biggest traffic problem." Fortunately, said the magazine, the city was also hard at work on "the world's biggest solution to that problem": a four-level interchange at the junction of the Pasadena, Hollywood, Santa Ana, and Harbor freeways. The $5 million interchange, the world's first quadruple-stacked interchange, formed part of a planned new grid of freeways that when completed would knit the region together. "The special nature of the Los Angeles traffic problem and its special urgency arise from the fact that Los Angeles is a decade or so ahead of other cities in its automotive culture," explained *Life*. To illustrate this fact, it cited the example of Brentwood advertising man Austin Peterson, who drove thirty miles to work each day for his job. The grind was worth it, however, because at day's end he could kick back at his half-acre, eight-room, country-style rancho. A photograph shows him doing just that: reading the paper on a lounge chair on his patio with his wife as their young son rides a tricycle. In the background of the shot is his convertible in the driveway.

Peterson needed his convertible, or at least wheels of some sort, because "the Angeleno who has no car is as helpless as an upside down turtle." One reason for this was the spread-out nature of the city: 450 square miles and 5,680 miles of streets patrolled by the biggest motorcycle force in the world. Growth in Los Angeles was no longer concentrated in the old Spring Street downtown core, and had not been for some time. Instead it was rolling north to the San Fernando Valley, east to San

Bernardino and Riverside, south to Long Beach and Santa Ana—"horizontally rather than vertically," as Carey McWilliams observed.

McWilliams, the distinguished writer and editor, was not alone in noticing something else that was going on in his home state. Everyone else noticed it too, and on certain days you'd have to be nose-free not to notice it.

It stunk. The air stunk.

Not only that, you could *see* it. A thing that is supposed to be invisible had developed a brownish or yellowish color. It made your eyes water too. Older people hacked and coughed and had a hard time breathing because of it.

"Smog and fumes accumulate for days in the basin and remain trapped in the basin, unable to escape," wrote McWilliams in 1949. "No problem of the postwar period has occasioned more agitation and discussion in Los Angeles than the problem of 'smog,' which is far from being solved today."

Not only was the problem far from being solved, nobody knew exactly what was causing it. What people did know was that "smog"—another new coinage, a combination of the words smoke and fog—or something resembling it had been around a long, long time, dating back centuries to the Tongva and Chumash Indians who lived in the area. The smoke from their campfires choked the basin to such a degree that Spanish settlers referred to it as "the Valley of the Smoke." By the late nineteenth century much had changed in the Los Angeles Basin, but not the occasional smoky pall that hung in the sky. A visitor in 1868 wrote in the San Francisco *Alta* that "the atmosphere has been so filled with smoke as to confine the vision to a small circumference."

In the early 1900s, after the arrival of automobiles, people were still remarking upon this phenomenon. "Queer chugging noises filled the air and the acrid smoke from burnt gasoline floated over the ancient Mission and the little adobes that nestled around it," said a playgoer at the opening night of a 1912 play in San Gabriel. "It was the first big outpouring of automobiles that San Gabriel had ever had." People surely connected those queer chugging noises with the acrid smoke in the air, but there simply weren't enough automobiles around yet to raise alarm. In the 1920s and '30s industrial sources received most of the blame for the smoke that appeared in Los Angeles and then blew east toward Riverside and other inland areas.

Then, in the midst of war, the bad air became impossible to ignore. "The year 1943 is generally accepted as the one during which smog as it is now known began to become a menace in Los Angeles County," wrote a reporter (from the vantage point of 1951). In September 1943 Los Angeles experienced a daylight dimout caused by the smoke clouds in the air. "Thousands of eyes smarted," said one account. "Many wept, sneezed and coughed. Throughout the downtown area and into the foothills the fumes spread their irritation."

With other urgent matters to attend to, southern Californians had to set this one aside for a while. But after the war people turned their attention to it. Those in the tourist industry were especially alarmed. "People came here for the sun and the climate," said Stephen Royce, president of the Huntington Hotel Company in

Pasadena. "Air pollution was affecting our sunshine." Backed by the Los Angeles County Board of Supervisors, the Los Angeles County Citizens' Committee on Air Pollution, of which Royce was chair, consisted of business, community, and government representatives. It crafted and successfully lobbied for a law that created, in 1946, the Los Angeles County Pollution Control District, the first pollution control agency in the nation.

Farmers, manufacturers, railroads, lumber companies, oil producers, and others opposed the district and challenged its right to regulate their business activities. The fight shifted to Sacramento and the heated debate continued over the Collier-Burns highway bill which, along with raising taxes, authorized counties to adopt, monitor, and enforce anti-pollution measures and form pollution control districts of their own. Lawsuits and more political wrangling ensued. But the courts upheld the legal basis for these districts, and other counties in the state followed the lead of Los Angeles and formed air pollution control districts of their own. Other cities around the country also struggling with pollution problems closely followed what was going on out West, and Los Angeles became the model for similar pollution control districts across the United States.

Still, no city in America produced smog like Los Angeles. On certain days it was miserable, but on other days it was nowhere to be seen. Why? What was the reason for this? It was a mystery.

Enter Dr. Arie J. Haagen-Smit, a biochemist at Carl Breer's old school, the California Institute of Technology in Pasadena. Born in the Netherlands, a pleasant, relentlessly optimistic scientist, "Haagy," as his friends called him, was the least likely hero of his age. He was not an anti-hero but he was not a traditional sort of hero either. And some regarded him as a villain.

He first arrived in the United States in 1936 to deliver a biochemistry lecture at Harvard. The next year he accepted an invitation from Caltech to join its faculty and moved to Pasadena with his wife. Asked once about his scientific interests, he said, "My interest was life. Why does a plant grow? Why does a fly have red eyes?" He was not a smog expert at first; there were, in fact, no smog experts anywhere when he began his research in the field, not even among the Nobel Prize winners on the Caltech faculty. Early on Stephen Royce and the Los Angeles County Citizens' Committee on Air Pollution had approached Caltech to see if anyone there could explain all this haze in the sky, but the professors only had ideas and no real proof. Finally the pollution control district asked Haagen-Smit, who agreed to look into the matter. After all, he had to breathe the air too.

"No one could miss it in those days—that stinking cloud that rolled across the landscape every afternoon," he said. "I felt it would not be difficult to find out what smog was. So I began."

Working basically by himself in his laboratory at Caltech, Haagen-Smit reproduced smog in a test tube. Said a news account, "He took a glass of ordinary thermal-cracked gasoline and passed ozone over it; nothing happened. He then took a glass of catalytic-cracked gasoline, passed the ozone over it, and smog was produced immediately. It smelled like smog, tasted like it, looked like it and made your eyes smart." But ozone, a volatile gas that occurs naturally in the atmosphere, did not by itself create smog. "The main villainous substances are hydrocarbons from gasoline and oxides of nitrogen from combustion processes. These two, activated by sunlight, set up the chain reaction of explosive forces that cause smog." Haagy himself could vouch for the explosive nature of these gases after a laboratory explosion knocked the lenses out of his eyeglasses. When he invited members of the pollution control board over to his lab for a demonstration, they watched as some inflated rubber balloons burst when oxidized with ozone. Then Haagen-Smit unleashed his smog-making machine on them and they ran from the room complaining about the stink and with their eyes stinging.

The local press trumpeted Dr. Haagen-Smit's 1950 findings as a major breakthrough. "How smog is produced and what it consists of have been discovered at last," said one report. "The greatest mystery of the smog has been solved," said another. But it's one thing to identify the chemical composition of smog; it's quite another to actually do something about it. As Haagen-Smit said, "Then the war began."

The first skirmishes centered on the smoke and fumes produced by oil refineries. But Haagen-Smit and his colleagues kept working the problem and determined that oil and other industries didn't deserve to shoulder all of the responsibility. "Automobiles themselves contribute as much to the smog problem as does the petroleum industry," he said. "One could draw the conclusion that automobiles and the petroleum industry are about equal contributors to the smog problem."

Individually a car was a small thing, but millions upon millions of them added up to a large thing indeed. Automobile exhausts were releasing hundreds of tons of pollutants into the air a day, and the sunlight turned these gasoline vapors into smog, which hung in the air due to the atmospheric condition known as "temperature inversion." This explained the age-old mystery of the Los Angeles Basin: why on some days the air was fine and on other days it was not. The cumulative impacts of smog, however, could not be ignored. It harmed people's health and damaged the environment and, said Dr. Haagen-Smit, their emissions needed to be curbed.

Many in the car industry attacked him, deriding his test tube–created smog as "Haagen-smog." Others ridiculed him as a "scientific Don Quixote" and challenged his methods and findings. His colleagues at Caltech and other pollution control advocates rallied to his side but, in one regard at least, Haagen-Smit suffered a grievous lapse of judgment. If, after making his breakthrough discovery, he had expected to return to his quiet laboratory life to find out why plants grow, it did not happen. Instead he became, said a reporter, "a one-man army against air pollution."

He and a fellow chemist, C. E. Bradley, developed a scientific method for measuring smog, comparing ozone levels with 1 million parts of air. When the ozone content in the air exceeded a certain level, similar to the "Spare the Air" alerts of today, the pollution control district asked citizens to drive less until conditions improved. Surprisingly perhaps, Haagen-Smit and his opponents in the auto industry agreed on one long-term fix for the problem: build more freeways. More freeways with fewer traffic stops would increase gas mileage and minimize acceleration and deceleration, thereby reducing the amount of gasoline fumes released in the atmosphere. In a report to the Pure Air Committee of Los Angeles, Haagen-Smit argued for "a radical revision of the transportation system" that included "freeway expansion to promote a less interrupted traffic flow and a more systematic encouragement of share-the-ride programs."

By this time, however, California's ambitious highway-building program had stalled due to a lack of money. The Collier-Burns gas tax revenue had helped some, but the job was too big for state and local jurisdictions to foot the bill themselves. They needed federal help. In June 1956 President Dwight Eisenhower signed the $33 billion Federal Highway Act to create the national interstate highway system. Ike's 1919 military road trip across the country had given him a firsthand look at how bad America's roads were, but his belief in the value of an interstate system stemmed more from his experience as Supreme Commander of the Allied Forces in World War II when he saw how quickly and efficiently the German army used the autobahns to move troops, vehicles, and weapons. The interstate system was an outgrowth, really, of Carl Fisher's Lincoln Highway dream, but instead of one Main Street for America it would create lots of them, improving commerce in the country and providing vital communications and transportation links in the event of a nuclear or other attack on American soil.

People instantly grasped the significance of this measure, regarding it, with the 1916 federal highway bill, as "one of the two most important milestones in American highway history." Its immediate impact was to release lots of money to the states—in California's case, $400 million over three years, including money pitched in by state and local sources. The effect was to take all the proposed highway projects that had been sitting in drawers, all those that had been started but never finished, all those that needed improvements or extensions, all those that had been stopped or delayed for whatever reason, and give them the green light. "Now, with the 1956 bill just passed," said a California business executive, "we are about to experience an acceleration of that program on a scale never in the past considered possible."

Which was what happened. The interstate highway system became "the largest public works project in history," as one analyst put it. In southern California alone, the Harbor, Golden State, Ventura, and Hollywood freeways were finished, and the Santa Ana and San Diego freeways were built. Most Americans, who were sick of being stuck in traffic, welcomed this "new era of the freeway," as a headline writer called it, and approved of putting it on a fast track.* Still, a minority view held that putting down all this asphalt to carry all these vehicles that dirtied up the air and cut into the land maybe had some drawbacks to it. These feelings of

---

* During this time Elmer Botts, a chemist with Caltrans, developed a pavement marker to help drivers see the lane stripes better at night and in bad weather. But when these raised and brightly painted markers were put down on the asphalt, something unexpected happened: drivers accidentally ran over them and the jolt made them more alert behind the wheel. "Botts' dots" have since become a safety feature on highways around the state and nation.

disillusionment grew over time and surely contributed to the widespread social unrest that roiled the country during the Vietnam War era of the 1960s. In his 1958 collection of poems, *A Coney Island of the Mind*, San Francisco Beat poet Lawrence Ferlinghetti expressed his disenchantment with "a concrete continent / spaced with bland billboards / illustrating imbecile illusions of happiness." More expressions of unhappiness came from a prominent Los Angeles urban affairs reporter, William C. Stewart: "Today the wail of the ambulance, smog, violence and the auto that seems bent upon controlling our lives appear to have betrayed the promise of order and power that once symbolized the city."

One transportation option enjoyed by Easterners, interurban rail, did not exist for the most part in California. But in 1957 the governor and state legislature approved the creation of the San Francisco Bay Area Rapid Transit District, a network of trains intended to provide a mass-transit alternative to the car. Still, fifteen years would elapse before BART would begin running trains and carrying passengers, and then only in three counties: Alameda, Contra Costa, and San Francisco. Residents without a car in the rest of the Bay Area and around California mostly took the bus or shared rides to work with someone who was driving. Meanwhile, the smog problem kept getting worse.

Delegates to the 1958 National Conference on Air Pollution in Washington, D.C., expressed "mounting alarm in many cities over the smog problem," said a wire service report. Smog was not restricted to California by any means, but it was worse there than anywhere else in the country. Los Angeles, San Francisco, Sacramento, and Fresno had all suffered severe smog over the summer. A group of Californians, including state and local politicians, public health officials, scientists, and Dr. Haagen-Smit, attended this conference, urging the federal government to join the fight against smog and to push the auto industry to move faster in its efforts to combat it. Auto industry representatives also attended the conference, arguing that they were being unfairly targeted for the problem and that they had spent $5 million in recent years to develop anti-smog controls on their vehicles. But this hardly satisfied the California group, one of whom charged that "the automobile industry has not yet fulfilled its great responsibility in controlling the health-destroying pollutants from motor vehicle exhausts. In the public interest the industry should strive for a healthier car [rather] than a bigger and more powerful car."

Haagen-Smit remained at the center of this controversy for the next two decades. "The people have a right to clean air," he said. "Perhaps I can help." And so he did, serving on a presidential task force on air pollution and winning every major scientific award except the Nobel Prize. In 1959 he sat on an advisory panel that urged California to form a pollution control agency for automobiles. The Motor Vehicle Pollution Control Board formed in 1960, and Haagen-Smit was one of its original members. Over the next years the board oversaw a number of national firsts—controls on hydrocarbon crankcase emissions and tailpipe emissions, and smog-control devices for automobiles—and its leadership spurred the creation of the Environmental Protection Agency and the passage of the federal Clean Air Act in

1970. In 1967 California merged the Motor Vehicle Pollution Control Board with another agency and formed the Air Resources Board, which continues to monitor air pollution and other environmental issues in the state. Governor Ronald Reagan appointed Dr. Haagen-Smit to be its first chairman, a position he held for the next five years. Many give him credit for holding the agency together in its early years, when under siege by its critics.

When Haagen-Smit died in 1977, a Chrysler executive who had fought with him many times over the years paid him one of the highest compliments. "He was once my judge and jury," he said, "because I am an automobile man. But never did I doubt his competence, integrity or humanity." A reporter added that "Haagen-Smit stood in the center of a crossfire. On one side, industrialists charged him with being too tough. On the other, environmentalists accused him of being too soft." Throughout it all the Dutch immigrant remained stubbornly, even defiantly optimistic, believing that society would find an answer to this massive problem that, in a very real sense, could be reduced to the size of a test tube.

THIRTY-TWO

Spirit of America

Throughout these years of optimism and pessimism, of constancy and upheaval, of change and renewal, of peace and war, Americans experimented with automobiles. This has been true of this country since the inception of automobiles, up to and including the present moment. Sometimes these experiments end in joy and accomplishment. Sometimes they end in sorrow and failure. But always this exploring, this seeking.

In August 1962 Craig Breedlove, a dark-haired twenty-five-year-old Californian with movie-star good looks, prepared to test the limits, once again, of how fast an automobile could travel. Only this automobile, called "Spirit of America," was different than all the others that had challenged the speed records of the past. Its power derived from a General Electric J-47 jet aircraft engine capable of generating 4,250 pounds of thrust.

Not only did the Spirit of America have a jet engine, it only had three wheels—two in back, one in front. Breedlove had decided on this approach "because the jet engine lent itself to that type of car," he said.

Breedlove's unconventional approach triggered admiration but also skepticism when the Spirit of America went on display early in August at a sponsor and press reception at the Wilshire Country Club in Los Angeles. The car, if one could call it that—some argued it was really a motorcycle or a tricycle—had yet to make a run to test the grandness of its ambitions against its performance. Could a three-wheeled jetmobile surpass the world land speed record of 394.194 miles per hour? It was anybody's guess.

But if looks meant anything, the Spirit of America had it in the bag. Master Indianapolis 500 builder Quinn Epperly of Gardena had crafted its swooping black nose and aerodynamic thirty-five-foot-long white fiberglass body. Both massive and refined, the vehicle stood six feet high, eleven feet wide, and weighed three tons. Lockheed Aircraft engineer Walt Sheehan had designed its ten-foot-long air ducts. Each of its three tires contained 250 pounds of nitrogen gas. Despite its imposing size, the Spirit of America had a lightness to it that made it seem capable of taking off the ground. On its white tail fin was a black stripe; inside the stripe was a decal of the American flag. Located amidships atop the vehicle, the driver's seat and instrument panel resembled those of a jet cockpit. The sportswriter Bill Dredge said that the Spirit of America "looks like an F-104 jet fighter plane shorn of its wings," also describing it, more colorfully, as "a pencil-shaped buzz bomb."

The other focus of attention at the reception was the man behind "the most radical try of its kind in the history of the land speed trials." Charming and boyishly handsome in a suit and tie, Breedlove reminded Dredge of Cary Grant in the ease with which he handled questions and relations with his two major sponsors, Shell Oil and Goodyear Tire and Rubber. The Spirit of America had cost two hundred and fifty thousand dollars to design, engineer, and build, and the two companies had furnished much of that sum despite the fact that Breedlove had no real track record in land speed record attempts. "It's not easy for a guy with no college education to go to a company and get them to believe in your idea," he explained. "I was trying to sell a program that would wind up costing hundreds of thousands of dollars. A lot of people thought I'd never make it. There were times when I didn't think I'd make it myself."

The enterprise, he admitted, was "a way-out scheme," a scheme that had originated during a time in his life when he felt stuck as a human being. "I didn't think I was accomplishing anything," he said. "I wanted to try to do something more important."

That something important became the LSR, as aficionados refer to the land speed record, which John Cobb set way back in 1947. Fifteen years was too long, in Breedlove's view, for a record of such magnitude to stay in the books. Furthermore, he said, it was held by an Englishman, and that simply did not cut it. Born in Los Angeles, raised in Mar Vista, living in Culver City, Breedlove was an American through and through. He felt it was time to bring the record back to the land of Barney Oldfield and Tommy Milton and Frankie Lockhart and the other great American speed pioneers of the past.

Growing up near Venice on the shores of the Pacific, the young Breedlove enjoyed the familiar hot-rod boyhood of machines, machines, machines, buying his first car when he was thirteen. Even at that age he was in thick with a local car club, the Igniters, which consisted mainly of a bunch of sixteen- and seventeen-year-olds who took a shine to the kid and let him ride along with them for an early taste of the boulevard life circa 1949. That was when the youngest Igniter started socking his allowance away and asking his parents for money, not presents, at Christmas so he could buy a car. When he turned thirteen on March 23, 1950, his piggy bank held forty-five dollars in bills and change—not enough, alas, to pull the trick off. But his mother and father came through with a birthday present of thirty dollars cash, which added up to seventy-five dollars, enough for him to buy a beat-down '34 Ford that looked like a million bucks in his eyes.

"Of course, I was [too] young to drive," he recalled. "I had to promise I'd just work on the car. Well, I took that car completely apart. Every piece. It was all over the place. I bought hot rod magazines and read all about hopping up cars. I bought special gears for the rear end and installed them. I cleaned the frame and repainted it.

I got a supercharged '48 flathead Merc engine. About all I wanted to do was work on that car. But I didn't have any idea at all of driving."

Three long years later, after he turned sixteen, he took his '34 Ford with the '48 flathead Merc out to the speed trials at El Mirage Dry Lake. But Breedlove didn't come to race; another guy was supposed to do that for him. "El Mirage sort of scared me," he said. "Everybody said it was a tricky course." The other guy was overbooked, though, committed to racing too many cars in violation of the rules of the Southern California Timing Association. That left the job to the reluctant teen, who proceeded to set a class record of 142 miles per hour on his first run in the desert. From then on he started developing ideas about driving.

Breedlove competed at the dry lakes, the Saugus drags, and other places, supplementing his racing education with auto shop and drafting courses at Venice High. After graduating in 1955 he got a job at a local speed shop. He had talents, to be sure, but not the kind that made him interested in a four-year college education. So he drifted a little, leaving the speed shop to install air conditioners and then abandoning that job to clerk at an auto parts store. He felt frustrated because all this drifting seemed to be taking him away from racing, which was what he loved.

In the meantime the California speed scene was booming. El Mirage remained a happening spot (as it does today), new drag strips were opening all over, and tracks such as Laguna Seca and Riverside International were in full bloom.* Equally enticing was the new Land of Speed that had been discovered to the east. Actually, red-hots had been making speed runs on the salt flats of the Great Salt Lake Desert since the advent of the Model T. And Bonneville had gained a reputation around the world as the best place on earth to go fast by the time another speed-loving Englishman, Malcolm Campbell, had become the first man to exceed 300 miles per hour there in 1935. But it wasn't until after World War II, when a couple of go-go Californians got involved, that Bonneville became a regular stop on the national speed circuit. In 1949, *Hot Rod*'s Robert Petersen and future National Hot Rod Association founder Wally Parks went to Utah to meet with the Salt Lake Chamber of Commerce and the Bonneville Speedway Association to pitch them on the idea of an annual speed meet. The groups saw the merits of the plan, and in August of that year Bonneville hosted the first national speed trials, which came to be known as Bonneville Speed Week.

The first speed week, organized by the SCTA, featured forty-seven hot rods, all but two from hot rod–happy California. By the next August the trials had turned into the "World Series of hot-rodding," with hundreds of hop-ups from around the country crashing the formerly all-California party. Three cars broke 200 miles per hour. The fastest was the So-Cal Streamliner, sponsored by Alex Xydias's speed shop. Xydias served as wrenchman and Dean Batchelor drove; its time was 208.92 miles per hour.

Over the years many more California hot-shoes guys gravitated to the salt flats, one of the greatest being Mickey Thompson. Sporting a full head of thick dark hair

---

* Sears Point Raceway opened in Sonoma County later in the decade; it's now Infineon Raceway. Riverside International was razed in the 1980s for a shopping center. The premier track in southern California today is the California Speedway (renamed the Auto Club Speedway) in Fontana.

and dark eyebrows, the Alhambra-born Thompson, the son of a policeman, nearly set a class record when he was fifteen at El Mirage in a souped-up Model A. This earned him a rep as having the fastest car in his high school, and if anyone wished to challenge his title he was happy to oblige. His debut at the salt flats came in 1952 when, in his early twenties, he clocked 194 miles per hour at Speed Week. Afterward he returned home to his regular job as a pressman for the *Los Angles Times*.

Mickey could drive anything, but especially things that went straight and fast. In 1958, already a drag-racing hero, he posted a new record of 294 miles per hour for his class of vehicles at Bonneville. Notable about this mark besides the speed was the engine used: a modified Chrysler Hemi. Engines built by Chrysler and Cadillac and, most importantly, the V-8 introduced by Chevrolet in 1955, were not only luring hot-rodders away from their traditional power plant of choice, the flathead Ford V-8, but also drastically changing hot rodding itself. In the old days hot-rodders built their cars on the cheap using parts from a speed shop or junkyard. But with the mass production of the Chevy V-8, Chrysler Hemi, and other engines, "it became a simple matter to buy an off-the-shelf engine which, with very minor alterations, would produce more power than we used to get from a flathead V-8 or a four-banger after weeks, months, or maybe years of experimentation," said Dean Batchelor. "By the end of the 1950s one could buy a new car from a dealer that was faster than most of the hot rods we made ourselves a decade earlier."

Another change in hot-rodding involved money and all the opportunities and challenges that come with it. Hot-rodding wasn't just a bunch of kids racing on the street for bragging rights and pink slips anymore, although there were still lots of kids who did that. Car manufacturers, oil companies, tire companies, and many others in the auto industry saw hot-rodding, racing, and customizing as excellent ways to promote and advertise their products, especially to the young. The outlaw image of hot-rodders and their four-banger Fords helped to gussy up the staid reputation of Ford Motor Company. The Big Three had all made major investments in their new, more powerful engines, and to showcase them they sponsored Indianapolis 500 racing, drag racing, and other forms of the sport. It was now pricier and more complicated to compete at the highest levels. The stakes had gone up, as had the speeds of the cars.

Mickey Thompson took his first shot at the world land speed record in 1959; the attempt combined backyard do-it-yourself hot-rod ingenuity with the corporate know-how and resources of Mobil and Goodyear. The inspiration for the try came from Thompson, who had built the frame for his Challenger using steel tubing salvaged from a junkyard. Goodyear kicked in money and expertise; two of its employees, a chemist and an engineer, created special, near-treadless tires to hold the fantastic speeds the car would be traveling. Production on the 2,800-horsepower Challenger with its four Pontiac engines was so hurried that for its grand unveiling at the Beverly Hilton Hotel in Beverly Hills in early August, the car hadn't even been painted yet. But it made it to Bonneville in time for Speed Week, primed, painted and ready to rumble. And rumble it did. Its average two-run speed of 345.33 m.p.h.

made it the fastest car that had ever raced at Speed Week. Nevertheless, it fell far short of the prize Thompson really wanted, and he and Challenger returned to Utah the next year to get it.

On September 9, 1960, in his first run at the salt flats, Thompson went 406.60 miles per hour—the first American to go faster than 400 miles per hour on land. But the Challenger's drive shaft went askew, and he couldn't make a second run to qualify for a land speed record. Lacking this, Thompson's 406.60 did not count officially, and he returned to Los Angeles in frustration. Two years later he came back to Bonneville only to encounter more frustration, as the Challenger fared poorly and did not threaten Cobb's mark. This ended his attempt for the land speed record, a minor blip in a life otherwise rich with accomplishment. Thompson set scores of racing records, managed the Lions Drag Strip in Wilmington and another in Fontana, held numerous patents for automobile innovations, and became a successful businessman. His life ended in ugly circumstances in 1988 when two hooded men murdered him and his wife, Trudy, at their Bradbury, California, home. A former business partner of Thompson's was later found guilty and sent to prison for hiring the killers and ordering the murders.

The year 1962 marked the end of Mickey Thompson's land speed record quest and the beginning of Craig Breedlove's. In the late fifties Breedlove was working at Douglas Aircraft in Santa Monica, learning the engineering techniques that he was applying to the cars he was racing and building. But the job, like every other one he'd had, seemed to be a dead-end street until eventually he found the ideal situation: firefighter in Costa Mesa. The money was decent, he liked the other guys at the station, and the work was occasionally rewarding. Over time, though, it turned into more of the same old thing. Restless and bored, he kept looking for something that would give his life more meaning, something that drew on his talents and experiences and yet was bigger than himself and his personal desires. Finally he settled on a goal that had been around since 1898 when Gaston de Chasselloup-Laubat of France drove a battery-powered electric car 39.25 miles per hour, faster than any automobile had ever gone before. This was it, he felt, this was what he was meant to do.

He quit his fireman's job, went to work in the garage behind his bungalow in Culver City, and pitched Shell and Goodyear on his plans. With their resources behind him, more doors opened for Breedlove, although it surprised him to find that some of his fellow hot-rodders did not approve of what he was doing. They didn't think it was right or fair to couple an automobile with a jet engine—that an automobile was, by definition, "a piston-driven car where the power is transferred through the wheels." John Cobb drove a piston machine; so did Mickey Thompson. For that matter every hot-rodder at Bonneville Speed Week used a piston-driven machine; the rules required it. No rocket thrust propulsion was allowed, and the jet car hybrids of Breedlove and others raced at a different time of the season and belonged to a different racing category.

This was one reason why some people weren't displeased when, after its grand unveiling at the Wilshire Country Club in 1962, the Spirit of America failed miserably in its first try at Bonneville. The brakes and steering did not operate correctly and the nose had partially lifted off the ground at speed. Breedlove never got close to either Cobb's or Thompson's performances, and when he came back home to Culver City he found himself the butt of jokes and snide comments.

"There was a lot of ridicule," he said. "It was hard for people to understand why I'd quit my job to take on something like this."

One of those people was his first wife, and their marriage ended in divorce. Two more who couldn't understand him were his mother and father. They worried, first and foremost, that their son was going to kill himself, and even if he survived he'd still end up with nothing, and for what? Just to be called "the fastest man alive"? What was the difference, ultimately, between 394 and 400? Or 400 and 406? Or 400 and 500, for that matter? Numbers—that was all they were, nothing more. Sportswriters often spoke in terms of breaking the "barrier" of 400 miles per hour. But what barrier? Where? No barrier existed except for the one in people's minds.

"My parents thought I might turn into a bum," said Breedlove in his matter-of-fact way. "My dad thought I was heading for a big disappointment that could ruin my life. One time he got so upset about it he kicked me out of his house."

Goodyear and Shell stuck with him, though, and Breedlove focused on the nuts-and-bolts details that would determine success or failure. He and his team overhauled the brakes and steering on the Spirit of America. As for the tendency of its nose to take flight, he sought out the advice of aircraft industry aerodynamicists, who proved to be of no use at all. The jets they designed went 400 miles per hour in the thin upper atmosphere, where conditions were much different than on the ground. "Friend," they told Breedlove, "when you get over 150 miles per hour on the ground, you're on your own."

Nor did wind tunnel tests help any. Falling back on their own knowledge and instincts and what they had learned at Bonneville the year before, Team Breedlove beefed up the car some and lengthened it a little, and installed an anti-lift device in the nose. Power was an obviously important asset, but so were stability and control. "The course is one hundred feet wide but at the higher speeds it seems like about two feet," Breedlove said. "And the black line on the salt can look like it was drawn with a pencil."

On August 5, 1963, a new, improved Spirit of America went 388.47 miles per hour on Breedlove's first run down that long thin black line. That put him within a few ticks of the record, and on his second run he annihilated it: 428.37, faster than anyone had ever traveled on land before. His two-way average of 407.45 returned the world land speed record to Yankee hands, even if the world's racing organizations couldn't quite agree on it. Though the tricycle was a time-honored design dating back to the earliest motorcars ever made, the International Automobile Federation rejected Breedlove's LSR because the Spirit of America had three wheels, not four. But the United States Auto Club sanctioned the mark, and so did the International Motorcycle Federation, which decreed that the world's fastest car was also the world's fastest motorcycle.

Asked about this dispute, Breedlove said, "All I'm really interested in is the world land speed record, no matter what it's made in."

As it happened, some other people were interested in that record too, and they were going after it with the same determination and skill as the Californians. In October 1964, Tom Green, an Indiana engineer, came to Bonneville and drove his jet-powered Wingfoot Express 413.19 miles per hour, eclipsing Breedlove's mark. Then, three days later, Art Arfons, a gifted do-it-yourself hot-rodder from Ohio, retired Green's record by going 434.18 miles per hour in his Green Monster, another jet-powered vehicle.

A week later, Breedlove and his sixteen-man crew showed up on the salt with the idea of taking the record back. The Spirit of America's first run on October 13 was barely adequate: 422.59. But its second run of 498.13 blew down the house. Breedlove's two-run average of 468.71 shoved Arfons and Green back in line and set up a run for the next big speed barrier: 500 miles per hour.

The Spirit of America went after it two days later. Its first run of 513.33 was smooth and trouble-free. So was its second, in fact, until it passed through the electronically timed mile, marking it as an official run. That was when disaster struck.

Afterward Breedlove said that the steering went out on his car and for that reason he did not release his drag chutes. Other accounts said that both his primary and backup chutes malfunctioned. In any event, he could not stop or steer a seven-thousand-pound steel and fiberglass projectile traveling at 540 miles per hour. When the chutes didn't open he clamped down on his wheel brakes. They snapped under the pressure. Then he hit his back-up braking device and it failed too.

At its top speed the Spirit of America reportedly moved faster than a .30 caliber bullet shot from a rifle. Under such circumstances it was impossible for Breedlove to react fast enough to save himself. And even if he could have reacted in time, there was nothing he could do anyhow. He no longer controlled the vehicle; it controlled him. All he could do was sit and hang on with his heart pounding against the wall of his chest.

The Spirit of America hurtled beyond the hard-pack area designated for the speed trials, "spinning and skidding" across the salt flats. One mile passed. Then another. The car had slowed—if you want to call it that—to 300 miles per hour, and it was still out of control, hurtling out of bounds. "The Spirit of America veered to the left, snapped off a utility pole like a splinter, shot up an incline, soared a six-foot dike and landed, nose down, in a pool of salt water—three miles from the course." The salt water it landed in was an eighteen-foot-deep canal near Highway 40 (now Interstate 80). It hit it at an estimated 200 miles per hour and immediately started to sink. Breedlove's parents had worried about him for many reasons. One worry they surely did not have was that he would become the first person to drown while chasing the world land speed record. But their son pushed off the canopy and got free of the sinking capsule that suddenly resembled a coffin.

He swam to the side of the canal and crawled up onto the ground. He was unhurt, shaking, disoriented. The first two rescuers to reach him said he appeared to be in a "slight stage of hysteria." "Just let me kiss the ground," he told them. "I almost drowned in that thing."

When he got to his feet and looked back at his car, he could not believe what he saw. "Look at my racer!" he kept saying. "Look at my racer!" Nearly all of it—tires, cockpit, most of its body—was submerged. About the only thing visible above the surface of the water was its tail fin with the decal of the Stars and Stripes.

Gradually he calmed down enough to make a joke. "For my next trick I will set myself afire," he said to those in his crew and the others who had come rushing to the site. And by the time the Goodyear representative arrived, his mind had clicked back into its normal groove. "I'm all right, baby," he said to him. "What's the speed?"

Fast, baby, fast. Before he lost control he flew through the timing station at 539.89 miles per hour, completing a two-run average of 526.27. Breedlove had done it—had become the first 500-mile-an-hour man!—although it turned out to be a short-lived celebration. Two weeks later, surviving a blown-out tire that made him briefly lose control of his car too, Art Arfons clocked 536.71 and took back the record that Breedlove had taken from him.

This flurry of records and close calls ended Bonneville's speed racing season for the year, although not the questions about what these two men were doing, and why. Breedlove usually shrugged off such questions, referring to the tremendous concentration it takes to drive a car traveling faster than a speeding bullet. "When I'm strapped in and the engine's lit," he said, "I'm too busy keeping my eyes on the course to worry about anything else." Adding, "Once I close the canopy, it's all business. You've got 20,000 horsepower by the tail and you better hang on." Bob Thomas, a writer who covered Breedlove during this period, had this to say about his reluctance to discuss matters of life and death: "It never pays to ask a mountain climber why he challenges a mountain. The answer is always the same, 'Because it's there.' By the same token, never ask a man why he attempts to break the land speed record—or his neck. His answer will be as vague. He's not really sure either."

Breedlove's attempts to either break the record or his neck turned him into a national celebrity, and in 1964 he made close to one hundred thousand dollars in endorsements and personal appearances. His parents dropped their opposition and came over to his way of thinking. He had remarried and was living with his wife, Lee, and their five children in Palos Verdes. Asked about the danger her husband put himself in, Lee Breedlove was philosophical. "This is what he wants to do," she said in a matter-of-fact way that resembled Craig's. Put him in a motorized vehicle of any kind, she added, and he was going to want to drive it *fast*.

So this was part of the appeal of what was going on in the desert: Two go-for-broke hot-rodders, Breedlove and Arfons, dueling each other like a pair of Old West gunfighters. Let the best man win. The loser gets left in the dirt.

Both were married with families. By the standards of some, they were potentially throwing their lives away in a useless, wasteful spectacle. Ask them what they were doing and why, and they didn't even know precisely and couldn't explain it.

But this, too, was part of the appeal of the thing: the lunatic audaciousness of their shared dream, a dream that could easily end in the nightmare of death or horrific injury. Then there were their horses, those two frighteningly beautiful machines they were riding. Both the Spirit of America and the Green Monster represented the height of automotive science, engineering, machinery, and jet-age technology. Both were marketing and promotional marvels, an unashamed and gaudy mix of Madison Avenue and Hollywood commercialism. And both seemed capable of doing what seemed impossible at the time—going faster than the speed of sound. Supersonic rocket planes had broken the sound barrier many years before, but no one had ever done it on land. Based on the air temperature and other factors, experts estimated the sound barrier at Bonneville to be 720 miles per hour. But mystery and superstition surrounded this invisible wall. If a car broke the sound barrier, some wondered, would it shatter into pieces? Typically Breedlove dismissed such worries, saying that a car would not disintegrate, that if it was traveling 720 miles per hour all that meant was that it was going 10 miles per hour faster than 710.

Breedlove and Arfons weren't just trying to break speed records but challenging conventional notions of time and space. Seventy-five years ago, in a world of kerosene lamps and Concord coaches and oiled dirt roads, these machines barely existed. Now, in a crazy but cold-sober coming together of commercialism and adventure and science and vision and nature and technology and ambition and dreams and work and love and brains and courage, these machines were practically transporting human beings into another dimension. It was positively mind-expanding.

George Lucas, an imaginative young film student at the University of Southern California, was among the many people who came to the desert to watch the speed duels. More than just a casual spectator, he was *into* it. He belonged to a group of speed record enthusiasts known as the Salt Bears. The Salt Bears came to Bonneville from around California and the United States much the same way that people traveled to Cape Canaveral to watch the rocket ships blast off in America's attempt to put a man on the moon. Lucas had a keen appreciation of the risks that Arfons and Breedlove were taking because he had almost died in a car crash as a teenager. In Modesto, where he grew up, Lucas loved hot rods and cruising the boulevards around town. "I went through all that stuff, drove the cars, bought liquor, chased girls," he said, admitting he got such a charge out of driving fast that he was "always on the edge of getting killed." On a June day in 1962 he nearly crossed over that edge when his Fiat sports car broadsided a Chevy Impala on a country road outside of town. The other driver escaped injury, but not Lucas, who was knocked unconscious when his Fiat barrel-rolled into a walnut tree. An ambulance took him to the hospital where he recovered, certain in the knowledge that he never would have woken up if his car hadn't had a roll bar and he hadn't been using his seat belt. The picture of his totaled Fiat appeared the next day in the *Modesto Bee*.

Despite the accident, Lucas retained his love for fast-moving machines, and no machines in the world moved faster across the ground than the ones at Bonneville. He worked as an assistant cameraman for a company that was making a documentary about the land speed record attempts, and when Lucas graduated from USC he turned to film as a career, writing, directing, and producing movies. His second film, *American Graffiti,* was based on his youthful cruising days in Modesto. It was a colossal hit that spurred a national revival of interest in custom hot rods and the teenage chic of the 1950s and early '60s. Audiences adored it, although its popularity did not match that of his *Star Wars* blockbusters. One movie in the *Star Wars* series, *The Phantom Menace,* contains a sequence in which brightly colored airborne pods race wildly across the desert. The similarity between this sequence, the most inspired in the movie, and the land speed record chases of the 1960s is not coincidental.

The duel between Breedlove and Arfons resumed in the fall of 1965 with the Californian getting out of the box first, breaking the Ohioan's record with a two-run benchmark of 555.48 miles per hour on November 2. His wingless jet had been rebuilt from the year before. Now with four wheels and weighing eight thousand pounds, a full ton more than its predecessor, and an upgraded J-79 General Electric jet engine to match Arfons's, the blue-and-white Spirit of America Sonic I represented the next generation of jet-powered vehicles. On its first run its nose began to lift off the ground just as the air speed indicator was reading 600 miles per hour. Breedlove released his braking parachute, which failed. This forced him to go to his disc brakes, which worked. After rolling to a stop in a mushy area about two miles past the timing area, he said, "Thank God for good brakes. Just say I'm lucky."

Two days later, on November 4, Lee Breedlove borrowed her husband's car and set a new women's land speed record, averaging 308.56 miles per hour on her two runs. This may have been why she was so tolerant of Craig's itch for speed; she had been bitten by the bug too.

Three days after her, Art Arfons, whose wife was pregnant with their third child, reclaimed the world record with an average time of 576.55. But on his second run something went haywire with the engine and smoke billowed out of the car and filled the inside of the cockpit. For a moment Arfons thought the belching Green Monster was going to flip. "I knew if it rolled I was a goner," he said. But it didn't roll and he brought it to a safe stop, then popped the canopy and scrambled out before the smoke overwhelmed him.

Five days after that, Bob Summers of Ontario, another all-out southern California hot-rodder, snuck in a land speed record of his own. He wasn't driving on jet power; he had one of those old-fashioned piston-driven machines. His Goldenrod car, juiced by four Chrysler Hemi engines, booked 409.47 miles per hour to set a record in its class.

Meanwhile, as all this activity was going on, Craig Breedlove was gearing up for a new assault on time and space. After his earlier problems he and his pit crew had enlarged the nose to force it to remain earthbound. Then his wife took it out for her record run and everything checked out fine. But his speeds would be twice as fast as hers and the upward pressure on the nose would be that much greater, so there was still uncertainty about it. The only way to see if it was going to work was to do it.

On November 15, 1965, Breedlove took his first run in the Spirit of America Sonic I at about 8:30 in the morning. Its time: 593.17 miles per hour. There was no doubt he'd break Arfons's record; the question was would he get 600? He did. He finished in a rush at 608.201 for an average of 600.60, making him the first person to break 600 miles per hour and 500 miles per hour and to average 400 miles per hour on two runs.

"That 600 is about a thousand times better than 599," he said. "Boy, it's a great feeling."

With the smoking Green Monster having sustained irreparable damage and unable to mount another challenge, this meant that the duel in the desert was done for the year. But Breedlove wasn't taking any chances. Upon returning to Los Angeles he told a reporter that he was going to keep the Spirit of America lean and mean, just in case a retooled Green Monster reared its head again and he had to go back to the salt flats. "That record is too hard to get not to stay ready," he said. "I want to hang onto it this time."

He also mentioned how he was thinking about retiring from land speed racing and getting into water speed racing, another interest of his. He and his team had been working on a new jet-powered speedboat, to be called "Aqua America." Its preliminary design was finished, and construction on it was ready to start. An Englishman currently held the world water speed record of 277 miles per hour, and Breedlove said he wanted to bring that record back to America too.

EPILOGUE

As sometimes happens with people of achievement, Craig Breedlove's reach exceeded his grasp in terms of water racing, and he never set any world water speed records as he did on land. But his 1965 time of 600.60 miles per hour in the Spirit of America remained the standard in world land speed racing until it was surpassed five years later by a man who was not, as one might guess, his great rival Art Arfons. The Ohio hot-rodder faded from the speed racing scene after that near-disastrous final run in the Green Monster and never seriously challenged the LSR again. The end of the Breedlove-Arfons duels also largely marked the end of major corporate involvement in these speed quests. Without big dollars from their sponsors, it became very difficult for Breedlove and Arfons—and all those who wished to challenge them—to race these fabulously fast and expensive machines.

Nevertheless, on October 7, 1970, a thirty-year-old Californian, Gary Gabelich, drove the rocket-powered Blue Flame, sponsored by the Institute of Gas Technology, to a new land speed record of 622.28 miles per hour at Bonneville, cracking Breedlove's mark. Gabelich's record stood for thirteen years until an Englishman, Richard Noble, went 633.468 in his Thrust2 jet car. Gabelich, who raced at Lions Drag Strip in Wilmington and many other California tracks, lived to see his record broken—and not much more after that. He died in a motorcycle crash in 1984.

Gabelich set his record at the Bonneville Salt Flats, but Noble broke it at a different place: Black Rock Desert in northeast Nevada. Due to commercial salt mining and other reasons, surface conditions have deteriorated at Bonneville and it no longer hosts the fastest jetmobiles on earth. Even so, piston-driven, non-jet-powered cars still race at the salt flats and set astonishing speed records in their classes. Bonneville Speed Week, hosted by the Southern California Timing Association, remains a thriving annual event. The SCTA also sponsors a "Save the Salt" campaign to preserve and protect Bonneville for future racing and recreation.

But for world land speed record attempts, the place to go now is Black Rock, the site of the yearly Burning Man Festival. And Black Rock was where Craig Breedlove, in 1996, resumed an old quest: taking the record away from an Englishman and returning it to the United States. Then approaching sixty, Breedlove had made enough money selling real estate to afford the luxury of acting young again. His powers of persuasion had clearly not deserted him either because he convinced some patriotic-minded corporations to back him financially. Moving his base of operations to the small Delta town of Rio Vista, he and his team revamped and rejuvenated the Spirit of America III, as he called it. At its first run at Black Rock in 1996, the 45,000-horsepower car with a J-79 jet engine reached 675 miles per hour before a crosswind hit it and pushed it violently out of control. "I thought, this is it," said Breedlove, recalling his reaction at that moment. "I've just bought the farm." But he hung in there and the Spirit of America III eventually rolled to a peaceful stop a few miles off course.

While Breedlove's time beat Richard Noble's, it did not count officially because Spirit of America III could not make a second run due to mechanical damage. This left an opening for the Englishman, who had been spurred to action by the news that the great American land speed racer was taking a crack at his record. Noble reformed his team, updated his car, and renamed it the ThrustSSC, hiring fellow countryman Andy Green to drive it. They returned to Black Rock in the fall of 1997 and did the unthinkable: in September Green became the first to go faster than 700 miles per hour. The next month, on October 15, he broke the sound barrier with a run of 760.343 miles per hour—the current world land speed record. To date Green is the only person in history to travel at supersonic speeds on land. Nevertheless, Breedlove has not entirely abandoned the idea of doing it as well, and since he is only in his early seventies, it is too soon to count him out.

Of all the major figures profiled in this book, Breedlove is in the minority at least in one respect: He is still alive. And long may he flourish. We say the same for George Barris, Dan Gurney, Carroll Shelby, Alex Xydias, and other living members of the original Hot Rod Generation. But many in this generation have passed on, as have, of course, those from the generations before them. This would be sad except that, in the words of Fresno's William Saroyan, in the time of their lives, these men and women truly lived. May the same thing be said for all of us, when our time comes.

And what would these late, great personalities think about the state of automobiles in California and the United States today? It's pure speculation, but one thing is certain: They were all strong individuals, and they would surely hold strong opinions that reflected their own individual experiences and own ways of thinking. That said, they would be truly shocked, I believe, at the state of the American car industry today. These once-mighty companies, which have meant so much to this country, fallen on such hard times with such uncertain futures. Equally dismaying to them would be the state of our energy affairs. In 1950 the United States was energy independent, at least so far as gas and oil were concerned, whereas today we import up to 70 percent of the oil we use from foreign countries.

If innovators such as Fred Offenhauser and Harry A. Miller were alive today, it's a good bet they would be involved, somehow, in producing more energy-efficient vehicles. Saving gasoline and finding the most efficient gasoline mixtures are, and have always been, essential to racing. Besides racing, these men also experimented with passenger cars, and it would likely not surprise them to hear that a California company, Tesla Motors of San Carlos, is seeking to produce a high-mileage, high-powered electric sports car. It remains to be seen if the highly publicized Tesla venture will succeed, or if electrics or any of the alternative fuel vehicles now being discussed to replace gasoline engines will live up to the high expectations placed upon them by their supporters, but one thing is sure: Many of the ideas for new types of vehicles and new ways of doing things will come from individuals, experimenting with their friends in the dark creative ferment of their garages.

In these matters and all others having to do with car trends, it is also a safe bet that California will lead the way, or at least be at the front of the pack. To test one of its experimental hydrogen cars, Honda let a southern California family drive it around for two years, the thinking being that if you truly wished to see how an experimental vehicle ran in real-world conditions, give it to a family in Los Angeles. *They'll* show you. Similarly, in the early 1990s, when Starbucks wished to test-market its idea for drive-through coffee shops, where did they build the first ones? Southern California, naturally. When the idea proved successful there, Starbucks rolled it out into other areas of the country.

Southern California remains a center of automotive design in the United States. Most of the major automobile companies have design studios there, and these studios have hatched some of the best automobile creations of recent years, including the Volkswagen New Beetle and Audi TT, Volkswagen/Audi Design Center, Santa Monica; the BMW Z4, BMW Designworks/USA, in the old stagecoach stop of Newbury Park; the Chrysler Pacifica and Chrysler 300, Daimler-Chrysler, Carlsbad; the Nissan Urge concept car (with the X-Box 360 inside), Nissan Design America, La Jolla; and the diesel-electric hybrid Ford Reflex, Ford Motor's California Advance Production Creation Group, Irvine. Many of the designers at these studios hail from the Art Center College of Design in Pasadena, one of the leading industrial-design schools in the world.

It will not come as a shock to anyone who has seen a movie recently that the Hollywood tradition of chasing cars around on screen and cracking them up remains alive and well. It doesn't really matter what the cars of tomorrow will run on—gas, electric, hybrid, plug-in hybrid, hydrogen, ethanol, solar—moviemakers are going to find ways to create mayhem with them. The 2001 film *The Fast and the Furious* helped to popularize the "tuners" car trend. Generally speaking, tuners are revved-up Japanese imports that are driven fast by revved-up teenagers. Begun originally in Japan, the craze quickly got picked up and pushed to its limits by southern California teens who started customizing their Toyotas and Hondas and racing them on the streets. As with hot rods and low-riders, tuners have generated a mini-industry of clubs, races, magazines, websites, books, movies, video games and accessories.

MTV's *Pimp My Ride*, shot in the Los Angeles area, and *Monster Garage*, featuring Long Beach biker Jesse James, are two television programs that, like the oldtime *77 Sunset Strip*, with Kookie and his custom hot rod, celebrate new forms of alien motor life from planet California.

The California imported sports car scene, begun in the late 1940s and '50s, shows no signs of slowing down either. Los Angeles is the undisputed American capital of super-expensive imports: Mercedes, Ferraris, Lamborghinis, and Bugatis, each costing hundreds of thousands of dollars and sometimes into the millions. This was dramatized most spectacularly by the 2006 crash of an Enzo Ferrari on the Pacific Coast Highway in Malibu. One of only four hundred such cars in the world, the Enzo Ferrari crashed into a phone pole at 160 miles per hour. Its driver lived to tell the tale, but the tale he told police had some holes in it. He claimed that he was only a passenger in the car and that the man who was really behind the wheel had escaped into the hills after the crack-up. This man—the one and only person in the totaled Ferrari; there was no passenger—was later charged with theft and other crimes.

Begun in 1977 and still flourishing today, the annual Long Beach Grand Prix is a descendant of the old Santa Monica Road Race and the early 1950s California sports car scene: an international cast of characters driving very fast machines around the streets of the city. San Jose also hosted a Grand Prix event that has since been discontinued.

Not every California motor trend can be classified as wonderful or benign, of course. Despite the efforts of the Air Resources Board and other government agencies, California's air consistently ranks among the worst in the country. Parking and traffic cause more headaches than ever, and road safety remains an awful problem. Americans worry about crime, terrorism, war, disease, earthquakes, fire, hurricanes, economic hardship, global warming, chemical and environmental hazards, and accidents, but the most dangerous thing they do, on a daily basis, is climb into an automobile. In 2006 more than forty-two thousand Americans died in traffic accidents. This includes cars, trucks, and motorcycles, and drivers, passengers, pedestrians, bicyclists, and bystanders. That same year more than twelve hundred Californians were killed in car accidents caused by drunk drivers.

Many personalities have passed through these pages, and every effort has been made to sum up their stories in the text. One person whose story has not been told in full, however, is the one who started the book: Carl Breer. This book covers many decades and several generations but really takes place over the course of one man's lifetime, that man being Breer. He was a teenager when he built his homemade steamer in Los Angeles in 1901 during the first great wave of automobile experimentation. Then, after working for California car companies and graduating from Caltech and Stanford, he went east to be in on the ground floor of the creation of the Chrysler Corporation. At Chrysler he pioneered hydraulic brakes and aerodynamic automobile design and used his considerable talents during World War II to help defend freedom and defeat tyranny. His engineering team at Chrysler undertook more than a thousand projects for the United States Armed Forces, such as the design and building of aircraft engines and engines for Sherman and Pershing tanks. After the war Breer's family participated in a minor but not insignificant event in Los Angeles history. One of Carl's older brothers was Henry Breer who, like Carl, was born on South San Pedro Street in the first brick house in the city. But unlike Carl, Henry did not chase the hot new early–twentieth-century trend of automobiles. Instead he followed the path of his blacksmith father, Iron Louis Breer, and became a harness maker for wagons and carts. Henry opened a shop on Aliso Street and worked as a harness maker for nearly sixty years until May 21, 1945, when he shut the doors for the last time and walked away. His shop was the last in Los Angeles to make harnesses. Five days after he retired, Henry died of natural causes at the age of seventy-five.

In the 1950s Carl Breer also retired, to spend more time with his wife of many years at their suburban Grosse Point, Michigan home and to write his memoirs. He had raised a family and had children and grandchildren. He had formed friendships that had stayed with him all his life, meanwhile doing work that had brought him great success, the respect of his peers, and much enjoyment and personal satisfaction. He had contributed to the advancement of a great if flawed machine that had helped to build a great if flawed nation. It was time to hand the wheel over to the next generation, and so he did.

One thing he never lost track of throughout his life was that old steam chariot, the one he had let his friend and mentor Mr. Fisher drive on its second day of operation and that Mr. Fisher, to his embarrassment, ran into a ditch. But Breer restored the car to running order, took it on fishing trips with his brother to the San Gabriel Mountains, and squired girls around town in it. After he went to Stanford and ultimately to Detroit, he left it in the care of his parents. After they died his sister kept it at her house. Nearing the end of his run with Chrysler, Breer naturally began to think back on his beginnings, and in the early 1940s he had the car restored to its ancient luster. In 1946, after the end of World War II, Breer and his youngest son Tom rode the refurbished steamer in a jubilee parade on the streets of Detroit. For the occasion Breer wore a motoring hat, goggles, and gloves that he had kept since boyhood. He handled the tiller and his son pushed the foot button that triggered the steam whistle. "Every time the whistle blew as we drove along," said Breer, "the crowd would let out a shriek and holler."

Of all the cars he designed and was involved with, none of them ever meant as much to him as that roofless one-seater with the two-cylinder double-acting steam engine. It was the car he built and drove when he was young, and it was the car that reminded him of the sweetness of youth and the swiftness of time's passage. That steamer wasn't just a machine, it was a piece of him. It represented a piece of his life and his past, and what he felt for it was something close to love.

Breer died in 1970. After his death his family donated the steamer to the Petersen Automotive Museum in Los Angeles. It is on display today. It is the first exhibit that visitors see when they enter the museum's section on southern California.

ACKNOWLEDGMENTS

This book came about only through the efforts of many people. Bob McNeely, board chairman of the California Historical Society, originated the idea for it, and to him I am most grateful. This has been without doubt the most challenging and compelling project I've ever done. Stephen Becker, formerly with the California Historical Society, got the ball rolling, and David Crosson, its executive director, picked it up and kept it going. Without these three and Malcolm Margolin, this book would not exist. Malcolm, publisher and sage of Heyday Books, was also present at its creation and helped to foster its development. Jeannine Gendar did what many editors at other publishing houses no longer do: she edited. Her suggestions for changes and trims helped tighten the book, and I appreciate her thought and care. Many thanks to everyone else at Heyday for all their excellent work and contributions in editing, photo research, design and many other areas, especially Gayle Wattawa, Lisa K. Manwill, and Diane Lee.

When I began research on this book, practically the first place I went was Blackhawk Museum in Danville, where auto historians Fred Zimmerman and Fred Kern kindly and patiently shared their expertise with me. Diane Curry of the Hayward Area Historical Society provided me with articles about early East Bay motoring and one of her enthusiasms, the Oakland Speedway. I spent a very pleasant afternoon learning about farm vehicles at the Hays Antique Truck Museum in Woodland. At the Towe Automotive Museum in Sacramento, the "Old Schoolmaster" Bill Millard filled me in on Sacramento automobile culture. Janet Baker, Tracey Panek, and especially John Goepel of the AAA of Northern California, Nevada, and Utah in San Francisco answered my questions and provided help as needed. Goepel, an editor and writer who has since retired from the organization, read the *Wheels of Change* manuscript prior to publication, and his research on the old automobile palaces of Van Ness served as the basis for my writing on that subject.

This book would have been a far, far different work, and not nearly as complete, without the contributions of Morgan Yates of the Automobile Club of Southern California in Los Angeles. Like John Goepel, Yates read the manuscript before publication and did an outstanding job of catching mistakes and adding editorial suggestions to improve the book. Morgan also tipped me off to the online historical archives of the *Los Angeles Times*, which proved invaluable to me.

The *Los Angeles Times* deserves high praise for opening up its archives to the public and writers like myself. Many are quick to remind us of the old saw that if we ignore history, we're condemned to repeat the mistakes of the past. But so much of what we know about history today is based on inaccurate or incomplete information. By putting their archives into a scrollable, searchable online database, and making it available to the public, the *Times* and other newspapers provide an immense public service that helps to correct the historical record and any lingering falsehoods and mistaken impressions we may have about the past.

Many thanks to JoAnn Carlson and everyone at the Southern California Timing Association. My day of watching the time trials at El Mirage Dry Lake was one of the most enjoyable I had while researching the book. That day at El Mirage I spent with my friend Bob Newlon. He and his wife, Shoba, let me stay at their house in Malibu while I drove around to see other Los Angeles automobile sights. On other trips to Los Angeles—needless to say, for this book, I spent a good chunk of time there—I stayed with Gary and Sherry Grillo and their daughters in Silver Lake. One night they took me to the happening Friday-night hot rod spot of Bob's Big Boy in Burbank, which was a total hoot. On other trips to the Southland I saw a 1953 Jaguar XK on display at the San Diego Automotive Museum in Balboa Park, ate at the vintage McDonald's in Downey, saw the storied Pomona Speedway, admired the lineup of dragsters at the Wally Parks Motorsports Museum, walked downtown Los Angeles to see where Carl Breer lived and rode his bicycle, imagined the long-gone Gilmore Stadium on the site of the current Farmer's Market, toured the Miracle Mile, and logged several productive and enjoyable hours at the Petersen Automotive Museum.

Others who have read chapters and made corrections and comments are Harold Peters of the Miller/Offenhauser Historical Society and Richard Earl, Harley Earl's grandson. Both men operate excellent websites on their respective passions. Martha A. Crosley Graham helped me dig out information on early Los Angeles personalities through her website. Captain Larry Schneider, Fire Station 50, Los Angeles Fire Department, pointed me to an 1890s Edison film showing traffic on Spring Street before the arrival of the automobile.

Laura Verlaque at the Pasadena History Museum generously sent me articles about Lester Whitman and Eugene Hammond and early Pasadena motoring history. Nilda Rego's historical column in the *Contra Costa Times* has proved useful to me many times, and Bobbi Vierra of the St. Helena Public Library helped me find an 1896 magazine piece by David Starr Jordan that I was trying to hunt down. Susan Goldstein of the San Francisco Public Library gave me leads on John Meyer, and Tami Suzuki also helped in this regard. To get a sense of what it must have been like to drive the first gas motorcar in California, I walked around Meyer's old neighborhood in Noe Valley. From there I went to Tom Frye, the curator emeritus of the Oakland Museum of California, which is the home of Meyer's Pioneer today. The Oakland Museum's art curator, Phil Linhares, is a hot rod buff, and his hot rod show at the Bedford Gallery in Walnut Creek gave me insights and a whole host of cool cars to look at.

Speaking of cool cars, I saw lots more at the Good Guys custom show in Pleasanton, where another good friend of mine, Dan Crouch, shared his knowledge and love for these machines. Dan and I also took in the NHRA drags at Infineon Raceway one warm August afternoon in Sonoma. With my brother Dave I ventured down to the historic car races at Laguna Seca (starring that ancient road warrior, the Blitzen Benz), followed by a meal of fried artichokes at the Giant Artichoke in Castroville, an example of "giant object" architecture with its gargantuan artichoke out front. After a tour of Seventeen Mile Drive and the old Pebble Beach Road Race, my family and I joined my father-in-law Bruno Kaiser for a rousing night of dirt track racing at the Ocean Speedway in Watsonville. To borrow a phrase that is usually applied to baseball, if you wish to understand the heart and soul of America, go to a dirt track race in a small town in farm country.

Gregory Franzwa, author and publisher of Patrice Press and an expert on the Lincoln Highway, knows all about small towns in the countryside. I took copious notes during his talk at the Vallejo Naval and Historical Museum. Franzwa researches his Lincoln Highway books the best way one can: by driving. This was what I did with this book too, driving thousands of miles around the state over the past three years—east and west, north and south. One time, based on a Franzwa tip, we headed down to the Duarte garage, a restored early-1900s gas station in Livermore. When we got there, it was closed and all we could do was press our noses to the windows and peer inside. But that's the way it goes with historical research. Sometimes you find what you're looking for, and sometimes you peer through a dusty window, hoping for a glimpse. But you have to follow the trails wherever they lead. And if you want to learn about cars and driving, you've got to hit the road.

For accompanying me on many of those road trips, I must thank my daughter Annie, my sons Hank and Gabe and my wife, Jennifer. Jennifer reads everything I write before the publisher sees it, and she helps me in every way possible. I couldn't do any of this without her.

Finally, I must thank, above all, the newspaper reporters and columnists whose work I drew from to write this book. Most of them, like the people they were writing about, are long gone now, but their work endures and with continued access to it, it will remain a gift to future generations. For the most part these writers did not make history, but they were the ones who recorded it and wrote it down. Without them our world, and our understanding of the world, would be much the poorer for it.

BIBLIOGRAPHY

Books and Articles

Adams, Ansel. *An Autobiography.* Boston, Mass.: Little, Brown and Company, 1985.

Adler, Dennis. *The Art of the Sports Car: The Greatest Designs of the Twentieth Century.* New York: HarperResource, 2002.

Ambrose, Stephen E. *Citizen Soldiers.* New York: Simon and Schuster, 1997.

———. *D-Day.* New York: Simon and Schuster, 1994.

Basinger, Jeanne. *Silent Stars.* New York: Knopf, 1999.

Batchelor, Dean. *The American Hot Rod.* Osceola, Wisc.: Motorbooks International, 1995.

———. *Harrah's Automobile Collection: One Man's Tribute to the Great Automobiles of the World.* Pontiac, Mich.: GP Publishing, 1984.

Bayley, Stephen. *Harley Earl and the Dream Machine.* New York: Knopf, 1983.

Beal, Richard A. *Highway 17: The Road to Santa Cruz.* Aptos, Calif.: Pacific Group, 1991.

Bell, James D. "Companion Car to Cadillac," *Automobile Quarterly,* Vol. 5, No. 3, Winter 1967.

Berg, A. Scott. *Lindbergh.* New York: Berkley Books, 1998.

Bergerud, Eric M. *Fire in the Sky: The Air War in the Pacific.* Boulder, Colo.: Westview Press, 2001.

Biddle, Wayne. *Barons of the Sky: From Early Flight to Strategic Warfare.* New York: Henry Holt and Company, 1991.

Borgeson, Griffith. *The Golden Age of the American Racing Machine.* New York: Bonanza Books, 1966.

———. "Madness at Muroc: The Great Duesenberg-Mercedes Match Race," *Automobile Quarterly,* Vol. 18, No. 3, Fall 1980.

———. "1950 National Roadster Show," in Editors, *The Best of Hot Rod Magazine, 1949–1959.*

Bottles, Scott L. *Los Angeles and the Automobile.* Berkeley: University of California Press, 1987.

Boyne, Walter J. *Beyond the Horizons: The Lockheed Story.* New York: St. Martin's Press, 1998.

Bradley, James. *Flyboys.* Boston: Little, Brown and Company, 2003.

Breer, Carl, with Anthony Yanik. *The Birth of Chrysler Corporation and Its Engineering Legacy.* Danvers, Md.: Society of Automotive Engineers, 1995.

Brilliant, Ashleigh. *The Great Car Craze: How Southern California Collided with the Automobile in the 1920s.* Santa Barbara: Woodbridge Press, 1989.

Brinkley, Douglas. *Wheels for the World: Henry Ford, His Company, and a Century of Progress.* New York: Viking, 2003.

Burgess, John W., and Briggs Cunningham. *Connoisseur's Choice: Racing, Sports and Touring Cars.* New York: Walker and Co., 1979.

Butler, John L. *First Highways of America.* Iola, Wisc.: Krause Publications, 1994.

Catlin, Russ. "The Great Vail," *Automobile Quarterly,* Vol. 15, No. 4, Winter 1977.

Caughey, John Walton. *California.* Englewood Cliffs, N.J.: Prentice Hall, 1953.

Caughey, John and LaRee. *Los Angeles: Biography of a City.* Berkeley: University of California Press, 1976.

Clee, Paul. *Before Hollywood: From Shadow Play to the Silver Screen.* New York: Clarion Books, 2005.

Conde, John A. *Cars with Personalities.* Keego Harbor, Mich.: Arnold-Potter Publishing, 1982.

Cotter, Tom. *The Cobra in the Barn: Great Stories of Automotive Archaeology.* St. Paul, Minn.: MBI, 2005.

Curcio, Vincent. *Chrysler: The Life and Times of an Automotive Pioneer.* New York: Oxford University Press, 2000.

Darrin, Howard. "Disaster Is My Business," *Automobile Quarterly,* Vol. 7, No. 1, Summer 1968.

Davidson, Donald. "George Salih's Little Beauty," *Monterey Historic Automobile Races Program,* August 2007.

Davis, David. *Play by Play: Los Angeles Sports Photography, 1890–1989.* Los Angeles: Angel City Press, 2004.

DeWitt, John. *Cool Cars, High Art: The Rise of Kustom Kulture.* Jackson, Miss.: University Press of Mississippi, 2001.

Didion, Joan. *Where I Was From.* New York: Knopf, 2003.

———. *The White Album.* New York: Simon and Schuster, 1979.

Dunne, Florence. *John Steinbeck: America's Author.* Berkeley Heights, N.J.: Enslow Publishers, 2000.

Durrell, Lawrence. *The Henry Miller Reader.* New York: New Directions, 1950.

Earl, Harley. "Harley Earl Recalls LaSalle," *Automobile Quarterly,* Vol. 5, No. 3, Winter 1967.

———. "I Dream Automobiles," *Saturday Evening Post,* August 7, 1954, pp. 19, 82.

East, E. E., and H. F. Holley. "Traffic Survey, Los Angeles Metropolitan Area 1937." Los Angeles: Automobile Club of Southern California, 1937.

Editors. *The Best of Hot Rod Magazine, 1949–1959*, St. Paul, Minn.: Motorbooks International, 2003.

Egan, Timothy. *The Worst Hard Time.* New York: Houghton-Mifflin, 2006.

Eisenhower, Dwight D. *At Ease: Stories I Tell to Friends.* New York: Doubleday and Company, 1967.

Fenster, Julie M. *Race of the Century: The Heroic True Story of the 1908 New York to Paris Auto Race.* New York: Crown, 2005.

Ford, John Anson. "Smog Settles Over Los Angeles," in Caughey, *California.*

Foster, Mark S. *Henry J. Kaiser: Builder in the Modern American West.* Austin: University of Texas Press, 1989.

Fowler, Gene, and Bill Crawford. *Border Radio.* Austin: University of Texas Press, 2002.

Fox, Stephen. "The Strange Triumph of Abner Doble," *Invention and Technology Magazine,* Vol. 14, No. 1, Summer 1998.

Fradkin, Philip L. *The Great Earthquake and Firestorms of 1906*. Berkeley: University of California Press, 2005.

Ganahl, Pat. *The American Custom Car*. St. Paul, Minn.: MBI, 2001.

Gehring, Wes D. *James Dean: Rebel with a Cause*. Indianapolis: Indiana Historical Society Press, 2005.

Georgano, G. N. *A History of Sports Cars*. New York: Bonanza Books, 1970.

Gish, Lillian, and Ann Pinchot. *The Movies, Mr. Griffith, and Me*. Englewood Cliffs, N.J.: Prentice Hall, 1969.

Groome, Kevin, and Jo Liana King. *The Pioneer*. San Francisco: J. L. King, 1990.

Gross, Ken. "Bridging Old and New: Bohman and Schwartz Custom Cadillac," *Automobile Quarterly*, Vol. 33, No. 2, September 1994.

———. "Death Be Not Proud," in Cotter, *The Cobra in the Barn*.

Gunnell, John, ed. *Standard Catalog of American Cars, 1946–1975*. Iola, Wisc.: Krause Publications, 1982.

Harris, Warren G. *Clark Gable: A Biography*. New York: Harmony Books, 2002.

———. *Gable and Lombard*. New York: Simon and Schuster, 1974.

Harrison, George. "Roads and Highways of California," *California's Magazine*, Vol. 1, July 1915.

Hart, James D. *A Companion to California*. Berkeley: University of California Press, 1987.

Hayes, Derek. *Historical Atlas of California*. Berkeley: University of California Press, 2007.

Hendry, Maurice D. "The Steam Odyssey of Abner Doble," *Automobile Quarterly*, Vol. 8, No. 1, Summer 1969.

Hess, Alan. *Googie Redux: Ultramodern Roadside Architecture*. San Francisco: Chronicle Books, 2004.

———. *Rancho Deluxe: Rustic Dreams and Real Western Living*. San Francisco: Chronicle Books, 2000.

Hillenbrand, Laura. *Seabiscuit*. New York: Ballantine Books, 2001.

Hiney, Tom. *Raymond Chandler: A Biography*. New York: Atlantic Monthly Press, 1997.

Hirohata, Bob. "Kross Kountry in a Kustom," *Rod and Custom*, October 1953.

Hoag, Gael S. *A Complete Official Road Guide of the Lincoln Highway, Fifth Edition, 1924*. Facsimile reprint edition. Tucson, Ariz: Patrice Press,1993.

Hokanson, Drake. *The Lincoln Highway: Main Street Across America*. Iowa City: University of Iowa Press, 1988.

Irvine, R.C., Marsden Manson, and J. L. Maude. "Biennial Report of the Bureau of Highways, 1895–1896." Sacramento: State of California, 1896.

Janis, Maria Cooper. *Gary Cooper Off Camera: A Daughter Remembers*. New York: Harry Abrams, 1999.

Jeffers, H. Paul. *Ace of Aces: The Life of Capt. Eddie Rickenbacker*. New York: Ballantine, 2003.

Jordan, David Starr. *California and the Californians*. San Francisco: Robertson, 1907. Published in *Atlantic Monthly,* Nov. 1898.

Kerouac, Jack. *On the Road*. New York: Penguin, 1976. Reprint of the Viking Compass Edition, 1959.

Kimes, Beverly Rae. *The Star and the Laurel: The Centennial History of Daimler, Mercedes, and Benz*. Montvale, N.J.: Mercedes-Benz, 1986.

Kimes, Beverly Rae, and Henry Austin Clark. *Standard Catalog of American Cars, 1805–1942.* Iola, Wisc.: Krause Publications, 1985.

Leffingwell, Randy. *Caterpillar.* St. Paul, Minn.: MBI, 1994. Supplied by Diane Curry, Hayward Area Historical Society.

Liebs, Chester H. *Main Street to Miracle Mile: American Roadside Architecture.* Baltimore: Johns Hopkins University Press, 1985, 1995.

Loomis, Frederic. *Miner, Preacher, Doctor, Teacher.* Walnut Creek, Calif.: Hardscratch Press, 2000.

Lorimer, Michael. "Super 8 Victoria: Queen of the Darrin Packards," *Automobile Quarterly*, Vol. 7, No. 1, Summer 1968.

Louvish, Simon. *Keystone: The Life and Clowns of Mack Sennett.* New York: Faber and Faber, 2003.

Lynch, Michael T. "The Rise and Fall of the Indianapolis Roadster," *Monterey Historic Automobile Races Program*, August 2007.

MacMinn, Strother. "Fifties Finest: Hits of the Design Decade," *Automobile Quarterly*, Vol. 25, No. 1, 1987.

McConnell, Curt. *Coast to Coast by Automobile: The Pioneering Trips, 1899–1908.* Stanford, Calif.: Stanford University Press, 2000.

———. *A Reliable Car and a Woman Who Knows It: The First Coast-to-Coast Auto Trips by Women, 1899–1916.* Jefferson, N.C.: McFarland and Company, 2000.

McCullough, David G., ed. *The American Heritage Picture Dictionary of World War II.* New York: American Heritage Publishing, 1966.

McWilliams, Carey. *California: The Great Exception.* Berkeley: University of California Press, 1999.

———. *Fool's Paradise.* Berkeley: Heyday Books, 2001.

Meyers, Jeffrey. *Gary Cooper: An American Hero.* New York: William Morrow, 1998.

Miller, Henry. "Automotive Passacaglia," in Durrell, *The Henry Miller Reader.*

Mitchell, S. L. "The Automobile in California Life and Industry," *California's Magazine*, Vol. 1, July 1915.

Motter, Tom. *A History of the Oakland Speedway, 1931–1941.* Rancho Cordova, Calif.: Vintage Images, 2002.

Nadeau, Remi. "Enter the Moviemakers," in Caughey, *Los Angeles.*

Nolan, William F. *Barney Oldfield: The Life and Times of America's Legendary Speed King.* Carpinteria, Calif.: Brown Fox Books, 2002. Reprint, New York: G. P. Putnam's Sons, 1961.

———. *Phil Hill: Yankee Champion*, New York: G. P. Putnam's Sons, 1962.

———. "Ralph De Palma," *Automobile Quarterly*, Vol. 2, No. 3, Fall 1968.

Norris, Frank. *The Octopus.* 1901. Reprint, New York: Penguin Books, 1986.

Olin, Spencer C., Jr. *California's Prodigal Sons: Hiram Johnson and the Progressives, 1911–1917.* Berkeley: University of California Press, 1968.

Osmer, Harold L. *Where They Raced Lap Two: Auto Racing Venues in Southern California, 1900–2000.* Chatsworth, Calif.: Harold L. Osmer Publishing, 2000.

Parks, Wally. "Bonneville Nationals 1950," in Editors, *The Best of Hot Rod Magazine, 1949–1959.*

Penland, Paige R. *Lowrider: History, Pride, Culture.* St. Paul, Minn.: MBI, 2003.

Perry, George. *James Dean.* London: DK Publishing, 2005.

Pollock, Dale. *Skywalking: The Life and Films of George Lucas.* Hollywood: Samuel French, 1990.

Ramsey, Alice. *Alice's Drive.* Tucson, Ariz.: Patrice Press, 2005. Reprinted as *Veil, Duster, and Tire Iron*, with annotations and notes by Gregory M. Franzwa. Pasadena: Castle Press, 1961.

Rawls, James J., and Walton Bean. *California: An Interpretive History.* San Francisco: McGraw-Hill, 1998.

Rider, Fremont. *Rider's California: A Guide-Book for Travelers.* New York: Macmillan, 1925.

Riggs, L. Spencer. "Building the Offy," *Automobile Quarterly,* Vol. 31, No. 3, Spring 1993.

———. "The Fifty-Year Reign of the Immortal Offy," *Automobile Quarterly,* Vol. 31, No. 3, Spring 1993.

Rittenhouse, Jack D. *American Horse-Drawn Vehicles.* New York: Bonanza Books, 1948.

Rowsome, Frank, Jr *The Verse by the Side of the Road.* New York: Plume Books, 1965.

Ruddock, Ken. "Automobiles and Expositions: Affairs to Remember," *Automobile Quarterly*, Vol. 31, No. 3, Spring 1993.

Sandford, Christopher. *McQueen.* New York: Taylor Trade Publishing, 2003.

Scalzo, Joe. "The Glamour Years of Racing on the West Coast," *Automobile Quarterly*, Vol. 19, No. 2, second quarter, 1981.

Scharff, Virginia. *Taking the Wheel: Women and the Coming of the Motor Age.* Albuquerque: University of New Mexico Press, 1991.

Scott, Harrison Irving. *The Ridge Route: The Road that United California.* Torrance, Calif.: Torrance, 2003.

Siecyk, C. R., ed. *Kustom Kulture: Von Dutch, Ed "Big Daddy" Roth, Robert Williams, and Others.* San Francisco: Last Gasp, Laguna Art Museum, 1993.

Sloan, Alfred P. *My Years with General Motors.* New York: Bantam Doubleday Dell, 1963.

Stein, Gertrude. *Everybody's Autobiography.* New York: Random House, 1937. Reprint, Cooper Square Publishers, 1971.

Stein, Ralph. *The Treasury of the Automobile.* New York: Golden Press, 1961.

Steinbeck, John. *Bombs Away: The Story of a Bomber Team.* New York: Viking Press, 1942.

———. *Cannery Row.* New York: Viking Press, 1945.

Storke, Thomas M., and Walter Tompkins. *California Editor.* Santa Barbara: News-Press Publishing Company, 1966.

Talley-Jones, Kathy, and Letitia Burns-O'Connor. *The Road Ahead: The Automobile Club of Southern California, 1900–2000.* Los Angeles: Automobile Club of Southern California, 2000.

Terrill, Marshall. *Steve McQueen: Portrait of an American Rebel.* New York: Donald I. Fine, 1993.

Todd, Frank Morton. *The Story of the Panama Pacific International Exposition.* New York: G. P. Putnam's Sons, 1921.

Turner, Ted, and John Sparks. *The Spirit of the Road: 100 Years of the California State Automobile Association.* San Francisco: Via Books, 2000.

Ulmann, Alec. "Mercedes: The Man Behind the Name," *Automobile Quarterly,* Vol. 5, No. 3, Winter 1967.

Wallis, Michael. *Route 66: The Mother Road.* New York: St. Martin's Press, 1990.

Washington, Rosemary. *Racing's Fast Little Cars.* Minneapolis: Lerner Publications, 1980.

Watson, Aldren A. *The Blacksmith, Ironworker, and Farrier.* New York: W. W. Norton and Company, 1977.

White, Gordon Eliot. *Lost Race Tracks: Treasures of Automobile Racing.* Hudson, Wisc.: Iconografix, 2002.

———. *The Marvelous Mechanical Designs of Harry A. Miller.* Hudson, Wisc.: Iconografix, 2004.

Witzel, Michael Karl. *The American Gas Station.* Osceola, Wisc.: MBI, 1992.

———. *Gas Stations Coast to Coast.* MBI, 2000.

———. *Route 66 Remembered.* MBI, 1996.

Wolfe, Tom. *Kandy-Kolored Tangerine-Flake Streamline Baby.* New York: Farrar, Straus and Giroux, 1965.

———. *The Pump House Gang.* New York: Farrar, Straus and Giroux, 1968.

———. *The Right Stuff Illustrated.* New York: Farrar, Straus and Giroux, 1979.

Yagoda, Ben. *Will Rogers: A Biography.* New York: HarperCollins West, 1994.

Yallop, David A. *The Day the Laughter Stopped.* New York: St. Martin's Press, 1976.

Yates, Brock. *The Critical Path: Inventing an Automobile and Reinventing a Corporation.* Boston: Little, Brown, 1996.

———. *The Hot Rod: Resurrection of a Legend.* St. Paul, Minn.: MBI, 2003.

———. *World's Greatest Outlaw Road Race.* St. Paul, Minn.: MBI, 2002.

Yeager, Chuck, and Charles Leerhsen. *Press On! Further Adventures in the Good Life.* New York: Bantam, 1988.

Newspapers

Battle Creek (Michigan) Enquirer

Contra Costa Times

Detroit News

Hayward Daily Review

Las Vegas Review-Journal

Los Angeles Times

New York Times

Pasadena Star-News

Riverside News-Enterprise

San Francisco Chronicle

Magazines

The Automobile

Automobile Quarterly

Bulb Horn Magazine
Car and Driver
Drive Magazine
Holiday
Hot Rod Magazine
Indy Car Series Magazine
Life
Motorland
Saturday Evening Post
Touring Topics
Westways

Websites

Allamericanracers.com
Americanheritage.com
Arizonaracinghistory.com
Art Center College of Design, artcenter.edu
Theautochannel.com
Automobile Safety Improvements, web.bryant.edu/~ehu/h364proj/sprg_97/dirksen/index.htm
Automotivehalloffame.org
Bay Area Radio Museum, bayarearadio.org
Bell Auto Parts official website, bell-autoparts.com
California Biography Project, history.sloco.net
California Digital Library, cdlib.org
California Highway Patrol, chp.ca.gov
California Historian, californiahistorian.org
Classic Car-Nection, car-nection.org
Corbis.com
Cragar.com
Earthsignals.com
ESPN, espn.go.com
Fatality Analysis Reporting System, www-fars.nhtsa.dot.gov/Main/index.aspx
Filmmonthly.com
Hagginmuseum.org
Hays Antique Truck Museum, truckmuseum.org
Hickoksports.com
Highwayhost.org
History of Lincoln Heights, lincolnheightsla.com
Hot Rod Magazine, hotrod.com
Internet Movie Database, imdb.com
International Motorsports Hall of Fame, motorsportshalloffame.com

John Heinz website, johnheinzlegacy.com
Los Angeles Fire Department Historical Archive, lafire.com
Library of Congress, American Memory, memory.loc.gov
Mazda Raceway [at] Laguna Seca, laguna-seca.com
McDonald's: The Historic Site, route-66.com/mcdonalds
Miller/Offenhauser Historical Society, milleroffy.com
Museum of the City of San Francisco, sfmuseum.org
National Aviation Hall of Fame, nationalaviation.com
National Corvette Museum, corvettemuseum.com
National Hot Rod Association, nhra.com
National Park Service, nps.org
New York Times, nytimes.com
Official Carroll Shelby Website, carrollshelby.com
Official Harley Earl Website, carofthecentury.com
Old Yeller II: 1959 Balchowsky Buick Special, oldyeller2.com
Oldradio.com
Petersen Automotive Museum, petersenmuseum.org
Prewarbuick.com
Ridgeroute.com
Salon.com
San Diego Historical Society, sandiegohistory.org
Santa Clarita Valley History in Pictures, scvhistory.com
Sunsetsaga.com
Time magazine, time.com
Trojan Family Magazine, University of Southern California, usc.edu/dept/pubrel/trojan_family
Vernacular Language North, verlang.com
Wikipedia, wikipedia.org

SOURCE NOTES

AP = Associated Press
LAT = *Los Angeles Times*
SFC = *San Francisco Chronicle*
UPI = United Press International

Chapter 1: Blacksmith's Son

"We would build": Breer, *The Birth of Chrysler Corporation*, p. 11/**Empire Steam Laundry:** Exhibit placard, Petersen Automotive Museum, observed by author, Feb. 2007/**A few blocks away:** The location of the rail yards in relation to the Breer smithy are based on a walking tour by the author and close study of a 1900 map of Los Angeles published by George F. Cram, Chicago. This map is on public view in the basement History section of the central branch of the Los Angeles Public Library. /**Here cometh the iceman:** Rittenhouse, *American Horse-Drawn Vehicles*, pp. 76–78. Vehicle descriptions are drawn from illustrations on these pages. /**all manner of other vehicles:** "South Spring Street, Los Angeles, Cal." This twenty-seven-second film shot by Edison Motion Pictures on February 24, 1898, shows Spring Street traffic. Library of Congress, American Memory, www.memory.loc.gov. /**The habitués of this park:** "At the City's Gates," *LAT,* Mar. 4, 1901, p. 9. The other quotes describing Elysian Park are from this article and its unnamed correspondent as well. /**"As we walked around":** Breer, *The Birth of Chrysler Corporation,* p. 11/**"thrilled to learn":** Ibid. /**"Before I left":** Ibid., p. 12/**"except for a few sleepy policemen":** "Without Horses, Gasoline Carriage Invented in Los Angeles," *LAT,* May 31, 1897, p. 3. The quotes describing the maiden run of the Erie-Sturgis are taken from this article. /**"burned out":** "Testing the Carriage," *LAT,* June 3, 1897, p. 8/**Mainly it sat:** "Speed Trial Postponed," *LAT,* June 4, 1897, p. 14/**"a light and graceful":** "A Horseless Carriage," *LAT,* July 25, 1899, p. 7/**spotted all around town:** "Horseless Carriage Record," *LAT,* Sept. 10, 1899, p. D1/ **Though it was a little inconvenient:** Author conversation with Fred Zimmerman, auto historian, Blackhawk Museum, Danville, Calif. /**two-cylinder, double-acting:** Breer, *The Birth of Chrysler Corporation,* p. 13/**"I asked if I":** Ibid. /**"proud I was":** Ibid., p. 14/ **forged the steel crankshaft:** Exhibit placard, Petersen Automotive Museum, observed by author, Feb. 2007/**Kodak picture of Carl:** Breer, *The Birth of Chrysler*, photograph, p. 14/**"Finally the day arrived"**: Ibid., p. 15/**"I never wanted that":** Ibid., p. 17

Chapter 2: A Day at the Races

"The sense of freedom": Breer, *The Birth of Chrysler,* p. xii/**"the exhilaration of being your own master":** Ibid./**The storekeepers who carried gasoline:** Ibid., p. 18/**a roomier building:** "Automobile Factory for Los Angeles," *LAT,* May 8, 1902, p. A5/**a starchy tuxedo:** Breer, *The Birth of Chrysler,* p. 19/**"A quick exploration":** Ibid./**"Southern California's first hot-rodder":** Osmer, *Where They Raced Lap Two*, p. 69/**a talented Riverside car man:** "Automobile Factory Sure in Riverside," *LAT,* Aug. 24, 1902, p. 8/**"Our factory is open":** Advertisement, *LAT,* Mar. 6, 1907, p. 16/**Nearby on Bruno Street:** Kimes and Clark, *Standard Catalog,* p. 1451/**Stewart's Automobile Machine Works:** Ibid., p. 1322/**Electric Carriage Works:** Ibid., p. 609/**"the Smithmobile":** Ibid., p. 1277/**"the Shepmobile":** Ibid., p. 1265/**"the Rocket":** Ibid., p. 1222/**"Police Officer J. E. Fay":** "Policeman Built Horseless Carriage," *LAT,* Oct. 13, 1901, p. B5/**"It is interesting to live in the time":** "The Auto's Fight for the Highway," *LAT*, Aug. 11, 1901, p. C3/**royal sum of twenty-four hundred dollars:** "The Auto's Fight for the Highway," *LAT,* Aug. 11, 1901, p. C3. All prices and names come from this article./**a sixty-five-member brass band:** Nolan, *Barney Oldfield*, p. 47/**their Kingpin Chauffeur:** "All Records To Go Today," *LAT,* Nov. 22, 1903, p. B1/**"How do I feel to ride faster than the wind?":** "How the Auto Will Dash in Los Angeles," *LAT,* Nov. 1, 1903, p. B1/**"If anybody will tell you within forty rods":** "At the Races," *LAT,* Oct. 25, 1900, p. I11/**"uncertain as a flea's movements":** Ibid./**head-to-head show-down:** "At the Races," *LAT,* Oct. 27, 1900, p. I8/**"The edible accompaniment served with drinks":** Ibid./**Chamber of Commerce passed a resolution:** "Reckless Driving," *LAT,* Oct. 16, 1902, p. A1/**police on bicycles:** "Twenty Years Ago in Motordom," *LAT,* June 21, 1925, p. I13. The speed trap anecdote is also from this article./**"We just jump in":** "How the Auto Will Dash in Los Angeles," *LAT,* Nov. 1, 1903, p. B1/**"The mist of dust":** Ibid./**"it seemed as if he must scrape the paint":** "Thousands Cheer Barney and Bullet," *LAT,* Nov. 21, 1903, p. A1/**"if Barney's hat":** Ibid./**"It looked this way":** Ibid./**"All sensation is exaggerated":** "How the Auto Will Dash in Los Angeles," *LAT,* Nov. 1, 1903, p. B1

Chapter 3: The Impossible Journey

born and raised in Maine: McConnell, *Coast to Coast by Automobile*, p. 152/**De Dion Bouton:** "Long Automobile Trip," *LAT*, June 23, 1901, p. B7/**Two San Jose brothers:** Frank J. Taylor, "Yosemite's All Year Highway," *Motorland*, July 1926, reprinted in Turner and Sparks, *The Spirit of the Road*, p. 55/**artist, photographer, and prominent member:** "Auto in Yosemite," *LAT*, June 26, 1900, p. 12/**In one of the few photographs:** Talley-Jones and Burns-O'Connor, *The Road Ahead*, p. 31/**How Lester looked:** Photographs of Whitman in 1903, Pasadena Museum of History/**"a jovial, adventure-seeking":** John S. Hammond II, "From Sea to Sea in 1903 in a Curved Dash Oldsmobile," in McConnell, *Coast to Coast by Automobile*, p. 152/**"I am always up to something":** "First Vehicle Up Mountain," *LAT,* June 2, 1907, p. VIII2/**covered about one thousand miles:** "Long

Automobile Trip," *LAT,* June 23, 1901, p. B7/**"My fellow autoist:"** McConnell, *Coast to Coast by Automobile,* p. 150/**"He could lift any wheel:"** Ibid./**on Delacy Street:** Pasadena City Directory, 1904, Pasadena Museum of History/**ride the trolley home:** John S. Hammond II, "Historic Trip Recalled," *Pasadena Star-News*, Sept. 21, 1973, p. D1/**wrote a letter to Ransom E. Olds:** Ibid./**"an ordinary Oldsmobile":** "Another Club Run," *LAT,* July 24, 1903, p. 11/**"L. L. Whitman and E. Hammond":** *The Automobile*, July 18, 1903, p. 72/**drove it down to San Pedro harbor:** "By Auto Across Rockies," *LAT,* July 2, 1903, p. 15/**In his late teens:** McConnell, *Coast to Coast by Automobile,* p. 63/**At the first sight of reporters:** Ibid. p. 98/**accidentally destroyed:** Ibid., p. 106/**Their solution:** Ibid., p. 111/**"a country of nothing but sage brush":** "Another Club Run," *LAT,* July 24, 1903, p. 11/**In his advance planning:** John S. Hammond II, "Historic Trip Recalled," *Pasadena Star-News,* Sept. 21, 1973, p. D1/**"Outfitting included a 100-foot":** John S. Hammond II, "The Whitman-Hammond Curved Dash Olds," *Bulb Horn Magazine*, May–June 1978, p. 18/**dip their wheels into the Pacific:** McConnell, *Coast to Coast by Automobile,* p. 153/ **another photo op:** Ibid., p. 154/**"Without benefit of printed":** John S. Hammond II, "Historic Trip Recalled," *Pasadena Star-News,* Sept. 21, 1973, p. D1/**cut down a small pine:** McConnell, *Coast to Coast by Automobile,* p. 157/**"the car of the future":** Ibid., p. 187/**ex–bicycle repairman:** Kimes and Clark, *Standard Catalog,* p. 614/**"searchlights":** "Record Pair Now on Road," *LAT,* June 15, 1905, p. II3/**tried to recapture the record:** "Whitman After Auto Record," *LAT,* July 11, 1905, p. II3

Chapter 4: San Francisco

only New York, Chicago: "Many Motors in Angel City," *LAT,* Jan. 3, 1909, p. V12/**"The traffic consisted":** "From Horses to Motors," *LAT,* Aug. 24, 1948, p. 15. The article looks back on traffic problems in the early 1900s./**Police controlled the traffic:** Ibid./**"essentially a horse-keeping":** Turner and Sparks, *The Spirit of the Road,* p. 13/ **Mrs. Arthur Sears of Santa Cruz:** Beal, *Highway 17,* p. 74/**"It is no longer safe":** "The Auto's Fight for the Highway," *LAT,* Aug. 11, 1901, p. C3/**sponsored rallies and races:** "Club Run To Be Held Next Sunday," *SFC,* Apr. 17, 1906, p. 8/**more rigorous law enforcement:** "Auto Club Asks Enforcement of Laws," *SFC,* Apr. 15, 1906, p. 49/ **Enlisting the aid:** Turner and Sparks, *The Spirit of the Road,* p. 18/**"The policeman's most frequent":** "Runaways and Glory: Will Passing of Horse Affect Cops?" *LAT,* Mar. 3, 1901, p. C3/**"An amateur chauffeur almost caused":** "Women and Auto in Flames," *SFC,* Apr. 15, 1906, p. 18/**"Miss Morrish is well known":** Ibid./**"Well, I was smitten":** Leffingwell, *Caterpillar,* p. 36./**"I constructed a second":** Ibid./**bought a horse's head:** Hayward Centennials Committee, "Hayward: The First 100 Years," Hayward Area Historical Society, 1975./**seven horsepower engine:** Kimes and Clark, *Standard Catalog,* p. 117/**original home factory:** "San Leandro Plant Shuts," *LAT,* May 6, 1985, p. E2/**"A favorite stunt":** William Klinger, "Pioneering Automobile Insurance," *San Francisco News Letter,* Sept. 5, 1925, reprinted on the Museum of the City of San Francisco's website, http://www.sfmuseum.org/hist/autos.html/**"walked around the summer resort":** Ibid./

drained it of gasoline: Groome and King, *The Pioneer*, p. 10/**A German immigrant:** Photograph, ibid., p. 4/**J. L. Hicks Gas Engine:** Ibid., p. 5/**"Meyer's Folly":** Ibid., p. 7/ **an addition in front:** Author's observation, on a walking tour of this area, Aug. 2006/**a small metal plate:** Author's observation, visit to the Oakland Museum of California, Mar. 2006/**"J. A. Meyer, Machinist and Engineer":** Groome and King, *The Pioneer,* p. 12/**"devil wagons":** From a *SFC* report quoted in Fradkin, *The Great Earthquake*, p. 102/**"The machines did whatever":** Ibid./**Pioneer Auto:** Advertisement, *SFC,* Apr. 15, 1906, p. 49/**local distributor of Columbias:** Columbia Advertisement, *SFC,* Apr. 5, 1906, p. 8/**"the finest automobile station":** "White Steamer versus Gasoline," advertisement, *SFC,* Apr. 5, 1906, p. 8/**"The car moved and rocked":** J. C. Cunningham, "Earthquake," *Motorland,* Mar.–Apr. 1967, pp. 36–39. All quotes from Cunningham are from this article./**"the Pioneer's finest hour":** Groome and King, *The Pioneer,* p. 11/**"I got out the old, faithful transcontinental car":** McConnell, *Coast to Coast by Automobile*, p. 231/**"Miss Dollie Hyland":** Personal ad, *SFC,* Apr. 23, 1906, p. 5/**a Knox truck carrying cans:** J. C. Cunningham, "Earthquake," *Motorland,* Mar.–Apr. 1967, p. 38/**"Keep Out of the Way":** "Keep Out of the Way of the Automobiles," *SFC,* Apr. 22, 1906, p. 2

Chapter 5: Suddenly Shrinking State

Sunset Automobile Company: Kimes and Clark, *Standard Catalog,* p. 1369/**appeared on the front page:** "Will Attempt to Lower His Record," *SFC,* Aug. 3, 1906, p. 9/**"a particularly opportune way":** Quoted in McConnell, *Coast to Coast by Automobile*, p. 232/**Since it had been raining:** "L. L. Whitman to Start this Evening on Transcontinental Tour," *SFC,* Aug. 2, 1906, p. 8/**"a man to do things":** McConnell, *Coast to Coast by Automobile,* p. 260/**"the original speed merchants":** "Many Autos After Glory," *LAT,* July 8, 1905, p. II3/**the first to reach the top:** L. L. Whitman, "First Vehicle Up Mountain," *LAT,* June 2, 1907, p. VIII2/**"There are probably more automobiles":** Quoted in Dorothy K. Hassler, "The Great Pasadena-Altadena Hill Climb," *Westways*, Jan. 1962, p. 30/**Also on South Main:** Display ads, *LAT,* Oct. 9, 1906, p. I6/**California covered a geographical area:** "Good Roads in California," *LAT,* Dec. 8, 1896, p. 6/**as "impulsive," Fenner:** "For Blood and Ducats Is Race," *LAT,* July 28, 1906, p. II3/**"holding up the reputation":** "Reo Man Ready to Race," *LAT,* July 26, 1906, p. II3/**challenged a Santa Fe passenger:** "Auto Beats Overland in Wild Night Run," *LAT,* Oct. 27, 1907, p. VIII3/**"He is sincere":** "Wild Race on Desert Waste," *LAT,* Oct. 4, 1908, p. VI2/**30 hours, 36 minutes:** Jim and Nancy Schaut, "The Cactus Derby: LA to Phoenix," http://arizonaracinghistory.com/cactusderbyintro.htm/**"We hit the sand on the beach":** "Twelve Hours to San Diego," *LAT,* July 9, 1905, p. III4. Hanshue is not identified in this article, but he made this run for Shettler, who hired him many times as an endurance driver, and it's a safe bet he said these things./**"A snake would have":** Ibid./**"So I coasted":** Ibid./**"muddy and rather heavy":** "Motor Makes Speed," *LAT,* Feb. 18, 1908, p. I6/**Following the new road signs:** "Inland Route Has Charms," *LAT,* Mar. 1, 1908, p. VIII2/**nearby Hotel Brewster:** "Renton Runs Road Measure," *LAT,* Aug. 15, 1909, p. VI2/**"What becomes of the men":** Bert Smith, "Road

Record Race Thrills," *LAT,* Dec. 11, 1910, p. VII1/**to the Mojave Desert and back:** "To Desert and Return," *LAT,* Aug. 22, 1905, p. II3/**His most sensational race:** "Clean Sweep of Records," *LAT,* Apr. 15, 1908, p. I6/**"Crowds on the streets of Fresno":** Ibid./ **moved to San Francisco:** "Match Train with Motor," *LAT,* Sept. 12, 1909, p. VI2/**a betting pool of ten thousand dollars:** "Car Against Car, Men Against Men, Both Against Nature, Today's Race," *LAT,* Mar. 28, 1907, p. II1/**"a visionary look in his eyes":** Lynn Rogers, "Automotive Highlights," *LAT,* July 2, 1939, p. 11/**believed in the power:** "Earle C. Anthony, Auto and Radio Pioneer, Dies," *LAT,* Aug. 8, 1961, p. B1/**mechanically minded:** Barry Mishkind, "Earle C. Anthony Drives KFI to Fame," Jan. 10, 1996, http://www.oldradio.com/archives/stations/LA/kfi.htm/**"I will tell you a secret":** "Quotes from the Motoring Past," *Westways,* Dec. 1950, p. 70. The description of Anthony in his bowler hat is drawn from a photo that appears with this article./**"To everybody's surprise":** Lynn Rogers, "Automotive Highlights," *LAT,* July 2, 1939, p. 11/**The very definition of:** "Juvenile Journalism," *LAT,* Dec. 30, 1894, p. 9/**"The aurora borealis":** "Cups Awarded in Auto Run," *LAT,* July 3, 1906, p. II10/**"finished in apple green":** "Marvel More Not Killed," *LAT,* Oct. 16, 1906, p. I7/**"We do not care to risk":** Dorothy K. Hassler, "The Great Pasadena-Altadena Hill Climb," *Westways,* Jan. 1962, p. 31/**the planned route:** "We May See Great Race," *LAT,* Jan. 5, 1908, p. VIII2/**posted a large American map:** "New York to Paris Run," *LAT,* Feb. 16, 1908, p. VIII2/**When Earle C. Anthony heard:** "World Race Route Varied," *LAT,* Mar. 19, 1908, p. II1/**announced to the press:** "Enthusiasts Disappointed," *LAT,* Mar. 23, 1908, p. I4/**"hot as a furnace":** "A Readiness to Greet Cars," *LAT,* Mar. 22, 1908, p. VIII1/**"Reports that the car":** "Hail to the Chief," *LAT,* Mar. 22, 1908, p. VIII1/**escort that included:** Ibid./**"Thomas Flyer, America's Winner":** Fenster, *Race of the Century*, p. 205/**"the hour of the automobile":** Ibid., p. 208/**"thousands of people":** "Crowds Cheer Racing Crew," *LAT,* Mar. 25, 1908, p. I3/**"At North Main Street a crowd":** "Glad Greeting Here for Italian Racer," *LAT,* Apr. 1, 1908, p. II1

Chapter 6: Machine Politics

"There was great unspoken": Ramsey, *Alice's Drive*, p. 127/**"The Sierra range confronted":** Ibid./**"First a long pull":** Ibid./**"The carburetor was feeling":** Ibid./**"To give the engine":** Ibid./**"Majestic sugar pines, Douglas firs":** Ibid., p. 129/**the cut-glass cups:** Ibid. p. 50–51/**"I was born mechanical":** Ibid., p. 16/**a noisy, road-hogging Pierce-Arrow:** Ibid, p. 34/**"It wasn't exactly":** Ibid./**"the little daughter":** McConnell, *A Reliable Car*, p. 54/**"Women can handle":** Ibid./**"Driving was a guy thing":** Author conversation with Fred Zimmerman, auto historian, Blackhawk Auto Museum, Danville, Calif., Nov. 2005/**Another challenge was the hand–crank starter:** Franzwa, in Ramsey, *Alice's Drive*, p. 8/**"Danger to a woman's fair complexion":** Camille Aimee, "Beauty Hints for Fair Drivers," *The California Motorist,* Sept. 1917, reprinted in Turner and Sparks, *The Spirit of the Road*, p. 50/**"The latest handbag":** Ibid./**"Our fair-weather hats":** Ramsey, *Alice's Drive,* p. 14/**"Near Hayward a terrific

wind": Ibid., p. 34/**"Woman Motorist of the Century":** Franzwa, in Ramsey, *Alice's Drive,* p. 138/**"I'm probably happiest":** McConnell, *A Reliable Car,* p. 59/**"Covina was just being built up":** Ibid./**"a lot of hooey":** "W. Covina Motorist Defends Her Kind," *LAT,* June 16, 1966, p. SG4/**"The cross-country trip":** "Hairpins, Chewing Gum Kept Car Going in '09 Coast to Coast Epic," *LAT,* Feb. 19, 1961, p. A14/**"There's an enormous wildcat":** McConnell, *A Reliable Car,* p. 94/**"Without preamble I jumped in":** Ibid./**revealing in her autobiography:** Ibid./**"Kick the Southern Pacific":** Olin, *California's Prodigal Sons,* p. 26/**"soulless Force":** Norris, *The Octopus,* 1901, p. 51/**"The [road] franchise is frequently":** Irvine, Manson, and Maude, "Biennial Report of the Bureau of Highways, 1895–1896," p. 34/**"How well I remember":** Storke and Tompkins, *California Editor*, p. 180/**"In a red automobile":** Ibid./**"Johnson's campaign":** Hart, *A Companion to California*, p. 249/**For the College Equal Suffrage League's:** Scharff, *Taking the Wheel*, p. 80/**"swept down in automobiles":** "More of the Smile than the Shout," *LAT,* Oct. 11, 1911, p. II1/**"It was a new sort of machine politics":** Ibid.

Chapter 7: Barney and Friends

a girl by the name: Nolan, *Barney Oldfield,* p. 61/**horse named after him:** Ibid./**"I believe in God":** "Speed King's Wife to Ride with Him on Record Run," *LAT,* Dec. 4, 1910, p. VII5/**"drives like a madman":** Ibid./**rode in airplanes:** "Nothing to It, Says Mrs. Barney," *LAT,* Jan. 15, 1915, p. III1/**"transportation determines":** "San Diego Biographies: John D. Spreckels," San Diego Historical Society, http://sandiegohistory.org/bio/spreckels/spreckels.htm/**"San Diego is the only city":** "San Diego's Boulevard System," *Touring Topics,* May 1909, p. 9/**"surfaced with decomposed granite":** Ibid./**pricey housing subdivision:** Ibid./**"The track is two miles around":** "Racing Game Is Boosted," *LAT,* Feb. 17, 1907, p. III2/**"Five racing cars":** Ibid./**"just for fun":** "Oldfield's Fast Time," *LAT,* Mar. 20, 1907, p. II11/**arm bandaged from an injury:** "World Record by Oldfield," *LAT,* Apr. 22, 1907, p. II3/**"cupid race":** "Slow Time on Berdoo Track," *LAT,* Apr. 28, 1907, p. II2/**a first for an American gas racecar:** Nolan, *Barney Oldfield,* p. 84/**"I shifted into high":** Nolan, *Barney Oldfield,* p. 86/**first board track in the world***:* Yates, *The Hot Rod*, p. 37/**"the greatest motorcar ever":** "Dutch Benny Almost Flies," *LAT,* Apr. 3, 1910, p. VII1/**"a roaring, plunging":** Ibid./**Records started falling:** "Motordrome," *Touring Topics,* May 1910, p. 15/**"Throughout the race":** Ibid./**"As it rushed":** Ibid./**"cheered itself":** Ibid./**Johnson...who loved cars:** Nolan, *Barney Oldfield,* p. 75/**announced his comeback event:** Bert C. Smith, "Barney Oldfield to Drive in Santa Monica Race," *LAT,* Apr. 7, 1912/**Ocean Front Boulevard:** White, *Lost Race Tracks,* p. 22. Course description based on map./**Crowd estimates:** R. A. Wynne, "Awed Throng Cheers Winner," *LAT,* May 5, 1912, p. VII7/**"the farmer in the country":** "Saturday the Tenth," *Touring Topics,* Aug. 1909, p. 5/**Ancient Arabic Order of the Mystic Shrine:** "Shriners from All Parts World at Santa Monica," *LAT,* Mar. 10, 1912, p. VII10/**nearly all the pre-race excitement:** "World Record in Big Race," *LAT,* Apr. 28, 1912, p. VII2/**"Bert,...if it was like you":** Bert C. Smith, "Fast Work Makes Big

Race," *LAT,* May 3, 1912, p. III1/**"Never was a more":** Bert C. Smith, "New World Motor Champion," *LAT,* May 5, 1912, p. VII1/**First out of the smoke:** Ibid./**"Brown on the Benz":** Ibid./**Starting in fourth position:** "Entrants and Order of Start," *LAT,* May 4, 1912, p. II9/**"He realized in a second":** R. A. Wynne, "Awed Throng Cheers Winner," *LAT,* May 5, 1912, p. V111

Chapter 8: The Original Hollywood Fast-Car Guy

"An occasional ride": "No Vacation for Mack Sennett," *LAT,* June 6, 1915, p. VII23/ **Sterling ties her to the railroad tracks:** "With the Photoplayers," *LAT,* Feb. 20, 1913, p. III4/**"That sweater-swaddled figure":** "At the Stage Door," *LAT,* Mar. 19, 1915, p. III4/**"Of the machines that changed":** Rawls and Bean, *California*, p. 296/**"When I came to the Pacific Coast":** "Credit Given to Motor Car," *LAT,* Feb. 2, 1915, p. VII9/ **in full costume and makeup:** Ibid./**"Take the auto away":** Ibid./**"Comparatively little":** Ibid./**"A squad of auto repair experts":** "With the Photoplayers," *LAT,* Feb. 20, 1913, p. III4/**"Where's a bridge":** "Locating Locations Locally," *LAT,* Oct. 27, 1915, p. III3/**"One day last week":** "Motor Stars Among Films," *LAT,* Oct. 11, 1914, p. VII8/**"Four o'clock rising":** Gish and Pinchot, *The Movies, Mr. Griffith, and Me*, p. 90/**"Not only touring cars for the people":** "Autos Help the Movies," *LAT,* Sept. 28, 1913, p. VII5/**The Balboa Feature Film Company:**"LA Picture Players Invest Millions in Machines," *LAT,* July 11, 1915, p. VI2. Details on the use of machines by the studios come from this article./**"The motion picture people":** "Credit Given to Motor Car," *LAT,* Feb. 2, 1915, p. VII9/**in front of the Keystone lot:** "With the Photoplayers," *LAT,* Mar. 12, 1913, p. III4/**"We got us a spectacle, kids!"** Remi Nadeau, "Enter the Moviemakers," in Caughey, *Los Angeles*, p. 258/**"the man whose work first presented us":** Basinger, *Silent Stars*, p. 65/**crashed into things:** "Mishap Keeps Doctor Busy," *LAT,* May 6, 1914, p. II2/**"Mack Sennett, the Keystone director":** "With the Photoplayers," *LAT,* Feb. 20, 1913, p. III4. All quotes from this article.

Chapter 9: Shows of Wonder

once planted a story: Nolan, *Barney Oldfield*, p. 131/**his first-ever airplane ride:** Jeffers, *Ace of Aces*, p. 39/**averaging 65.3 miles per hour:** Johnny McDonald, "The Great Point Loma Road Race," sunsetsaga.com/**Western Union telegraph key:** "Panama-California Exposition," San Diego Historical Society, http://www.sandiegohistory.org/pan-cal/sdexpo32.htm/**owned and designed by Clyde Osborn:** Kimes and Clark, *Standard Catalog*, p. 479 /**"scout car":** "San Diego Run Sets Attendance Record," *Touring Topics,* May 1915, p. 12/**"With a single stop":** Ibid./**"Although southern California":** Ibid., p. 11/**spent more than a year driving:** Kristin Tilford, "Signs of the Times," Automobile Club of Southern California brochure/**"In 1913 practically the only":** Hoag, *A Complete*

Official Road Guide of the Lincoln Highway, p. 108/**"the first modern transcontinental highway":** Eisenhower, *At Ease*, p. 386/**first coast-to-coast truck delivery:** Don Hays, "1910 Alco," Hays Antique Truck Museum, http://www.truckmuseum.org/1910alco.html/**"The Panama-Pacific International Exposition":** Laura E. Soulliere, "Historic Roads in the National Park System," National Park Service, Oct. 1995, p. 7/**"What we lacked in white-flaked":** "Race Across the Country," *LAT,* Feb. 21, 1915, p. VII3/**"Can you tell me":** Hokanson, *The Lincoln Highway,* p. 30/**pressed a button in the White House:** "First Great Exposition Opened by Radio Waves," *LAT,* Feb. 21, 1915, p. I4/ **More than 425,000 people:** "425,000 Persons See Opening," *LAT,* Feb. 23, 1915, p. I2/ **eighty thousand exhibits in dozens of pavilions:** "San Francisco Exposition Nears Completion," *Touring Topics,* Feb. 1915, p. 23/**"the most comprehensive":** Jeanne Redman, "All Buildings Filled with Fair Exhibits," *LAT,* Mar. 15, 1915, p. I2/**the world's largest frame building:** "San Francisco Exposition Nears Completion," *Touring Topics,* Feb. 1915, p. 23/**a scary four-mile course:** White, *Lost Race Tracks* , p. 19/**"There probably never was":** "Speed Demons Buzz in Vanderbilt Cup Today," *LAT,* Feb. 22, 1915, p. III1/**cracked 100 miles per hour:** Ibid./**England's Dario Resta:** "Resta and Wilcox Win Again in San Francisco Auto Classic," *LAT,* Mar. 7, 1915, p. VII1/**"turned turtle at the right-angle":** "Running Story of Vanderbilit," *LAT,* Mar. 7, 1915, p. VII10/**one hundred thousand spectators**: Jeanne Redman, "A Girl's Impressions of the Vanderbilt Cup Race," *LAT,* Mar. 7, 1915, p. VII1/**"This is a scene of indefinable beauty":** Ibid./**"An exhibit of horse-drawn vehicles":** Todd, "Individual Transportation," in *The Story of the Panama Pacific International Exposition*, Vol. 4, p. 246/**"the fastest growing industry":** Hillenbrand, *Seabiscuit*, p. 9/**"No doubt the largest":** "Motor Display Great Feature," *LAT,* Jan. 31, 1915, p. VII5/**"The greatest automobile show":** "Exposition Auto Show the World's Greatest," *LAT,* May 2, 1915, p. VIII6/**Location 783 in Block 11:** "Motor Display Great Feature," *LAT,* Jan. 31, 1915, p. VII5/**"a specially made polished steel chassis":** Ibid./**"a very beautiful Packard":** Todd, "Individual Transportation," in *The Story of the Panama Pacific International Exposition,* Vol. 4, p. 248/**"three trucks on display":** "Exposition Auto Show the World's Greatest," *LAT,* May 2, 1915, p. VIII6/**"Studebaker Auto Delivery Vehicle":** Nilda Rego, "Fred Galindo's Challenge," *Contra Costa Times,* Nov. 15, 2005/**"The exposition was large":** Adams, *An Autobiography*, p. 18/**"One day Mr. Born":** Ibid., p. 16/**Kodak Box Brownie:** Ibid., p. 53/**"It skirts thousand feet precipices":** "500,000 Ridge Road Engineering Masterpiece," *Touring Topics*, Dec. 1915, p. 7/**"one of the most remarkable engineering":** Scott, *The Ridge Route*, p. 77/**"I think the reason for the rapid growth":** Mitchell, "The Automobile in California Life and Industry," *California's Magazine,* p. 224/**forsaking his old Locomobile steamer:** "Governor to Travel Well," *LAT,* Mar. 14, 1915, p. VII6/**"the new model, eight-cylinder V-type":** "Exposition Auto Show the World's Greatest," *LAT,* May 2, 1915, p. VIII6/ **enterprising automobile man:** "Volney S. Beardsley," *Los Angeles County Biography and Sketches, 1915,* California Biography Project, www.history.sloco.net, with a research assist from Martha A. Crosley Graham/**Minnie drove a Beardsley:** "Local-Made Car Scores," *LAT,* July 11, 1915, p. VI6/**gas was cheap:** "One Dollar Is Price of Oil," *LAT,* Apr. 3, 1910, VI7/**"bulk depots":** Witzel, *The American Gas Station*, p. 13/**earful of gas:** Ibid., p.

15/**"This plant was one of the main show places":** Todd, "Individual Transportation," in *The Story of the Panama Pacific International Exposition,* Vol. 4, p. 247/**"Within four minutes":** Ibid./**$675 per vehicle:** Nilda Rego, "Fred Galindo's Challenge," *Contra Costa Times,* Nov. 15, 2005;**"High-Priced Quality in a Low-Priced Car":** Advertisement, *LAT,* Dec. 19, 1909, p. VIII4/**"one of the roughest and worst":** "Ford Times," 1913, reprinted in Butler, *First Highways of America*, p. 212

Chapter 10: Wheelboys

Richmond Tank Depot: "Ford Motor Company Assembly Plant," National Park Service, http://www.nps.gov/history/nr/travel/wwIIbayarea/for.htm/**closed in the early 1990s:** "Last Auto Factory in Southern California Closed by GM," *New York Times,* Aug. 28, 1992/ **thousands watching from the waterfront:** "Beachey's Final Thrill Costs Him His Life," *LAT,* Mar. 15, 1915, p. I1/**"the hail-fellow well-met type":** Biddle, *Barons of the Sky* , p. 150/**"Speed...had a visceral":** Boyne, *Beyond the Horizons*, p. 3/**Malcolm first started thinking:** Ibid., p. 4/**"demonstrator":** Ibid./**"none of this bothered":** Ibid., p. 6/**"It was partly nerve":** Ibid./**"not a new experience":** "Allan Lockheed," National Aviation Hall of Fame, http://nationalaviation.blade6.donet.com/components/content_manager_v02/view_nahf/htdocs/menu_ps.asp?NodeID=-1449208259&group_ID=1134656385&Parent_ID=-1/**most colorful adventures:** Boyne, *Beyond the Horizons,* p. 10/**bullet holes:** Ibid./**400 block of State Street:** Storke and Tompkins, *California Editor*, p. 229/**"Entirely self-taught":** Ibid., p. 230/**"stop the car on a dime":** Boyne, *Beyond the Horizons,* p. 16/**all-wheel hydraulic braking system:** Stephen Dirksen, "History of American Technology," Automobile Safety Improvements, http://web.bryant.edu/~ehu/h364proj/sprg_97/dirksen/brakes.html/**"an everyman's plane":** Boyne, *Beyond the Horizons,* p. 16/**"wizards":** Curcio, *Chrysler,* p. 351/**Raised in farm country Kansas:** Biddle, *Barons of the Sky,* p. 44/**began selling Maxwells:** Ibid., p. 45/**stopped in to see Martin:** McConnell, *A Reliable Car,* p. 96/**"There is an ever-increasing field":** "Automobiles and Airships," *LAT,* Jan. 16, 1910, p. VI4/**"motion picture, the phonograph":** "Advent of Intimate Theater," *LAT,* May 17, 1912, p. III4/**a prairie schooner west:** Author interview with Richard Earl, Feb. 21, 2006/**"Have you seen our oval glass":** Display ad, *LAT,* Dec. 8, 1907, p. VIII5/**"A young man of considerable altitude":** "We'll Make 'Em Right Here," *LAT,* Jan. 14, 1919, p. III1/**"nickel trim and a mohair top":** Biddle, *Barons of the Sky,* p. 61/**A photograph of Harley:** Photograph, Official Harley Earl Website, carofthecentury.com

Chapter 11: Long and Low

"the public interest, long taken away": "First After War Auto Show Closes," *LAT,* Jan. 19, 1919, VI1/**featured two hundred passenger cars:** William M. Henry, "Great Motor Show Opens Today," *LAT,* Jan. 11, 1919, p. VI1/**"Beautifully gowned women with**

their escorts": William M. Henry, "Crowds Stream into Huge Tented Salon," *LAT,* Jan. 12, 1919, p. VI1/**"oily-tongued salesmen":** Ibid./**"Home-grown talent is occupying":** William M. Henry, "We'll Make 'Em Right Here," *LAT,* Jan. 14, 1919, p. III1/**"sporting and rakish":** Kimes and Clark, *Standard,* p. 113/**"introduced wire wheels to the Pacific Coast":** Ibid./**"Perhaps the most startling local models":** William M. Henry, "We'll Make 'Em Right Here," *LAT,* Jan. 14, 1919, p. III1/**"would make the most blasé New Yorker":** William M. Henry, "Great Motor Show Opens Today," *LAT,* Jan. 11, 1919, p. VI1/**"About the classiest thing":** William M. Henry, "We'll Make 'Em Right Here," *LAT,* Jan. 14, 1919, p. III1/**"some of their showmanship":** "I Dream Automobiles," *Saturday Evening Post*, Aug. 7, 1954, p. 82/**"He had lots of interaction":** Author interview with Richard Earl, Feb. 2006/**"builders and designers of automobile bodies":** Earl Automobile Works business card, Official Harley Earl Website, carofthecentury.com/**"a little hole in the wall":** "I Dream Automobiles," *Saturday Evening Post,* Aug. 7, 1954, p. 82/**"Since childhood":** MacMinn, "Fifties Finest," *Automobile Quarterly*, p. 75/**"This made it possible":** Curcio, *Chrysler,* p. 351/**"What was most important":** Robert Ackerman quoted in Curcio, *Chrysler,* p. 353. Ackerman is writing here about one of Harley's later designs, the LaSalle, but it applies to his California creations too./**"Harley would do a clay model":** Author interview with Richard Earl, Feb. 2006/**"America's first professional car stylist":** Bayley, *Harley Earl and the Dream Machine*, pp. 24–25/**"My primary purpose for twenty-eight years":** "I Dream Automobiles," *Saturday Evening Post,* Aug. 7, 1954, p. 82/**"If you wouldn't like to own":** "Some Class to this Body," *LAT,* May 11, 1919, p. VI3/**"the classiest creation":** Ibid./**"It is a special":** Ibid./**"the car is upholstered":** Ibid./**sponsoring Cadillacs in attention-getting:** "Many Entries for Big Races," *LAT,* May 9, 1909, p. VI3/**thirty-nine hours after it had left:** "Cadillac Smashes Record," *Touring Topics*, Jan. 1911, p. 15/**casual, easygoing business style:** "Auto Industry Feels Loss," *LAT,* Sept. 9, 1934, p. D4/**Governor Johnson's new Cadillac:** "Governor to Travel Well," *LAT,* Mar. 14, 1915, p. VII6/**Cadillac introduced the electric:** "Nine Hundred Cadillac Mark," *LAT,* May 25, 1913, p. VII5/**Balding and with glasses:** Photograph, "Buys Big Body Factory," *LAT,* July 13, 1919, p. V18/**"had a personal habit":** KSFO 560 AM, Bay Area Radio Musuem, bayarearadio.org/**"the largest business of its kind":** "Buys Big Body Factory," *LAT,* July 13, 1919, p. V18/**"We will create as well as build":** Ibid./**"With an idea of learning":** Ibid./**Mary's brother Jack:** Photographs of Pickford's and other star cars from Don Lee's 1920 catalog, Classic Car-Nection, http://www.car-nection.com/yann/Dbas_txt/Drm20-24.htm/**his development deal at Paramount**: "Arbuckle's Extras," *LAT,* June 30, 1918, VI6

Chapter 12: The Go-Fast Kid

"The Fashion Parade": Howard Angus, "Races Prove Thrillers," *LAT,* July 21, 1919, p. I6/**"In the 15-mile race":** Ibid./**"The handkerchief waving":** Ibid./**"Cecil de Mille [sic]":** Ibid./**at the junction of Wilshire:** Osmer, *Where They Raced Lap Two*, p. 22/**"It was beautiful, and we spared":** Quoted in Borgeson, *The Golden Age*, p. 30/

the shorthand name for the speedway: "The Los Angeles Speedway," *LAT,* Jan. 18, 1920, p. V1/**"the most elegant wooden speedway":** Yates, *The Hot Rod*, p. 38/**"An entirely new color scheme":** "Await Speedway Opening," *LAT,* Feb. 15, 1920, p. VI1/**"What probably will":** Ibid./**stipulated in Prince's contract:** "Murphy Burns Up Track," *LAT,* Feb. 27, 1920, p. III1/**"The competition…will be warm enough":** "The Los Angeles Speedway," *LAT,* Jan. 18, 1920, p. V1/**With the backing of Firestone:** Nolan, *Barney Oldfield*, p. 181/**Oldfield Motor Corporation:** Kimes and Clark, *Standard Catalog*, p. 985/**the person by his side:** "Death Ends Career of Barney Oldfield," *LAT,* Oct. 5, 1946, p. A1/**"I walked down under the stand":** Harry Williams, "Murphy Wins Cyclonic Opening Race," *LAT,* Feb. 29, 1920, p. I1. Descriptions of Murphy's win at Beverly later in chapter are also from this article./**"quite simply the greatest creative":** Griffith Borgeson, *Miller*, from the Miller/Offenhauser Historical Society, milleroffy.com/**"inventor-engineer with a wizard's touch for motors":** Nolan, *Barney Oldfield,* p. 174/**"just a backyard lean-to":** Borgeson, *The Golden Age*, p. 107/**"I was headquartered at Miller's":** Ibid., p. 181/**A web of cables:** Photograph in White, *The Marvelous Mechanical Designs*, p. 11/**the engine for the last plane:** Borgeson, *The Golden Age,* p. 111/**"fantastically advanced":** White, *The Marvelous Mechanical Designs,* p. 13/**"the most fully streamlined vehicle":** Borgeson, *The Golden Age*, p. 113/**"a nightmare version of a U-boat":** Nolan, *Barney Oldfield,* p. 175/**put butcher paper:** Photograph in White, *The Marvelous Mechanical Designs,* p. 17/**"a frail, slight Irish youth":** "Angelenos Mourn Pilot," *LAT,* Sept. 16, 1924, p. B1/**in the Boyle Heights section:** Paul Lowry, "Rabbit Punches," *LAT,* Apr. 28, 1928/**married at St. Francis Hotel:** Catlin, "The Great Vail," *Automobile Quarterly,* p. 344/**Jimmy did it again:** "Murphy Wins Fresno Race," *LAT,* Oct. 13, 1920, p. I8/**"the hottest thing in wheels":** "Miller History," Miller/Offenhauser Historical Society, http://milleroffy.com/Racing%20History.htm/**"a combined jewelry and race car":** Borgeson, *The Golden Age,* p. 79/**"It has to be a Miller-Murphy affair":** "Gives Credit to Engineer," *LAT,* June 11, 1922, p. VI2/**"I truly believe":** Ibid./**"unassuming, unpretentious":** Joseph Scott of the Knights of Columbus quoted in "Rites for Murphy Today," *LAT,* Sept. 22, 1924, p. A1/**"a sweet, clean, lovable character":** A. M. Young, manager of the Los Angeles Speedway Association, quoted in "Los Angelenos Mourn Pilot," *LAT,* Sept. 16, 1924, p. B1/**canary yellow Durant with a cat-quick:** "Murphy Steps On It," *LAT,* Oct. 29, 1922, p. VIII2/**"fat clubhouse cigar":** Paul Lowry, "Milton's New Baby Go Fast Machine," *LAT,* Mar. 11, 1923, p. VI1/**"the originator, in the United States":** "Miller History," Miller/Offenhauser Historical Society, http://milleroffy.com/Racing%20History.htm/**"moved American racing vehicles":** White, *The Marvelous Mechanical Designs*/**"like tamale carts":** Paul Lowry, "Harry Miller Is King of Race Car Builders," *LAT,* June 3, 1923, p. VI1/**change his sparkplugs eighteen times:** "Jimmy Murphy Plans a Trip," *LAT,* June 8, 1923, p. III1/**that crazy-sweet moment:** Ibid./**nearly twice as many points:** "Jimmy Murphy Piles Up Healthy Lead," *LAT,* July 21, 1924, p. I1/**"forced its way through the hood":** "Jimmy Murphy Dies in Race," *LAT,* Sept. 16, 1924, p. B/**"His back and neck":** Ibid./**One wire service photo:** "When Death Rode with Jimmy Murphy," *LAT,* Sept. 22, 1924, p. 9/**"All that is mortal":** Paul Lowry, "Pals Sob at Jimmy's Bier," *LAT,* Sept. 20, 1924, p. 3/**An honor guard of Knights:** "Murphy's Body

Due Tomorrow," *LAT,* Sept. 18, 1924, p. 12/**"Jimmy Murphy, before God and Man":** "Jimmy Murphy at Rest," *LAT,* Sept. 23, 1924, p. A2

Chapter 13: Something Happening Here

"There is nothing so marking": "High Ideals of Masonry Extolled," *LAT,* Oct. 20, 1924, p. A3/**The Interchurch World Movement:** Brilliant, *The Great Car Craze*, p. 58/**"We now have a thousand":** Ibid., p. 57/**"Everybody who is anybody":** Rider, *Rider's California*, p. 22/**"In California, all traffic":** Report, United States Bureau of Public Roads and the California Highway Committee, 1922, p. 23/**More than a million Californians:** Ibid., p. 202. Statistics compiled by Ashleigh Brilliant from the California Department of Motor Vehicles, the Automobile Manufacturer's Association, and other sources./**"From whatever angle":** Ernest McCaffey, ibid., p. 27/**"The significance of the automobile":** Rockwell Hunt, 1929, ibid., p. 25/**"We are a fast-moving nation":** William Klinger, "Pioneering Automobile Insurance," *San Francisco News Letter,* Sept. 5, 1925, reprinted on Museum of the City of San Francisco's website, http://www.sfmuseum.org/hist/autos.html/**"one of the greatest labor-saving devices":** Rawls and Bean, *California*, p. 296/**rented saddle horses for a couple bucks:** Storke and Tompkins, *California Editor*, p. 62/**"It is almost unbelievable":** "Growth of Auto Row Keeps Pace with City in Last 20 Years," *LAT,* Nov. 29, 1925, p. G1/**"auto-hogs":** Bottles, *Los Angeles and the Automobile*, p. 71/**"The day when the automobile":** Brilliant, *The Great Car Craze,* p. 73/**"There is no longer any argument":** "Car Apiece Predicted by Dealer," *LAT,* Dec. 21, 1924, p. G9/**"the future would be tied":** Exhibit, Petersen Automotive Museum, Los Angeles. Observed by author, spring 2006/**more female motorists:** "Many Women Motorists," *LAT,* Mar. 14, 1920, p. VI3/**"It is a perpetual surprise":** William Robson, 1925, Brilliant, p. 40/**"The working man, and the man":** Ernest McGaffey, ibid., p. 30/**a term first coined by:** "Increase Your Capital" display ad, *LAT,* Jan. 27, 1929, p. F2/**"Los Angeles in particular":** Liebs, *Main Street to Miracle Mile*, p. 123/**"where the use of the automobile":** Rawls and Bean, *California,* p. 293/**"Hot dog stands and unsightly shacks":** Brilliant, *The Great Car Craze,* p. 137/**"324 billboards, 74 filling stations":** Ibid., p. 141/**"The trend of American tourist traffic":** Hoag, *A Complete Official Road Guide of the Lincoln Highway, Fifth Edition, 1924*, p. 179/**"When a man buys an automobile":** "The Private Garage Question," *Touring Topics,* May 1910, p. 9/**"Men who know very little":** Ibid./**"The automobile is the undoing":** Dr. Emory S. Bogardus, 1929, Brilliant, p. 34/**"I fear that the automobile":** Jackson Graves, ibid., p. 36/**"The practice of making love":** Editorial, *LAT,* 1921, ibid., p. 31/**"the triumvirate of hell":** Scharff, *Taking the Wheel*, p. 138/**"Never before in human history":** Brilliant, *The Great Car Craze,* p. 78/**"Every American soon took it":** Caughey, *California*, p. 486/**vice president of Leach:** "Leach Engines Set Fast Pace," *LAT,* Dec. 18, 1921, p. VI11/**"The world never had seen":** Borgeson, *The Golden Age*, p. 194/**"If Harry Miller had done nothing more":** "Miller History," Miller/Offenhauser Historical Society, http://miller-offy.com/Racing%20History.htm/**"look like something the cat":** Bill Henry, "Alumni of Auto Row," *LAT,* Mar. 30, 1930, p. F5/**"He was doing things":** Sloan, *My Years with General Motors*, p. 268/**"companion car to the Cadillac":** Bell, "Companion Car to Cadillac," *Automobile Quarterly*, p. 305/**"the first American mass-produced automobile":** Ibid./**"execute something distinctively":** "Harley Earl of Car Factory in Los Angeles," *LAT,* May 15, 1927, p. G9/**"When you are a designer":** Earl, "Harley Earl Recalls LaSalle," *Automobile Quarterly*, p. 313/**"I didn't want to take":** Ibid./**"The self-confident young Californian":** Brinkley, *Wheels for the World*, p. 399/**"a production automobile":**Sloan, *My Years with General Motors*, p. 269/**"the most beautiful of cars":** Bell, "Companion Car to Cadillac," *Automobile Quarterly*, p. 305/**"intangible essence that sets":** Ibid./**"The original LaSalle was a watershed":** Curcio, *Chrysler*, p. 352/**"the man who designed the LaSalle":** "Harley Earl of Car Factory in Los Angeles," *LAT,* May 15, 1927, p. G9/**"We designed and planned":** Ibid./**"With woman's ever increasing":** Ibid.

Chapter 14: The Big Three

Charles Howard knew Harley: Author interview with Richard Earl, May 2007/**"the largest automobile distributing organization":** "All California Is Vacationing," *LAT,* Aug. 15, 1920, p. VII1/**"If you are not qualified":** "White Steamer versus Gasoline" advertisement, *SFC*, Apr. 5, 1906, p. 8/**"The day of the horse is past":** Charles Howard quoted in Hillenbrand, *Seabiscuit*, p. 9/**"had the feel of a giant":** Hillenbrand, *Seabiscuit*, p. 3/**"Donning a gridiron helmet":** Ibid., p. 8/**"He could climb anything":** "Compares Race to Old Scraps," *LAT,* Feb. 22, 1920, p. V12/**battled Leon Shettler:** "Electric Font Blazes Bright," *LAT,* Jan. 28, 1909, p. I6/**When the Howards needed more:** "Buick Men on Their Toes," *LAT,* Mar. 11, 1913, p. II2/**"fully equipped with tops":** "Record Buick Shipment Now on Way to Howard," *LAT,* Jan. 7, 1912, p. VII2/**"There is no question":** "Women Ready for This Car," *LAT,* Oct. 5, 1913, p. VII2/**Whatever the trend:** Bert C. Smith, "Sensational Dash into Night," *LAT,* June 29, 1913, p. VII1/**could have thrown him in jail:** Albert Mroz, "Charles S. Howard: Buick Salesman of the Century," http://www.prewarbuick.com/features/charles_s_howard/**a Howard-sponsored Buick:** "Coupe Grabs Fast Record," *LAT,* Jan. 21, 1921, p. VI2/**In July of that same year:** "First Over Tioga Pass," *LAT,* July 10, 1921, p. VII1/**the road to the new Lake Arrowhead:** Paul Lowry, "New Scenic Road Connects Los Angeles with the Thrills of Winter Sports," *LAT,* Dec. 10, 1922, p. VI1/**new five-hundred-thousand-dollar Buick showroom:** "Crowds Throng Giant Building," *LAT,* Feb. 17, 1924, p. F5/**consisted of 150,000 square feet:** "Ground Is Broken for Mammoth Howard Building," *LAT,* Oct. 24, 1923, p. VI2/**"Radio...came to the state":** Caughey, *California*, p. 486/**he read an article:** Barry Mishkind, "Earle C. Anthony Drives KFI to Fame," Jan. 10, 1996, http://www.oldradio.com/archives/stations/LA/kfi.htm/**"the new radio division":** Display ad, *LAT,* July 28, 1922, p. II10/**"Last night at home":** Ibid./**traveled to France:** "Chauffeurs Are Cheap," *LAT,* Oct. 15, 1922, p. VI8/**"That very first night":** Witzel, *Gas Stations Coast to Coast*, p. 14/**"one of the most powerful":** "KFI Will Build Larger Station," *LAT,*

June 22, 1924, p. A11/**The orange KFI stamp:** Marvin Collins, "Early KFI Historical Photos," http://www.earthsignals.com/Collins/0021/**"Never at a loss":** Conde, *Cars with Personalities*, p. 32/**"This is KFI":** Barry Mishkind, "Earle C. Anthony Drives KFI to Fame," Jan. 10, 1996, http://www.oldradio.com/archives/stations/LA/kfi.htm/**"working in the gloom":** Robert Mix, "Packard Automobile Showroom," Vernacular Language North, http://www.verlang.com/sfbay0004ref_slideshow_bm_sf_02.html#Packard/**"the queen of the Van Ness Avenue":** Ibid./**"an Aladdin's palace":** Ibid./**Keaton tire and rubber shop:** The information on Van Ness Avenue car dealerships comes from the historical research of auto historian John Goepel/**The front of this 1921 ten-story:** These and other observations of the Lee and Packard buildings are from a walk taken by the author, July 2007/**"not to be outdone":** Roger M. Grace, *Riverside News-Enterprise,* Sept. 12, 2002/**"I designed the 1929 Buick":** Sloan, *My Years with General Motors*, p. 273/**"an advocate for change":** Ibid., p. 271/**"was unaware of what":** Ibid., p. 273

Chapter 15: The Curious Case of Doble Steam Motors

"You can design": Quoted in Sloan, *My Years with General Motors,* p. 278/**One of its first customers:** Brinkley, *Wheels for the World,* p. 359/**"Intellectually he was the equal":** Hendry, "The Steam Odyssey of Abner Doble," *Automobile Quarterly*, p. 45/**"impatient of academic education":** Ibid./**"high-strung and sensitive":** Stephen Fox, "The Strange Triumph of Abner Doble," *Invention and Technology Magazine,* americanheritage.com/**Abner resembled a college intellectual:** Photograph in Andy Patterson, "The Magnificent Doble," http://ghlin2.greenhills.net/~apatter/doble.html/**"It was...an encounter":** Hendry, "The Steam Odyssey of Abner Doble," *Automobile Quarterly,* p. 45/**"rethought, and in most cases":** Stephen Fox, "The Strange Triumph of Abner Doble," *Invention and Technology Magazine,* p. 2/**travel fifteen hundred miles:** Hendry, "The Steam Odyssey of Abner Doble," *Automobile Quarterly,* p. 48/**"within two and a half days the mail":** Advertisement, *LAT,* Aug. 30, 1922, p. I7/**Another explanation cites:** Stephen Fox, "The Strange Triumph of Abner Doble," *Invention and Technology Magazine*, p. 1/**"We don't have that kind of work":** Hendry, "The Steam Odyssey of Abner Doble," *Automobile Quarterly,* p. 51/**"the ultimate steam car":** Advertisement, *LAT,* Sept. 11, 1922, p. II11/**with his wavy hair combed:** Photograph in Hendry, "The Steam Odyssey of Abner Doble," *Automobile Quarterly,* p. 48/**"There was a mysterious majesty":** Quoted in Stephen Fox, "The Strange Triumph of Abner Doble," *Invention and Technology Magazine,* p. 1/**"promptly at 2:25 Saturday afternoon":** Advertisement, *LAT,* Sept. 11, 1922, p. II11/**"Come to the Doble Showroom":** Ibid./**Tally's Broadway Theatre:** Advertisement, *LAT,* Feb. 24, 1923, p. I15/**"Grand Avenue hill":** From the *Los Angeles Express*, quoted in Hendry, "The Steam Odyssey of Abner Doble," *Automobile Quarterly,* p. 52/**"the boiler roared to life":** Hendry, "The Steam Odyssey of Abner Doble," *Automobile Quarterly,* p. 4/**"The Model E was essentially":** Ibid./**a Superior Court judge:** "Doble Fails to Block Trial," *LAT,*

Dec. 23, 1925, p. 3/**"It was revealed that":** "Doble Car Firm Head Convicted," *LAT,* Feb. 20, 1926, p. 4/**"unscrupulous":** Ibid./**The justices decided:** "Doble Free in Stock Charge," *LAT,* Apr. 29, 1928, p. 11/**"lifelong tendency":** Stephen Fox, "The Strange Triumph of Abner Doble," *Invention and Technology Magazine,* p. 4/**"a state of the art":** "Abner Doble," http://automotivehalloffame.org/honors/index.php?cmd=view&id=45&type=inductees/**"the last and finest flowering":** Stephen Fox, "The Strange Triumph of Abner Doble," *Invention and Technology Magazine,* p. 4/**"The present pre-eminence":** Quoted in Stephen Fox, "The Strange Triumph of Abner Doble," *Invention and Technology Magazine,* p. 4/**"he was not remotely":** Borgeson, *The Golden Age,* p. 67/**"one of the world's major":** "Miller Engine in Merger Deal," *LAT,* Oct. 10, 1929, p. I4/**break ground on a new building:** "Expansion of Firm Outlined," *LAT,* Nov. 3, 1929, p. D5/**"mechanical genius":** "Miller, Famous Auto Designer, Dies in Detroit," *LAT,* May 4, 1943, p. A2/**"I went down and talked with Miller":** Quoted in Borgeson, *The Golden Age,* p. 108/**"the original Miller engineer":** Ed Winfield quoted in Borgeson, *The Golden Age,* p. 81/**"an amazing measure of the substance":** Borgeson, *The Golden Age,* p. 77

Chapter 16: Blood on the Tracks

"pee-wees": "Midget Racers After Records, *LAT,* Sept. 14, 1933, p. A11/**"pint-sized petrol burners":** "Good Things Come in Small Packages," *LAT,* July 4, 1934, p. A7/**"go-buggies," "hot roller skates":** "Midget Racing Cars to Hold Calcium Tonight," *LAT,* May 31, 1934, p. A12/**"bantam buzz wagons":** Bill Henry, "Bill Henry Says," *LAT,* July 5, 1934, p. A9/**Nineteen-year-old Billy Betteridge:** "Midget Racers Clash Tonight," *LAT,* Feb. 8, 1934, p. A12/**Everything about it:** Kimes and Clark, *Standard Catalog,* p. 117/**"Midget racing":** Bill Henry, "Bill Henry Says," *LAT,* July 5, 1934, p. A9/**"the whole bughouse idea":** Ibid./**"you can't drink the stuff":** Ibid./**"the mad man of the short":** "Two Midgets," *LAT,* Oct. 31, 1934, p. 8/**After Curly Mills bested Happy:** "Miller Wins in Midget Grind," *LAT,* June 15, 1934, p. A13/**Pee Wee Distarce responded:** Osmer, *Where They Raced Lap Two,* p. 77/**"formerly engineers for the famed":** "Mighty Midget Racer to Make Debut," *LAT,* Sept. 27, 1934, p. A13/**"the most important development":** Ibid./**larger than what had run at the Indianapolis:** "New Midget Racing Autos," *LAT,* Sept. 23, 1934, p. E4/**Betteridge said he was dumping:** "New Mighty Midget Amazes," *LAT,* Oct. 7, 1934, p. F2/**"menace":** "Midget War Looms," *LAT,* Nov. 6, 1934, p. A10/**"Mortemore's passing":** Braven Dyer, "Crash Hats Ordered for Midget Drivers," *LAT,* Oct. 30, 1934, p. A13/**"Why don't all the drivers":** Ibid. The results of the poll also come from this article./**"Gordon and Triplett, running close together":** "Two Killed in Race Crash," *LAT,* Mar. 5, 1934, p. 1/**"easy practice spin":** "Reinke Killed as Car Turns Over," *LAT,* Apr. 12, 1934, p. A11/**Durant Motor Company:** Motter, *A History of the Oakland Speedway,* p. 2/**A southern Californian:** Ibid., p. 130/**"Failure to comply immediately":** Ibid., p. 31. All quotes from Warren come from this text./**"the Miracle Man":** "Sam Palmer,

Race Driver, Hurt in Highway Crash," *LAT,* May 9, 1934/**"At high speeds:** "Auto's Toll Disclosed," *LAT,* June 11, 1934, p. A1/**"the dominant influence":** "Death, the Speeder," *LAT,* June 25, 1934, p. A4/**"Thus it is seen":** Ibid./**"No man or woman":** "Auto's Toll Disclosed," *LAT,* June 11, 1934, p. A1/**"California still has the country's":** Ibid./**"Bay Shore Highway":** Ibid./**automobile industry associations:** "Auto Industry Pledges Support," *LAT,* Mar. 15, 1936, p. F4/**"The officer who hands you":** "Palo Alto Aims Driver at Warning Speeders," *LAT,* Mar. 21, 1936, p. 12/**hauling down fourteen thousand offenders:** "Auto Deaths Still Soar," *LAT,* Oct. 23, 1934, p. A1/**"made of light, comfortable":** Motter, *A History of the Oakland Speedway,* p. 17/**"as he was coming high":** Bob Ray, "Gordon Killed in Ascot Race Crash," *LAT,* Jan. 27, 1936, p. A9/**"I remember that":** Maurice Holladay letter to History of Lincoln Heights website about Legion Ascot Speedway, http://www.lincolnheightsla.com/ascot/**"Widow Weeps as Mate Dies":** Osmer, *Where They Raced Lap Two,* p. 37/**"A rising crescendo":** "Fans Mourn Two Deaths," *LAT,* Jan. 28, 1936, p. A9/**Scammell, an ex–restaurant:** "Inquest for Race Pilots," *LAT,* Jan. 29, 1936, p. A12/**demanded improvements at Legion:** "Ascot Must Alter Oval," *LAT,* Feb. 29, 1936, p. 16/**In April a fire:** "Ascot Grandstand Falls Prey to Flames," *LAT,* Apr. 27, 1936, p. A2/**experiment with roll bars:** Motter, *A History of the Oakland Speedway,* p. 80

Chapter 17: Hopped Up

"From the block down": Andy Hamilton, "Speed Made in Los Angeles," *LAT,* May 24, 1936, p. I3/**"America's No. 1 builder":** Ibid./**"couldn't or wouldn't pronounce Calvino":** Ibid./**"check ticket":** Chandler, *Farewell My Lovely,* p. 44. Although this source is a novel, its author, a longtime southern Californian, knew the Ridge Route well./**"Miller was well known":** Andy Hamilton, "Speed Made in Los Angeles," *LAT,* May 24, 1936, p. I3/**"Driving like a wild man":** Ibid./**"there never was an Offenhauser":** Quoted in Riggs, "The Fifty-Year Reign of the Immortal Offy," *Automobile Quarterly*, p. 90/**"The fifty year reign":** Ibid./**"'Hopping up' light stock cars":** "Hopping Up of Autos New Southland Fad," *LAT,* Jan. 15, 1938, p. I4/**"I drove it 55 miles":** Batchelor, *Harrah's Automobile Collection*, p. 3/**"midnight auto supply":** Batchelor, *The American Hot Rod,* p. 16/**"spent a considerable amount":** Batchelor, *Harrah's Automobile Collection*, p. 3/**"Get rid of the shills":** Ibid., p. 4/**"prodigiously charming":** Fenster, *Race of the Century*, p. 352/**"Your Honor, I have just bought":** "Judge Lists Speed Alibis," *LAT,* Feb. 23, 1936, p. A1. All the excuses come from this article./**on Glenoaks Boulevard:** Batchelor, *The American Hot Rod*, p. 160/**Dana Burk, the mayor of:** "Honk! Honk! To Auto Paradise," *LAT,* Sept. 11, 1906, p. I6/**"a strange ship":** Ibid./**"Once on the glassy":** Ibid./**"California has all the rest":** Ibid./**road signs, posted by:** Frank B. Howe, "Milton Uncorks Speed," *LAT,* Apr. 4, 1924, p. B1/**Having run out of:** Ibid./**"Certainly never in the history":** "Milton Sets Two World's Records," *LAT,* Apr. 5, 1924, p. 9/**"From the finish line":** Ibid./**"one of the true geniuses":** Yates, *The Hot Rod*, p. 43/ **When he started racing at Legion:** Paul Lowry, "Rabbit Punches," *LAT,* Apr. 28, 1928,

p. 9/**"What little money":** Borgeson, *The Golden Age,* p. 242/**"No one ever sat":** Ibid., p. 243/**"All I think of":** Ibid., p. 244/**"Because of his youth":** "Lockhart Is Doped to Win," *LAT,* Sept. 13, 1924, p. I6/**"has to have his whiskers":** Braven Dyer, "Lockhart Star of Ascot Race," *LAT,* Oct. 27, 1924, p. I1/**"The most spectacular mile":** Quoted in Borgeson, *The Golden Age*, p. 247/**On his first run Lockhart:** "He Has Set Up Another World Speed Record," *LAT,* Apr. 17, 1927, p. G16/**hit a soft spot in the sand:** Borgeson, *The Golden Age,* p. 255/**"one of the greatest":** Ibid., p. 239/**In 1930 Shorty Cantlon:** "Small Car Record Broken," *LAT,* Apr. 20, 1930, p. F5/**none other than Outdoor Franklin:** "Speed Trials Given De Soto," *LAT,* Apr. 19, 1931, p. E3/**When Stubby Stubblefield:** "New World Records Established," *LAT,* May 29, 1932, p. D2/**Earl Gilmore, who attended:** "Speed Records Being Hung Up," *LAT,* July 10, 1932, p. D3/**a Ford Model A sedan:** "Muroc Scene of Test," *LAT,* Mar. 11, 1928, p. G7/**the Flyer drove:** "Ford Sets Speed Mark," *LAT,* Mar. 29, 1931, p. E2/**with rules governing such modifications:** "Amateurs Vie in Race Today," *LAT,* June 25, 1933, p. E4/**"I see we both like:** Batchelor, *American Hot Rod*, p. 31. All quotes in this passage are from this book.

Chapter 18: Gable and Lombard

The Packard cost: Adler, *The Art of the Sports Car,* p. 23/**"was but one of hundreds":** Yates, *The Hot Rod*, p. 52/**"Clark has talked about nothing":** Batchelor, *The American Hot Rod*, p. 31/**His father bought a Model T:** Harris, *Clark Gable*, p. 6/**"We used to bum":** Ibid., p. 38/**"What is a hitchhiker?":** Brilliant, *The Great Car Craze*, p. 54/**"He was so clean":** Harris, *Clark Gable,* p. 6/**"There was a competition":** Fred Kern, historian, email to author, Feb. 20, 2006/**"Cars, cars, cars":** Janis, *Gary Cooper Off Camera*, p. 120/**His daughter tells a story:** Ibid./**canary yellow and robin's egg blue:** Grace Kingsley, "Hobnobbing with Hollywood," *LAT,* Mar. 23, 1933, p. 7/**"would take his favorite car":** Janis, *Gary Cooper Off Camera,* p. 120/**He drove a new Mercedes SSK:** Borgeson, "Madness at Muroc," *Automobile Quarterly*, p. 288/**His mansion, known as "Cordhaven":** Shashank Bengali, "Williams the Conqueror," *USC Trojan Family Magazine,* Spring 2004, http://www.usc.edu/dept/pubrel/trojan_family/spring04/williams1.html/**"lower, lighter, smaller":** Borgeson, "Madness at Muroc," *Automobile Quarterly,* p. 287/**Skipping the long bus ride:** Ibid./**Miller, who participated in the testing:** "Forty Speed Records Shattered," *LAT,* Jan. 22, 1933, p. D3/**"Oh I can't see him":** Yallop, *The Day the Laughter Stopped*, p. 100/**rolling start:** Borgeson, "Madness at Muroc," *Automobile Quarterly,* p. 288/**poured on the coal:** Ibid., p. 292/**who in 1935 earned:** Meyers, *Gary Cooper*, p. 110/**"a short 125-inch wheelbase":** Fred Kern, historian, email to author/**"Who do you think you are":** Harris, *Gable and Lombard*, p. 145/**she ventured over to a local junkyard:** Ibid., p. 26/**she expected him to pick her up:** Ibid./**"interesting cars for interesting people":** Gross, "Bridging Old and New" *Automobile Quarterly*, p. 6/**Gable himself participated:** Fred Kern, historian, email to author/**"Packing their wedding clothes":** Harris, *Gable and Lombard*, p. 104. The story of their elopement derives from this book, pp. 104–106.

Chapter 19: 1942

"conception of the car": Kimes and Clark, *Standard Catalog, p.* 1097/**"wildly voluptuous":** Batchelor, *Harrah's Automobile Collection,* p. 206/**Looking out of narrow:** Ibid./**Entering an in-house design contest:** Fred Kern, historian, email to author, Feb. 21, 2006/**one story of Mix's death:** Author conversation with Fred Zimmerman, automobile historian, Blackhawk Automotive Museum, Danville, Calif., Jan. 2006/**carrying six grand in cash:** Basinger, *Silent Stars,* p. 199/**black mohair:** Ibid./**she left Los Angeles:** Harris, *Gable and Lombard*, p. 150/**who flew to Las Vegas:** "Clark Gable Paces Floor and Broods," *LAT,* Jan. 20, 1942, p. A2/**sent it off to Canada:** Exhibit placard, Blackhawk Automotive Museum, Sept. 28, 2007/**"Blackouts became more than fiction":** Maury Godchaux, "Year Since Pearl Harbor Transforms Los Angeles," *LAT,* Dec. 7, 1942, p. 10. Other quotes from Godchaux also from this article./**dimout rules:** "More Trouble for Motorists," editorial, *LAT,* Sept. 28, 1942, p. A4/**"Rubber...is indispensable":** Harvey S. Firestone, "The Rubber Situation," Firestone advertisement, *LAT,* Dec. 30, 1941, p. 7/**"the dependence of this country":** Ibid./**"For the time being":** "Auto Tire Rationing to Start Jan. 4," *LAT,* Dec. 18, 1941, p. 1/**"from attic to cellar":** "Treasure Hunt Urged," *LAT,* Jan. 28, 1942, p. A1/**"old stoves, pieces of plumbing":** "Scrap Drive Will Start Tomorrow," *LAT,* Aug. 16, 1942, p. A1/**"The public tonight":** AP, "Government May Seize Civilians' Tires," *LAT,* Mar. 6, 1942, p. 1/**"There is no sense":** Ibid./**one thousand Japanese American men:** Tom Cameron, "Auto Caravan and Train Take 1,000 Japs in Voluntary Mass Migration," *LAT,* Mar. 24, 1942, p. 1/**"in good humor but still holding":** Ibid./**"the automobile junk capital":** "Scrap Iron Drive Starts," *LAT,* Mar. 5, 1942, p. A1/**Even waste fats:** "Salvage Chief Makes Plea," *LAT,* May 8, 1943, p. A1/**"had a feeling of a proud participation":** Maury Godchaux, "Year Since Pearl Harbor Transforms Los Angeles," *LAT,* Dec. 7, 1942, p. 10/**With this loss:** McCullough, ed. *The American Heritage Dictionary of World War II*, p. 185/**"the first summer":** "Many Small Businesses to Feel Rationing Pinch," *LAT,* May 17, 1942, p. A14/**A national poll conducted:** "Nation Divided on Gas Rationing," *LAT,* Aug. 8, 1942, p. 6/**"In view of the fact":** "State Chamber of Commerce Fights Coast Gas Rationing," *LAT,* June 6, 1942/**"a super-abundance of motor fuel":** Howard Kegley, "California Oil News," *LAT,* May 22, 1942, p. 26/**"not trying to save rubber":** "Confiscation Looms If Things Get Worse," *LAT,* July 8, 1942, p. 1/**the voluntary campaign confused:** "Check Discloses City Motorists Burn Rubber," *LAT,* Aug. 8, 1942, p. A1/**"It is an unpatriotic act":** "Public Aroused by Speed Data," *LAT,* Aug. 14, 1942, p. A1/**"unique transportation problem":** "Western Tire Need Stressed," *LAT,* Sept. 3, 1942, p. A2/**in part because they lived:** "No Escape from Gas Rationing," editorial, *LAT,* Sept. 13, 1942, p. A4/**"were the automobile wheels":** "Western Tire Need Stressed," *LAT,* Sept. 3, 1942, p. A2/**"necessary driving":** "U.S. to Ration Gas Over Nation," *LAT,* Sept. 11, 1942, p. 1/**oversaw the distribution:** "Forms for Gas Rationing," *LAT,* Nov. 3, 1942, p. A1/**An "A" coupon book:** "Half of Autoists Get Gas Books," *LAT,* Nov. 20, 1942, p. 1/**"There either be a complete breakdown":** "Gas Rationing Goes in Effect Today," *LAT,* Dec. 1, 1942, p. 1/**"It's like a submarine":** "Why Worry? Asks Driver of Old Detroit Electric," *LAT,* Nov. 25, 1942, p. A2

Chapter 20: Abner of California

one time he and Ed Le Tourneau: Batchelor, *The American Hot Rod,* p. 75/**"slick-looking car":** Ibid., p. 81/**"They're gonna wanta":** Ibid./**"Instead of cussing out":** "Lee Side o' LA," *LAT,* Mar. 4, 1941, p. A4. The following two quotes also come from this article./**known as Lockheed Air Terminal:** "Newsman Tells Burbank History," *LAT,* Dec. 26, 1944, p. A4/**his usual Sunday routine:** Batchelor, *The American Hot Rod,* p. 23/**"Beer up before":** Ibid., p. 16/**to the Hollywood Palladium:** Ibid., p. 24/**"the dream life":** Ambrose, *Citizen Soldiers*, p. 232/**an easing of the dimout rules:** "Dimout Bans Will Be Eased," *LAT,* Sept. 19, 1943, p. 1/**Veda Orr took over:** Ibid., p. 22/**"final inspectors":** William L. Wright, "Women at Work for Victory," *LAT,* Jan. 10, 1943, p. G4/**"Back in peacetime":** Ruth Cowan, "WAACs Who Drive Jeeps," *LAT,* Feb. 7, 1943, p. 3/**women civilians were commanding:** "Ten Women Put to Work as Army Truck Drivers," *LAT,* Nov. 2, 1942, p. 1/**"When the boy husbands":** Ambrose, *D-Day*, p. 488/ **production surpassed:** "Americans Exceed British in Production," *LAT,* June 11, 1942, p. 7/**257,000 tanks, jeeps, and other vehicles":** "Right Down Our Alley," *LAT,* Aug. 29, 1944, p. A4/**8,000 planes a month:** "Plane Cutback Expected to be 2,000 Monthly," *LAT,* May 2, 1945, p. 8/**three quarters of world's automobiles:** John Grinspan, "The Jeep, the Humvee, and How War Has Changed," Aug. 1, 2007, http://www.americanheritage.com/events/articles/web/20070801-jeep-humvee-wwII-iraq.shtml/**the brass rolled out jeeps:** "War Bond Salesmen, with Help of Army, Convince Shoppers," *LAT,* Sept. 12. 1942, p. A3/**"Hepcats and alligators":** "The Jeep—Dance or Plain Torture," *LAT,* Sept. 27, 1942, p. F15/**one motor vehicle for every nintey men:** Lynn Rogers, "Automotive Highlights," *LAT,* Mar. 19, 1944, p. A3. Other statistics here also from this article./**"Abner of California":** Steinbeck, *Bombs Away,* p. 145/**"The first car I remember":** John Steinbeck, "Jalopies I Cursed and Loved," *Holiday,* 1954, in Florence Dunne, *John Steinbeck*, p. 16/**"used it for five years and sold it":** Steinbeck, *Cannery Row*, p. 63. All quotes about Lee Chong's truck from this page./**"Most of the babies of this period":** Ibid., p. 69/**hosted extensive tank training:** "Age-Old Silence of Desert Broken," *LAT,* Apr. 21, 1942/**"he talked to motors":** Steinbeck, *Bombs Away*, p. 145/**"long chin":** Ibid./**"He had a way":** Ibid., p. 147/**"When Abner enlisted":** Ibid., p. 146/**"In nearly every small town":** Ibid., p. 145/**"People trusted Abner":** Ibid./**"Two generations of young men":** Ibid., p. 29/**"For the Allied Air Forces":** Bergerud, *Fire in the Sky: The Air War in the Pacific*, p. 317/**"Japan, by contrast":** Bradley, *Flyboys*, p. 80/**"No army in the world":** Ambrose, *Citizen Soldiers*, p. 64/**Instead of "defense":** Maury Godchaux, "Year Since Pearl Harbor Transforms Los Angeles," *LAT,* Dec. 7, 1942, p. 10

Chapter 21: The Great American Road Trip

"Why don't you write": Wallis, *Route 66*, p. 13/**"But I was not a very good pupil":** Ibid., p. 9/**"I told my mother":** Ibid., p. 11/**"Get your kicks":** Ibid., p. 13/**"putting the song together":** Ibid./**South Madison Avenue:** Pasadena City Directory, 1906–1907, Pasadena Museum of History/**"looking out of the car windows":** Jacob Murdock quoted in McConnell, *Coast to Coast by Automobile*, p. 269/**"California's Sahara":** "The Need of Desert Signs," *Touring Topics,* Aug. 1909, p. 27/**"terra incognito":** McConnell, *Coast to Coast by Automobile,* p. 27/**"a vast lack of everything":** Ibid., p. 278/**"latest United States survey":** Ibid., p. 279/**"As noontime drew near":** Ibid., p. 279. In his book Jacob Murdock did not name the female member of the party who wrote this account, but it was almost certainly Anna./**"By this time":** Ibid./**"when we got out our field glasses":** Ibid./**She left Los Angeles:** McConnell, *A Reliable Car,* p. 101/**"if I had pluck enough":** Ibid., p. 104/**"I was going to prove":** Ibid./**"Gracious. I can beat that":** Ibid., p. 133/**"khaki riding breeches":** Ibid., p. 137/**"Had I not been steeled":** Ibid., p. 144/**Evangeline Lindbergh and her son:** Berg, *Lindbergh*, p. 46. The Lindbergh account derives from pp. 46–48./**a family from Michigan:** Loomis, *Miner, Preacher, Doctor, Teacher*, p. 11/**"Transcontinental touring":** Ibid., p. 127/**"especially for those":** Ibid./**"we saw party after party":** Ibid., p. 129/**"We shall never forget":** Ibid., p. 133/**near Fabiola Hospital:** Ibid., p. 140/**"There were moments":** Eisenhower, *At Ease*, p. 167/**"the best":** Ibid., p. 166/**"Does Your Husband":** Rowsome, Jr., *The Verse by the Side of the Road,* p. 73/**"Said Juliet":** Ibid., p. 92/**"Covers a Multitude" and "Pays Dividends":** Ibid., pp. 46–47/**"Okies and Dogs":** Egan, *The Worst Hard Time*, p. 235/**"the mother road":** Steinbeck, *The Grapes of Wrath,* p. 160/**"a drive yourself car":** Stein, *Everybody's Autobiography*, p. 261/**"I am always afraid of precipices":** Ibid., p. 285/**"It was frightening":** Ibid., p. 288/**"nightmare trip":** Miller, in Durrell, *The Henry Miller Reader,* p. 178/**"There's one thing":** Ibid., p. 179/**"They all have something":** Ibid., p. 180/**"take it for granted":** Ibid./**"Route 66. The name":** Wallis, *Route 66*, p. 232/**Troup idolized Cole:** Ibid., p. 13/**"I never realized":** Ibid., p. 15

Chapter 22: Outlaws of Speed

"It was a grand time": Batchelor, *The American Hot Rod,* p. 63/**"the greatest years":** Ibid., p. 71/**"but by God":** Ibid., p. 63/**"Life couldn't have been":** Ibid./**"Wanna try it out?":** Ibid., p. 45. The story of the race is on pp. 45–46./**The racing Spalding brothers:** Ibid., p. 20/**an estimated 27 million:** Lynn Rogers, "Automotive Highlights," *LAT,* Nov. 18, 1945, p. 12/**by war's end:** Ibid./**three of every ten cars:** Lynn Rogers, "Automotive Highlights," *LAT,* Apr. 4, 1943, p. A12/**Nearly 10 million cars:** Lynn Rogers, "Automotive Highlights," *LAT,* Nov. 18, 1945, p. 12/**12 million Americans:** Ibid./**Complaints about traffic:** "If They're Caught, Punish Them," *LAT,* Dec. 28, 1946, p. A4/**the thirty-eight Americans:** "U.S. Traffic to Kill 38,000 in Single Year," *LAT,* Apr. 4, 1946, p. 1/**up significantly from:** "If They're Caught, Punish Them," *LAT,* Dec. 28, 1946, p. A4/**"poor man's rockets":** Al Wolf, "Sportraits," *LAT,* June 18, 1948, p. A10/**"stripped down on the outside":** Ibid./**Parts builder Vic Edelbrock:** Batchelor, *The American Hot Rod,* p. 66. All the locations of the speed shops come from here./**the first woman to compete:** Ibid., p. 68/**new owner, Roy Richter:** "Racing's General Store," Bell Auto Parts official website, http://www.bell-autoparts.com/general.html/**"thousands of young men":** Yates, *The Hot Rod*, p. 51/ **Hudson of Riverside:** Batchelor, *The American Hot Rod,* p. 73/**"Rebuilding of standard":** Lynn Rogers, "Automotive Highlights," *LAT,* May 26, 1946, p. 8/**"Most are mechanically":** Al Wolf, "Sportraits," *LAT,* June 18, 1948, p. A10/**"that let down the bars":** Lee Shippey, "Leeside," *LAT,* Dec. 14, 1946, p. A4/**"Every motor vehicle":** Batchelor, *The American Hot Rod,* p. 67/**Another bill in 1945:** Ibid./**"any person or persons":** "Change in Law Asked to Curb 'Hot-Rod' Races," *LAT,* Oct. 27, 1946, p. 1/**"We'd all be at the Picadilly":** Wolfe, *Kandy-Kolored Tangerine-Flake Streamline Baby,* p. 88/**"Then you really saw something":** Ibid., pp. 88–89/**"Four Corners":** Batchelor, *The American Hot Rod,* p. 13/**The Solemint store:** Ibid./**"the problem of local schoolboys":** "Safety Plan Advanced for 'Hot Rod' Fans," *LAT,* June 21, 1946, p. 7

Chapter 23: Hot Rod Nation

"part airplane": Display ad, *LAT,* Jan. 18, 1948, p. 14/**"Miss Safety First":**"Models of Hot Rods on Displays at Show," *LAT,* Jan. 24, 1948, p. A1/**"taking the veil of semi-secrecy":** "First Annual Hot Rod Exposition," *Hot Rod Magazine,* Jan. 1948, p. 14/**"who a few moments":** Ibid., p. 1/**"Right from the beginning":** Ken Gross, "Pete Petersen: Remembering Pete," *Hot Rod Magazine*, 2007, http://www.hotrod.com/thehistoryof/113_0708_pete_petersen/index.html/**"What do you think?":** Batchelor, *The American Hot Rod*, p. 179/**"the doorknocker type":** Ken Gross, "Pete Petersen: Remembering Pete," *Hot Rod Magazine*, 2007, http://www.hotrod.com/thehistoryof/113_0708_pete_petersen/index.html/**"At first, I'd go":** Ibid./ **the Throttlers car club met:** Batchelor, *The American Hot Rod,* p. 117/**"That's how we got enough money:** Ken Gross, "Pete Petersen: Remembering Pete," *Hot Rod Magazine*, 2007, http://www.hotrod.com/thehistoryof/113_0708_pete_petersen/index.html/**"gave every ounce":** Dick Messer quoted in "*Hot Rod, Motor Trend* Founder Petersen Dies," Mar. 23, 2007, National Hot Rod Association, http://www.nhra.com/content/news/19207.htm/**"Long regarded as a screwball diversion":** "First Annual Hot Rod Exposition," *Hot Rod Magazine*, Jan. 1948, p. 14/**"a dazzling, chrome-plated":** Ibid./**KMPC Radio broadcast:** "Your Radio Today," *LAT,* Jan. 25, 1948, p. 12/**"A tall man with a deep voice":** Shav Glick, "Wally Parks, Drag Racing's Father Figure, Dies at 94," *LAT,* Sept. 30, 2007/**"drag race" in print:** Batchelor, *The American Hot Rod,* p. 159. Following quotes are also from this page./**"the world's first jeep rod":** "Wally Parks," International Motorsports Hall of Fame, http://www.motorsportshalloffame.com/halloffame/1992/Wally_Parks_main.htm/**"We weren't planning":** "NHRA Founder Wally Parks, Patriarch of Drag Racing, Dies at Age 94," Sept. 28, 2007, National Hot Rod Association, http://www.nhra.com/content/news.asp?articleid=24561/**"not only to prevent injuries":** "Original Hot Rod Group Pledges Safety Aid," *LAT,* Sept. 20, 1948, p. 19/**"unfortunate":** Ibid./**"That's what they were called":** Ken Gross, "Pete Petersen: Remembering Pete," *Hot Rod Magazine*, 2007, http://www.hotrod.com/thehistoryof/113_0708_pete_petersen/index.html/**"If it weren't for *Hot Rod*":**

Ibid. / **"throughout the world":** Editorial, *Hot Rod Magazine*, Jan. 1948, p. 3/ **"A guy named Johnny Johnson":** DeWitt, *Cool Cars, High Art*, p. 19/ **"A red '32 Ford five window":** Ibid. / **"gasoline-powered dreams":** Dick Messer quoted in "*Hot Rod, Motor Trend* Founder Petersen Dies," Mar. 23, 2007, National Hot Rod Association, http://www.nhra.com/content/news/19207.htm/ **"the helter skelter jalopy class":** "Los Angeles News in Brief," *LAT,* Jan. 23, 1948, p. A3/ **"Their biggest fight":** Jack Curnow, "Hot Rod Show Exhibits Far Beyond Back-Yard Garage Jalopy," *LAT,* Jan. 27, 1949, p. C3/ **driven by Wally Parks:** "Cream of Hot Rod Crop Exhibited at Armory," *LAT,* Jan. 22, 1949, p. A5/ **"He never lost":** Ken Gross, "Pete Petersen: Remembering Pete," *Hot Rod Magazine*, 2007, http://www.hotrod.com/thehistoryof/113_0708_pete_petersen/index.html/ **McGregor had just finished:** Ken Gross, "Death Be Not Proud," in Cotter, *The Cobra in the Barn*, p. 236. These and other details about the crash come from this article and "Crash of Hot Rod Racers," *LAT,* May 23, 1949, p. 1/ **"the magazine for a motoring world":** "*Hot Rod, Motor Trend* Founder Petersen Dies," Mar. 23, 2007, National Hot Rod Association, http://www.nhra.com/content/news/19207.htm/ **"The once-roundly condemned":** "Californian's Hot Rod Feature of Tulsa Show," *LAT,* Nov. 12, 1950, p. C28/ **Gordon Browning of the Los Angeles:** "Gordon Browning," *Drive Magazine,* Mar. 2006, p. 35/ **"When?":** Dennis Hevesi, "Robert Petersen, Publisher of Auto Buff Magazines, Dies at 80," *New York Times,* Mar. 27, 2007, http://www.nytimes.com/2007/03/27/business/media/27petersen.html?_r=1&oref=slogin

Chapter 24: Enchanted Kingdom

a different group of race car: "Sports Cars Race at Santa Ana," *LAT,* June 24, 1950, p. B3/ **"The construction gives":** "Southland Called Sports Car Capital," *LAT,* Nov. 9, 1952, p. A13/ **the No. 1 American market:** "Motorama Exposition Opens Here," *LAT,* Oct. 25, 1953, p. A14/ **a two-and-a-half-mile layout:** Jack Curnow, "Sports Cars Roar Today in Road Race," *LAT,* June 25, 1950, p. B14/ **"Beverly Hills sportsman":** Ibid. / **121.95 miles per hour:** Batchelor, *The American Hot Rod*, p. 14/ **"us-versus-them attitude":** Ibid., p. 131/ **"huffing and chuffing":** Ibid., p. 132/ **"howling screech":** Ibid. / **Confounding the handicappers:** Jack Curnow, "Richter Captures Santa Ana Race," *LAT,* June 26, 1950, p. C4/ **"It's an accepted fact":** Lamm, "Dean Batchelor Tribute," *The American Hot Rod*, p. 7/ **came to California as a baby:** Nolan, *Phil Hill*, p. 19/ **"I was far more interested":** Ibid., p. 20/ **"This was during the Depression":** Ibid., p. 21/ **"foolishly happy":** Ibid. / **"I'd begin pestering":** Ibid. / **"in absolutely amazing condition":** Ibid. / **"an unconscious effort":** Ibid., p. 26/ **"swagger and smoke":** Ibid. / **"I had an identity":** Ibid., p. 31/ **"the dash with the big round tach":** Ibid., p. 33/ **"generally acknowledged the fastest":** Jack Curnow, "Sports Cars Roar Today in Road Race," *LAT,* June 25, 1950, p. B14/ **"Into the first tricky S-turn":** Jack Curnow, "Richter Captures Santa Ana Race," *LAT,* June 26, 1950, p. C4/ **"I was always aware":** Nolan, *Phil Hill*, p. 39/ **"the most theatrical style":** Scalzo, "The Glamour Years of Racing on the West Coast," *Automobile Quarterly*, p. 132/ **The 2.4-mile layout:** The course description stems from a close observation of the map in White, *Lost*

Race Tracks, p. 20/**"the reverberations":** Art Lauring, "From the Pits," *LAT,* Apr. 8, 1956, p. A30/**"hazardous and difficult art":** Nolan, *Phil Hill,* p. 14/**"Long Lead":** Ibid., p. 15/**"his own brakes were rapidly failing":** Ibid./**became his brother-in-law:** Ibid., p. 28/**44 minutes, 8 seconds:** "Jaguar Takes Road Race at Pebble Beach," *LAT,* Nov. 6, 1950, p. C4/**"color, pageantry, showmanship":** Art Lauring, "From the Pits," *LAT,* Apr. 8, 1956, p. A30/**sunny desert oasis:** "Hill Favored in Race at Palm Springs," *LAT,* Mar. 23, 1952, p. A11/**"pretzel circuit":** "Sports Car Specialists Race at Santa Barbara," *LAT,* May 28, 1955, p. C5/**"romance, splendor":** Scalzo, "The Glamour Years of Racing on the West Coast," *Automobile Quarterly,* p. 129/**"More than ninety thousand people":** "Pollock Snags Race Before 90,000 Fans," *LAT,* June 1, 1952, p. B11/**The only excitement:** "Torrey Pines Race Captured by Hill," *LAT,* July 21, 1952, p. C3

Chapter 25: The Car of Tomorrow

hosted a swank party: James Coop, "Skylarking," *LAT,* Nov. 10, 1952, p. B2/**"one of the world's most famous":** "Southland Called Sports Car Capital," *LAT,* Nov. 9, 1952, p. A13/**"the internationally known":** "Kaiser-Darren Will Be Shown," *LAT,* June 20, 1954, p. A18/**"Paris' brilliant Howard Darrin":** Display ad, *LAT,* June 25, 1954, p. C2/**"We had one thing":** Darrin, "Disaster Is My Business," *Automobile Quarterly*, p. 60/**"The three things":** Ibid., p. 67/**"She specified only":** Ibid./**Super 8 Victoria:** Lorimer, "Super 8 Victoria: Queen of the Darrin Packards," *Automobile Quarterly*, Summer 1968/**"He was like an early":** Author conversation with Fred Zimmerman, auto historian, Blackhawk Museum, Danville, Calif., Feb. 2005/**"it was the car to have":** Batchelor, *Harrah's Automobile Collection,* p. 175/**dependable, low-cost car:** Foster, *Henry J. Kaiser,* p. 144/**"Kaiser at first envisioned":** Ibid., p. 3/**"logistical and other problems":** Ibid., p. 143/**"appeared in the trade paper":** Ibid., p. 142/**"The boss...enjoyed driving":** Ibid./**profit of $17 million:** Ibid., p. 149/**executives charged GM:** Ibid./**"overpriced and out of date":** Ibid., p. 157/**"So I signed a contract":** Darrin, "Disaster Is My Business," *Automobile Quartery*, p. 67/**"the motorcar of the future":** Bill Henry, "By the Way," *LAT,* Jan. 3, 1951, p. A1/**"the car of tomorrow":** "Dream Auto Unveiled by LA Designer," *LAT,* Sept. 13, 1952, p. 10/**which Harley designed himself:** Conversation with Richard Earl, May 2008/**"Mies van der Rohe chairs":** *Battle Creek (Michigan) Enquirer*, May 19, 1929/**extra suits of light blue:** Bayley, *Harley Earl and the Dream Machine*, p. 12/**Some mistakenly thought:** Darrin, "Disaster Is My Business," *Automobile Quarterly*, p. 64/**"first designer to attain such heights":** Sloan, *My Years with General Motors*, p. 77/**power, automatic transmission:** Ibid., p. 264/**"twin Allison engines":** Ibid., p. 278/**"When I saw those two rudders":** "Harley J. Earl Dies," *Detroit News,* Apr. 10, 1969/**"There is a touch of Oldfield":** "I Dream Automobiles," *Saturday Evening Post,* Aug. 7, 1954, p. 82/**a full-size model:** Batchelor, *Harrah's Automobile Collection,* p. 121/**"Harley Earl is the father":** Harley Earl page in the "Corvette Hall of Fame," National Corvette Museum, http://www.corvettemuseum.com/library-archives/hof/earl.shtml/**"one of the first Americans to take delivery":** Batchelor, *Harrah's Automobile Collection,* p. 122

Chapter 26: Bob Hirohata's Wild Ride

"I am a very happy man": Hiney, *Raymond Chandler,* p. 181/**"Wandering up and down":** Ibid./**rigged up a two-way speaker system:** "Esther Snyder Dies," *Contra Costa Times,* Aug. 7, 2006, p. A10/**"Speedee Service System":** "History of the Historic Site of the Original McDonald's in San Bernardino," McDonald's: The Historic Site, route-66.com/mcdonalds/**"All American meal":** From a 1955 placard posted at the Downey McDonald's, observed by the author, Dec. 2006/**"Big Boy Burger, the original":** Photograph in Witzel, *Route 66 Remembered*, p. 99/**"the billboard raised":** Hess, *Googie Redux,* p. 86/**"one of the most significant":** William H. Honan, "Wayne McAllister, 92, Architect for a Car Culture," *New York Times,* Apr. 3, 2000/**"on the level like any other building":** Douglas Haskell quoted in Hess, *Googie Redux,* p. 66/**"This is Googie":** Ibid., p. 68/**"a lot of upward hard-driving":** Wolfe, *The Pump House Gang*, p. 125/**"influenced by the automobile":** "Wayne McAllister, a Pioneer Strip Architect, Dies after Fall," *Las Vegas Review-Journal,* Apr. 1, 2000/**Near the top of the arches:** Author's observation, Dec. 2006/**"the fastest growing community":** McWilliams, *California,* p. 14/**"the commercial strip":** Hess, *Googie Redux,* p. 19/**"little car":** Washington, *Racing's Fast Little Cars*, p. 5/**"teardrop-shaped, 13-foot canvas":** Witzel, *Route 66 Remembered*, p. 146/**"power lines cut":** Liebs, *Main Street to Miracle Mile,* p. 189/**the second self-serve in California:** Author interview with Jerry Cummings, Robinson Oil Corporation advisor, Dec. 2007/**"Five or six pretty girls":** Quoted in Liebs, *Main Street to Miracle Mile,* p. 108/**"a strictly local phenomenon":** Ibid./**"California's newest contribution":** Ibid./**the wings of an airplane:** Cecilia Rasmussen, "A Daredevil Pilot and Angel Falls," *LAT,* July 2, 2006, p. B2/**biggest screen in the world:** Petersen Museum exhibit, observed by author, June 2006/**"Out on Pico Boulevard":** Liebs, *Main Street to Miracle Mile,* p. 155/**"You see, an auto's a lot more":** Ibid., p. 159/**"was chopped":** Al Carr, "George Barris: Penknives to Winners," *LAT,* July 30, 1970, p. C5/**"lowering the top of the car":** Tom Wolfe, *Kandy-Kolored Tangerine-Flake Streamline Baby*, p. 89/**carved car models:** Al Carr, "George Barris: Penknives to Winners," *LAT,* July 30, 1970, p. C5/**hammered pot lids:** Ibid./**"She'd go to open":** Gary Schultz, "Interview with George Barris," Apr. 22, 2004, http://www.filmmonthly.com/Profiles/Articles/GBarris/GBarris.html/**"They wanted me":** Wolfe, *Kandy-Kolored Tangerine-Flake Streamline Baby*, p. 89/**"the father of customizing":** Petersen Automotive Museum, petersenmuseum.org/**"He did all his work":** Dick Bertolucci quoted in Ganahl, *The American Custom Car,* p. 23. Bertolucci's next quote is also from this page./**"He is a good example of a kid":** Wolfe, *Kandy-Kolored Tangerine-Flake Streamline Baby*, p. 82/**"creating forms":** Ibid., p. 83/**"the teenage netherworld":** Ibid., p. 92/**"They could tell me":** Wolfe, *Kandy-Kolored Tangerine-Flake Streamline Baby*, p. 90/**"lifted some twenty designs":** Ibid./**"If there was any one marked trend":** Griffith Borgeson, "1950 National Roadster Show," *The Best of Hot Rod*, p. 31/**More juried shows around the state:** Ganahl, *The American Custom Car,* p. 61/**For as long as he could remember:** Hirohata, "Kross Kountry in a Kustom," *Rod and Custom*, p. 10/**"When I picked up the car":** Ibid./**"The top was chopped":** Ibid./**"looked like a couple of narrow":** Wolfe, *Kandy-Kolored Tangerine-Flake*

Streamline Baby, p. 90. Wolfe is speaking here about Barris customs in general, but this look certainly applies to the Hirohata Merc./**"We loaded the luggage":** Hirohata, "Kross Kountry in a Kustom," *Rod and Custom*, p. 12/**"I couldn't even get out":** Ibid.

Chapter 27: Indianapolis Takeover

"astounded at the speeds": Hirohata, "Kross Kountry in a Kustom," *Rod and Custom*, p. 63/**"didn't feel quite right":** Jack Curnow, "Holland Sizzles with 137.868 Mark," *LAT,* May 25, 1953, p. C1/**hopped aboard the Ray Crawford:** Ibid./**"Dressed in a manner":** Jack Curnow, "Frustrated as Racer, Aggie Turns Promoter," *LAT,* Feb. 5, 1950, p. 39/**"The Armenian Beau Brummell":** Ibid./**"You can own it":** Ibid./**"It's a saga":** Ibid./**Freddie Agabashian drove it:** "Agabashian Nabs Auto Title," *LAT,* Oct. 31, 1949, p. C4/**"the Shish-kebab kids":** Jack Curnow, "Drivers on Edge Awaiting Start," *LAT,* May 30, 1950, p. C1/**"the sleek, technologically advanced":** "Car Built by Angeleno for '52 500-Miler," *LAT,* May 31, 1953, p. B11/ **all of them "honed their skills":** Yates, *The Hot Rod,* p. 62–63/**"flip-flopped all the way":** Al Wolf, "Sportraits," *LAT,* July 27, 1950, p. C2/**Mantz had run the Agajanian:** "M Boys Go as Entry Today," *LAT,* Mar. 13, 1949, p. 29/**"smackeroo":** Jack Curnow, "Parsons Indianapolis Victor Over 345 Miles," *LAT,* May 31, 1950, p. C1/ **raked in one hundred thousand dollars:** "Southland's Indianapolis Cut $100,00," *LAT,* June 2, 1950, p. C2/**purse-paying midget races:** Bill Millard, Towe Museum, Sacramento, email to author, Mar. 20, 2007/**"The Cow Palace was dangerous":** "Former Indy Chaps Roared at Hayward," *Hayward Daily Review,* May 19, 1969/**"sit forward in our seats":** Dick Hyland, "The Hyland Fling," *LAT,* May 1, 1946, p. 11/**"I felt sure I'd crash":** Nolan, *Phil Hill*, p. 37/**nineteen Golden Staters:** Jack Curnow, "Holland Sizzles with 137.868 Mark," *LAT,* May 25, 1953, p. C1/**"two-seated buggy":** AP, "Vukovich's Death Stuns Home Town," *LAT,* May 31, 1955, p. C2/**his father committed suicide:** Lisette Hilton, "Vukovich Was a Fearless Racing Legend," http://sports.espn.go.com/espn/classic/bio/news/story?page=Vukovich_Bill/**"Don't tangle with me":** Ibid./**"the Mad Russian":** Jack Curnow, "Billy Vukovich Nips Faulkner in 75-Lap Race," *LAT,* May 13, 1949, p. C3/**"One of the toughest":** Jack Curnow, "Enigma to Racing Fraternity," *LAT,* May 31, 1955, p. C1/**"He could do anything":** Ibid./**"hot dog kid":** Jack Curnow, "Ruttman Roars to Record '500' Victory," *LAT,* May 31, 1952, p. B1/**"the Rich Kids" [and] "Whiz Kids"** Michael T. Lynch, "The Rise and Fall of the Indianapolis Roadster," *Monterey Historic Automobile Races Program,* Aug. 2007, p. 74/**"Between Ruttman and Vukovich":** Jack Curnow, "Ruttman Roars to Record '500' Victory," *LAT,* May 31, 1952, p. B1/**broken steering column pin:** "Vukovich Wins Pole Position," *LAT,* May 18, 1953, p. C1/**175,000 people turned out:** "Expect 175,000," *LAT,* Mar. 28, 1953, p. C2/**Vukovich, in No. 14:** Photograph caption, AP, "Bill Vukovich Winning the Indianapolis 500," May 30, 1953, corbis.com, U1225800INP/**"the finest I've ever seen":** Jack Curnow, "Vukovich Pockets $89,496 Jackpot," *LAT,* June 1, 1953, p. C1/**"If they think this is hot":** Michael T. Lynch, "The

Rise and Fall of the Indianapolis Roadster," *Monterey Historic Automobile Races Program,* Aug. 2007, p. 73/**"We were so happy":** AP, "Vukie's Victory Brings Tears, Elation, Relief," *LAT,* May 31, 1953. All the family quotes come from this article.

Chapter 28: Twelve Months

go to Indianapolis to see: Perry, *James Dean*, p. 152/**town of Salinas:** "Salinas of 1917 Built at Warners," *LAT,* Mar. 11, 1955, p. 20/**"At once a roughneck":** Phillip K. Scheuer, "Kazan Has Another Offbeat Film Classic," *LAT,* Jan. 23, 1955, p. D1/**"the most exciting young actor":** "Two Films Set for Elizabeth Taylor," *LAT,* Jan. 31, 1955, p. 20/**"I can't remember":** Hedda Hopper, "Ex-Farm Boy Is Making Hay in Movies," *LAT,* Mar. 27, 1955, p. E3/**"He arrived on the dot":** Ibid./**"My whole life":** Ibid./**twenty thousand fans:** "McAfee's Ferrari Wins Speed Duel," *LAT,* May 30, 1955, p. C3/**"James Dean, Hollywood actor":** Art Lauring, "McAfee Wins Desert Race in Ferrari," *LAT,* Mar. 28, 1955, p. C4/**two other promising young actors:** Phillip K. Scheuer, "A Town Called Hollywood," *LAT,* Apr. 3, 1955, p. E2/**the last practice lap of the day:** "Ayulo Critically Injured in Crash," *LAT,* May 17, 1953, p. C3/**"came down the main straightaway":** Ibid./**wife and four-year-old daughter:** "Ayulo Rites Set Monday," *LAT,* May 20, 1955, p. C3/**"Witnesses said Ayulo":** "Driver Manny Ayulo Dies of Injuries," *LAT,* May 18, 1955, p. C1/**"chose to take the wall":** Jack Curnow, "Enigma to Racing Fraternity," *LAT,* May 31, 1955, p. C1/**"Vukovich's sleek dark blue":** "Vukie Called Shot," *LAT,* May 30, 1955, p. C2/**"raced into the backyard":** AP, "Vukovich's Death Stuns Home Town," *LAT,* May 31, 1955, p. C2/**"Many residents who had been":** Ibid./**"The badly burned Hopkins Special":** Caption, Wire Service, Bettmann/Corbis, June 4, 1955, corbis.com/**looking on "helplessly":** Caption, Wire Service, Bettmann/Corbis, June 1, 1955, corbis.com/**"Billy didn't burn":** "Vukovich's Body Will Be Returned," *LAT,* June 1, 1955, p. C3/**"probably dead":** "Funeral Rites Held," *LAT,* June 2, 1955, p. 35/**"The shock was almost":** AP, "Vukovich's Death Stuns Home Town," *LAT*, May 31, 1955, p. C2/**out-of-control Mercedes racecar:** "Race Car Plows into Crowd, At Least 70 Killed," *LAT,* June 12, 1955, p. 1/**including Santa Monica's Phil Hill:** Ibid./**"her Morgenson Special swerved":** "Woman Killed in Torrey Pines Race," *LAT,* July 11, 1955, p. 1. Information on Kowalski comes from this article./**"This is a drag race":** "Behind the Cameras," *Rebel Without a Cause,* Two-Disc Special Edition DVD, Warner Brothers, 1955. All the quotes from the Young-Dean interview come from this program./**his Porsche blew a piston:** Perry, *James Dean*, p. 152/**"Motor racing...had become":** Perry, *James Dean,* p. 11/**"a tiny vehicle":** Ibid., p. 18/**The car scared Ursula Andress:** Ibid., p. 186/**"at the last minute":** "Film Star James Dean Killed in Auto Crash," *LAT,* Oct. 1, 1955, p. 1/ **long ride to Paso Robles:** "Death Premonition by Dean Recalled," *LAT,* Oct. 2, 1955, p. A/**declared to be accidental:** "Death of Dean, Actor, Listed as Accidental," *LAT,* Oct. 12, 1955, p. 5/**"neither man had his safety belt":** Ibid./**"the sense of real loss":** Phillip K. Scheuer, "James Dean Cheats Death in Bit of Film Irony," *LAT,* Oct. 30, 1955, p. E2/**when his car flipped:** "Jack McGrath Killed," *LAT,* Nov. 7, 1955, p. C1/**Faulkner's**

car blew a tire: "Faulkner, Ernie McAfee Die in Auto Crashes," *LAT,* Apr. 23, 1956, p. C1/**"Listen," he said":** Ibid./**"Whether you slip":** Ibid./**"The car was buckled":** "Faulkner, Ernie McAfee Die in Auto Crashes," *LAT,* Apr. 23, 1956, p. C1/**"quiet, unassuming":** Ibid./**Services for McAfee:** "Final Rites Today for Ernie McAfee," *LAT,* Apr. 25, 1956, p. 35/**Faulkner's rites:** "Walt Faulkner Services Set," *LAT,* Apr. 24, 1956, p. C1/**"a true champion":** "Billy Vukovich Memorial Rite in Fresno," *LAT,* May 31, 1956, p. C3/**"his accomplishments, his courage":** Ibid.

Chapter 29: Comeback

Eight Californians*:* "Californians Take First Eight Places," *LAT,* May 31, 1956, p. C1/**a lousy twenty-two seconds:** Will Grimsley, "Flaherty Beats Hanks by 22 Seconds," AP, *LAT,* May 31, 1956, p. C1/**jumped over a guardrail:** "Race Driver Sweikert Dies in Crash," *LAT,* June 18, 1956, p. 1/**"Rangy, curly-haired":** Ibid./**his wife, Dolores:** "Bob Sweikert Rites Pending," *LAT,* June 19, 1956, p. C2/**"because it was no longer":** "Jack McGrath Killed," *LAT,* Nov. 7, 1955, p. C1/**Montgomery Air Field:** "Sports Car Races Set," *LAT,* July 1, 1956, p. B16/**"Certain things are apparent":** Art Lauring, "From the Pits," *LAT,* Apr. 29, 1956, p. A25/**entered into negotiations:** "SCRAMP Was the Beginning," Mazda Raceway [at] Laguna Seca, laguna-seca.com/**"virtually worthless with respect":** Oct. 6, 1957, publication of SCCA, quoted in Bob Hagin, "An Unheralded Auto Safety Pioneer," Jan. 29, 2001, http://www.theautochannel.com/news/writers/bhagin/2001/fs0105.html/**"force vectors at a single point":** Brock Yates, "Reinventing the Wheel," *Car and Driver,* 1993, http://www.cragar.com/history/reinventing_the_wheel.pdf/**stopped selling his old brands:** Brock Yates, "Reinventing the Wheel," *Car and Driver,* 1993, http://www.cragar.com/history/reinventing_the_wheel.pdf/**"No one can calculate":** Bob Hagin, "An Unheralded Auto Safety Pioneer," Jan. 29, 2001, http://www.theautochannel.com/news/writers/bhagin/2001/fs0105.html/**"Impact Auto Saf-Tee Belt":** Batchelor, *The American Hot Rod*, p. 65/**"the hairy-eyed tempters":** Art Lauring, "From the Pits," *LAT,* May 29, 1955, p. C12/**challenging 3.5-mile loop:** "Raceway Slates Opener April 27," *LAT,* Mar. 21, 1957, p. C2/**Ginther put his foot down:** Art Lauring, "From the Pits," *LAT,* July 14, 1957, p. A23/**championship stock car race:** Jack Curnow, "Jerry Unser Drives to Riverside Victory," *LAT,* Dec. 2, 1957, p. C1/**"more like a chemical engineer":** Dick Hyland, "The Hyland Fling," *LAT,* May 1, 1946, p. 11/**"There's Sam":** Jack Curnow, "The Thin Man Finally Gets Fat," *LAT,* May 31, 1957, p. C5/**increase aircraft engine horsepower:** Dick Hyland, "The Hyland Fling," *LAT,* May 1, 1946, p. 11/**"I began doodling":** Donald Davidson, "George Salih's Little Beauty," *Monterey Historic Automobile Races Program*, Aug. 2007, p. 64/**"in a nearly flat position":** Braven Dyer, "Sports Parade," *LAT,* May 27, 1957, p. C1/**chief wrenchman for the winning:** Michael T. Lynch, "The Rise and Fall of the Indianapolis Roadster," *Monterey Historic Automobile Races Program*, Aug. 2007, p. 74/**called everyone he met:** Donald Davidson, "George Salih's Little Beauty," *Monterey Historic Automobile Races Program,* Aug. 2007, p. 65/**these five men:** Display placard, Petersen Automotive Museum, observed by author, Mar. 2006/**"I felt this**

car could do": "Sam Hanks Finished with 500," *LAT,* May 31, 1957, p. C5/**"It looked strange":** "Sweet and Low," *Time,* June 10, 1957, http://www.time.com/time/magazine/article/0,9171,937469,00.html/**Averaging a record:** "Hanks Shatters Marks in '500' Win," *LAT,* May 31, 1957, p. C1/**"the most popular win":** Donald Davidson, "George Salih's Little Beauty," *Monterey Historic Automobile Races Program,* Aug. 2007, p. 65/**"This is the only ambition":** "Sweet and Low," *Time,* June 10, 1957, http://www.time.com/time/magazine/article/0,9171,937469,00.html/**"to third place":** Jack Curnow, "Jerry Unser Drives to Riverside Victory," *LAT,* Dec. 2, 1957, p. C1/**"You think of everything":** Ibid./**"It seems hard to comprehend":** Ibid.

Chapter 30: McQueen

"I don't want to sound": *Indy Car Series Magazine,* Sept. 2005, p. 45/**"If you were in a race":** Ibid./**His first sports car race:** "Biography: Dan Gurney," http://allamerican-racers.com/bio.html/**"the most formidable sports car":** Adler, *The Art of the Sports Car,* p. 215/**a twelve-acre site south:** Jim Race, "Shelby the Factory," caferace.com/ **for $5.5 million:** Michael Taylor, "Think Big," *SFC,* Jan. 28, 2007, p. J6/**"a thirty-two-year-old Texas oilman":** Art Lauring, "Shelby Wins Torrey Pines Feature," *LAT,* July 11, 1955/**launched his Euopean Grand Prix career:** "History," Official Carroll Shelby Website, http://www.carrollshelby.com/history.html/**"the world's greatest sports car racing event":** Display ad, *LAT,* Sept. 4, 1958, p. B1/**"The toast of Europe":** "Hill Arrives Tomorrow," *LAT,* Sept. 18, 1958, p. C4/**misspelled his name as "Guerney":** "Times-Mirror Stages Sports Car Classic," *LAT,* July 25, 1958, p. C1/**"can do everything":** Jeanne Hoffman, "Beat Up Buick," *LAT,* Oct. 7, 1958, p. C5/**"We can replace anything":** Ernie Nagamatsu, "The History of Max and Ina Balchowsky and Old Yeller II," Old Yeller II: 1959 Balchowsky Buick Special, http://oldyeller2.com/history.html/**"Free Advice With Purchases":** Jeanne Hoffman, "Beat Up Buick," *LAT,* Oct. 7, 1958, p. C5/**"a tossed salad":** Ibid./**"amazing amalgam":** Batchelor, *The American Hot Rod,* p. 134/**"Like its canine namesake":** Scalzo, "The Glamour Years of Racing on the West Coast," *Automobile Quarterly,* p. 136/**"one of their best weekends ever":** Bill Dredge, "Balchowsky Pulls Major Upset at Santa Barbara," *LAT,* Aug. 31, 1958, p. A6/**delighted all twenty thousand of the spectators:** Bill Dredge, "Balchowsky Wins Road Race," *LAT,* Sept. 1, 1958, p. C3/**"I observed Ol' Yeller":** Scalzo, "The Glamour Years of Racing on the West Coast," *Automobile Quarterly,* p. 137/**Balchowsky and Old Yeller qualified seventh:** Bill Dredge, "Two Reventlow Grand Prix Cars Qualify," *LAT,* Oct. 12, 1958, p. 1/**"Daigh got off the mark":** Bill Dredge, "70,000 See Daigh Win Grand Prix," *LAT,* Oct. 13, 1958, p. 1. Other events in the race derive from this article./**"a hometown Riverside boy":** Ibid./**"not a single person":** Ibid./**"adult Western":** Boots Lebaron, "New Adult Western Series Star Owes Maturity to Active and Varied Life," *LAT,* Sept. 21, 1958, p. G7/**"His restless manner":** Ibid./**"worked on a tanker":** Ibid./**"Off the set his loves":** Ibid./**in January a show-business column:** Jean McMurphy, "From Shirley Temple to Peter Gunn," *LAT,* Jan. 4, 1959, p. G2/**he and Clark Gable:** "Concours Next

Sunday," *LAT,* Mar. 8, 1959, p. A16/**"Around the studios everybody":** Terrill, *Steve McQueen,* p. 66/**Novice Production:** Bob Thomas, "Miles Wins Sports Race Feature," *LAT,* May 31, 1959, p. C6/**"forty of the hard-to-beat":** "Sports Cars Race at Santa Barbara," *LAT,* May 30, 1959, p. A5/**"That was the worst thing":** Bob Thomas, "Actor Steve McQueen Happiest When He's Racing," *LAT,* May 20, 1962, p. G8/**the *Times* ran a picture:** Bob Thomas, "McAfee and Miles Figure 1-2," *LAT,* Aug. 23, 1959, p. C7/**"The studio kept putting out":** Bob Thomas, "Actor Steve McQueen Happiest When He's Racing," *LAT,* May 20, 1962, p. G8/**the time separating:** Bob Thomas, "Krause Drives to Victory," *LAT,* Sept. 6, 1959, p. B4/**"Steve McQueen's hotter":** Hedda Hopper, "McQueen Impresses in *Never So Few,*" *LAT,* Oct. 29, 1959, p. C8/**"I never have gotten a thrill":** Aleene Barnes, "Steve McQueen Stays Busy," *LAT,* May 22, 1960, p. N2/**leaving a couple of months before production:** Hedda Hopper, "Entertainment," *LAT,* Aug. 10, 1961, p. B12/**"I would follow Stirling":** Bob Thomas, "Actor Steve McQueen Happiest When He's Racing," *LAT,* May 20, 1962, p. G8

Chapter 31: Heroes and Anti-Heroes

"one of the new folk heroes": John Wasserman, *SFC,* Mar. 30, 1968, reprinted in *SFC* Datebook, Aug. 12, 2007, p. 14/**"Randall is associated":** Boots Lebaron, "New Adult Western Series Star Owes Maturity to Active and Varied Life," *LAT,* Sept. 21, 1958, p. G7/**"gave birth to bike culture":** William M. Welch, *USA Today,* Apr. 5, 2006, p. 4A/**"with its millions":** Kerouac, *On the Road*, p. 107/**go to midget:** Ibid., p. 44/**"a travel bureau car":** Ibid., p. 181/**"a Frisco taxi-jitney":** Ibid., p. 205/**disliked driving:** Ibid., p. 121/**wrecked '37 Ford:** Ibid., p. 265/**Firestone tire shop:** Ibid., p. 186/**1.6 million Volkswagen Beetles:** Tad Burness, "Auto Album," *Contra Costa Times,* Apr. 13, 2008/**reupholstered Liberace's Cadillac:** Al Carr, "George Barris: Penknives to Winners," *LAT,* July 30, 1970, p. C5/**"candy apple red":** Exhibit placard, Oakland Museum of California, observed by author, May 2006/**"The Mystery Car":** Ibid./**"the size of a good NFL":** Joel Siegel, "Once Upon a Time," *LAT,* Oct. 10, 1971, p. W7/**"began jury-rigging a simple system":** Paige R. Penland, *Lowrider*/**"the automobile is used":** E. E. East and M. F. Holley, "Traffic Survey, Los Angeles Metropolitan Area 1937," p. 27/**"the problem has not":** Ibid., p. 7/**"The growing street":** Ibid., p. 27/**"a marvel of innovation":** Bob Pool, "Pasadena Freeway Is Headed for Immortality," *LAT,* n.d. Courtesy of the Pasadena Museum of History/**"a modern state highway":** Chester G. Hanson, "Road Measure Signed," *LAT,* June 24, 1947, p. 1/**"the world's biggest traffic problem":** "City Against Auto," *Life,* July 11, 1949, p. 79. All quotes come from this article, pp. 79–84./**"horizontally rather than":** McWilliams, *California*, p. 238/**"Smog and fumes":** Ibid., p. 245/**"Queer chugging noises":** McWilliams, *Fool's Paradise,* p. 11/**"The year 1943 is":** Ed Ainsworth, "Raw Gasoline Vapors Believed Partial Cause of Smog Irritation," *LAT,* Jan. 18, 1951, p. A1/**"Thousands of eyes smarted":** Ford, "Smog Settles Over Los Angeles," in McWilliams, *California*, p. 383/**"People came here":** "Man Who Organized the First Campaign," *LAT,* Nov. 19, 1953, p. A5/**"My**

interest was life": Al Martinez, "Haagen-Smit, Pioneer in Study of Smog, Dies at 76," *LAT,* Mar. 19, 1977, p. A1/**"No one could miss it":** Ibid./**"He took a glass":** Ibid./**"The main villainous substances":** "Mystery Cloaking Smog Birth Ends," *LAT,* May 2, 1952, p. A1/**a laboratory explosion:** Ibid./**"How smog is produced":** William S. Barton, "Puzzle of Smog Production Solved by Caltech Scientist," *LAT,* Nov. 20, 1950/**"The greatest mystery":** "Mystery Cloaking Smog Birth Ends," *LAT,* May 2, 1952, p. A1/**"Then the war":** Al Martinez, "Haagen-Smit, Pioneer in Study of Smog, Dies at 76," *LAT,* Mar. 19, 1977, p. A1/**"Automobiles themselves":** William S. Barton, "Autos Held Large Smog Contributor," *LAT,* May 26, 1952, p. A1/**harmed people's health:** "Car Exhausts Blamed for Irritants," *LAT,* Oct. 5, 1953, p. 11/**"scientific Don Quixote":** Al Martinez, "Haagen-Smit, Pioneer in Study of Smog, Dies at 76," *LAT,* Mar. 19, 1977, p. A1/**"a one-man army":** Ibid./**He and a fellow chemist:** "Less Driving, Burning Urged in Smog Fight," *LAT,* May 13, 1955, p.1/**"a radical revision":** "Car Exhausts Blamed for Irritants," *LAT,* Oct. 5, 1953, p. 11/**"one of the two most important":** "U.S. Act to Speed Freeways," *LAT,* June 28, 1956, p. 2/**"Now, with the 1956 bill just passed":** Ibid./**"the largest public works project":** "Highway," *LAT,* July 10, 1966, p. D9/**"Harbor, Golden State, Ventura":** William C. Stewart, "New Era of the Freeway," *LAT,* Jan. 2, 1959, p. 75/**"new era of the freeway":** Ibid./**"Today the wail of the ambulance":** William C. Stewart, "Can Urban Chaos Be Prevented Here?" *LAT,* Oct. 15, 1957, p. A1/**"mounting alarm":** "Californian to Lead U.S. Smog Talks," *LAT,* Oct. 13, 1958, p. B1/**"the automobile industry has not yet fulfilled":** Supervisor Warren Dorn quoted in Don Shannon, "Southlanders Scold Auto Industry," *LAT,* Nov. 19, 1958, p. 2/**"The people have":** Al Martinez, "Haagen-Smit, Pioneer in Study of Smog, Dies at 76," *LAT,* Mar. 19, 1977, p. A1/**sat on an advisory panel:** "State Commission on Auto Smog Proposed," *LAT,* Dec. 18, 1959, p. 28/**one of its original members:** Al Thrasher, "Brown Names State Smog Control Board," *LAT,* May 27, 1960, p. B1/**"He was once my judge and jury":** Al Martinez, "Haagen-Smit, Pioneer in Study of Smog, Dies at 76," *LAT,* Dec. 18, 1959, p. 28/**"Haagen-Smit stood":** Ibid.

Chapter 32: Spirit of America

"because the jet engine": Al Wolf, "Lots of Throttle Left," *LAT,* Aug. 10, 1963, p. A3/**"the most radical":** Bill Dredge, "Jet-Powered Racing Car Prepared," *LAT,* Aug. 5, 1962, p. M7/**"looks like a F-104 jet fighter":** Bill Dredge, "Culver City Man in Jet Engine Race," *LAT,* July 8, 1962, p. H8/**"It's not easy for a guy":** Charles Maher, "Money, Prestige or Madness?" *LAT,* Dec. 5, 1965, p. J8/**"a way-out scheme":** Ibid./**"I didn't think":** Ibid./**"Of course, I was young":** Ibid./**"El Mirage sort of scared me":** Ibid./**"the World Series":** Shav Glick, "Speed Seasons the Bonneville Salt," *LAT,* Oct. 3, 1979, p. F1/**Three cars broke 200 miles an hour:** Wally Parks, "Bonneville Nationals 1950," *The Best of Hot Rod Magazine*, p. 41/**"a piston-driven car":** Shav Glick, "Land Speed Record," *LAT,* Sept. 9, 1979, p. C13/**"There was a lot of ridicule:** Ibid./**"My parents thought":** Ibid./**"Friend...when you get":** Ibid./**"The course is one hundred feet**

wide": "Record Seeker," UPI, *LAT,* Aug. 3, 1963, p. A5/**"All I'm really interested in":** Al Wolf, "Lots of Throttle Left," *LAT,* Aug. 10, 1963, p. A3/**first run on Oct. 13:** "Breedlove Zips 468.72 for Record!" UPI, *LAT,* Oct. 14, 1964, p. B1/**"The Spirit of America veered":** Shav Glick, "Speed Seasons the Bonneville Salt," *LAT,* Oct. 3, 1979, p. F1/**"Just let me kiss":** "Breedlove Breaks Record—Crashes," UPI, *LAT,* Oct. 16, 1964, p. B1. The other quotes from the accident are taken from this article./**surviving a blown-out tire:** "Arfons Regains Land Speed Record," UPI, *LAT,* Oct. 28, 1964, p. B1/**"When I'm strapped in":** "L.A. Man Sets 407 M.P.H. Speed Mark," UPI, *LAT,* Aug. 6, 1963, p. C1/**"Once I close the canopy":** Charles Maher, "Money, Prestige or Madness?" *LAT,* Dec. 5, 1965, p. J8/**"It never pays":** Bob Thomas, "The Why Doesn't Matter," *LAT,* Mar. 14, 1965, p. N8/**"This is what he wants":** Charles Maher, "Money, Prestige or Madness?" *LAT,* Dec. 5, 1965, p. J8/**I went through all that":** George Lucas, interview, "Production Notes," *American Grafitti* DVD/**the next day in the *Modesto Bee:*** Ibid./**out of the box first:** "Breedlove Guns New Jet to Record 555 MPH," *LAT,* Nov. 3, 1965, p. B1/**"Thank God for good brakes":** "Breedlove Crashes at 600 MPH—and Lives," *LAT,* Oct. 21, 1965, p. B1/**"I knew if it rolled":** "Art Arfons Boosts World Speed Mark to 576 MPH," *LAT,* Nov. 8, 1965, p. B1/**"That 600 is":** "Breedlove Breaks Record," *LAT,* Nov. 16, 1965, p. B1/**"That record is":** Bob Thomas, "Breedlove Turning to Speedboats," *LAT,* Nov. 23, 1965, p. B5/**"Aqua America":** Ibid.

Epilogue

Moving his base of operations: Michael Mattis, "Craig Breedlove," July 31, 1999, http://www.salon.com/people/rewind/1999/07/31/breedlove/**"I thought, This is it":** Ibid./**Noble reformed his team:** Ibid./**He died in a motorcycle crash:** "Gary Gabelich, Land Speed Record Driver, Dies in Motorcycle Accident," *LAT,* Jan. 27, 1984, p. D8/**Honda let a southern California family:** Norman Mayersohn, "Hydrogen Car Is Here, a Bit Ahead of Its Time," *New York Times*, Dec. 9, 2007, p. 11/**when Starbucks wished:** Elizabeth M. Gillespie, "Starbucks Drive-Throughs Bring an Even Quicker Java Fix," *Contra Costa Times,* Dec. 27, 2005, p. C1/**a center of automotive design:** Fred Kern, historian, email to author, Feb. 2006/**the tale he told police:** Christina Almeida, AP, *Contra Costa Times,* Apr. 15, 2006, p. A9/**California's air consistently:** "California Air Ranks Among Worst in Country," *Contra Costa Times,* Mar. 23, 2006, p. A11/**more than forty-two thousand Americans:** Fatality Analysis Reporting System, National Statistics 2006, http://www-fars.nhtsa.dot.gov/Main/index.aspx/**twelve hundred Californians:** "Stop the Subsidy of Drunk Driving," *SFC,* June 11, 2008, p. B9/**died of natural causes:** "Harness Maker Quits, Dies Five Days Later," *LAT,* May 30, 1945, p. A9/**"Every time the whistle":** Breer memo, photos, California Digital Library, content.cdlib.org

INDEX

A

B

C

D

E

F

G

H

I

J

K

L

M

N

O

P

Q

R

S

T

U

V

W

Y

Z

ABOUT THE AUTHOR

Kevin Nelson is the author of eighteen books. His most recent, *Operation Bullpen: The Inside Story of the Biggest Forgery Scam in American History*, is currently under development to be a motion picture. Another highly praised book of his, *The Golden Game: The Story of California Baseball*, published by Heyday Books, was named one of the top ten books of the year by the *San Francisco Chronicle* and National Public Radio. Nelson devoted three years to researching and writing *Wheels of Change*, driving thousands of miles around California on road trips to car shows, car museums, car clubs, racetracks, the El Mirage dry lakes area, and other significant spots in the state's automotive history. He lives in the Bay Area with his wife and children. Contact him at kln@KevinNelsonWriter.com.

CALIFORNIA
HISTORICAL
SOCIETY

This book has been deemed important to the preservation and interpretation of California history and is published jointly by Heyday Books and The California Historical Society.

Founded in 1871, the California Historical Society (CHS) inspires and empowers Californians to make the past a meaningful part of their contemporary lives. CHS is the designated official historical society of the State of California, with corporate offices in San Francisco. CHS fulfills its mission throughout the state by:

- Fostering scholarship
- Promoting and enhancing history education in California
- Stimulating public exploration on the meaning of the past in contemporary life

Scholarship. CHS maintains and shares one of the four major research collections on California history, including some of the most cherished and valuable documents and images of California's past. *California History* remains one of the most respected state history journals in the country, with an enviable record of introducing groundbreaking scholarship and challenging interpretations.

History Education. The *California History Timeline Online* (http://www.californiahistoricalsociety.org/timeline) has become an invaluable web-based tool for classroom history teachers. CHS is one of the leading organizations in a broad-based network addressing the needs of classroom history and social science educators.

Public Programs. CHS has pioneered the presentation and discussion of critical issues in history that impact our daily lives. In recent years, CHS has expanded public service through partnerships with other organizations throughout the state, such as the Bancroft Library, Chinese Historical Society of America, Autry National Center, and University of Southern California.

Please consider joining the California Historical Society. Members receive:

- *California History*, a quarterly journal published by CHS since 1922
- *California Chronicle*, a quarterly newsletter highlighting CHS activities that keeps members up to date on programs, events, and exhibits.
- Special invitations to events throughout California
- Reciprocal admission benefits to hundreds of museums and historical societies throughout California and the United States

To become a member of the California Historical Society, please write to: California Historical Society, 678 Mission St., San Francisco, CA 94105, or call (415) 357-1848, ext. 229, or join online at www.californiahistoricalsociety.org.

Heyday Books is committed to preserving ancient forests and natural resources. We elected to print this title on 30% post consumer recycled paper, processed chlorine free. As a result, for this printing, we have saved:

36 Trees (40' tall and 6-8" diameter)
16,553 Gallons of Wastewater
11 million BTU's of Total Energy
1,005 Pounds of Solid Waste
3,437 Pounds of Greenhouse Gases

Heyday Books made this paper choice because our printer, Thomson-Shore, Inc., is a member of Green Press Initiative, a nonprofit program dedicated to supporting authors, publishers, and suppliers in their efforts to reduce their use of fiber obtained from endangered forests.

For more information, visit www.greenpressinitiative.org

Environmental impact estimates were made using the Environmental Defense Paper Calculator. For more information visit: www.papercalculator.org.